Textbooks in Language Sciences

In this series:

1. Müller, Stefan. Grammatical theory: From transformational grammar to constraint-based approaches.
2. Schäfer, Roland. Einführung in die grammatische Beschreibung des Deutschen.
3. Freitas, Maria João & Ana Lúcia Santos (eds.). Aquisição de língua materna e não materna: Questões gerais e dados do português.
4. Roussarie, Laurent. Sémantique formelle: Introduction à la grammaire de Montague.
5. Kroeger, Paul. Analyzing meaning: An introduction to semantics and pragmatics.
6. Ferreira, Marcelo. Curso de semântica formal.
7. Stefanowitsch, Anatol. Corpus linguistics: A guide to the methodology.

ISSN: 2364-6209

Corpus linguistics

A guide to the methodology

Anatol Stefanowitsch

Stefanowitsch, Anatol. 2020. *Corpus linguistics: A guide to the methodology* (Textbooks in Language Sciences 7). Berlin: Language Science Press.
This title can be downloaded at:
http://langsci-press.org/catalog/book/148

ISBN: 978-3-96110-224-2 (Digital)
978-3-96110-225-9 (Hardcover)
978-3-96110-226-6 (Softcover)
ISSN: 2364-6209
DOI:10.5281/zenodo.3735822
Source code available from www.github.com/langsci/148
Collaborative reading: paperhive.org/documents/remote?type=langsci&id=148

Cover and concept of design: Ulrike Harbort
Typesetting: Anatol Stefanowitsch, Felix Kopecky
Proofreading: Adrien Barbaresi, Ahmet Bilal Özdemir, Alena Witzlack, Alexandr Rosen, Andreas Hölzl, Andreea Calude, Aniefon Daniel, Bev Erasmus, Bojana Bašaragin, Carmen Jany, Guohua Zhang, Harald Ulland, Hella Olbertz, Ivelina Stoyanova, Ivica Jeđud, Jakub Sláma, Jeroen van de Weijer, José Luis Poblete, Katja Politt, Lachlan Mackenzie, Luigi Talamo, Marie Stará, Marijana Janjic, Melanie Röthlisberger, Monika Czerepowicka, Richard Griscom, Tamara Schmidt, Ulrike Demske, Vadim Kimmelman, Viola Wiegand
Open reviewing: Daniel Kaufman, Daniel Riaño, Emiel van Miltenburg, Sebastian Nordhoff, Stefano Coretta, Susanne Flach
Fonts: Libertinus, Arimo, DejaVu Sans Mono
Typesetting software: XƎLaTeX

Language Science Press
Xhain
Grünberger Str. 16
10243 Berlin, Germany
langsci-press.org
Storage and cataloguing done by FU Berlin

To Lena, Jannes, Elisabeth and Nora –

may you build a world in which knowledge is free.

Contents

Preface

This book has been a long time in the making (the first version of the first chapter has the date stamp 2005-08-04, 11:30) and as the field of corpus linguistics and my own perspective on this field developed over this time span, many thoughts accumulated, that I intended to put into the preface when the time would come to publish. Now that this time is finally there, I feel that there is not much left to say that I have not already said in the book itself.

However, given that there is, by now, a large number of corpus-linguistic textbooks available, ranging from the very decent to the excellent, a few words seem in order to explain why I feel that it makes sense to publish another one. The main reason is that I have found, in my many years of teaching corpus linguistics, that most available textbooks are either too general or too specific. On the one hand, there are textbooks that provide excellent discussions of the history of corpus linguistics or the history of corpus design, or that discuss the epistemological status of corpus data in a field that has been dominated far too long by generative linguistic ideas about what does and does not constitute linguistic evidence. On the other hand, there are textbooks that focus one or more specific corpus-based techniques, discussing very specific phenomena (often the research interests of the textbook authors themselves) using a narrow range of techniques (often involving specific software solutions).

What I would have wanted and needed when I took my first steps into corpus linguistic research as a student is an introductory textbook that focuses on methodological issues – on how to approach the study of language based on usage data and what problems to expect and circumvent. A book that discusses the history and epistemology of corpus linguistics only to the extent necessary to grasp these methodological issues and that presents case studies of a broad range of linguistic phenomena from a coherent methodological perspective. This book is my attempt to write such a textbook.

The first part of the book begins with an almost obligatory chapter on the need for corpus data (a left-over from a time when corpus linguistics was still somewhat of a fringe discipline). I then present what I take to be the methodological foundations that distinguish corpus linguistics from other, superficially similar methodological frameworks, and discuss the steps necessary to build concrete research projects on these foundations – formulating the research question, operationalizing the relevant constructs and deriving quantitative predictions, extracting and annotating data, evaluating the results statistically and drawing conclusions. The second part of the book presents a range of case studies from the domains of lexicology, grammar, text linguistics and metaphor, including variationist and diachronic perspectives. These case studies are drawn from the vast body of corpus linguistic research literature published over the last thirty years, but they are all methodologically deconstructed and explicitly reconstructed in terms of the methodological framework developed in the first part of the book.

While I refrain from introducing specific research tools (e.g. in the form of specific concordancing or statistics software), I have tried to base these case studies on publicly available corpora to allow readers to replicate them using whatever tools they have at their disposal. I also provide supplementary online material, including information about the corpora and corpus queries used as well as, in many cases, the full data sets on which the case studies are based. At the time of publication, the supplementary online material is available as a zip file via http://stefanowitsch.net/clm/clm_v01.zip and https://osf.io/89mgv and as a repository on GitHub via https://github.com/astefanowitsch/clm_v01. I hope that it will remain available at least at one of these locations for the foreseeable future. Feel free to host the material in additional locations.

I hope that the specific perspective taken in this book, along with the case studies and the possibility to study the full data sets, will help both beginning and seasoned researchers gain an understanding of the underlying logic of corpus linguistic research. If not – the book is free as in beer, so at least you will not have wasted any money on it. It is also free as in speech – the Creative Commons license under which it is published allows you to modify and build on the content, remixing it into the textbook *you* would have wanted and needed.

Berlin, 8th March 2020

Acknowledgments

This book was written, with interruptions, over a period of 15 years, during which I used many versions of it in my seminars and communicated with dozens of colleagues about methodological issues I came up against in writing it. My thanks go to my students at the Universität Bremen, the Universität Hamburg and the Freie Universität Berlin and to Harald Baayen, Claudia Baldermann, Michael Barlow, Timothy Colleman, Alice Deignan, Holger Diessel, Stefan Evert, Kerstin Fischer, Susanne Flach, Adele Goldberg, Juliana Goschler, Stefan Gries, Beate Hampe, Stefan Hartmann, Thomas Herbst, Jürgen Hermes, Martin Hilpert, Veronika Koller, Jeong-Hwa Lee, Yoo Yung Lee, Britta Mondorf, Carlos Nash, Erich Neuwirth, Klaus-Uwe Panther, Günter Radden, Alexander Rauhut, Ada Rohde, Doris Schönefeld, Peter Uhrig, Daniel Wiechmann, Stefanie Wulff, Hilary Young, Arne Zeschel, and to everyone I have forgotten here. A few of these people deserve a more detailed mention for the substantial roles they played in the emergence of this book. Klaus-Uwe Panther and Günter Radden encouraged my first steps into corpus linguistics when supervising my master's thesis, and Michael Barlow continued this encouragement during my time as a Ph.D. student at Rice University. My fellow student Ada Rohde and I spent many hours sifting through concordances for our dissertations and discussing questions of retrieval and annotation over a beer or two. My collaboration with Stefan Gries during the first decade of the new millennium was an exciting and most instructive time in my research career. Susanne Flach read and commented on every chapter of the final version of the book, which I started preparing in 2014, and she also introduced me to the excellent Corpus Workbench environment, without which the book would have taken another 15 years. Yoo Yung Lee proof-read the manuscript and checked many of the queries. Two anonymous reviewers, one of whom revealed himself to be Stefan Hartmann, provided stern but constructive comments on the manuscript. Stefan Müller's founding of the open-access Language Science Press provided me with an incentive to finally get serious about finishing this book, and Felix Kopecky and Sebastian Nordhoff always remained friendly and supportive when LaTeX drove me to dispair. Finally, Juliana Goschler has been, and continues to be, a wonderful colleague and the light of my life.

1 The need for corpus data

Broadly speaking, science is the study of some aspect of the (physical, natural or social) world by means of systematic observation and experimentation, and linguistics is the scientific study of those aspects of the world that we summarize under the label *language*. Again very broadly, these encompass, first, language *systems* (sets of linguistic elements and rules for combining them) as well as mental representations of these systems, and second, *expressions* of these systems (spoken and written utterances) as well as mental and motorsensory processes involved in the production and perception of these expressions. Some linguists study only the linguistic system, others study only linguistic expressions. Some linguists study linguistic systems as formal entities, others study them as mental representations. Some linguists study linguistic expressions in their social and/or cultural contexts, others study them in the context of production and comprehension processes. Everyone should agree that whatever aspect of language we study and from whatever perspective we do so, if we are doing so scientifically, observation and experimentation should have a role to play.

Let us define a corpus somewhat crudely as a large collection of authentic text (i.e., samples of language produced in genuine communicative situations), and corpus linguistics as any form of linguistic inquiry based on data derived from such a corpus. We will refine these definitions in the next chapter to a point where they can serve as the foundation for a methodological framework, but they will suffice for now.

Defined in this way, corpora clearly constitute recorded observations of language behavior, so their place in linguistic research seems so obvious that anyone unfamiliar with the last sixty years of mainstream linguistic theorizing will wonder why their use would have to be justified at all. I cannot think of any other scientific discipline whose textbook authors would feel compelled to begin their exposition by defending the use of observational data, and yet corpus linguistics textbooks often do exactly that.

The reasons for this defensive stance can be found in the history of the field, which until relatively recently has been dominated by researchers interested mainly in language as a formal system and/or a mental representation of such a system. Among these researchers, the role of corpus data, and the observation of linguistic behavior more generally is highly controversial. While there are formalists who have discovered (or are beginning to discover) the potential of corpus data for their research, much of the formalist literature has been, and continues to be, at best dismissive of corpus data, at worst openly hostile. Corpus data are attacked as being inherently flawed in ways and to an extent that leaves them with no conceivable use at all in linguistic inquiry.

In this literature, the method proposed instead is that of *intuiting* linguistic data. Put simply, intuiting data means inventing sentences exemplifying the phenomenon under investigation and then judging their *grammaticality* (roughly, whether the sentence is a possible sentence of the language in question). To put it mildly, inventing one's own data is a rather subjective procedure, so, again, anyone unfamiliar with the last sixty years of linguistic theorizing might wonder why such a procedure was proposed in the first place and why anyone would consider it superior to the use of corpus data.

Readers familiar with this discussion or readers already convinced of the need for corpus data may skip this chapter, as it will not be referenced extensively in the remainder of this book. For all others, a discussion of both issues – the alleged uselessness of corpus data and the alleged superiority of intuited data – seems indispensable, if only to put them to rest in order to concentrate, throughout the rest of this book, on the vast potential of corpus linguistics and the exciting avenues of research that it opens up.

Section 1.1 will discuss four major points of criticisms leveled at corpus data. As arguments against corpus data, they are easily defused, but they do point to aspects of corpora and corpus linguistic methods that must be kept in mind when designing linguistic research projects. Section 1.2 will discuss intuited data in more detail and show that it does not solve any of the problems associated (rightly or wrongly) with corpus data. Instead, as Section 1.3 will show, intuited data actually creates a number of additional problems. Still, intuitions we have about our native language (or other languages we speak well) can nevertheless be useful in linguistic research – as long as we do not confuse them with "data".

1.1 Arguments against corpus data

The four major points of criticism leveled at the use of corpus data in linguistic research are the following:

1. corpora are usage data and thus of no use in studying linguistic knowledge;
2. corpora and the data derived from them are necessarily incomplete;

3. corpora contain only linguistic forms (represented as graphemic strings), but no information about the semantics, pragmatics, etc. of these forms; and

4. corpora do not contain negative evidence, i.e., they can only tell us what is possible in a given language, but not what is not possible.

I will discuss the first three points in the remainder of this section. A fruitful discussion of the fourth point requires a basic understanding of statistics, which will be provided in Chapters 5 and 6, so I will postpone it and come back to it in Chapter 8.

1.1.1 Corpus data as usage data

The first point of criticism is the most fundamental one: if corpus data cannot tell us anything about our object of study, there is no reason to use them at all. It is no coincidence that this argument is typically made by proponents of generative syntactic theories, who place much importance on the distinction between what they call *performance* (roughly, the production and perception of linguistic expressions) and *competence* (roughly, the mental representation of the linguistic system). Noam Chomsky, one of the first proponents of generative linguistics, argued early on that the exclusive goal of linguistics should be to model competence, and that, therefore, corpora have no place in serious linguistic analysis:

> The speaker has represented in his brain a grammar that gives an ideal account of the structure of the sentences of his language, but, when actually faced with the task of speaking or "understanding", many other factors act upon his underlying linguistic competence to produce actual performance. He may be confused or have several things in mind, change his plans in midstream, etc. Since this is obviously the condition of most actual linguistic performance, *a direct record – an actual corpus – is almost useless, as it stands, for linguistic analysis of any but the most superficial kind* (Chomsky 1964: 36, emphasis mine).

This argument may seem plausible at first glance, but it is based on at least one of two assumptions that do not hold up to closer scrutiny: first, that there is an impenetrable bi-directional barrier between competence and performance, and second, that the influence of confounding factors on linguistic performance cannot be identified in the data.

The assumption of a barrier between competence and performance is a central axiom in generative linguistics, which famously assumes that language acquisition depends on input only minimally, with an innate "universal grammar" doing most of the work. This assumption has been called into question by a wealth of recent research on language acquisition (see Tomasello 2003 for an overview). But even if we accept the claim that linguistic competence is not derived from linguistic usage, it would seem implausible to accept the converse claim that linguistic usage does not reflect linguistic competence (if it did not, this would raise the question what we need linguistic competence for at all).

This is where the second assumption comes into play. If we believe that linguistic competence is at least broadly reflected in linguistic performance, as I assume any but the most hardcore generativist theoreticians do, then it should be possible to model linguistic knowledge based on observations of language use – unless there are unidentifiable confounding factors distorting performance, making it impossible to determine which aspects of performance are reflections of competence and which are not. Obviously, confounding factors exist – the confusion and the plan-changes that Chomsky mentions, but also others like tiredness, drunkenness and all the other external influences that potentially interfere with speech production. However, there is no reason to believe that these factors and their distorting influence cannot be identified and taken into account when drawing conclusions from linguistic corpora.[1]

Corpus linguistics is in the same situation as any other empirical science with respect to the task of deducing underlying principles from specific manifestations influenced by other factors. For example, Chomsky has repeatedly likened linguistics to physics, but physicists searching for gravitational waves do not reject the idea of observational data on the basis of the argument that there are "many other factors acting upon fluctuations in gravity" and that therefore "a direct record of such fluctuations is almost useless". Instead, they attempt to identify these factors and subtract them from their measurements.

In any case, the gap between linguistic usage and linguistic knowledge would be an argument against corpus data only if there were a way of accessing linguistic knowledge directly and without the interference of other factors. Sometimes, intuited data is claimed to fit this description, but as I will discuss in Section 1.2.1, not even Chomsky himself subscribes to this position.

[1]In fact, there is an entire strand of experimental and corpus-based research that not only takes disfluencies, hesitation, repairs and similar phenomena into account, but actually treats them as object of study in their own right. The body of literature produced by this research is so large that it makes little sense to even begin citing it in detail here, but cf. Kjellmer (2003), Corley & Stewart (2008) and Gilquin & De Cock (2011) for corpus-based approaches.

1.1.2 The incompleteness of corpora

Next, let us look at the argument that corpora are necessarily incomplete, also a long-standing argument in Chomskyan linguistics:

> [I]t is obvious that the set of grammatical sentences cannot be identified with any particular corpus of utterances obtained by the linguist in field work. Any grammar of a language will project the finite and somewhat accidental corpus of observed utterances to a set (presumably infinite) of grammatical utterances (Chomsky 1957: 15).

Let us set aside for now the problems associated with the idea of grammaticality and simply replace the word *grammatical* with *conventionally occurring* (an equation that Chomsky explicitly rejects). Even the resulting, somewhat weaker statement is quite clearly true, and will remain true no matter how large a corpus we are dealing with. Corpora are incomplete in at least two ways.

First, corpora – no matter how large – are obviously finite, and thus they can never contain examples of every linguistic phenomenon. As an example, consider the construction [*it doesn't matter the* N] (as in the lines *It doesn't matter the colour of the car / But what goes on beneath the bonnet* from the Billy Bragg song *A Lover Sings*).[2] There is ample evidence that this is a construction of British English. First, Bragg, a speaker of British English, uses it in a song; second, most native speakers of English will readily provide examples if asked; third, as the examples in (1) show, a simple web query for ⟨ `"it doesn't matter the"` ⟩ will retrieve hits that have clearly been produced by native speakers of British English and other varieties (note that I enclose corpus queries in angled brackets in order to distinguish them from the linguistic expressions that they are meant to retrieve from the corpus):

(1) a. *It doesn't matter the reasons* people go and see a film as long as they go and see it. (thenorthernecho.co.uk)

b. Remember, *it doesn't matter the size of your garden*, or if you live in a flat, there are still lots of small changes you can make that will benefit wildlife. (avonwildlifetrust.org.uk)

[2]Note that this really is a grammatical construction in its own right, i.e., it is not a case of right-dislocation (as in *It doesn't matter, the color* or *It is not important, the color*). In cases of right-dislocation, the pronoun and the dislocated noun phrase are co-referential and there is an intonation break before the NP (in standard English orthographies, there is a comma before the NP). In the construction in question, the pronoun and the NP are not co-referential (*it* functions as a dummy subject) and there is no intonation break (cf. Michaelis & Lambrecht 1996 for a detailed (non-corpus-based) analysis of the very similar [*it BE amazing the* N]).

c. *It doesn't matter the context.* In the end, trust is about the person extending it. (clocurto.us)

d. *It doesn't matter the color of the uniform*, we all work for the greater good. (fw.ky.gov)

However, the largest currently publicly available linguistic corpus of British English, the one-hundred-million-word British National Corpus, does not contain a single instance of this construction. This is unlikely to be due to the fact that the construction is limited to an informal style, as the BNC contains a reasonable amount of informal language. Instead, it seems more likely that the construction is simply too infrequent to occur in a sample of one hundred million words of text. Thus, someone studying the construction might wrongly conclude that it does not exist in British English on the basis of the BNC.

Second, linguistic usage is not homogeneous but varies across situations (think of the kind of variation referred to by terms such as *dialect, sociolect, genre, register, style* etc., which I will discuss in more detail in Section 2.1 below). Clearly, it is, for all intents and purposes, impossible to include this variation in its entirety in a given corpus. This is a problem not only for studies that are interested in linguistic variation but also for studies in core areas such as lexis and grammar: many linguistic patterns are limited to certain varieties, and a corpus that does not contain a particular language variety cannot contain examples of a pattern limited to that variety. For example, the verb *croak* in the sense 'die' is usually used intransitively, but there is one variety in which it also occurs transitively. Consider the following representative examples:

(2) a. Because he was a skunk and a stool pigeon ... I *croaked* him just as he was goin' to call the bulls with a police whistle ... (Veiller, *Within the Law*)

b. [Use] your bean. If I had *croaked the guy* and frisked his wallet, would I have left my signature all over it? (Stout, *Some Buried Cesar*)

c. I recall pointing to the loaded double-barreled shotgun on my wall and replying, with a smile, that I would *croak at least two of them* before they got away. (Thompson, *Hell's Angels*)

Very roughly, we might characterize this variety as *tough guy talk*, or perhaps *tough guy talk as portrayed in crime fiction* (I have never come across an example outside of this (sub-)genre). Neither of these varieties is prominent among the text categories represented in the BNC, and therefore the transitive use of *croak* 'die' does not occur in this corpus.[3]

The incompleteness of linguistic corpora must therefore be accepted and kept in mind when designing and using such a corpus (something I will discuss in detail in the next chapter). However, it is not an argument against the use of corpora, since *any* collection of data is necessarily incomplete. One important aspect of scientific work is to build general models from incomplete data and refine them as more data becomes available. The incompleteness of observational data is not seen as an argument against its use in other disciplines, and the argument gained currency in linguistics only because it was largely accepted that intuited data are more complete. I will argue in Section 1.2.2, however, that this is not the case.

1.1.3 The absence of meaning in corpora

Finally, let us turn to the argument that corpora do not contain information about the semantics, pragmatics, etc. of the linguistic expressions they contain. Lest anyone get the impression that it is only Chomskyan linguists who reject corpus data, consider the following statement of this argument by George Lakoff, an avowed anti-Chomskyan:

> Corpus linguistics can only provide you with utterances (or written letter sequences or character sequences or sign assemblages). To do cognitive linguistics with corpus data, you need to interpret the data – to give it meaning. The meaning doesn't occur in the corpus data. Thus, introspection is always used in any cognitive analysis of language [...] (Lakoff 2004).

Lakoff (and others putting forward this argument) are certainly right: if the corpus itself was all we had, corpus linguistics would be reduced to the detection of formal patterns (such as recurring combinations) in otherwise meaningless strings of symbols.

There are cases where this is the best we can do, namely, when dealing with documents in an unknown or unidentifiable language. An example is the *Phaistos disc*, a clay disk discovered in 1908 in Crete. The disc contains a series of symbols that appear to be pictographs (but may, of course, have purely phonological value), arranged in an inward spiral. These pictographs may or may not

[3] A kind of pseudo-transitive use with a dummy object does occur, however: *He croaked it* meaning 'he died', and of course the major use of *croak* ('to speak with a creaky voice') occurs transitively.

present a writing system, and no one knows what language, if any, they may represent (in fact, it is not even clear whether the disc is genuine or a fake). However, this has not stopped a number of scholars from linguistics and related fields from identifying a number of intriguing patterns in the series of pictographs and some general parallels to known writing systems (see Robinson (2002: ch. 11) for a fairly in-depth popular account). Some of the results of this research are suggestive and may one day enable us to identify the underlying language and even decipher the message, but until someone does so, there is no way of knowing if the theories are even on the right track.

It hardly seems desirable to put ourselves in the position of a Phaistos disc scholar artificially, by excluding from our research designs our knowledge of English (or whatever other language our corpus contains); it is quite obvious that we should, as Lakoff (2004) says, interpret the data in the course of our analysis. But does this mean that we are using introspection in the same way as someone inventing sentences and judging their grammaticality?

I think not. We need to distinguish two different kinds of introspection: (i) *intuiting*, i.e. practice of introspectively accessing one's linguistic experience in order to create sentences and assign grammaticality judgments to them; and (ii) *interpreting*, i.e. the practice of assigning an interpretation (in semantic and pragmatic terms) to an utterance. These are two very different activities, and there is good reason to believe that speakers are better at the second activity than at the first: interpreting linguistic utterances is a natural activity – speakers must interpret everything they hear or read in order to understand it; inventing sentences and judging their grammaticality is *not* a natural activity – speakers never do it outside of papers on grammatical theory. Thus, one can take the position that interpretation has a place in linguistic research but intuition does not. Nevertheless, interpretation is a subjective activity and there are strict procedures that must be followed when including its results in a research design. This issue will be discussed in more detail in Chapter 4.

As with the two points of criticism discussed in the preceding subsections, the problem of interpretation would be an argument against the use of corpus data only if there were a method that avoids interpretation completely or that at least allows for interpretation to be made objective.

1.2 Intuition

Intuited data would not be the only alternative to corpus data, but it is the one proposed and used by critics of the latter, so let us look more closely at this practice. Given the importance of grammaticality judgments, one might expect them to have been studied extensively to determine exactly what it is that people are doing when they are making such judgments. Surprisingly, this is not the case, and the few studies that do exist are hardly ever acknowledged as potentially problematic by those linguists that routinely rely on them, let alone discussed with respect to their place in scientific methodology.

One of the few explicit discussions is found in Jackendoff (1994). Jackendoff introduces the practice of intuiting grammaticality judgments as follows:

> [A]mong the kinds of experiments that can be done on language, one kind is very simple, reliable, and cheap: *simply present native speakers of a language with a sentence or phrase, and ask them to judge whether or not it is grammatical in their language or whether it can have some particular meaning.* [...] The idea is that although we can't observe the mental grammar of English itself, we *can* observe the judgments of grammaticality and meaning that are produced by using it (Jackendoff 1994: 47, emphasis mine).

This statement is representative of the general assumptions underlying the practice of grammaticality judgments in generative linguistics (and many other frameworks) in two ways: first, in that it presents individual grammaticality judgments as a kind of scientific experiment on a par with more sophisticated experiments, and second, in that it presents grammaticality judgments as a direct reflection of a speaker's mental representation of the language in question.

Jackendoff briefly touches upon a crucial problem of the first assumption:

> Ideally, we might want to check these experiments out by asking large numbers of people under controlled circumstances, and so forth. But in fact the method is so reliable that, for a very good first approximation, linguists tend to trust their own judgments and those of their colleagues (Jackendoff 1994: 48).

It is certainly true that linguists trust their own judgments, but that does not mean, of course, that this trust is justified. There is little evidence that individual grammaticality judgments are reliable: in the linguistic literature, grammaticality judgments of the same sentences by different authors often differ considerably and the few studies that have investigated the reliability of grammaticality judgments have consistently shown that such judgments display too much variation within and across speakers to use them as linguistic data (cf., e.g., Schütze (1996) (reissued under a Creative-Commons license by Language Science Press in 2016), esp. Ch. 3 on factors influencing grammaticality judgments, and Cowart (1997)).

The attraction of grammaticality judgments lies not so much in their reliability, then, but in the ease with which they can be collected, and Jackendoff is very explicit about this when he says that

> other kinds of experiments can be used to explore properties of the mental grammar [...] Their disadvantage is their relative inefficiency: it takes a great deal of time to set up the experiment. By contrast, when the experiment consists of making judgments of grammaticality, there is nothing simpler than devising and judging some more sentences (Jackendoff 1994: 49).

However, the fact that something can be done quickly and effortlessly does not make it a good scientific method. If one is serious about using grammaticality judgments – and there are research questions that are not easily addressed without them –, then these judgments must be made as reliable as possible; among other things, this involves the two aspects mentioned by Jackendoff in passing: first, asking large numbers of speakers (or at least more than one) and, second, controlling the circumstances under which they are asked (cf. Schütze 1996 and Cowart 1997 for detailed suggestions as to how this is to be done and Bender 2005 for an interesting alternative; cf. also Section 4.2.3 in Chapter 4). In order to distinguish such empirically collected introspective data from data intuited by the researcher, I will refer to the former as *elicitation data* and continue to reserve for the latter the term *intuition* or *intuited "data"*.

In sum, there are serious problems with the reliability of linguistic intuition in general, a point I will briefly return to in Section 1.3. In the case of isolated judgments *by the researchers themselves*, these problems are compounded by two additional ones: first, the researchers are language experts, whose judgments will hardly be representative of the average native speaker – as Ronald Langacker has quipped (in an example sentence meant to illustrate syntactic complexity): "Linguists are no different from any other people who spend nineteen hours a day pondering the complexity of grammar [...]" (Langacker 1973: 109). Second, they will usually know what it is that they want to prove, and this will distort their judgments. Thus, expert judgments should be used with extreme caution (cf. Labov 1996) if at all (Schütze 1996), instead of serving as the default methodology in linguistics.

Let us return to the second assumption in the passage quoted above – that grammaticality judgments are transparently related to the mental grammar of the speaker producing them. In particular, let us discuss whether intuited "data" fare better than corpus data in terms of the three major points of criticism discussed in the preceding section:

1. Are intuited "data" a more direct reflection of linguistic knowledge (competence) than corpus data;
2. are intuited "data" more complete than corpus data; and
3. do intuited "data" contain information about the semantics, pragmatics, etc. of these forms.

1.2.1 Intuition as performance

The most fundamental point of criticism leveled against corpus data concerns the claim that since corpora are samples of language use ("performance"), they are useless in the study of linguistic knowledge ("competence"). I argued in Section 1.1.1 above that this claim makes sense only in the context of rather implausible assumptions concerning linguistic knowledge and linguistic usage, but even if we accept these assumptions, the question remains whether intuited judgments are different from corpus data in this respect.

It seems obvious that both inventing sentences and judging their grammaticality are kinds of behavior and, as such, performance in the generative linguistics sense. In fact, Chomsky himself admits this:

> [W]hen we study competence – the speaker-hearer's knowledge of his language – we may make use of his reports and his behavior as evidence, but we must be careful not to confuse "evidence" with the abstract constructs that we develop on the basis of evidence and try to justify in terms of evidence. [...] Since *performance – in particular, judgments about sentences – obviously involves many factors apart from competence*, one cannot accept as an absolute principle that the speaker's judgments will give an accurate account of his knowledge. (Chomsky 1972: 187, emphasis mine).

There is little to add to this statement, other than to emphasize that if it is possible to construct a model of linguistic competence on the basis of intuited judgments that involve factors other than competence, it should also be possible to do so on the basis of corpus data that involve factors other than competence, and the competence/performance argument against corpus data collapses.

1.2.2 The incompleteness of intuition

Next, let us turn to the issue of incompleteness. As discussed in Section 1.1.2, corpus data are necessarily incomplete, both in a quantitative sense (since every corpus is finite in size) and in a qualitative sense (since even the most carefully constructed corpus is skewed with respect to the language varieties it contains). This incompleteness is not an argument against using corpora as such, but it might be an argument in favor of intuited judgments if there was reason to believe that they are more complete.

To my knowledge, this issue has never been empirically addressed, and it would be difficult to do so, since there is no complete data set against which intuited judgments could be compared. However, it seems implausible to assume that such judgments are more complete than corpus data. First, just like a corpus, the linguistic experience of a speaker is finite and any mental generalizations based on this experience will be partial in the same way that generalizations based on corpus data must be partial (although it must be admitted that the linguistic experience a native speaker gathers over a lifetime exceeds even a large corpus like the BNC in terms of quantity). Second, just like a corpus, a speaker's linguistic experience is limited to certain language varieties: most English speakers have never been to confession or planned an illegal activity, for example, which means they will lack knowledge of certain linguistic structures typical of these situations.

To exemplify this point, consider that many speakers of English are unaware of the fact that there is a use of the verb *bring* that has the valency pattern (or subcategorization frame) [*bring* $\text{NP}_{\text{LIQUID}}$ [$_{\text{PP}}$ *to the boil*]] (in British English) or [*bring* $\text{NP}_{\text{LIQUID}}$ [$_{\text{PP}}$ *to a boil*]] (in American English). This use is essentially limited to a single genre, – recipes: of the 145 matches in the BNC, 142 occur in recipes and the remaining three in narrative descriptions of someone following a recipe. Thus, a native speaker of English who never reads cookbooks or cooking-related journals and websites and never watches cooking shows on television can go through their whole life without encountering the verb *bring* used in this way. When describing the grammatical behavior of the verb *bring* based on their intuition, this use would not occur to them, and if they were asked to judge the grammaticality of a sentence like *Half-fill a large pan with water and bring to the boil* [BNC A7D], they would judge it ungrammatical. Thus, this valency pattern would be absent from their description in the same way that transitive *croak* 'die' or [*it doesn't matter the* N] would be absent from a grammatical description based on the BNC (where, as we saw in Section 1.1.2, these patterns do not occur).

If this example seems too speculative, consider Culicover's analysis of the phrase *no matter* (Culicover 1999: 106f.). Culicover is an excellent linguist by any standard, but he bases his intricate argument concerning the unpredictable nature of the phrase *no matter* on the claim that the construction [*it doesn't matter the* N] is ungrammatical. If he had consulted the BNC, he might be excused for coming to this wrong conclusion, but he reaches it without consulting a corpus at all, based solely on his native-speaker intuition.[4]

1.2.3 Intuitions about form and meaning

Finally, let us turn to the question whether intuited "data" contain information about meaning. At first glance, the answer to this question would appear to be an obvious "yes": if I make up a sentence, of course I know what that sentence means. However, a closer look shows that matters are more complex and the answer is less obvious.

Constructing a sentence and interpreting a sentence are two separate activities. As a consequence, I do *not* actually know what my constructed sentence means, but only what I *think* it means. While I may rightly consider myself the final authority on the *intended* meaning of a sentence that I myself have produced, my interpretation ceases to be privileged in this way once the issue is no longer my intention, but the interpretation that my constructed sentence would conventionally receive in a particular speech community. In other words, the interpretation of a constructed sentence is subjective in the same way that the interpretation of a sentence found in a corpus is subjective. In fact, interpreting other people's utterances, as we must do in corpus linguistic research, may actually lead to more intersubjectively stable results, as interpreting other people's utterances is a more natural activity than interpreting our own: the former is what we routinely engage in in communicative situations, the latter, while not exactly unnatural, is a rather exceptional activity.

On the other hand, it is very difficult *not* to interpret a sentence, but that is exactly what I would have to do in intuiting grammaticality judgments – judging a sentence to be grammatical or ungrammatical is supposed to be a judgment purely about form, dependent on meaning only insofar as that meaning is relevant to the grammatical structure. Consider the examples in (3):

(3) a. When she'd first moved in she hadn't cared about anything, certainly not her surroundings – they had been the least of her problems – and *if the villagers hadn't so kindly donated her furnishings* she'd probably still be existing in empty rooms. (BNC H9V)

[4]Culicover is a speaker of American English, so if he were writing his book today, he might check the 450-Million-word Corpus of Contemporary American English (COCA), first released in 2008, instead of the BNC. If he did, he would find a dozen or more instances of the construction, depending which version he were to use – for example *It doesn't matter the number of zeros they attach to it*, from a 1997 transcript of ABC Nightline –, so he would not have to rely on his incomplete native-speaker intuition.

b. [$_{VP}$ *donated* [$_{NP}$ *her*] [$_{NP}$ *furnishings*]]
c. [$_{VP}$ *donated* [$_{NP}$ [$_{DET}$ *her*] [$_{N}$ *furnishings*]]]
d. Please have a look at our wish-list and see if you can *donate us a plant* we need. (headway-cambs.org.uk)

The grammaticality of the clause *[T]he villagers [...] donated her furnishings* in (3a) can be judged for its grammaticality only after disambiguating between the meanings associated with the structures in (3b) and (3c).

The structure in (3b) is a ditransitive, which is widely agreed to be impossible with *donate* (but see Stefanowitsch 2007a), so the sentence would be judged ungrammatical under this reading by the vast majority of English speakers. The structure in (3c), in contrast, is a simple transitive, which is one of the two most frequent valency patterns for *donate,* so the sentence would be judged grammatical by all English speakers. The same would obviously be true if the sentence was constructed rather than taken from a corpus.

But the semantic considerations that increase or decrease our willingness to judge an utterance as grammatical are frequently more subtle than the difference between the readings in (3b) and (3c).

Consider the example in (3d), which contains a clear example of *donate* with the supposedly ungrammatical ditransitive valency pattern. Since this is an authentic example, we cannot simply declare it ungrammatical; instead, we must look for properties that distinguish this example from more typical uses of *donate* and try to arrive an an explanation for such exceptional, but possible uses. In Stefanowitsch (2007a), looking at a number of such exceptional uses, I suggest that they may be made possible by the highly untypical sense in which the verb *donate* is used here. In (3d) and other ditransitive uses, *donate* refers to a direct transfer of something relatively valueless from one individual to another in a situation of personal contact. This is very different from the typical use, where a sum of money is transferred from an individual to an organization without personal contact. If this were an intuited example, I might judge it grammatical (at least marginally so) for similar reasons, while another researcher, unaware of my subtle reconceptualization, would judge it ungrammatical, leading to no insights whatsoever into the semantics of the verb *donate* or the valency patterns it occurs in.

1.3 Intuition data vs. corpus data

As the preceding section has shown, intuited judgments are just as vulnerable as corpus data as far as the major points of criticism leveled at the latter are concerned. In fact, I have tried to argue that they are, in some respects, more vulnerable to these criticisms. For those readers who are not yet convinced of the need for corpus data, let me compare the quality of intuited "data" and corpus data in terms of two aspects that are considered much more crucial in methodological discussions outside of linguistics than those discussed above:

1. data reliability (roughly, how sure can we be that other people will arrive at the same set of data using the same procedures);
2. data validity or epistemological status of the data (roughly, how well do we understand what real world phenomenon the data correspond to);[5]

As to the first criterion, note that the problem is not that intuition "data" are necessarily wrong. Very often, intuitive judgments turn out to agree very well with more objective kinds of evidence, and this should not come as a surprise. After all, as native speakers of a language, or even as advanced foreign-language speakers, we have considerable experience with using that language actively (speaking and writing) and passively (listening and reading). It would thus be surprising if we were categorically unable to make statements about the probability of occurrence of a particular expression.

Instead, the problem is that we have no way of determining introspectively whether a particular piece of intuited "data" is correct or not. To decide this, we need objective evidence, obtained either by serious experiments (including elicitation experiments) or by corpus-linguistic methods. But if that is the case, the question is why we need intuition "data" in the first place. In other words, intuition "data" are simply not reliable.

The second criterion provides an even more important argument, perhaps *the* most important argument, against the practice of intuiting. Note that even if we manage to solve the problem of reliability (as systematic elicitation from a representative sample of speakers does to some extent), the epistemological status of intuitive data remains completely unclear. This is particularly evident in the

[5]Readers who are well-versed in methodological issues are asked to excuse this somewhat abbreviated use of the term *validity*; there are, of course, a range of uses in the philosophy of science and methodological theory for the term validity (we will encounter a different use from the one here in Chapters 2.3 and 4).

case of grammaticality judgments: we simply do not know what it means to say that a sentence is "grammatical" or "ungrammatical", i.e., whether grammaticality is a property of natural languages or their mental representations in the first place. It is not entirely implausible to doubt this (cf. Sampson 1987), and even if one does not, one would have to offer a theoretically well-founded definition of what grammaticality is and one would have to show how it is measured by grammaticality judgments. Neither task has been satisfactorily undertaken.

In contrast, the epistemological status of a corpus datum is crystal clear: it is (a graphemic representation of) something that a specific speaker has said or written on a specific occasion in a specific situation. Statements that go beyond a specific speaker, a specific occasion or a specific situation must, of course, be inferred from these data; this is difficult and there is a constant risk that we get it wrong. However, inferring general principles from specific cases is one of the central tasks of all scientific research and the history of any discipline is full of inferences that turned out to be wrong. Intuited data may create the illusion that we can jump to generalizations directly and without the risk of errors. The fact that corpus data do not allow us to maintain this illusion does not make them inferior to intuition, it makes them superior. More importantly, it makes them normal observational data, no different from observational data in any other discipline.

To put it bluntly, then, intuition "data" are less reliable and less valid than corpus data, and they are just as incomplete and in need of interpretation. Does this mean that intuition "data" should be banned completely from linguistics? The answer is no, but not straightforwardly.

On the one hand, we would deprive ourselves of a potentially very rich source of information by dogmatically abandoning the use of our linguistic intuition (native-speaker or not). On the other hand, given the unreliability and questionable epistemological status of intuition data, we cannot simply use them, as some corpus linguists suggest (e.g. McEnery & Wilson 2001: 19), to augment our corpus data. The problem is that any mixed data set (i.e. any set containing both corpus data and intuition "data") will only be as valid, reliable, and complete as the weakest subset of data it contains. We have already established that intuition "data" and corpus data are both incomplete, thus a mixed set will still be incomplete (albeit perhaps less incomplete than a pure set), so nothing much is gained. Instead, the mixed set will simply inherit the lack of validity and reliability from the intuition "data", and thus its quality will actually be *lowered* by the inclusion of these.

The solution to this problem is quite simple. While intuited information about linguistic patterns fails to meet even the most basic requirements for scientific data, it meets every requirement for scientific *hypotheses*. A hypothesis has to be neither reliable, nor valid (in the sense of the term used here), nor complete. In fact, these words do not have any meaning if we apply them to hypotheses – the only requirement a hypothesis must meet is that of *testability* (as discussed further Chapter 3). There is nothing wrong with introspectively accessing our experience as a native speaker of a language (or a non-native one at that), provided we treat the results of our introspection as hypotheses about the meaning or probability of occurrence rather than as facts.

Since there are no standards of purity for hypotheses, it is also unproblematic to mix intuition and corpus data in order to come up with more fine-grained hypotheses (cf. in this context Aston & Burnard 1998: 143), as long as we then *test* our hypothesis on a pure data set that does not include the corpus-data used in generating it in the first place.

1.4 Corpus data in other sub-disciplines of linguistics

Before we conclude our discussion of the supposed weaknesses of corpus data and the supposed strengths of intuited judgments, it should be pointed out that this discussion is limited largely to the field of grammatical theory. This in itself would be surprising if intuited judgments were indeed superior to corpus evidence: after all, the distinction between linguistic behavior and linguistic knowledge is potentially relevant in other areas of linguistic inquiry, too. Yet, no other sub-discipline of linguistics has attempted to make a strong case against observation and for intuited "data".

In some cases, we could argue that this is due to the fact that intuited judgments are simply not available. In language acquisition or in historical linguistics, for example, researchers could not use their intuition even if they wanted to, since not even the most fervent defendants of intuited judgments would want to argue that speakers have meaningful intuitions about earlier stages of their own linguistic competence or their native language as a whole. For language acquisition research, corpus data and, to a certain extent, psycholinguistic experiments are the only sources of data available, and historical linguists must rely completely on textual evidence.

In dialectology and sociolinguistics, however, the situation is slightly different: at least those researchers whose linguistic repertoire encompasses more than one dialect or sociolect (which is not at all unusual), could, in principle, attempt to use intuition data to investigate regional or social variation. To my knowledge, however, nobody has attempted to do this. There are, of course, descriptions of individual dialects that are based on introspective data – the description of the grammar of African-American English in Green (2002) is an impressive example. But in the study of actual *variation*, systematically collected survey data (e.g. Labov et al. 2006) and corpus data in conjunction with multivariate statistics (e.g. Tagliamonte 2006) were considered the natural choice of data long before their potential was recognized in other areas of linguistics.

The same is true of conversation and discourse analysis. One could theoretically argue that our knowledge of our native language encompasses knowledge about the structure of discourse and that this knowledge should be accessible to introspection in the same way as our knowledge of grammar. However, again, no conversation or discourse analyst has ever actually taken this line of argumentation, relying instead on authentic usage data.[6]

Even lexicographers, who could theoretically base their descriptions of the meaning and grammatical behavior of words entirely on the introspectively accessed knowledge of their native language have not generally done so. Beginning with the Oxford English Dictionary (OED), dictionary entries have been based at least in part on *citations* – authentic usage examples of the word in question (see Chapter 2).

If the incompleteness of linguistic corpora or the fact that corpus data have to be interpreted were serious arguments against their use, these sub-disciplines of linguistics should not exist, or at least, they should not have yielded any useful insights into the nature of language change, language acquisition, language variation, the structure of linguistic interactions or the lexicon. Yet all of these disciplines have, in fact, yielded insightful descriptive and explanatory models of their respective research objects.

The question remains, then, why grammatical theory is the only sub-discipline of linguistics whose practitioners have rejected the common practice of building models of underlying principles on careful analyses of observable phenomena. If I were willing to speculate, I would consider the possibility that the rejection of corpora and corpus-linguistic methods in (some schools of) grammatical theorizing are based mostly on a desire to avoid having to deal with actual data, which *are* messy, incomplete and often frustrating, and that the arguments against the use of such data are, essentially, post-hoc rationalizations. But whatever the case

[6]Perhaps Speech Act Theory could be seen as an attempt at discourse analysis on the basis of intuition data: its claims are often based on short snippets of invented conversations. The difference between intuition data and authentic usage data is nicely demonstrated by the contrast between the relatively broad but superficial view of linguistic interaction found in philosophical pragmatics and the rich and detailed view of linguistic interaction found in Conversation Analysis (e.g. Sacks et al. 1974, Sacks 1992) and other discourse-analytic traditions.

may be, we will, at this point, simply stop worrying about the wholesale rejection of corpus linguistics by some researchers until the time that they come up with a convincing argument for this rejection, and turn to a question more pertinent to this book: what exactly constitutes corpus linguistics?

2 What is corpus linguistics?

Although corpus-based studies of language structure can look back on a tradition of at least a hundred years, there is no general agreement as to what exactly constitutes corpus linguistics. This is due in part to the fact that the hundred-year tradition is not an unbroken one. As we saw in the preceding chapter, corpora fell out of favor just as linguistics grew into an academic discipline in its own right and as a result, corpus-based studies of language were relegated to the margins of the field. While the work on corpora and corpus-linguistic methods never ceased, it has returned to a more central place in linguistic methodology only relatively recently. It should therefore come as no surprise that it has not, so far, consolidated into a homogeneous methodological framework. More generally, linguistics itself, with a tradition that reaches back to antiquity, has remained notoriously heterogeneous discipline with little agreement among researchers even with respect to fundamental questions such as what aspects of language constitute their object of study (recall the brief remarks at the beginning of the preceding chapter). It is not surprising, then, that they do not agree how their object of study should be approached methodologically and how it might be modeled theoretically. Given this lack of agreement, it is highly unlikely that a unified methodology will emerge in the field any time soon.

On the one hand, this heterogeneity is a good thing. The dogmatism that comes with monolithic theoretical and methodological frameworks can be stifling to the curiosity that drives scientific progress, especially in the humanities and social sciences which are, by and large, less mature descriptively and theoretically than the natural sciences. On the other hand, after more than a century of scientific inquiry in the modern sense, there should no longer be any serious disagreement as to its fundamental procedures, and there is no reason not to apply these procedures within the language sciences. Thus, I will attempt in this chapter to sketch out a broad, and, I believe, ultimately uncontroversial characterization of corpus linguistics as an instance of the scientific method. I will develop this proposal by successively considering and dismissing alternative characterizations of corpus linguistics. My aim in doing so is not to delegitimize these alternative characterizations, but to point out ways in which they are incomplete unless they are embedded in a principled set of ideas as to what it means to study language scientifically.

Let us begin by considering a characterization of corpus linguistics from a classic textbook:

> Corpus linguistics is perhaps best described for the moment in simple terms as the study of language based on examples of "real life" language use. (McEnery & Wilson 2001: 1).

This definition is uncontroversial in that any research method that does not fall under it would not be regarded as corpus linguistics. However, it is also very broad, covering many methodological approaches that would not be described as corpus linguistics even by their own practitioners (such as discourse analysis or citation-based lexicography). Some otherwise similar definitions of corpus linguistics attempt to be more specific in that they define corpus linguistics as "the compilation and analysis of corpora." (Cheng 2012: 6, cf. also Meyer 2002: xi), suggesting that there is a particular form of recording "real-life language use" called a *corpus*.

The first chapter of this book started with a similar definition, characterizing corpus linguistics as "as any form of linguistic inquiry based on data derived from [...] a corpus", where *corpus* was defined as "a large collection of authentic text". In order to distinguish corpus linguistics proper from other observational methods in linguistics, we must first refine this definition of a linguistic corpus; this will be our concern in Section 2.1. We must then take a closer look at what it means to study language on the basis of a corpus; this will be our concern in Section 2.2.

2.1 The linguistic corpus

The term *corpus* has slightly different meanings in different academic disciplines. It generally refers to a collection of texts; in literature studies, this collection may consist of the works of a particular author (e.g. all plays by William Shakespeare) or a particular genre and period (e.g. all 18th century novels); in theology, it may be (a particular translation of) the Bible. In field linguistics, it refers to any collection of data (whether narrative texts or individual sentences) elicited for the purpose of linguistic research, frequently with a particular research question in mind (cf. Sebba & Fligelstone 1994: 769).

In corpus linguistics, the term is used differently – it refers to a collection of samples of language use with the following properties:

- the instances of language use contained in it are *authentic*;

- the collection is *representative* of the language or language variety under investigation;
- the collection is *large*.

In addition, the texts in such a collection are often (but not always) *annotated* in order to enhance their potential for linguistic analysis. In particular, they may contain information about paralinguistic aspects of the original data (intonation, font style, etc.), linguistic properties of the utterances (parts of speech, syntactic structure), and demographic information about the speakers/writers.

To distinguish this type of collection from other collections of texts, we will refer to it as a *linguistic corpus*, and the term *corpus* will always refer to a linguistic corpus in this book unless specified otherwise.

Let us now discuss each of these criteria in turn, beginning with authenticity.

2.1.1 Authenticity

The word *authenticity* has a range of meanings that could be applied to language – it can mean that a speaker or writer speaks true to their character (*He has found his authentic voice*), or to the character of the group they belong to (*She is the authentic voice of her generation*), that a particular piece of language is correctly attributed (*This is not an authentic Lincoln quote*), or that speech is direct and truthful (*the authentic language of ordinary people*).

In the context of corpus linguistics (and often of linguistics in general), *authenticity* refers much more broadly to what McEnery & Wilson (2001) call "real life language use". As Sinclair puts it, an authentic corpus is one in which

> [a]ll the material is gathered from the genuine communications of people going about their normal business. Anything which involves the linguist beyond the minimum disruption required to acquire the data is reason for declaring a special corpus. (Sinclair 1996a)

In other words, *authentic* language is language produced for the purpose of communication, not for linguistic analysis or even with the knowledge that it might be used for such a purpose. It is language that is not, as it were, performed for the linguist based on what speakers believe constitutes "good" or "proper" language. This is a very broad view of authenticity, since people may be performing inauthentic language for reasons other than the presence of a linguist – but such performances are regarded by linguists as something people will do naturally from time to time and that can and must be studied as an aspect of language use. In contrast, performances for the linguist are assumed to distort language behavior in ways that makes them unsuitable for linguistic analysis.

In the case of written language, the criterion of authenticity is easy to satisfy. Writing samples can be collected after the fact, so that there is no way for the speakers to know that their language will come under scientific observation. In the case of spoken language, the "minimum disruption" that Sinclair mentions becomes relevant. We will return to this issue and its consequences for authenticity presently, but first let us discuss some general problems with the corpus linguist's broad notion of authenticity.

Widdowson (2000), in the context of discussing the use of corpora in the language classroom, casts doubt on the notion of authenticity for what seems, at first, to be a rather philosophical reason:

> The texts which are collected in a corpus have a reflected reality: they are only real because of the presupposed reality of the discourses of which they are a trace. This is decontexualized language, which is why it is only partially real. If the language is to be realized as use, it has to be recontextualized. (Widdowson 2000: 7)

In some sense, it is obvious that the texts in a corpus (in fact, all texts) are only fully authentic as long as they are part of an authentic communicative situation. A sample of spoken language is only authentic as part of the larger conversation it is part of, a sample of newspaper language is only authentic as long as it is produced in a newsroom and processed by a reader in the natural context of a newspaper or news site for the purposes of informing themselves about the news, and so on. Thus, the very act of taking a sample of language and including it in a corpus removes its authenticity.

This rather abstract point has very practical consequences, however. First, any text, spoken or written, will lose not only its communicative context (the discourse of which it was originally a part), but also some of its linguistic and paralinguistic properties when it becomes part of a corpus. This is most obvious in the case of transcribed spoken data, where the very act of transcription means that aspects like tone of voice, intonation, subtle aspects of pronunciation, facial expressions, gestures, etc. are replaced by simplified descriptions or omitted altogether. It is also true for written texts, where, for example, visual information about the font, its color and size, the position of the text on the page, and the tactile properties of the paper are removed or replaced by descriptions (see further Section 2.1.4 below).

The corpus linguist can attempt to supply the missing information introspectively, "recontextualizing" the text, as Widdowson puts it. But since they are not in an authentic setting (and often not a member of the same cultural and demographic group as the original or originally intended hearer/reader), this recontextualization can approximate authenticity at best.

Second, texts, whether written or spoken, may contain errors that were present in the original production or that were introduced by editing before publication or by the process of preparing them for inclusion in the corpus (cf. also Emons 1997). As long as the errors are present in the language sample before it is included in the corpus, they are not, in themselves, problematic: errors are part of language use and must be studied as such (in fact, the study of errors has yielded crucial insights into language processing, cf., for example, Fromkin 1973 and Fromkin 1980). The problem is that the decision as to whether some bit of language contains an error is one that the researcher must make by reconceptualizing the speaker and their intentions in the original context, a reconceptualization that makes authenticity impossible to determine.

This does not mean that corpora cannot be used. It simply means that limits of authenticity have to be kept in mind. With respect to spoken language, however, there is a more serious problem – Sinclair's "minimum disruption".

The problem is that in observational studies no disruption is ever minimal – as soon as the investigator is present in person or in the minds of the observed, we get what is known as the "observer's paradox": we want to observe people (or other animate beings) behaving as they would if they were not observed – in the case of gathering spoken language data, we want to observe speakers interacting linguistically as they would if no linguist was in sight.

In some areas of study, it is possible to circumvent this problem by hiding (or installing hidden recording devices), but in the case of human language users this is impossible: it is unethical as well as illegal in most jurisdictions to record people without their knowledge. Speakers must typically give written consent before the data collection can begin, and there is usually a recording device in plain view that will constantly remind them that they are being recorded.

This knowledge will invariably introduce a degree of inauthenticity into the data. Take the following excerpts from the *Bergen Corpus of London Teenage Language* (COLT). In the excerpt in (1), the speakers are talking about the recording device itself, something they would not do in other circumstances:

(1) A: Josie?
B: Yeah. [laughs] I'm not filming you, I'm just taping you. [...]
A: Yeah, I'll take your little toy and smash it to pieces!
C: Mm. Take these back to your class. [COLT B132611]

In the excerpt in (2), speaker A explains to their interlocutor the fact that the conversation they are having will be used for linguistic research:

(2) A: Were you here when I got that?
B: No what is it? A: It's for the erm, [...] language course. Language, survey. [...]
B: Who gave it to you?
A: Erm this lady from the, University of Bergen.
B: So how d'ya how does it work?
A: Erm you you speak into it and erm, records, gotta record conversations between people. [COLT B141708]

A speaker's knowledge that they are being recorded for the purposes of linguistic analysis is bound to distort the data even further. In example (3), there is evidence for such a distortion – the speakers are performing explicitly for the recording device:

(3) C: Ooh look, there's Nick!
A: Is there any music on that?
B: A few things I taped off the radio.
A: Alright then. Right. I wa..., I just want true things. He told me he dumped you is that true?
C: [laughs]
B: No it is not true. I protest. [COLT B132611]

Speaker A asks for "true things" and then imitates an interview situation, which speaker B takes up by using the somewhat formal phrase *I protest*, which they presumably would not use in an authentic conversation about their love life.

Obviously, such distortions will be more or less problematic depending on our research question. Level of formality (style) may be easier to manipulate in performing for the linguist than pronunciation, which is easier to manipulate than morphological or syntactic behavior. However, the fact remains that spoken data in corpora are hardly ever authentic in the corpus-linguistic sense (unless it is based on recordings of public language use, for example, from television or the radio), and the researcher must rely, again, on an attempt to recontextualize the data based on their own experience as a language user in order to identify possible distortions. There is no objective way of judging the degree of distortion introduced by the presence of an observer, since we do not have a sufficiently broad range of surreptitiously recorded data for comparison.

There is one famous exception to the observer's paradox in spoken language data: the so-called Nixon Tapes – illegal surreptitious recordings of conversation in the executive offices of the White House and the headquarters of the opposing Democratic Party produced at the request of the Republican President Richard Nixon between February 1971 and July 1973. Many of these tapes are now available as digitized sound files and/or transcripts (see, for example, Nichter 2007). In addition to the interest they hold for historians, they form the largest available corpus of truly authentic spoken language.

However, even these recordings are too limited in size and topic area as well as in the diversity of speakers recorded (mainly older white American males), to serve as a standard against which to compare other collections of spoken data.

The ethical and legal problems in recording unobserved spoken language cannot be circumvented, but their impact on the authenticity of the recorded language can be lessened in various ways – for example, by getting general consent from speakers, but not telling them when precisely they will be recorded.

Researchers may sometimes deliberately choose to depart from authenticity in the corpus-linguistic sense if their research design or the phenomenon under investigation requires it. A researcher may be interested in a phenomenon that is so rare in most situations that even the largest available corpora do not contain a sufficient number of cases. These may be structural phenomena (like the pattern [*It doesn't matter the* N] or transitive *croak*, discussed in the previous chapter), or unusual communicative situations (for example, human-machine interaction).

In such cases, it may be necessary to switch methods and use some kind of grammaticality judgments after all, but it may also be possible to elicit these phenomena in what we could call semi-authentic settings. For example, researchers interested in motion verbs often do not have the means (or the patience) to collect these verbs from general corpora, or corpora may not contain a sufficiently broad range of descriptions of motion events with particular properties. Such descriptions are sometimes elicited by asking speakers to describe movie snippets or narrate a story from a picture book (cf. e.g. Berman & Slobin 1994; Strömqvist & Verhoeven 2003). Human-machine interaction is sometimes elicited in so-called "Wizard of Oz" experiments, where people believe they are talking to a robot, but the robot is actually controlled by one of the researchers (cf. e.g. Georgila et al. 2010).

Such semi-structured elicitation techniques may also be used where a phenomenon is frequent enough in a typical corpus, but where the researcher wants to vary certain aspects systematically, or where the researcher wants to achieve comparability across speakers or even across languages.

These are sometimes good reasons for eliciting a special-purpose corpus rather than collecting naturally occurring text. Still, the stimulus-response design of elicitation is obviously influenced by experimental paradigms used in psychology. Thus, studies based on such corpora must be regarded as falling somewhere between corpus linguistics and psycholinguistics and they must therefore meet the design criteria of both corpus linguistic and psycholinguistic research designs.

2.1.2 Representativeness

Put simply, a representative sample is a subset of a population that is identical to the population as a whole with respect to the distribution of the phenomenon under investigation. Thus, for a corpus (a sample of language use) to be representative of a particular language, the distribution of linguistic phenomena (words, grammatical structures, etc.) would have to be identical to their distribution in the language as a whole (or in the variety under investigation, see further below).

The way that corpus creators typically aim to achieve this is by including in the corpus different manifestations of the language it is meant to represent in proportions that reflect their incidence in the speech community in question. Such a corpus is sometimes referred to as a *balanced* corpus.

Before we can discuss this in more detail, a terminological note is in order. You may have noted that in the preceding discussion I have repeatedly used terms like *language variety, genre, register* and *style* for different manifestations of language. The precise usage of these terms notoriously vary across subdisciplines of linguistics and individual researchers, including the creators of corpora.

In this book, I use *language variety* to refer to any form of language delineable from other forms along cultural, linguistic or demographic criteria. In other words, I use it as a superordinate term for text-linguistic terms like *genre, register, style*, and *medium* as well as sociolinguistic terms like *dialect, sociolect*, etc. With respect to what I am calling *text-linguistic* terms here, I follow the usage suggestions synthesized by Lee (2001) and use *genre* for culturally defined and recognized varieties, *register* for varieties characterized by a particular "functional configuration" (roughly, a bundle of linguistic features associated with a particular social function), *style* to refer to the degrees of formality (e.g. formal, informal, colloquial, humorous, etc.), and *medium* to refer to the material manifestation (essentially, spoken and written with subtypes of these). I use the term *topic (area)* to refer to the content of texts or the discourse domain from which they come. When a particular variety, defined by one or more of the dimensions just mentioned, is included in a given corpus, I refer to it as a *text category* of that corpus.

For a corpus to be representative (or "balanced"), its text categories should accurately reflect both quantitatively and qualitatively the language varieties found in the speech community whose language is represented in the corpus. However, it is clear that this is an ideal that is impossible to achieve in reality for at least four reasons.

First, for most potentially relevant parameters we simply do not know how they are distributed in the population. We may know the distribution of some of the most important demographic variables (e.g. sex, age, education), but we simply do not know the overall distribution of spoken vs. written language, press language vs. literary language, texts and conversations about particular topics, etc.

Second, even if we did know, it is not clear that all manifestations of language use shape and/or represent the linguistic system in the same way, simply because we do not know how widely they are received. For example, emails may be responsible for a larger share of written language produced in a given time span than news sites, but each email is typically read by a handful of people at the most, while some news texts may be read by millions of people (and others not at all).

Third, in a related point, speech communities are not homogeneous, so defining balance based on the proportion of language varieties in the speech community may not yield a realistic representation of the language even if it were possible: every member of the speech community takes part in different communicative situations involving different language varieties. Some people read more than others, and among these some read mostly newspapers, others mostly novels; some people watch parliamentary debates on TV all day, others mainly talk to customers in the bakery where they work. In other words, the proportion of language varieties that speakers encounter varies, requiring a notion of balance based on the incidence of language varieties *in the linguistic experience of a typical speaker*. This, in turn, requires a definition of what constitutes a typical speaker in a given speech community. Such a definition may be possible, but to my knowledge, does not exist so far.

Finally, there are language varieties that are impossible to sample for practical reasons – for example, pillow talk (which speakers will be unwilling to share because they consider it too private), religious confessions or lawyer-client conversations (which speakers are prevented from sharing because they are privileged), and the planning of illegal activities (which speakers will want to keep secret in order to avoid lengthy prison terms).

Representativeness or balancedness also plays a role if we do not aim at investigating a language as a whole, but are instead interested in a particular variety. In this case, the corpus will be deliberately skewed so as to contain only samples of the variety under investigation. However, if we plan to generalize our results to that variety as a whole, the corpus must be representative of that variety. This is sometimes overlooked. For example, there are studies of political rhetoric that are based on speeches by just a handful of political leaders (cf., e.g., Charteris-Black 2006; 2005) or studies of romantic metaphor based on a single Shakespeare play (Barcelona Sánchez 1995). While such studies can be insightful with respect to the language of the individuals included in the corpus, their results are unlikely to be generalizable even within the narrow variety under investigation (political speeches, romantic tragedies). Thus, they belong to the field of literary criticism or stylistics much more clearly than to the field of linguistics.

Given the problems discussed above, it seems impossible to create a linguistic corpus meeting the criterion of representativeness. In fact, while there are very well-thought out approaches to approximating representativeness (cf., e.g., Biber 1993), it is fair to say that most corpus creators never really try. Let us see what they do instead.

The first linguistic corpus in our sense was the Brown University Standard Corpus of Present-Day American English (generally referred to as BROWN). It is made up exclusively of edited prose published in the year 1961, so it clearly does not attempt to be representative of American English in general, but only of a particular kind of written American English in a narrow time span. This is legitimate if the goal is to investigate that particular variety, but if the corpus were meant to represent the standard language in general (which the corpus creators explicitly deny), it would force us to accept a very narrow understanding of *standard*.

The BROWN corpus consists of 500 samples of approximately 2000 words each, drawn from a number of different language varieties, as shown in Table 2.1.

The first level of sampling is, roughly, by genre: there are 286 samples of non-fiction, 126 samples of fiction and 88 samples of press texts. There is no reason to believe that this corresponds proportionally to the total number of words produced in these language varieties in the USA in 1961. There is also no reason to believe that the distribution corresponds proportionally to the incidence of these language varieties in the linguistic experience of a typical speaker. This is true all the more so when we take into account the second level of sampling within these

Table 2.1: Composition of the BROWN corpus

Genre	Subgenre/Topic Area		Samples
Non-Fiction	Religion	Books	7
		Periodicals	6
		Tracts	4
	Skills and Hobbies	Books	2
		Periodicals	34
	Popular Lore	Books	23
		Periodicals	25
	Belles Lettres, Biography, Memoirs, etc.	Books	38
		Periodicals	37
	Miscellaneous	Government Documents	24
		Foundation Reports	2
		Industry Reports	2
		College Catalog	1
		Industry House organ	1
	Learned	Natural Sciences	12
		Medicine	5
		Mathematics	4
		Social and Behavioral Sciences	14
		Political Science, Law, Education	15
		Humanities	18
		Technology and Engineering	12
Fiction	General	Novels	20
		Short Stories	9
	Mystery and Detective	Novels	20
		Short Stories	4
	Science Fiction	Novels	3
		Short Stories	3
	Adventure and Western	Novels	15
		Short Stories	14
	Romance and Love Story	Novels	14
		Short Stories	15
	Humor	Novels	3
		Essays, etc.	6
Press	Reportage	Political	14
		Sports	7
		Society	3
		Spot News	9
		Financial	4
		Cultural	7
	Editorial	Institutional	10
		Personal	10
		Letters to the Editor	7
	Reviews (theatre, books, music, dance)		17

genres, which uses a mixture of sub-genres (such as reportage or editorial in the press category or novels and short stories in the fiction category), and topic areas (such as Romance, Natural Science or Sports). Clearly the number of samples included for these categories is not based on statistics of their proportion in the language as a whole. Intuitively, there may be a rough correlation in some cases: newspapers publish more reportage than editorials, people (or at least academics like those that built the corpus) generally read more mystery fiction than science fiction, etc. The creators of the BROWN corpus are quite open about the fact that their corpus design is not a representative sample of (written) American English. They describe the collection procedure as follows:

> The selection procedure was in two phases: an initial subjective classification and decision as to how many samples of each category would be used, followed by a random selection of the actual samples within each category. In most categories the holding of the Brown University Library and the Providence Athenaeum were treated as the universe from which the random selections were made. But for certain categories it was necessary to go beyond these two collections. For the daily press, for example, the list of American newspapers of which the New York Public Library keeps microfilms files was used (with the addition of the Providence Journal). Certain categories of chiefly ephemeral material necessitated rather arbitrary decisions; some periodical materials in the categories Skills and Hobbies and Popular Lore were chosen from the contents of one of the largest second-hand magazine stores in New York City. (Francis & Kučera 1979)

If anything, the BROWN corpus is representative of the holdings of the libraries mentioned, although even this representativeness is limited in two ways. First, by the unsystematic additions mentioned in the quote, and second, by the sampling procedure applied.

Although this sampling procedure is explicitly acknowledged to be "subjective" by the creators of the BROWN corpus, their description suggests that their design was guided by a general desire for balance:

> The list of main categories and their subdivisions was drawn up at a conference held at Brown University in February 1963. The participants in the conference also independently gave their opinions as to the number of samples there should be in each category. These figures were averaged to obtain the preliminary set of figures used. A few changes were later made

> on the basis of experience gained in making the selections. Finer subdivision was based on proportional amounts of actual publication during 1961. (Francis & Kučera 1979)

This procedure combines elements from both interpretations of representativeness discussed above. First, it involves the opinions (i.e., intuitions) of a number of people concerning the proportional relevance of certain sub-genres and/or topic areas. The fact that these opinions were "averaged" suggests that the corpus creators wanted to achieve a certain degree of intersubjectivity. This idea is not completely wrongheaded, although it is doubtful that speakers have reliable intuitions in this area. In addition, the participants of the conference mentioned did not exactly constitute a group of typical speakers or a cross-section of the American English speech community: they consisted of six academics with backgrounds in linguistics, education and psychology – five men and one woman; four Americans, one Brit and one Czech; all of them white and middle-aged (the youngest was 36, the oldest 59). No doubt, a different group of researchers – let alone a random sample of speakers – following the procedure described would arrive at a very different corpus design.

Second, the procedure involves an attempt to capture the proportion of language varieties in actual publication – this proportion was determined on the basis of the American Book Publishing Record, a reference work containing publication information on all books published in the USA in a given year. Whether this is, in fact, a comprehensive source is unclear, and anyway, it can only be used in the selection of excerpts from books. Basing the estimation of the proportion of language varieties on a different source would, again, have yielded a very different corpus design. For example, the copyright registrations for 1961 suggest that the category of periodicals is severely underrepresented relative to the category of books – there are roughly the same number of copyright registrations for the two language varieties, but there are one-and-a-half times as many excerpts from books as from periodicals in the BROWN corpus.

Despite these shortcomings, the BROWN corpus set standards, inspiring a host of corpora of different varieties of English using the same design – for example, the Lancaster-Oslo/Bergen Corpus (LOB) containing British English from 1961, the Freiburg Brown (FROWN) and Freiburg LOB (FLOB) corpora of American and British English respectively from 1991, the Wellington Corpus of Written New Zealand English, and the Kolhapur Corpus (Indian English). The success of the BROWN design was partly due to the fact that being able to study strictly comparable corpora of different varieties is useful regardless of their design. However, if the design had been widely felt to be completely off-target, researchers would not have used it as a basis for the substantial effort involved in corpus creation.

More recent corpora at first glance appear to take a more principled approach to representativeness or balance. Most importantly, they typically include not just written language, but also spoken language. However, a closer look reveals that this is the only real change. For example, the BNC Baby, a four-million-word subset of the 100-million-word British National Corpus (BNC), includes approximately one million words each from the text categories spoken conversation, written academic language, written prose fiction and written newspaper language (Table 2.2 shows the design in detail). Obviously, this design does not correspond to the linguistic experience of a typical speaker, who is unlikely to be exposed to academic writing and whose exposure to written language is unlikely to be three times as large as their exposure to spoken language. The design also does not correspond in any obvious way to the actual amount of language produced on average in the four categories or the subcategories of academic and newspaper language. Despite this, the BNC Baby, and the BNC itself, which is even more drastically skewed towards edited written language, are extremely successful corpora that are still widely used a quarter-century after the first release of the BNC.

Even what I would consider the most serious approach to date to creating a balanced corpus design, the sampling schema of the International Corpus of English (ICE), is unlikely to be substantially closer to constituting a representative sample of English language use (see Table 2.3).

It puts a stronger emphasis on spoken language – sixty percent of the corpus are spoken text categories, although two thirds of these are public language use, while for most of us private language use is likely to account for more of our linguistic experience. It also includes a much broader range of written text categories than previous corpora, including not just edited writing but also student writing and letters.

Linguists would probably agree that the design of the ICE corpora is "more representative" than that of the BNC Baby, which is in turn "more representative" than that of the BROWN corpus and its offspring. However, in light of the above discussion of representativeness, there is little reason to believe that any of these corpora, or the many others that fall somewhere between BROWN and ICE, even come close to approximating a random sample of (a given variety of) English in terms of the text categories they contain and the proportions with which they are represented.

This raises the question as to why corpus creators go to the trouble of attempting to create representative corpora at all, and why some corpora seem to be more successful attempts than others.

Table 2.2: Composition of the BNC Baby corpus

Medium	Genre	Subgenre	Topic area	Samples	Words
Spoken	Conversation			30	1 017 025
Written	Academic		Humanities/Arts	7	224 872
			Medicine	2	89 821
			Nat. Science	6	215 549
			Politics/Law/Education	6	195 836
			Soc. Science	7	209 645
			Technology/Engineering	2	77 533
	Fiction	Prose		25	1 010 279
	Newspapers	Nat. Broadsheet	Arts	9	36 603
			Commerce	7	64 162
			Editorial	1	8821
			Miscellaneous	25	121 194
			Report	3	48 190
			Science	5	18 245
			Social	13	34 516
			Sports	3	36 796
		Other	Arts	3	43 687
			Commerce	5	89 170
			Report	7	232 739
			Science	7	13 616
			Social	8	94 676
		Tabloid		1	121 252

It seems to me that, in fact, corpus creators are not striving for representativeness at all. The impossibility of this task is widely acknowledged in corpus linguistics. Instead, they seem to interpret balance in terms of the related but distinct property *diversity*. While corpora will always be skewed relative to the overall population of texts and language varieties in a speech community, the undesirable effects of this skew can be alleviated by including in the corpus as broad a range of varieties as is realistic, either in general or in the context of a given research project.

Unless language structure and language use are infinitely variable (which, at a given point in time, they are clearly not), increasing the diversity of the sample will increase representativeness even if the corpus design is not strictly proportional to the incidence of text varieties or types of speakers found in the speech community. It is important to acknowledge that this does not mean that diversity and representativeness are the same thing, but given that representative corpora are practically (and perhaps theoretically) impossible to create, diversity is a workable and justifiable proxy.

Table 2.3: Composition of the ICE corpora

Medium		Situation/Genre		Samples
Spoken	Dialogues	Private	Face-to-face conversations	90
			Phone calls	10
		Public	Classroom lessons	20
			Broadcast discussions	20
			Broadcast interviews	10
			Parliamentary debates	10
			Legal cross-examinations	10
			Business transactions	10
	Monologues	Unscripted	Spontaneous commentaries	20
			Unscripted speeches	30
			Demonstrations	10
			Legal presentations	10
		Scripted	Broadcast news	20
			Broadcast talks	20
			Non-broadcast talks	10
Written	Non-printed	Student writing	Student essays	10
			Exam scripts	10
		Letters	Social letters	15
			Business letters	15
	Printed	Academic writing	Humanities	10
			Social Sciences	10
			Natural Sciences	10
			Technology	10
		Popular writing	Humanities	10
			Social Sciences	10
			Natural Sciences	10
			Technology	10
		Reportage	Press news reports	20
		Instructional writing	Administrative writing	10
			Skills/Hobbies	10
		Persuasive writing	Press editorials	10
		Creative writing	Novels and short stories	10

2.1.3 Size

Like diversity, corpus size is also assumed, more or less explicitly, to contribute to representativeness (e.g. McEnery & Wilson 2001: 78; Biber 2006: 251). The extent of the relationship is difficult to assess. Obviously, sample size does correlate with representativeness to some extent: if our corpus were to contain the totality of all manifestations of a language (or variety of a language), it would necessarily be representative, and this representativeness would not drop to zero immediately if we were to decrease the sample size. However, it would drop rather rapidly – if we exclude one percent of the totality of all texts produced in a given language, entire language varieties may already be missing. For example, the Library of Congress holds around 38 million print materials, roughly half of them in English. A search for *cooking* in the main catalogue yields 7638 items that presumably include all cookbooks in the collection. This means that cookbooks make up no more than 0.04 percent of printed English ($^{7638}/_{19000000} = 0.000402$). Thus, they could quickly be lost in their entirety when the sample size drops substantially below the size of the population as a whole. And when a genre (or a language variety in general) goes missing from our sample, at least some linguistic phenomena will disappear along with it – such as the expression [*bring* $\text{NP}_{\text{LIQUID}}$ [$_{\text{PP}}$ *to the/a boil*]], which, as discussed in Chapter 1, is exclusive to cookbooks.[1]

In the age of the World Wide Web, corpus size is practically limited only by technical considerations. For example, the English data in the *Google N-Grams* data base are derived from a trillion-word corpus (cf. Franz & Brants 2006). In quantitative terms, this represents many times the linguistic input that a single person would receive in their lifetime: an average reader can read between 200 and 250 words per minute, so it would take them between 7500 and 9500 years of non-stop reading to get through the entire corpus. However, even this corpus contains only a tiny fraction of written English, let alone of English as a whole. Even more crucially, in terms of language varieties, it is limited to a narrow section of published written English and does not capture the input of any actual speaker of English at all.

There are several projects gathering very large corpora on a broader range of web-accessible text. These corpora are certainly impressive in terms of their size, even though they typically contain mere billions rather than trillions of

[1]The expression actually occurs once in the BROWN corpus, which includes one 2000 word sample from a cookbook, over-representing this genre by a factor of five, but not at all in the LOB corpus. Thus, someone investigating the LOB corpus might not include this expression in their description of English at all, someone comparing the two corpora would wrongly conclude that it is limited to American English.

words. However, their size is the only argument in their favor, as their creators and their users must not only give up any pretense that they are dealing with a representative corpus, but must contend with a situation in which they have no idea what texts and language varieties the corpus contains and how much of it was produced by speakers of English (or by human beings rather than bots).

These corpora certainly have their uses, but they push the definition of a linguistic corpus in the sense discussed above to their limit. To what extent they are representative cannot be determined. On the one hand, corpus size correlates with representativeness only to the extent that we take corpus diversity into account. On the other hand, assuming (as we did above) that language structure and use are not infinitely variable, size will correlate with the representativeness of a corpus at least to some extent with respect to particular linguistic phenomena (especially frequent phenomena, such as general vocabulary, and/or highly productive processes such as derivational morphology and major grammatical structures).

There is no principled answer to the question "How large must a linguistic corpus be?", except, perhaps, an honest "It is impossible to say" (Renouf 1987: 130). However, there are two practical answers. The more modest answer is that it must be large enough to contain a sample of instances of the phenomenon under investigation that is large enough for analysis (we will discuss what this means in Chapters 5 and 6). The less modest answer is that it must be large enough to contain sufficiently large samples of every grammatical structure, vocabulary item, etc. Given that an ever increasing number of texts from a broad range of language varieties is becoming accessible via the web, the second answer may not actually be as immodest as it sounds.

Current corpora that at least make an honest attempt at diversity currently range from one million (e.g. the ICE corpora mentioned above) to about half a billion (e.g. the COCA mentioned in the preceding chapter). Looking at the published corpus-linguistic literature, my impression is that for most linguistic phenomena that researchers are likely to want to investigate, these corpus sizes seem sufficient. Let us take this broad range as characterizing a linguistic corpus for practical purposes.

2.1.4 Annotations

Minimally, a linguistic corpus consists simply of a large, diverse collection of files containing authentic language samples as raw text, but more often than not, corpus creators add one or more of three broad types of annotation:

1. information about paralinguistic features of the text such as font style, size and color, capitalization, special characters, etc. (for written texts), and intonation, overlapping speech, length of pauses, etc. (for spoken text);

2. information about linguistic features, such as parts of speech, lemmas or grammatical structure;

3. information about the producers of the text (speaker demographics like age, sex, education) or the circumstances of its production (genre, medium, situation).

In this section, we will illustrate these types of annotation and discuss their practical implications as well as their relation to the criterion of authenticity, beginning with paralinguistic features, whose omission was already hinted at as a problem for authenticity in Section 2.1.1 above.

For example, Figure 2.1 shows a passage of transcribed speech from the Santa Barbara Corpus of Spoken American English (SBCSAE).

```
 ... <PAR<P what was I gonna say.
 .. I forgot what I was think- --
LENORE: You sai[d you never] made the horseshoes,
LYNNE: [gonna say] P>PAR>.
LENORE: but,
LYNNE: ... (H) Well,
 % .. %w- u=m,
 %= when we put em on a horse's hoof,
 all we do,
 (H) they're already made.
 .. they're round.
 .. we pick out a size.
 .. you know we'd,
 like look at the horse's hoof,
 and say,
 okay,
 (H) this is a double-aught.
```

Figure 2.1: Paralinguistic features of spoken language in the SBCSAE

The speech is transcribed more or less in standard orthography, with some paralinguistic features indicated by various means. For example, the beginning of a passage of "attenuated" (soft, low-volume) speech is indicated by the sequence `<P`, and the end by `P>`. Audible breathing is transcribed as `(H)`, lengthening is indicated by an equals sign (as in `u=m` in the seventh line) and pauses are represented as sequences of dots (two for a short pause, three for a long pause). Finally, overlapping speech, a typical feature of spoken language, is shown by square brackets, as in the third and fourth line. Other features of spoken language are not represented in detail in (this version of) the SBCSAE. Most notably, intonation is only indicated to the extent that each line represents one intonation unit (i.e. a stretch of speech with a single, coherent intonation contour), and that a period and a comma at the end of a line indicate a "terminative" and a "continuative" prosody respectively.

In contrast, consider the London-Lund Corpus of Spoken English (LLC), an excerpt from which is shown in Figure 2.2.

```
4 5 17 1400 1 2 c 11 *^have you !still _got the _little* !gr\/ey /
4 5 17 1400 1 1 c 11 'one# - - /
4 5 17 1410 1 1 b 11 [@:] . ^which one`s th\at# /
4 5 17 1420 1 1 b 11 the ^one that`s ex'pecting a f\/oal# . /
4 5 17 1430 1 1 b 11 +we`ve ^st\/ill 'got her#+ /
4 5 17 1440 1 1 c 11 +well I ^saw a+ !dear little :f\oal in the 'field# /
4 5 17 1450 1 1 b 11 ^oh n\o# /
4 5 17 1460 1 1 b 11 we ^haven`t got h/im# . /
4 5 17 1470 1 1 b 11 ^h\e got s/old# - - /
4 5 17 1480 1 1 b 11 ^went to 'be a a 'nuisance to 'somebody /else# - /
4 5 18 1490 1 1 a 11 (giggles . ) ^[/\m]# . /
4 5 18 1500 1 1 a 11 are you ^making a !pr\ofit on `em# /
4 5 18 1510 1 1 b 11 ^n/o# /
4 5 18 1520 1 1 b 20 *(laughs - )* /
4 5 18 1530 1 1 a 11 *^n\/o#* . /
4 5 18 1540 1 1 a 11 ^\oh# /
4 5 18 1550 1 1 b 11 ^never !make a 'profit on ((a)) p/ony# /
4 5 18 1560 1 1 a 11 ^n\o# /
4 5 18 1570 1 1 a 11 I ^th/ought so# /
4 5 18 1580 1 1 a 11 well they ^take up . e!nough . gr\/ass# /
4 5 19 1590 1 1 a 11 ^d\on`t they# . /
4 5 19 1600 1 1 b 11 ^y=es# /
4 5 19 1610 1 1 b 11 ^w=ell# - /
4 5 19 1620 1 1 b 11 ^we just l/ook at them# . /
```

Figure 2.2: Paralinguistic features of spoken language in the LLC

Like the SBCAE, the LLC also indicates overlapping speech (enclosing it in plus signs as in lines 1430 and 1440 or in asterisks, as in lines 1520 and 1530), pauses (a period for a "brief" pause, single hyphen for a pause the length of one "stress unit" and two hyphens for longer pauses), and intonation units, called "tone units" by the corpus creators (with a caret marking the onset and the number sign marking the end).

In addition, however, intonation contours are recorded in detail preceding the vowel of the prosodically most prominent syllable using the equals sign and rightward and leftward slashes: = stands for "level tone", / for "rise", \ for "fall", \/ for "(rise-)fall-rise" and /\ for "(fall-)rise-fall". A colon indicates that the following syllable is higher than the preceding one, an exclamation mark indicates that it is very high. Occasionally, the LLC uses phonetic transcription to indicate an unexpected pronunciation or vocalizations that have no standard spelling (like the `[@:]` in line 1410 which stands for a long schwa).

The two corpora differ in their use of symbols to annotate certain features, for example:

- the LLC indicates overlap by asterisks and plus signs, the SBCSAE by square brackets, which, in turn, are used in the LLC to mark "subordinate tone units" or phonetic transcriptions;
- the LLC uses periods and hyphens to indicate pauses, the SBCSAE uses only periods, with hyphens used to indicate that an intonation unit is truncated;
- intonation units are enclosed by the symbols ^ and # in the LLC and by line breaks in the SBCSAE;
- lengthening is shown by an equals sign in the SBCSAE and by a colon following a vowel in the LLC.

Thus, even where the two corpora *annotate* the same features of speech in the transcriptions, they *code* these features differently.

Such differences are important to understand for anyone working with the these corpora, as they will influence the way in which we have to search the corpus (see further Section 4.1.1 below) – before working with a corpus, one should always read the full manual. More importantly, such differences reflect different, sometimes incompatible theories of what features of spoken language are relevant, and at what level of detail. The SBCSAE and the LLC cannot easily be combined into a larger corpus, since they mark prosodic features at very different levels of detail. The LLC gives detailed information about pitch and intonation contours absent from the SBCSAE; in contrast, the SBCSAE contains information about volume and audible breathing that is absent from the LLC.

Written language, too, has paralinguistic features that are potentially relevant to linguistic research. Consider the excerpt from the LOB corpus in Figure 2.3.

```
A07 94 |^And, of course, 29-year-old Gerry, to whom \0Mme Kilian Hennessy
A07 95 has remained so loyal, will continue to partner him henceforth.
A07 96 |^Problem horse Mossreeba even defied Johnny Gilbert's skill in the
A07 97 Metropolitan Hurdle.
A07 98 **[BEGIN INDENTATION**]
A07 99 |^He struck the front after jumping the last but as Keith Piggott
A07 100 says: ^*"He'll come and beat *1anything, *0 but as soon as he gets his
A07 101 head in front up it goes*- and he doesn't want to know.**"
A07 102 **[END INDENTATION**]
```

Figure 2.3: Paralinguistic features of written language in the LOB corpus

The word *anything* in line 100 was set in italics in the original text; this is indicated by the sequences `*1`, which stands for "begin italic" and `*0`, which stands for "begin lower case (roman)" and thus ends the stretch set in italics. The original text also contained typographic quotes, which are not contained in the ASCII encoding used for the corpus. Thus, the sequence `*"` in line 100 stands for "begin double quotes" and the sequence `**"` in line 101 stands for "end double quotes". ASCII also does not contain the dash symbol, so the sequence `*-` indicates a dash. Finally, paragraph boundaries are indicated by a sequence of three blank spaces followed by the pipe symbol | (as in lines 96 and 99), and more complex text features like indentation are represented by descriptive tags, enclosed in square brackets preceded by two asterisks (as in line 98 and 102, which signal the beginning and end of an indented passage).

Additionally, the corpus contains markup pertaining not to the appearance of the text but to its linguistic properties. For example, the word *Mme* in line 94 is an abbreviation, indicated in the corpus by the sequence `\0` preceding it. This may not seem to contribute important information in this particular case, but it is useful where abbreviations end in a period (as they often do), because it serves to disambiguate such periods from sentence-final ones. Sentence boundaries are also marked explicitly: each sentence begins with a caret symbol ^.

Other corpora (and other versions of the LOB corpus) contain more detailed linguistic markup. Most commonly, they contain information about the word class of each word, represented in the form of a so-called "part-of-speech (or POS) tags". Figure 2.4 shows a passage from the BROWN corpus, where these POS tags take the form of sequences of uppercase letters and symbols, attached to the end of each word by an underscore (for example, `_AT` for articles, `_NN` for singular nouns, `_*` for the negative particle *not*, etc.). Note that sentence boundaries are also marked, in this case by a pipe symbol (used for paragraph boundaries in the LOB) followed by the sequence SN and an id number.

```
|SN12:30 the_AT fact_NN that_CS Jess's_NP\$ horse_NN had_HVD not_*
been_BEN returned_VBN to_IN its_PP\$ stall_NN could_MD indicate_VB
that_CS Diane's_NP\$ information_NN had_HVD been_BEN wrong_JJ ,_,
but_CC Curt_NP didn't_DOD* interpret_VB it_PPO this_DT way_NN ._.
|SN12:31 a_AT man_NN like_CS Jess_NP would_MD want_VB to_TO have_HV
a_AT ready_JJ means_NNS of_IN escape_NN in_IN case_NN it_PPS was_BEDZ
needed_VBN ._.
```

Figure 2.4: Structural features in the BROWN corpus

Other linguistic features that are sometimes recorded in (written and spoken) corpora are the lemmas of each word and (less often) the syntactic structure of the sentences (corpora with syntactic annotation are sometimes referred to as *treebanks*). When more than one variable is annotated in a corpus, the corpus is typically structured as shown in Figure 2.5, with one word per line and different columns for the different types of annotation (more recently, the markup language XML is used in addition to or instead of this format).

Annotations of paralinguistic or linguistic features in a corpus impact its authenticity in complex ways.

On the one hand, including information concerning paralinguistic features makes a corpus more authentic than it would be if this information was simply discarded. After all, this information represents aspects of the original speech events from which the corpus is derived and is necessary to ensure a reconceptualization of the data that approximates these events as closely as possible.

On the other hand, this information is necessarily biased by the interests and theoretical perspectives of the corpus creators. By splitting the spoken corpora into intonation units, for example, the creators assume that there are such units

ID	POS	Word	Lemma	Grammar
N12:0280.42	AT	The	the	[O[S[Ns:s.
N12:0290.03	NN1n	fact	fact	.
N12:0290.06	CST	that	that	[Fn.
N12:0290.09	NP1f	Jess	Jess	[Ns:S[G[Nns.Nns]
N12:0290.12	GG	+<apos>s	-	.G]
N12:0290.15	NN1c	horse	horse	.Ns:S]
N12:0290.18	VHD	had	have	[Vdefp.
N12:0290.21	XX	not	not	.
N12:0290.24	VBN	been	be	.
N12:0290.27	VVNv	returned	return	.Vdefp]
N12:0290.30	IIt	to	to	[P:q.
N12:0290.33	APPGh1	its	its	[Ns.
N12:0290.39	NN1c	stall	stall	.Ns]P:q]Fn]Ns:s]
N12:0290.42	VMd	could	can	[Vdc.
N12:0290.48	VV0t	indicate	indicate	.Vdc]
N12:0300.03	CST	that	that	[Fn:o.
N12:0300.06	NP1f	Diane	Diane	[Ns:s[G[Nns.Nns]
N12:0300.09	GG	+<apos>s	-	.G]
N12:0300.12	NN1u	information	information	.Ns:s]
N12:0300.15	VHD	had	have	[Vdfb.
N12:0300.18	VBN	been	be	.Vdfb]
N12:0300.21	JJ	wrong	wrong	[J:e.J:e]Fn:o]
N12:0300.24	YC	+,	-	.
N12:0300.27	CCB	but	but	[S+.
N12:0300.30	NP1m	Curt	Curt	[Nns:s.Nns:s]
N12:0300.33	VDD	did	do	[Vde.
N12:0300.39	XX	+n<apos>t	not	.
N12:0300.42	VV0v	interpret	interpret	.Vde]
N12:0310.03	PPH1	it	it	[Ni:o.Ni:o]
N12:0310.06	DD1i	this	this	[Ns:h.
N12:0310.09	NNL1n	way	way	.Ns:h]S+]S]
N12:0310.12	YF	+.	-	.

Figure 2.5: Example of a corpus with complex annotation (SUSANNE corpus)

and that they are a relevant category in the study of spoken language. They will also identify these units based on particular theoretical and methodological assumptions, which means that different creators will come to different decisions. The same is true of other aspects of spoken and written language. Researchers using these corpora are then forced to accept the assumptions and decisions of the corpus creators (or they must try to work around them).

This problem is even more obvious in the case of linguistic annotation. There may be disagreements as to how and at what level of detail intonation should be described, for example, but it is relatively uncontroversial that it consists of changes in pitch. In contrast, it is highly controversial how many parts of speech there are and how they should be identified, or how the structure even of simple sentences is best described and represented. Accepting (or working around) the corpus creators' assumptions and decisions concerning POS tags and annotations of syntactic structure may seriously limit or distort researcher's use of corpora.

Also, while it is clear that speakers are at some level aware of intonation, pauses, indentation, roman vs. italic fonts, etc., it is much less clear that they are aware of parts of speech and grammatical structures. Thus, the former play a legitimate role in reconceptualizing authentic speech situations, while the latter arguably do not. Note also that while linguistic markup is often a precondition for an efficient retrieval of data, error in markup may hide certain phenomena systematically (see further Chapter 4, especially Section 4.1.1).

Finally, corpora typically give some information about the texts they contain – so-called *metadata*. These may be recorded in a manual, a separate computer-readable document or directly in the corpus files to which they pertain. Typical metadata are language variety (in terms of genre, medium topic area, etc., as described in Section 2.1.2 above), the origin of the text (for example, speaker/writer, year of production and or publication), and demographic information about the speaker/writer (sex, age, social class, geographical origin, sometimes also level of education, profession, religious affiliation, etc.). Metadata may also pertain to the structure of the corpus itself, like the file names, line numbers and sentence or utterance ids in the examples cited above.

Metadata are also crucial in recontextualizing corpus data and in designing certain kinds of research projects, but they, too, depend on assumptions and choices made by corpus creators and should not be uncritically accepted by researchers using a given corpus.

2.2 Towards a definition of corpus linguistics

Having characterized the linguistic corpus in its ideal form, we can now reformulate the definition of corpus linguistics cited at the beginning of this chapter as follows:

> Definition (First attempt)
> Corpus linguistics is the investigation of linguistic phenomena *on the basis of linguistic corpora.*

This definition is more specific with respect to the data used in corpus linguistics and will exclude certain variants of discourse analysis, text linguistics, and other fields working with authentic language data (whether such a strict exclusion is a good thing is a question we will briefly return to at the end of this chapter).

However, the definition says nothing about the *way* in which these data are to be investigated. Crucially, it would cover a procedure in which the linguistic corpus essentially serves as a giant citation file, that the researcher scours, more or less systematically, for examples of a given linguistic phenomenon.

This procedure of basing linguistic analyses on citations has a long tradition in descriptive English linguistics, going back at least to Otto Jespersen's seven-volume Modern English Grammar on Historical Principles (Jespersen 1909). It played a particularly important role in the context of dictionary making. The Oxford English Dictionary (Simpson & Weiner 1989) is the first and probably still the most famous example of a citation-based dictionary of English. For the first two editions, it relied on citations sent in by volunteers (cf. Winchester 2003 for a popular account). In its current third edition, its editors actively search corpora and other text collections (including the Google Books index) for citations.

A fairly stringent implementation of this method is described in the following passage from the FAQ web page of the Merriam-Webster Online Dictionary:

> Each day most Merriam-Webster editors devote an hour or two to reading a cross section of published material, including books, newspapers, magazines, and electronic publications; in our office this activity is called "reading and marking." The editors scour the texts in search of [...] anything that might help in deciding if a word belongs in the dictionary, understanding what it means, and determining typical usage. Any word of interest is marked, along with surrounding context that offers insight into its form and use. [...] The marked passages are then input into a computer system and stored both in machine-readable form and on 3″× 5″slips of paper to create *citations.* (Merriam-Webster 2014)

The "cross-section of published material" referred to in this passage is heavily skewed towards particular varieties of formal written language. Given that people will typically consult dictionaries to look up unfamiliar words they encounter in writing, this may be a reasonable choice to make, although it should be pointed out that modern dictionaries are often based on more diverse linguistic corpora.

But let us assume, for the moment, that the cross-section of published material read by the editors of Merriam Webster's dictionary counts as a linguistic corpus. Given this assumption, the procedure described here clearly falls under our definition of corpus linguistics. Interestingly, the publishers of Merriam Webster's even refer to their procedure as "study[ing] the language as it's used" (Merriam-Webster 2014), a characterization that is very close to McEnery and Wilson's definition of corpus linguistics as the "study of language based on examples of 'real life' language use".

Collecting citations is perfectly legitimate. It may serve to show that a particular linguistic phenomenon existed at a particular point in time – one reason for basing the OED on citations was and is to identify the first recorded use of each word. It may also serve to show that a particular linguistic phenomenon exists at all, for example, if that phenomenon is considered ungrammatical (as in the case of [*it doesn't matter the* N], discussed in the previous chapter).

However, the method of collecting citations cannot be regarded as a scientific method except for the purpose of proving the existence of a phenomenon, and hence does not constitute corpus linguistics proper. While the procedure described by the makers of Merriam Webster's sounds relatively methodical and organized, it is obvious that the editors will be guided in their selection by many factors that would be hard to control even if one were fully aware of them, such as their personal interests, their sense of esthetics, the intensity with which they have thought about some uses of a word as opposed to others, etc.

This can result in a substantial bias in the resulting data base even if the method is applied systematically, a bias that will be reflected in the results of the linguistic analysis, i.e. the definitions and example sentences in the dictionary. To pick a random example: The word of the day on Merriam-Webster's website at the time of writing is *implacable*, defined as "not capable of being appeased, significantly changed, or mitigated" (Merriam-Webster, sv. implacable). The entry gives two examples for the use of this word (cf. 4a, b), and the word-of-the-day message gives two more (shown in 4c, d in abbreviated form):

(4) a. He has an implacable hatred for his political opponents.

b. an implacable judge who knew in his bones that the cover-up extended to the highest levels of government

c. ...the implacable laws of the universe are of interest to me.

d. Through his audacity, his vision, and his implacable faith in his future success...

Except for *hatred*, the nouns modified by *implacable* in these examples are not at all representative of actual usage. The lemmas most frequently modified by *implacable* in the 450-million-word Corpus of Contemporary American English (COCA) are *enemy* and *foe*, followed at some distance by *force*, *hostility*, *opposition*, *will*, and the *hatred* found in (4a). Thus, it seems that *implacable* is used most frequently in contexts describing adversarial human relationships, while the examples that the editors of the Merriam-Websters selected as typical deal mostly with adversarial abstract forces. Perhaps this distortion is due to the materials the editors searched, perhaps the examples struck the editors as citation-worthy precisely because they are slightly unusual, or because they appealed to them esthetically (they all have a certain kind of rhetorical flourish).[2]

Contrast the performance of the citation-based method with the more strictly corpus-based method used by the Longman Dictionary of English, which illustrates the adjective *implacable* with the representative examples in (5a,b):

(5) a. implacable enemies

b. The government faces implacable opposition on the issue of nuclear waste. (LDCE, s.v. *implacable*)

Obviously, the method of citation collection becomes worse the more opportunistically the examples are collected: the researcher will not only focus on examples that they happen to notice, they may also selectively focus on examples that they intuitively deem particularly relevant or representative. In the worst case, they will consciously perform an introspection-based analysis of a phenomenon and then scour the corpus for examples that support this analysis; we could call this method *corpus-illustrated* linguistics (cf. Tummers et al. 2005). In the case of spoken examples that are overheard and then recorded after the fact, there is an additional problem: researchers will write down what they thought they heard, not what they actually heard.[3]

[2]This kind of distortion means that it is dangerous to base analyses on examples included in citation-based dictionaries; but Mair (cf. 2004), who shows that, given an appropriately constrained research design, the dangers of an unsystematically collected citation base can be circumvented (see Section 8.2.5.3 below).

[3]As anyone who has ever tried to transcribe spoken data, this implicit distortion of data is a problem even where the data is available as a recording: transcribers of spoken data are forever struggling with it. Just record a minute of spoken language and try to transcribe it exactly – you will be surprised how frequently you transcribe something that is similar, but not identical to what is on the tape.

The use of corpus examples for illustrative purposes has become somewhat fashionable among researchers who largely depend on introspective "data" otherwise. While it is probably an improvement over the practice of simply inventing data, it has a fundamental weakness: it does not ensure that the data selected by the researcher are actually representative of the phenomenon under investigation. In other words, corpus-illustrated linguistics simply replaces introspectively *invented* data with introspectively *selected* data and thus inherits the fallibility of the introspective method discussed in the previous chapter.

Since overcoming the fallibility of introspective data is one of the central motivations for using corpora in the first place, the analysis of a given phenomenon must not be based on a haphazard sample of instances that the researcher happened to notice while reading or, even worse, by searching the corpus for specific examples. The whole point of constructing corpora as representative samples of a language or variety is that they will yield representative samples of particular linguistic phenomena in that language or variety. The best way to achieve this is to draw a *complete* sample of the phenomenon in question, i.e. to retrieve all instances of it from the corpus (issues of retrieval are discussed in detail in Chapter 4). These instances must then be analyzed systematically, i.e., according to a single set of criteria. This leads to the following definition (cf. Biber & Reppen 2015: 2, Cook 2003: 78):

> Definition (Second attempt)
> Corpus linguistics is the *complete and systematic* investigation of linguistic phenomena on the basis of linguistic corpora.

As was mentioned in the preceding section, linguistic corpora are currently between one million and half a billion words in size, while web-based corpora can contain up to a trillion words. As a consequence, it is usually impossible to extract a complete sample of a given phenomenon manually, and this has lead to a widespread use of computers and corpus linguistic software applications in the field.[4]

In fact, corpus technology has become so central that it is sometimes seen as a defining aspect of corpus linguistics. One corpus linguistics textbook opens

[4]Note, however, that sometimes manual extraction is the only option – cf. Colleman (2006; 2009), who manually searched a 1-million word corpus of Dutch in order to extract all ditransitive clauses. To convey a rough idea of the work load involved in this kind of manual extraction: it took Colleman ten full work days to go through the entire corpus (Colleman, pers. comm.), which means his reading speed was fairly close to the 200 words typical for an average reader, an impressive feat given that he was scanning the corpus for a particular phenomenon.

with the sentence "The main part of this book consists of a series of case studies which involve the use of corpora and corpus analysis technology" (Partington 1998: 1), and another observes that "[c]orpus linguistics is [...] now inextricably linked to the computer" (Kennedy 1998: 5); a third textbook explicitly includes the "extensive use of computers for analysis, using both automatic and interactive techniques" as one of four defining criteria of corpus linguistics Biber et al. (1998: 4). This perspective is summarized in the following definition:

> Definition (Third attempt, Version 1)
> Corpus linguistics is the investigation of linguistic phenomena *on the basis of computer-readable linguistic corpora using corpus analysis software.*

However, the usefulness of this approach is limited. It is true that there are scientific disciplines that are so heavily dependent upon a particular technology that they could not exist without it – for example, radio astronomy (which requires a radio telescope) or radiology (which requires an x-ray machine). However, even in such cases we would hardly want to claim that the technology in question can serve as a defining criterion: one can use the same technology in ways that do not qualify as belonging to the respective discipline. For example, a spy might use a radio telescope to intercept enemy transmissions, and an engineer may use an x-ray machine to detect fractures in a steel girder, but that does not make the spy a radio astronomer or the engineer a radiologist.

Clearly, even a discipline that relies crucially on a particular technology cannot be defined by the technology itself but by the uses to which it puts that technology. If anything, we must thus replace the reference to corpus analysis software by a reference to what that software typically does.

Software packages for corpus analysis vary in capability, but they all allow us to search a corpus for a particular (set of) linguistic expression(s) (typically word forms), by formulating a *query* using query languages of various degrees of abstractness and complexity, and they all display the results (or *hits*) of that query. Specifically, most of these software packages have the following functions:

1. they produce *KWIC (Key Word In Context) concordances,* i.e. they display the hits for our query in their immediate context, defined in terms of a particular number of words or characters to the left and the right (see Figure 2.6 for a KWIC concordance of the noun *time*) – they are often referred to as *concordancers* because of this functionality;

2. they identify *collocates* of a given expression, i.e. word forms that occur in a certain position relative to the hits; these words are typically listed in the

order of frequency with which they occur in the position in question (see Table 2.4 for a list of collocates of the noun *time* in a span of three words to the left and right);

3. they produce *frequency lists*, i.e. lists of all character strings in a given corpus listed in the order of their frequency of occurrence (see Table 2.5 for the forty most frequent strings (word forms and punctuation marks) in the BNC Baby).

Note that concordancers differ with respect to their ability to deal with annotation – there are few standards in annotation, especially in older corpora and even the emerging XML-based standards, or wide-spread conventions like the column format shown in Figure 2.5 above are not implemented in many of the widely available software packages.

Let us briefly look at why the three functions listed above might be useful in corpus linguistic research (we will discuss them in more detail in later chapters).

A concordance provides a quick overview of the typical usage of a particular (set of) word forms or more complex linguistic expressions. The occurrences are presented in random order in Figure 2.6, but corpus-linguistic software packages typically allow the researcher to sort concordances in various ways, for example, by the first word to the left or to the right; this will give us an even better idea as to what the typical usage contexts for the expression under investigation are.

Collocate lists are a useful way of summarizing the contexts of a linguistic expression. For example, the collocate list in the column marked L1 in Table 2.4 will show us at a glance what words typically directly precede the string *time*. The determiners *the* and *this* are presumably due to the fact that we are dealing with a noun, but the adjectives *first*, *same*, *long*, *some*, *last*, *every* and *next* are related specifically to the meaning of the noun *time*; the high frequency of the prepositions *at*, *by*, *for* and *in* in the column marked L2 (two words to the left of the node word *time*) not only gives us additional information about the meaning and phraseology associated with the word *time*, it also tells us that *time* frequently occurs in prepositional phrases in general.

Finally, frequency lists provide useful information about the distribution of word forms (and, in the case of written language, punctuation marks) in a particular corpus. This can be useful, for example, in comparing the structural properties or typical contents of different language varieties (see further Chapter 10). It is also useful in assessing which collocates of a particular word are frequent only because they are frequent in the corpus in general, and which collocates actually tell us something interesting about a particular word.

Table 2.4: Collocates of *time* in a span of three words to the left and to the right

L3		L2		L1			R1		R2		R3	
for	335	the	851	the	1032		.	950	the	427	.	294
.	322	at	572	this	380		,	661	?	168	,	255
at	292	a	361	first	320		to	351	i	141	the	212
,	227	all	226	of	242		of	258	.	137	to	120
a	170	.	196	same	240		and	223	and	118	a	118
the	130	by	192	a	239		for	190	you	104	it	112
it	121	,	162	long	224		in	184	it	102	was	107
to	100	of	154	some	200		i	177	a	96	and	92
and	89	for	148	last	180		he	136	he	92	i	86
in	89	it	117	every	134		?	122	,	91	you	76
was	85	in	93	in	113		you	120	was	87	in	75
is	78	’s	68	that	111		when	118	had	80	?	71
’s	68	and	65	what	108		the	90	but	70	of	64
have	59			next	83		we	88	to	69	’s	59
that	58			any	72		is	85	?	64	is	59
had	55			one	65		as	78	she	58	?	58
?	52			’s	64		it	70	they	57	he	58
				no	63		they	70	that	56	had	53
				from	57		she	69	in	55		
							that	64				
							was	50				

Table 2.5: The forty most frequent strings in the BNC Baby

.	226 990	that	51 976	on	29 258	do	20 433
,	212 502	you	49 346	n’t	27 672	at	20 164
the	211 148	’s	48 063	be	24 865	not	19 983
of	100 874	is	40 508	with	24 533	had	19 453
to	94 772	?	38 422	as	24 171	we	18 834
and	94 469	was	37 087	have	23 093	are	18 474
a	88 277	‘	36 831	[unclear]	21 879	this	18 393
in	69 121	he	36 217	but	21 209	there	17 585
it	60 647	’	34 994	they	21 177	his	17 447
i	59 827	for	31 784	she	21 121	by	17 201

```
st sight to take an unconscionably long [time] . A common fallacy is the attempt to as
s with Arsenal . ' Graham reckons it 's [time] his side went gunning for trophies agai
ough I did n't , he he , I did n't have [time] to ask him what the hell he 'd been up
was really impressed . I think the last [time] I came I had erm a chicken thing . A ch
 away . No Ann would have him the whole [time] . Yeah well [unclear] Your mum would n'
arch 1921 . He had been unwell for some [time] and had now gone into a state of collap
te the planned population in five years [time] . So what are you gon na multiply that
tempt to make a coding time and content [time] the same ) . 10 Conclusion I have stres
 hearer and for the analyst most of the [time] . Most of the time , things will indeed
in good faith and was reasonable at the [time] it was prepared . The bank gave conside
 he had something on his mind the whole [time] . ' ` Perhaps he was thinking of his wr
ctices of commercial architects because [time] and time again they come up with the go
nyway . ' From then on Augusto , at the [time] an economist with the World Bank , and
This may be my last free night for some [time] . ' ` I do n't think they 'd be in any
 two reasons . Firstly , the passage of [time] provides more and more experience and t
go . The horse was racing for the first [time] for Epsom trainer Roger Ingram having p
imes better and you would do it all the [time] , right Mm I mean basically you say the
ther , we 'll see you in a fortnight 's [time] . ' ` Perhaps then , ' said Viola , who
 granny does it and she 's got loads of [time] . She sits there and does them twice as
 pig , fattened up in woods in half the [time] and costing well under an eighth of the
ike to be [unclear] like that , all the [time] ! Yeah . I said they wo n't bloody lock
es in various biological groups through [time] are most usefully analysed in terms of
 ? Er do you want your dinner at dinner [time] or [unclear] No I do n't know what I 'v
 But they always around about Christmas [time] . My mam reckons that the You can put t
inversion , i.e. of one descriptor at a [time] , but they are generally provided and e
```

Figure 2.6: KWIC concordance (random sample) of the noun *time* (BNC Baby)

Note, for example, that the collocate frequency lists on the right side of the word *time* are more similar to the general frequency list than those on the left side, suggesting that the noun *time* has a stronger influence on the words preceding it than on the words following it (see further Chapter 7).

Given the widespread implementation of these three techniques, they are obviously central to corpus linguistics research, so we might amend the definition above as follows (a similar definition is implied by Kennedy (1998: 244–258)):

> Definition (Third attempt, Version 2)
> Corpus linguistics is the investigation of linguistic phenomena *on the basis of concordances, collocations, and frequency lists.*

Two problems remain with this definition. The first problem is that the requirements of systematicity and completeness that were introduced in the second definition are missing. This can be remedied by combining the second and third definition as follows:

> Definition (Combined second and third attempt)
> Corpus linguistics is the *complete and systematic* investigation of linguistic phenomena on the basis of linguistic corpora *using concordances, collocations, and frequency lists.*

The second problem is that including a list of specific techniques in the definition of a discipline seems undesirable, no matter how central these techniques are. First, such a list will necessarily be finite and will thus limit the imagination of future researchers. Second, and more importantly, it presents the techniques in question as an arbitrary set, while it would clearly be desirable to characterize them in terms that capture the *reasons* for their central role in the discipline.

What concordances, collocate lists and frequency lists have in common is that they are all ways of studying the distribution of linguistic elements in a corpus. Thus, we could define corpus linguistics as follows:

> Definition (Fourth attempt)
> Corpus linguistics is the complete and systematic investigation of the *distribution of linguistic phenomena* in a linguistic corpus.

On the one hand, this definition subsumes the previous two definitions: If we assume that corpus linguistics is essentially the study of the distribution of linguistic phenomena in a linguistic corpus, we immediately understand the central role of the techniques described above: (i) KWIC concordances are a way of displaying the distribution of an expression across different syntagmatic contexts; (ii) collocation tables summarize the distribution of lexical items with respect to other lexical items in quantitative terms, and (iii) frequency lists summarize the overall quantitative distribution of lexical items in a given corpus.

On the other hand, the definition is not limited to these techniques but can be applied open-endedly on all levels of language and to all kinds of distributions. This definition is close to the understanding of corpus linguistics that this book will advance, but it must still be narrowed down somewhat.

First, it must not be misunderstood to suggest that studying the distribution of linguistic phenomena is an end in itself in corpus linguistics. Fillmore (1992: 35) presents a caricature of a corpus linguist who is "busy determining the relative frequencies of the eleven parts of speech as the first word of a sentence versus as the second word of a sentence". Of course, there is nothing intrinsically wrong with such a research project: when large electronically readable corpora and the computing power to access them became available in the late 1950s, linguists became aware of a vast range of stochastic regularities of natural languages that had previously been difficult or impossible to detect and that are certainly worthy of study. Narrowing our definition to this stochastic perspective would give us the following:

> Definition (Fourth attempt, stochastic interpretation)
> Corpus linguistics is the investigation of *the statistical properties of language.*

However, while the statistical properties of language are a worthwhile and actively researched area, they are not the primary object of research in corpus linguistics. Instead, the definition just given captures an important aspect of a discipline referred to as *statistical* or *stochastic natural language processing* (Manning & Schütze 1999 is a good, if somewhat dense introduction to this field).

Stochastic natural language processing and corpus linguistics are closely related fields that have frequently profited from each other (see, e.g., Kennedy 1998: 5); it is understandable, therefore, that they are sometimes conflated (see, e.g., Sebba & Fligelstone 1994: 769). However, the two disciplines are best regarded as overlapping but separate research programs with very different research interests.

Corpus linguistics, as its name suggests, is part of linguistics and thus focuses on linguistic research questions that may include, but are in no way limited to the stochastic properties of language. Adding this perspective to our definition, we get the following:

> Definition (Fourth attempt, *linguistic interpretation*)
> Corpus linguistics is the investigation *of linguistic research questions* based on the complete and systematic analysis of the distribution of linguistic phenomena in a linguistic corpus.

This is a fairly accurate definition, in the sense that it describes the actual practice of a large body of corpus-linguistic research in a way that distinguishes it from similar kinds of research. It is not suitable as a final characterization of corpus linguistics yet, as the phrase "distribution of linguistic phenomena" is still somewhat vague. The next section will explicate this phrase.

2.3 Corpus linguistics as a scientific method

Say we have noticed that English speakers use two different words for the forward-facing window of a car: some say *windscreen*, some say *windshield*. It is a genuinely linguistic question, what factor or factors explain this variation. In line with the definition above, we would now try to determine their distribution in a corpus. Since the word is not very frequent, assume that we combine four corpora that we happen to have available, namely the BROWN, FROWN, LOB and FLOB corpora mentioned in Section 2.1.2 above. We find that *windscreen* occurs 12 times and *windshield* occurs 13 times.

That the two words have roughly the same frequency in our corpus, while undeniably a fact about their distribution, is not very enlightening. If our combined corpus were representative, we could at least conclude that neither of the two words is dominant.

Looking at the grammatical contexts also does not tell us much: both words are almost always preceded by the definite article *the*, sometimes by a possessive pronoun or the indefinite article *a*. Both words occur frequently in the PP [*through* NP], sometimes preceded by a verb of seeing, which is not surprising given that they refer to a type of window. The distributional fact that the two words occur in very similar grammatical contexts is more enlightening: it suggests that we are, indeed, dealing with synonyms. However, it does not provide an answer to the question *why* there should be two words for the same thing.

It is only when we look at the distribution across the four corpora, that we find a possible answer: *windscreen* occurs exclusively in the LOB and FLOB corpora, while *windshield* occurs exclusively in the BROWN and FROWN corpora. The first two are corpora of British English, the second two are corpora of American English; thus, we can hypothesize that we are dealing with dialectal variation. In other words: we had to investigate differences in the distribution of linguistic phenomena *under different conditions* in order to arrive at a potential answer to our research question.

Taking this into account, we can now posit the following final definition of corpus linguistics:

> Definition (Final Version)
> Corpus linguistics is the investigation of linguistic research questions that have been framed *in terms of the conditional distribution of linguistic phenomena* in a *linguistic corpus*.

The remainder of Part I of this book will expand this definition into a guideline for conducting corpus linguistic research. The following is a brief overview.

Any scientific research project begins, obviously, with the choice of an object of research – some fragment of reality that we wish to investigate –, and a research question – something about this fragment of reality that we would like to know.

Since reality does not come pre-packaged and labeled, the first step in formulating the research question involves describing the object of research in terms of *constructs* – theoretical concepts corresponding to those aspects of reality that we plan to include. These concepts will be provided in part by the state of the art in our field of research, including, but not limited to, the specific model(s) that we may choose to work with. More often than not, however, our models will not provide fully explicated constructs for the description of every aspect of the object of research. In this case, we must provide such explications.

In corpus linguistics, the object of research will usually involve one or more aspects of language structure or language use, but it may also involve aspects of our psychological, social or cultural reality that are merely *reflected* in language (a point we will return to in some of the case studies presented in Part II of this book). In addition, the object of research may involve one or more aspects of extralinguistic reality, most importantly demographic properties of the speaker(s) such as geographical location, sex, age, ethnicity, social status, financial background, education, knowledge of other languages, etc. None of these phenomena are difficult to characterize meaningfully as long as we are doing so in very broad terms, but none of them have generally agreed-upon definitions either, and no single theoretical framework will provide a coherent model encompassing all of them. It is up to the researcher to provide such definitions and to justify them in the context of a specific research question.

Once the object of research is properly delineated and explicated, the second step is to state our research question in terms of our constructs. This always involves a relationship between at least two theoretical constructs: one construct, whose properties we want to explain (the *explicandum*), and one construct that we believe might provide the explanation (the *explicans*). In corpus linguistics, the explicandum is typically some aspect of language structure and/or use, while the explicans may be some other aspect of language structure or use (such as the presence or absence of a particular linguistic element, a particular position in a discourse, etc.), or some language external factor (such as the speaker's sex or age, the relationship between speaker and hearer, etc.).

In empirical research, the explicandum is referred to as the *dependent variable* and the explicans as the *independent variable* – note that these terms are actually quite transparent: if we want to explain X in terms of Y, then X must be (potentially) dependent on Y. Each of the variables must have at least two possible *values.* In the simplest case, these values could be the presence vs. the absence of instances of the construct, in more complex cases, the values would correspond to different (classes of) instances of the construct. In the example above, the dependent variable is Word for the Forward-Facing Window of a Car with the values windshield and windscreen; the independent variable is Variety of English with the values british and american (from now on, variables will be typographically represented by small caps with capitalization, their values will be represented by all small caps).[5] The formulation of research questions will be discussed in detail in Chapter 3, Section 3.1.

The third step in a research project is to derive a testable prediction from the hypothesis. Crucially, this involves defining our constructs in a way that allows us to measure them, i.e., to identify them reliably in our data. This process, which is referred to as *operationalization*, is far from trivial, since even well-defined and agreed-upon aspects of language structure or use cannot be straightforwardly read off the data. We will return to operationalization in detail in Chapter 3, Section 3.2.

The fourth step consists in collecting data – in the case of corpus linguistics, in *retrieving* them from a corpus. Thus, we must formulate one or more queries that will retrieve all (or a representative sample of) cases of the phenomenon under investigation. Once retrieved, the data must, in a fifth step, be categorized according to the values of the variables involved. In the context of corpus linguistics, this means *annotating* them according to an annotation scheme containing the operational definitions. Retrieval and annotation are discussed in detail in Chapter 4.

The fifth and final step of a research project consists in evaluating the data with respect to our prediction. Note that in the simple example presented here, the conditional distribution is a matter of all-or-nothing: all instances of *windscreen* occur in the British part of the corpus and all instances of *windshield* occur in the American part. There is a categorical difference between the two words with respect to the conditions under which they occur (at least in our corpora). In

[5]Some additional examples may help to grasp the notion of variables and values. For example, the variable Interruption has two values, presence (an interruption occurs) vs. absence, (no interruption occurs). The variable Sex, in lay terms, also has two values (male vs. female). In contrast, the value of the variable Gender is language dependent: in French or Spanish it has two values (masculine vs. feminine), in German or Russian it has three (masculine vs. feminine vs. neuter) and there are languages with even more values for this variable. The variable Voice has two to four values in English, depending on the way that this construct is defined in a given model (most models of English would see active and passive as values of the variable Voice, some models would also include the middle construction, and a few models might even include the antipassive).

contrast, the two words do not differ at all with respect to the grammatical contexts in which they occur. The evaluation of such cases is discussed in Chapter 3, Section 3.1.2.

Categorical distributions are only the limiting case of a quantitative distribution: two (or more) words (or other linguistic phenomena) may also show *relative* differences in their distribution across conditions. For example, the words *railway* and *railroad* show clear differences in their distribution across the combined corpus used above: *railway* occurs 118 times in the British part compared to only 16 times in the American part, while *railroad* occurs 96 times in the American part but only 3 times in the British part. Intuitively, this tells us something very similar about the words in question: they also seem to be dialectal variants, even though the difference between the dialects is gradual rather than absolute in this case. Given that very little is absolute when it comes to human behavior, it will come as no surprise that gradual differences in distribution will turn out to be much more common in language (and thus, more important to linguistic research) than absolute differences. Chapters 5 and 6 will discuss in detail how such cases can be dealt with. For now, note that both categorical and relative conditional distributions are covered by the final version of our definition.

Note also that many of the aspects that were proposed as defining criteria in previous definitions need no longer be included once we adopt our final version, since they are presupposed by this definition: conditional distributions (whether they differ in relative or absolute terms) are only meaningful if they are based on the complete data base (hence the criterion of *completeness*); conditional distributions can only be assessed if the data are carefully categorized according to the relevant conditions (hence the criterion of *systematicity*); distributions (especially relative ones) are more reliable if they are based on a large data set (hence the preference for large electronically stored corpora that are accessed via appropriate software applications); and often – but not always – the standard procedures for accessing corpora (*concordances, collocate lists, frequency lists*) are a natural step towards identifying the relevant distributions in the first place. However, these preconditions are not self-serving, and hence they cannot themselves form the defining basis of a methodological framework: they are only motivated by the definition just given.

Finally, note that our final definition does distinguish corpus linguistics from other kinds of observational methods, such as text linguistics, discourse analysis, variationist sociolinguistics, etc., but it does so in a way that allows us to recognize the overlaps between these methods. This is highly desirable given that these methods are fundamentally based on the same assumptions as to how language can and should be studied (namely on the basis of authentic instances of language use), and that they are likely to face similar methodological problems.

3 Corpus linguistics as a scientific method

At the end of the previous chapter, we defined corpus linguistics as "the investigation of linguistic research questions that have been framed in terms of the conditional distribution of linguistic phenomena in a linguistic corpus" and briefly discussed the individual steps necessary to conduct research on the basis of this discussion.

In this chapter, we will look in more detail at the logic and practice of formulating and testing research questions (Sections 3.1.1 and 3.1.2). We will then discuss the notion of operationalization in some detail (Section 3.2) before closing with some general remarks about the place of hypothesis testing in scientific research practice (Section 3.3).

3.1 The scientific hypothesis

Broadly speaking, there are two ways in which we can state our research question: first, in the form of an actual *question* such as "Is there a relationship between X and Y?" or "What is the relationship between X and Y?"; second, in the form of a specific *hypothesis* concerning the relationship between two variables, such as "all X are Y" or "X leads to Y".

The first way entails a relatively open-minded approach to our data. We might have some general expectation of what we will find, but we would put them aside and simply start collecting observations and look for patterns. If we find such patterns, we might use them to propose a provisional generalization, which we successively confirm, modify or replace on the basis of additional observations until we are satisfied that we have found the broadest generalization that our data will allow – this will then be the answer to our research question.

This so-called *inductive* approach was famously rejected by the Austrian-British philosopher Karl Popper for reasons that will become clear below, but after a period of disrepute it has been making a strong comeback in many disciplines in recent years due to the increasing availability of massive amounts of data and of tools that can search for correlations in these data within a reasonable time frame (think of the current buzz word "big data"). Such massive amounts of data allow us to take an extremely inductive approach – essentially just asking "What relationships exist in my data?" – and still arrive at reliable generalizations. Of course, matters are somewhat more complex, since, as discussed at the end of the previous chapter, theoretical constructs cannot directly be read off our data. But the fact remains that, used in the right way, inductive research designs have their applications. In corpus linguistics, large amounts of data have been available for some time (as mentioned in the previous chapter, the size even of corpora striving for some kind of balance is approaching half-a-billion words), and inductive approaches are used routinely and with insightful consequences (Sinclair 1991 is an excellent example).

The second way of stating research questions entails a more focused way of approaching our data. We state our hypothesis before looking at any data, and then limit our observations just to those that will help us determine the truth of this hypothesis (which is far from trivial, as we will see presently). This so-called *deductive* approach is generally seen as the standard way of conducting research (at least ideally – actual research by actual people tends to be a bit messier even conceptually).

We will generally take a deductive approach in this book, but it will frequently include inductive (exploratory) excursions, as induction is a often useful in itself (for example, in situations where we do not know enough to state a useful working hypothesis or where our aim is mainly descriptive) or in the context of deductive research (where a first exploratory phase might involve inductive research as a way of generating hypotheses). We will see elements of inductive research in some of the case studies in Part II of this book.

3.1.1 Stating hypotheses

As indicated above, scientific hypotheses are typically statements relating two variables, but in order to understand what makes such statements special, let us take a step back and look at the simpler statement in (1):

(1) The English language has a word for the forward-facing window of a car.

Let us assume, for the moment, that we agree on the existence of something called *car* that has something accurately and unambiguously described by 'forward-facing window', and that we agree on the meaning of "English" and "language X has a word for Y". How could we prove the statement in (1) to be true?

There is only one way: we have to find the word in question. We could, for example, describe the concept Forward-Facing Window of Car to a native speaker or show them a picture of one, and ask them what it is called (a method used in traditional dialectology and field linguistics). Or we could search a corpus for all passages mentioning cars and hope that one of them mentions the forward-facing window; alternatively, we could search for grammatical contexts in which we might expect the word to be used, such as ⟨ `through the NOUN of POSS.PRON car` ⟩ (see Section 4.1 in Chapter 4 on how such a query would have to be constructed). Or we could check whether other people have already found the word, for example by searching the definitions of an electronic dictionary. If we find a word referring to the forward-facing window of a car, we have thereby proven its existence – we have *verified* the statement in (1).

But how could we *falsify* the statment, i.e., how could we prove that English does *not* have a word for the forward-facing window of a car? The answer is simple: we can't. As discussed extensively in Chapter 1, both native-speaker knowledge and corpora are necessarily finite. Thus, if we ask a speaker to tell us what the forward-facing window of car is called and they don't know, this may be because there is no such word, or because they do not know this word (for example, because they are deeply uninterested in cars). If we do not find a word in our corpus, this may be because there is no such word in English, or because the word just happens to be absent from our corpus, or because it does occur in the corpus but we missed it. If we do not find a word in our dictionary, this may be because there is no such word, or because the dictionary-makers failed to include it, or because we missed it (for example, because the definition is phrased so oddly that we did not think to look for it – as in the Oxford English Dictionary, which defines *windscreen* somewhat quaintly as "a screen for protection from the wind, now esp. in front of the driver's seat on a motor-car" (OED, sv. *windscreen*)). No matter how extensively we have searched for something (e.g. a word for a particular concept), the fact that we have not found it does not mean that it does not exist.

The statement in (1) is a so-called "existential statement" (it could be rephrased as "There exists at least one x such that x is a word of English and x refers to the forward-facing window of a car"). Existential statements can (potentially) be verified, but they can never be falsified. Their verifiability depends on a crucial condition hinted at above: that all words used in the statement refer to entities that actually exist and that we agree on what these entities are. Put simply, the statement in (1) rests on a number of additional existential statements, such as

"Languages exist", "Words exist", "At least one language has words", "Words refer to things", "English is a language", etc.

There are research questions that take the form of existential statements. For example, in 2016 the astronomers Konstantin Batygin and Michael E. Brown proposed the existence of a ninth planet (tenth, if you cannot let go of Pluto) in our solar system (Batygin & Brown 2016). The existence of such a planet would explain certain apparent irregularities in the orbits of Kuiper belt objects, so the hypothesis is not without foundation and may well turn out to be true. However, until someone actually finds this planet, we have no reason to believe *or not to believe* that such a planet exists (the irregularities that Planet Nine is supposed to account for have other possible explanations, cf., e.g. Shankman et al. 2017). Essentially, its existence is an article of faith, something that should clearly be avoided in science.[1]

Nevertheless, existential statements play a crucial role in scientific enquiry – note that we make existential statements every time we postulate and define a construct. As pointed out above, the statement in (1) rests, for example, on the statement "Words exist". This is an existential statement, whose precise content depends on how our model defines words. One frequently-proposed definition is that words are "the smallest units that can form an utterance on their own" (Matthews 2014: 436), so "Words exist" could be rephrased as "There is at least one x such that x can form an utterance on its own" (which assumes an additional existential statement defining *utterance*, and so on). In other words, scientific enquiry rests on a large number of existential statements that are themselves rarely questioned as long as they are useful in postulating meaningful hypotheses about our research objects.

But if scientific hypotheses are not (or only rarely) existential statements, what are they instead? As indicated at the end of the previous and the beginning of the current chapter, they are statements postulating *relationships* between constructs, rather than their existence. The minimal model within which such a hypothesis can be stated is visualized schematically in the *cross table* (or *contingency table*) in Table 3.1.

There must be (at least) two constructs, one of which we want to explain (the *dependent* variable), and one which we believe provides an explanation (the *independent* variable). Each variable has (at least) two values. The dimensions of

[1] Which is not to say that existential statements in science cannot lead to a happy ending – consider the case of the so-called *Higgs boson*, a particle with a mass of 125.09 GeV/c^2 and a charge and spin of 0, first proposed by the physicist Peter Higgs and five colleagues in 1964. In 2012, two experiments at the Large Hadron Collider in Geneva finally measured such a particle, thus verifying this hypothesis.

Table 3.1: A contingency table

		Dependent Var.	
		value 1	value 2
Independent Var.	value 1	$IV_1 \cap DV_1$	$IV_1 \cap DV_2$
	value 2	$IV_2 \cap DV_1$	$IV_2 \cap DV_2$

the table represent the variables (with a loose convention to show the values of the independent variable in the table rows and the values of the dependent variables in the table columns, the cells represent all possible *intersections* (i.e., combinations) of their values (these are represented here, and on occasion in the remainder of the book, by the symbol ∩)).

The simplest cases of such hypotheses (in Popper's view, the only legitimate case) are so-called *universal statements*. A text-book example of such a statement is *All swans are white* (Popper 1959), where the two constructs are Animal, with the values swan and non-swan and Color, with the values white and non-white. The hypothesis *All swans are white* amounts to the prediction that the intersection swan ∩ white exists, while the intersection swan ∩ non-white does not exist – it makes no predictions about the other two intersections.

Our speculation concerning the distribution of the words *windscreen* and *windshield*, discussed in the previous chapter, essentially consists of the two universal statements, given in (2) and (3):

(2) All occurrences of the word *windscreen* are British English.
(or, more formally, "For all x, if x is the word *windscreen* then x is (a word of) British English")

(3) All occurrences of the word *windshield* are American English.
(or, more formally, "For all x, if x is the word *windshield* then x is (a word of) American English")

Note that the statements in (2) and (3) could be true or false independently of each other (and note also that we are assuming a rather simple model of English, with British and American English as the only varieties).

How would we test (either one or both of) these hypotheses? Naively, we might attempt to verify them, as we would in the case of existential statements. This attempt would be doomed, however, as Popper (1963) forcefully argues.

If we treat the statements in (2) and (3) analogously to the existential statement in (1), we might be tempted to look for positive evidence only, i.e., for evidence that appears to support the claim. For example, we might search a corpus of British English for instances of *windscreen* and a corpus of American English for instances of *windshield.* As mentioned at the end of the previous chapter, the corresponding quieries will indeed turn up cases of *windscreen* in British English and of *windshield* in American English.

If we were dealing with existential statements, this would be a plausible strategy and the results would tell us, that the respective words exist in the respective variety. However, with respect to the universal statements in (2) and (3), the results tell us nothing. Consider Table 3.2, which is a visual representation of the hypotheses in (2) and (3).

Table 3.2: A contingency table with binary values for the intersections

		Forward-Facing Car Window	
		windscreen	*windshield*
Variety	british	✓	✗
	american	✗	✓

What we would have looked for in our naive attempt to verify our hypotheses are only those cases that *should* exist (i.e., the intersections indicated by checkmarks in Table 3.2). But if we find such examples, this does not tell us anything with respect to (2) and (3): we would get the same result if both words occur in both varieties. As Popper puts it, "[i]t is easy to obtain confirmations, or verifications, for nearly every theory [i.e., hypothesis, A.S.] – if we look for confirmations" (Popper 1963: 36).

Obviously, we also have to look for those cases that should *not* exist (i.e., the intersections indicated by crosses in Table 3.2): the prediction derived from (2) and (3) is that *windscreen* should occur *exclusively* in British English corpora and that *windshield* should occur *exclusively* in American English corpora.

Even if we approach our data less naively and find that our data conform fully to the hypothesized distribution in Table 3.2, there are two reasons why this does not count as verification.

First, the distribution could be due to some difference between the corpora other than the dialectal varieties they represent – it could, for example, be due to stylistic preferences of the authors, or the house styles of the publishing houses whose texts are included in the corpora. There are, after all, only a handful of texts in LOB and BROWN that mention either of the two words at all (three in each corpus).

Second, and more importantly, even if such confounding variables could be ruled out, no amount of data following the distribution in Table 3.2 could ever verify the hypotheses: no matter how many cases of *windscreen* we find in British but not American English and of *windshield* in American but not in British English, we can never conclude that the former *cannot* occur in American or the latter in British English. No matter how many observations we make, we cannot exclude the possibility that our next observation will be of the word *windscreen* in American English or of the word *windshield* in British English. This would be true even if we could somehow look at the entirety of British and American English at any given point in time, because new instances of the two varieties are being created all the time.

In other words, we cannot verify the hypotheses in (2) and (3) at all. In contrast, we only have to find a single example of *windshield* in British or *windscreen* in American English to *falsify* them. Universal statements are a kind of mirror-image of existential statements. We can verify the latter (in theory) by finding the entity whose existence we claim (such as Planet Nine in our solar system or a word for the forward-facing window of a car in English), but we cannot falsify them by *not* finding this entity. In contrast, we can falsify the former (in theory) by finding the intersection of values whose existence we deny (such as non-white swans or the word *windscreen* in American English), but we cannot verify them by finding intersections whose existence we affirm.

Thus, to test a scientific hypothesis, we have to specify cases that should not exist if the hypothesis were true, and then do our best to find such cases. As Popper puts it: "Every 'good' scientific theory is a prohibition: it forbids certain things to happen", and "[e]very genuine *test* of a theory is an attempt to falsify it, or to refute it" (Popper 1963: 36).

The harder we try to find such cases but fail to do so, the more certain we can be that our hypothesis is correct. But no matter how hard we look, we must learn to accept that we can never be absolutely certain: in science, a "fact" is simply a hypothesis that has not yet been falsified. This may seem disappointing, but science has made substantial advances despite (or perhaps because) scientists accept that there is no certainty when it comes to truth. In contrast, a single counterexample will give us the certainty that our hypothesis is false. Incidentally, our attempts to falsify a hypothesis will often turn up evidence that appears to confirm it – for example, the more data we search in an attempt to find examples of the word *windshield* in British English, the more cases of *windscreen* we will come across. It would be strange to disregard this confirming evidence, and even Popper does not ask us to: however, he insists that in order to count as confirming evidence (or "corroborating evidence", as he calls it), it must be the result of “a serious but unsuccessful attempt to falsify the theory” (Popper 1963: 36).

In our example, we would have to take the largest corpora of British and American English we can find and search them for counterexamples to our hypothesis (i.e., the intersections marked by crosses in Table 3.2). As long as we do not find them (and as long as we find corroborating evidence in the process), we are justified in *assuming* a dialectal difference, but we are never justified in claiming to have proven such a difference. Incidentally, we do indeed find such counterexamples in this case if we increase our samples: The 100-million word British National Corpus contains 33 cases of the word *windshield* (as opposed to 451 cases of *windscreen*), though some of them refer to forward-facing windows of aircraft rather than cars; conversely the 450-million-word Corpus of Current American English contains 205 cases of *windscreen* (as opposed to 2909 cases of *windshield*).

3.1.2 Testing hypotheses: From counterexamples to probabilities

We have limited the discussion of scientific hypotheses to the simple case of universal statements so far, and in the traditional Popperian philosophy of science, these are the only statements that truly qualify as scientific hypotheses. In corpus linguistics (and the social sciences more generally), hypotheses of this type are the exception rather than the norm – we are more likely to deal with statements about tendencies (think *Most swans are white* or *Most examples of windscreen are British English*), where the search for counterexamples is not a viable research strategy.

They may, however, inform corpus-based syntactic argumentation (cf. Meurers (2005), Meurers & Müller (2009), Noël (2003) for excellent examples of such studies, cf. also Case Study 8.2.7.1 in Chapter 8), and of course they have played a major role in traditional, intuition-based linguistic argumentation. Thus, a brief discussion of counterexamples will be useful both in its own right and in setting the stage for the discussion of hypotheses concerning tendencies. For expository reasons, I will continue to use the case of dialectal variation as an example, but the issues discussed apply to all corpus-linguistic research questions.

In the case of *windscreen* and *windshield*, we actually find counterexamples once we increase the sample size sufficiently, but there is still an overwhelming number of cases that follow our predictions. What do we make of such a situation?

Take another well-known lexical difference between British and American English: the distilled petroleum used to fuel cars is referred to as *petrol* in British

English and *gasoline* in American English. A search in the four corpora used above yields the frequencies of occurrence shown in Table 3.3.

Table 3.3: *Petrol* vs. *gasoline*

		Distilled Petroleum	
		petrol	*gas*
Variety	british	21	0
	american	1	20

In other words, the distribution is almost identical to that for the words *windscreen* and *windshield* – except for one counterexample, where *petrol* occurs in the American part of the corpus (specifically, in the FROWN corpus). In other words, it seems that our hypothesis is falsified at least with respect to the word *petrol*. Of course, this is true only if we are genuinely dealing with a counterexample, so let us take a closer look at the example in question, which turns out to be from the novel *Eye of the Storm* by Jack Higgins:

(4) He was in Dorking within half an hour. He passed straight through and continued toward Horsham, finally pulling into a petrol station about five miles outside. (Higgins, *Eye of the Storm*)

Now, Jack Higgins is a pseudonym used by the novelist Harry Patterson for some of his novels – and Patterson is British (he was born in Newcastle upon Tyne and grew up in Belfast and Leeds). In other words, his novel was erroneously included in the FROWN corpus, presumably because it was published by an American publisher. Thus, we can discount the counterexample and maintain our original hypothesis. Misclassified data are only one reason to discount a counterexample, other reasons include intentional deviant linguistic behavior (for example, an American speaker may imitate a British speaker or a British speaker may have picked up some American vocabulary on a visit to the United States); a more complex reason is discussed below.

Note that there are two problems with the strategy of checking counterexamples individually to determine whether they are genuine counterexample or not. First, we only checked the example that looked like a counterexample – we did not check all the examples that fit our hypothesis. However, these examples could, of course, also contain cases of misclassified data, which would lead to additional counterexamples. Of course, we could theoretically check all examples, as there are only 42 examples overall. However, the larger our corpus is (and most corpus-linguistic research requires corpora that are much larger than the four million words used here), the less feasible it becomes to do so.

The second problem is that we were lucky, in this case, that the counterexample came from a novel by a well-known author, whose biographical information is easily available. But linguistic corpora do not (and cannot) contain only well-known authors, and so checking the individual demographic data for every speaker in a corpus may be difficult to impossible. Finally, some language varieties cannot be attributed to a single speaker at all – political speeches are often written by a team of speech writers that may or may not include the person delivering the speech, newspaper articles may include text from a number of journalists and press agencies, published texts in general are typically proof-read by people other than the author, and so forth.

Let us look at a more complex example, the words for the (typically elevated) paved path at the side of a road provided for pedestrians. Dictionaries typically tell us, that this is called *pavement* in British English and *sidewalk* in American English, for example, the OALD:

(5) a. pavement *noun* [...]
1 [countable] (*British English*) (*North American English* sidewalk) a flat part at the side of a road for people to walk on [OALD]

b. sidewalk *noun* [...]
(*North American English*) (*British English* pavement) a flat part at the side of a road for people to walk on [OALD]

A query for the two words (in all their potential morphological and orthographic variants) against the LOB and FLOB corpora (British English) and BROWN and FROWN corpora (American English) yields the results shown in Table 3.4.

Table 3.4: *Pavement* vs. *sidewalk*

		Paved roadside path	
		pavement	*sidewalk*
Variety	british	37	4
	american	22	43

In this case, we are not dealing with a single counterexample. Instead, there are four apparent counterexamples where *sidewalk* occurs in British English, and 22 apparent counterexamples where *pavement* occurs in American English.

In the case of *sidewalk*, it seems at least possible that a closer inspection of the four cases in British English would show them to be only apparent counterexamples, due, for example, to misclassified texts. In the case of the 22 cases of *pavement* in American English, this is less likely. Let us look at both cases in turn.

Here are all four examples of *sidewalk* in British English, along with their author and title of the original source as quoted in the manuals of the corresponding corpora:

(6) a. One persistent taxi follows him through the street, crawling by the sidewalk...
(LOB E09: Wilfrid T. F. Castle, *Stamps of Lebanon's Dog River*)

b. "Keep that black devil away from Rusty or you'll have a sick horse on your hands," he warned, and leaped to the wooden sidewalk.
(LOB N07: Bert Cloos, *Drury*)

c. There was a small boy on the sidewalk selling melons.
(FLOB K24: Linda Waterman, *Bad Connection.*)

d. Joe, my love, the snowflakes fell on the sidewalk.
(FLOB K25: Christine McNeill, *The Lesson.*)

Not much can be found about Wilfrid T.F. (Thomas Froggatt) Castle, other than that he wrote several books about postal stamps and about history, including the history of English parish churches, all published by British publishers. There is a deceased estate notice under the name Wilfrid Thomas Froggatt Castle that gives his last address in Somerset (The Stationery Office 1999). If this is the same person, it seems likely that he was British and that (6a) is a genuinely British English use of *sidewalk*.

Bert Cloos is the author of a handful of western novels with titles like *Sangre India*, *Skirmish* and *Injun Blood*. Again, very little can be found out about him, but he is mentioned in the Los Angeles Times from May 2, 1963 (p. 38), which refers to him as "Bert Cloos of Encinitas". Since Encinitas is in California, Bert Cloos may, in fact, be an American author who ended up in the LOB by mistake – but, of course, Brits may also live in California, so there is no way of determining this. Clearly, though, the novels in question are all set in the US, so whether Cloos is American or not, he is presumably using American English in (6b) above.

For the authors of (6c, d), Linda Waterman and Christine McNeill, no biographical information can be found at all. Waterman's story was published in a British student magazine, but this in itself is no evidence of anything. The story is set in Latin America, so there may be a conscious effort to evoke American English.

In McNeill's case there is some evidence that she is British: she uses some words that are typically British, such as *dressing gown* (AmE *(bath)robe*) and *breadbin* (AmE *breadbox*), so it is plausible that she is British. Like Waterman's story, hers was published in a British magazine. Interestingly, however, the scene in which the word is used is set in the United States, so she, too, might be consciously evoking American English. To sum up, we have one example that was likely produced by an American speaker, and three that were likely produced by British speakers, although two of these were probably evoking American English. Which of these examples we may safely discount, however, remains difficult to say.

Turning to *pavement* in American English, it would be possible to check the origin of the speakers of all 22 cases with the same attention to detail, but it is questionable that the results would be worth the time invested: as pointed out, it is unlikely that there are so many misclassified examples in the American corpora.

On closer inspection, however, it becomes apparent that we may be dealing with a different type of exception here: the word *pavement* has additional senses to the one cited in (5a) above, one of which does exist in American English. Here is the remainder of the relevant dictionary entry:

(7) a. 2 [*countable, uncountable*] (*British English*) any area of flat stones on the ground
b. 3 [*uncountable*] (*North American English*) the surface of a road (OALD)

Since neither of these meanings is relevant for the issue of British and American words for pedestrian paths next to a road, they cannot be treated as counterexamples in our context. In other words, we have to look at all hits for *pavement* and annotate them for their appropriate meaning. This in itself is a nontrivial task, which we will discuss in more detail in Chapters 4 and 5. Take the example in (8):

(8) [H]e could see the police radio car as he rounded the corner and slammed on the brakes. He did not bother with his radio – there would be time for that later – but as he scrambled out on the *pavement* he saw the filling station and the public telephone booth … (BROWN L 18)

Even with quite a large context, this example is compatible with a reading of *pavement* as 'road surface' or as 'pedestrian path'. If it came from a British text, we would not hesitate to assign the latter reading, but since it comes from an American text (the novel *Error of Judgment* by the American author George Harmon Coxe), we might lean towards erring on the side of caution and annotate it as 'road surface'. Alas, the side of "caution" here is the side suggested by the very hypothesis we are trying to falsify – we would be basing our categorization circularly on what we are expecting to find in the data.

A more intensive search of novels by American authors in the Google Books archive (which is larger than the BROWN corpus by many orders of magnitude), turns up clear cases of the word *pavement* with the meaning of *sidewalk*, for example, this passage from a novel by American author Mary Roberts Rinehart:

(9) He had fallen asleep in his buggy, and had wakened to find old Nettie drawing him slowly down the main street of the town, pursuing an erratic but homeward course, while the people on the pavements watched and smiled. (Mary Roberts Rinehart, *The Breaking Point*, Ch. 10)

Since this reading exists, then, we have found a counterexample to our hypothesis and can reject it.

But what does this mean for our data from the BROWN corpus – is there really nothing to be learned from this sample concerning our hypothesis? Let us say we truly wanted to err on the side of caution, i.e. on the side that goes *against* our hypothesis, and assign the meaning of *sidewalk* to Coxe's novel too. Let us further assume that we can assign all other uses of *pavement* in the sample to the reading 'paved surface', and that two of the four examples of *sidewalk* in the British English corpus are genuine counterexamples. This would give us the distribution shown in Table 3.5.

Table 3.5: Pavement vs. sidewalk (corrected)

		Paved roadside path	
		pavement	*sidewalk*
Variety	british	37	2
	american	1	43

Given this distribution, would we really want to claim that it is wrong to assign *pavement* to British and *sidewalk* to American English on the basis that there are a few possible counterexamples? More generally, is falsification by counterexample a plausible research strategy for corpus linguistics?

There are several reasons why the answer to this question must be "no". First, we can rarely say with any certainty whether we are dealing with true counterexamples or whether the apparent counterexamples are due to errors in the construction of the corpus or in our classification. This turned out to be surprisingly difficult even with respect to a comparatively straightforward issue like the distribution of vocabulary across major dialectal boundaries. Imagine how much more difficult it would have been with grammatical phenomena. For example, the LOB corpus contains (10a):

(10) a. We must not be rattled into surrender, but we must not – and I am not – be afraid of negotiation. (LOB A05)

b. We must not be rattled into surrender, but we must not be – and I am not – afraid of negotiation. (Macmillan 1961)

There is what seems to be an agreement error in (10a), that is due to the fact that the appositional *and I am not* is inserted before the auxiliary *be*, leading to the ungrammatical *am not be*. But how do we know it is ungrammatical, since it occurs in a corpus? In this case, we are in luck, because the example is quoted from a speech by the former British Prime Minister Harold Macmillan, and the original transcript shows that he actually said (10b). But not every speaker in a corpus is a prime minister, just as not every speaker is a well-known author, so it will not usually be possible to get independent evidence for a particular example. Take (11), which represents a slightly more widespread agreement "error":

(11) It is, however, reported that the tariff on textiles and cars imported from the Common Market are to be reduced by 10 percent. (LOB A15)

Here, the auxiliary *be* should agree with its singular subject *tarrif*, but instead, the plural form occurs. There is no way to find out who wrote it and whether they intended to use the singular form but were confused by the embedded plural NP *textiles and cars* (a likely explanation). Thus, we would have to discard it based on our intuition that it constitutes an error (the LOB creators actually mark it as such, but I have argued at length in Chapter 1 why this would defeat the point of using a corpus in the first place), or we would have to accept it as a counterexample to the generalization that singular subjects take singular verbs (which we are unlikely to want to give up based on a single example).

In theoretical terms, this may not be a definitive argument against the idea of falsification by counterexample. We could argue that we simply have to make sure that there are no errors in the construction of our corpus and that we have to classify all hits correctly as constituting a genuine counterexample or not. However, in actual practice this is impossible. We can (and must) try to minimize errors in our data and our classification, but we can never get rid of them completely (this is true not only in corpus-linguistics but in any discipline).

Second, even if our data and our classification were error-free, human behavior is less deterministic than the physical processes Popper had in mind when he elevated counterexamples to the sole acceptable evidence in science. Even in a simple case like word choice, there may be many reasons why a speaker may produce an exceptional utterance – evoking a variety other than their own (as in the examples above), unintentionally or intentionally using a word that they would not normally use because their interlocutor has used it, temporarily slipping into a variety that they used to speak as a child but no longer do, etc. With more complex linguistic behavior, such as producing particular grammatical structures, there will be additional reasons for exceptional behavior: planning errors, choosing a different formulation in mid-sentence, tiredness, etc. – all the kinds of things classified as performance errors in traditional grammatical theory.

In other words, our measurements will never be perfect and speakers will never behave perfectly consistently. This means that we cannot use a single counterexample (or even a handful of counterexamples) as a basis for rejecting a hypothesis, *even if that hypothesis is stated in terms of a universal statement.*

However, as pointed out above, many (if not most) hypotheses in corpus linguistics do not take the form of universal statements ("All X's are Y", "Z's always do Y", etc.), but in terms of tendencies or preferences ("X's tend to be Y", "Z's prefer Y", etc.). For example, there are a number of prepositions and/or adverbs in English that contain the morpheme *-ward* or *-wards*, such as *afterward(s)*, *backward(s)*, *downward(s)*, *inward(s)*, *outward(s)* and *toward(s)*. These two morphemes are essentially allomorphs of a single suffix that are in free variation: they have the same etymology (*-wards* simply includes a lexicalized genitive ending), they have both existed throughout the recorded history of English and there is no discernible difference in meaning between them. However, many dictionaries claim that the forms ending in *-s* are *preferred* in British English and the ones without the *-s* are *preferred* in American English.

We can turn this claim into a hypothesis involving two variables (Variety and Suffix Variant), but not one of the type "All x are y". Instead, we would have to state it along the lines of (12) and (13):

(12) Most occurrences of the suffix *-wards* are British English.

(13) Most occurrences of the suffix *-ward* are American English.

Clearly, counterexamples are irrelevant to these statements. Finding an example like (14a) in a corpus of American English does not disprove the hypothesis that the use in (14b) would be preferred or more typical:

(14) a. [T]he tall young buffalo hunter pushed open the swing doors and walked *towards* the bar. (BROWN N)

b. Then Angelina turned and with an easy grace walked *toward* the kitchen. (BROWN K)

Instead, we have to state our prediction in relative terms. Generally speaking, we should expect to find more cases of *-wards* than of *-ward* in British English and more of *-ward* than of *-wards* in American English, as visualized in Table 3.6 (where the circles of different sizes represent different frequencies of occurrence).

Table 3.6: A contingency table with graded values for the intersections

		Suffix Variant	
		-ward	*-wards*
Variety	british	∘	○
	american	○	∘

We will return to the issue of how to phrase predictions in quantitative terms in Chapter 5. Of course, phrasing predictions in quantitative terms raises additional questions: How large must a difference in quantity be in order to count as evidence in favor of a hypothesis that is stated in terms of *preferences* or *tendencies*? And, given that our task is to try to falsify our hypothesis, how can this be done if counterexamples cannot do the trick? In order to answer such questions, we need a different approach to hypothesis testing, namely *statistical hypothesis testing*. This approach will be discussed in detail in Chapter 6.

There is another issue that we must turn to first, though – that of defining our variables and their values in such a way that we can identify them in our data. We saw even in the simple cases discussed above that this is not a trivial matter. For example, we defined American English as "the language occurring in the BROWN and FROWN corpora", but we saw that the FROWN corpus contains at least one misclassified text by a British author, and we also saw that it is questionable to assume that all and only speakers of American English produce the language we would want to call "American English" (recall the uses of *sidewalk* by British speakers). Thus, nobody would want to claim that our definition accurately reflects linguistic reality. Similarly, we assumed that it was possible, in principle, to recognize which of several senses of a word (such as *pavement*) we are dealing with in a given instance from the corpus; we saw that this assumption runs into difficulties very quickly, raising the more general question of how to categorize instances of linguistic phenomena in corpora. These are just two examples of the larger problem of *operationalization*, to which we will turn in the next section.

3.2 Operationalization

The discussion so far has shown some of the practical challenges posed even by a simple construct like VARIETY with seemingly obvious values such as BRITISH and AMERICAN. However, there is a more fundamental, and more challenging issue to consider: As hinted at in Section 3.1.1, we are essentially making (sets of) existential statements when we postulate such constructs. All examples discussed above simply assumed the existence of something called "British English" and "American English", concepts that in turn presuppose the existence of something called "English" and of the properties "British" and "American". But if we claim the existence of these constructs, we must define them; what is more, we must define them in a way that enables us (and others) to find them in the real world (in our case, in samples of language use). We must provide what is referred to as *operational* definitions.

3.2.1 Operational definitions

Put simply, an operational definition of a construct is an explicit and unambiguous description of a set of operations that are performed to identify and measure that construct. This makes operational definitions fundamentally different from our every-day understanding of what a definition is.

Take an example from physics, the property HARDNESS. A typical dictionary definition of the word *hard* is the following (the abbreviations refer to dictionaries, see Study Notes to the current chapter):

(15) **1** FIRM TO TOUCH firm, stiff, and difficult to press down, break, or cut [≠ soft] (LDCE, s.v. *hard*, cf. also the virtually identical definitions in CALD, MW and OALD)

This definition corresponds quite closely to our experiential understanding of what it means to be *hard*. However, for a physicist or an engineer interested in the hardness of different materials, it is not immediately useful: *firm* and *stiff* are simply loose synonyms of *hard*, and *soft* is an antonym – they do not help in understanding hardness, let alone in finding hardness in the real world. The remainder of the definition is more promising: it should be possible to determine the hardness of a material by pressing it down, breaking or cutting it and noting how difficult this is. However, before, say, "pressing down" can be used as an operational definition, at least three questions need to be asked: first, what type of object is to be used for pressing (what material it is made of and what shape it has); second, how much pressure is to be applied; and third, how the "difficulty" of pressing down is to be determined.

There are a number of hardness tests that differ mainly along the answers they provide to these questions (cf. Herrmann (2011) and Wiederhorn et al. (2011) for a discussion of hardness tests). One commonly used group of tests is based on the size of the indentation that an object (the "indenter") leaves when pressed into some material. One such test is the *Vickers Hardness Test*, which specifies the indenter as a diamond with the shape of a square-based pyramid with an angle of 136°, and the test force as ranging between or 49.3 to 980.7 newtons (the exact force must be specified every time a measurement is reported). *Hardness* is then defined as follows (cf. Herrmann 2011: 43):

(16) $$\mathrm{HV} = \frac{0.102 \times F}{A}$$

F is the load in newtons, A is the surface of the indentation, and 0.102 is a constant that converts newtons into kilopond (this is necessary because the Vickers Hardness Test used to measure the test force in kilopond before the newton became the internationally recognized unit of force).

Unlike the dictionary definition quoted above, *Vickers Hardness (HV)* is an operational definition of hardness: it specifies a procedure that leads to a number representing the hardness of a material. This operational definition is partly motivated by our experiential understanding of hardness in the same way as (part of) the dictionary definition ("difficult to press down"), but in other aspects, it is arbitrary. For example, one could use indenters that differ in shape or material, and indeed there are other widely used tests that do this: the *Brinell Hardness Test* uses a hardmetal ball with a diameter that may differ depending on the material to be tested, and the *Knoop Hardness Test* uses a diamond indenter with a rhombic-based pyramid shape. One could also use a different measure of "difficulty of pressing down": for example, some tests use the rebound energy of an object dropped onto the material from a particular height.

Obviously, each of these tests will give a different result when applied to the same material, and some of them cannot be applied to particular materials (for example, materials that are too flexible for the indenter to leave an indentation, or materials that are so brittle that they will fracture during testing). More crucially, none of them attempt to capture the "nature" of hardness; instead, they are meant to turn *hardness* into something that is close enough to our understanding of what it means to be *hard*, yet at the same time reliably measurable.

Take another example: in psychiatry, it is necessary to identify mental disorders in order to determine what (if any) treatment may be necessary for a given patient. But clearly, just like the hardness of materials, mental disorders are not directly accessible. Consider, for example, the following dictionary definition of *schizophrenia*:

(17) a serious mental illness in which someone cannot understand what is real and what is imaginary [CALD, s.v. *schizophrenia*, see again the very similar definitions in LDCE, MW and OALD].

Although matters are actually substantially more complicated, let us assume that this definition captures the essence of schizophrenia. As a basis for diagnosis, it is useless. The main problem is that "understanding what is real" is a mental process that cannot be observed or measured directly (a second problem is that everyone may be momentarily confused on occasion with regard to whether something is real or not, for example, when we are tired or drunk).

In psychiatry, mental disorders are therefore operationally defined in terms of certain behaviors. For example, the fourth edition of the *Diagnostic and Statistical Manual of Mental Disorders* (DSM-IV), used by psychiatrists and psychologists in the United States to diagnose schizophrenia, classifies an individual as schizophrenic if they (i) display at least two of the following symptoms: "delusions", "hallucinations", "disorganized speech", "grossly disorganized or catatonic behavior" and "affective flattening", "poverty of speech" or "lack of motivation"; and if they (ii) function "markedly below the level achieved prior to the onset" in areas "such as work, interpersonal relations, or self-care"; and if (iii) these symptoms can be observed over a period of at least one month and show effects over a period of at least six months; and if (iv) similar diagnoses (such as schizoaffective disorder) and substance abuse and medication can be ruled out (APA 2000).

This definition of schizophrenia is much less objective than that of physical hardness, which is partly due to the fact that human behavior is more complex and less comprehensively understood than the mechanical properties of materials, and partly due to the fact that psychology and psychiatry are less mature disciplines than physics. However, it is an operational definition in the sense that it effectively presents a check-list of observable phenomena that is used to determine the presence of an unobservable phenomenon. As in the case of hardness tests, there is no single operational definition – the *International Statistical Classification of Diseases and Related Health Problems* used by European psychologists and psychiatrists offers a different definition that overlaps with that of the DSM-IV but places more emphasis on (and is more specific with respect to) mental symptoms and less emphasis on social behaviors.

As should have become clear, operational definitions do not (and do not attempt to) capture the "essence" of the things or phenomena they define. We cannot say that the Vickers Hardness number "is" hardness or that the DSM-IV list of symptoms "is" schizophrenia. They are simply ways of measuring or diagnosing these phenomena. Consequently, it is pointless to ask whether operational definitions are "correct" or "incorrect" – they are simply useful in a particular context. However, this does not mean that any operational definition is as good as any other. A good operational definition must have two properties: it must be *reliable* and *valid.*

A definition is *reliable* to the degree that different researchers can use it at different times and all get the same results; this objectivity (or at least intersubjectivity) is one of the primary motivations for operationalization in the first place. Obviously, the reliability of operational definitions will vary depending on the degree of subjective judgment involved: while *Vickers Hardness* is extremely reliable, depending only on whether the apparatus is in good working order and the procedure is followed correctly, the DSM-IV definition of *schizophrenia* is much less reliable, depending, to some extent irreducibly, on the opinions and experience of the person applying it. Especially in the latter case it is important to test the reliability of an operational definition empirically, i.e. to let different people apply it and see to what extent they get the same results (see further Chapter 4).

A definition is *valid* to the degree that it actually measures what it is supposed to measure. Thus, we assume that there are such phenomena as "hardness" or "schizophrenia" and that they may be more or less accurately captured by an operational definition. Validity is clearly a very problematic concept: since phenomena can only be measured by operational definitions, it would be circular to assess the quality of the same definitions on the basis of these measures. One indirect indication of validity is consistency (e.g., the phenomena identified by the definition share a number of additional properties not mentioned in the definition), but to a large extent, the validity of operationalizations is likely to be assessed on the basis of plausibility arguments. The more complex and the less directly accessible a construct is, the more problematic the concept of validity becomes: While everyone would agree that there is such a thing as HARDNESS, this is much less clear in the case of SCHIZOPHRENIA: it is not unusual for psychiatric diagnoses to be reclassified (for example, what was *Asperger's syndrome* in the DSM-IV became part of *autism spectrum disorder* in the DSM-V) or to be dropped altogether (as was the case with *homosexuality*, which was treated as a mental disorder by the DSM-II until 1974). Thus, operational definitions may *create* the construct they are merely meant to measure; it is therefore important to keep in mind that even a construct that has been operationally defined is still just a construct, i.e. part of a theory of reality rather than part of reality itself.

3.2.2 Examples of operationalization in corpus linguistics

Corpus linguistics is no different from other scientific disciplines: it is impossible to conduct any corpus-based research without operational definitions. However, this does not mean that researchers are necessarily aware that this is what they are doing. In corpus-based research, we find roughly three different situations:

1. operational definitions may already be part of the corpus and be accepted (more or less implicitly) by the researcher, as is frequently the case with tokenization (which constitutes an operational definition of *token* that presupposes a particular theory of what constitutes a word), or with part-of-speech tagging (which constitutes an operational definition of word classes), but also with metadata, including the corpus design itself (which typically constitutes a series of operational definitions of language varieties);

2. operational definitions may remain completely implicit, i.e. the researcher simply identifies and categorizes phenomena on the basis of their (professional but unspoken) understanding of the subject matter without any indication as to how they proceeded;

3. operational definitions and the procedure by which they have been applied may be explicitly stated.

There may be linguistic phenomena, whose definition is so uncontroversial that it seems justified to simply assume and/or apply it without any discussion at all – for example, when identifying occurrences of a specific word like *sidewalk*. But even here, it is important to state explicitly which orthographic strings were searched for and why. As soon as matters get a little more complex, implicitly applied definitions are unacceptable because unless we state exactly how we identified and categorized a particular phenomenon, nobody will be able to interpret our results correctly, let alone reproduce or replicate them or transfer them to a different set of data.

For example, the English possessive construction is a fairly simple and uncontroversial grammatical structure. In written English it consists either of the sequence [NOUN_1 + ' + *s* + zero or more ADJECTIVEs + NOUN_2] (where the entire noun phrase that includes NOUN_1 is part of the construction) , or [NOUN_1 + ' + zero or more ADJECTIVEs + NOUN_2] (if the noun ends in s and is not a surname), or [POSS. PRONOUN + zero or more ADJECTIVEs + NOUN]. These sequences seem easy enough to identify in a corpus (or in a list of hits for appropriately constructed queries), so a researcher studying the possessive may not even mention how they defined this construction. The following examples show that matters are more complex, however:

(18) a. We are a *women's college*, one of only 46 *women's colleges* in the United States and Canada (womenscollege.du.edu)

b. That wasn't too far from Fifth Street, and should allow him to make *Scotty's Bar* by midnight. (BROWN L05)

c. *My Opera* was the virtual community for Opera web browser users. (Wikipedia, s.v. *My Opera*)

d. 'Oh *my God*!' she heard Mike mutter under his breath, and she laughed at his discomfort. (BNC HGM)

e. The following day she caught an early train from *King's Cross* station and set off on the two-hundred-mile journey north. (BNC JXT)

f. The true tack traveller would spend *his/her honeymoon* in a motel, on a heart-shaped water bed. (BNC AAV)

While all of these cases have the form of the possessive construction and match the strings above, opinions may differ on whether they should be included in a sample of English possessive constructions. Example (18a) is a so-called *possessive compound*, a lexicalized possessive construction that functions like a conventional compound and could be treated as a single word. In examples (18b and c), the possessive construction is a proper name. Concerning the latter: if we want to include it, we would have to decide whether also to include proper names where possessive pronoun and noun are spelled as a single word, as in *MySpace* (the name of an online social network now lost in history). Example (18d) is similar in that *my God* is used almost like a proper name; in addition, it is part of a fixed phrase. Example (18e) is a geographical name; here, the problem is that such names are increasingly spelled without an apostrophe, often by conscious decisions by government institutions (see Swaine 2009; Newman 2013). If we want to include them, we have to decide whether also to include spellings without the apostrophe (such as 19), and how to find them in the corpus:

(19) His mother's luggage had arrived at *Kings Cross* Station in London, and of course nobody collected it. (BNC H9U)

Finally, (18f) is a regular possessive construction, but it contains two pronouns separated by a slash; we would have to decide whether to count these as one or as two cases of the construction.

These are just some of the problems we face even with a very simple grammatical structure. Thus, if we were to study the possessive construction (or any other structure), we would have to state precisely which potential instances of a structure we include. In other words, our operational definition needs to include a list of cases that may occur in the data together with a statement of whether – and why – to include them or not.

Likewise, it may be plausible in certain contexts to use operational definitions already present in the data without further discussion. If we accept graphemic or even orthographic representations of language (which corpus linguists do, most of the time), then we also accept some of the definitions that come along with orthography, for example concerning the question what constitutes a word. For many research questions, it may be irrelevant whether the orthographic word correlates with a linguistic word in all cases (whether it does depends to a large extent on the specific linguistic model we adopt), so we may simply accept this correspondence as a pre-theoretical fact. But there are research questions, for example concerning the mean length of clauses, utterances, etc., where this becomes relevant and we may have to define the notion of word in a different way. At the very least, we should acknowledge that we are accepting a graphemic or orthographic definition despite the fact that it may not have a linguistic basis.

Similarly, there may be situations where we simply accept the part-of-speech tagging or the syntactic annotation in a corpus, but given that there is no agreed-upon theory of word classes, let alone of syntactic structures, this can be problematic in some situations. At the very least, it is crucial to understand that tagging and other kinds of annotation are the result of applying operational definitions by other researchers and if we use tags or other forms of annotation, we must familiarize ourselves with these definitions by reading the fine manuals that typically accompany the corpus. These manuals and other literature provided by corpus creators must be read and cited like all other literature, and we must clarify in the description of our research design why and to what extent we rely on the operationalizations described in these materials.

Let us look at five examples of frequently used corpus linguistic operationalizations that demonstrate various aspects of the issues sketched out above.

3.2.2.1 Parts of speech

Let us begin with a brief discussion of tokenization and part-of-speech (POS) tagging, two phenomena whose operational definitions are typically decided on and applied by the corpus makers and implicitly accepted by the researchers using a corpus. We saw an example of POS tagging in Figure 2.4 in Chapter 2, but let us look at examples from different corpora. Examples (20a–c) are taken from the BROWN, LOB and FROWN corpora, which share a common corpus design in order to be used comparatively, examples (20d) is from the British National Corpus (the POS tags are shown separated from the word by a slash for consistency, they are encoded in the actual corpora in very different ways):

(20) a. `a/AT young/JJ man/NN doesn't/DOZ* like/VB to/TO be/BE driven/VBN up/RP in/IN front/NN of/IN a/AT school/NN in/IN a/AT car/NN driven/VBN by/IN a/AT girl/NN who/WPS isn't/BEZ* even/RB in/IN a/AT higher/JJR class/NN than/CS he/PPS is/BEZ ,/, and/CC is/BEZ also/RB a/AT girl/NN ./.` (BROWN A30)

b. `none/PN of/IN these/DTS wines/NNS should/MD cost/VB much/RB over/RB 8/CD s/NNU per/IN bottle/NN ,/, but/CC do/DO n't/XNOT roast/VB them/PP3OS in/IN front/IN" of/IN" the/ATI fire/NN ./.` (LOB E19)

c. `Someone/PN1 had/VVHD to/TO give/VVI Marie/NP1 a/AT1 hand/NN1 down/RP ,/YCOM but/CCB she/PPHS1 did/VADD n't/XX feel/VVI like/II asking/VVG for/IF help/NN1 in/II31 front/II32 of/II33 the/AT still/JJ assembled/JJ press/NN1 ./YSTP` (FLOB P26)

d. `What/DTQ I/PNP feel/VVB you/PNP are/VBB saying/VVG to/PRP me/PNP is/VBZ that/CJT this/DT0 previous/AJ0 relationship/NN1 is/VBZ something/PNI you/PNP do/VDB n't/XX0 want/VVI to/TO0 talk/VVI about/PRP in/PRP front/NN1 of/PRF Tom/NP0 ./PUN` (BNC CB8)

Note that each corpus has its own set of POS tags (called a *tagset*), i.e., its own theory of word classes. In some cases, this is merely a matter of labels. For example, all tagsets have the word class "uninflected adjective", but it is labeled `JJ` in BROWN and FLOB and `AJ0` in the BNC; all corpora seem to recognize the word-class "infinitive marker" (with only one member, *to*), but it is labeled `TO` in BROWN and FLOB, and `TO0` in the BNC; all corpora seem to make a difference between auxiliaries like *be* and *do* and other verbs, but the label for *do* is `DO` in BROWN and LOB, `VAD...` in FROWN and `VD...` in the BNC. The ellipsis in these tags indicates that additional letters may follow to distinguish subcategories, such as tense. Again, the corpora seem to recognize the same subcategories: for example, third person forms are signaled by a `Z` in BROWN and the BNC.

In other cases, the categories themselves differ. For example, in BROWN, all prepositions are labeled `IN`, while the BNC distinguishes *of* from other prepositions by labeling the former `PRF` and the latter `PRP`; FLOB has a special tag for the preposition *for*, `IF`; LOB labels all coordinating conjunctions `CC`, FLOB has a special tag for *BUT*, `CCB`. More drastically, LOB and FLOB treat some sequences of orthographic words as multi-word tokens belonging to a single word class: *in front of* is treated as a preposition in LOB and FLOB, indicated by labeling all three words `IN` (LOB) and `II` (FLOB), with an additional indication that they are part of a sequence: LOB attaches straight double quotes to the second and third word, FLOB adds a `3` to indicate that they are part of a three word sequence and then a number indicating their position in the sequence. Such tag sequences, called *ditto tags* make sense only if you believe that the individual parts in a multi-word expression lose their independent word-class membership. Even then, we have to check very carefully, which particular multi-word sequences are treated like this and decide whether we agree. The makers of BROWN and the BNC obviously had a more traditional view of word classes, simply treating *in front of* as a sequence of a preposition, a noun, and another preposition (BROWN) or specifically the subcategory *of* (BNC).

Ditto tags are a way of tokenizing the corpus at orthographic word boundaries while allowing words to span more than one token. But tokenization itself also differs across corpora. For example, BROWN tokenizes only at orthographic word boundaries (white space or punctuation), while the other three corpora also tokenize at clitic boundaries. They all treat the *n't* in words like `don't`, `doesn't`, etc. as separate tokens, labeling it `XNOT` (LOB), `XX` (FLOB) and `XX0` (BNC), while BROWN simply indicates that a word contains this clitic by attaching an asterisk to the end of the POS tag (other clitics, like *'ll*, *'s*, etc. are treated similarly).

It is clear, then, that tokenization and part-of-speech tagging are not inherent in the text itself, but are the result of decisions by the corpus makers. But in what sense can these decisions be said to constitute operational definitions? There are two different answers to this question. The first answer is that the theories of tokenization and word classes are (usually) explicitly described in the corpus manual itself or in a guide as to how to apply the tag set. A good example of the latter is Santorini (1990), the most-widely cited tagging guideline for the PENN tagset developed for the PENN treebank but now widely used.

As an example, consider the instructions for the POS tags `DT` and `JJ`, beginning with the former:

> **Determiner – DT** This category includes the articles *a(n), every, no* and *the*, the indefinite determiners *another, any* and *some, each, either* (as in *either way*), *neither* (as in *neither decision*), *that, these, this* and *those*, and instances of *all* and *both* when they do not precede a determiner or possessive pronoun (as in *all roads* or *both times*). (Instances of *all* or *both* that do precede a determiner or possessive pronoun are tagged as predeterminers (PDT).) Since any noun phrase can contain at most one determiner, the fact that *such* can occur together with a determiner (as in *the only such case*) means that it should be tagged as an adjective (JJ), unless it precedes a determiner, as in *such a good time*, in which case it is a predeterminer (PDT). (Santorini 1990: 2)

The instructions rely to some extent on undefined categories (such as *article, indefinite determiner*, etc.). In the case of a closed class like "determiners", they get around the need to define them by listing their members. In the case of open-class items like "adjectives", this is not possible, so it is assumed that the annotator knows what the corpus makers mean and the instruction only lists two special cases that might cause confusion:

> **Adjective – JJ** Hyphenated compounds that are used as modifiers are tagged as adjectives (JJ).
>
> EXAMPLES: happy-go-lucky/JJ one-of-a-kind/JJ run-of-the-mill/JJ
>
> Ordinal numbers are tagged as adjectives (JJ), as are compounds of the form *n-th X-est*, like *fourth-largest.* (Santorini 1990: 1)

Note that special cases are also listed in the definition of `DT`, which contains a discussion of grammatical contexts under which the words listed at the beginning of the definition should instead be tagged as predeterminers (`PDT`) or adjectives (`JJ`). There is also an entire section in the tagging guidelines that deals with special, exceptional or generally unclear cases, as an example, consider the passage distinguishing uses of certain words as conjunctions (`CC`) and determiners (`DT`):

> **CC or DT** When they are the first members of the double conjunctions *both ... and, either ... or* and *neither ... nor, both, either* and *neither* are tagged as coordinating conjunctions (CC), not as determiners (DT).

> EXAMPLES: Either/DT child could sing.
>
> But:
>
> Either/CC a boy could sing or/CC a girl could dance.
>
> Either/CC a boy or/CC a girl could sing.
>
> Either/CC a boy or/CC girl could sing.
>
> Be aware that *either* or *neither* can sometimes function as determiners (DT) even in the presence of *or* or *nor*. EXAMPLE: Either/DT boy or/CC girl could sing. (Santorini 1990: 7)

The mixture of reliance on generally accepted terminology, word lists and illustrations is typical of tagging guidelines (and, as we saw in Section 3.2, of annotation schemes in general). Nevertheless, such tagging guidelines can probably be applied with a relatively high degree of interrater reliability (although I am not aware of a study testing this), but they require considerable skill and experience (try to annotate a passage from your favorite novel or a short newspaper article to see how quickly you run into problems that require some very deep thinking).

However, POS tagging is not usually done by skilled, experienced annotators, bringing us to the second, completely different way in which POS tags are based on operational definitions. The usual way in which corpora are annotated for parts of speech is by processing them using a specialized software application called *tagger* (a good example is the Tree Tagger (Schmid 1994), which can be downloaded, studied and used relatively freely).

Put simply, these taggers work as follows: For each word, they take into account the probabilities with which the word is tagged as `A`, `B`, `C`, etc., and the probability that a word tagged as `A`, `B`, `C` should occur at this point given the tag assigned to the preceding word. The tagger essentially multiplies both probabilities and then chooses the tag with the highest joint probability. As an example, consider the word *cost* in (20b), the beginning of which I repeat here:

(21) `none/PN of/IN these/DTS wines/NNS should/MD cost/VB much/RB over/RB 8/CD s/NNU per/IN bottle/NN`

The wordform *cost* has a probability of 0.73 (73 percent) of representing a noun and a probability of 0.27 (27 percent) of representing a verb. If the tagger simply went by these probabilities, it would assign the tag `NN`. However, the probability that modal verb is followed by a noun is 0.01 (1 percent), while the probability that it is followed by a verb is 0.8 (80 percent). The tagger now multiplies the probabilities for *noun* ($0.73 \times 0.01 = 0.0072$) and for *verb* ($0.27 \times 0.8 = 0.216$). Since the latter is much higher, the tagger will tag the word (correctly, in this case, as a verb).

But how does the tagger know these probabilities? It has to "learn" them from a corpus that has been annotated by hand by skilled, experienced annotators based on a reliable, valid annotation scheme. Obviously, the larger this corpus, the more accurate the probabilities, the more likely that the tagger will be correct. I will return to this point presently, but first, note that in corpora which have been POS tagged automatically, the tagger itself and the probabilities it uses are the operational definition. In terms of reliability, this is a good thing: If we apply the same tagger to the same text several times, it will give us the same result every time.

In terms of validity, this is a bad thing in two ways: first, because the tagger assigns tags based on learned probabilities rather than definitions. This is likely to work better in some situations than in others, which means that incorrectly assigned tags will not be distributed randomly across parts of speech. For example, *the* is unlikely to be tagged incorrectly, as it is always a determiner, but *that* is more likely to be tagged incorrectly, as it is a conjunction about two thirds of the time and a determiner about one third of the time. Likewise, *horse* is unlikely to be tagged incorrectly as it is a noun 99 percent of the time, but *riding* is more likely to be tagged incorrectly, as it is a noun about 15 percent of the time and a verb about 85 percent of the time. A sequence like *the horse* is almost certain to be tagged correctly, but a sequence like *that riding* much less so. What is worse, in the latter case, whether *riding* will be tagged correctly depends on whether *that* has been tagged correctly. If *that* has been tagged as a determiner, *riding* will be (correctly) tagged as a noun, as verbs never follow determiners and the joint probability that it is a verb will be zero. In contrast, if *that* has been tagged as a conjunction, the tagger will tag *riding* as a verb: conjunctions are followed by verbs with a probability of 0.16 and by nouns with a probability of 0.11, and so the joint probability that it is a verb ($0.16 \times 0.85 = 0.136$) is higher than the joint probability that it is a noun ($0.11 \times 0.67 = 0.0165$). This will not always be the right decision, as (22) shows:

(22) [W]e did like to make it quite clear during our er discussions that riding of horses on the highway is a matter for the TVP (BNC JS8)

In short, some classes of word forms (like *ing*-forms of verbs) are more difficult to tag correctly than others, so incorrectly assigned tags will cluster around such cases. This can lead to considerable distortions in the tagging of specific words and grammatical constructions. For example, in the BNC, the word form *regard* is systematically tagged incorrectly as a verb in the complex prepositions *with regard to* and *in regard to*, but is correctly tagged as a noun in most instances of the phrase *in high regard*. In other words, particular linguistic phenomena will be severely misrepresented in the results of corpus queries based on automatically assigned tags or parse trees.

Sometimes the probabilities of two possible tags are very close. In these cases, some taggers will stoically assign the more probable tag even if the difference in probabilities is small. Other taggers will assign so-called *ambiguity* or *portmanteau tags*, as in the following example from the BNC:

(23) `Ford/NP0-NN1 faces/NN2-VVZ strike/VVB-NN1 over/AVP-PRP pay/NN1-VVB deal/NN1-VVB ./PUN` (BNC AAC)

First, such cases must obviously be kept in mind when constructing queries: the query ⟨ `VBB` ⟩ will miss the word *strike* in this sentence (as will the query ⟨ `NN1` ⟩). In order to find words with ambiguity tags, we have to indicate that the ag we are interested in may be preceded or followed by another tag (one such way is provided by regular expressions, see Section 4.1 below). Second, such cases demonstrate vividly why the two operational definitions of parts of speech – by tagging guide line and by tagger – are fundamentally different: no human annotator, even one with a very sketchy tagging guideline, would produce the annotation in (23). On the other hand, it is simply not feasible to annotate a 100-million-word corpus using human annotators (though advances in crowd-sourcing technology may change this), so we are stuck with a choice between using a tagger or having no POS annotation at all.

Existing taggers tend to have an accuracy of around 95 to 97 percent. For example, it has been estimated (Leech et al. 1994) that 1.5 percent of all words in the BNC are tagged incorrectly. In a further 3.5 percent, the automatic tagger was not able to make a decision, assigning ambiguity tags (as shown in (23) above).

This leaves 95 percent of the words in the corpus tagged correctly and unambiguously. As impressive as this sounds at first, a closer look reveals two problems. First, an accuracy of 95 percent means that roughly one word in 20 is tagged incorrectly. Assuming a mean sentence length of 20 words (actual estimates range from 16 to 22), every sentence contains on average one incorrectly or ambiguously tagged word. Second, as pointed out above, some (classes of) word forms are more difficult to tag correctly, so the five percent mistagged or ambiguously tagged words will not be spread randomly through the data.

3.2.2.2 Length

There is a wide range of phenomena that has been claimed and/or shown to be related to the *weight* of linguistic units (syllables, words or phrases) – word-order phenomena following the principle "light before heavy", such as the dative alternation (Thompson & Koide 1987), particle placement (Chen 1986), *s*-possessive (or "genitive") and *of*-construction (Deane 1987) and frozen binominals (Sobkowiak 1993), to name just a few. In the context of such claims, *weight* is sometimes understood to refer to structural complexity, sometimes to length, and sometimes to both. Since complexity is often difficult to define, it is, in fact, frequently operationalized in terms of length, but let us first look at the difficulty of defining length in its own right and briefly return to complexity below.

Let us begin with words. Clearly, words differ in length – everyone would agree that the word *stun* is shorter than the word *flabbergast*. There are a number of ways in which we could operationalize Word Length, all of which would allow us to confirm this difference in length:

- as "number of letters" (cf., e.g., Wulff 2003), in which case *flabbergast* has a length of 11 and *stun* has a length of 4;
- as "number of phonemes" (cf., e.g., Sobkowiak 1993), in which case *flabbergast* has a length of 9 (BrE /ˈflæbəgɑːst/ and AmE /flæbɚgæst/), and *stun* has a length of 4 (BrE and AmE /stʌn/);
- as "number of syllables" (cf., e.g., Sobkowiak 1993, Stefanowitsch 2003), in which case *flabbergast* has a length of 3 and *stun* has a length of 1.

While all three operationalizations give us comparable results in the case of these two words, they will diverge in other cases. Take *disconcert*, which has the same length as *flabbergast* when measured in terms of phonemes (it has nine; BrE /dɪskənsɜt/ and AmE /dɪskənsɝːt/) or syllables (three), but it is shorter when measured in terms of letters (ten). Or take *shock*, which has the same length as *stun* when measured in syllables (one), but is longer when measured in letters (5 vs. 4) and shorter when measured in phonemes (3 vs. 4; BrE /ʃɑk/ and AmE /ʃɑːk/). Or take *amaze*, which has the same length as *shock* in terms of letters (five), but is longer in terms of phonemes (4 or 5, depending on how we analyze the diphthong in /əmeɪz/) and syllables (2 vs. 1).[2]

[2]Note that I have limited the discussion here to definitions of length that make sense in the domain of traditional linguistic corpora; there are other definitions, such as phonetic length

Clearly, none of these three definitions is "correct" – they simply measure different ways in which a word may have (phonological or graphemic) length. Which one to use depends on a number of factors, including first, what aspect of word length is relevant in the context of a particular research project (this is the question of validity), and second, to what extent are they practical to apply (this is the question of reliability). The question of reliability is a simple one: "number of letters" is the most reliably measurable factor assuming that we are dealing with written language or with spoken language transcribed using standard orthography; "number of phonemes" can be measured less reliably, as it requires that data be transcribed phonemically (which leaves more room for interpretation than orthography) or, in the case of written data, converted from an orthographic to a phonemic representation (which requires assumptions about which the language variety and level of formality the writer in question would have used if they had been speaking the text); "number of syllables" also requires such assumptions.

The question of validity is less easy to answer: if we are dealing with language that was produced in the written medium, "number of letters" may seem like a valid measure, but writers may be "speaking internally" as they write, in which case orthographic length would play a marginal role in stylistic and/or processing-based choices. Whether phonemic length or syllabic length are the more valid measure may depend on particular research questions (if rhythmic considerations are potentially relevant, syllables are the more valid measure), but also on particular languages; for example, Cutler et al. (1986) have shown that speakers of French (and other so-called syllable-timed languages) process words syllabically, in which case phonemic length would never play a role, while En-

(time it took to pronounce an instance of the word in a specific situation), or mean phonetic length (time it takes to pronounce the word on average). For example, the pronunciation samples of the CALD, as measured by playing them in the browser Chrome (Version 32.0.1700.102 for Mac OSX) and recording them using the software Audacity (Version 2.0.3 for Mac OSX) on a MacBook Air with a 1.8 GHz Intel Core i5 processor and running OS X version 10.8.5 and then using Audacity's timing function, have the following lengths: *flabbergast* BrE 0.929s, AmE 0.906s and *stun* BrE 0.534s, AmE 0.482s. The reason I described the hardware and software I used in so much detail is that they are likely to have influenced the measured length in addition to the fact that different speakers will produce words at different lengths on different occasions; thus, calculating meaningful mean pronunciation lengths would be a very time- and resource-intensive procedure even if we decided that it was the most valid measure of Word Length in the context of a particular research project. I am not aware of any corpus-linguistic study that has used this definition of word length; however, there are versions of the SWITCHBOARD corpus (a corpus of transcribed telephone conversations) that contain information about phonetic length, and these have been used to study properties of spoken language (e.g. Greenberg et al. 1996; 2003).

glish (and other stress-timed languages) process them phonemically (in which case it depends on the phenomenon, which of the measures are more valid).[3]

Finally, note that of course phonemic and/or syllabic length correlate with orthographic length to some extent (in languages with phonemic and syllabic scripts), so we might use the easily and reliably measured orthographic length as an operational definition of phonemic and/or syllabic length and assume that mismatches will be infrequent enough to be lost in the statistical noise (cf. Wulff 2003).

When we want to measure the length of linguistic units above word level, e.g. phrases, we can choose all of the above methods, but additionally or instead we can (and more typically do) count the number of words and/or constituents (cf. e.g. Gries (2003a) for a comparison of syllables and words as a measure of length). Here, we have to decide whether to count orthographic words (which is very reliable but may or may not be valid), or phonological words (which is less reliable, as it depends on our theory of what constitutes a phonological word).

As mentioned at the beginning of this subsection, *weight* is sometimes understood to refer to structural complexity rather than length. The question how to measure structural complexity has been addressed in some detail in the case of phrases, where it has been suggested that Complexity could be operationalized as "number of nodes" in the tree diagram modeling the structure of the phrase (cf. Wasow & Arnold 2003). Such a definition has a high validity, as "number of nodes" directly corresponds to a central aspect of what it means for a phrase to be syntactically complex, but as tree diagrams are highly theory-dependent, the reliability across linguistic frameworks is low.

Structural complexity can also be operationalized at various levels for words. The number of nodes could be counted in a phonological description of a word. For example, two words with the same number of syllables may differ in the complexity of those syllables: *amaze* and *astound* both have two syllables, but the second syllable of *amaze* follows a simple CVC pattern, while that of *astound* has the much more complex CCVCC pattern. The number of nodes could also be counted in the morphological structure of a word. In this case, all of the words mentioned above would have a length of one, except *disconcert*, which has a length of 2 (*dis* + *concert*).

[3]The difference between these two language types is that in stress-timed languages, the time between two stressed syllables tends to be constant regardless of the number of unstressed syllables in between, while in syllable-timed languages every syllable takes about the same time to pronounce. This suggests an additional possibility for measuring length in stress-timed languages, namely the number of stressed syllables. Again, I am not aware of any study that has discussed the operationalization of word length at this level of detail.

Due to the practical and theoretical difficulties of defining and measuring complexity, the vast majority of corpus-based studies operationalize Weight in terms of some measure of Word Length even if they theoretically conceptualize it in terms of complexity. Since complexity and length correlate to some extent, this is a justifiable simplification in most cases. In any case, it is a good example of how a phenomenon and its operational definition may be more or less closely related.

3.2.2.3 Discourse status

The notion of "topical", "old", or "given" information plays an important role in many areas of grammar, such as pronominal reference, voice, and constituent order in general. Definitions of this construct vary quite drastically across researchers and frameworks, but there is a simple basis for operational definitions of Topicality in terms of "referential distance", proposed by Talmy Givón:

(24) Referential Distance [...] assesses the gap between the previous occurrence in the discourse of a referent/topic and its current occurrence in a clause, where it is marked by a particular grammatical *coding device*. The gap is thus expressed in terms of *number of clauses to the left*. The minimal value that can be assigned is thus 1 clause [...] (Givón 1983: 13)

This is not quite an operational definition yet, as it cannot be applied reliably without a specification of the notions *clause* and *coding device*. Both notions are to some extent theory-dependent, and even within a particular theory they have to be defined in the context of the above definition of referential distance in a way that makes them identifiable.

With respect to *coding devices*, it has to be specified whether only overt references (by lexical nouns, proper names and pronouns) are counted, or whether covert references (by structural and/or semantic positions in the clause that are not phonologically realized) are included, and if so, which kinds of covert references. With respect to *clauses*, it has to be specified what counts as a clause, and it has to be specified how complex clauses are to be counted.

A concrete example may demonstrate the complexity of these decisions. Let us assume that we are interested in determining the referential distance of the pronouns in the following example, all of which refer to the person named *Joan* (verbs and other elements potentially forming the core of a clause have been indexed with numbers for ease of reference in the subsequent discussion):

(25) *Joan*, though Anne's junior$_1$ by a year and not yet fully accustomed$_2$ to the ways of the nobility, was$_3$ by far the more worldly-wise of the two. *She* watched$_4$, listened$_5$, learned$_6$ and assessed$_7$, speaking$_8$ only when spoken$_9$ to in general – whilst all the while making$_{10}$ *her* plans and looking$_{11}$ to the future... Enchanted$_{12}$ at first by *her* good fortune in becoming$_{13}$ Anne Mowbray's companion, grateful$_{14}$ for the benefits showered$_{15}$ upon *her*, *Joan* rapidly became$_{16}$ accustomed to her new role. (BNC CCD)

Let us assume the traditional definition of a clause as a finite verb and its dependents and let us assume that only overt references are counted. If we apply these definitions very narrowly, we would put the referential distance between the initial mention of Joan and the first pronominal reference at 1, as *Joan* is a dependent of *was* in clause (25$_3$) and there are no other finite verbs between this mention and the pronoun *she*. A broader definition of *clause* along the lines of "a unit expressing a complete proposition" however, might include the structures (25$_1$) (*though Anne's junior by a year*) and (25$_2$) (*not yet fully accustomed to the ways of the nobility*) in which case the referential distance would be 3 (a similar problem is posed by the potential clauses (25$_{12}$) and (25$_{14}$), which do not contain finite verbs but do express complete propositions). Note that if we also count the NP *the two* as including reference to the person named *Joan*, the distance to *she* would be 1, regardless of how the clauses are counted.

In fact, the structures (25$_1$) and (25$_2$) pose an additional problem: they are dependent clauses whose logical subject, although it is not expressed, is clearly coreferential with *Joan*. It depends on our theory whether these covert logical subjects are treated as elements of grammatical and/or semantic structure; if they are, we would have to include them in the count.

The differences that decisions about covert mentions can make are even more obvious when calculating the referential distance of the second pronoun, *her* (in *her plans*). Again, assuming that every finite verb and its dependents form a clause the distance between *her* and the previous use *she* is six clauses (25$_4$ to 25$_9$). However, in all six clauses, the logical subject is also *Joan*. If we include these as *mentions*, the referential distance is 1 again (*her good fortune* is part of the clause (25$_{12}$) and the previous mention would be the covert reference by the logical subject of clause (25$_{11}$)).

Finally, note that I have assumed a very flat, sequential understanding of "number of clauses" counting every finite verb separately. However, one could argue that the sequence *She watched$_4$, listened$_5$, learned$_6$ and assessed$_7$* is actually a single clause with four coordinated verb phrases sharing the subject *she*, that *speaking$_8$ only when spoken$_9$ to in general* is a single clause consisting of a matrix clause and an embedded adverbial clause, and that this clause itself is dependent on the clause with the four verb phrases. Thus, the sequence from (25_4) to (25_9) can be seen as consisting of six, two or even just one clause, depending on how we decide to count clauses in the context of referential distance.

Obviously, there is no “right” or “wrong” way to count clauses; what matters is that we specify a way of counting clauses that can be reliably applied and that is valid with respect to what we are trying to measure. With respect to reliability, obviously the simpler our specification, the better (simply counting every verb, whether finite or not, might be a good compromise between the two definitions mentioned above). With respect to validity, things are more complicated: referential distance is meant to measure the degree of activation of a referent, and different assumptions about the hierarchical structure of the clauses in question are going to have an impact on our assumptions concerning the activation of the entities referred to by them.

Since specifying what counts as a clause and what does not is fairly complex, it might be worth thinking about more objective, less theory-dependent measures of distance, such as the number of (orthographic) words between two mentions (I am not aware of studies that do this, but finding out to what extent the results correlate with clause-based measures of various kinds seems worthwhile).

For practical as well as for theoretical reasons, it is plausible to introduce a cut-off point for the number of clauses we search for a previous mention of a referent: practically, it will become too time consuming to search beyond a certain point, theoretically, it is arguable to what extent a distant previous occurrence of a referent contributes to the current information status. Givón (1983) originally set this cut-off point at 20 clauses, but there are also studies setting it at ten or even at three clauses. Clearly, there is no “correct” number of clauses, but there is empirical evidence that the relevant distinctions are those between a referential distance of 1, between 2 and 3, and > 3 (cf. Givón 1992).

Note that, as an operational definition of “topicality” or “givenness”, it will miss a range of referents that are “topical” or “given”. For example, there are referents that are present in the minds of speakers because they are physically present in the speech situation, or because they constitute salient shared knowledge for them, or because they talked about them at a previous occasion, or because they were mentioned prior to the cut-off point. Such referents may already be “given” at the point that they are first mentioned in the discourse.

Conversely, the definition may wrongly classify referents as discourse-active. For example, in conversational data an entity may be referred to by one speaker but be missed or misunderstood by the hearer, in which case it will not constitute given information to the hearer (Givón originally intended the measure for narrative data only, where this problem will not occur).

Both Word Length and Discourse Status are phenomena that can be defined in relatively objective, quantifiable terms – not quite as objectively as physical Hardness, perhaps, but with a comparable degree of rigor. Like Hardness measures, they do not access reality directly and are dependent on a number of assumptions and decisions, but providing that these are stated sufficiently explicitly, they can be applied almost automatically. While Word Length and Discourse Status are not the only such phenomena, they are not typical either. Most phenomena that are of interest to linguists (and thus, to corpus linguists) require operational definitions that are more heavily dependent on interpretation. Let us look at two such phenomena, Word Sense and Animacy.

3.2.2.4 Word senses

Although we often pretend that corpora contain words, they actually contain graphemic strings. Sometimes, such a string is in a relatively unique relationship with a particular word. For example, *sidewalk* is normally spelled as an uninterrupted sequence of the character *S* or *s* followed by the characters *i, d, e, w, a, l* and *k*, or as an uninterrupted sequence of the characters *S, I, D, E, W, A, L* and *K*, so (assuming that the corpus does not contain hyphens inserted at the end of a line when breaking the word across lines), there are just three orthographic forms; also, the word always has the same meaning. This is not the case for *pavement*, which, as we saw, has several meanings that (while clearly etymologically related), must be distinguished.

In these cases, the most common operationalization strategy found in corpus linguistics is reference to a dictionary or lexical database. In other words, the researcher will go through the concordance and assign every instance of the orthographic string in question to one word-sense category posited in the corresponding lexical entry. A resource frequently used in such cases is the WordNet database (cf. Fellbaum 1998, see also Study Notes). This is a sort of electronic dictionary that includes not just definitions of different word senses but also information about lexical relationships, etc.; but let us focus on the word senses. For *pavement*, the entry looks like this:

(26) a. S: (n) pavement#1, paving#2 (the paved surface of a thoroughfare)
b. S: (n) paving#1, pavement#2, paving material#1 (material used to pave an area)
c. S: (n) sidewalk#1, pavement#3 (walk consisting of a paved area for pedestrians; usually beside a street or roadway)

There are three senses of *pavement*, as shown by the numbers attached, and in each case there are synonyms. Of course, in order to turn this into an operational definition, we need to specify a procedure that allows us to assign the hits in our corpus to these categories. For example, we could try to replace the word *pavement* by a unique synonym and see whether this changes the meaning. But even this, as we saw in Section 3.1.2 above, may be quite difficult.

There is an additional problem: We are relying on someone else's decisions about which uses of a word constitute different senses. In the case of *pavement*, this is fairly uncontroversial, but consider the entry for the noun *bank*:

(27)
a. bank#1 (sloping land (especially the slope beside a body of water))
b. bank#2, depository financial institution#1, bank#2, banking concern#1, banking company#1 (a financial institution that accepts deposits and channels the money into lending activities)
c. bank#3 (a long ridge or pile)
d. bank#4 (an arrangement of similar objects in a row or in tiers)
e. bank#5 (a supply or stock held in reserve for future use (especially in emergencies))
f. bank#6 (the funds held by a gambling house or the dealer in some gambling games)
g. bank#7, cant#2, camber#2 (a slope in the turn of a road or track; the outside is higher than the inside in order to reduce the effects of centrifugal force)
h. savings bank#2, coin bank#1, money box#1, bank#8 (a container (usually with a slot in the top) for keeping money at home)
i. bank#9, bank building#1 (a building in which the business of banking transacted)
j. bank#10 (a flight maneuver; aircraft tips laterally about its longitudinal axis (especially in turning))

While everyone will presumably agree that (27a) and (27b) are separate senses (or even separate words, i.e. homonyms), it is less clear whether everyone would distinguish (27b) from (27i) and/or (27f); or (27e) and (27f), or even (27a) and (27g). In these cases, one could argue that we are just dealing with contextual variants of a single underlying meaning.

Thus, we have the choice of coming up with our own set of senses (which has the advantage that it will fit more precisely into the general theoretical framework we are working in and that we might find it easier to apply), or we can stick with an established set of senses such as that proposed by WordNet, which has the advantage that it is maximally transparent to other researchers and that we cannot subconsciously make it fit our own preconceptions, thus distorting our results in the direction of our hypothesis. In either case, we must make the set of senses and the criteria for applying them transparent, and in either case we are dealing with an operational definition that does not correspond directly with reality (if only because word senses tend to form a continuum rather than a set of discrete categories in actual language use).

3.2.2.5 Animacy

The animacy of the referents of noun phrases plays a role in a range of grammatical processes in many languages. In English, for example, it has been argued (and shown) to be involved in the grammatical alternations already discussed above, in other languages it is involved in grammatical gender, in alignment systems, etc.

The simplest distinction in the domain of ANIMACY would be the following:

(28) ANIMATE VS. INANIMATE

Dictionary definitions typically treat *animate* as a rough synonym of *alive* (OALD and CALD define it as "having life"), and *inanimate* as a rough synonym of *not alive*, normally in the sense of not being capable of having life, like, for example, a rock ("having none of the characteristics of life that an animal or plant has", CALD, see also OALD), but sometimes additionally in the sense of being *no longer alive* ("dead or appearing to be dead", OALD).

The basic distinction in (28) looks simple, so that any competent speaker of a language should be able to categorize the referents of nouns in a text accordingly. On second thought, however, it is more complex than it seems. For example, what about dead bodies or carcasses? The fact that dictionaries disagree as to whether these are *inanimate* shows that this is not a straightforward question that calls for a decision before the nouns in a given corpus could be categorized reliably.

Let us assume for the moment that *animate* is defined as "potentially having life" and thus includes dead bodies and carcasses. This does not solve all problems: For example, how should body parts, organs or individual cells be categorized? They "have life" in the sense that they are *part* of something alive, but they are not, in themselves, living beings. In fact, in order to count as an *animate* being in a communicatively relevant sense, an entity has to display some degree of intentional agency. This raises the question of whether, for example, plants, jellyfish, bacteria, viruses or prions should be categorized as animate.

Sometimes, the dimension of intentionality/agency is implicitly recognized as playing a crucial role, leading to a three-way categorization such as that in (29):

(29) HUMAN VS. OTHER ANIMATE VS. INANIMATE

If ANIMACY is treated as a matter of degree, we might want to introduce further distinctions in the domain of animates, such as HIGHER ANIMALS, LOWER ANIMALS, PLANTS, MICRO-ORGANISMS. However, the distinction between HUMANS and OTHER ANIMATES introduces additional problems. For example, how should we categorize animals that are linguistically represented as quasi-human, like the bonobo Kanzi, or a dog or a cat that is treated by their owner as though it has human intelligence? If we categorize them as OTHER ANIMATE, what about fictional talking animals like the Big Bad Wolf and the Three Little Pigs? And what about fully fictional entities, such as gods, ghosts, dwarves, dragons or unicorns? Are they, respectively, humans and animals, even though they do not, in fact exist? Clearly, we treat them conceptually as such, so unless we follow an extremely objectivist semantics, they should be categorized accordingly – but this is not something we can simply assume implicitly.

A slightly different problem is posed by robots (fictional ones that have quasi-human or quasi-animal capacities and real ones, that do not). Should these be treated as HUMANS/ANIMATE? If so, what about other kinds of "intelligent" machines (again, fictional ones with quasi-human capacities, like HAL 9000 from Arthur C. Clarke's *Space Odyssey* series, or real ones without such capacities, like the laptop on which I am writing this book)? And what about organizations (when they are metonymically treated as agents, and when they are not)? We might want to categorize robots, machines and organizations as human/animate in contexts where they are treated as having human or animal intelligence and agency, and as inanimate where they are not. In other words, our categorization of a referent may change depending on context.

Sometimes studies involving animacy introduce additional categories in the INANIMATE domain. One distinction that is often made is that between concrete and abstract, yielding the four-way categorization in (30):

(30) HUMAN VS. ANIMATE VS. CONCRETE INANIMATE VS. ABSTRACT INANIMATE

The distinction between concrete and abstract raises the practical issue where to draw the line (for example, is *electricity* concrete?). It also raises a deeper issue that we will return to: are we still dealing with a single dimension? Are abstract inanimate entities (say, *marriage* or *Wednesday*) really less "animate" than concrete entities like a *wedding ring* or a *calendar*? And are `animate` and `abstract` incompatible, or would it not make sense to treat the referents of words like *god*, *demon*, *unicorn*, etc. as `abstract animate`?

3.2.2.6 Interim summary

We have seen that operational definitions in corpus linguistics may differ substantially in terms of their objectivity. Some operational definitions, like those for length and discourse status, are almost comparable to physical measures like *Vickers Hardness* in terms of objectivity and quantitativeness. Others, like those for word senses or animacy are more like the definitions in the DSM or the ICD in that they leave room for interpretation, and thus for subjective choices, no matter how precise the instructions for the identification of individual categories are. Unfortunately, the latter type of operational definition is more common in linguistics (and the social sciences in general), but there are procedures to deal with the problem of subjectiveness at least to some extent. We will return to these procedures in detail in the next chapter.

3.3 Hypotheses in context: The research cycle

Let us conclude this chapter with a brief discussion of the role that hypothesis testing plays within a given strand of research, i.e., within the context of a set of research projects dealing with a particular research question (or a set of such questions), starting, again, with Karl Popper. Popper is sometimes portrayed as advocating an almost mindless version of falsificationism, where researchers randomly pull hypotheses out of thin air and test them until they are falsified, then start again with a new randomly invented hypothesis.

Popper's actual discussions are closer to actual scientific practice. It is true that in terms of scientific logic, the only requirement of a hypothesis is that it is testable (i.e., falsifiable), but in scientific practice, it must typically meet two additional criteria: first, it must be a potentially insightful explanation of a particular research problem, and second, it must take into account previous research (if such research exists). It is also true that falsification is central to Popperian research logic, but not as a mindless slashing of ideas, but as a process of error elimination. Popper describes the entire process using the following schematic representation (Popper 1970: 3):

(31) $\mathrm{P}_1 \rightarrow \mathrm{TT} \rightarrow \mathrm{EE} \rightarrow \mathrm{P}_2$

In this schema, P_1 stands for a research question (a "problem"), *TT* stands for a hypothesis (a "tentative theory"), *EE* for the attempt to falsify the hypothesis ("error elimination") by testing, but also by "critical discussion", and P_2 stands for new or additional problems and research questions arising from the falsification process.[4] Popper also acknowledges that it is good research practice to entertain several hypotheses at once, if there is more than one promising explanation for a problem situation, expanding his formula as follows:

(32)
$$\mathrm{P}_1 \begin{array}{l} \nearrow \ \mathrm{TT}_a \rightarrow \mathrm{EE}_a \rightarrow \mathrm{P}_{2a} \\ \rightarrow \ \mathrm{TT}_b \rightarrow \mathrm{EE}_b \rightarrow \mathrm{P}_{2b} \\ \searrow \ \mathrm{TT}_n \rightarrow \mathrm{EE}_n \rightarrow \mathrm{P}_{2n} \end{array}$$

He explicitly acknowledges that falsification, while central, is not the only criterion by which science proceeds: if there are several unfalsified hypotheses, we may also assess them based on which promises the most insightful explanation or which produces the most interesting additional hypotheses (Popper 1970: 3).

Crucially, (31) and (32) suggest a *cyclic* and *incremental* approach to research: the status quo in a given field is the result of a long process of producing new hypotheses and eliminating errors, and it will, in turn, serve as a basis for more new hypotheses (and more errors which need to be eliminated). This incremental cyclicity can actually be observed in scientific disciplines. In some, like physics or psychology, researchers make this very explicit, publishing research in the form of series of experiments attempting to falsify certain existing hypotheses and corroborating others, typically building on earlier experiments by others or themselves and closing with open questions and avenues of future research. In other disciplines, like the more humanities-leaning social sciences including (corpus) linguistics, the cycle is typically less explicit, but viewed from a distance, researchers also follow this procedure, summarizing the ideas of previous authors (sometimes to epic lengths) and then adding more or less substantial data and arguments of their own.

Fleshing out Popper's basic schema in (31) above, drawing together the points discussed in this and the previous chapter, we can represent this cycle as shown in Figure 3.1.

Research begins with a general question – something that intrigues an individual or a group of researchers. The part of reality to which this question pertains is then modeled, i.e., described in terms of theoretical constructs, enabling us to formulate, first, a more specific research question, and often, second, a hypothesis.

[4]Of course, Popper did not invent, or claim to have invented, this procedure. He was simply explicating what he thought successful scientists were, and ought to be, doing (Rudolph (2005) traces the explicit recognition of this procedure to John Dewey's still very readable *How we think* (Dewey 1910), which contains insightful illustrations).

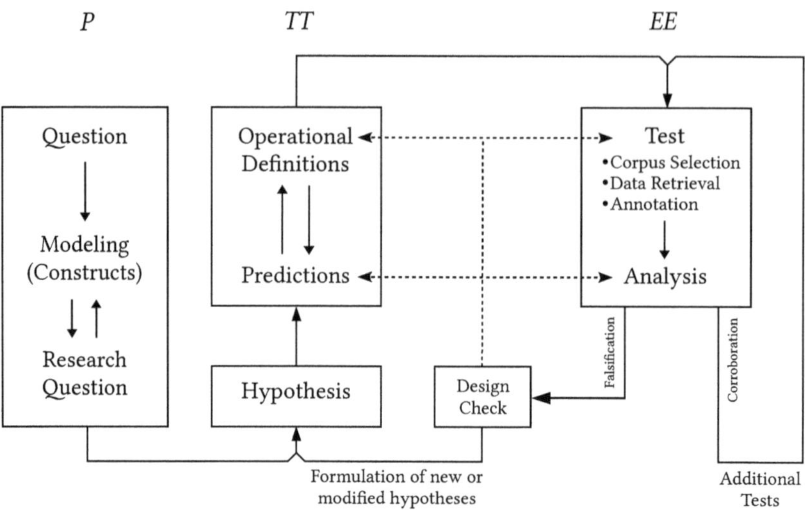

Figure 3.1: The scientific research cycle

There is nothing automatic about these steps – they are typically characterized by lengthy critical discussion, false starts or wild speculation, until testable hypotheses emerge (in some disciplines, this stage has not yet been, and in some cases probably never will be reached). Next, predictions must be derived, requiring operational definitions of the constructs posited previously. This may require some back and forth between formulating predictions and providing sufficiently precise operationalizations.

Next, the predictions must be tested – in the case of corpus linguistics, corpora must be selected and data must be retrieved and annotated, something we will discuss in detail in the next chapter. Then the data are analyzed with respect to the hypothesis. If they corroborate the hypothesis (or at least fail to falsify it), this is not the end of the process: with Popper, we should only begin to accept evidence as corroborating when it emerges from repeated attempts to falsify the hypothesis. Thus, additional tests must be, and typically are, devised. If the results of any test falsify the hypothesis, this does not, of course, lead to its immediate rejection. After all, we have typically arrived at our hypothesis based on good arguments, and so researchers will typically perform what we could call a "design check" on their experiment, looking closely at their predictions to see if they really follow from the hypothesis, the operational definitions to see whether they are reliable and valid with respect to the constructs they represent, and the test itself to determine whether there are errors or confounding variables in the data selection and analysis. If potential problems are found, they will be fixed and the test will be repeated. Only if it fails repeatedly will researchers abandon (or modify) the hypothesis.

The repeated testing, and especially the modification of a hypothesis is inherently dangerous, as we might be so attached to our hypothesis that we will keep testing it long after we should have given it up, or that we will try to save it by changing it just enough that our test will no longer falsify it, or by making it completely untestable (cf. Popper 1963: 37). This must, of course, be avoided, but so must throwing out a hypothesis, or an entire model, on the basis of a single falsification event. Occasionally, especially in half-mature disciplines like linguistics, models morph into competing schools of thought, each vigorously defended by its adherents even in the face of a growing number of phenomena that they fail to account for. In such cases, a radical break in the research cycles within these models may be necessary to make any headway at all – a so-called "paradigm shifts" occurs. This means that researchers abandon the current model wholesale and start from scratch based on different initial assumptions (see Kuhn 1962). Corpus linguistics with its explicit recognition that generalizations about the language system can and must be deduced from language usage may present such a paradigm shift with respect to the intuition-driven generative models.

Finally, note that the scientific research cycle is not only incremental, with each new hypothesis and each new test building on previous research, but that it is also collaborative, with one researcher or group of researchers picking up where another left off. This collaborative nature of research requires researchers to be maximally transparent with respect to their research designs, laying open their data and methods in sufficient detail for other researchers to understand exactly what prediction was tested, how the constructs in question were operationalized, how data were retrieved and analyzed. Again, this is the norm in disciplines like experimental physics and psychology, but not so much so in the more humanities-leaning disciplines, which tend to put the focus on ideas and arguments rather than methods. We will deal with data retrieval and annotation in the next chapter and return to the issue of methodological transparency at the end of it.

4 Data retrieval and annotation

Traditionally, many corpus-linguistic studies use the (orthographic) word form as their starting point. This is at least in part due to the fact that corpora consist of text that is represented as a sequence of word forms, and that, consequently, word forms are easy to retrieve. As briefly discussed in Chapter 2, concordancing software allows us to query the corpus for a string of characters and displays the result as a list of hits in context.

As we saw when discussing the case of *pavement* in Chapter 3, a corpus query for a string of characters like ⟨ `pavement` ⟩ may give us more than we want – it will return not only hits corresponding to the word sense 'pedestrian footpath', which we could contrast with the synonym *sidewalk*, but also those corresponding to the word sense 'hard surface' (which we could contrast with the synonym *paving*).

The query may, at the same time, give us *less* than we want, because it would only return the singular form of the word and only if it is spelled entirely in lower case. A study of the word (in either or both of its senses) would obviously require that we look at the *lemma* PAVEMENT, comprising at least the word forms *pavement* (singular), *pavements* (plural) and, depending on how the corpus is prepared, *pavement's* (possessive). It also requires that we include in our query all possible graphemic variants, comprising at least cases in lower case, with an initial capital (*Pavement, Pavements, Pavement's*, e.g. at the beginning of a sentence), or in all caps (*PAVEMENT, PAVEMENTS, PAVEMENT'S)*, but, depending on the corpus, also hyphenated cases occurring at a line break (e.g. *pave-¶ment*, with ¶ standing for the line break).

In Chapter 3, we implicitly treated the second issue as a problem of *retrieval*, noting in passing that we queried our corpus in such a way as to capture all variants of the lemma PAVEMENT. We treated the first issue as a problem of categorization – we went through the results of our query one by one, determining from the context, which of the senses of *pavement* we were likely dealing with. In the context of a research project, our decisions would be recorded together with the data in some way – we would *annotate* the data, using an agreed-upon *code* for each of the categories (e.g., word senses).

Retrieval is a non-trivial issue even when dealing with individual lexical items whose orthographic representations are not ambiguous. The more complex the phenomena under investigation are, the more complex these issues become, requiring careful thought and a number of decisions concerning an almost inevitable trade-off between the quality of the results and the time needed to retrieve them. This issue will be dealt with in Section 4.1. We already saw that the issue of data annotation is extremely complex even in the case of individual lexical items, and the preceding chapter discussed some more complicated examples. This issue will be dealt with in more detail in Section 4.2.

4.1 Retrieval

Broadly speaking, there are two ways of searching a corpus for a particular linguistic phenomenon: manually (i.e., by reading the texts contained in it, noting down each instance of the phenomenon in question) or automatically (i.e., by using a computer program to run a query on a machine-readable version of the texts). As discussed in Chapter 2, there may be cases where there is no readily apparent alternative to a fully manual search, and we will come back to such cases below.

However, as also discussed in Chapter 2, software-aided queries are the default in modern corpus linguistics, and so we take these as a starting point of our discussion.

4.1.1 Corpus queries

There is a range of more or less specialized commercial and non-commercial concordancing programs designed specifically for corpus linguistic research, and there are many other software packages that may be repurposed to the task of searching text corpora even though they are not specifically designed for corpus-linguistic research. Finally, there are scripting languages like Perl, Python and R, with a learning curve that is not forbiddingly steep, that can be used to write programs capable of searching text corpora (ranging from very simple two-liners to very complex solutions). Which of these solutions are available to you and suitable to your research project is not for me to say, so the following discussion will largely abstract away from such specifics.

The power of software-aided searches depends on two things: first, on the annotation contained in the corpus itself and second, on the pattern-matching capacities of the software used to access them. In the simplest case (which we assumed to hold in the examples discussed in the previous chapter), a corpus will contain plain text in a standard orthography and the software will be able to find passages matching a specific string of characters. Essentially, this is something every word processor is capable of.

Most concordancing programs can do more than this, however. For example, they typically allow the researcher to formulate queries that match not just one string, but a class of strings. One fairly standardized way of achieving this is by using so-called *regular expressions* – strings that may contain not just simple characters, but also symbols referring to classes of characters or symbols affecting the interpretation of characters. For example, the lexeme *sidewalk*, has (at least) six possible orthographic representations: *sidewalk, side-walk, Sidewalk, Side-walk, sidewalks, side-walks, Sidewalks* and *Side-walks* (in older texts, it is sometimes spelled as two separate words, which means that we have to add at least *side walk, side walks, Side walk* and *Side walks* when investigating such texts). In order to retrieve all occurrences of the lexeme, we could perform a separate query for each of these strings, but I actually queried the string in (1a); a second example of regular expressions is (1b), which represents one way of searching for all inflected forms and spelling variants of the verb *synthesize* (as long as they are in lower case):

(1) a. `[Ss]ide[- ]?walks?`
    b. `synthesi[sz]e?[ds]?(ing)?`

Any group of characters in square brackets is treated as a class, which means that any one of them will be treated as a match, and the question mark means "zero or one of the preceding characters". This means that the pattern in (1a) will match an upper- or lower-case *S*, followed by *i*, *d*, and *e*, followed by zero or one occurrence of a hyphen or a blank space, followed by *w*, *a*, *l*, and *k*, followed by zero or one occurrence of *s*. This matches all the variants of the word. For (1b), the [sz] ensures that both the British spelling (with an *s*) and the American spelling (with a *z*) are found. The question mark after *e* ensures that both the forms with an *e* (*synthesize, synthesizes, synthesized*) and that without one (*synthesizing*) are matched. Next, the string matches zero to one occurrence of a *d* or an *s* followed by zero or one occurrence of the string *ing* (because it is enclosed in parentheses, it is treated as a unit for the purposes of the following question mark.

Regular expressions allow us to formulate the kind of complex and abstract queries that we are likely to need when searching for words (rather than individual word forms) and even more so when searching for more complex expressions. But even the simple example in (1) demonstrates a problem with such queries:

they quickly overgeneralize. The pattern would also, for example, match some non-existing forms, like *synthesizding*, and, more crucially, it will match existing forms that we may not want to include in our search results, like the noun *synthesis* (see further Section 4.1.2).

The benefits of being able to define complex queries become even more obvious if our corpus contains annotations in addition to the original text, as discussed in Section 2.1.4 of Chapter 2. If the corpus contains part-of-speech tags, for example, this will allow us to search (within limits) for grammatical structures. For example, assume that there is a part-of-speech tag attached to the end of every word by an underscore (as in the BROWN corpus, see Figure 2.4 in Chapter 2) and that the tags are as shown in (2) (following the sometimes rather nontransparent BROWN naming conventions). We could then search for prepositional phrases using a pattern like the one in (3):

(2)

preposition	`_IN`
articles	`_AT`
adjectives	`_JJ` (uninflected)
	`_JJR` (comparative)
	`_JJT` (superlative)
nouns	`_NN` (common singular nouns)
	`_NNS` (common plural nouns)
	`_NN$` (common nouns with possessive clitic)
	`_NP` (proper names)
	`_NP$` (proper nouns with possessive clitic)

(3)

```
\S+_IN   (\S+_AT)?   (\S+_JJ[RT]?)*   (\S+_N[PN][S$]?)+
   1          2             3                   4
```

An asterisk means "zero or more", a plus means "one or more", and \S means "any non-whitespace character", the meaning of the other symbols is as before. The pattern in (3) matches the following sequence:

1. any word (i.e., sequence of non-whitespace characters) tagged as a preposition, followed by

2. zero or one occurrence of a word tagged as an article that is preceded by a whitespace, followed by

3. zero or more occurrences of a word tagged as an adjective (again preceded by a whitespace), including comparatives and superlatives – note that the JJ tag may be followed by zero or one occurrence of a *T* or an *R*), followed by

4. one or more words (again, preceded by a whitespace) that are tagged as a noun or proper name (note the square bracket containing the N for common nouns and the P for proper nouns), including plural forms and possessive forms (note that NN or NP tags may be followed by zero or one occurrence of an S or a $).

The query in (3) makes use of the annotation in the corpus (in this case, the part-of-speech tagging), but it does so in a somewhat cumbersome way by treating word forms and the tags attached to them as strings. As shown in Figure 2.5 in Chapter 2, corpora often contain multiple annotations for each word form – part of speech, lemma, in some cases even grammatical structure. Some concordance programs, such as the widely-used open-source Corpus Workbench (including its web-based version CQPweb) (cf. Evert & Hardie 2011) or the Sketch Engine and its open-source variant NoSketch engine (cf. Kilgarriff et al. 2014) are able to "understand" the structure of such annotations and offer a query syntax that allows the researcher to refer to this structure directly.

The two programs just mentioned share a query syntax called *CQP* (for "Corpus Query Processor") in the Corpus Workbench and *CQL* (for "Corpus Query Language") in the (No)Sketch Engine. This syntax is very powerful, allowing us to query the corpus for tokens or sequences of tokens at any level of annotation. It is also very transparent: each token is represented as a value-attribute pair in square brackets, as shown in (4):

(4) `[attribute="value"]`

The attribute refers to the level of annotation (e.g. `word`, `pos`, `lemma` or whatever else the makers of a corpus have called their annotations), the value refers to what we are looking for. For example, a query for the different forms of the word *synthesize* (cf. (1) above) would look as shown in (5a), or, if the corpus contains information about the lemma of each word form, as shown in (5b), and the query for PPs in (3) would look as shown in (5c):

(5) a. `[word="synthesi[sz]e?[ds]?(ing)?"]`
 b. `[lemma="synthesize"]`
 c. `[pos="IN"] [pos="AT"]? [pos="JJ[RT]"] [pos="N[PN][S$]?"]+`

As you can see, we can use regular expressions inside the values for the attributes, and we can use the asterisk, question mark and plus outside the token to indicate that the query should match "zero or more", "zero or one" and "one or more" tokens with the specified properties. Note that CQP syntax is case sensitive, so for example (5a) would only return hits that are in lower case. If we want the query to be case-insensitive, we have to attach `%c` to the relevant values.

We can also combine two or more attribute-value pairs inside a pair of square brackets to search for tokens satisfying particular conditions at different levels of annotation. For example, (6a) will find all instances of the word form *walk* tagged as a verb, while (6b) will find all instances tagged as a noun. We can also address different levels of annotation at different positions in a query. For example, (6c) will find all instances of the word form *walk* followed by a word tagged as a preposition, and (6d) corresponds to the query ⟨ `through the NOUN of POSS.PRON car` ⟩ mentioned in Section 3.1.1 of Chapter 3 (note the `%c` that makes all queries for words case-insensitive):

(6) a. `[word="walk"%c & pos="VB"]`
b. `[word="walk"%c & pos="NN"]`
c. `[word="walk"%c] [pos="IN"]`
d. `[word="through"%c] [word="the"%c] [pos="NNS?"] [word="of"%c] [pos="PP$"] [word="car"%c]`

This query syntax is so transparent and widely used that we will treat it as a standard in the remainder of the book and use it to describe queries. This is obviously useful if you are using one of the systems mentioned above, but if not, the transparency of the syntax should allow you to translate the query into whatever possibilities your concordancer offers you. When talking about a query in a particular corpus, I will use the annotation (e.g., the part-of-speech tags) used in that corpus, when talking about queries in general, I will use generic values like *noun* or *prep.*, shown in lower case to indicate that they do not correspond to a particular corpus annotation.

Of course, even the most powerful query syntax can only work with what is there. Retrieving instances of phrasal categories based on part-of-speech annotation is only possible to a certain extent: even a complex query like that in (5c) or in (3) will not return all prepositional phrases. These queries will not, for example, match cases where the adjective is preceded by one or more quantifiers (tagged `_QT` in the BROWN corpus), adverbs (tagged `_RB`), or combinations of the two. It will also not return cases with pronouns instead of nouns. These and other issues can be fixed by augmenting the query accordingly, although the increasing complexity will bring problems of its own, to which we will return in the next subsection.

Other problems are impossible to fix; for example, if the noun phrase inside the PP contains another PP, the pattern will not recognize it as belonging to the NP but will treat it as a new match and there is nothing we can do about this, since there is no difference between the sequence of POS tags in a structures like (7a), where the PP *off the kitchen* is a complement of the noun *room* and as such is part of the NP inside the first PP, and (7b), where the PP *at a party* is an adjunct of the verb *standing* and as such is not part of the NP preceding it:

(7) a. A mill stands *in a room off the kitchen.* (BROWN F04)
    b. He remembered the first time he saw her, standing *across the room at a party.* (BROWN P28)

In order to distinguish these cases in a query, we need a corpus annotated not just for parts of speech but also for syntactic structure (sometimes referred to as a *treebank*), like the SUSANNE corpus briefly discussed in Section 2.1.4 of Chapter 2 above.

4.1.2 Precision and recall

In arriving at the definition of corpus linguistics adopted in this book, we stressed the need to investigate linguistic phenomena exhaustively, which we took to mean "taking into account all examples of the phenomenon in question" (cf. Chapter 2). In order to take into account all examples of a phenomenon, we have to retrieve them first. However, as we saw in the preceding section and in Chapter 3, it is not always possible to define a corpus query in a way that will retrieve all and only the occurrences of a particular phenomenon. Instead, a query can have four possible outcomes: it may

1. include hits that are instances of the phenomenon we are looking for (these are referred to as a *true positives* or *hits*, but note that we are using the word *hit* in a broader sense to mean "anything returned as a result of a query");
2. include hits that are not instances of our phenomenon (these are referred to as a *false positives*);
3. fail to include instances of our phenomenon (these are referred to as a *false negatives* or *misses*); or
4. fail to include strings that are not instances of our phenomenon (this is referred to as a *true negative*).

Table 4.1 summarizes these outcomes (¬ stands for "not").

Table 4.1: Four possible outcomes of a corpus query for a given phenomenon X

		Search result	
		Included	Not included
Corpus	X	True positive (*hit*)	False negative (*miss*)
	¬ X	False positive (*false alarm*)	True negative (*correct rejection*)

Obviously, the first case (true positive) and the fourth case (true negative) are desirable outcomes: we want our search results to include all instances of the phenomenon under investigation and exclude everything that is not such an instance. The second case (false negative) and the third case (false positive) are undesirable outcomes: we do not want our query to miss instances of the phenomenon in question and we do not want our search results to incorrectly include strings that are not instances of it.

We can describe the quality of a data set that we have retrieved from a corpus in terms of two measures. First, the proportion of positives (i.e., strings returned by our query) that are true positives; this is referred to as *precision*, or as the *positive predictive value*, cf. (8a). Second, the proportion of all instances of our phenomenon that are true positives (i.e., that were actually returned by our query; this is referred to as *recall*, cf. (8b):[1]

(8) a. $$\text{Precision} = \frac{\text{True Positives}}{\text{True Positives} + \text{False Positives}}$$

[1]There are two additional measures that are important in other areas of empirical research but do not play a central role in corpus-linguistic data retrieval. First, the *specificity* or true negative rate – the proportion of negatives that are incorrectly included in our data (i.e. false negatives); second, *negative predictive value* – the proportion of negatives (i.e., cases not included in our search) that are true negatives (i.e., that are correctly rejected). These measures play a role in situations where a negative outcome of a test is relevant (for example, with medical diagnoses); in corpus linguistics, this is generally not the case. There are also various scores that combine individual measures to give us an overall idea of the accuracy of a test, for example, the *F1 score*, defined as the harmonic mean of precision and recall. Such scores are useful in information retrieval or machine learning, but less so in corpus-linguistic research projects, where precision and recall must typically be assessed independently of, and weighed against, each other.

$$\text{b. Recall} = \frac{\text{True Positives}}{\text{True Positives} + \text{False Negatives}}$$

Ideally, the value of both measures should be 1, i.e., our data should include all cases of the phenomenon under investigation (a recall rate of 100 percent) and it should include nothing that is not a case of this phenomenon (a precision of 100 percent). However, unless we carefully search our corpus manually (a possibility I will return to below), there is typically a trade-off between the two. Either we devise a query that matches only clear cases of the phenomenon we are interested in (high precision) but that will miss many less clear cases (low recall). Or we devise a query that matches as many potential cases as possible (high recall), but that will include many cases that are not instances of our phenomenon (low precision).

Let us look at a specific example, the English ditransitive construction, and let us assume that we have an untagged and unparsed corpus. How could we retrieve instances of the ditransitive? As the first object of a ditransitive is usually a pronoun (in the objective case) and the second a lexical NP (see, for example, Thompson & Koide 1987), one possibility would be to search for a pronoun followed by a determiner (i.e., for any member of the set of strings in (9a)), followed by any member of the set of strings in (9b)). This gives us the query in (9c), which is long, but not very complex:

(9) a. *me, you, him, her, it, us, them*
   b. *the, a, an, this, that, these, those, some, many, lots, my, your, his, her, its, our, their, something, anything*
   c. `[word="(me|you|him|her|it|us|them)"%c] [word="(the|a|an|this|that|these|those|some|many|lots|my|your|his|her|its|our|their|something|anything)"%c]`

Let us apply this query (which is actually used in Colleman & De Clerck 2011) to a freely available sample from the British Component of the International Corpus of English mentioned in Chapter 2 above (see the Study Notes to the current chapter for details). This corpus has been manually annotated, amongst other things, for argument structure, so that we can check the results of our query against this annotation.

There are 36 ditransitive clauses in the sample, thirteen of which are returned by our query. There are also 2838 clauses that are not ditransitive, 14 of which are also returned by our query. Table 4.2 shows the results of the query in terms of true and false positives and negatives.

Table 4.2: Comparison of the search results

		Search result		
		Included	Not included	Total
Corpus	Ditransitive	13 *true positives*	23 *false negatives*	36
	¬ Ditransitive	14 *false positives*	2824 *true negatives*	2838
	Total	27	2847	2874

We can now calculate precision and recall rate of our query:

(10) a. Precision $= \frac{13}{27} = 0.48$

b. Recall $= \frac{13}{36} = 0.36$

Clearly, neither precision nor recall are particularly impressive. Let us look at the reasons for this, beginning with precision.

While the sequence of a pronoun and a determiner is typical for (one type of) ditransitive clause, it is not unique to the ditransitive, as the following false positives of our query show:

(11) a. ... one of the experiences that went towards making me a Christian...
b. I still ring her a lot.
c. I told her that I'd had to take these tablets
d. It seems to me that they they tend to come from
e. Do you need your caffeine fix before you this

Two other typical structures characterized by the sequence pronoun-determiner are object-complement clauses (cf. 11a) and clauses with quantifying noun phrases (cf. 11b). In addition, some of the strings in (9b) above are ambiguous, i.e., they can represent parts of speech other than determiner; for example, *that* can be a conjunction, as in (9c), which otherwise fits the description of a ditransitive, and in (11d), which does not. Finally, especially in spoken corpora, there may be fragments that match particular search criteria only accidentally (cf. 11e). Obviously, a corpus tagged for parts of speech could improve the precision of our search results somewhat, by excluding cases like (9c–d), but others, like (9a), could never be excluded, since they are identical to the ditransitive as far as the sequence of parts-of-speech is concerned.

Of course, it is relatively trivial, in principle, to increase the precision of our search results: we can manually discard all false positives, which would increase precision to the maximum value of 1. Typically, our data will have to be manually annotated for various criteria anyway, allowing us to discard false positives in the process. However, the larger our data set, the more time consuming this will become, so precision should always be a consideration even at the stage of data retrieval.

Let us now look at the reasons for the recall rate, which is even worse than the precision. There are, roughly speaking, four types of ditransitive structures that our query misses, exemplified in (12a–e):

(12) a. How much money have they given you?
  b. The centre [...] has also been granted a three-year repayment freeze.
  c. He gave the young couple his blessing.
  d. They have just given me enough to last this year.
  e. He finds himself [...] offering Gradiva flowers.

The first group of cases are those where the second object does not appear in its canonical position, for example in interrogatives and other cases of left-dislocation (cf. 12a), or passives (12b). The second group of cases are those where word order is canonical, but either the first object (12c) or the second object (12d) or both (12e) do not correspond to the query.

Note that, unlike precision, the recall rate of a query cannot be increased after the data have been extracted from the corpus. Thus, an important aspect in constructing a query is to annotate a random sample of our corpus manual for the phenomenon we are interested in, and then to check our query against this manual annotation. This will not only tell us how good or bad the recall of our query is, it will also provide information about the most frequent cases we are missing. Once we know this, we can try to revise our query to take these cases into account. In a POS-tagged corpus, we could, for example, search for a sequence of a pronoun and a noun in addition to the sequence pronoun-determiner that we used above, which would give us cases like (12d), or we could search for forms of *be* followed by a past participle followed by a determiner or noun, which would give us passives like those in (12b).

In some cases, however, there may not be any additional patterns that we can reasonably search for. In the present example with an untagged corpus, for example, there is no additional pattern that seems in any way promising. In such cases, we have two options for dealing with low recall: First, we can check (in our manually annotated subcorpus) whether the data that were recalled differ from the data that were not recalled in any way that is relevant for our research question. If this is not the case, we might decide to continue working with a low recall and hope that our results are still generalizable – Colleman & De Clerck (2011), for example, are mainly interested in the question which classes of verbs were used ditransitively at what time in the history of English, a question that they were able to discuss insightfully based on the subset of ditransitives matching their query.

If our data *do* differ along one or more of the dimensions relevant to our research project, we might have to increase the recall at the expense of precision and spend more time weeding out false positives. In the most extreme case, this might entail extracting the data manually, so let us return to this possibility in light of the current example.

4.1.3 Manual, semi-manual and automatic searches

In theory, the highest quality search results would always be achieved by a kind of close reading, i.e. a careful word-by-word (or phrase-by-phrase, clause-by-clause) inspection of the corpus. As already discussed in Chapter 2, this may sometimes be the only feasible option, either because automatic retrieval is difficult (as in the case of searching for ditransitives in an untagged corpus), or because an automatic retrieval is impossible (e.g., because the phenomenon we are interested in does not have any consistent formal properties, a point we will return to presently).

As discussed above, in the case of words and in at least some cases of grammatical structures, the quality of automatic searches may be increased by using a corpus annotated automatically with part-of-speech tags, phrase tags or even grammatical structures. As discussed in Section 3.2.2.1 of Chapter 3, this brings with it its own problems, as automatic tagging and grammatical parsing are far from perfect. Still, an automatically annotated corpus will frequently allow us to define searches whose precision and recall are higher than in the example above.

In the case of many other phenomena, however, automatic annotation is simply not possible, or yields a quality so low that it simply does not make sense to base queries on it. For example, linguistic metaphors are almost impossible to identify automatically, as they have little or no properties that systematically set them apart from literal language. Consider the following examples of the metaphors ANGER IS HEAT and ANGER IS A (HOT) LIQUID (from Lakoff & Kövecses 1987: 203):

(13) a. Boy, am I burned up.
b. He's just letting off steam.
c. I had reached the boiling point.

The first problem is that while the expressions in (13a–c) may refer to feelings of anger or rage, they can also occur in their literal meaning, as the corresponding authentic examples in (14a–c) show:

(14) a. "Now, after I am burned up," he said, snatching my wrist, "and the fire is out, you *must* scatter the ashes. ..." (Anne Rice, *The Vampire Lestat*)
b. As soon as the driver saw the train which had been hidden by the curve, he let off steam and checked the engine... (Galignani, *Accident on the Paris and Orleans Railway*)
c. Heat water in saucepan on highest setting until you reach the boiling point and it starts to boil gently. (www.sugarfreestevia.net)

Obviously, there is no query that would find the examples in (13) but not those in (14). In contrast, it is very easy for a human to recognize the examples in (14) as literal. If we are explicitly interested in metaphors involving liquids and/or heat, we could choose a semi-manual approach, first extracting all instances of words from the field of liquids and/or heat and then discarding all cases that are not metaphorical. This kind of approach is used quite fruitfully, for example, by Deignan (2005), amongst others.

If we are interested in metaphors of anger in general, however, this approach will not work, since we have no way of knowing beforehand which semantic fields to include in our query. This is precisely the situation where exhaustive retrieval can only be achieved by a manual corpus search, i.e., by reading the entire corpus and deciding for each word, phrase or clause, whether it constitutes an example of the phenomenon we are looking for. Thus, it is not surprising that many corpus-linguistic studies on metaphor are based on manual searches (see, for example, Semino & Masci (1996) or Jäkel (1997) for very thorough early studies of this kind).

However, as mentioned in Chapter 2, manual searches are very time-consuming and this limits their practical applicability: either we search large corpora, in which case manual searching is going to take more time and human resources than are realistically available, or we perform the search in a realistic time-frame and with the human resources realistically available, in which case we have to limit the size of our corpus so severely that the search results can no longer be considered representative of the language as a whole. Thus, manual searches are useful mainly in the context of research projects looking at a linguistic phenomenon in some clearly defined subtype of language (for example, metaphor in political speeches, see Charteris-Black 2005).

When searching corpora for such hard-to-retrieve phenomena, it may sometimes be possible to limit the analysis usefully to a subset of the available data, as shown in the previous subsection, where limiting the query for the ditransitive to active declarative clauses with canonical word order still yielded potentially useful results. It depends on the phenomenon and the imagination of the researcher to find such easier-to-retrieve subsets.

To take up the example of metaphors introduced above, consider the examples in (15), which are quite close in meaning to the corresponding examples in (13a–c) above (also from Lakoff & Kövecses 1987: 189, 203):

(15) a. He was consumed by his anger.
b. He was filled with anger.
c. She was brimming with rage.

In these cases, the PPs *by/with anger/rage* make it clear that *consume*, *(be) filled* and *brimming* are not used literally. If we limit ourselves just to metaphorical expressions of this type, i.e. expressions that explicitly mention both semantic fields involved in the metaphorical expression, it becomes possible to retrieve metaphors of anger semi-automatically. We could construct a query that would retrieve all instances of the lemmas ANGER, RAGE, FURY, and other synonyms of *anger*, and then select those results that also contain (within the same clause or within a window of a given number of words) vocabulary from domains like 'liquids', 'heat', 'containers', etc. This can be done manually by going through the concordance line by line (see, e.g., Tissari (2003) and Stefanowitsch (2004; 2006c), cf. also Section 11.2.2 of Chapter 11), or automatically by running a second query on the results of the first (or by running a complex query for words from both semantic fields at the same time, see Martin 2006). The first approach is more useful if we are interested in metaphors involving any semantic domain in addition to 'anger', the second approach is more useful (because more economical) in cases where we are interested in metaphors involving specific semantic domains.

Limiting the focus to a subset of cases sharing a particular formal feature is a feasible strategy in other areas of linguistics, too. For example, Heyd (2016) wants to investigate "narratives of belonging" – roughly, stretches of discourse in which members of a diaspora community talk about shared life experiences for the purpose of affirming their community membership. At first glance, this is the kind of potentially fuzzy concept that should give corpus linguists nightmares, even after Heyd (2016: 292) operationalizes it in terms of four relatively narrow criteria that the content of a stretch of discourse must fulfill in order to count as an example. Briefly, it must refer to experiences of the speaker themselves, it must mention actual specific events, it must contain language referring to some aspect of migration, and it must contain an evaluation of the events narrated. Obviously it is impossible to search a corpus based on these criteria. Therefore, Heyd chooses a two-step strategy (Heyd 2016: 294): first, she queries her corpus for the strings *born in*, *moved to* and *grew up in*, which are very basic, presumably wide-spread ways of mentioning central aspects of one's personal migration biography, and second, she assesses the stretches of discourse within which these strings occur on the basis of her criteria, discarding those that do not fulfill all four of them (this step is somewhere between retrieval and annotation).

As in the example of the ditransitive construction discussed above, retrieval strategies like those used by Stefanowitsch (2006c) and Heyd (2016) are useful where we can plausibly argue – or better yet, show – that the results are comparable to the results we would get if we extracted the phenomenon completely.

In cases, where the phenomenon in question does not have any consistent formal features that would allow us to construct a query, and cannot plausibly be restricted to a subset that does have such features, a mixed strategy of elicitation and corpus query may be possible. For example, Levin (2014) is interested in what he calls the "Bathroom Formula", which he defines as "clauses and phrases expressing speakers' need to leave any ongoing activity in order to go to the bathroom" Levin (2014: 2), i.e. to the toilet (sorry to offend American sensitivities[2]). This speech act is realized by phrases as diverse as (16a–c):

(16) a. I need a pee. (BNC A74)
  b. I have to go to the bathroom. (BNC CEX)
  c. I'm off to powder my nose. (BNC FP6)

There is no way to search for these expressions (and others with the same function) unless you are willing to read through the entire BNC – or unless you already know what to look for. Levin (2014) chooses a strategy based on the latter: he first assembles a list of expressions from the research literature on euphemisms and complement this by asking five native speakers for additional examples. He then searches for these phrases and analyzes their distribution across varieties and demographic variables like gender and class/social stratum.

[2]See Manning & Melchiori (1974), who show that the word *toilet* is very upsetting even to American college students.

Of course, this query will miss any expressions that were not part of their initial list, but the *conditional distribution* of those expressions that are included may still yield interesting results – we can still learn something about which of these expressions are preferred in a particular variety, by a particular group of speakers, in a particular situation, etc.

If we assemble our initial list of expressions systematically, perhaps from a larger number of native speakers that are representative of the speech community in question in terms of regional origin, sex, age group, educational background, etc., we should end up with a representative sample of expressions to base our query on. If we make our query flexible enough, we will likely even capture additional variants of these expressions. If other strategies are not available, this is certainly a feasible approach. Of course, this approach only works with relatively routinized speech event categories like the Bathroom Formula – greetings and farewells, asking for the time, proposing marriage, etc. – which, while they do not have any invariable formal features, do not vary infinitely either.

To sum up, it depends on the phenomenon under investigation and on the research question whether we can take an automatic or at least a semi-automatic approach or whether we have to resort to manual data extraction. Obviously, the more completely we can extract our object of research from the corpus, the better.

4.2 Annotating

Once the data have been extracted from the corpus (and, if necessary, false positives have been removed), they typically have to be annotated in terms of the variables relevant for the research question. In some cases, the variables and their values will be provided externally; they may, for example, follow from the structure of the corpus itself, as in the case of BRITISH ENGLISH VS. AMERICAN ENGLISH defined as "occurring in the LOB corpus" and "occurring in the BROWN corpus" respectively. In other cases, the variables and their values may have been operationalized in terms of criteria that can be applied objectively (as in the case of LENGTH defined as "number of letters"). In most cases, however, some degree of interpretation will be involved (as in the case of ANIMACY or the metaphors discussed above). Whatever the case, we need an annotation scheme – an explicit statement of the operational definitions applied. Of course, such an annotation scheme is especially important in cases where interpretative judgments are involved in categorizing the data. In this case, the annotation scheme should contain not just operational definitions, but also explicit guidelines as to how these definitions should be applied to the corpus data. These guidelines must be explicit enough to ensure a high degree of agreement if different annotators (sometimes also referred to as *coders* or *raters* apply it to the same data. Let us look at each of these aspects in some detail.

4.2.1 Annotating as interpretation

First of all, it is necessary to understand that the categorization of corpus data is an interpretative process in the first place. This is true regardless of the kind of category.

Even externally given categories typically receive a specific interpretation in the context of a specific research project. In the simplest case, this consists in accepting the operational definitions used by the makers of a particular corpus (as well as the interpretative judgments made in applying them). Take the example of BRITISH ENGLISH and AMERICAN ENGLISH used in Chapters 3 and 2: If we accept the idea that the LOB corpus contains "British English" we are accepting an interpretation of language varieties that is based on geographical criteria: British English means "the English spoken by people who live (perhaps also: who were born and grew up) in the British Isles".

Or take the example of SEX, one of the demographic speaker variables included in many modern corpora: By accepting the values of this variable, that the corpus provides (typically MALE and FEMALE), we are accepting a specific interpretation of what it means to be "male" or "female". In some corpora, this may be the interpretation of the speakers themselves (i.e., the corpus creators may have asked the speakers to specify their sex), in other cases this may be the interpretation of the corpus creators (based, for example, on the first names of the speakers or on the assessment of whoever collected the data). For many speakers in a corpus, these different interpretations will presumably match, so that we can accept whatever interpretation was used as an approximation of our own operation definition of SEX. But in research projects that are based on a specific understanding of SEX (for example, as a purely biological, a purely social or a purely psychological category), simply accepting the (often unstated) operational definition used by the corpus creators may distort our results substantially. The same is true of other demographic variables, like education, income, social class, etc., which are often defined on a "common sense" basis that does not hold up to the current state of sociological research.

Interpretation also plays a role in the case of seemingly objective criteria. Even though a criterion such as "number of letters" is largely self-explanatory, there are cases requiring interpretative judgments that may vary across researchers. In the absence of clear instructions they may not know, among other things, whether to treat ligatures as one or two letters, whether apostrophes or word-internal hyphens are supposed to count as letters, or how to deal with spelling variants (for example, in the BNC the noun *programme* also occurs in the variant *program* that is shorter by two letters). This kind of orthographic variation is very typical of older stages of English (before there was a somewhat standardized orthography), which causes problems not only for retrieval (cf. the discussion in Section 4.1.1 above, cf. also Barnbrook (1996), Section 8.2 for more detailed discussion), but also for a reasonable application of the criterion "number of letters".

In such cases, the role of interpretation can be reduced by including explicit instructions for dealing with potentially unclear cases. However, we may not have thought of all potentially unclear cases before we start annotating our data, which means that we may have to amend our annotation scheme as we go along. In this case, it is important to check whether our amendments have an effect on the data we have already annotated, and to re-annotate them if necessary.

In cases of less objective criteria (such as Animacy discussed in Section 3.2.2.5 of Chapter 3), the role of interpretation is obvious. No matter how explicit our annotation scheme, we will come across cases that are not covered and will require individual decisions; and even the clear cases are always based on an interpretative judgment. As mentioned in Chapter 1, this is not necessarily undesirable in the same way that intuitive judgements about acceptability are undesirable; interpreting linguistic utterances is a natural activity in the context of using language. Thus, if our operational definitions of the relevant variables and values are close to the definitions speakers implicitly apply in everyday linguistic interactions, we may get a high degree of agreement even in the absence of an explicit annotation scheme,[3] and certainly, operational definitions should strive to retain some degree of linguistic naturalness in the sense of being anchored in interpretation processes that plausibly occur in language processing.

4.2.2 Annotation schemes

We can think of a linguistic annotation scheme as a comprehensive operational definition for a particular variable, with detailed instructions as to how the values of this variable should be assigned to linguistic data (in our case, corpus data, but annotation schemes are also needed to categorize experimentally elicited linguistic data). The annotation scheme would typically also include a *coding scheme*,

[3]In fact, it may be worth exploring, within a corpus-linguistic framework, ways of annotating data that are based entirely on implicit decisions by untrained speakers; specifically, I am thinking here of the kinds of association tasks and sorting tasks often used in psycholinguistic studies of word meaning.

specifying the labels by which these categories are to be represented. For example, the distinctions between different degrees of Animacy need to be defined in a way that allows us to identify them in corpus data (this is the annotation scheme, cf. below), and the scheme needs to specify names for these categories (for example, the category containing animate entities could be labelled by the codes ANIMATE, ANIM, #01, CAT:8472, etc. – as long as we know what the label stands for, we can choose it randomly).

In order to keep different research projects in a particular area comparable, it is desirable to create annotation and coding schemes independently of a particular research project. However, the field of corpus linguistics is not well-established and methodologically mature enough yet to have yielded uncontroversial and widely applicable annotation schemes for most linguistic phenomena. There are some exceptions, such as the part-of-speech tag sets and the parsing schemes used by various wide-spread automatic taggers and parsers, which have become de facto standards by virtue of being easily applied to new data; there are also some substantial attempts to create annotation schemes for the manual annotation of phenomena like topicality (cf. Givón 1983), animacy (cf. Zaenen et al. 2004), and the grammatical description of English sentences (e.g. Sampson 1995).

Whenever it is feasible, we should use existing annotation schemes instead of creating our own – searching the literature for such schemes should be a routine step in the planning of a research project. Often, however, such a search will come up empty, or existing annotation schemes will not be suitable for the specific data we plan to use or they may be incompatible with our theoretical assumptions. In these cases, we have to create our own annotation schemes.

The first step in creating an annotation scheme for a particular variable consists in deciding on a set of values that this variable may take. As the example of Animacy in Chapter 3) shows, this decision is loosely constrained by our general operational definition, but the ultimate decision is up to us and must be justified within the context of our theoretical assumptions and our specific research question.

There are, in addition, several general criteria that the set of values for any variable must meet. First, they must be non-overlapping. This may seem obvious, but it is not at all unusual, for example, to find continuous dimensions split up into overlapping categories, as in the following quotation:

> Hunters aged 15–25 years old participated more in non-consumptive activities than those aged 25–35 and 45–65 ($P < 0.05$), as were those aged 35–45 compared to those 55–65 years old ($P < 0.05$). (Ericsson & Heberlein 2002: 304).

Here, the authors obviously summarized the ages of their subjects into the following four classes: (I) 25–35, (II) 35–45, (III) 45–55 and (IV) 55–65: thus, subjects aged 35 could be assigned to class I or class II, subjects aged 45 to class II or class III, and subjects aged 55 to class III or class IV. This must be avoided, as different annotators might make different decisions, and as other researchers attempting to replicate the research will not know how we categorized such cases.

Second, the variable should be defined such that it does not conflate properties that are potentially independent of each other, as this will lead to a set of values that do not fall along a single dimension. As an example, consider the so-called *Silverstein Hierarchy* used to categorize nouns for (inherent) Topicality (after Deane 1987: 67):

(17) 1st person pronoun
2nd person pronoun
3rd person pronoun
3rd person demonstrative
Proper name
Kin-Term
Human and animate NP
Concrete object
Container
Location
Perceivable
Abstract

Note, first, that there is a lot of overlap in this annotation scheme. For example, a first or second person pronoun will always refer to a human or animate NP and a third person pronoun will frequently do so, as will a proper name or a kin term. Similarly, a container is a concrete object and can also be a location, and everything above the category "Perceivable" is also perceivable. This overlap can only be dealt with by an instruction of the kind that every nominal expression should be put into the topmost applicable category; in other words, we need to add an "except for expressions that also fit into one of the categories above" to every category label.

Secondly, although the Silverstein Hierarchy may superficially give the impression of providing values of a single variable that could be called Topicality, it is actually a mixture of several quite different variables and their possible values. One attempt of disentangling these variables and giving them each a set of plausible values is the following:

(18) a. Type of Nominal Expression:
PRONOUN > PROPER NAME > KINSHIP TERMS > LEXICAL NP

b. Discourse Role:
SPEAKER > HEARER > OTHER (NEAR > FAR)

c. Animacy/Agency:
HUMAN > ANIMATE > INANIMATE

d. Concreteness:
TOUCHABLE > NON-TOUCHABLE CONCRETE > ABSTRACT

e. Gestalt Status:
OBJECT > CONTAINER > LOCATION

Given this set of variables, it is possible to describe all categories of the Silverstein Hierarchy as a combination of values of these variables, for example:

(19) a. 1st Person Pronoun:
PRONOUN + SPEAKER + HUMAN + TOUCHABLE + OBJECT

b. Concrete Object:
LEXICAL NP + OTHER + INANIMATE + TOUCHABLE + OBJECT

The set of variables in (18) also allows us to differentiate between expressions that the Silverstein Hierarchy lumps together, for example, a 3rd person pronoun could be categorized as (20a), (20b), (20c) or (20d), depending on whether it referred to a *mouse*, a *rock*, *air* or *democracy*:

(20) a. PRONOUN + OTHER + ANIMATE + TOUCHABLE + OBJECT

b. PRONOUN + OTHER + INANIMATE + TOUCHABLE + OBJECT

c. PRONOUN + OTHER + INANIMATE + NON-TOUCHABLE + OBJECT (or perhaps LOCATION, cf. *in the air*)

d. PRONOUN + OTHER + INANIMATE + ABSTRACT + OBJECT (or perhaps LOCATION, cf. the locative preposition in the phrase *in a democracy*)

There are two advantages of this more complex annotation scheme. First, it allows a more principled categorization of individual expressions: the variables and their values are easier to define and there are fewer unclear cases. Second, it would allow us to determine empirically which of the variables are actually relevant in the context of a given research question, as irrelevant variables will not show a skew in their distribution across different conditions. Originally, the Silverstein Hierarchy was meant to allow for a principled description of split ergative systems; it is possible, that the specific conflation of variables is suitable for this task. However, it is an open question whether the same conflation of variables is also suitable for the analysis of other phenomena. If we were to apply it as is, we would not be able to tell whether this is the case. Thus, we should always define our variables in terms of a single dimension and deal with complex concepts (like Topicality) by analyzing the data in terms of a set of such variables.

After defining a variable (or set of variables) and deciding on the type and number of values, the second step in creating an annotation scheme consists in defining what belongs into each category. Where necessary, this should be done in the form of a decision procedure.

For example, the annotation scheme for Animacy mentioned in Chapter 3 (Garretson 2004; Zaenen et al. 2004) has the categories human and organization (among others). The category human is relatively self-explanatory, as we tend to have a good intuition about what constitutes a human. Nevertheless, the annotation scheme spells out that it does not matter by what linguistic means humans are referred to (e.g., proper names, common nouns including kinship terms, and pronouns) and that dead, fictional or potential future humans are included as well as "humanoid entities like gods, elves, ghosts, and androids".

The category organization is much more complex to apply consistently, since there is no intuitively accessible and generally accepted understanding of what constitutes an organization. In particular, it needs to be specified what distinguishes an organization from other groups of human beings (that are to be categorized as human according to the annotation scheme). The annotation scheme defines an organization as a referent involving "more than one human" with "some degree of group identity". It then provides the following hierarchy of properties that a group of humans may have (where each property implies the presence of all properties below its position in the hierarchy):

(21) +/– chartered/official
+/– temporally stable
+/– collective voice/purpose
+/– collective action
+/– collective

It then states that "any group of humans at + collective voice or higher" should be categorized as organization, while those below should simply be annotated as human. By listing properties that a group must have to count as an organization in the sense of the annotation scheme, the decision is simplified considerably, and by providing a decision procedure, the number of unclear cases is reduced. The annotation scheme also illustrates the use of the hierarchy:

> Thus, while "the posse" would be an ORG, "the mob" might not be, depending on whether we see the mob as having a collective purpose. "The crowd" would not be considered ORG, but rather simply HUMAN.

Whether or not to include such specific examples is a question that must be answered in the context of particular research projects. One advantage is that examples may help the annotators understand the annotation scheme. A disadvantage is that examples may be understood as prototypical cases against which the referents in the data are to be matched, which may lead annotators to ignore the definitions and decision procedures.

The third step, discussed in detail in the next section, consists in testing the reliability of our annotation scheme. When we are satisfied that the scheme can be reliably applied to the data, the final step is the annotation itself.

4.2.3 The reliability of annotation schemes

In some cases, we may be able to define our variables in such a way that they can be annotated automatically. For example, if we define WORD LENGTH in terms of "number of letters", we could write a simple computer program to go through our corpus, count the letters in each word and attach the value as a tag. Since computers are good at counting, it would be easy to ensure that such a program is completely accurate in its decisions. We could also, for example, create a list of the 2500 most frequent nouns in English and their ANIMACY values, and write a program that goes through a tagged corpus and, whenever it encounters a word tagged as a noun, looks up this value and attaches it to the word as a tag. In this case, the accuracy is likely to be much lower, as the program would not be able to distinguish between different word senses, for example assigning the label ANIMATE to the word *horse* regardless of whether it refers to an actual horse, a hobby horse (which should be annotated as INANIMATE or ABSTRACT depending on whether an actual or a metaphorical hobby horse is referred to) or whether it occurs in the idiom STRAIGHT FROM THE HORSE'S MOUTH (where it would presumably have to be annotated as HUMAN, if at all).

In these more complex cases, we can, and should, assess the quality of the automatic annotation in the same way in which we would assess the quality of the results returned by a particular query, in terms of precision and recall (cf. Section 4.1.2, Table 4.1). In the context of annotating data, a true positive result for a particular value would be a case where that value has been assigned to a corpus example correctly, a false positive would be a case where that value has been assigned incorrectly, a false negative would be a case where the value has not been assigned although it should have been, and a true negative would be a case where the value has not been assigned and should not have been assigned.

This assumes, however, that we can determine with a high degree of certainty what the correct value would be in each case. The examples discussed in this chapter show, however, that this decision itself often involves a certain degree of interpretation – even an explicit and detailed annotation scheme has to be applied by individuals based on their understanding of the instructions contained in it and the data to which they are to be applied. Thus, a certain degree of subjectivity cannot be avoided, but we need to minimize the subjective aspect of interpretation as much as possible.

The most obvious way of doing this is to have (at least) two different annotators apply the annotation scheme to the data – if our measurements cannot be made objective (and, as should be clear by now, they rarely can in linguistics), this will at least allow us to ensure that they are intersubjectively reliable.

One approach would be to have the entire data set annotated by two annotators independently on the basis of the same annotation scheme. We could then identify all cases in which the two annotators did not assign the same value and determine where the disagreement came from. Obvious possibilities include cases that are not covered by the annotation scheme at all, cases where the definitions in the annotation scheme are too vague to apply or too ambiguous to make a principled decision, and cases where one of the annotators has misunderstood the corpus example or made a mistake due to inattention. Where the annotation scheme is to blame, it could be revised accordingly and re-applied to all unclear cases. Where an annotator is at fault, they could correct their annotation decision. At the end of this process we would have a carefully annotated data set with no (or very few) unclear cases left.

However, in practice there are two problems with this procedure. First, it is extremely time-consuming, which will often make it difficult to impossible to find a second annotator. Second, discussing all unclear cases but not the apparently clear cases holds the danger that the former will be annotated according to different criteria than the latter.

Both problems can be solved (or at least alleviated) by testing the annotation scheme on a smaller dataset using two annotators and calculating its reliability across annotators. If this so-called interrater reliability is sufficiently high, the annotation scheme can safely be applied to the actual data set by a single annotator. If not, it needs to be made more explicit and applied to a new set of test data by two annotators; this process must be repeated until the interrater reliability is satisfactory.

A frequently used measure of interrater reliability in designs with two annotators is Cohen's κ (Cohen 1960), which can range from 0 ("no agreement") to 1 ("complete agreement"). It is calculated as shown in (22):[4]

(22) $$\kappa = \frac{p_o - p_e}{1 - p_e}$$

In this formula, p_o is the relative observed agreement between the raters (i.e. the percentage of cases where both raters have assigned the same category) and p_e is the relative expected agreement (i.e. the percentage of cases where they should have agreed by chance).

Table 4.3 shows a situation where the two raters assign one of the two categories X or Y. Here, p_o would be the sum of *n*(X, X) and *n*(Y, Y), divided by the sum of all annotation; p_e can be calculated in various ways, a straightforward one will be introduced below.

Table 4.3: A contingency table for two raters and two categories

		Rater 2	
		category x	Category x
Rater 1	category x	*n*(x, x)	*n*(x, y)
	category y	*n*(y, x)	*n*(y, y)

Let us look at a concrete case. In English, many semantic relations can be expressed by more than one linguistic structure. A prominent example is 'possession', which can be expressed in two main ways: either by the *s*-possessive (traditionally referred to as "genitive") with the modifier marked by the clitic *'s* (cf. 23a), or by the *of*-construction, with the modifier as a prepositional object of the preposition *of* (cf. 23b):

(23) a. a tired horse's plodding step (BROWN K13)
b. every leaping stride of the horse (BROWN N02)

Let us assume that we want to investigate the factors determining the choice between these two constructions (as we will do in Chapters 5 and 6). In order to do so, we need to identify the subset of constructions with *of* that actually

[4]For more than two raters, there is a more general version of this metric, referred to as Fleiss' κ (Fleiss 1971), but as it is typically difficult even to find a second annotator, we will stick with the simpler measure here.

correspond to the *s*-possessive semantically – note that the *of*-construction encodes a wide range of relations, including many – for example quantification or partition – that are never expressed by an *s*-possessive. This means that we must manually go through the hits for the *of*-construction in our data and decide whether the relation encoded could also be encoded by an *s*-posessive. Let us use the term "*of*-possessive" for these cases. Ideally, we would do this by searching a large corpus for actual examples of paraphrases with the *s*-possessive, but let us assume that this is too time-consuming (a fair assumption in many research contexts) and that we want to rely on introspective judgments instead.

We might formulate a simple annotation scheme like the following:

> For each case of the structure [(DET_i) (AP_i) N_i *of* NP_j], paraphrase it as an *s*-possessive of the form [NP_j *'s* (APi) N_i] (for example, *the leaping stride of the horse* becomes *the horse's leaping stride*). If the result sounds like something a speaker of English would use, assign the label POSS, if not, assign the label *other.*

In most cases, following this instruction should yield a fairly straightforward response, but there are more difficult cases. Consider (24a, b) and (25a, b), where the paraphrase sounds decidedly odd:

(24) a. a lack of unity
b. ?? unity's lack

(25) a. the concept of unity
b. ?? unity's concept

At first glance, neither of them seems to be paraphraseable, so they would both be assigned the value OTHER according to our annotation scheme. However, in a context that strongly favors *s*-possessives – namely, where the possessor is realised as a possessive determiner –, the paraphrase of (24a) sounds acceptable, while (25a) still sounds odd:

(26) a. Unity is important, and *its lack* can be a problem.
b. ?? Unity is important, so *its concept* must be taught early.

Thus, we might want to expand our annotation scheme as follows:

For each case of the structure [(DET_i) (AP_i) N_i *of* NP_j],

1. paraphrase it as an *s*-possessive of the form [NP_j *'s* (AP_i) N_i] (for example, *the leaping stride of the horse* becomes *the horse's leaping stride*). If the result sounds like something a speaker of English would use, assign the label POSS. If not,
2. replace NP_j by a possessive determiner (for example, *the horse's leaping stride* becomes *its leaping stride* and construct a coordinated sentence with NP*j* as the subject of the first conjunct and [$PDET_j$ (AP_i) N_i] as the subject of the second conjunct (for example, *The horse tired and its leaping stride shortened.* If the *s*-possessive sounds like something a speaker of English would use in this context, assign the label *poss*,) if not, assign the label OTHER.

Obviously, it is no simple task to invent a meaningful context of the form required by these instructions and then deciding whether the result is acceptable. In other words, it is not obvious that this is a very reliable operationalization of the construct *OF*-POSSESSIVE, and it would not be surprising if speakers' introspective judgments varied too drastically to yield useful results.

Table 4.4 shows a random sample of *of*-constructions from the BROWN corpus (with cases that have a quantifying noun like *lot* or *bit* instead of a regular noun as N_i already removed. The introspective judgments were derived by two different raters (both trained linguists who wish to remain anonymous) based on the instructions above. The tabulated data for both annotators are shown in Table 4.5.

As discussed above, the relative observed agreement is the percentage of cases both raters chose POSS or both raters chose OTHER, i.e.

$$p_o = \frac{18+9}{18+2+1+9} = \frac{27}{30} = 0.9$$

The relative expected agreement, i.e. the probability that both raters agree in their choice between POSS or OTHER by chance, can be determined as follows (we will return to this issue in the next chapter and keep it simple here). RATER 1 chose POSS with a probability of $20/30 = 0.6667$ (i.e., 66.67 percent of the time) and OTHER with a probability of $10/30 = 0.3333$ (i.e., 33.33 percent of the time). RATER 2 chose POSS with a probability of $19/30 = 0.6333$, and OTHER with a probability of $11/30 = 0.3667$.

The joint probability that both raters will choose POSS by chance is the product of their individual probabilities of doing so, i.e. $0.6667 \times 0.6333 = 0.4222$; for no it is $0.3333 \times 0.3667 = 0.1222$. Adding these two probabilities gives us the overall probability that the raters will agree by chance: $0.4222 + 0.1222 = 0.5444$.

Table 4.4: Paraphraseablility ratings for a sample of *of*-constructions by two raters

Example	Rater 1	Rater 2
the wintry homeland of his fathers	POSS	POSS
August of 1960	OTHER	OTHER
on the side of the law	POSS	POSS
the guardians of our precious liberty	POSS	POSS
the board of directors	OTHER	OTHER
the label of un-American	OTHER	OTHER
the lack of consciousness	POSS	POSS
a direct consequence of observations	POSS	POSS
the side of the stall	POSS	POSS
the end of the afternoon	POSS	POSS
the crew of a trawler	POSS	POSS
children of military personnel	POSS	POSS
a large group of people	OTHER	OTHER
the feeding of the fluid (into the manometer)	POSS	OTHER
the spirit of the mad genius	POSS	POSS
economical means of control	POSS	OTHER
(in) violation of the Fifth Amendment	OTHER	OTHER
the announcement of a special achievement award	POSS	POSS
the concept of unity	OTHER	OTHER
(in) honor of its commander	POSS	POSS
the blood group of the donor	POSS	POSS
a box of ammunition	OTHER	OTHER
the odor of decay	POSS	POSS
the surge of nationalism	OTHER	OTHER
a fair knowledge of the English language	OTHER	POSS
the resignation of Neil Duffy	POSS	POSS
various levels of competence	OTHER	OTHER
the invasion of Cuba	POSS	POSS
the advancement of all people	POSS	POSS
the novelty of such a gathering	POSS	POSS

Table 4.5: Count of judgments from Table 4.4

		Rater 2		
		poss	other	Total
Rater 1	poss	18	2	20
	other	1	9	10
	Total	19	11	30

We can now calculate the interrater reliability for the data in Table 4.4 using the formula in (22) above:

$$\kappa = \frac{0.7667 - 0.5444}{1 - 0.5444} = 0.7805$$

There are various suggestions as to what value of κ is to be taken as satisfactory. One reasonable suggestion (following McHugh 2012) is shown in Table 4.6; according to this table, our annotation scheme is good enough to achieve "strong" agreement between raters, and hence presumably good enough to use in a corpus linguistic research study (what is "good enough" obviously depends on the risk posed by cases where there is no agreement in classification).

Table 4.6: Interpretation of κ values

κ	Level of agreement
0–0.20	None
0.21–0.39	Minimal
0.40–0.59	Weak
0.60–0.79	Moderate
0.80–0.90	Strong
> 0.90	Almost Perfect

4.2.4 Reproducibility

Scientific research is collaborative and incremental in nature, with researchers building on and extending each other's work. As discussed in the previous chapter in Section 3.3, this requires that we be transparent with respect to our data and methods to an extent that allows other researchers to reproduce our results. This is referred to as *reproducibility* and/or (with a different focus, *replicability*) – since there is some variation in how these terms are used, let us briefly switch to more specific, non-conventional terminology.

The minimal requirement of an incremental and collaborative research cycle is what we might call *retraceability*: our description of the research design and the associated procedures must be explicit and detailed enough for another researcher to retrace and check for correctness each step of our analysis and when provided with all our research materials (i.e., the corpora, the raw extracted data and the annotated data) and all other resources used (such as our annotation scheme and the software used in the extraction and statistical analysis of the data) and all our research notes, intermediate calculations, etc. In other words, our research project must be documented in sufficient detail for others to make sure that we arrived at our results via the procedures that we claim to have used, and to identify possible problems in our data and/or procedure. Thus retraceability is closely related to the idea of accountability in accounting.

Going slightly beyond retraceability, we can formulate a requirement which we might call *reconstructibility*: given all materials and resources, the description of our procedure must be detailed enough to ensure that a researcher independently applying this procedure to the same data using the same resources, but without access to our research notes, intermediate results, etc., should arrive at the same result.

Both of the requirements just described fall within the range of what is referred to as reproducibility. Obviously, as long as our data and other resources (and, if relevant, our research notes and intermediate results) are available, reproducibility is largely a matter of providing a sufficiently explicit and fine-grained description of the steps by which we arrived at our results. However, in actual practice it is surprisingly difficult to achieve reproducibility even if our research design does not involve any manual data extraction or annotation (see Stefanowitsch (2018) for an attempt). As soon as our design includes steps that involve manual extraction or annotation, it may still be retraceable, but it will no longer be reconstructible; however, if we ensure that our extraction methods and annotation scheme(s) have a high interrater reliability, an attempt at reconstruction should at least lead to very similar results.

Matters become even more difficult if our data or other resources are not accessible, for example, if we use a corpus or software constructed specifically for our research project that we cannot share publicly due to copyright restrictions, or if our corpus contains sensitive information such that sharing it would endanger individuals, violate non-disclosure agreements, constitute high treason, etc.

In such a case, our research will not be reproducible (retraceable or reconstructible), which is why we should avoid this situation. If it cannot be avoided, however, our research should still meet a requirement that we might call *transferability*: the description of our materials, resources and procedures must be detailed enough for other researchers to transfer it to similar materials and resources and arrive at a similar result. This is broadly what *replicability* refers to, but the term may also be used in an extended sense to situations where a researcher attempts to replicate our results and conclusions rather than our entire research design. Obviously, research designs that meet the criterion of reproducibility are also transferable, but not vice versa.

In the context of the scientific research cycle, reproducibility and replicability are crucial: a researcher building on previous research must be able to reconstruct this research in order to determine its quality and thus the extent to which our results can be taken to corroborate our hypotheses. They must also be able to reconstruct the research in order to build on it in a meaningful way, for example by adapting our methods to other kinds of data, new hypotheses or other linguistic phenomena.

Say, for example, a researcher wanted to extend the analysis of the words *windscreen* and *windshield* presented in Chapter 3, Section 3.1 to other varieties of English. The first step would be to reconstruct our analysis (if they had access to the LOB, BROWN, FLOB and FROWN corpora), or to adapt it (for example, to the BNC and COCA, briefly mentioned at the end of our analysis). However, with the information provided in Chapter 3, this would be very difficult. First, there was no mention of which version of the LOB, BROWN, FLOB and FROWN was used (there are at least two official releases, one that was commercially available from an organization called ICAME and a different one that is available via the CLARIN network, and each of those releases contains different versions of each corpus). Second, there was no mention of the exact queries used – obviously, the words can be spelled in a range of ways, including at least *WINDSCREEN, WIND SCREEN, WIND-SCREEN, Windscreen, Wind screen, Wind Screen, Wind-screen, Wind-Screen, windscreen, wind screen* and *wind-screen* for WINDSCREEN, and the corresponding variants for WINDSHIELD. This range of graphemic variants can be searched for in different ways depending what annotation the respective version of the corpus contains, what software was used to access it and how we want to formulate our query. None of this information was provided in Chapter 3. Finally, nothing was said about how the total number of hits was calculated, which is not a problem in the case of a simple mathematical operation like addition, but which can quickly become relevant in the case of procedures and software used to evaluate the results statistically (as discussed in the next chapter).

It would not be surprising if a researcher attempting to reconstruct our analysis would get different results. This is not a purely theoretical possibility even with such a simple research design – you will often find that even word frequencies reported for a given corpus in the literature will not correspond to what your own query of the same corpus yields. Obviously, the more complex the phenomenon, the more difficult it will be to guess what query or queries a researcher has used if they do not tell us. And if the data had to be annotated in any way more complex than "number of letters", that annotation will be difficult to reconstruct even if an annotation scheme is provided, and impossible to reconstruct if this is not the case.

Unfortunately, corpus linguists have long paid insufficient attention to this (and I include much of my own research in this criticism). It is high time that this change and that corpus linguists make an honest effort to describe their designs in sufficient detail to make them reproducible (in all senses discussed above). In many disciplines, it is becoming customary to provide raw data, categorized data, computer scripts, etc. in the form of *supplementary materials* with every research article. This is not yet standard in corpus linguistics, but it is a good idea to plan and document your research as though it already were.

4.2.5 Data storage

We will conclude this chapter with a discussion of a point that may, at first, appear merely practical but that is crucial in carrying out corpus-linguistic research (and that has some methodological repercussions, too): the question of how to store our data and annotation decisions. There are broadly two ways of doing so: first, in the corpus itself, and second, in a separate database of some sort.

The first option is routinely chosen in the case of automatically annotated variables like Part of Speech, as in the passage from the BROWN corpus cited in Figure 2.4 in Chapter 2, repeated here partially as (27):

(27) `the_AT fact_NN that_CS Jess's_NP$ horse_NN had_HVD not_* been_BEN returned_VBN to_IN its_PP$ stall_NN could_MD indicate_VB that_CS Diane's_NP$ information_NN had_HVD been_BEN wrong_JJ ,_, but_CC Curt_NP didn't_DOD* interpret_VB it_PPO this_DT way_NN ._.` (BROWN N12)

Here, the annotation (i.e., the part-of-speech tags) are attached to the data they refer to (i.e., words) by an underscore (recall that alternatively, a vertical format with words in the first and tags in the second column is frequently used, as are various kinds of XML notation).

The second option is more typically chosen in the case of annotations added in the context of a specific research project (especially if they are added manually): the data are extracted, stored in a separate file, and then annotated. Frequently, spreadsheet applications are used to store the corpus data and annotation decisions, as in the example in Figure 4.1, where possessive pronouns and nouns are annotated for NOMINAL TYPE, ANIMACY and CONCRETENESS:

	A	B	C	D	E
1	**Example**	**Source File**	**Word**	**Nom. Type**	**Animacy**
2	Jess's horse	N 12	Jess	proper name	human
3	its stall	N 12	it	pronoun	animate
4	Diane's information	N 12	Diane	proper name	human

Figure 4.1: Example of a raw data table

The first line contains labels that tell us what information is found in each column respectively. This should include the example itself (either as shown in Figure 4.1, or in the form of a KWIC concordance line) and meta-information such as what corpus and/or corpus file the example was extracted from. Crucially, it will include the relevant variables. Each subsequent line contains one observation (i.e., one hit and the appropriate values of each variable). This format – one column for each variable, and one line for each example – is referred to as a *raw data table*. It is the standard way of recording measurements in all empirical sciences and we should adhere to it strictly, as it ensures that the *structure* of the data is retained.

In particular, we should never store our data in summarized form, for example, as shown in Figure 4.2.

	A	B	C	D	E
1	**Noun Type**	pronoun	proper name	noun	
2		1	2	0	
3	**Animacy**	human	animate	inanimate	
4		2	1	0	

Figure 4.2: Data stored in summarized form

There is simply no need to store data in this form – if we need this kind of summary, it can be created automatically from a raw data table like that in Figure 4.1 – all major spreadsheet applications and statistical software packages have this functionality. What is more, statistics software packages require a raw data table of the kind shown in Figure 4.1 as input for most kinds of statistical analysis.

As mentioned above, however, the format of storage is not simply a practical matter, but a methodological one. If we did store our data in the form shown in Figure 4.2 straight away, we would irreversibly destroy the relationship between the corpus hits and the different annotations applied to them. In other words, we would have no way of telling which combinations of variables actually occurred in the data. In Figure 4.2, for example, we cannot tell whether the pronoun referred to one one of the human referents or to the animate referent. Even if we do not need to know these relationships in the context of a given research project (or initially believe we will not), we should avoid this situation, as we do not know what additional questions may come up in the course of our research that do require this information.

Since quantitative analysis always requires a raw data table, we might conclude that it is the only useful way of recording our annotation decisions. However, there are cases where it may be more useful to record them in the form of annotations in (a copy of) the original corpus instead, i.e., analogously to automatically added annotations. For example, the information in Figure 4.1 could be recorded in the corpus itself in the same way that part-of-speech tags are, i.e., we could add an Animacy label to every nominal element in our corpus in the format used for POS tags by the original version of the BROWN corpus, as shown in (28):

(28) `the_AT fact_NN_`**`abstract`**` that_CS Jess's_NP$_`**`human`**` horse_NN_`**`animate`**` had_HVD not_* been_BEN returned_VBN to_IN its_PP$_`**`animate`**` stall_NN_`**`inanimate`**` could_MD indicate_VB that_CS Diane's_NP$_`**`human`**` information_NN_`**`abstract`**` had_HVD been_BEN wrong_JJ ,_, but_CC Curt_NP_`**`human`**` didn't_DOD* interpret_VB it_PPO_`**`inanimate`**` this_DT way_NN_`**`inanimate`**` ._.`

From a corpus annotated in this way, we can always create a raw data list like that in Figure 4.1 by searching for possessives and then separating the hits into the word itself, the Part-of-Speech label and the Animacy annotation (this can be done manually, or with the help of regular expressions in a text editor or with a few lines of code in a scripting language like Perl or Python).

The advantage would be that we, or other researchers, could also use our annotated data for research projects concerned with completely different research questions. Thus, if we are dealing with a variable that is likely to be of general interest, we should consider the possibility of annotating the corpus itself, instead of first extracting the relevant data to a raw data table and annotating them afterwards. While the direct annotation of corpus files is rare in corpus linguistics, it has become the preferred strategy in various fields concerned with qualitative analysis of textual data. There are open-source and commercial software packages dedicated to this task. They typically allow the user to define a set of annotation categories with appropriate codes, import a text file, and then assign the codes to a word or larger textual unit by selecting it with the mouse and then clicking a button for the appropriate code that is then added (often in XML format) to the imported text. This strategy has the additional advantage that one can view one's annotated examples in their original context (which may be necessary when annotating additional variables later). However, the available software packages are geared towards the analysis of individual texts and do not let the user to work comfortably with large corpora.

5 Quantifying research questions

Recall, once again, that at the end of Chapter 2, we defined corpus linguistics as

> the investigation of linguistic research questions that have been framed in terms of the conditional distribution of linguistic phenomena in a linguistic corpus.

We discussed the fact that this definition covers cases of hypotheses phrased in absolute terms, i.e. cases where the distribution of a phenomenon across different conditions is a matter of all or nothing (as in "All speakers of American English refer to the front window of a car as *windshield*; all speakers of British English refer to it as *windscreen*") as well as cases where the distribution is a matter of more-or-less (as in "British English speakers prefer the word *railway* over *railroad* when referring to train tracks; American English speakers prefer *railroad* over *railway*" or "More British speakers refer to networks of train tracks as *railway* instead of *railroad*; more American English speakers refer to them as *railroad* instead of *railway*").

In the case of hypotheses stated in terms of more-or-less, predictions must be stated in quantitative terms which in turn means that our data have to be quantified in some way so that we can compare them to our predictions. In this chapter, we will discuss in more detail how this is done when dealing with different types of data.

Specifically, we will discuss three types of data (or *levels of measurement*) that we might encounter in the process of quantifying the (annotated) results of a corpus query (Section 5.1): nominal data (discussed in more detail in Section 5.2), ordinal (or rank) data (discussed in more detail in Section 5.3, and cardinal data (discussed in more detail in Section 5.4. These discussions, summarized in Section 5.5, will lay the ground work for the introduction to statistical hypothesis testing presented in the next chapter.

5.1 Types of data

In order to illustrate these types of data, let us turn to a linguistic phenomenon that is more complex than the distribution of words across varieties, and closer to the kind of phenomenon actually of interest to corpus linguists: that of the two English possessive constructions introduced in Section 4.2.3 of Chapter 4 above. As discussed there, the two constructions can often be used seemingly interchangeably, as in (1a, b):

(1) a. *The city's museums* are treasure houses of inspiring objects from all eras and cultures. (www.res.org.uk)

b. Today one can find the monuments and artifacts from all of these eras in *the museums of the city*. (www.travelhouseuk.co.uk)

However, there are limits to this interchangeability. First, there are a number of relations that are exclusively encoded by the *of*-construction, such as quantities (both generic, as in *a couple/bit/lot of*, and in terms of measures, as in *six miles/years/gallons of*), type relations (*a kind/type/sort/class of*) and composition or constitution (*a mixture of water and whisky, a dress of silk*, etc.) (cf., e.g., Stefanowitsch 2003).

Second, and more interestingly, even where a relation *can* be expressed by both constructions, there is often a preference for one or the other in a given context. A number of factors underlying these preferences have been suggested and investigated using quantitative corpus-linguistic methods. Among these, there are three that are widely agreed upon to have an influence, namely the givenness, animacy and weight of the modifier. These three factors nicely illustrate the levels of measurement mentioned above, so we will look at each of them in some detail.

(a) Givenness Following the principle of Functional Sentence Perspective, the *s*-possessive will be preferred if the modifier (the phrase marked by *'s* or *of*) refers to given information, while the construction with *of* will be preferred if the modifier is new (Standwell 1982). Thus, (2a) and (3a) sound more natural than (2b) and (3b) respectively:

(2) a. In New York, we visited *the city's* many museums.

b. ?? In New York, we visited the many museums *of the city*.

(3) a. The Guggenheim is much larger than the museums *of other major cities*.

b. ?? The Guggenheim is much larger than *other major cities'* museums.

(b) Animacy Since animate referents tend to be more topical than inanimate ones and more topical elements tend to precede less topical ones, if the modifier is animate, the *s*-possessive will be preferred, if it is inanimate, the construction with *of* will be preferred (cf. Quirk et al. 1972: 192–203; Deane 1987):

(4) a. *Solomon R. Guggenheim's* collection contains some fine paintings.
    b. ?? The collection *of Solomon R. Guggenheim* contains some fine paintings.

(5) a. The collection *of the Guggenheim museum* contains some fine paintings.
    b. ?? *The Guggenheim museum's* collection contains some fine paintings.

(c) Length Since short constituents generally precede long constituents, if the modifier is short, the *s*-possessive will be preferred, if it is long, the construction with *of* will be preferred (Altenberg 1980):

(6) a. *The museum's* collection is stunning.
    b. ?? The collection *of the museum* is stunning.

(7) a. The collection *of the most famous museum in New York* is stunning.
    b. ?? *The most famous museum in New York's* collection is stunning.

In the case of all three factors, we are dealing with hypotheses concerning preferences rather than absolute difference. None of the examples with question marks are ungrammatical and all of them could conceivably occur; they just sound a little bit odd. Thus, the predictions we can derive from each hypothesis must be stated and tested in terms of relative rather than absolute differences – they all involve predictions stated in terms more-or-less rather than all-or-nothing. Relative quantitative differences are expressed and dealt with in different ways depending on the type of data they involve.

5.1.1 Nominal data

A nominal variable is a variable whose values are labels for categories that have no intrinsic order with respect to each other (i.e., there is no aspect of their definition that would allow us to put them in a natural order) – for example, Sex, Nationality or Native Language. If we categorize data in terms of such a nominal variable, the only way to quantify them is to count the number of observations of each category in a given sample and express the result in absolute frequencies (i.e., raw numbers) or relative frequencies (such as percentages). For example, in the population of the world in 2005, there were 92 million native speakers of german and 75 million speakers of french.

We cannot *rank* the values of nominal variables based on intrinsic criteria. For example, we cannot rank the German language higher than the French language on the basis of any intrinsic property of German and French. They are simply two different manifestations of the phenomenon Language, part of an unordered set including all human languages.

That we cannot rank them based on intrinsic criteria does not mean that we cannot rank them at all. For example, we could rank them by number of speakers worldwide (in which case, as the numbers cited above show, German ranks above French). We could also rank them by the number of countries in which they are an official language (in which case French, which has official status in 29 countries, ranks above German, with an official status in only 6 countries). But the number of native speakers or the number of countries where a language has an official status is not an intrinsic property of that language – German would still be German if its number of speakers was reduced by half by an asteroid strike, and French would still be French if it lost its official status in all 29 countries). In other words, we are not really ranking french and german as values of Language at all; instead, we are ranking values of the variables Size of Native Speech Community and Number of Countries with Official Language X respectively.

We also cannot calculate mean values ("averages") between the values of nominal variables. We cannot claim, for example, that Javanese is the mean of German and French because the number of Javanese native speakers falls (roughly) halfway between that of German and French native speakers. Again, what we would be calculating a mean of is the values of the variable Size of Native Speech Community, and while it makes a sort of sense to say that the mean of the values number of french native speakers and number of german native speakers was 83.5 in 2005, it does not make sense to refer to this mean as number of javanese speakers.

With respect to the three hypotheses concerning the distribution of the *s*-possessive and the *of*-possessive, it is obvious that they all involve at least one nominal variable – the constructions themselves. These are essentially values of a variable we could call Type of Possessive Construction. We could categorize all grammatical expressions of possession in a corpus in terms of the values *s*-possessive and *of*-possessive, count them and express the result in terms of absolute or relative frequencies. For example, the *s*-possessive occurs 22 193 times in the BROWN corpus (excluding proper names and instances of the double *s*-possessive), and the *of*-possessive occurs 17 800 times.[1]

[1]This is an estimate; it would take too long to go through all 36 406 occurrences of *of* and identify those that occur in the structure relevant here, so I categorized a random subsample of 500 hits of *of* and generalized the proportion of *of*-possessives vs. other uses of *of* to the total number of hits for *of*.

As with the example of the variable Native Language above, we can rank the constructions (i.e., the values of the variable Type of Possessive Construction) in terms of their frequency (the *s*-possessive is more frequent), but again we are not ranking these values based on an intrinsic criterion but on an extrinsic one: their corpus frequency in one particular corpus. We can also calculate their mean frequency (19 996.50), but again, this is not a mean of the two constructions, but of their frequencies in one particular corpus.

5.1.2 Ordinal data

An ordinal variable is a variable whose values are labels for categories that *do* have an intrinsic order with respect to each other but that cannot be expressed in terms of natural numbers. In other words, ordinal variables are variables that are defined in such a way that some aspect of their definition allows us to order them without reference to an extrinsic criterion, but that does not give us any information about the distance (or degree of difference) between one category and the next. If we categorize data in terms of such an ordinal variable, we can treat them accordingly (i.e., we can rank them), or we can treat them like nominal data by simply ignoring their inherent order (i.e., we can still count the number of observations for each value and report absolute or relative frequencies). We cannot calculate mean values.

Some typical examples of ordinal variables are demographic variables like Education or (in the appropriate sub-demographic) Military Rank, but also School Grades and the kind of ratings often found in questionnaires (both of which are, however, often treated as though they were cardinal data, see below).

For example, academic degrees are intrinsically ordered: it is part of the definition of a PhD degree that it ranks higher than a master's degree, which in turn ranks higher than a bachelor's degree. Thus, we can easily rank speakers in a sample of university graduates based on the highest degree they have completed. We can also simply count the number of PhDs, MAs, and BAs and ignore the ordering of the degrees. But we cannot calculate a mean: if five speakers in our sample of ten speakers have a PhD and five have a BA, this does not allow us to claim that all of them have an MA degree on average. The first important reason for this is that the size of the difference in terms of skills and knowledge that separates a BA from an MA is not the same as that separating an MA from a PhD: in Europe, one typically studies two years for an MA, but it typically takes three to five years to complete a PhD. The second important reason is that the values of ordinal variables typically differ along more than one dimension: while it is true that a PhD is a higher degree than an MA, which is a higher degree than a BA, the three degrees also differ in terms of specialization (from a relatively broad BA to a very narrow PhD), and the PhD degree differs from the two other degrees qualitatively: a BA and an MA primarily show that one has acquired knowledge and (more or less practical skills), but a PhD primarily shows that one has acquired research skills.

With respect to the three hypotheses concerning the distribution of the *s*-possessive and the *of*-possessive, clearly Animacy is an ordinal variable, at least if we think of it in terms of a scale, as we did in Chapter 3, Section 3.2. Recall that a simple animacy scale might look like this:

(8) animate > inanimate > abstract

On this scale, animate ranks higher than inanimate which ranks higher than abstract in terms of the property we are calling Animacy, and this ranking is determined by the scale itself, not by any extrinsic criteria.

This means that we could categorize and rank all nouns in a corpus according to their animacy. But again, we cannot calculate a mean. If we have 50 human nouns and 50 abstract nouns, we cannot say that we have 100 nouns with a mean value of inanimate. Again, this is because we have no way of knowing whether, in terms of animacy, the difference between animate and inanimate is the same quantitatively as that between inanimate and abstract, but also, because we are, again, dealing with qualitative as well as quantitative differences: the difference between animate and inanimate on the one hand and abstract on the other is that the first two have physical existence; and the difference between animate on the one hand and inanimate and abstract on the other is that animates are potentially alive and the other two are not. In other words, our scale is really a combination of at least two dimensions.

Again, we could ignore the intrinsic order of the values on our Animacy scale and simply treat them as nominal data, i.e., count them and report the frequency with which each value occurs in our data. Potentially ordinal data are actually frequently treated like nominal data in corpus linguistics (cf. Section 5.3.2), and with complex scales combining a range of different dimensions, this is probably a good idea; but ordinal data also have a useful place in quantitative corpus linguistics.

5.1.3 Cardinal data

Cardinal variables are variables whose values are numerical measurements along a particular dimension. In other words, they are intrinsically ordered (like ordinal data), but not because some aspect of their definition allows us to order them, but because of their nature as numbers. Also, the distance between any two measurements is precisely known and can directly be expressed as a number itself. This means that we can perform any arithmetic operation on cardinal data – crucially, we can calculate means. Of course, we can also treat cardinal data like rank data by ignoring all of their mathematical properties other than their order, and we can also treat them as nominal data.

Typical cases of cardinal variables are demographic variables like Age or Income. For example, we can categorize a sample of speakers by their age and then calculate the mean age of our sample. If our sample contains five 50-year-olds and five 30-year-olds, it makes perfect sense to say that the mean age in our sample is 40; we might need additional information to distinguish between this sample and another sample that consists of 5 41-year-olds and 5 39-year-olds, that would also have a mean age of 40 (cf. Chapter 6), but the mean itself is meaningful, because the distance between 30 and 40 is the same as that between 40 and 50 and all measurements involve just a single dimension (age).

With respect to the two possessives, the variables Length and Givenness are cardinal variables. It should be obvious that we can calculate the mean length of words or other constituents in a corpus, a particular sample, a particular position in a grammatical construction, etc.

As mentioned above, we can also treat cardinal data like ordinal data. This may sometimes actually be necessary for mathematical reasons (see Chapter 6 below); in other cases, we may want to transform cardinal data to ordinal data based on theoretical considerations.

For example, the measure of Referential Distance discussed in Chapter 3, Section 3.2 yields cardinal data ranging from 0 to whatever maximum distance we decide on and it would be possible, and reasonable, to calculate the mean referential distance of a particular type of referring expression. However Givón (1992: 20f) argues that we should actually think of referential distance as ordinal data: as most referring expressions consistently have a referential distance of either 0–1, or 2–3, or larger than 3, he suggests converting measures of Referential Distance into just three categories: minimal gap (0–1), small gap (2–3) and long gap (> 3). Once we have done this, we can no longer calculate a mean, because the categories are no longer equivalent in size or distance, but we can still rank them. Of course, we can also treat them as nominal data, simply counting the number of referring expressions in the categories minimal gap, small gap and long gap.

5.1.4 Interim summary

In the preceding three subsections, we have repeatedly mentioned concepts like *frequency*, *percentage*, *rank* and *mean*. In the following three sections, we will introduce these concepts in more detail, providing a solid foundation of descriptive statistical measures for nominal, ordinal and cardinal data.

Note, however, that most research designs, including those useful for investigating the hypotheses about the two possessive constructions, involve (at least) two variables: (at least) one independent variable and (at least) one dependent variable. Even our definition of corpus linguistics makes reference to this fact when it states that research questions should be framed such that it enables us to answer them by looking at the distribution of linguistic phenomena across different conditions.

Since such conditions are most likely to be nominal in character (a set of language varieties, groups of speakers, grammatical constructions, etc.), we will limit the discussion to combinations of variables where at least one variable is nominal, i.e., (a) designs with two nominal variables, (b) designs with one nominal and one ordinal variable, and (c) designs with one nominal and one cardinal variable. Logically, there are three additional designs, namely designs with (d) two ordinal variables, (e) two cardinal variables or (f) one ordinal and one cardinal variable. For such cases, we would need different variants of correlation analysis, which we will not discuss in this book in any detail (but there are pointers to the relevant literature in the Study Notes to Chapter 6 and we will touch upon such designs in some of the Case Studies in Part II of this book).

5.2 Descriptive statistics for nominal data

Most examples we have looked at so far in this book involved two nominal variables: the independent variable VARIETY (with the values BRITISH ENGLISH VS. AMERICAN ENGLISH) and a dependent variable consisting of some linguistic alternation (mostly regional synonyms of some lexicalized concept). Thus, this kind of research design should already be somewhat familiar.

For a closer look, we will apply it to the first of the three hypotheses introduced in the preceding section, which is restated here with the background assumption from which it is derived:

(9) Assumption: Discourse-old items occur before discourse-new items.
Hypothesis: The *S*-POSSESSIVE will be used when the modifier is DISCOURSE-OLD, the *OF*-POSSESSIVE will be used when the modifier is DISCOURSE-NEW.

Note that the terms S-POSSESSIVE and OF-POSSESSIVE are typeset in small caps in these hypotheses. This is done in order to show that they are values of a variable in a particular research design, based on a particular theoretical construct. As such, these values must, of course, be given operational definitions (also, the construct upon which the variable is based should be explicated with reference to a particular model of language, but this would lead us too far from the purpose of this chapter and so I will assume that the phenomenon "English nominal possession" is self-explanatory).

The definitions I used were the following:

(10) a. S-POSSESSIVE: A construction consisting of a possessive pronoun or a noun phrase marked by the clitic *'s* modifying a noun following it, where the construction as a whole is not a proper name.

b. OF-POSSESSIVE: A construction consisting of a noun modified by a prepositional phrase with *of*, where the construction as a whole encodes a relation that could theoretically also be encoded by the S-POSSESSIVE and is not a proper name.

Proper names (such as *Scotty's Bar* or *District of Columbia*) are excluded in both cases because they are fixed and could not vary. Therefore, they will not be subject to any restrictions concerning givenness, animacy or length.

To turn these definitions into *operational* definitions, we need to provide the specific queries used to extract the data, including a description of those aspects of corpus annotation used in formulating these queries. We also need annotation schemes detailing how to distinguish proper names from other uses and how to identify *of*-constructions that encode relations that could also be encoded by the *s*-possessive.

The *s*-possessive is easy to extract if we use the tagging present in the BROWN corpus: words with the possessive clitic (i.e. *'s*, or just *'* for words whose stem ends in *s*) as well as possessive pronouns are annotated with tags ending in the dollar sign $, so a query for words tagged in this way will retrieve all cases with high precision and recall. For the *of*-possessive, extraction is more difficult – the safest way seems to be to search for words tagged as nouns followed by the preposition *of*, which already excludes uses like [*most of* NP] (where the quantifying expression is tagged as a post-determiner) [*because of* NP], [*afraid of* NP], etc.

The annotation of the results for proper name or common noun status can be done in various ways – in some corpora (but not in the BROWN corpus), the POS tags may help, in others, we might use capitalization as a hint, etc. The annotation for whether or not an *of*-construction encodes a relation that could also be encoded by an *s*-possessive can be done as discussed in Section 4.2.3 of Chapter 4.

Using these operationalizations for the purposes of the case studies in this chapter, I retrieved and annotated a one-percent sample of each construction (the constructions are so frequent that even one percent leaves us with 222 *s*- and 178 *of*-possessives (the full data set for the studies presented in this and the following two subsections can be found in the Supplementary Online Material, file HKD3).

Next, the values DISCOURSE-OLD and DISCOURSE-NEW have to be operationalized. This could be done using the measure of referential distance discussed in Section 3.2 of Chapter 3, which (in slightly different versions) is the most frequently used operationalization in corpus linguistics. Since we want to demonstrate a design with two nominal variables, however, and in order to illustrate that constructs can be operationalized in different ways, I will use a different, somewhat indirect operationalization. It is well established that pronouns tend to refer to old information, whereas new information must be introduced using common nouns in full lexical NPs. Thus, we can assume a correlation between the construct DISCOURSE-OLD and the construct PRONOUN on the one hand, and the construct DISCOURSE-NEW and the construct COMMON NOUN on the other.

This correlation is not perfect, as common nouns can also encode old information, so using PART OF SPEECH OF NOMINAL EXPRESSION as an operational definition for GIVENNESS is somewhat crude in terms of validity, but the advantage is that it yields a highly reliable, easy-to-annotate definition: we can use the part-of-speech tagging to annotate our sample automatically.

We can now state the following quantitative prediction based on our hypothesis:

(11) Prediction: There will be more cases of the S-POSSESSIVE with DISCOURSE-OLD modifiers than with DISCOURSE-NEW modifiers, and more cases of the *OF*-POSSESSIVE with discourse-new modifiers than with DISCOURSE-OLD modifiers.

Table 5.1 shows the absolute frequencies of the parts of speech of the modifier in both constructions (examples with proper names were discarded, as the givenness of proper names in discourse is less predictable than that of pronouns and common nouns).

Such a table, examples of which we have already seen in previous chapters, is referred to as a *contingency table*. In this case, the contingency table consists

Table 5.1: Part of speech of the modifier in the *s*-possessive and the *of*-possessive

		Possessive		
		s-possessive	of-possessive	Total
Givenness	old	180	3	183
	new	20	153	173
	Total	200	156	356

of four cells showing the frequencies of the four intersections of the variables Givenness, (with the values new, i.e. "pronoun", and old, i.e. "common noun" and Possessive (with the values s and of); in other words, it is a two-by-two table. Possessive is presented as the dependent variable here, since logically the hypothesis is that the information status of the modifier influences the choice of construction, but mathematically it does not matter in contingency tables what we treat as the dependent or independent variable.

In addition, there are two cells showing the *row totals* (the sum of all cells in a given row) and the *column totals* (the sum of all cells in a given column), and one cell showing the *table total* (the sum of all four intersections). The row and column totals for a given cell are referred to as the *marginal frequencies* for that cell.

5.2.1 Percentages

The frequencies in Table 5.1 are fairly easy to interpret in this case, because the differences in frequency are very clear. However, we should be wary of basing our assesment of corpus data directly on raw frequencies in a contingency table. These can be very misleading, especially if the marginal frequencies of the variables differ substantially, which in this case, they do: the *s*-possessive is more frequent overall than the *of*-possessive and discourse-old modifiers (i.e., pronouns) are slightly more frequent overall than discourse-new ones (i.e., common nouns).

Thus, it is generally useful to convert the absolute frequencies to relative frequencies, abstracting away from the differences in marginal frequencies. In order to convert an absolute frequency n into a relative one, we simply divide it by the total number of cases N of which it is a part. This gives us a decimal fraction expressing the frequency as a proportion of 1. If we want a percentage instead, we multiply this decimal fraction by 100, thus expressing our frequency as a proportion of 100.

For example, if we have a group of 31 students studying some foreign language and six of them study German, the percentage of students studying German is

$$\frac{6}{31} = 0.1935.$$

Multiplying this by 100, we get

$$0.1953 \times 100 = 19.35\%$$

In other words, a percentage is just another way of expressing a decimal fraction, which is just another way of expressing a fraction, all of which are (among other things) ways of expressing relative frequencies (i.e., proportions). In academic papers, it is common to report relative frequencies as decimal fractions rather than as percentages, so we will follow this practice here.

If we want to convert the absolute frequencies in Table 5.1 into relative frequencies, we first have to decide what the relevant total *N* is. There are three possibilities, all of which are useful in some way: we can divide each cell by its column total, by its row total or by the table total. Table 5.2 shows the results for all three possibilities.

The column proportions can be related to our prediction most straightforwardly: based on our hypothesis, we predicted that in our sample a majority of *s*-possessives should have modifiers that refer to discourse-old information and, conversely a majority of *of*-possessives should have modifiers that refer to discourse-new information.

The relevance of the row proportions is less clear in this case. We might predict, based on our hypothesis, that the majority of modifiers referring to old information should occur in *s*-possessives and the majority of modifiers referring to new information should occur in *of*-possessives.

This is the case in Table 5.2, and this is certainly compatible with our hypothesis. However, if it were not the case, this could also be compatible with our hypothesis. Note that the constructions differ in frequency, with the *of*-possessive being only three-quarters as frequent as the *s*-possessive. Now imagine the difference was ten to one instead of four to three. In this case, we might well find that the majority of both old and new modifiers occurs in the *s*-possessives, simply because there are so many more *s*-possessives than *of*-possessives. We would, however, expect the majority to be larger in the case of old modifiers than in the case of new modifiers. In other words, even if we are looking at row percentages, the relevant comparisons are across rows, not within rows.

Table 5.2: Absolute and relative frequencies of the modifier's givenness (as reflected in its part of speech) in the English possessive constructions

			Possessive		
			S-possessive	*of*-possessive	Total
Discourse Status	old	*Abs.*	180	3	183
		Rel. (Col.)	0.9000	0.0192	–
		Rel. (Row)	0.9836	0.0164	1.0000
		Rel. (Tab.)	0.5056	0.0084	0.5140
	new	*Abs.*	20	153	173
		Rel. (Col.)	0.1000	0.9808	–
		Rel. (Row)	0.1156	0.8844	1.0000
		Rel. (Tab.)	0.0562	0.4298	0.4860
	Total	*Abs.*	200	156	356
		Rel. (Col.)	1.0000	1.0000	1.0000
		Rel. (Row)	–	–	1.0000
		Rel. (Tab.)	0.5618	0.4382	1.0000

Whether column or row proportions are more relevant to a hypothesis depends, of course, on the way variables are arranged in the table: if we rotate the table such that the variable Possessive ends up in the rows, then the row proportions would be more relevant. When interpreting proportions in a contingency table, we have to find those that actually relate to our hypothesis. In any case, the interpretation of both row and column proportions requires us to choose one value of one of our variables and compare it across the two values of the other variable, and then compare this comparison to a comparison of the other value of that variable. If that sounds complicated, this is because it *is* complicated.

It would be less confusing if we had a way of taking into account both values of both variables at the same time. The table proportions allow this to some extent. The way our hypothesis is phrased, we would expect a majority of cases to instantiate the intersections s-possessive ∩ discourse-old and *of*-possessive ∩ discourse-new, with a minority of cases instantiating the other two intersections. In Table 5.2, this is clearly the case: the intersection s-possessive ∩ discourse-old contains more than fifty percent of all cases, the intersection *of*-possessive ∩ discourse-new well over 40 percent. Again, if the marginal frequencies differ more extremely, so may the table percentages in the relevant intersections. We could imagine a situation, for example, where 90 percent of the cases fell into the intersection S-POSSESSIVE ∩ DISCOURSE-OLD and 10 percent in the intersection *OF*-POSSESSIVE ∩ DISCOURSE-NEW – this would still be a corroboratation of our hypothesis.

While relative frequencies (whether expressed as decimal fractions or as percentages) are, with due care, more easily interpretable than absolute frequencies, they have two disadvantages. First, by abstracting away from the absolute frequencies, we lose valuable information: we would interpret a distribution such as that in Table 5.3 differently, if we knew that it was based on a sample on just 35 instead of 356 corpus hits. Second, it provides no sense of how different our observed distribution is from the distribution that we would expect if there was no relation between our two variables, i.e., if the values were distributed randomly. Thus, instead of (or in addition to) using relative frequencies, we should compare the *observed* absolute frequencies of the intersections of our variables with the *expected* absolute frequencies, i.e., the absolute frequencies we would expect if there was a random relationship between the variables. This comparison between observed and expected frequencies also provides a foundation for inferential statistics, discussed in Chapter 6.

5.2.2 Observed and expected frequencies

So how do we determine the expected frequencies of the intersections of our variables? Consider the textbook example of a random process: flipping a coin onto a hard surface. Ignoring the theoretical and extremely remote possibility that the coin will land, and remain standing, on its edge, there are two possible outcomes, *heads* and *tails*. If the coin has not been manipulated in some clever way, for example, by making one side heavier than the other, the probability for heads and tails is 0.5 (or fifty percent) each (such a coin is called a *fair coin* in statistics).

From these probabilities, we can calculate the expected frequency of heads and tails in a series of coin flips. If we flip the coin ten times, we expect five heads and five tails, because $0.5 \times 10 = 5$. If we flip the coin 42 times, the expected frequency is 21 for heads and 21 for tails (0.5×42), and so on. In the real world, we would of course expect some variation (more on this in Chapter 6), so *expected frequency* refers to a theoretical expectation derived by multiplying the probability of an event by the total number of observations.

So how do we transfer this logic to a contingency table like Table 5.1? Naively, we might assume that the expected frequencies for each cell can be determined by taking the total number of observations and dividing it by four: if the data were distributed randomly, each intersection of values should have about the same frequency (just like, when tossing a coin, each side should come up roughly the same number of times). However, this would only be the case if all marginal frequencies were the same, for example, if our sample contained fifty S-POSSESSIVES and fifty *OF*-POSSESSIVES and fifty of the modifiers were discourse old (i.e. pronouns) and fifty of them were discourse-new (i.e. common nouns). But this is not the case: there are more discourse-old modifiers than discourse-new ones (183 vs. 173) and there are more *s*-possessives than *of*-possessives (200 vs. 156).

These marginal frequencies of our variables and their values are a fact about our data that must be taken as a given when calculating the expected frequencies: our hypothesis says nothing about the overall frequency of the two constructions or the overall frequency of discourse-old and discourse-new modifiers, but only about the frequencies with which these values should co-occur. In other words, the question we must answer is the following: Given that the *s*- and the *of*-possessive occur 200 and 156 times respectively and given that there are 183 discourse-old modifiers and 173 discourse-new modifiers, how frequently would each combination these values occur by chance?

Put like this, the answer is conceptually quite simple: the marginal frequencies should be distributed across the intersections of our variables such that the relative frequencies in each row should be the same as those of the row total and the relative frequencies in each column should be the same as those of the column total.

For example, 56.18 percent of all possessive constructions in our sample are *s*-possessives and 43.82 percent are *of*-possessives; if there were a random relationship between type of construction and givenness of the modifier, we should find the same proportions for the 183 constructions with old modifiers, i.e. 183 × 0.5618 = 102.81 *s*-possessives and 183 × 0.4382 = 80.19 *of*-possessives. Likewise, there are 173 constructions with new modifiers, so 173 × 0.5618 = 97.19 of them should be *s*-possessives and 173 × 0.4382 = 75.81 of them should be *of*-possessives. The same goes for the columns: 51.4 percent of all constructions have old modifiers and 41.6 percent have new modifiers. If there were a random relationship between type of construction and givenness of the modifier, we should find the same proportions for both types of possessive construction: there should be 200 × 0.514 = 102.8 *s*-possessives with old modifiers and 97.2 with new modifiers, as well as 156 × 0.514 = 80.18 *of*-possessives with old modifiers and 156 × 0.486 = 75.82 *of*-possessives with new modifiers. Note that the expected frequencies for each intersection are the same whether we use the total row percentages or the total column percentages: the small differences are due to rounding errors.

To avoid rounding errors, we should not actually convert the row and column totals to percentages at all, but use the following much simpler way of calculating the expected frequencies: for each cell, we simply multiply its marginal frequencies and divide the result by the table total as shown in Table 5.3; note that we are using the standard convention of using O to refer to observed frequencies, E to refer to expected frequencies, and subscripts to refer to rows and columns. The convention for these subscripts is as follows: use *1* for the first row or column, *2* for the second row or column, and T for the row or column total, and give the index for the row before that of the column. For example, E_{21} refers to the expected frequency of the cell in the second row and the first column, O_{1T} refers to the total of the first row, and so on.

Table 5.3: Calculating expected frequencies from observed frequencies

		Dependent Variable		
		value 1	value 2	Total
Independent Variable	value 1	$E_{11} = \frac{O_{T1} \times O_{1T}}{O_{TT}}$	$E_{12} = \frac{O_{T2} \times O_{1T}}{O_{TT}}$	O_{1T}
	value 2	$E_{21} = \frac{O_{T1} \times O_{2T}}{O_{TT}}$	$E_{22} = \frac{O_{T2} \times O_{2T}}{O_{TT}}$	O_{2T}
	Total	O_{T1}	O_{T2}	O_{TT}

Applying this procedure to our observed frequencies yields the results shown in Table 5.4. One should always report nominal data in this way, i.e., giving both the observed and the expected frequencies in the form of a contingency table.

We can now compare the observed and expected frequencies of each intersection to see whether the difference conforms to our quantitative prediction. This is clearly the case: for the intersections *s*-possessive ∩ discourse-old and *of*-possessive ∩ discourse-new, the observed frequencies are higher than the expected ones, for the intersections *s*-possessive ∩ discourse-new and *of*-possessive ∩ discourse-old, the observed frequencies are lower than the expected ones.

This conditional distribution seems to corroborate our hypothesis. However, note that it does not yet prove or disprove anything, since, as mentioned above, we would never expect a real-world distribution of events to match the expected distribution perfectly. We will return to this issue in Chapter 6.

Table 5.4: Observed and expected frequencies of old and new modifiers in the *s*- and the *of*-possessive

			Possessive		
			s-possessive	of-possessive	Total
Discourse Status	old	*Obs.*	180	3	183
		Exp.	102.81	80.19	
	new	*Obs.*	20	153	173
		Exp.	97.19	75.81	
	Total	*Obs.*	200	156	356

5.3 Descriptive statistics for ordinal data

Let us turn, next, to a design with one nominal and one ordinal variable: a test of the second of the three hypotheses introduced at the beginning of this chapter. Again, it is restated here together with the background assumption from which it is derived:

(12) Assumption: Animate items occur before inanimate items.
Hypothesis: The s-possessive will be used when the modifier is high in Animacy, the of-possessive will be used when the modifier is low in Animacy.

The constructions are operationalized as before. The data used are based on the same data set, except that cases with proper names are now included. For expository reasons, we are going to look at a ten-percent subsample of the full sample, giving us 22 *s*-possessives and 17 *of*-possessives.

Animacy was operationally defined in terms of the annotation scheme shown in Table 5.5 (based on Zaenen et al. 2004).

As pointed out above, Animacy hierarchies are a classic example of ordinal data, as the categories can be ordered (although there may be some disagreement about the exact order), but we cannot say anything about the distance between one category and the next, and there is more than one conceptual dimension involved (I ordered them according to dimensions like "potential for life", "touchability" and "conceptual independence").

Table 5.5: A simple annotation scheme for ANIMACY

ANIMACY CATEGORY		Definition	Rank
HUMAN	(HUM)	Real or fictional humans and human-like beings	1
ORGANIZATION	(ORG)	Groups of humans acting with a common purpose	2
OTHER ANIMATE	(ANI)	Real or fictional animals, animal-like beings and plants	3
HUMAN ATTRIBUTE	(HAT)	Body parts, organs, etc. of humans	4
CONCRETE TOUCHABLE	(CCT)	Physical entities that are incapable of life and can be touched	5
CONCRETE NONTOUCHABLE	(CCN)	Physical entities that are incapable of life and cannot be touched	6
LOCATION	(LOC)	Physical places and regions	7
TIME	(TIM)	Points in and periods of time	8
EVENT	(EVT)	Events	9
ABSTRACT	(ABS)	Other abstract entities	10

We can now formulate the following prediction:

(13) Prediction: The modifiers of the S-POSSESSIVE will tend to occur high on the ANIMACY scale, the modifiers of the *OF*-POSSESSIVE will tend to occur low on the ANIMACY scale.

Note that phrased like this, it is not yet a quantitative prediction, since "tend to" is not a mathematical concept. While *frequency* for nominal data and *mean* (or "average") for cardinal data are used in everyday language with something close to their mathematical meaning, we do not have an everyday word for dealing with differences in ordinal data. We will return to this point presently, but first, let us look at the data impressionistically. Table 5.6 shows the annotated sample (cases are listed in the order in which they occurred in the corpus).

A simple way of finding out whether the data conform to our prediction would be to sort the entire data set by the rank assigned to the examples and check whether the *s*-possessives cluster near the top of the list and the *of*-possessives near the bottom. Table 5.7 shows this ranking.

Table 5.7 shows that the data conform to our hypothesis: among the cases whose modifiers have an animacy of rank 1 to 3, *s*-possessives dominate, among those with a modifier of rank 4 to 10, *of*-possessives make up an overwhelming majority.

However, we need a less impressionistic way of summarizing data sets coded as ordinal variables, since not all data set will be as straightforwardly interpretable as this one. So let us turn to the question of an appropriate descriptive statistic for ordinal data.

Table 5.6: A sample of *s*- and *of*-possessives annotated for ANIMACY (BROWN)

No.	Example	ANIMACY	Rank
(a)	S-POSSESSIVE		
1	*its [administration] policy*	ORG	2
2	*her professional roles*	HUM	1
3	*their burden*	HUM	1
4	*its [word] musical frame*	CCN	6
5	*its [sect] metaphysic*	ORG	2
6	*your management climate*	ORG	2
7	*their families*	HUM	1
8	*Lumumba's death*	HUM	1
9	*his arts or culture*	HUM	1
10	*her life*	HUM	1
11	*its [monument] reputation*	CCT	5
12	*their impulses and desires*	HUM	1
13	*its [board] members' duties*	ORG	2
14	*our national economy*	ORG	2
15	*the convict's climactic reappearance*	HUM	1
16	*its [bird] wing*	ANI	3
17	*her father*	HUM	1
18	*his voice*	HUM	1
19	*her brain*	HUM	1
20	*his brown face*	HUM	1
21	*his expansiveness*	HUM	1
22	*its [snake] black, forked tongue*	ANI	3
23	*the novelist's carping phrase*	HUM	1
(b)	OF-POSSESSIVE		
1	*the invasion of Cuba*	LOC	8
2	*a joint session of Congress*	ORG	2
3	*[...] enemies of peaceful coexistence*	EVT	7
4	*the word of God*	HUM	1
5	*the volume of the cylinder opening [...]*	CCT	5
6	*the depths of the fourth dimension*	ABS	10
7	*the views of George Washington*	HUM	1
8	*all the details of the pattern*	ABS	10
9	*the makers of constitutions*	CCN	6
10	*the extent of ethical robotism*	ABS	10
11	*the number of new [...] construction projects [...]*	CCT	5
12	*the expanding [...] economy of the 1960's*	TIM	9
13	*hyalinization of [...] glomerular arterioles*	HAT	4
14	*the possible forms of nonverbal expression*	EVT	7
15	*the maintenance of social stratification [...]*	ABS	10
16	*knowledge of the environment*	CCT	5
17	*the bow of the nearest skiff*	CCT	5
18	*the corner of the car*	CCT	5

Table 5.7: The annotated sample from Table 5.6 ordered by animacy rank

			(contd.)		
Anim.	Type	No.	Anim.	Type	No.
1	S	(a 2)	4	OF	(b 13)
1	S	(a 3)	5	S	(a 11)
1	S	(a 7)	5	OF	(b 5)
1	S	(a 8)	5	OF	(b 11)
1	S	(a 9)	5	OF	(b 16)
1	S	(a 10)	5	OF	(b 17)
1	S	(a 12)	5	OF	(b 18)
1	S	(a 15)	6	S	(a 4)
1	S	(a 17)	6	OF	(b 9)
1	S	(a 18)	7	OF	(b 3)
1	S	(a 19)	7	OF	(b 14)
1	S	(a 20)	8	OF	(b 1)
1	S	(a 21)	9	OF	(b 12)
1	S	(a 23)	10	OF	(b 6)
1	OF	(b 4)	10	OF	(b 8)
1	OF	(b 7)	10	OF	(b 10)
2	S	(a 1)	10	OF	(b 15)
2	S	(a 5)			
2	S	(a 6)			
2	S	(a 13)			
2	S	(a 14)			
2	OF	(b 2)			
3	S	(a 16)			
3	S	(a 22)			

5.3.1 Medians

As explained above, we cannot calculate a mean for a set of ordinal values, but we can do something similar. The idea behind calculating a mean value is, essentially, to provide a kind of mid-point around which a set of values is distributed – it is a so-called measure of *central tendency*. Thus, if we cannot calculate a mean, the next best thing is to simply list our data ordered from highest to lowest and find the value in the middle of that list. This value is known as the *median* – a value that splits a sample or population into a higher and a lower portion of equal sizes.

For example, the rank values for the Animacy of our sample of *s*-possessives are shown in Figure 5.1a. There are 23 values, thus the median is the twelfth value in the series (marked by a dot labeled M) – there are 11 values above it and eleven below it. The twelfth values in the series is a 1, so the median value of *s*-possessive modifiers in our sample is 1 (or HUMAN).

(a)
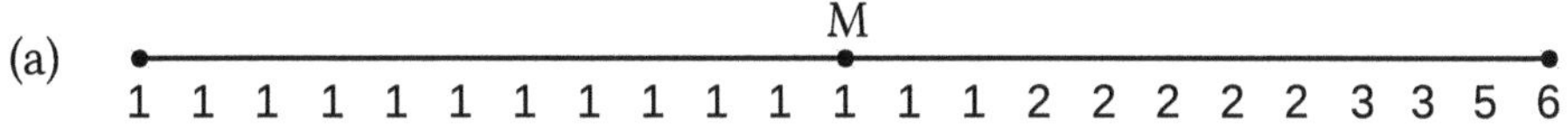

(b)
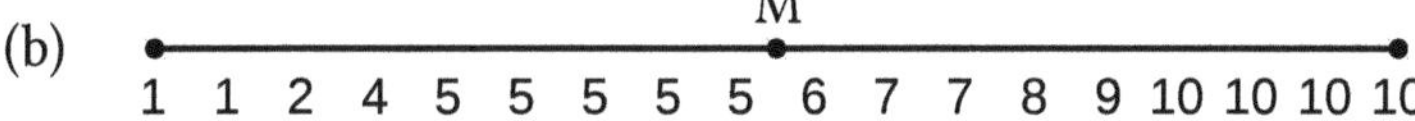

Figure 5.1: Medians for (a) the *s*-possessives and (b) the *of*-possessives in Table 5.7

If the sample consists of an even number of data points, we simply calculate the mean between the two values that lie in the middle of the ordered data set. For example, the rank values for the Animacy of our sample of *of*-possessives are shown in Figure 5.1b. There are 18 values, so the median falls between the ninth and the tenth value (marked again by a dot labeled M). The ninth and tenth value are 5 and 6 respectively, so the median for the *of*-possessive modifiers is $(5+6)/2 =$ 5.5 (i.e., it falls between CONCRETE TOUCHABLE and CONCRETE NONTOUCHABLE).

Using the idea of a median, we can now rephrase our prediction in quantitative terms:

(14) Prediction: The modifiers of the S-POSSESSIVE will have a higher median on the ANIMACY scale than the modifiers of the *OF*-POSSESSIVE.

Our data conform to this prediction, as 1 is higher on the scale than 5.5. As before, this does not prove or disprove anything, as, again, we would expect some random variation. Again, we will return to this issue in Chapter 6.

5.3.2 Frequency lists and mode

Recall that I mentioned above the possibility of treating ordinal data like nominal data. Table 5.8 shows the relative frequencies for each animacy category, (alternatively, we could also calculate expected frequencies in the way described in Section 5.3 above).

Table 5.8: Relative frequencies for the Animacy values of possessive modifiers

Animacy		s-possessive		of-possessive	
Rank	Category	Abs.	Rel.	Abs.	Rel.
1	human	14	0.609	2	0.111
2	organization	5	0.217	1	0.056
3	other animate	2	0.087	0	–
4	human attribute	0	–	1	0.056
5	concrete touchable	1	0.043	5	0.279
6	concrete nontouchable	1	0.043	1	0.056
7	location	0	–	1	0.056
8	time	0	–	1	0.056
9	event	0	–	2	0.111
10	abstract	0	–	4	0.222
Total		23	1.000	18	1.000

This table also nicely shows the preference of the *s*-possessive for animate modifiers (human, organization, other animate) and the preference of the *of*-possessive for the categories lower on the hierarchy. The table also shows, however, that the modifiers of the *of*-possessive are much more evenly distributed across the entire Animacy scale than those of the *s*-possessive.

For completeness' sake, let me point out that there is a third measure of central tendency, that is especially suited to nominal data (but can also be applied to ordinal and cardinal data): the *mode*. The mode is simply the most frequent value in a sample, so the modifiers of the *of*-possessive have a mode of 5 (or concrete touchable) and those of the *s*-possessive have a mode of 1 (or human) with respect to animacy (similarly, we could have said that the mode of *s*-possessive modifiers is discourse-old and the mode of *of*-possessive modifiers is discourse-new). There may be more than one mode in a given sample.

For example, if we had found just a single additional modifier of the type ABSTRACT in the sample above (which could easily have happened), its frequency would also be five; in this case, the *of*-possessive modifier would have two modes (CONCRETE TOUCHABLE and ABSTRACT).

The concept of *mode* may seem useful in cases where we are looking for a single value by which to characterize a set of nominal data, but on closer inspection it turns out that it does not actually tell us very much: it tells us what the most frequent value is, but it does not tell us how much more frequent that value is than the next most frequent one, how many other values occur in the data at all, etc. Thus, it is always preferable to report the frequencies of all values, and, in fact, I have never come across a corpus-linguistic study reporting modes.

5.4 Descriptive statistics for cardinal data

Let us turn, finally, to a design with one nominal and one cardinal variable: a test of the third of the three hypotheses introduced at the beginning of this chapter. Again, it is restated here together with the background assumption from which it is derived:

(15) Assumption: Short items tend to occur toward the beginning of a constituent, long items tend to occur at the end.

Hypothesis: The S-POSSESSIVE will be used with short modifiers, the *OF*-POSSESSIVE will be used with long modifiers.

The constructions are operationalized as before. The data used are based on the same data set as before, except that cases with proper names and pronouns are excluded. The reason for this is that we already know from the first case study that pronouns, which we used as an operational definition of OLD INFORMATION prefer the *s*-possessive. Since all pronouns are very short (regardless of whether we measure their length in terms of words, syllables or letters), including them would bias our data in favor of the hypothesis. This left 20 cases of the *s*-possessive and 154 cases of the *of*-possessive. To get samples of roughly equal size for expository clarity, let us select every sixth case of the *of*-possessive, giving us 25 cases (note that in a real study, there would be no good reason to create such roughly equal sample sizes – we would simply use all the data we have).

The variable LENGTH was defined operationally as "number of orthographic words". We can now state the following prediction:

(16) Prediction: The mean length of modifiers of the s-POSSESSIVE should be smaller than that of the modifiers of the *OF*-POSSESSIVE.

Table 5.9 shows the length of head and modifier for all cases in our sample.

5.4.1 Means

How to calculate a mean (more precisely, an arithmetic mean) should be common knowledge, but for completeness' sake, the formula is given in (17):

(17) $$\bar{x}_{arithm} = \frac{1}{n}\sum_{i=1}^{n} x_i = \frac{x_1 + x_2 + ... + x_n}{n}$$

In other words, in order to calculate the mean of a set of values $x_1, x_2, ..., x_n$ of size n, we add up all values and divide them by n (or multiply them by $1/n$, which is the same thing).

Since we have stated our hypothesis and the corresponding prediction only in terms of the modifier, we should first make sure that the heads of the two possessives do not differ greatly in length: if they did, any differences we find for the modifiers could simply be related to the fact that one of the constructions may be longer in general than the other. Adding up all 20 values for the *s*-possessive heads gives us a total of 57, so the mean is $57/20 = 2.85$. Adding up all 25 values of the *of*-possessive heads gives us a total of 59, so the mean is $59/25 = 2.36$. We have, as yet, no way of telling whether this difference could be due to chance, but the two values are so close together that we will assume so for now. In fact, note that there is one obvious outlier (a value that is much bigger than the others: example (a 1) in Table 5.9 has a head that is 14 words long. If we assume that this is somehow exceptional and remove this value, we get a mean length of $43/19 = 2.26$, which is almost identical to the mean length of the *of*-possessive's modifiers.

If we apply the same formula to the modifiers, however, we find that they differ substantially: the mean length of the *s*-possessive modifiers is $38/20 = 1.9$, while the mean length of the *of*-possessive's modifiers is more than twice as much, namely $112/25 = 4.48$. Even if we remove the obvious outlier, example (b 18) in Table 5.9, the *of*-possessive's modifiers are twice as long as those of the *s*-possessive, namely $92/24 = 3.83$.

Table 5.9: A sample of *s*- and *of*-possessives annotated for length of head and modifier (BROWN)

No.	Example	Modifier	Head
(a)	S-POSSESSIVE		
1	*the government's special ceremonies at Memorial University honoring distinguished sons and daughters of the island province*	2	14
2	*the year's grist of nearly 15,000 book titles*	2	6
3	*a burgomaster's Beethoven*	2	1
4	*the world's finest fall coloring*	2	3
5	*a standard internist's text*	3	1
6	*mom's apple pie*	1	2
7	*the Square's historic value*	2	2
8	*his mother's urging*	2	1
9	*the Department's recommendation*	2	1
10	*the posse's approach*	2	1
11	*ladies' fashions*	1	1
12	*the convict's climactic reappearance in London*	2	4
13	*industry's main criticism of the Navy's antisubmarine effort*	1	7
14	*the town marshal's office*	3	1
15	*the pool's edge*	2	1
16	*man's tongue*	1	1
17	*an egotist's rage for fame*	2	3
18	*a women's floor*	2	1
19	*these shores' peculiar powers of stimulation*	2	4
20	*the novelist's carping phrase*	2	2
(b)	OF-POSSESSIVE		
1	*the announcement last week of the forthcoming encounter*	3	4
2	*the necessity of interpretation by a Biblical scholar*	5	2
3	*his portrayal of an edgy head-in-the-clouds artist*	4	2
4	*a lack of unity of purpose and respect for heroic leadership*	8	2
5	*the death throes of men who were shot before the paredon*	7	3
6	*lack of rainfall*	1	1
7	*the amazing variety and power of reactions, attitudes, and emotions precipitated by the nude form*	9	5
8	*the wet end of the cork*	2	3
9	*the constitution of his home state of Massachusetts*	5	2
10	*the spirit of the mad genius from Baker Street*	6	2
11	*Ann's own description of the scene*	2	3
12	*considerable criticism of its length*	2	2
13	*the exaltations of combat*	1	2
14	*the existence of Prandtl numbers reaching values of more than unity*	8	2
15	*the outstanding standard bearer of Mr. Brown's tradition for accuracy*	5	4
16	*the growth of senile individuals*	2	2
17	*the totality of singular lines*	2	2
18	*a consequence of the severe condition of perceived threat that persists unabated for the anxious child in an ambiguous sort of school environment*	20	2
19	*the lead of the Russians*	2	2
20	*costs of service*	1	1
21	*ineffective dispersion of stock ownership*	2	2
22	*the value of a for the major portion of the knife*	8	2
23	*the eyes of the Lord's servants*	3	2
24	*the high ridge of the mountains*	2	3
25	*the pirouette of his arms*	2	2

5.5 Summary

We have looked at three case studies, one involving nominal, one ordinal and one cardinal data. In each case, we were able to state a hypothesis and derive a quantitative prediction from it. Using appropriate descriptive statistics (percentages, observed and expected frequencies, modes, medians and means), we were able to determine that the data conform to these predictions – i.e., that the quantitative distribution of the values of the variables Givenness (measured by Part of Speech, Animacy and Length across the conditions *s*-possessive and *of*-possessive fits the predictions formulated.

However, these distributions by themselves do not prove (or, more precisely, *fail to disprove*) the hypotheses for two related reasons. First, the predictions are stated in relative terms, i.e. in terms of more-or-less, but they do not tell us *how much* more or less we should expect to observe. Second, we do not know, and currently have no way of determining, whether the more-or-less that we observe reflects real differences in distribution, or whether it falls within the range of random variation that we always expect when observing tendencies. More generally, we do not know how to apply the Popperian all-or-nothing research logic to quantitative predictions. All this will be the topic of the next chapter.

6 Significance testing

As discussed extensively in Chapter 3, scientific hypotheses that are stated in terms of universal statements can only be falsified (proven to be false), but never verified (proven to be true). This insight is the basis for the Popperian idea of a research cycle where the researcher formulates a hypothesis and then attempts to falsify it. If they manage to do so, the hypothesis has to be rejected and replaced by a new hypothesis. As long as they do not manage to do so, they may continue to treat it as a useful working hypothesis. They may even take the repeated failure to falsify a hypothesis as corroborating evidence for its correctness. If the hypothesis can be formulated in such a way that it could be falsified by a counterexample (and if it is clear what would count as a counterexample), this procedure seems fairly straightforward.

However, as also discussed in Chapter 3, many if not most hypotheses in corpus linguistics have to be formulated in relative terms – like those introduced in Chapter 5. As discussed in Section 3.1.2, individual counterexamples are irrelevant in this case: if my hypothesis is that most swans are white, this does not preclude the existence of differently-colored swans, so the hypothesis is not falsified if we come across a black swan in the course of our investigation. In this chapter, we will discuss how relative statements can be investigated within the scientific framework introduced in Chapter 3.

6.1 Statistical hypothesis testing

Obviously, if our hypothesis is stated in terms of proportions rather than absolutes, we must also look at our data in terms of proportions rather than absolutes. A single counterexample will not disprove our hypothesis, but what if the majority cases we come across are counterexamples? For example, if we found more black swans than white swans, would this not falsify our hypothesis that most swans are white? The answer is: not quite. With a hypothesis stated in absolute terms, it is easy to specify how many counterexamples we need to disprove it: one. If we find just one black swan, then it cannot be true that all swans are white, regardless of how many swans we have looked at and how many swans there are.

But with a hypothesis stated in terms of proportions, matters are different: even if the majority or even all of the cases in our data contradict it, this does not preclude the possibility that our hypothesis is true – our data will always just constitute a sample, and there is no telling whether this sample corresponds to the totality of cases from which it was drawn. Even if most or all of the swans we observe are black, this may simply be an unfortunate accident – in the total population of swans, the majority could still be white. (By the same reasoning, of course, a hypothesis is not verified if our sample consists exclusively of cases that corroborate it, since this does not preclude the possibility that in the total population, counterexamples are the majority).

So if relative statements cannot be falsified, and if (like universal statements) they cannot be verified, what can we do? There are various answers to this question, all based in probability theory (i.e., statistics). The most widely-used and broadly-accepted of these, and the one we adopt in this book, is an approach sometimes referred to as "Null Hypothesis Significance Testing".[1]

In this approach, which I will refer to simply as *statistical hypothesis testing*, the problem of the non-falsifiability of quantitative hypotheses is solved in an indirect but rather elegant way. Note that with respect to any two variables, there are two broad possibilities concerning their distribution in a population: the distribution could be random (meaning that there is no relationship between the values of the two variables), or it could be non-random (meaning that one value of one variable is more probable to occur with a particular value of the other variable). For example, it could be the case that swans are randomly black or white, or it could be the case that they are more probable to have one of these colors. If the latter is true, there are, again, two broad possibilities: the data could agree with our hypothesis, or they could disagree with it. For example, it could be the case that there are more white swans than black swans (corroborating our hypothesis), or that there are more black swans than white swans (falsifying our hypothesis).

[1]It should be mentioned that there is a small but vocal group of critics that have pointed out a range of real and apparent problems with Null-Hypothesis Significance Testing. In my view, there are three reasons that justify ignoring their criticism in a text book like this. First, they have not managed to convince a significant (pun intended) number of practitioners in any field using statistics, which may not constitute a theoretical argument against the criticism, but certainly a practical one. Second, most, if not all of the criticisms, pertain to the way in which Null Hypothesis Significance Testing is used and to the way in which the results are (mis-)interpreted in the view of the critics. Along with many other practitioners, and even some of the critics, I believe that the best response to this is to make sure we apply the method appropriately and interpret the results carefully, rather than to give up a near-universally used fruitful set of procedures. Third, it is not clear to me that the alternatives suggested by the critics are, on the whole, less problematic or less prone to abuse and misinterpretation.

Unless we have a very specific prediction as to exactly what proportion of our data should consist of counterexamples, we cannot draw any conclusions from a sample. For most research hypotheses, we cannot specify such an exact proportion – if our hypothesis is that Most swans are white, then "most" could mean anything from 50.01 percent to 99.99 percent. But as we will see in the next subsection, we can always specify the exact proportion of counterexamples that we would expect to find if there was a *random* relationship between our variables, and we can then use a sample whether such a random relationship holds (or rather, how probable it is to hold).

Statistical hypothesis testing utilizes this fact by formulating not one, but two hypotheses – first, a research hypothesis postulating a relationship between two variables (like "Most swans are white" or like the hypotheses introduced in Chapter 5), also referred to as H_1 or *alternative hypothesis*; second, the hypothesis that there is a random relationship between the variables mentioned in the research hypothesis, also referred to as H_0 or *null hypothesis.* We then attempt to falsify the *null hypothesis* and to show that the data conform to the alternative hypothesis.

In a first step, this involves turning the null hypothesis and the alternative hypothesis are turned into quantitative predictions concerning the intersections of the variables, as schematically shown in (1a, b):

(1) a. Null hypothesis (H_0): There is no relationship between Variable A and Variable B.

Prediction: The data should be distributed randomly across the intersections of A and B; i.e., the frequency/medians/means of the intersections should not differ from those expected by chance.

b. Alternative hypothesis (H_1): There is a relationship between Variable A and Variable B such that some value(s) of A tend to co-occur with some value(s) of B.

Prediction: The data should be distributed non-randomly across the intersections of A and B; i.e., the frequency/medians/means of some the intersections should be higher and/or lower than those expected by chance.

Once we have formulated our research hypothesis and the corresponding null hypothesis in this way (and once we have operationalized the constructs used in formulating them), we collect, annotate and quantify the relevant data, as discussed in the preceding chapter.

The crucial step in terms of statistical significance testing then consists in determining whether the observed distribution differs from the distribution we would expect if the null hypothesis were true – if the values of our variables were distributed randomly in the data. Of course, it is not enough to observe a difference – a certain amount of variation is to be expected even if there is no relationship between our variables. As will be discussed in detail in the next section, we must determine whether the difference is large enough to assume that it does not fall within the range of variation that could occur randomly. If we are satisfied that this is the case, we can (provisionally) reject the null hypothesis. If not, we must (provisionally) reject our research hypothesis.

In a third step (or in parallel with the second step), we must determine whether the data conform to our research hypothesis, or, more precisely, whether they differ from the prediction of H_0 *in the direction predicted by H_1*. If they do (for example, if there are more white swans than black swans), we can (provisionally) accept our research hypothesis, i.e., we can continue to use it as a working hypothesis in the same way that we would continue to use an absolute hypothesis in this way as long as we do not find a counterexample. If the data differ from the prediction of H_0 in the *opposite* direction to that predicted by our research hypothesis – for example, if there are more black than white swans – we must, of course, also reject our research hypothesis, and treat the unexpected result as a new problem to be investigated further.

Let us now turn to a more detailed discussion of probabilities, random variation and how statistics can be used to (potentially) reject null hypotheses.

6.2 Probabilities and significance testing

Recall the example of a coin that is flipped onto a hard surface: every time we flip it, there is a fifty percent probability that it will come down heads, and a fifty percent probability that it will come down tails. From this it follows, for example, that if we flip a coin ten times, the expected outcome is five heads and five tails. However, as pointed out in the last chapter, this is only a theoretical expectation derived from the probabilities of each individual outcome. In reality, every outcome – from ten heads to ten tails is *possible*, as each flip of the coin is an independent event.

Intuitively, we know this: if we flip a coin ten times, we do not really expect it to come down heads and tails exactly five times each but we accept a certain amount of variation. However, the greater the imbalance between heads and tails, the less willing we will be to accept it as a result of chance. In other words, we would not be surprised if the coin came down heads six times and tails four times, or even heads seven times and tails three times, but we might already be slightly surprised if it came down heads eight times and tails only twice, and we would certainly be surprised to get a series of ten heads and no tails.

Let us look at the reasons for this surprise, beginning with a much shorter series of just two coin flips. There are four possible outcomes of such a series:

(2) a. heads – heads
    b. heads – tails
    c. tails – heads
    d. tails – tails

Obviously, none of these outcomes is more or less probable than the others: since there are four possible outcomes, they each have a probability of $1/4 = 0.25$ (i.e., 25 percent, we will be using the decimal notation for percentages from here on). Alternatively, we can calculate the probability of each series by multiplying the probability of the individual events in each series, i.e. $0.5 \times 0.5 = 0.25$.

Crucially, however, there are differences in the probability of getting a particular *set* of results (i.e, a particular number of heads and regardless of the order they occur in): There is only one possibility of getting two heads (2a) and one of getting two tails (2d), but there are two possibilities of getting one head and one tail (2b, c). We calculate the probability of a particular set by adding up the probabilities of all possible series that will lead to this set. Thus, the probabilities for the sets {heads, heads} and {tails, tails} are 0.25 each, while the probability for the set {heads, tails}, corresponding to the series heads–tails and tails–heads, is $0.25 + 0.25 = 0.5$.

This kind of coin-flip logic (also known as probability theory), can be utilized in evaluating quantitative hypotheses that have been stated in quantitative terms. Take the larger set of ten coin flips mentioned at the beginning of this section: now, there are eleven potential outcomes, shown in Table 6.1.

Again, these outcomes differ with respect to their probability. The third column of Table 6.1 gives us the number of different series corresponding to each set.[2] For example, there is only one way to get a set consisting of heads only: the coin must come down showing heads every single time. There are ten different ways of getting one heads and nine tails: The coin must come down heads the

[2]You may remember having heard of Pascal's triangle, which, among more sophisticated things, lets us calculate the number of different ways in which we can get a particular combination of heads and tails for a given number of coin flips: the third column of Table 6.1 corresponds to line 11 of this triangle. If you don't remember, no worries, we will not need it.

Table 6.1: Possible sets of ten coin flips

	Unordered Set	No. of Series	Probability
1	{0 heads, 10 tails}	1	0.000 977
2	{1 heads, 9 tails}	10	0.009 766
3	{2 heads, 8 tails}	45	0.043 945
4	{3 heads, 7 tails}	120	0.117 188
5	{4 heads, 6 tails}	210	0.205 078
6	{5 heads, 5 tails}	252	0.246 094
7	{6 heads, 4 tails}	210	0.205 078
8	{7 heads, 3 tails}	120	0.117 188
9	{8 heads, 2 tails}	45	0.043 945
10	{9 heads, 1 tails}	10	0.009 766
11	{10 heads, 0 tails}	1	0.000 977

first or second or third or fourth or fifth or sixth or seventh or eighth or ninth or tenth time, and tails the rest of the time. Next, there are forty-five different ways of getting two heads and eight tails, which I am not going to list here (but you may want to, as an exercise), and so on. The fourth column contains the same information, expressed in terms of relative frequencies: there are 1024 different series of ten coin flips, so the probability of getting, for example, two heads and eight tails is $45/1024 = 0.043945$.

The basic idea behind statistical hypothesis testing is simple: we calculate the probability of the result that we have observed. The lower this probability is, the less likely it is to have come about by chance and the more probable is it that we will be right if we reject the null hypothesis. For example, if we observed a series of ten heads and zero tails, we know that the likelihood that the deviation from the expected result of five heads and five tails is due to chance is 0.000977 (i.e. roughly a tenth of a percent). This tenth of a percent is also the probability that we are wrong if we reject the null hypothesis and claim that the coin is not behaving randomly (for example, that it is manipulated in some way).

If we observed one heads and nine tails, we would know that the likelihood that this deviation from the expected result is 0.009766 (i.e. almost one percent). Thus we might think that, again, if we reject the null hypothesis, this is the probability that we are wrong. However, we must add to this the probability of getting ten heads and zero tails. The reason for this is that if we accept a result of 1:9 as evidence for a non-random distribution, we would also accept the even more extreme result of 0:10. So the probability that we are wrong in rejecting the null hypothesis is 0.000977 + 0.009766 = 0.010743. In other words: the probability that we are wrong in rejecting the null hypothesis is always the probability of the observed result plus the probabilities of all results that deviate from the null hypothesis even further in the direction of the observed frequency. This is called the *probability of error* (or simply *p*-value) in statistics.

It must be mentioned at this point that some researchers (especially opponents of null-hypothesis statistical significance testing) disagree that *p* can be interpreted as the probability that we are wrong in rejecting the null hypothesis, raising enough of a controversy to force the American Statistical Association to take an official stand on the meaning of *p*:

> Informally, a *p*-value is the probability under a specified statistical model that a statistical summary of the data (e.g., the sample mean difference between two compared groups) would be equal to or more extreme than its observed value. (Wasserstein & Lazar 2016: 131)

Although this is the informal version of their definition, it may be completely incomprehensible at first glance, but it is actually just a summary of the discussion above: the "specified statistical model" in our case is the null hypothesis, i.e., the hypothesis that our data have come about purely by chance. The *p*-value thus tells us how probable it is under this hypothesis that we would observe the result we have observed, or an even more extreme result.

It also tells us how likely we are wrong if we reject this null hypothesis: If our model (i.e. the null hypothesis) will occasionally produce our observed result (or a more extreme one), then we will be wrong in rejecting it at those occasions. The *p*-value tells us, how likely it is that we are dealing with such an occasion. Of course, it does *not* tell us how likely it is that the null hypothesis is actually true or false – we do not know this likelihood and we can never know it. Statistical hypotheses are no different in this respect from universal hypotheses. Even if we observe a result with a probability of one in a million, the null hypothesis could be true (as we might be dealing with this one-in-a-million event), and even if we observe a result with a probability of 999 999 in a million, the null hypothesis could be false (as our result could nevertheless have come about by chance). The *p*-value simply tells us how likely it is that our study – with all its potential faults, confounding variables, etc. – would produce the result we observe and thus how likely we are wrong *on the basis of this study* to reject the null hypothesis. This simply means that we should not start believing in our hypothesis until additional studies have rejected the null hypothesis – an individual study may lead us to wrongly reject the null hypothesis, but the more studies we conduct that allow us to reject the null hypothesis, the more justified we are in treating them as corroborating our research hypothesis.

By convention, probability of error of 0.05 (five percent) is considered to be the limit as far as acceptable risks are concerned in statistics – if $p < 0.05$ (i.e., if p is smaller than five percent), the result is said to be *statistically significant* (i.e., not due to chance), if it is larger, the result is said to be non-significant (i.e., likely due to chance). Table 6.2 shows additional levels of significance that are conventionally recognized.

Table 6.2: Interpretation of p-values

p-value	Level of significance
≥ 0.05	not significant
< 0.05	significant
< 0.01	very significant
< 0.001	highly significant

Obviously, these cut-off points are largely arbitrary (a point that is often criticized by opponents of null-hypothesis significance testing): it is strange to be confident in rejecting a null hypothesis if the probability of being wrong in doing so is five percent, but to refuse to reject it if the probability of being wrong is six percent (or, as two psychologists put it: “Surely, God loves the .06 nearly as much as the .05” (Rosnow & Rosenthal 1989: 1277)).

In real life, of course, researchers do not treat these cut-off points as absolute. Nobody would simply throw away a set of carefully collected data as soon as their calculations yielded a p-value of 0.06 or even 0.1. Some researchers actually report such results, calling p-values between 0.05 and 0.10 “marginally significant”, and although this is often frowned upon, there is nothing logically wrong with it. Even the majority of researchers who are unwilling to report such results would take them as an indicator that additional research might be in order (especially if there is a reasonable effect size, see further below).

They might re-check their operational definitions and the way they were applied, they might collect additional data in order to see whether a larger data set yields a lower probability of error, or they might replicate the study with a different data set. Note that this is perfectly legitimate, and completely in line with the research cycle sketched out in Section 3.3 – provided we retain all of our data. What we must not do, of course, is test different data sets until we find one that gives us a significant result, and then report just that result, ignoring all attempts that did not yield significant results. What we must also not do is collect an extremely large data set and then keep drawing samples from it until we happen to draw one that gives us a significant result. These practices are sometimes referred to as *p-hacking*, and they constitute a scientific fraud (imagine a a researcher who wants to corroborate their hypothesis that all swans are white and does so by simply ignoring all black swans they find).

Clearly, what probability of error one is willing to accept for any given study also depends on the nature of the study, the nature of the research design, and a general disposition to take or avoid risk. If mistakenly rejecting the null hypothesis were to endanger lives (for example, in a study of potential side-effects of a medical treatment), we might not be willing to accept a p-value of 0.05 or even 0.01.

Why would collecting additional data be a useful strategy, or, more generally speaking, why are corpus-linguists (and other scientists) often intent on making their samples as large as possible and/or feasible? Note that the probability of error depends not just on the proportion of the deviation, but also on the overall size of the sample. For example, if we observe a series of two heads and eight tails (i.e., twenty percent heads), the probability of error in rejecting the null hypothesis is $0.000977 + 0.009766 + 0.043945 = 0.054688$. However, if we observe a series of four heads and sixteen tails (again, twenty percent heads), the probability of error would be roughly ten times lower, namely 0.005909. The reason is the following: There are 1 048 576 possible series of twenty coin flips. There is still only one way of getting one head and nineteen tails, so the probability of getting one head and nineteen tails is $1/1048576 = 0.0000009536743$; however, there are already 20 ways of getting one tail and nineteen heads (so the probability is $20/1048576 = 0.000019$), 190 ways of getting two heads and eighteen tails ($p = 190/1048576 = 0.000181$), 1140 ways of getting three heads and seventeen tails ($p = 1140/1048576 = 0.001087$) and 4845 ways of getting four heads and sixteen tails ($p = 4845/1048576 = 0.004621$). And adding up these probabilities gives us 0.005909.

Most research designs in any discipline are more complicated than coin flipping, which involves just a single variable with two values. However, it is theoretically possible to generalize the coin-flipping logic to any research design, i.e., calculate the probabilities of all possible outcomes and add up the probabilities of the observed outcome and all outcomes that deviate from the expected outcome even further in the same direction. Most of the time, however, this is only a theoretical possibility, as the computations quickly become too complex to be performed in a reasonable time frame even by supercomputers, let alone by a standard-issue home computer or manually.

Therefore, many statistical methods use a kind of mathematical detour: they derive from the data a single value whose probability distribution is known – a so-called *test statistic.* Instead of calculating the probability of our observed outcome directly, we can then assess its probability by comparing the test statistic against its known distribution. Mathematically, this involves identifying its position on the respective distribution and, as we did above, adding up the probability of this position and all positions deviating further from a random distribution. In practice, we just have to look up the test statistic in a chart that will give us the corresponding probability of error (or *p*-value, as we will call it from now on).

In the following three sections, I will introduce three widely-used tests involving test statistics for the three types of data discussed in the previous section: the chi-square (χ^2) test for nominal data, the Wilcoxon-Mann-Whitney test (also known as Mann-Whitney *U* test or Wilcoxon rank sum test) for ordinal data, and Welch's *t*-test for cardinal data. I will also briefly discuss extensions of the χ^2 test for more complex research designs, including those involving more than two variables.

Given the vast range of corpus-linguistic research designs, these three tests will not always be the ideal choice. In many cases, there are more sophisticated statistical procedures which are better suited to the task at hand, be it for theoretical (mathematical or linguistic) or for practical reasons. However, the statistical tests introduced here have some advantages that make them ideal procedures for an initial statistical evaluation of results. For example, they are easy to perform: we don't need more than a paper and a pencil, or a calculator, if we want to speed up things, and they are also included as standard functions in widely-used spreadsheet applications. They are also relatively robust in situations where we should not really use them (a point I will return to below).

They are also ideal procedures for introducing statistics to novices. Again, they are easy to perform and do not require statistical software packages that are typically expensive and/or have a steep learning curve. They are also relatively transparent with respect to their underlying logic and the steps required to perform them. Thus, my purpose in introducing them in some detail here is at least as much to introduce the logic and the challenges of statistical analysis, as it is to provide basic tools for actual research.

I will not introduce the mathematical underpinnings of these tests, and I will mention alternative and/or more advanced procedures only in passing – this includes, at least for now, research designs where neither variable is nominal. In these cases, correlation tests are used, such as Pearson's product-moment correlations (if are dealing with two cardinal variables) and Spearman's rank correlation coefficient or the Kendall tau rank correlation coefficient (if one or both of our variables are ordinal).

I will not, in other words, do much more than scratch the surface of the vast discipline of statistics. In the Study Notes to this chapter, there are a number of suggestions for further reading that are useful for anyone interested in a deeper understanding of the issues introduced here, and obligatory for anyone serious about using statistical methods in their own research. While I will not be making reference to any statistical software applications, such applications are necessary for serious quantitative research; again, the Study Notes contain useful suggestions where to look.

6.3 Nominal data: The chi-square test

As mentioned in the preceding chapter, nominal data (or data that are best treated like nominal data) are the type of data most frequently encountered in corpus linguistics. I will therefore treat them in slightly more detail than the other two types, introducing different versions and (in the next chapter) extensions of the most widely used statistical test for nominal data, the *chi-square* (χ^2) *test*. This test in all its variants is extremely flexible; it is thus more useful across different research designs than many of the more specific and more sophisticated procedures (much like a Swiss army knife is an excellent all-purpose tool despite the fact that there is usually a better tool dedicated to a specific task at hand).

Despite its flexibility, there are two requirements that must be met in order for the χ^2 test to be applicable: first, no intersection of variables must have a frequency of zero in the data, and second, no more than twenty-five percent of the intersections must have frequencies lower than five. When these conditions are not met, an alternative test must be used instead (or we need to collect additional data).

6.3.1 Two-by-two designs

Let us begin with a two-by-two design and return to the case of discourse-old and discourse-new modifiers in the two English possessive constructions. Here is the research hypothesis again, paraphrased from (9) and (11) in Chapter 5:

(3) H_1: There is a relationship between Discourse Status and Type of Possessive such that the s-possessive is preferred when the modifier is discourse-old, the *of*-possessive is preferred when the modifier is discourse-new.

Prediction: There will be more cases of the S-POSSESSIVE with DISCOURSE-OLD modifiers than with DISCOURSE-NEW modifiers, and more cases of the *OF*-POSSESSIVE with discourse-new modifiers than with DISCOURSE-OLD modifiers.

The corresponding null hypothesis is stated in (4):

(4) H_0: There is no relationship between DISCOURSE STATUS and TYPE OF POSSESSIVE.

Prediction: Discourse-old and discourse-new modifiers will be distributed randomly across the two Possessive constructions.

We already reported the observed and expected frequencies in Table 5.4, but let us repeat them here as Table 6.3 for convenience in a slightly simplified form that we will be using from now on, with the expected frequencies shown in parentheses below the observed ones.

Table 6.3: Observed and expected frequencies of old and new modifiers in the *s*- and the *of*-possessive (= Table 5.4)

		POSSESSIVE		
		S-POSSESSIVE	*OF*-POSSESSIVE	Total
DISCOURSE STATUS	OLD	180 (102.81)	3 (80.19)	183
	NEW	20 (97.19)	153 (75.81)	173
	Total	200	156	356

In order to test our research hypothesis, we must show that the observed frequencies differ from the null hypothesis in the direction of our prediction. We already saw in Chapter 5 that this is the case: The null hypothesis predicts the expected frequencies, but there are more cases of *s*-possessives with old modifiers and *of*-possessives with new modifiers than expected. Next, we must apply the coin-flip logic and ask the question: "Given the sample size, how surprising is the difference between the expected frequencies (i.e., a perfectly random distribution) and the observed frequencies (i.e., the distribution we actually find in our data)?"

As mentioned above, the conceptually simplest way of doing this would be to compute all possible ways in which the marginal frequencies (the sums of the columns and rows) could be distributed across the four cells of our table and then check what proportion of these tables deviates from a perfectly random distribution at least as much as the table we have actually observed. For two-by-two tables, there is, in fact, a test that does this, the exact test (also called Fisher's exact test or, occasionally, Fisher-Yates exact test), and where the conditions for using the χ^2 test are not met, we should use it. But, as mentioned above, this test is difficult to perform without statistical software, and it is not available for tables larger than 2-by-2 anyway, so instead we will derive the χ^2 test statistic from the table.

First, we need to assess the magnitude of the differences between observed and expected frequencies. The simplest way of doing this would be to subtract the expected differences from the observed ones, giving us numbers that show for each cell the size of the deviation as well as its direction (i.e., are the observed frequencies higher or lower than the expected ones). For example, the values for Table 6.3 would be 77.19 for cell C_{11} (S-POSSESSIVE ∩ OLD), −77.19 for C_{21} (*OF*-POSSESSIVE ∩ OLD), −77.19 for C_{12} (*S*-POSSESSIVE ∩ NEW) and 77.19 for C_{22} (*OF*-POSSESSIVE ∩ NEW).

However, we want to derive a single measure from the table, so we need a measure of the overall deviation of the observed frequencies from the expected, not just a measure for the individual intersections. Obviously, adding up the differences of all intersections does not give us such a measure, as it would always be zero (since the marginal frequencies are fixed, any positive deviance in one cell will have a corresponding negative deviance in its neighboring cells). Second, subtracting the observed from the expected frequencies gives us the same number for each cell, when it is obvious that the actual magnitude of the deviation depends on the expected frequency. For example, a deviation of 77.19 is more substantial if the expected frequency is 75.81 than if the expected frequency is 102.81. In the first case, the observed frequency is more than a hundred percent higher than expected, in the second case, it is only 75 percent higher.

The first problem is solved by squaring the differences. This converts all deviations into positive numbers, and thus their sum will no longer be zero, and it has the additional effect of weighing larger deviations more strongly than smaller ones. The second problem is solved by dividing the squared difference by the expected frequencies. This will ensure that a deviation of a particular size will be weighed more heavily for a small expected frequency than for a large expected frequency. The values arrived at in this way are referred to as the *cell components of* χ^2 (or simply χ^2 *components*); the formulas for calculating the cell components in this way are shown in Table 6.4.

Table 6.4: Calculating χ^2 components for individual cells

		DEPENDENT VARIABLE	
		VALUE 1	VALUE 2
INDEPENDENT VARIABLE	VALUE 1	$\frac{(O_{11}-E_{11})^2}{E_{11}}$	$\frac{(O_{12}-E_{12})^2}{E_{12}}$
	VALUE 2	$\frac{(O_{21}-E_{21})^2}{E_{21}}$	$\frac{(O_{22}-E_{22})^2}{E_{22}}$

If we apply this procedure to Table 6.3, we get the components shown in Table 6.5.

Table 6.5: χ^2 components for Table 6.3

		POSSESSIVE	
		S-POSSESSIVE	*OF*-POSSESSIVE
DISCOURSE STATUS	OLD	$\frac{(180-102.81)^2}{102.81} = 57.96$	$\frac{(3-80.19)^2}{80.19} = 74.3$
	NEW	$\frac{(20-97.19)^2}{97.19} = 61.31$	$\frac{(153-75.81)^2}{75.81} = 78.6$

The degree of deviance from the expected frequencies for the entire table can then be calculated by adding up the χ^2 components. For Table 7.3, the χ^2 value (χ^2) is 272.16. This value can now be used to determine the probability of error by checking it against a table like that in Section 14.1 in the Statistical Tables at the end of this book.

Before we can do so, there is a final technical point to make. Note that the degree of variation in a given table that is expected to occur by chance depends quite heavily on the size of the table. The bigger the table, the higher the number of cells that can vary independently of other cells without changing the marginal sums (i.e., without changing the overall distribution). The number of such cells that a table contains is referred to as the number of *degrees of freedom* of the table. In the case of a two-by-two table, there is just one such cell: if we change any single cell, we must automatically adjust the other three cells in order to keep the marginal sums constant. Thus, a two-by-two table has one degree of freedom.

The general formula for determining the degrees of freedom of a table is the following, where N_{rows} is the number of rows and N_{column} is the number of columns:

(5) $\mathrm{df} = (\mathrm{N}_{\mathrm{rows}} - 1) \times (\mathrm{N}_{\mathrm{columns}} - 1)$

Significance levels of χ^2 values differ depending on how many degrees of freedom a table has, so we always need to determine the degrees of freedom before we can determine the *p*-value. Turning to the table of χ^2 values in Section 14.1, we first find the row for one degree of freedom (this is the first row); we then check whether our χ^2-value is larger than that required for the level of significance that we are after. In our case, the value of 272.16 is much higher than the χ^2 value required for a significance level of 0.001 at one degree of freedom, which is 10.83. Thus, we can say that the differences in Table 6.3 are *statistically highly significant.* The results of a χ^2 test are conventionally reported in the following format:

(6) Format for reporting the results of a χ^2 test
(χ^2 = [chi-square value], df = [deg. of freedom], $p <$ (or $>$) [sig. level])

In the present case, the analysis might be summarized along the following lines: "This study has shown that *s*-possessives are preferred when the modifier is discourse-old while *of*-possessives are preferred when the modifier is discourse-new. The differences between the constructions are highly significant ($\chi^2 = 272.16, \mathrm{df} = 1, p < 0.001$)".

A potential danger to this way of formulating the results is the meaning of the word *significant.* In statistical terminology, this word simply means that the results obtained in a study based on one particular sample are unlikely to be due to chance and can therefore be generalized, with some degree of certainty, to the entire population. In contrast, in every-day usage the word means something along the lines of 'having an important effect or influence' (LDCE, s.v. *significant*). Because of this every-day use, it is easy to equate statistical significance with theoretical importance. However, there are at least three reasons why this equation must be avoided.

First, and perhaps most obviously, statistical significance has nothing to do with the validity of the operational definitions used in our research design. In our case, this validity is reasonably high, provided that we limit our conclusions to written English. As a related point, statistical significance has nothing to do with the quality of our data. If we have chosen unrepresentative data or if we have extracted or annotated our data sloppily, the statistical significance of the results is meaningless.

Second, statistical significance has nothing to do with theoretical relevance. Put simply, if we have no theoretical model in which the results can be interpreted meaningfully, statistical significance does not add to our understanding of the object of research. If, for example, we had shown that the preference for the two possessives differed significantly depending on the font in which a modifier is printed, rather than on the discourse status of the modifier, there is not much that we conclude from our findings.[3]

Third, and perhaps least obviously but most importantly, statistical significance does not actually tell us anything about the importance of the relationship we have observed. A relationship may be highly significant (i.e., generalizable with a high degree of certainty) and still be extremely weak. Put differently, statistical significance is not typically an indicator of the strength of the association.[4]

To solve the last problem, we can calculate a so-called measure of *effect size*, which, as its name suggests, indicates the size of the effect that our independent variable has on the dependent variable. For two-by-two contingency tables with categorical data, there is a widely-used measure referred to as ϕ (*phi*) that is calculated as follows:

(7) $$\phi = \sqrt{\frac{\chi^2}{O_{TT}}}$$

In our example, this formula gives us

$$\phi = \sqrt{\frac{272.16}{356}} = 0.8744$$

[3]This problem cannot be dismissed as lightly as this example may suggest: it points to a fundamental difficulty in doing science. Note that if we *did* find that the font has an influence on the choice of possessive, we would most likely dismiss this finding as a random fluke despite its statistical significance. And we may well be right, since even a level of significance of $p < 0.001$ does not preclude the possibility that the observed frequencies are due to chance. In contrast, an influence of the discourse status of the modifier makes sense because discourse status has been shown to have effects in many areas of grammar, and thus we are unlikely to question such an influence. In other words, our judgment of what is and is not plausible will influence our interpretation of our empirical results even if they are statistically significant. Alternatively, we could take every result seriously and look for a possible explanation, which will then typically require further investigation. For example, we might hypothesize that there is a relationship between font and level of formality, and the latter has been shown to have an influence on the choice of possessive constructions (Jucker 1993).

[4]This statement must be qualified to a certain degree: given the right research design, statistical significance may actually be a very reasonable indicator of association strength (cf. e.g. Stefanowitsch & Gries 2003, Gries & Stefanowitsch 2004 for discussion). However, in most contexts we are well advised to keep statistical significance and association strength conceptually separate.

The ϕ-value is a so-called correlation coefficient, whose interpretation can be very subtle (especially when it comes to comparing two or more of them), but we will content ourselves with two relatively simple ways of interpreting them.

First, there are generally agreed-upon verbal descriptions for different ranges that the value of a correlation coefficient may have (similarly to the verbal descriptions of p-values discussed above. These descriptions are shown in Table 6.6.

Table 6.6: Conventional interpretation of correlation coefficients

Absolute Value	Interpretation
0	No relationship
0.01–0.10	Very weak
0.11–0.25	Weak
0.26–0.50	Moderate
0.51–0.75	Strong
0.76–0.99	Very strong
1	Perfect association

Our ϕ-value of 0.8744 falls into the *very strong* category, which is unusual in uncontrolled observational research, and which suggests that Discourse Status is indeed a very important factor in the choice of Possessive constructions in English.

Exactly how much of the variance in the use of the two possessives is accounted for by the discourse status of the modifier can be determined by looking at the square of the ϕ coefficient: the square of a correlation coefficient generally tells us what proportion of the distribution of the dependent variable we can account for on the basis of the independent variable (or, more generally, what proportion of the variance our design has captured). In our case, $\phi^2 = (0.8744 \times 0.8744) = 0.7645$. In other words, the variable Discourse Status explains roughly three quarters of the variance in the use of the Possessive constructions – if, that is, our operational definition actually captures the discourse status of the modifier, and nothing else. A more precise way of reporting the results from our study would be something like the following "This study has shown a strong and statistically highly significant influence of Discourse Status on the choice of possessive construction: *s*-possessives are preferred when the modifier is discourse-old (defined in this study as being realized by a pronoun) while *of*-possessives are preferred when the modifier is discourse-new (defined in this study as being realized by a lexical NP) ($\chi^2 = 272.16, \text{df} = 1, p < 0.001, \phi^2 = 0.7645$)".

Unfortunately, studies in corpus linguistics (and in the social sciences in general) often fail to report effect sizes, but we can usually calculate them from the data provided, and one should make a habit of doing so. Many effects reported in the literature are actually somewhat weaker than the significance levels might lead us to believe.

6.3.2 One-by-*n* designs

In the vast majority of corpus linguistic research issues, we will be dealing with designs that are at least bivariate (i.e., that involve the intersection of at least *two* variables), like the one discussed in the preceding section. However, once in a while we may need to test a *univariate* distribution for significance (i.e., a distribution of values of a single variable regardless of any specific condition). We may, for instance, have annotated an entire corpus for a particular speaker variable (such as sex), and we may now want to know whether the corpus is actually balanced with respect to this variable.

Consider the following example: the spoken part of the BNC contains language produced by 1317 female speakers and 2311 male speakers (as well as 1494 speakers whose sex is unknown, which we will ignore here). In order to determine whether the BNC can be considered a balanced corpus with respect to Speaker Sex, we can compare this observed distribution of speakers to the expected one more or less exactly in the way described in the previous sections except that we have two alternative ways of calculating the expected frequencies.

First, we could simply take the total number of elements and divide it by the number of categories (values), on the assumption that "random" distribution means that every category should occur with the same frequency. In this case, the expected number of male and female speakers would be [Total Number of Speakers / Sex Categories], i.e. $3628/2 = 1814$. We can now calculate the χ^2 components just as we did in the preceding sections, using the formula $((O - E)^2)/E$. Table 6.7 shows the results.

Adding up the components gives us a χ^2 value of 272.34. A one-by-two table has one degree of freedom (if we vary one cell, we have to adjust the other one automatically to keep the marginal sum constant). Checking the appropriate row in the table in Section 14.1, we can see that this value is much higher than the 10.83 required for a significance level of 0.01. Thus, we can say that "the BNC corpus contains a significantly higher proportion of male speakers than expected by chance ($\chi^2 = 272.34, \text{df} = 1, p < 0.001$)" – in other words, the corpus is not balanced well with respect to the variable Speaker Sex (note that since this is a test of proportions rather than correlations, we cannot calculate a phi value here).

Table 6.7: Observed and expected frequencies of Speaker Sex in the BNC (based on the assumption of equal proportions)

		Observed	Expected	χ^2
Sex	female	1317	1814	$\frac{(1317-1814)^2}{1814} = 136.17$
	male	2311	1814	$\frac{(2311-1814)^2}{1814} = 136.17$
	Total	3628		272.34

The second way of deriving expected frequencies for a univariate distribution is from prior knowledge concerning the distribution of the values in general. In our case, we could find out the proportion of men and women in the relevant population and then derive the expected frequencies for our table by assuming that they follow this proportion. The relevant population in this case is that of the United Kingdom between 1991 and 1994, when the BNC was assembled. According to the World Bank, the women made up 51.4 percent and men 48.6 percent of the total population at that time, so the expected frequencies of male and female speakers in the corpus are as shown in Table 6.8.

Table 6.8: Observed and expected frequencies of Speaker Sex in the BNC (based on the proportions in the general population)

		Observed	Expected	χ^2
Sex	female	1317	$3628 \times 0.514 = 1864.79$	$\frac{(1317-1864.79)^2}{1864.79} = 160.92$
	male	2311	$3628 \times 0.486 = 1763.21$	$\frac{(2311-1763.21)^2}{1763.21} = 170.19$
	Total	3628		331.1

Clearly, the empirical distribution in this case closely resembles our hypothesized equal distribution, and thus the results are very similar – since there are slightly more women than men in the population, their underrepresentation in the corpus is even more signficant.

Incidentally, the BNC not only contains speech by more male speakers than female speakers, it also includes more speech by male than by female speakers:

men contribute 5 654 348 words, women contribute 3 825 804. I will leave it as an exercise to the reader to determine whether and in what direction these frequencies differ from what would be expected either under an assumption of equal proportions or given the proportion of female and male speakers in the corpus.

In the case of speaker sex it does not make much of a difference how we derive the expected frequencies, as men and women make up roughly half of the population each. For variables where such an even distribution of values does not exist, the differences between these two procedures can be quite drastic. As an example, consider Table 6.9, which lists the observed distribution of the speakers in the spoken part of the BNC across age groups (excluding speakers whose age is not recorded), together with the expected frequencies on the assumption of equal proportions, and the expected frequencies based on the distribution of speakers across age groups in the real world. The distribution of age groups in the population of the UK between 1991 and 1994 is taken from the website of the Office for National Statistics, averaged across the four years and cumulated to correspond to the age groups recorded in the BNC.

Table 6.9: Observed and expected frequencies of Speaker Age in the BNC

			Equal Proportions		Population Proportions	
Age	Obs.	p(Pop.)	Expected	χ^2	Expected	χ^2
0–14	255	0.1938	$\frac{1978}{6} = 329.67$	16.91	$255 \times 0.1938 = 383.32$	42.96
15–24	300	0.1351	$\frac{1978}{6} = 329.67$	2.67	$300 \times 0.1351 = 267.17$	4.03
25–34	346	0.1565	$\frac{1978}{6} = 329.67$	0.81	$346 \times 0.1565 = 309.61$	4.28
35–44	331	0.1351	$\frac{1978}{6} = 329.67$	0.01	$331 \times 0.1351 = 267.29$	15.18
45–59	433	0.1719	$\frac{1978}{6} = 329.67$	32.39	$433 \times 0.1719 = 340.02$	25.42
60+	313	0.2076	$\frac{1978}{6} = 329.67$	0.84	$313 \times 0.2076 = 410.58$	23.19
Total	1978	1		53.63		115.07

Adding up the χ^2 components gives us an overall χ^2 value of 53.63 in the first case and 115.07 in the second case. For univariate tables, df = (Number of Values − 1), so Table 6.9 has four degrees of freedom (we can vary four cells independently and then simply adjust the fifth to keep the marginal sum constant). The required χ^2 value for a 0.001-level of significance at four degrees of freedom is 18.47: clearly, whichever way we calculate the expected frequencies, the differences between observed and expected are highly significant. However, the distribution of age groups in the corpus is much closer to the assumption of equal proportions than to the actual proportions in the population; also, the conclusions we will draw concerning the over- or underrepresentation of individual categories will be very different. In the first case, for example, we might be led to believe that the age group 34–44 is fairly represented while the age group 15–24 is underrepresented. In the second case, we see that in fact both age groups are overrepresented. In this case, there is a clear argument for using empirically derived expected frequencies: the categories differ in terms of the age span each of them covers, so even if we thought that the distribution of ages in the population is homogeneous, we would not expect all categories to have the same size.

The exact alternative to the univariate χ^2 test with a two-level variable is the *binomial* test, which we used (without calling it that), in our coin-flip example in Section 6.2 above and which is included as a predefined function in many major spreadsheet applications and in R; for one-by-n tables, there is a multinomial test also available in R and other statistics packages.

6.4 Ordinal data: The Mann-Whitney *U*-test

Where one variable is nominal (more precisely, nominal with two values) and one is ordinal, the most widely used test statistic is the Mann-Whitney *U*-test (also called Wilcoxon rank sum test).

Let us return to the case study of the animacy of modifiers in the two English possessive constructions. Here is the research hypothesis again, from (12) and (13) in Chapter 5:

(8) H_1: The S-POSSESSIVE will be used when the modifier is high in ANIMACY, the OF-POSSESSIVE will be used when the modifier is low in ANIMACY.

Prediction: The modifiers of the S-POSSESSIVE will have a higher median on the ANIMACY scale than the the modifiers of the OF-POSSESSIVE.

The corresponding null hypothesis is stated in (9):

(9) H_0: There is no relationship between ANIMACY and TYPE OF POSSESSIVE.

Prediction: There will be no difference between the medians of the modifiers of the S-POSSESSIVE and the OF-POSSESSIVE on the ANIMACY scale.

The median animacy of all modifiers in our sample taken together is 2,[5] so the H_0 predicts that the medians of *s*-possessive and the *of*-possessive should

[5] There are 41 data points in our sample, whose ranks are the following: 1, 1, 1, 1, 1, 1, 1, 1, 1, 1, 1, 1, 1, 1, 1, 2, 2, 2, 2, 2, 2, 3, 3, 4, 5, 5, 5, 5, 5, 5, 6, 6, 7, 7, 8, 9, 10, 10, 10, 10. The twenty-first item on the list is a 2, so this is the median.

also be 2. Recall that the observed median animacy in our sample was 1 for the *s*-possessive and 5 for the *of*-possessive, which deviates from the prediction of the H_0 in the direction of our H_1. However, as in the case of nominal data, a certain amount of deviation from the null hypothesis will occur due to chance, so we need a test statistic that will tell us how likely our observed result is. For ordinal data, this test statistic is the U value, which is calculated as follows.

In a first step, we have to determine the rank order of the data points in our sample. For expository reasons, let us distinguish between the rank value and the rank position of a data point: the rank value is the ordinal value it received during annotation (in our case, its value on the Animacy scale), its rank position is the position it occupies in an ordered list of all data points. If every rank value occurred only once in our sample, rank value and rank position would be the same. However, there are 41 data points in our sample, so the rank positions will range from 1 to 41, and there are only 10 rank values in our annotation scheme for Animacy. This means that at least some rank values will occur more than once, which is a typical situation for corpus-linguistic research involving ordinal data. Table 6.10 shows all data points in our sample together with their rank position.

Every rank value except 4, 8 and 9 occurs more than once; for example, there are sixteen cases that have an Animacy rank value of 1 and six cases that have a rank value of 2, two cases that have a rank value of 3, and so on. This means we cannot simply assign rank positions from 1 to 41 to our examples, as there is no way of deciding which of the sixteen examples with the rank value 1 should receive the rank position 1, 2, 3, etc. Instead, these 16 examples as a group share the range of ranks from 1 to 16, so each example gets the mean rank position of this range. There are sixteen cases with rank value 1, to their mean rank is

$$\frac{1+2+3+4+5+6+7+8+9+10+11+12+13+14+15+16}{16} = \frac{136}{16} = 8.5$$

The first example with the rank value 2 occurs in line 17 of the table, so it would receive the rank position 17. However, there are five more examples with the same rank value, so again we calculate the mean rank position of the range from rank 17 to 22, which is

$$\frac{17+18+19+20+21+22}{6} = \frac{117}{16} = 19.5$$

Repeating this process for all examples yields the rank positions shown in the second column in Table 6.10.

Table 6.10: Annotated sample from Table 5.6 with animacy rank and position (cf. Table 5.7)

Anim.	Pos.	Type	No.	*(contd.)* Anim.	Pos.	Type	No.
1	8.5	S	(a 2)	4	25	OF	(b 13)
1	8.5	S	(a 3)	5	28.5	S	(a 11)
1	8.5	S	(a 7)	5	28.5	OF	(b 5)
1	8.5	S	(a 8)	5	28.5	OF	(b 11)
1	8.5	S	(a 9)	5	28.5	OF	(b 16)
1	8.5	S	(a 10)	5	28.5	OF	(b 17)
1	8.5	S	(a 12)	5	28.5	OF	(b 18)
1	8.5	S	(a 15)	6	32.5	S	(a 4)
1	8.5	S	(a 17)	6	32.5	OF	(b 9)
1	8.5	S	(a 18)	7	34.5	OF	(b 3)
1	8.5	S	(a 19)	7	34.5	OF	(b 14)
1	8.5	S	(a 20)	8	36.0	OF	(b 1)
1	8.5	S	(a 21)	9	37.0	OF	(b 12)
1	8.5	S	(a 23)	10	39.5	OF	(b 6)
1	8.5	OF	(b 4)	10	39.5	OF	(b 8)
1	8.5	OF	(b 7)	10	39.5	OF	(b 10)
2	19.5	S	(a 1)	10	39.5	OF	(b 15)
2	19.5	S	(a 5)				
2	19.5	S	(a 6)				
2	19.5	S	(a 13)				
2	19.5	S	(a 14)				
2	19.5	OF	(b 2)				
3	23.5	S	(a 16)				
3	23.5	S	(a 22)				

Once we have determined the rank position of each data point, we separate them into two subsamples corresponding to the values of the nominal variable Type of Possessive again, as in Table 6.11. We then calculate rank sum R for each group, which is simply the sum of their rank positions, and we count the number of data points N in each group.

Table 6.11: Animacy ranks and positions and rank sums for the sample of possessives

S-POSSESSIVE				*OF*-POSSESSIVE			
Anim.	Pos.	Type	Example	Anim.	Pos.	Type	Example
2	19.5	*s*	(a 1)	8	36.0	*OF*	(b 1)
1	8.5	*s*	(a 2)	2	19.5	*OF*	(b 2)
1	8.5	*s*	(a 3)	7	34.5	*OF*	(b 3)
6	32.5	*s*	(a 4)	1	8.5	*OF*	(b 4)
2	19.5	*s*	(a 5)	5	28.5	*OF*	(b 5)
2	19.5	*s*	(a 6)	10	39.5	*OF*	(b 6)
1	8.5	*s*	(a 7)	1	8.5	*OF*	(b 7)
1	8.5	*s*	(a 8)	10	39.5	*OF*	(b 8)
1	8.5	*s*	(a 9)	6	32.5	*OF*	(b 9)
1	8.5	*s*	(a 10)	10	39.5	*OF*	(b 10)
5	28.5	*s*	(a 11)	5	28.5	*OF*	(b 11)
1	8.5	*s*	(a 12)	9	37.0	*OF*	(b 12)
2	19.5	*s*	(a 13)	4	25.0	*OF*	(b 13)
2	19.5	*s*	(a 14)	7	34.5	*OF*	(b 14)
1	8.5	*s*	(a 15)	10	39.5	*OF*	(b 15)
3	23.5	*s*	(a 16)	5	28.5	*OF*	(b 16)
1	8.5	*s*	(a 17)	5	28.5	*OF*	(b 17)
1	8.5	*s*	(a 18)	5	28.5	*OF*	(b 18)
1	8.5	*s*	(a 19)				
1	8.5	*s*	(a 20)				
1	8.5	*s*	(a 21)				
3	23.5	*s*	(a 22)				
1	8.5	*s*	(a 23)				
R	324.5			R	536.5		
N	23			N	18		

The rank sum and the number of data points for each sample allow us to calculate the U values for both group using the following simple formulas:

(10) a. $U_1 = (N_1 \times N_2) + \frac{N_1 \times (N_1+1)}{2} - R_1$

b. $U_2 = (N_1 \times N_2) + \frac{N_2 \times (N_2+1)}{2} - R_2$

Applying these formulas to the measures for the *s*-possessive (10a) and *of*-possessive (10b) respectively, we get the U values

$$U_1 = (23 \times 18) + \frac{23 \times (23 + 1)}{2} - 324.5 = 365.5$$

and

$$U_2 = (23 \times 18) + \frac{18 \times (18 + 1)}{2} - 536.5 = 48.5$$

The U value for the entire data set is always the smaller of the two U values. In our case this is U_2, so our U value is 48.5. This value can now be compared against its known distribution in the same way as the χ^2 value for nominal data. In our case, this means looking it up in the table in Section 14.3 in the Statistical Tables at the end of this book, which tells us that the p-value for this U value is smaller than 0.001 – the difference between the *s*- and the *of*-possessive is, again, highly significant. The Mann-Whitney U test may be reported as follows:

(11) *Format for reporting the results of a Mann-Whitney test*
(U = [U value], N_1 = [N_1], N_2 = [N_2], $p <$ (or $>$) [sig. level]).

Thus, we could report the results of this case study as follows: "This study has shown that *s*-possessives are preferred when the modifier is high in animacy, while *of*-possessives are preferred when the modifier is low in animacy. A Mann-Whitney test shows that the differences between the constructions are highly significant ($U = 48.5, N_1 = 18, N_2 = 23, p < 0.001$)".

6.5 Inferential statistics for cardinal data

Where one variable is nominal (more precisely, nominal with two values) and one is cardinal, the a widely-used test is the t-test, of which there are two well-known versions, Welch's t-test and Student's t-test, that differ in terms of the requirements that the data must meet in order for them to be applicable. In the following, I will introduce Welch's t-test, which can be applied more broadly, although it still has some requirements that I will return to below.

6.5.1 Welch's *t*-test

Let us return to the case study of the length of modifiers in the two English possessive constructions. Here is the research hypothesis again, paraphrased slightly from (15) and (16) in Chapter 5:

(12) H_1: The S-POSSESSIVE will be used with short modifiers, the *OF*-POSSESSIVE will be used with long modifiers.

Prediction: The mean LENGTH (in "number of words") of modifiers of the S-POSSESSIVE should be smaller than that of the modifiers of the *OF*-POSSESSIVE.

The corresponding null hypothesis is stated in (13):

(13) H_0: There is no relationship between LENGTH and TYPE OF POSSESSIVE.

Prediction: There will be no difference between the mean length of the modifiers of the S-POSSESSIVE and the *OF*-POSSESSIVE.

Table 6.12 shows the length in number of words for the modifiers of the *s*- and *of*-possessives (as already reported in Table 5.9), together with a number of additional pieces of information that we will turn to next.

First, note that one case that was still included in Table 5.9 is missing: Example (b 19) from that Table, which had a modifier of length 20. This is treated here as a so-called *outlier*, i.e., a value that is so far away from the mean that it can be considered an exception. There are different opinions on if and when outliers should be removed that we will not discuss here, but for expository reasons alone it is reasonable here to remove it (and for our results, it would not have made a difference if we had kept it).

In order to calculate Welch's *t*-test, we determine three values on the basis of our measurements of LENGTH: the number of measurements *N*, the mean length for each group ($\overline{x}$), and a value called "sample variance" (s^2). The number of measurements is easy to determine – we just count the cases in each group: 20 *s*-possessives and 24 *of*-possessives. We already calculated the mean lengths in Chapter 5: for the *s*-possessive, the mean length is 1.9 words, for the *of*-possessive it is 3.83 words. As we already discussed in Chapter 5, this difference conforms to our hypothesis: *s*-possessives are, on average, shorter than *of*-possessives.

The question is, again, how likely it is that this difference is due to chance. When comparing group means, the crucial question we must ask in order to determine this is how large the variation is within each group of measurements: put simply, the more widely the measurements within each group vary, the more likely it is that the differences across groups have come about by chance.

Table 6.12: Length of the modifier in the sample of *s*- and *of*-possessives from Table 5.9

S-POSSESSIVE				OF-POSSESSIVE			
No.	Length	$(x-\overline{x})$	$(x-\overline{x})^2$	No.	Length	$(x-\overline{x})$	$(x-\overline{x})^2$
(a 1)	2	0.10	0.01	(b 1)	3	−0.83	0.69
(a 2)	2	0.10	0.01	(b 2)	5	1.17	1.36
(a 3)	2	0.10	0.01	(b 3)	4	0.17	0.03
(a 4)	2	0.10	0.01	(b 4)	8	4.17	17.36
(a 5)	3	1.10	1.21	(b 5)	7	3.17	10.03
(a 6)	1	−0.90	0.81	(b 6)	1	−2.83	8.03
(a 7)	2	0.10	0.01	(b 7)	9	5.17	26.69
(a 8)	2	0.10	0.01	(b 8)	2	−1.83	3.36
(a 9)	2	0.10	0.01	(b 9)	5	1.17	1.36
(a 10)	2	0.10	0.01	(b 10)	6	2.17	4.69
(a 11)	1	−0.90	0.81	(b 11)	2	−1.83	3.36
(a 12)	2	0.10	0.01	(b 12)	2	−1.83	3.36
(a 13)	1	−0.90	0.81	(b 13)	1	−2.83	8.03
(a 14)	3	1.10	1.21	(b 14)	8	4.17	17.36
(a 15)	2	0.10	0.01	(b 15)	5	1.17	1.36
(a 16)	1	−0.90	0.81	(b 16)	2	−1.83	3.36
(a 17)	2	0.10	0.01	(b 17)	2	−1.83	3.36
(a 18)	2	0.10	0.01	(b 19)	2	−1.83	3.36
(a 19)	2	0.10	0.01	(b 20)	1	−2.83	8.03
(a 20)	2	0.10	0.01	(b 21)	2	−1.83	3.36
				(b 22)	8	4.17	17.36
				(b 23)	3	−0.83	0.69
				(b 24)	2	−1.83	3.36
				(b 25)	2	−1.83	3.36
N	20			N	24		
Total	58	0		Total	92	0	
$\overline{x}$	1.9			$\overline{x}$	3.8333		
s^2			0.3053	s^2			6.67

The first step in assessing the variation consists in determining for each measurement, how far away it is from its group mean. Thus, we simply subtract each measurement for the S-POSSESSIVE from the group mean of 1.9, and each measurement for the OF-POSSESSIVE from the group mean of 3.83. The results are shown in the third column of each sub-table in Table 6.12. However, we do not want to know how much each single measurement deviates from the mean, but how far the group S-POSSESSIVE or OF-POSSESSIVE as a whole varies around the mean. Obviously, adding up all individual values is not going to be helpful: as in the case of observed and expected frequencies of nominal data, the result would always be zero. So we use the same trick we used there, and calculate the square of each value – making them all positive and weighting larger deviations more heavily. The results of this are shown in the fourth column of each sub-table. We then calculate the mean of these values for each group, but instead of adding up all values and dividing them by the number of cases, we add them up and divide them by the total number of cases minus one. This is referred to as the sample variance:

(14) $$s^2 = \frac{\sum_{i=1}^{n}(x_i - \overline{x})^2}{n - 1}$$

The sample variances themselves cannot be very easily interpreted (see further below), but we can use them to calculate our test statistic, the *t*-value, using the following formula ($\overline{x}$ stands for the group mean, s^2 stands for the sample variance, and N stands for the number of cases; the subscripts 1 and 2 indicate the two subsamples:

(15) $$t_{\text{Welch}} = \frac{\overline{x}_1 - \overline{x}_2}{\sqrt{\frac{s_1^2}{N_1} + \frac{s_2^2}{N_2}}}$$

Note that this formula assumes that the measures with the subscript 1 are from the larger of the two samples (if we don't pay attention to this, however, all that happens is that we get a negative *t*-value, whose negative sign we can simply ignore). In our case, the sample of *of*-possessives is the larger one, giving us:

$$t_{\text{Welch}} = \frac{3.8333 - 1.9}{\sqrt{\frac{6.6667}{24} + \frac{0.3053}{20}}} = 3.5714$$

As should be familiar by now, we compare this *t*-value against its distribution to determine the probability of error (i.e., we look it up in the table in Section 14.4

in the Statistical Tables at the end of this book. Before we can do so, however, we need to determine the degrees of freedom of our sample. This is done using the following formula:

(16)
$$\mathrm{df} \approx \frac{\left(\frac{s_1^2}{N_1} + \frac{s_2^2}{N_2}\right)^2}{\frac{s_1^4}{N_1^2\,\mathrm{df}_1} + \frac{s_2^4}{N_2^2\,\mathrm{df}_2}}$$

Again, the subscripts indicate the sub-samples, s^2 is the sample variance, and N is the number of items the degrees of freedom for the two groups (df_1 and df_2) are defined as $N - 1$. If we apply the formula to our data, we get the following:

$$\mathrm{df} \approx \frac{\left(\frac{6.6667}{24} + \frac{0.3053}{20}\right)^2}{\frac{6.6667^2}{24^2 \times (24-1)} + \frac{0.3053^2}{20^2 \times (20-1)}} = 25.5038$$

As we can see in the table of critical values, the t-value is smaller than 0.01. A t-test should be reported in the following format:

(17) *Format for reporting the results of a t test*
(t([deg. freedom]) = [t value], p < (or >) [sig. level]).

Thus, a straightforward way of reporting our results would be something like this: "This study has shown that for modifiers that are realized by lexical NPs, *s*-possessives are preferred when the modifier is short, while *of*-possessives are preferred when the modifier is long. The difference between the constructions is very significant ($t(25.50) = 3.5714$, $p < 0.01$)".

As pointed out above, the value for the sample variance does not, in itself, tell us very much. We can convert it into something called the *sample standard deviation*, however, by taking its square root. The standard deviation is an indicator of the amount of variation in a sample (or sub-sample) that is frequently reported; it is good practice to report standard deviations whenever we report means.

Finally, note that, again, the significance level does not tell us anything about the size of the effect, so we should calculate an effect size separately. The most widely-used effect size for data analyzed with a t-test is Cohen's *d*, also referred to as the standardized mean difference. There are several ways to calculate it, the simplest one is the following, where σ is the standard deviation of the entire sample:

(18) $$d = \frac{\overline{x_1} - \overline{x_2}}{\sigma}$$

For our case study, this gives us

$$d = \frac{3.8333 - 1.9}{2.1562} = 0.8966$$

This standardized mean difference can be converted to a correlation coefficient by the formula in (19):

(19) $$r = \frac{d}{\sqrt{d^2 + \frac{(N_1+N_2)^2}{N_1 \times N_2}}}$$

For our case study, this gives us

$$r = \frac{0.8966}{\sqrt{0.8966^2 + \frac{(24+20)^2}{24 \times 20}}} = 0.4077$$

Since this is a correlation coefficient, it can be interpreted as described in Table 6.6 above. It falls into the *moderate* range, so a more comprehensive way of summarizing the results of this case study would be the following: "This study has shown that length has a moderate, statistically significant influence on the choice of possessive constructions with lexical NPs in modifier position: *s*-possessives are preferred when the modifier is short, while *of*-possessives are preferred when the modifier is long. ($t(25.50) = 3.5714, p < 0.01, r = 0.41$)".

6.5.2 Normal distribution requirement

In the context of corpus linguistics, there is one fundamental problem with the *t*-test in any of its variants: it requires data that follow what is called the *normal distribution.* Briefly, the normal distribution is a probability distribution where most measurements fall in the middle, decreasing on either side until they reach zero. Figure 6.1a shows some examples. As you can see, the curve may be narrower or wider (depending on the standard deviation) and it may be positioned at different points on the x axis (depending on the mean), but it is always a symmetrical bell curve.

You will often read that many natural phenomena approximate this distribution – examples mentioned in textbooks are, invariably, the size and weight of organisms, frequently other characteristics of organisms such as skin area, blood pressure or IQ, and occasionally social phenomena like test scores and salaries. Figure 6.1b show the distribution of body weight in a sample of swans collected for an environmental impact study (Fite 1979), and, indeed, it seems to follow,

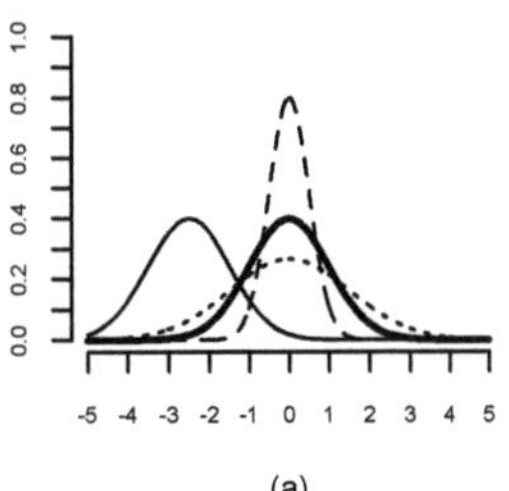

(a)

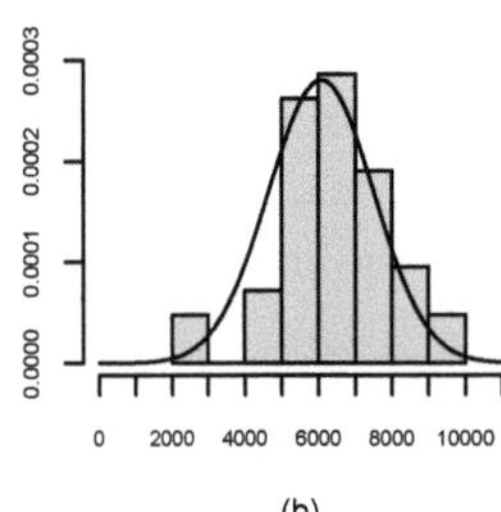

(b)

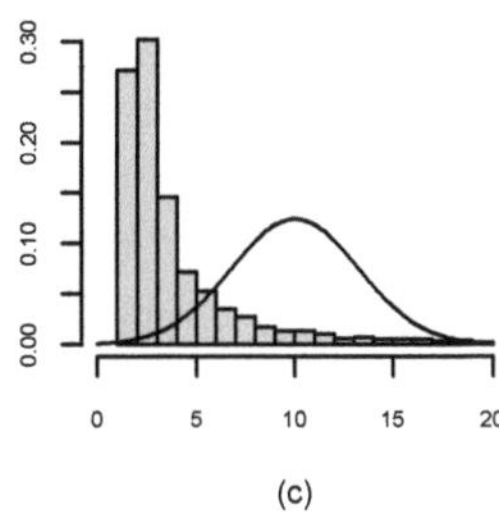

(c)

Figure 6.1: The normal distribution and linguistic data

roughly, a normal distribution if we compare it to the bell curve superimposed on the figure.

Unfortunately, cardinal measurements derived from language data (such as the length or of words, constituents, sentences, etc. or the distance to the last mention of a referent) are rarely (if ever) normally distributed (see, e.g., McEnery & Hardie 2012: 51). Figure 6.1c shows the distribution of the constituent length, in number of words, of *of*-phrases modifying nouns in the SUSANNE corpus (with *of*-phrases with a length of more than 20 words removed as outliers). As you can see, they do not follow a normal distribution at all – there are many more short *of*-phrases than long ones, shifting the distribution further to the left and making it much narrower than it should be.

There are three broad ways of dealing with this issue. First, we could ignore it and hope that the *t*-test is robust enough to yield meaningful results despite this violation of the normality requirement. If this seems like a bad idea, this is because it is fundamentally a bad idea – and statisticians warn against it categorically. However, many social scientists regularly adopt this approach – just like we did in the case study above. And in practice, this may be less of a problem than one might assume, since the *t*-test has been found to be fairly robust against violations of the normality requirement. However, we should not generally rely on this robustness, as linguistic data may depart from normality to quite an extreme degree. More generally, ignoring the prerequisites of a statistical procedure is not exactly good scientific practice – the only reason I did it above was so you would not be too shocked when you see it done in actual research (which, inevitably, you will).

Second, and more recommendably, we could try to make the data fit the normality requirement. One way in which this is sometimes achieved in the many cases where data do not follow the normal distribution is to log-transform the data (i.e., use the natural logarithm of the data instead of the data themselves). This often, but not always, causes the data to approximate a normal distribution more closely. However, this does not work in all cases (it would not, for example, bring the distribution in Figure 6.1c much closer to a normal distribution, and anyway, transforming data carries its own set of problems.

Thus, third, and most recommendably, we could try to find a way around having to use a t-test in the first place. One way of avoiding a t-test is to treat our non-normally distributed cardinal data as ordinal data, as described in Chapter 5. We can then use the Mann-Whitney U-test, which does not require a normal distribution of the data. I leave it as an exercise to the reader to apply this test to the data in Table 6.12 (you know you have succeeded if your result for U is 137, $p < 0.01$).

Another way of avoiding the t-test is to find an operationalization of the phenomenon under investigation that yields rank data, or, even better, nominal data in the first place. We could, for example, code the data in Table 6.12 in terms of a very simple nominal variable: LONGER CONSTITUENT (with the variables HEAD and MODIFIER). For each case, we simply determine whether the head is longer than the modifier (in which case we assign the value head) or whether the modifier is longer than the head (in which case we assign the value MODIFIER; we discard all cases where the two have the same length. This gives us Table 6.13.

Table 6.13: The influence of length on the choice between the two possessives

		POSSESSIVE		
		S-POSSESSIVE	*OF*-POSSESSIVE	Total
LONGER CONSTITUENT	HEAD	8 (6.3)	5 (6.7)	13
	MOD	8 (9.7)	12 (10.3)	20
	Total	16	17	33

The χ^2 value for this table is 0.7281, which at one degree of freedom means that the p value is larger than 0.05, so we would have to conclude that there is no influence of length on the choice of possessive construction. However, the deviations of the observed from the expected frequencies go in the right direction, so this may simply be due to the fact that our sample is too small (obviously, a serious corpus-linguistic study would not be based on just 33 cases).

The normal-distribution requirement is only one of several requirements that our data set must meet in order for particular statistical methods to be applicable.

For example, many procedures for comparing group means – including the more widely-used *Student t*-test – can only be applied if the two groups have the same variance (roughly, if the measurements in both groups are spread out from the group means to the same extent), and there are tests to tell us this (for example, the *F* test). Also, it makes a difference whether the two groups that we are comparing are independent of each other (as in the case studies presented here), or if they are dependent in that there is a correspondence between measures in the two groups. For example, if we wanted to compare the length of heads and modifiers in the *s*-possessive, we would have two groups that are dependent in that for any data point in one of the groups there is a corresponding data point in the other group that comes from the same corpus example. In this case, we would use a *paired* test (for example, the matched-pairs Wilcoxon test for ordinal data and Student's paired *t*-test for cardinal data).

6.6 Complex research designs

In Chapter 5 and in this chapter so far, we have restricted our discussion to the simplest possible research designs – cases where we are dealing with two variables with two values each. To conclude our discussion of statistical hypothesis testing, we will look at two cases of more complex designs – one with two variables that each have more than two values, and one with more than two variables.

6.6.1 Variables with more than two values

In our case studies involving the English possessive constructions, the dependent variable (Type of) Possessive was treated as binary – we assumed that it had two values, *s*-possessive and *of*-possessive. The dependent variables were more complex: the cardinal variable Length obviously has a potentially infinite number of values and the ordinal variable Animacy was treated as having ten values in our annotation scheme. The nominal value Discourse Status, was treated like a binary variable (although potentially it has an infinite number of values, too).

Frequently, perhaps even typically, corpus linguistic research questions will be more complex, and we will be confronted with designs where both the dependent and the independent variable will have (or be treated as having) more than two values. Since we are most likely to deal with nominal variables in corpus linguistics, we will discuss in detail an example where both variables are nominal.

In the preceding chapters we treated as *s*-possessive constructions where the modifier is a possessive pronoun as well as constructions where the modifier is a proper name or a noun with a possessive clitic. Given that the proportion of pronouns and nouns in general varies across language varieties (Biber et al. 1999), we might be interested to see whether the same is true for these three variants of the *s*-possessive. Our dependent variable MODIFIER OF *S*-POSSESSIVE would then have three values. The independent variable VARIETY, being heavily dependent on the model of language varieties we adopt – or rather, on the nature of the text categories included in our corpus – has an indefinite number of values. To keep things simple, let us distinguish just four broad text categories recognized in the British National Corpus (and many other corpora): SPOKEN, FICTION, NEWSPAPER and ACADEMIC. This gives us a four-by-three design.

Searching the BNC Baby for words tagged as possessive pronouns and for words tagged unambiguously as proper names or common nouns yields the observed frequencies shown in the first line of each row in Table 6.14.

Table 6.14: Types of modifiers in the *s*-possessive in different text categories

			POSSESSIVE MODIFIER			
			PRONOUN	PROPER NAME	NOUN	Total
VARIETY	SPOKEN	*Obs.*	9593	768	604	10 965
		Exp.	8378.38	1361.04	1225.58	
		χ^2-*Comp.*	176.08	258.40	315.25	
	FICTION	*Obs.*	23 755	2681	1998	28 434
		Exp.	21 726.49	3529.39	3178.12	
		χ^2-*Comp.*	189.39	203.94	438.21	
	NEWS	*Obs.*	12 857	4070	3585	20 512
		Exp.	15 673.27	2546.07	2292.66	
		χ^2-*Comp.*	506.04	912.14	728.47	
	ACADEMIC	*Obs.*	8533	1373	1820	11 726
		Exp.	8959.86	1455.50	1310.64	
		χ^2-*Comp.*	20.34	4.68	197.96	
	Total		54 738	8892	8007	71 637

The expected frequencies and the χ^2 components are arrived at in the same way as for the two-by-two tables in the preceding chapter. First, for each cell, the sum of the column in which the cell is located is multiplied by the sum of the row in which it is located, and the result is divided by the table sum. For example, for the top left cell, we get the expected frequency

$$\frac{54738 \times 10965}{71637} = 8378.38,$$

the expected frequencies are shown in the second line of each cell. Next, for each cell, we calculate the χ^2 component. For example, for the top left cell, we get

$$\frac{(9593 - 8378.38)^2}{8378.38} = 176.08,$$

the corresponding values are shown in the third line of each cell. Adding up the individual χ^2 components gives us a χ^2 value of 3950.89.

Using the formula given in (5) above, Table 6.14 has $(4-1)\times(3-1) = 6$ degrees of freedom. As the χ^2 table in Section 14.1, the required value for a significance level of 0.001 at 6 degrees of freedom is 22.46; the χ^2 value for Table 6.14 is much higher than this, thus, our results are highly significant. We could summarize our findings as follows: "The frequency of pronouns, proper names and nouns as modifiers of the *s*-possessive differs highly significantly across text categories ($\chi^2 = 473.73, \text{df} = 12, p < 0.001$)".

Recall that the mere fact of a significant association does not tell us anything about the strength of that association – we need a measure of effect size. In the preceding chapter, ϕ was introduced as an effect size for two-by-two tables (see 7). For larger tables, there is a generalized version of ϕ, referred to as *Cramer's V* (or, occasionally, as *Cramer's* ϕ or ϕ'), which is calculated as follows (N is the table sum, k is the number of rows or columns, whichever is smaller):

(20)
$$\text{Cramer's V} = \sqrt{\frac{\chi^2}{N \times (k-1)}}$$

For our table, this gives us:

$$\sqrt{\frac{3950.89}{71637 \times (3-1)}} = 0.1661$$

Recall that the square of a correlation coefficient tells us the proportion of the variance captured by our design, which, in this case, is 0.0275. In other words, VARIETY explains less than three percent of the distribution of *s*-possessor modifier types across language varieties; or "This study has shown a very weak but highly significant influence of language variety on the realization of *s*-possessor modifiers as pronouns, proper names or common nouns ($\chi^2 = 473.73, \text{df} = 12, p < 0.001, r = 0.0275$)."

Despite the weakness of the effect, this result confirms our expectation that general preferences for pronominal vs. nominal reference across language varieties is also reflected in preferences for types of modifiers in the *s*-possessive. However, with the increased size of the contingency table, it becomes more difficult to determine exactly where the effect is coming from. More precisely, it is no longer obvious at a glance which of the intersections of our two variables contribute to the overall significance of the result in what way and to what extent.

To determine in what way a particular intersection contributes to the overall result, we need to compare the observed and expected frequencies in each cell. For example, there are 9593 cases of *s*-possessives with pronominal modifiers in spoken language, where 8378.38 are expected, showing that pronominal modifiers are more frequent in spoken language than expected by chance. In contrast, there are 8533 such modifiers in academic language, where 8959.86 are expected, showing that they are less frequent in academic language than expecte by chance. This comparison is no different from that which we make for two-by-two tables, but with increasing degrees of freedom, the pattern becomes less predictable. It would be useful to visualize the relation between observed and expected frequencies for the entire table in a way that would allow us to take them in at a glance.

To determine to what extent a particular intersection contributes to the overall result, we need to look at the size of the χ^2 components – the larger the component, the greater its contribution to the overall χ^2 value. In fact, we can do more than simply compare the χ^2 components to each other – we can determine for each component, whether it, in itself, is statistically significant. In order to do so, we first imagine that the large contingency table (in our case, the 4-by-3 table) consists of a series of tables with a single cell each, each containing the result for a single intersection of our variables.

We now treat the χ^2 component as a χ^2 value in its own right, checking it for statistical significance in the same way as the overall χ^2 value. In order to do so, we first need to determine the degrees of freedom for our one-cell tables – obviously, this can only be 1. Checking the table of critical χ^2 values in Section 14.1, we find, for example, that the χ^2 component for the intersection PRONOUN ∩ SPOKEN, which is 176.08, is higher than the critical value 10.83, suggesting that this intersection's contribution is significant at $p < 0.001$.

However, matters are slightly more complex: by looking at each intersection separately, we are essentially treating each cell as an independent result – in our case, it is as if we had performed twelve tests instead of just one. Now, recall that levels of significance are based on probabilities of error – for example, $p = 0.05$ means, roughly, that there is a five percent likelihood that a result is due to chance. Obviously, the more tests we perform, the more likely it becomes that one of the results will, indeed, be due to chance – for example, if we had performed twenty tests, we would expect one of them to yield a significant result at the 5-percent level, because $20 \times 0.05 = 1.00$.

To avoid this situation, we have to correct the levels of significance when performing multiple tests on the same set of data. The simplest way of doing so is the so-called Bonferroni correction, which consists in dividing the conventionally agreed-upon significance levels by the number of tests we are performing. In the case of Table 6.14, this means dividing them by twelve, giving us significance levels of $^{0.05}/_{12} = 0.004167$ (significant), $^{0.01}/_{12} = 0.000833$ (very significant), and $^{0.001}/_{12} = 0.000083$ (highly significant).[6] Our table does not give the critical χ^2-values for these levels, but the value for the the intersection PRONOUN ∩ SPOKEN, 176.08, is larger than the value required for the next smaller level (0.00001, with a critical value of 24.28), so we can be certain that the contribution of this intersection is, indeed, highly significant. Again, it would be useful to summarize the degrees of significance in such a way that they can be assessed at a glance.

There is no standard way of representing the way in, and degree to, which each cell of a complex table contributes to the overall result, but the representation in Table 6.15 seems reasonable: in each cell, the first line contains either a plus (for "more frequent than expected") or a minus (for "less frequent than expected"); the second line contains the χ^2-component, and the third line contains the (corrected) level of significance (using the standard convention of representing them by asterisks – one for each level of significance).

This table presents the complex results at a single glance; they can now be interpreted. Some patterns now become obvious: For example, spoken language and fiction are most similar to each other – they both favor pronominal modifiers, while proper names and common nouns are disfavored, and the χ^2-components for these preferences are very similar. Also, if we posit a kind of gradient of referent familiarity from pronouns over proper names to nouns, we can place spoken language and fiction at one end, academic language at the other, and newspaper language somewhere in the middle.

6.6.2 Designs with more than two variables

Note that from a certain perspective the design in Table 6.15 is flawed: the variable VARIETY actually conflates at least two variables that are theoretically independent: MEDIUM (with the variables SPOKEN and WRITTEN, and DISCOURSE DO-

[6]It should be noted that the Bonferroni correction is extremely conservative, but it has the advantage of being very simple to apply (see Shaffer 1995 for an overview corrections for multiple testing, including many that are less conservative than the Bonferroni correction).

Table 6.15: Types of modifiers in the *s*-possessive in different text categories: Contributions of the individual intersections

		Possessive Modifier		
		PRONOUN	PROPER NAME	NOUN
Variety	SPOKEN	+ 176.08 *****	− 258.40 *****	− 315.25 *****
	FICTION	+ 189.39 *****	− 203.94 *****	− 438.21 *****
	NEWS	− 506.04 *****	+ 912.14 *****	+ 728.47 *****
	ACADEMIC	− 20.34 ****	− 4.68 n.s.	+ 197.96 *****

MAIN (in our design with the variables NEWS (RECOUNTING OF ACTUAL EVENTS), FICTION (RECOUNTING OF IMAGINARY EVENTS) and ACADEMIC (RECOUNTING OF SCIENTIFIC IDEAS, PROCEDURES AND RESULTS). These two variables are independent in that there is both written and spoken language to be found in each of these discourse domains. They are conflated in our variable Variety in that one of the four values is spoken and the other three are written language, and in that the text category SPOKEN is not differentiated by topic. There may be reasons to ignore this conflation *a priori*, as we have done – for example, our model may explicitly assume that differentiation by topic happens only in the written domain. But even then, it would be useful to treat Medium and Discourse Domain as independent variables, just in case our model is wrong in assuming this.

In contrast to all examples of research designs we have discussed so far, which involved just two variables and were thus *bivariate*, this design would be *multivariate*: there is more than one independent variable whose influcence on the dependent variable we wish to assess. Such multivariate research designs are often useful (or even necessary) even in cases where the variables in our design are not conflations of more basic variables.

In the study of language use, we will often – perhaps even typically – be confronted with a fragment of reality that is too complex to model in terms of just two variables.

In some cases, this may be obvious from the outset: we may suspect from previous research that a particular linguistic phenomenon depends on a range of factors, as in the case of the choice between the *s*- and the *of*-possessive, which we saw in the preceding chapters had long been hypothesized to be influenced by the animacy, the length and/or the givenness of the modifier.

In other cases, the multivariate nature of the phenomenon under investigation may emerge in the course of pursuing an initially bivariate design. For example, we may find that the independent variable under investigation has a statistically significant influence on our dependent variable, but that the effect size is very small, suggesting that the distribution of the phenomenon in our sample is conditioned by more than one influencing factor.

Even if we are pursuing a well-motivated bivariate research design and find a significant influence with a strong effect size, it may be useful to take additional potential influencing factors into account: since corpus data are typically unbalanced, there may be hidden correlations between the variable under investigation and other variables, that distort the distribution of the phenomenon in a way that suggests a significant influence where no such influence actually exists.

The next subsection will use the latter case to demonstrate the potential shortcomings of bivariate designs and the subsection following it will present a solution. Note that this solution is considerably more complex than the statistical procedures we have looked at so far and while it will be presented in sufficient detail to enable the reader in principle to apply it themselves, some additional reading will be highly advisable.

6.6.2.1 A danger of bivariate designs

In recent years, attention has turned to sociolinguistic factors potentially influencing the choice between the s-possessive and the of-construction. It has long been known that the level of formality has an influence (Jucker 1993, also Grafmiller 2014), but recently, more traditional sociolinguistic variables like Sex and Age have been investigated. The results suggest that the latter has an influence, while the former does not – for example, Jankowski & Tagliamonte (2014) find no influence of sex, but find that age has an influence under some conditions, with young speakers using the *s*-genitive more frequently than old speakers for organizations and places; Shih et al. (2015) find a similar, more general influence of age.

Let us take a look at the influence of Sex and Age on the choice between the two possessives in the spoken part of the BNC. Since it is known that women tend to use pronouns more than men do (see Case Study 10.2.3.1 in Chapter 10), let us exclude possessive pronouns and operationalize the s-possessive as "all tokens tagged POS in the BNC", which will capture the possessive clitic *'s* and zero possessives (on common nouns ending in alveolar fricatives). Since the spoken part of the BNC is too large to identify *of*-possessives manually, let us operationalize them somewhat crudely as "all uses of the preposition *of*"; this encompasses not just *of*-possessives, but also the quantifying and partitive *of*-constructions that we manually excluded in the preceding chapters, the complementation of adjectives like *aware* and *afraid*, verbs like *consist* and *dispose*, etc. On the one hand, this makes our case study less precise, on the other hand, any preference for *of*-constructions may just be a reflex of a general preference for the preposition *of*, in which case we would be excluding relevant data by focusing on *of*-constructions. Anyway, our main point will be one concerning statistical methodology, so it does not matter too much either way.

So, let us query all tokens tagged as possessives (POS) or the preposition of (PRF) in the spoken part of the BNC, discarding all hits for which the information about speaker sex or speaker age is missing. Let us further exclude the age range 0–14, as it may include children who have not fully acquired the grammar of the language, and the age range 60+ as too unspecific. To keep the design simple, let us recode all age classes between 15 and 44 years of age as young and the age range 45–59 als old (I fall into the latter, just in case someone thinks this category label discriminates people in their prime). Let us further accept the categorization of speakers into *male* and *female* that the makers of the BNC provide.

Table 6.16 shows the intersections of Construction and Sex in the results of this query.

Unlike the studies mentioned above, we find a clear influence of Sex on Construction, with female speakers preferring the s-possessive and male speakers preferring the *of*-construction(s). The difference is highly significant, although the effect size is rather weak ($\chi^2 = 773.55, \mathrm{df} = 1, p < 0.001, \phi = 0.1061$).

Next, let us look at the intersections of Construction and Sex in the results of our query, which are shown in Table 6.17.

Like previous studies, we find a significant effect of age, with younger speakers preferring the s-possessive and older speakers preferring the *of*-construction(s). Again, the difference is highly significant, but the effect is extremely weak ($\chi^2 = 58.73, \mathrm{df} = 1, p < 0.001, \phi = 0.02922$).

We might now be satisfied that both speaker age and speaker sex have an influence on the choice between the two constructions. However, there is a potential problem that we need to take into account: the values of the variables Sex and

Table 6.16: The influence of SEX on the choice between the two possessives

		CONSTRUCTION		
		POS	OF	Total
SEX	FEMALE	3483	20 419	23 902
		(2432.89)	(21 469.11)	
	MALE	3515	41 335	44 850
		(4565.11)	(40 284.89)	
	Total	6998	61 754	68 752

Table 6.17: The influence of AGE on the choice between the two possessives

		CONSTRUCTION		
		POS	OF	Total
AGE	OLD	2450	24 535	26 985
		(2746.70)	(24 238.30)	
	YOUNG	4548	37 219	41 767
		(4251.30)	(37 515.70)	
	Total	6998	61 754	68 752

AGE and their intersections are not necessarily distributed evenly in the subpart of the BNC used here; although the makers of the corpus were careful to include a broad range of speakers of all ages, sexes (and class memberships, ignored in our study), they did not attempt to balance all these demographic variables, let alone their intersections. So let us look at the intersection of SEX and AGE in the results of our query. These are shown in Table 6.18.

There are significantly fewer hits produced by old women and significantly more produced by young women in our sample, and, conversely, significantly fewer hits produced by young men and significantly more produced by old men. This overrepresentation of young women and old men is not limited to our sample, but characterizes the spoken part of the BNC in general, which should intrigue feminists and psychoanalysts; for us, it suffices to know that the asymmetries in our sample are highly significant, with an effect size larger than that of that in the preceding two tables ($\chi^2 = 2142.72, \mathrm{df} = 1, p < 0.001, \phi = 0.1765$).

Table 6.18: Sex and Age in the BNC

		Age		
		old	young	Total
Sex	female	6559 (9381.48)	17 343 (14 520.52)	23 902
	male	20 426 (17 603.52)	24 424 (27 246.48)	44 850
	Total	26 985	41 767	68 752

This correlation in the corpus of old and male on the one hand and young and female on the other may well be enough to distort the results such that a linguistic behavior typical for female speakers may be wrongly attributed to young speakers (or vice versa), and, correspondingly, a linguistic behavior typical for male speakers may be wrongly interpreted to old speakers (or vice versa). More generally, the danger of bivariate designs is that a variable we have chosen for investigation is correlated with one or more variables ignored in our research design, whose influence thus remains hidden. A very general precaution against this possibility is to make sure that the corpus (or our sample) is balanced with respect to all potentially confounding variables. In reality, this is difficult to achieve and may in fact be undesirable, since we might, for example, want our corpus (or sample) to reflect the real-world correlation of speaker variables).

Therefore, we need a way of including multiple independent variables in our research designs even if we are just interested in a single independent variable, but all the more so if we are interested in the influence of several independent variables. It may be the case, for example, that both Sex and Age influence the choice between *'s* and *of*, either in that the two effects add up, or in that they interact in more complex ways.

6.6.2.2 Configural frequency analysis

There is a range of multivariate statistical methods that are routinely used in corpus linguistics, such as the ANOVA mentioned at the end of the previous chapter for situations where the dependent variable is measured in terms of cardinal numbers, and various versions of logistic regression for situations where the dependent variable is ordinal or nominal.

In this book, I will introduce multivariate designs using *Configural Frequency Analysis* (CFA), a straightforward extension of the χ^2 test to designs with more than two nominal variables. This method has been used in psychology and psychiatry since the 1970s, and while it has never become very wide-spread, it has, in my opinion, a number of didactic advantages over other methods, when it comes to understanding multivariate research designs. Most importantly, it is conceptually very simple (if you understand the χ^2 test, you should be able to understand CFA), and the results are very transparent (they are presented as observed and expected frequencies of intersections of variables.

This does not mean that CFA is useful *only* as a didactic tool – it has been applied fruitfully to linguistic research issues, for example, in the study of language disorders (Lautsch et al. 1988), educational linguistics (Fujioka & Kennedy 1997), psycholinguistics (Hsu et al. 2000) and social psychology (Christmann et al. 2000). An early suggestion to apply it to corpus data is found in Schmilz (1983), but the first actual such applications that I am aware of are Gries (2002; 2004). Since Gries introduced the method to corpus linguistics, it has become a minor but nevertheless well-established corpus-linguistic research tool for a range of linguistic phenomena (see, e.g., Stefanowitsch & Gries 2005; 2008; Liu 2010; Goschler et al. 2013; Hoffmann 2014; Hilpert 2015; and others).

As hinted at above, in its simplest variant, configural frequency analysis is simply a χ^2 test on a contingency table with more than two dimensions. There is no logical limit to the number of dimensions, but if we insist on calculating this statistic manually (rather than, more realistically, letting a specialized software package do it for us), then a three-dimensional table is already quite complex to deal with. Thus, we will not go beyond three dimensions here or in the case studies in the second part of this book.

A three-dimensional contingency table would have the form of a cube, as shown in Figure 6.2. The smaller cube represents the cells on the far side of the big cube seen from the same perspective and the smallest cube represents the cell in the middle of the whole cube). As before, cells are labeled by subscripts: the first subscript stands for the values and totals of the dependent variable, the second for those of the first independent variable, and the third for those of the second independent variable.

While this kind of visualization is quite useful in grasping the notion of a three-dimensional contingency table, it would be awkward to use it as a basis for recording observed frequencies or calculating the expected frequencies. Thus, a possible two-dimensional representation is shown in Table 6.19. In this table, the first independent variable is shown in the rows, and the second independent variable is shown in the three blocks of three columns (these may be thought of as three "slices" of the cube in Figure 6.2), and the dependent variable is shown in the columns themselves.

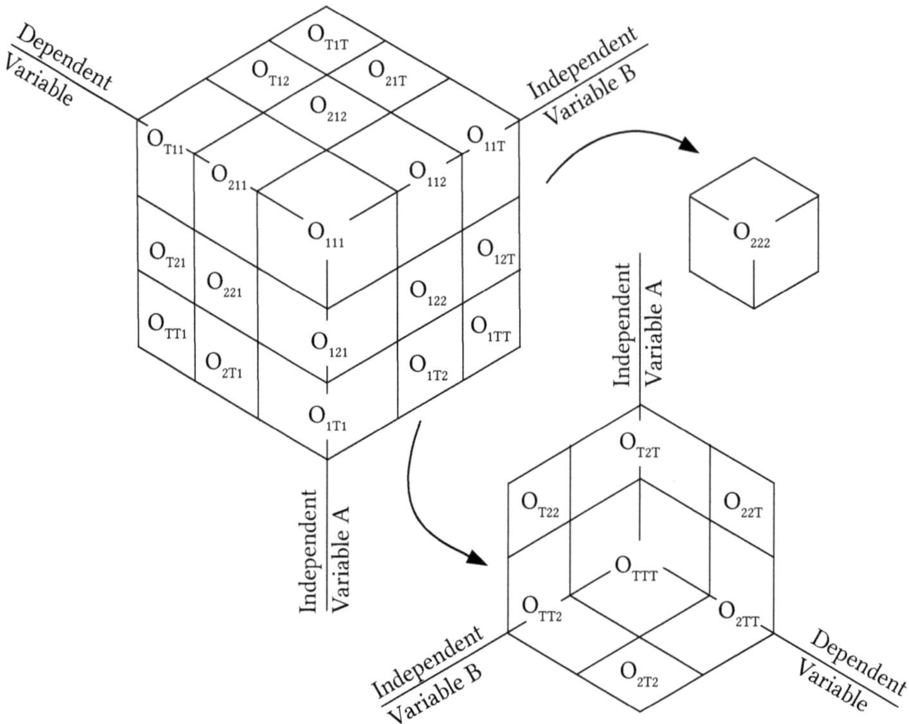

Figure 6.2: A three-dimensional contingency table

Table 6.19: A two-dimensional representation of a three-dimensional contingency table

	IV$_B$ 1			IV$_B$ 2			IV$_B$ Total		
	DV 1	DV 2	DV Total	DV 1	DV 2	DV Total	DV 1	DV 2	DV Total
IV$_A$ 1	O_{111}	O_{112}	O_{11T}	O_{121}	O_{122}	O_{12T}	O_{1T1}	O_{1T2}	O_{1TT}
IV$_A$ 2	O_{211}	O_{212}	O_{21T}	O_{221}	O_{222}	O_{22T}	O_{2T1}	O_{2T2}	O_{2TT}
IV$_A$ Total	O_{T11}	O_{T12}	O_{T1T}	O_{T21}	O_{T22}	O_{T2T}	O_{TT1}	O_{TT2}	O_{TTT}

Given this representation, the expected frequencies for each intersection of the three variables can now be calculated in a way that is similar (but not identical) to that used for two-dimensional tables. Table 6.20 shows the formulas for each cell as well as those marginal sums needed for the calculation.

Table 6.20: Calculating expected frequencies in a three-dimensional contingency table

	IV$_B$ 1			IV$_B$ 2			IV$_B$ Total		
	DV 1	DV 2	DV Total	DV 1	DV 2	DV Total	DV 1	DV 2	DV Total
IV$_A$ 1	$\frac{O_{T1T} \times O_{1TT} \times O_{TT1}}{O_{TTT}^2}$	$\frac{O_{T1T} \times O_{1TT} \times O_{TT2}}{O_{TTT}^2}$		$\frac{O_{T1T} \times O_{2TT} \times O_{TT1}}{O_{TTT}^2}$	$\frac{O_{T1T} \times O_{2TT} \times O_{TT2}}{O_{TTT}^2}$				
IV$_A$ 2	$\frac{O_{T2T} \times O_{1TT} \times O_{TT1}}{O_{TTT}^2}$	$\frac{O_{T2T} \times O_{1TT} \times O_{TT2}}{O_{TTT}^2}$		$\frac{O_{T2T} \times O_{2TT} \times O_{TT1}}{O_{TTT}^2}$	$\frac{O_{T2T} \times O_{2TT} \times O_{TT2}}{O_{TTT}^2}$				
IV$_A$ Total									

Once we have calculated the expected frequencies, we proceed exactly as before: we derive each cell's χ^2 component by the standard formula $(O-E)^2/E$ and then add up these components to give us an overall χ^2 value for the table, which can then be checked for significance. The degrees of freedom of a three-dimensional contingency table are calculated by the following formula (where k is the number of values of each variable and the subscripts refer to the variables themselves):

(21) $\mathrm{df} = (k_1 \times k_2 \times k_3) - (k_1 + k_2 + k_3) + 2$

In our case, each variable has two values, thus we get (2×2×2)−(2+2+2)+2 = 4. More interestingly, we can also look at the individual cells to determine whether their contribution to the overall value is significant). In this case, as before, each cell has one degree of freedom and the significance levels have to be adjusted for multiple testing. In CFA, an intersection of variables whose observed frequency is significantly higher than expected is referred to as a *type* and one whose observed frequency is significantly lower is referred to as an *antitype* (but if we do not like this terminology, we do not have to use it and can keep talking about "more or less frequent than expected", as we do with bivariate χ^2 tests).

Let us apply this method to the question described in the previous sub-section. Table 6.21 shows the observed and expected frequencies of the two possessive constructions by Speaker Age and Speaker Sex, as well as the corresponding χ^2 components.[7] For expository purposes, the table also shows for each cell the

[7]Note one important fact about multi-dimensional contingency tables that may be confusing: if we add up the expected frequencies of a given column, their sum will not usually correspond to the sum of the observed frequencies in that column (in contrast to two-dimensional tables, where this is necessarily the case). Instead, the sum of the observed and expected frequencies in each *slice* is identical.

significance level of these components (which is "highly significant" for almost all of them), and the direction of deviation from the expected frequencies (i.e., whether the intersection is a "type", marked by a plus sign, or an "antitype", marked by a minus sign).

Table 6.21: Sex, Age and Possessives Multivariate (BNC Spoken)

	FEMALE			MALE			
CONSTR.	YOUNG	OLD	Total	YOUNG	OLD	Total	Total
POS	*Obs.:* 2548 *Exp.:* 1477.99 χ^2: 774.65 *p:* *** *Type:* +	*Obs.:* 935 *Exp.:* 954.90 χ^2: 0.41 *p:* n.s. *Type:* –	3483	*Obs.:* 2000 *Exp.:* 2773.31 χ^2: 215.63 *p:* *** *Type:* –	*Obs.:* 1515 *Exp.:* 1791.79 χ^2: 42.76 *p:* *** *Type:* –	3515	6998
OF	*Obs.:* 14 795 *Exp.:* 13 042.53 χ^2: 235.47 *p:* *** *Type:* +	*Obs.:* 5624 *Exp.:* 8426.57 χ^2: 932.10 *p:* *** *Type:* –	20419	*Obs.:* 22 424 *Exp.:* 24 473.17 χ^2: 171.58 *p:* *** *Type:* –	*Obs.:* 18 911 *Exp.:* 15 811.73 χ^2: 607.49 *p:* *** *Type:* +	41335	61754
Total	17 343	6559	23 902	24 424	20 426	44 850	68752

Adding up the χ^2 components yields an overall χ^2 value of 2980.10, which, at four degrees of freedom, is highly significant. This tells us something we already expected from the individual pairwise comparisons of the three variables in the preceding section: there is a significant relationship among them. Of course, what we are interested in is what this relationship is and to answer this question, we need to look at the contributions to χ^2.

The result is very interesting. A careful inspection of the individual cells shows that age does *not*, in fact, have a significant influence. Young women use the *s*-possessive more frequently than expected and old women use it less (in the latter case, non-significantly), but young women also use the *of*-constructions significantly more frequently than expected and old women use it less. Crucially, young men use the *s*-possessive *less* frequently than expected, and old men use it more, but young men also use the *of*-construction less frequently than expected and old men use it more.

In other words, young women and old men use more of both constructions than young men and old women. A closer look at the contributions to χ^2 tells us that SEX, however, does still have an influence on the choice between the two constructions even when AGE is taken into account: for young women, the overuse of the *s*-possessive is more pronounced than that of the *of*-construction, while for old women, underuse of the *s*-possessive is less pronounced than underuse of the *of*-construction. In other words, taking into account that old women are underrepresented in the corpus compared to young women, there is a clear preference of all women for the *s*-possessive. Conversely, young men's underuse of the *s*-possessive is less pronounced than that of the *of*-construction, while old men's overuse of the *s*-possessive is less pronounced than their overuse of the *of*-construction. In other words, taking into account than young men are underrepresented in the corpus compared to old men, there is a clear preference of all men for the *of*-construction.

Armed with this new insight from our multivariate analysis, let us return to bivariate analyses, looking at each of the two variables while keeping the other constant. Table 6.22 shows the results of the four bivariate analyses this yields. Since we are performing four tests on the same set of data within the same research question, we have to correct for multiple testing by dividing the usual critical p-values by four, giving us $p < 0.0125$ for "significant", $p < 0.0025$ for "very significant" and $p < 0.00025$ for "highly significant". The exact p-values for each table are shown below, as is the effect size.

Table 6.22: Possessives, age and sex (BNC Spoken)

		Construction		
		POS	OF	Total
Sex	FEMALE	935	5624	6559
		(595.50)	(5963.50)	
	MALE	1515	18 911	20 426
		(1854.50)	(18 571.50)	
	Total	2450	24 535	26 985

(a) POSSESSIVE by SEX
OLD speakers only
($\chi^2 = 281.24, \text{df} = 1, p < 2.2 \times 10^{-16}, \phi = 0.1021$)

		Construction		
		POS	OF	Total
Sex	FEMALE	2548	14 795	17 343
		(1888.48)	(15 454.52)	
	MALE	2000	22 424	24 424
		(2659.52)	(21 764.48)	
	Total	4548	37 219	41 767

(b) POSSESSIVE by SEX
YOUNG speakers only
($\chi^2 x = 442.01, \text{df} = 1, p < 2.2 \times 10^{-16}, \phi = 0.1029$)

		Construction		
		POS	OF	Total
Age	OLD	935	5624	6559
		(955.78)	(5603.22)	
	YOUNG	2548	14 795	17 343
		(2527.22)	(14 815.78)	
	Total	3483	20 419	23 902

(c) POSSESSIVE by AGE
FEMALE speakers only
($\chi^2 = 0.72869, \text{df} = 1, p = 0.3933, \phi = 0.0055$)

		Construction		
		POS	OF	Total
Age	OLD	1515	18 911	20 426
		(1600.83)	(18 825.17)	
	YOUNG	2000	22 424	24 424
		(1914.17)	(22 509.83)	
	Total	3515	41 335	44 850

(d) POSSESSIVE by AGE
MALE speakers only
($\chi^2 = 9.1698, \text{df} = 1, p = 0.00246, \phi = 0.0143$)

Tables 6.22a and 6.22b show that the effect of SEX on the choice between the two constructions is highly significant both in the group of OLD speakers and in the group of YOUNG speakers, with effect sizes similar to those we found for the bivariate analysis for SPEAKER SEX in Table 6.16 in the preceding section. This effect seems to be genuine, or at least, it is not influenced by the hidden variable AGE (it may be influenced by CLASS or some other variable we have not included in our design).

In contrast, Tables 6.22a and 6.22b show that the effect of AGE that we saw in Table 6.17 in the preceding section disappears completely for women, with a *p*-value not even significant at uncorrected levels of significance. For men, it is still discernible, but only barely, with a *p*-value that indicates a very significant relationship at corrected levels of significance, but with an effect size that is close to zero. In other words, it may not be a genuine effect at all, but simply a consequence of the fact that the intersections of AGE and SEX are unevenly distributed in the corpus.

This section is intended to impress on the reader one thing: that looking at one potential variable influencing some phenomenon that we are interested in may not be enough. Multivariate research designs are becoming the norm rather than the exception, and rightly so. Excluding the danger of hidden variables is just one advantage of such designs – in many cases, it is sensible to include several independent variables simply because all of them potentially have an interesting influence on the phenomenon under investigation, or because there is just one particular combination of values of our variables that has an effect. In the second part of this volume, there are several case studies that use CFA and that illustrate these possibilities. One word of warning, however: the ability to include a large number of variables in our research designs should not lead us to do so for the sake of it. We should be able to justify, for each dependent variable we include, why we are including it and in what way we expect it to influence our independent variable.

7 Collocation

The (orthographic) word plays a central role in corpus linguistics. As suggested in Chapter 4, this is in no small part due to the fact that all corpora, whatever additional annotations may have been added, consist of orthographically represented language. This makes it easy to retrieve word forms. Every concordancing program offers the possibility to search for a string of characters – in fact, some are limited to this kind of query.

However, the focus on words is also due to the fact that the results of corpus linguistic research quickly showed that words (individually and in groups) are more interesting and show a more complex behavior than traditional, grammar-focused theories of language assumed. An area in which this is very obvious, and which has therefore become one of the most heavily researched areas in corpus linguistics, is the way in which words combine to form so-called *collocations*.

This chapter is dedicated entirely to the discussion of collocation. At first, this will seem like a somewhat abrupt shift from the topics and phenomena we have discussed so far – it may not even be immediately obvious how they fit into the definition of corpus linguistics as "the investigation of linguistic research questions that have been framed in terms of the conditional distribution of linguistic phenomena in a linguistic corpus", which was presented at the end of Chapter 2. However, a closer look will show that studying the co-occurrence of words and/or word forms is simply a special case of precisely this kind of research program.

7.1 Collocates

Trivially, texts are not random sequences of words. There are several factors influencing the likelihood of two (or more) words occurring next to each other.

First, the co-occurrence of words in a sequence is restricted by grammatical considerations. For example, a definite article cannot be followed by another definite article or a verb, but only by a noun, by an adjective modifying a noun, by an adverb modifying such an adjective or by a post-determiner. Likewise, a transitive verb requires a direct object in the form of a noun phrase, so – barring cases where the direct object is pre- or post-posed – it will be followed by a word that can occur at the beginning of a noun phrase (such as a pronoun, a determiner, an adjective or a noun).

Second, the co-occurrence of words is restricted by semantic considerations. For example, the transitive verb *drink* requires a direct object referring to a liquid, so it is probable that it will be followed by words like *water, beer, coffee, poison,* etc., and improbable that it will be followed by words like *bread, guitar, stone, democracy,* etc. Such restrictions are treated as a grammatical property of words (called *selection restrictions*) in some theories, but they may also be an expression of our world knowledge concerning the activity of drinking.

Finally, and related to the issue of world knowledge, the co-occurrence of words is restricted by topical considerations. Words will occur in sequences that correspond to the contents we are attempting to express, so it is probable that co-occurring content words will come from the same discourse domain.

However, it has long been noted that words are not distributed randomly even within the confines of grammar, lexical semantics, world knowledge, and communicative intent. Instead, a given word will have affinities to some words, and disaffinities to others, which we could not predict given a set of grammatical rules, a dictionary and a thought that needs to be expressed. One of the first principled discussions of this phenomenon is found in Firth (1957). Using the example of the word *ass* (in the sense of 'donkey'), he discusses the way in which what he calls *habitual collocations* contribute to the meaning of words:

> One of the meanings of *ass* is its habitual collocation with an immediately preceding *you silly*, and with other phrases of address or of personal reference. ... There are only limited possibilities of collocation with preceding adjectives, among which the commonest are *silly, obstinate, stupid, awful,* occasionally *egregious. Young* is much more frequently found than *old.* (Firth 1957: 194f).

Note that Firth, although writing well before the advent of corpus linguistics, refers explicitly to *frequency* as a characteristic of collocations. The possibility of using frequency as part of the definition of collocates, and thus as a way of identifying them, was quickly taken up. Halliday (1961) provides what is probably the first strictly quantitative definition (cf. also Church & Hanks (1990) for a more recent comprehensive quantitative discussion):

> Collocation is the syntagmatic association of lexical items, quantifiable, textually, as the probability that there will occur, at n removes (a distance of n lexical items) from an item x, the items a, b, c... Any given item thus enters into a range of collocation, the items with which it is collocated being ranged from more to less probable... (Halliday 1961: 276)

7.1.1 Collocation as a quantitative phenomenon

Essentially, then, collocation is just a special case of the quantitative corpus linguistic research design adopted in this book: to ask whether two words form a collocation (or: are collocates of each other) is to ask whether one of these words occurs in a given position more frequently than expected by chance under the condition that the other word occurs in a structurally or sequentially related position. In other words, we can decide whether two words *a* and *b* can be regarded as collocates on the basis of a contingency table like that in Table 7.1. The First Position in the sequence is treated as the dependent variable, with two values: the word we are interested in (here: word a), and all other words. The Second Position is treated as the independent variable, again, with two values: the word we are interested in (here: word b), and all other words (of course, it does not matter which word we treat as the dependent and which as the independent variable, unless our research design suggests a particular reason).[1]

Table 7.1: Collocation

		Second Position		
		word b	other words	Total
First Position	word a	a & b	a & other	a
	other words	other & b	other & other	other
	Total	b	other	corpus size

On the basis of such a table, we can determine the collocation status of a given word pair. For example, we can ask whether Firth was right with respect to the claim that *silly ass* is a collocation. The necessary data are shown in Table 7.2: As discussed above, the dependent variable is the First Position in the sequence, with the values silly and ¬silly (i.e., all words that are not *ass*); the independent variable is the Second Position in the sequence, with the values ass and ¬ass.

[1]Note that we are using the corpus size as the table total – strictly speaking, we should be using the total number of two-word sequences (bigrams) in the corpus, which will be lower: The last word in each file of our corpus will not have a word following it, so we would have to subtract the last word of each file – i.e., the number of files in our corpus – from the total. This is unlikely to make much of a difference in most cases, but the shorter the texts in our corpus are, the larger the difference will be. For example, in a corpus of tweets, which, at the time of writing, are limited to 280 characters, it might be better to correct the total number of bigrams in the way described.

Table 7.2: Co-occurrence of *silly* and *ass* in the BNC

		Second Position		
		ASS	¬ASS	Total
First Position	SILLY	7 (0.01)	2632 (2638.99)	2639
	¬SILLY	295 (301.99)	98 360 849 (98 360 842.01)	98 361 144
	Total	302	98 363 481	98 363 783

The combination *silly ass* is very rare in English, occurring just seven times in the 98 363 783 word BNC, but the expected frequencies in Table 7.2 show that this is vastly more frequent than should be the case if the words co-occurred randomly – in the latter case, the combination should have occurred just 0.01 times (i.e., not at all). The difference between the observed and the expected frequencies is highly significant ($\chi^2 = 6033.8$, $df = 1$, $p < 0.001$). Note that we are using the χ^2 test here because we are already familiar with it. However, this is not the most useful test for the purpose of identifying collocations, so we will discuss better options below.

Generally speaking, the goal of a quantitative collocation analysis is to identify, for a given word, those other words that are characteristic for its context of usage. Tables 7.1 and 7.2 present the most straightforward way of doing so: we simply compare the frequency with which two words co-occur to the frequencies with which they occur in the corpus in general. In other words, the two conditions across which we are investigating the distribution of a word are "next to a given other word" and "everywhere else". This means that the corpus itself functions as a kind of neutral control condition, albeit a somewhat indiscriminate one: comparing the frequency of a word next to some other word to its frequency in the entire rest of the corpus is a bit like comparing an experimental group of subjects that have been given a particular treatment to a control group consisting of all other people who happen to live in the same city.

Often, we will be interested in the distribution of a word across two specific conditions – in the case of collocation, the distribution across the immediate contexts of two semantically related words. It may be more insightful to compare adjectives occurring next to *ass* with those occurring next to the rough synonym *donkey* or the superordinate term *animal.* Obviously, the fact that *silly* occurs more frequently with *ass* than with *donkey* or *animal* is more interesting than the fact that *silly* occurs more frequently with *ass* than with *stone* or *democracy*. Likewise, the fact that *silly* occurs with *ass* more frequently than *childish* is more interesting than the fact that *silly* occurs with *ass* more frequently than *precious* or *parliamentary*.

In such cases, we can modify Table 7.1 as shown in Table 7.3 to identify the collocates that *differ* significantly between two words. There is no established term for such collocates, so we we will call them *differential collocates* here[2] (the method is based on Church et al. 1991).

Table 7.3: Identifying differential collocates

		Second Position		
		word b	word c	Total
First Position	word a	a & b	a & c	a
	other	other & b	other & c	other
	Total	b	c	sample size

Since the collocation *silly ass* and the word *ass* in general are so infrequent in the BNC, let us use a different noun to demonstrate the usefulness of this method, the word *game*. We can speak of *silly game(s)* or *childish game(s)*, but we may feel that the latter is more typical than the former. The relevant lemma frequencies to put this feeling to the test are shown in Table 7.4.

Table 7.4: *Childish game* vs. *silly game* (lemmas) in the BNC

		First Position		
		childish	silly	Total
Second Position	game	12 (6.18)	31 (36.82)	43
	¬game	431 (436.82)	2608 (2602.18)	3039
	Total	443	2639	3082

[2]Gries (2003b) and Gries & Stefanowitsch (2004) use the term *distinctive collocate*, which has been taken up by some authors; however, many other authors use the term *distinctive collocate* much more broadly to refer to *characteristic* collocates of a word.

The sequences *childish game(s)* and *silly game(s)* both occur in the BNC. Both combinations taken individually are significantly more frequent than expected (you may check this yourself using the frequencies from Table 7.4, the total lemma frequency of *game* in the BNC (20 627), and the total number of words in the BNC given in Table 7.2 above). The lemma sequence *silly game* is more frequent, which might lead us to assume that it is the stronger collocation. However, the direct comparison shows that this is due to the fact that *silly* is more frequent in general than *childish*, making the combination *silly game* more probable than the combination *childish game* even if the three words were distributed randomly. The difference between the observed and the expected frequencies suggests that *childish* is more strongly associated with *game(s)* than *silly*. The difference is significant ($\chi^2 = 6.49, \text{df} = 1, p < 0.05$).

Researchers differ with respect to what types of co-occurrence they focus on when identifying collocations. Some treat co-occurrence as a purely sequential phenomenon defining collocates as words that co-occur more frequently than expected within a given span. Some researchers require a span of 1 (i.e., the words must occur directly next to each other), but many allow larger spans (five words being a relatively typical span size).

Other researchers treat co-occurrence as a structural phenomenon, i.e., they define collocates as words that co-occur more frequently than expected in two related positions in a particular grammatical structure, for example, the adjective and noun positions in noun phrases of the form [Det Adj N] or the verb and noun position in transitive verb phrases of the form [V [$_{NP}$ (Det) (Adj) N]].[3] However, instead of limiting the definition to one of these possibilities, it seems more plausible to define the term appropriately in the context of a specific research question. In the examples above, we used a purely sequential definition that simply required words to occur next to each other, paying no attention to their word-class or structural relationship; given that we were looking at adjective-noun combinations, it would certainly have been reasonable to restrict our search parameters to adjectives modifying the noun *ass*, regardless of whether other adjectives intervened, for example in expressions like *silly old ass*, which our query would have missed if they occurred in the BNC (they do not).

It should have become clear that the designs in Tables 7.1 and 7.3 are essentially variants of the general research design introduced in previous chapters and used as the foundation of defining corpus linguistics: it has two variables,

[3]Note that such word-class specific collocations are sometimes referred to as *colligations*, although the term colligation usually refers to the co-occurrence of a word in the context of particular word classes, which is not the same.

Position 1 and Position 2, both of which have two values, namely word x vs. other words (or, in the case of differential collocates, word x vs. word y). The aim is to determine whether the value word a is more frequent for Position 1 under the condition that word b occurs in Position 2 than under the condition that other words (or a particular other word) occur in Position 2.

7.1.2 Methodological issues in collocation research

We may occasionally be interested in an individual pair of collocates, such as *silly ass*, or in a small set of such pairs, such as all adjective-noun pairs with *ass* as the noun. However, it is much more likely that we will be interested in large sets of collocate pairs, such as all adjective-noun pairs or even all word pairs in a given corpus. This has a number of methodological consequences concerning the practicability, the statistical evaluation and the epistemological status of collocation research.

a. Practicability. In practical terms, the analysis of large numbers of potential collocations requires creating a large number of contingency tables and subjecting them to the χ^2 test or some other appropriate statistical test. This becomes implausibly time-consuming very quickly and thus needs to be automated in some way.

There are concordancing programs that offer some built-in statistical tests, but they typically restrict our options quite severely, both in terms of the tests they allow us to perform and in terms of the data on which the tests are performed. Anyone who decides to become involved in collocation research (or some of the large-scale lexical research areas described in the next chapter), should get acquainted at least with the simple options of automatizing statistical testing offered by spreadsheet applications. Better yet, they should invest a few weeks (or, in the worst case, months) to learn a scripting language like Perl, Python or R (the latter being a combination of statistical software and programming environment that is ideal for almost any task that we are likely to come across as corpus linguists).

b. Statistical evaluation. In statistical terms, the analysis of large numbers of potential collocations requires us to keep in mind that we are now performing multiple significance tests on the same set of data. This means that we must adjust our significance levels. Think back to the example of coin-flipping: the probability of getting a series of one head and nine tails is 0.009765. If we flip a coin ten times and get this result, we could thus reject the null hypothesis with a probability of error of 0.010744, i.e., around 1 percent (because we would have to add the probability of getting ten tails, 0.000976). This is well below the level required to claim statistical significance. However, if we perform one hundred series of ten coin-flips and one of these series consists of one head and nine tails (or ten tails), we could not reject the null hypothesis with the same confidence, as a probability of 0.010744 means that we would expect one such series to occur by chance. This is not a problem as long as we do not accord this one result out of a hundred any special importance. However, if we were to identify a set of 100 collocations with *p*-values of 0.001 in a corpus, we *are* potentially treating all of them as important, even though it is very probable that at least one of them reached this level of significance by chance.

To avoid this, we have to correct our levels of significance when performing multiple tests on the same set of data. As discussed in Section 6.6.1 above, the simplest way to do this is the Bonferroni correction, which consists in dividing the conventionally agreed-upon significance levels by the number of tests we are performing. As noted in Section 6.6.1, this is an extremely conservative correction that might make it quite difficult for any given collocation to reach significance.

Of course, the question is how important the role of *p*-values is in a design where our main aim is to identify collocates and order them in terms of their collocation strength. I will turn to this point presently, but before I do so, let us discuss the third of the three consequences of large-scale testing for collocation, the methodological one.

c. Epistemological considerations. We have, up to this point, presented a very narrow view of the scientific process based (in a general way) on the Popperian research cycle where we formulate a research hypothesis and then test it (either directly, by looking for counterexamples, or, more commonly, by attempting to reject the corresponding null hypothesis). This is called the *deductive* method. However, as briefly discussed in Chapter 3, there is an alternative approach to scientific research that does not start with a hypothesis, but rather with general questions like "Do relationships exist between the constructs in my data?" and "If so, what are those relationships?". The research then consists in applying statistical procedures to large amounts of data and examining the results for interesting patterns. As electronic storage and computing power have become cheaper and more widely accessible, this approach – the *exploratory* or *inductive* approach – has become increasingly popular in all branches of science, particularly the social sciences. It would be surprising if corpus linguistics was an exception, and indeed, it is not. Especially the area of collocational research is typically exploratory.

In principle, there is nothing wrong with exploratory research – on the contrary, it would be unreasonable not to make use of the large amounts of language data and the vast computing power that has become available and accessible over the last thirty years. In fact, it is sometimes difficult to imagine a plausible hypothesis for collocational research projects. What hypothesis would we formulate before identifying all collocations in the LOB or some specialized corpus (e.g., a corpus of business correspondence, a corpus of flight-control communication or a corpus of learner language)?[4] Despite this, it is clear that the results of such a collocation analysis yield interesting data, both for practical purposes (building dictionaries or teaching materials for business English or aviation English, extracting terminology for the purpose of standardization, training natural-language processing systems) and for theoretical purposes (insights into the nature of situational language variation or even the nature of language in general).

But there is a danger, too: Most statistical procedures will produce *some* statistically significant result if we apply them to a large enough data set, and collocational methods certainly will. Unless we are interested exclusively in description, the crucial question is whether these results are meaningful. If we start with a hypothesis, we are restricted in our interpretation of the data by the need to relate our data to this hypothesis. If we do not start with a hypothesis, we can interpret our results without any restrictions, which, given the human propensity to see patterns everywhere, may lead to somewhat arbitrary post-hoc interpretations that could easily be changed, even reversed, if the results had been different and that therefore tell us very little about the phenomenon under investigation or language in general. Thus, it is probably a good idea to formulate at least some general expectations before doing a large-scale collocation analysis.

Even if we do start out with general expectations or even with a specific hypothesis, we will often discover additional facts about our phenomenon that go beyond what is relevant in the context of our original research question. For example, checking in the BNC Firth's claim that the most frequent collocates of *ass* are *silly*, *obstinate*, *stupid*, *awful* and *egregious* and that *young* is "much more frequent" than *old*, we find that *silly* is indeed the most frequent adjectival collocate, but that *obstinate*, *stupid* and *egregious* do not occur at all, that *awful* occurs only once, and that *young* and *old* both occur twice. Instead, frequent adjectival collocates (ignoring second-placed *wild*, which exclusively refers to actual donkeys), are *pompous* and *bad*. *Pompous* does not really fit with the semantics that Firth's adjectives suggest and could indicate that a semantic shift from 'stupidity' to 'self-importance' may have taken place between 1957 and 1991 (when the BNC was assembled).

[4] Of course we are making the implicit assumption that there *will* be collocates – in a sense, this is a hypothesis, since we could conceive of models of language that would not predict their existence (we might argue, for example, that at least some versions of generative grammar constitute such models). However, even if we accept this as a hypothesis, it is typically not the one we are interested in this kind of study.

This is, of course, a new hypothesis that can (and must) be investigated by comparing data from the 1950s and the 1990s. It has some initial plausibility in that the adjectives *blithering*, *hypocritical*, *monocled* and *opinionated* also co-occur with *ass* in the BNC but are not mentioned by Firth. However, it is crucial to treat this as a hypothesis rather than a result. The same goes for *bad ass* which suggests that the American sense of *ass* ('bottom') and/or the American adjective *badass* (which is often spelled as two separate words) may have begun to enter British English. In order to be tested, these ideas – and any ideas derived from an exploratory data analysis – have to be turned into testable hypotheses and the constructs involved have to be operationalized. Crucially, they must be tested on a new data set – if we were to circularly test them on the same data that they were derived from, we would obviously find them confirmed.

7.1.3 Effect sizes for collocations

As mentioned above, significance testing (while not without its uses) is not necessarily our primary concern when investigating collocations. Instead, researchers frequently need a way of assessing the *strength* of the association between two (or more) words, or, put differently, the effect size of their co-occurrence (recall from Chapter 6 that significance and effect size are not the same). A wide range of such association measures has been proposed and investigated. They are typically calculated on the basis of (some or all) the information contained in contingency tables like those in Tables 7.1 and 7.3 above.

Let us look at some of the most popular and/or most useful of these measures. I will represent the formulas with reference to the table in Table 7.5, i.e, O_{11} means the observed frequency of the top left cell, E_{11} its expected frequency, R_1 the first row total, C_2 the second column total, and so on. Note that second column would be labeled OTHER WORDS in the case of normal collocations, and WORD C in the case of differential collocations. The association measures can be applied to both kinds of design.

Table 7.5: A generic 2-by-2 table for collocation research

		SECOND POSITION		
		WORD B	OTHER/WORD C	Total
FIRST POSITION	WORD A	O_{11}	O_{12}	R_1
	OTHER WORDS	O_{21}	O_{22}	R_2
	Total	C_1	C_2	N

Now all we need is a good example to demonstrate the calculations. Let us use the adjective-noun sequence *good example* from the LOB corpus (but horse lovers need not fear, we will return to equine animals and their properties below).

Table 7.6: Co-occurrence of *good* and *example* in the LOB

		Second Position		
		example	¬example	Total
First Position	good	9 (0.2044)	836 (844.7956)	845
	¬good	236 (244.7956)	1 011 904 (1 011 895.2044)	1 012 140
	Total	245	1 012 740	1 012 985

Measures of collocation strength differ with respect to the data needed to calcuate them, their computational intensiveness and, crucially, the quality of their results. In particular, many measures, notably the ones easy to calculate, have a problem with rare collocations, especially if the individual words of which they consist are also rare. After we have introduced the measures, we will therefore compare their performance with a particular focus on the way in which they deal (or fail to deal) with such rare events.

7.1.3.1 Chi-square

The first association measure is an old acquaintance: the chi-square statistic, which we used extensively in Chapter 6 and in Section 7.1.1 above. I will not demonstrate it again, but the chi-square value for Table 7.6 would be 378.95 (at 1 degree of freedom this means that $p < 0.001$, but we are not concerned with p-values here).

Recall that the chi-square test statistic is not an effect size, but that it needs to be divided by the table total to turn it into one. As long as we are deriving all our collocation data from the same corpus, this will not make a difference, since the table total will always be the same. However, this is not always the case. Where table sizes differ, we might consider using the phi value instead. I am not aware of any research using phi as an association measure, and in fact the chi-square statistic itself is not used widely either. This is because it has a serious problem: recall that it cannot be applied if more than 20 percent of the cells of the contingency table contain expected frequencies smaller than 5 (in the case of collocates, this means not even one out of the four cells of the 2-by-2 table). One reason for this is that it dramatically overestimates the effect size and significance of such events, and of rare events in general. Since collocations are often relatively rare events, this makes the chi-square statistic a bad choice as an association measure.

7.1.3.2 Mutual Information

Mutual information is one of the oldest collocation measures, frequently used in computational linguistics and often implemented in collocation software. It is given in (1) in a version based on Church & Hanks (1990):[5]

(1) $$MI = \log_2\left(\frac{O_{11}}{E_{11}}\right)$$

Applying the formula to our table, we get the following:

$$\mathrm{MI} = \log_2\left(\frac{9}{0.2044}\right) = \log_2(44.03) = 5.46$$

In our case, we are looking at cases where WORD A and WORD B occur directly next to each other, i.e., the span size is 1. When looking at a larger span (which is often done in collocation research), the probability of encountering a particular collocate increases, because there are more slots that it could potentially occur in. The MI statistic can be adjusted for larger span sizes as follows (where S is the span size):

(2) $$\mathrm{MI} = \log_2\left(\frac{O_{11}}{E_{11} \times S}\right)$$

[5]A logarithm with a base b of a given number x is the power to which b must be raised to produce x, so, for example, $\log_{10}(2) = 0.30103$, because $10^{0.30103} = 2$. Most calculators offer at the very least a choice between the natural logarithm, where the base is the number e (approx. 2.7183) and the common logarithm, where the base is the number 10; many calculators and all major spreadsheet programs offer logarithms with any base. In the formula in (1), we need the logarithm with base 2; if this is not available, we can use the natural logarithm and divide the result by the natural logarithm of 2:

$$\mathrm{MI} = \frac{\log_e\left(\frac{O_{11}}{E_{11}}\right)}{\log_e(2)}$$

The mutual information measure suffers from the same problem as the χ^2 statistic: it overestimates the importance of rare events. Since it is still fairly widespread in collocational research, we may nevertheless need it in situations where we want to compare our own data to the results of published studies. However, note that there are versions of the MI measure that will give different results, so we need to make sure we are using the same version as the study we are comparing our results to. But unless there is a pressing reason, we should not use mutual information at all.

7.1.3.3 The log-likelihood ratio test

The *G* value of the log-likelihood ratio test is one of the most popular – perhaps *the* most popular – association measure in collocational research, found in many of the central studies in the field and often implemented in collocation software. The following is a frequently found form (Read & Cressie 1988: 134):

(3) $$G = 2\sum_{i=1}^{n} O_i \log_e\left(\frac{O_i}{E_i}\right)$$

In order to calculate the *G* measure, we calculate for each cell the natural logarithm of the observed frequency divided by the expected frequency and multiply it by the observed frequency. We then add up the results for all four cells and multiply the result by two. Note that if the observed frequency of a given cell is zero, the expression O_i/E_i will, of course, also be zero. Since the logarithm of zero is undefined, this would result in an error in the calculation. Thus, log(0) is simply defined as zero when applying the formula in (3).

Applying the formula in (3) to the data in Table 7.6, we get the following:

$$\begin{aligned} G = 2 \times & \left(9 \times \log_e\left(\frac{9}{0.2044}\right)\right) + \left(836 \times \log_e\left(\frac{836}{844.7956}\right)\right) \\ & + \left(236 \times \log_e\left(\frac{236}{244.7956}\right)\right) + \left(1011904 \times \log_e\left(\frac{1011904}{1011895.2044}\right)\right) \\ & = 2 \times ((34.0641) + (-8.7497) + (-8.6357) + (8.7956)) = 50.9489 \end{aligned}$$

The *G* value has long been known to be more reliable than the χ^2 test when dealing with small samples and small expected frequencies (Read & Cressie 1988: 134ff). This led Dunning (1993) to propose it as an association measure specifically to avoid the overestimation of rare events that plagues the χ^2 test, mutual information and other measures.

7.1.3.4 Minimum Sensitivity

Minimum sensitivity was proposed by Pedersen (1998) as potentially useful measure especially for the identification of associations between content words:

(4) $$\mathrm{MS} = \min\left(\frac{O_{11}}{R_1}, \frac{O_{11}}{C_1}\right)$$

We simply divide the observed frequency of a collocation by the frequency of the first word (R_1) and of the second word (C_1) and use the smaller of the two as the association measure. For the data in Table 7.6, this gives us the following:

$$\mathrm{MS} = \min\left(\frac{9}{836}, \frac{9}{236}\right) = \min(0.0108, 0.0381) = 0.0108$$

In addition to being extremely simple to calculate, it has the advantage of ranging from zero (words never occur together) to 1 (words always occur together); it was also argued by Wiechmann (2008) to correlate best with reading time data when applied to combinations of words and grammatical constructions (see Chapter 8). However, it also tends to overestimate the importance of rare collocations.

7.1.3.5 Fisher's exact test

Fisher's exact test was already mentioned in passing in Chapter 6 as an alternative to the χ^2 test that calculates the probability of error directly by adding up the probability of the observed distribution and all distributions that deviate from the null hypothesis further in the same direction. Pedersen (1996) suggests using this p-value as a measure of association because it does not make any assumptions about normality and is even better at dealing with rare events than G. Stefanowitsch & Gries (2003: 238–239) add that it has the advantage of taking into account both the magnitude of the deviation from the expected frequencies and the sample size.

There are some practical disadvantages to Fisher's exact test. First, it is computationally expensive – it cannot be calculated manually, except for very small tables, because it involves computing factorials, which become very large very quickly. For completeness' sake, here is (one version of) the formula:

(5) $$p_{\text{exact}} = \frac{R_1! \times R_2! \times C_1! \times C_2!}{O_{11}! \times O_{12}! \times O_{21}! \times O_{22}! \times N!}$$

Obviously, it is not feasible to apply this formula directly to the data in Table 7.6, because we cannot realistically calculate the factorials for 236 or 836, let alone 1 011 904. But if we could, we would find that the *p*-value for Table 7.6 is 0.000000000001188.

Spreadsheet applications do not usually offer Fisher's exact test, but all major statistics applications do. However, typically, the exact *p*-value is not reported beyond the limit of a certain number of decimal places. This means that there is often no way of ranking the most strongly associated collocates, because their *p*-values are smaller than this limit. For example, there are more than 100 collocates in the LOB corpus with a Fisher's exact *p*-value that is smaller than the smallest value that a standard-issue computer chip is capable of calculating, and more than 5000 collocates that have *p*-values that are smaller than what the standard implementation of Fisher's exact test in the statistical software package R will deliver. Since in research on collocations we often need to rank collocations in terms of their strength, this may become a problem.

7.1.3.6 A comparison of association measures

Let us see how the association measures compare using a data set of 20 potential collocations. Inspired by Firth's *silly ass*, they are all combinations of adjectives with equine animals. Table 7.7 shows the combinations and their frequencies in the BNC sorted by their raw frequency of occurrence (adjectives and nouns are shown in small caps here to stress that they are values of the variables Word A and Word B, but I will generally show them in italics in the remainder of the book in line with linguistic tradition).

All combinations are perfectly normal, grammatical adjective-noun pairs, meaningful not only in the specific context of their actual occurrence. However, I have selected them in such a way that they differ with respect to their status as potential collocations (in the sense of typical combinations of words). Some are compounds or compound like combinations (*rocking horse*, *Trojan horse*, and, in specialist discourse, *common zebra*). Some are the kind of semi-idiomatic combinations that Firth had in mind (*silly ass*, *pompous ass*). Some are very conventional combinations of nouns with an adjective denoting a property specific to that noun (*prancing horse*, *braying donkey*, *galloping horse* – the first of these being a conventional way of referring to the Ferrari brand mark logo). Some only give the appearance of semi-idiomatic combinations (*jumped-up jackass*, actually an unconventional variant of *jumped-up jack-in-office*; *dumb-fuck donkey*, actually an extremely rare phrase that occurs only once in the documented history of English, namely in the book *Trail of the Octopus: From Beirut to Lockerbie – Inside the DIA* and that probably sounds like an idiom because of the alliteration and the semantic relationship to *silly ass*; and *monocled ass*, which brings to mind *pompous ass* but is actually not a very conventional combination). Finally, there

Table 7.7: Some collocates of the form [ADJ N_{equine}] (BNC)

Word A	Word B	A with B	A without B	B without A	Neither
Trojan	horse(s)	37	73	12 198	98 351 475
rocking	horse(s)	34	168	12 201	98 351 380
new	horse(s)	21	113 540	12 214	98 238 008
galloping	horse(s)	17	110	12 218	98 351 438
silly	ass(es)	9	2630	340	98 360 804
prancing	horse(s)	6	17	12 229	98 351 531
pompous	ass(es)	5	250	344	98 363 184
common	zebra(s)	4	18 965	253	98 344 561
old	donkey(s)	3	52 433	643	98 310 704
old	mule(s)	3	52 433	316	98 311 031
young	zebra(s)	2	30 210	255	98 333 316
old	ass(es)	2	52 434	347	98 311 000
female	hinny(/-ies)	2	6620	17	98 357 144
braying	donkey(s)	2	9	644	98 363 128
monocled	ass(es)	1	5	348	98 363 429
large	mule(s)	1	34 228	318	98 329 236
jumped-up	jackass(es)	1	21	7	98 363 754
extinct	quagga(s)	1	428	4	98 363 350
dumb-fuck	donkey(s)	1	0	645	98 363 137
caparisoned	mule(s)	1	8	318	98 363 456

Supplementary Online Material: MNH4

are a number of fully compositional combinations that make sense but do not have any special status (*caparisoned mule, new horse, old donkey, young zebra, large mule, female hinny, extinct quagga*).

In addition, I have selected them to represent different types of frequency relations: some of them are (relatively) frequent, some of them very rare, for some of them the either the adjective or the noun is generally quite frequent, and for some of them neither of the two is frequent.

Table 7.8 shows the ranking of these twenty collocations by the five association measures discussed above. Simplifying somewhat, a good association measure should rank the conventionalized combinations highest (*rocking horse, Trojan horse, silly ass, pompous ass, prancing horse, braying donkey, galloping horse*), the distinctive sounding but non-conventionalized combinations somewhere in the middle (*jumped-up jackass, dumb-fuck donkey, old ass, monocled ass*) and the compositional combinations lowest (*common zebra, jumped-up jackass, dumb-fuck donkey, old ass, monocled ass*). *Common zebra* is difficult to predict – it is a conventionalized expression, but not in the general language.

Table 7.8: Comparison of selected association measures for collocates of the form [ADJ N_{equine}] (BNC)

Collocation	χ^2	Collocation	MI	Collocation	MS	Collocation	G	Collocation	Exact test
jumped-up jackass	558 883.30	*jumped-up jackass*	19.09	*jumped-up jackass*	0.045 455	*Trojan horse*	525.06	*Trojan horse*	7.78×10^{-116}
dumb-fuck donkey	152 264.90	*dumb-fuck donkey*	17.22	*pompous ass*	0.014 327	*rocking horse*	428.51	*rocking horse*	6.70×10^{-95}
Trojan horse	99 994.30	*monocled ass*	15.52	*silly ass*	0.003 410	*galloping horse*	205.79	*galloping horse*	2.13×10^{-46}
braying donkey	55 365.79	*extinct quagga*	15.48	*caparisoned mule*	0.003 135	*silly ass*	105.91	*silly ass*	1.34×10^{-24}
monocled ass	46 972.28	*caparisoned mule*	15.06	*braying donkey*	0.003 096	*prancing horse*	81.51	*prancing horse*	3.73×10^{-19}
rocking horse	45 946.30	*braying donkey*	14.76	*Trojan horse*	0.003 024	*pompous ass*	76.35	*pompous ass*	4.72×10^{-18}
extinct quagga	45 855.44	*pompous ass*	12.43	*monocled ass*	0.002 865	*braying donkey*	37.31	*braying donkey*	2.37×10^{-9}
caparisoned mule	34 259.27	*Trojan horse*	11.40	*rocking horse*	0.002 779	*common zebra*	27.29	*common zebra*	2.36×10^{-7}
pompous ass	27 622	*prancing horse*	11.03	*extinct quagga*	0.002 331	*female hinny*	25.64	*female hinny*	7.74×10^{-7}
galloping horse	18 263.01	*female hinny*	10.61	*dumb-fuck donkey*	0.001 548	*jumped-up jackass*	24.64	*jumped-up jackass*	1.79×10^{-6}
prancing horse	12 573.20	*rocking horse*	10.40	*galloping horse*	0.001 389	*dumb-fuck donkey*	23.87	*dumb-fuck donkey*	6.57×10^{-6}
silly ass	8633.06	*galloping horse*	10.07	*prancing horse*	0.000 490	*monocled ass*	19.69	*monocled ass*	2.13×10^{-5}
female hinny	3123.39	*silly ass*	9.91	*female hinny*	0.000 302	*extinct quagga*	19.68	*extinct quagga*	2.18×10^{-5}
common zebra	314.94	*common zebra*	6.33	*common zebra*	0.000 211	*caparisoned mule*	19.00	*caparisoned mule*	2.92×10^{-5}
old mule	47.12	*young zebra*	4.66	*new horse*	0.000 185	*old mule*	11.59	*old mule*	7.16×10^{-4}
young zebra	46.77	*old mule*	4.14	*young zebra*	0.000 066	*young zebra*	9.10	*young zebra*	2.95×10^{-3}
old donkey	20.49	*old ass*	3.43	*old donkey*	0.000 057	*old donkey*	7.69	*old donkey*	5.25×10^{-3}
old ass	17.70	*large mule*	3.17	*old mule*	0.000 057	*old ass*	5.88	*old ass*	1.53×10^{-2}
large mule	7.12	*old donkey*	3.12	*old ass*	0.000 038	*new horse*	2.91	*new horse*	5.15×10^{-2}
new horse	3.35	*new horse*	0.57	*large mule*	0.000 029	*large mule*	2.62	*large mule*	1.05×10^{-1}

All association measures fare quite well, generally speaking, with respect to the compositional expressions – these tend to occur in the lower third of all lists. Where there are exceptions, the χ^2 statistic, mutual information and minimum sensitivity rank rare cases higher than they should (e.g. *caparisoned mule*, *extinct quagga*), while the G and the p-value of Fisher's exact test rank frequent cases higher (e.g.*galloping horse*).

With respect to the non-compositional cases, χ^2 and mutual information are quite bad, overestimating rare combinations like *jumped-up jackass*, *dumb-fuck donkey* and *monocled ass*, while listing some of the clear cases of collocations much further down the list (*silly ass*, and, in the case of MI, *rocking horse*). Minimum sensitivity is much better, ranking most of the conventionalized cases in the top half of the list and the non-conventionalized ones further down (with the exception of *jumped-up jackass*, where both the individual words and their combination are very rare). The G and the Fisher p-value fare best (with no differences in their ranking of the expressions), listing the conventionalized cases at the top and the distinctive but non-conventionalized cases in the middle.

To demonstrate the problems that very rare events can cause (especially those where both the combination and each of the two words in isolation are very rare), imagine someone had used the phrase *tomfool onager* once in the BNC. Since neither the adjective *tomfool* (a synonym of *silly*) nor the noun *onager* (the name of the donkey sub-genus Equus hemionus, also known as *Asiatic* or *Asian wild ass*) occur in the BNC anywhere else, this would give us the distribution in Table 7.9.

Table 7.9: Fictive occurrence of *tomfool onager* in the BNC

		Second Position		
		ONAGER	¬ONAGER	Total
First Position	TOMFOOL	1 (0.00)	0 (1.00)	1
	¬TOMFOOL	0 (1.00)	98 363 782 (98 363 781.00)	98 363 782
	Total	1	98 363 782	98 363 783

Applying the formulas discussed above to this table gives us a χ^2 value of 98 364 000, an MI value of 26.55 and a minimum sensitivity value of 1, placing this (hypothetical) one-off combination at the top of the respective rankings by a wide margin. Again, the log-likelihood ratio test and Fisher's exact test are much better, putting in eighth place on both lists ($G = 36.81$, $p_{\text{exact}} = 1.02 \times 10^{-8}$).

Although the example is hypothetical, the problem is not. It uncovers a mathematical weakness of many commonly used association measures. From an empirical perspective, this would not necessarily be a problem, if cases like that in Table 7.9 were rare in linguistic corpora. However, they are not. The LOB corpus, for example, contains almost one thousand such cases, including some legitimate collocation candidates (like *herbal brews, casus belli* or *sub-tropical climates*), but mostly compositional combinations (*ungraceful typography, turbaned headdress, songs-of-Britain medley*), snippets of foreign languages (*freie Blicke, l'arbre rouge, palomita blanca*) and other things that are quite clearly not what we are looking for in collocation research. All of these will occur at the top of any collocate list created using statistics like χ^2, mutual information and minimum sensitivity. In large corpora, which are impossible to check for orthographical errors and/or errors introduced by tokenization, this list will also include hundreds of such errors (whose frequency of occurrence is low precisely because they are errors).

To sum up, when doing collocational research, we should use the best association measures available. For the time being, this is the p value of Fisher's exact test (if we have the means to calculate it), or *G* (if we don't, or if we prefer using a widely-accepted association measure). We will use *G* through much of the remainder of this book whenever dealing with collocations or collocation-like phenomena.

7.2 Case studies

In the following, we will look at some typical examples of collocation research, i.e. cases where both variables consist of (some part of) the lexicon and the values are individual words.

7.2.1 Collocation for its own sake

Research that is concerned exclusively with the collocates of individual words or the extraction of all collocations from a corpus falls into three broad types. First, there is a large body of research on the explorative extraction of collocations from corpora. This research is not usually interested in any particular collocation (or set of collocations), or in genuinely linguistic research questions; instead, the focus is on methods (ways of preprocessing corpora, which association measures to use, etc.). Second, there is an equally large body of applied research that results in lexical resources (dictionaries, teaching materials, etc.) rather than scientific studies on specific research questions. Third, there is a much smaller body of research that simply investigates the collocates of individual words or small sets of words. The perspective of these studies tends to be descriptive, often with the aim of showing the usefulness of collocation research for some application area.

The (relative) absence of theoretically more ambitious studies of the collocates of individual words may partly be due to the fact that words tend to be too idiosyncratic in their behavior to make their study theoretically attractive. However, this idiosyncrasy itself is, of course, theoretically interesting and so such studies hold an unrealized potential at least for areas like lexical semantics.

7.2.1.1 Case study: Degree adverbs

A typical example of a thorough descriptive study of the collocates of individual words is Kennedy (2003), which investigates the adjectival collocates of degree adverbs like *very*, *considerably*, *absolutely*, *heavily* and *terribly*. Noting that some of these adverbs appear to be relatively interchangeable with respect to the adjectives and verbs they modify, others are highly idiosyncratic, Kennedy identifies the adjectival and verbal collocates of 24 frequent degree adverbs in the BNC, extracting all words occurring in a span of two words to their left or right, and using mutual information to determine which of them are associated with each degree adverb.

Thus, as is typical for this kind of study, Kennedy adopts an exploratory perspective. The study involves two nominal variables: first, Degree Adverb, with 24 values corresponding to the 24 specific adverbs he selects; second, Adjective, with as many different potential values as there are different adjectives in the BNC (in exploratory studies, it is often the case that we do not know the values of at least one of the two variables in advance, but have to extract them from the data). As pointed out above, which of the two variables is the dependent one and which the independent one in studies like this depends on your research question: if you are interested in degree adverbs and want to explore which adjectives they co-occur with, it makes sense to treat Degree Adverb as the independent and Adjective as the dependent variable; if you are interested in adjectives and want to expore which degree adverbs they co-occur with, it makes sense to do it the other way around. Statistically, it does not make a difference, since our statistical tests for nominal data do not distinguish between dependent and independent variables.

Kennedy finds, first, that there are some degree adverbs that do not appear to have restrictions concerning the adjectives they occur with (for example, *very*, *re-*

ally and *particularly*). However, most degree adverbs are clearly associated with semantically restricted sets of adjectives. The restrictions are of three broad types. First, there are connotational restrictions (some adverbs are associated primarily with positive words (e.g. *perfectly*) or negative words (e.g. *utterly, totally*; on connotation cf. also Section 7.2.3). Second, there are specific semantic restrictions (for example, *incredibly*, which is associated with subjective judgments), sometimes relating transparently to the meaning of the adverb (for example, *badly*, which is associated with words denoting damage or *clearly*, which is associated with words denoting sensory perception). Finally, there are morphological restrictions (some adverbs are used frequently with words derived by particular suffixes, for example, *perfectly*, which is frequently found with words derived by *-able*/*-ible*, or *totally*, whose collocates often contain the prefix *un-*). Table 7.10 illustrates these findings for 5 of the 24 degree adverbs and their top 15 collocates.

Unlike Kennedy, I have used the *G* statistic of the log-likelihood ratio test,[6] and so the specific collocates differ from the ones he finds (generally, his lists include more low-frequency combinations, as expected given that he uses mutual information), but his observations concerning the semantic and morphological sets are generally confirmed.

This case study illustrates the exploratory design typical of collocational research as well as the kind of result that such studies yield and the observations possible on the basis of these results. By comparing the results reported here to Kennedy's, you may also gain a better understanding as to how different association measures may lead to different results.

7.2.2 Lexical relations

One area of lexical semantics where collocation data is used quite intensively is the study of lexical relations – most notably, (near) synonymy (Taylor 2003, cf. below), but also polysemy (e.g. Yarowsky 1993, investigating the idea that associations exist not between words but between particular senses of words) and antonymy (Justeson & Katz 1991, see below).

7.2.2.1 Case study: Near synonyms

Natural languages typically contain pairs (or larger sets) of words with very similar meanings, such as *big* and *large*, *begin* and *start* or *high* and *tall*. In isolation,

[6]Note that I will usually provide the frequencies for the cells O_{11}, O_{12}, O_{21} and O_{22} in tables like this, to allow you to check the calculations or to try out different association measures, but in this case lack of space prevents this. The complete dataset is part of the Supplementary Online Material, however).

Table 7.10: Selected degree adverbs and their collocates

INCREDIBLY		PERFECTLY		TOTALLY		COMPLETELY		BADLY	
Collocation	G	Collocation	G	Collocation	G	Collocation	G	Collocation	G
difficult	113.87	*normal*	989.49	*different*	3190.97	*different*	3965.12	*bruised*	573.27
lucky	95.58	*acceptable*	928.21	*dependent*	718.13	*new*	1242.61	*wrong*	410.49
fast	87.97	*clear*	880.93	*unacceptable*	706.93	*free*	404.43	*damaged*	217.62
beautiful	80.56	*happy*	822.98	*inadequate*	604.42	*wrong*	362.33	*beaten*	188.40
dangerous	77.75	*possible*	743.65	*wrong*	478.49	*unaware*	240.24	*hurt*	170.65
strong	68.13	*reasonable*	674.85	*unexpected*	459.52	*mad*	218.55	*injured*	141.80
stupid	65.32	*capable*	663.38	*unsuitable*	420.13	*refurbished*	184.58	*wounded*	138.48
efficient	61.84	*good*	545.89	*unaware*	345.90	*irrelevant*	178.25	*swollen*	113.92
simple	61.84	*adequate*	537.98	*opposed*	333.21	*separate*	172.60	*fitting*	106.13
low	59.14	*safe*	512.69	*new*	316.11	*independent*	149.81	*affected*	93.24
sexy	59.12	*natural*	469.62	*unnecessary*	303.03	*satisfied*	142.60	*broken*	71.49
naive	57.34	*competitive*	418.44	*irrelevant*	251.56	*innocent*	141.11	*mutilated*	70.78
expensive	56.66	*honest*	406.00	*alien*	251.06	*empty*	138.70	*burned*	62.07
hard	55.00	*balanced*	388.13	*confused*	249.15	*unknown*	137.75	*unstuck*	61.30
complicated	54.98	*well*	370.56	*blind*	247.58	*dry*	136.61	*lacerated*	58.56

Supplementary Online Material: LKTH

it is often difficult to tell what the difference in meaning is, especially since they are often interchangeable at least in some contexts. Obviously, the distribution of such pairs or sets with respect to other words in a corpus can provide insights into their similarities and differences.

One example of such a study is Taylor (2003), which investigates the synonym pair *high* and *tall* by identifying all instances of the two words in their subsense 'large vertical extent' in the LOB corpus and categorizing the words they modify into eleven semantic categories. These categories are based on semantic distinctions such as human vs. inanimate, buildings vs. other artifacts vs. natural entities, etc., which are expected *a priori* to play a role.

The study, while not strictly hypothesis-testing, is thus somewhat deductive. It involves two nominal variables; the independent variable TYPE OF ENTITY with eleven values shown in Table 7.11 and the dependent variable VERTICAL EXTENT ADJECTIVE with the values HIGH and TALL (assuming that people first choose something to talk about and then choose the appropriate adjective to describe it). Table 7.11 shows Taylor's results (he reports absolute and relative frequencies, which I have used to calculate expected frequencies and χ^2 components).

As we can see, there is little we can learn from this table, since the frequencies in the individual cells are simply too small to apply the χ^2 test to the table as a whole. The only χ^2 components that reach significance individually are those for the category HUMAN, which show that *tall* is preferred and *high* avoided with human referents. The sparsity of the data in the table is due to the fact that the analyzed sample is very small, and this problem is exacerbated by the fact that the little data available is spread across too many categories. The category labels are not well chosen either: they overlap substantially in several places (e.g., towers and walls are buildings, pieces of clothing are artifacts, etc.) and not all of them seem relevant to any expectation we might have about the words *high* and *tall*.

Taylor later cites earlier psycholinguistic research indicating that *tall* is used when the vertical dimension is prominent, is an acquired property and is a property of an individuated entity. It would thus have been better to categorize the corpus data according to these properties – in other words, a more strictly deductive approach would have been more promising given the small data set.

Alternatively, we can take a truly exploratory approach and look for differential collocates as described in Section 7.1.1 above – in this case, for differential noun collocates of the adjectives *high* and *tall*. This allows us to base our analysis on a much larger data set, as the nouns do not have to be categorized in advance. Table 7.12 shows the top 15 differential collocates of the two words in the BNC.

Table 7.11: Objects described as *tall* or *high* in the LOB corpus (adapted from Taylor 2003)

Noun Category	Adjective				Total
	tall		high		
humans	*Obs.:*	45	*Obs.:*	2	47
	Exp.:	22.91	*Exp.:*	24.09	
	χ^2:	21.31	χ^2:	20.26	
animals	*Obs.:*	0	*Obs.:*	1	1
	Exp.:	0.49	*Exp.:*	0.51	
	χ^2:	0.49	χ^2:	0.46	
plants, trees	*Obs.:*	7	*Obs.:*	3	10
	Exp.:	4.87	*Exp.:*	5.13	
	χ^2:	0.93	χ^2:	0.88	
buildings	*Obs.:*	3	*Obs.:*	10	13
	Exp.:	6.34	*Exp.:*	6.66	
	χ^2:	1.76	χ^2:	1.67	
walls, fences, etc	*Obs.:*	0	*Obs.:*	5	5
	Exp.:	2.44	*Exp.:*	2.56	
	χ^2:	2.44	χ^2:	2.32	
towers, statues, pillars, sticks	*Obs.:*	0	*Obs.:*	7	7
	Exp.:	3.41	*Exp.:*	3.59	
	χ^2:	3.41	χ^2:	3.24	
articles of clothing	*Obs.:*	0	*Obs.:*	7	7
	Exp.:	3.41	*Exp.:*	3.59	
	χ^2:	3.41	χ^2:	3.24	
miscellaneous artifacts	*Obs.:*	2	*Obs.:*	13	15
	Exp.:	7.31	*Exp.:*	7.69	
	χ^2:	3.86	χ^2:	3.67	
topographical features	*Obs.:*	0	*Obs.:*	5	5
	Exp.:	2.44	*Exp.:*	2.56	
	χ^2:	2.44	χ^2:	2.32	
other natural phenomena	*Obs.:*	0	*Obs.:*	5	5
	Exp.:	2.44	*Exp.:*	2.56	
	χ^2:	2.44	χ^2:	2.32	
uncertain reference	*Obs.:*	1	*Obs.:*	3	4
	Exp.:	1.95	*Exp.:*	2.05	
	χ^2:	0.46	χ^2:	0.44	
Total	58		61		119

Table 7.12: Differential collocates for *tall* and *high* in the BNC

COLLOCATE	Collocate with TALL	Collocate with HIGH	Other words with TALL	Other words with HIGH	*G*
Most strongly associated with *high*					
level	0	2741	1720	36 933	240.90
education	0	2499	1720	37 175	218.94
court	0	1863	1720	37 811	161.88
quality	0	1079	1720	38 595	92.83
standard	1	1163	1719	38 511	90.35
rate	0	922	1720	38 752	79.16
proportion	0	875	1720	38 799	75.08
street	1	810	1719	38 864	60.38
school	0	676	1720	38 998	57.86
price	0	642	1720	39 032	54.93
degree	0	638	1720	39 036	54.58
speed	0	547	1720	39 127	46.75
interest	0	493	1720	39 181	42.10
risk	0	431	1720	39 243	36.78
cost	0	387	1720	39 287	33.01
priority	0	374	1720	39 300	31.89
point	0	352	1720	39 322	30.01
unemployment	0	318	1720	39 356	27.10
temperature	0	305	1720	39 369	25.99
Most strongly associated with *tall*					
man	182	3	1538	39 671	1146.54
building	82	26	1638	39 648	408.35
tree	73	26	1647	39 648	355.52
boy	40	0	1680	39 674	255.36
glass	39	2	1681	39 672	233.14
woman	38	3	1682	39 671	221.34
ship	33	0	1687	39 674	210.54
girl	32	0	1688	39 674	204.15
figure	62	93	1658	39 581	195.58
chimney	28	8	1692	39 666	141.09
order	62	176	1658	39 498	138.01
dark	23	3	1697	39 671	128.27
grass	24	5	1696	39 669	126.76
tale	20	1	1700	39 673	119.50
window	34	41	1686	39 633	117.04
story	18	0	1702	39 674	114.69
tower	24	24	1696	39 650	88.47
plant	24	28	1696	39 646	83.57
person	13	0	1707	39 674	82.80
nave	9	0	1711	39 674	57.30

Supplementary Online Material: D9P4

The results for *tall* clearly support Taylor's ideas about the salience of the vertical dimension. The results for *high* show something Taylor could not have found, since he restricted his analysis to the subsense 'vertical dimension': when compared with tall, *high* is most strongly associated with quantities or positions in hierarchies and rankings. There are no spatial uses at all among its top differential collocates. This does not answer the question why we can use it spatially and in competition with *tall*, but it shows what general sense we would have to assume: one concerned not with the vertical extent as such, but with the magnitude of that extent (which, incidentally, Taylor notes in his conclusion).

This case study shows how the same question can be approached by a deductive or an inductive (exploratory) approach. The deductive approach can be more precise, but this depends on the appropriateness of the categories chosen *a priori* for annotating the data; it is also time consuming and therefore limited to relatively small data sets. In contrast, the inductive approach can be applied to a large data set because it requires no *a priori* annotation. It also does not require any choices concerning annotation categories; however, there may be a danger to project patterns into the data *post hoc*.

7.2.2.2 Case study: Antonymy

At first glance, we expect the relationship between antonyms to be a paradigmatic one, where only one or the other will occur in a given utterance. However, Charles & Miller (1989) suggest, based on the results of sorting tasks and on theoretical considerations, that, on the contrary, antonym pairs are frequently found in syntagmatic relationships, occurring together in the same clause or sentence. A number of corpus-linguistic studies have shown this to be the case (e.g. Justeson & Katz 1991, Justeson & Katz 1992, Fellbaum 1995; cf. also Gries & Otani 2010 for a study identifying antonym pairs based on their similarity in lexico-syntactic behavior).

There are differences in detail in these studies, but broadly speaking, they take a deductive approach: they choose a set of test words for which there is agreement as to what their antonyms are, search for these words in a corpus, and check whether their antonyms occur in the same sentence significantly more frequently than expected. The studies thus involve two nominal variables: SENTENCE (with the values CONTAINS TEST WORD and DOES NOT CONTAIN TEST WORD) and ANTONYM OF TEST WORD (with the values OCCURS IN SENTENCE and DOES NOT OCCUR IN SENTENCE). This seems like an unnecessarily complicated way of representing the kind of co-occurrence design used in the examples above, but I have chosen it to show that in this case sentences containing a particular word are used as the condition under which the occurrence of another word is investigated – a straightforward application of the general research design that defines quantitative corpus linguistics. Table 7.13 demonstrates the design using the adjectives *good* and *bad* (the numbers are, as always in this book, based on the tagged version of BROWN included with the ICAME collection and differ slightly from the ones reported in the studies discussed below).

Table 7.13: Sentential co-occurrence of *good* and *bad* in the BROWN corpus

		Bad		
		occurs	¬occurs	Total
Good	occurs	16 (1.57)	687 (701.43)	703
	¬occurs	110 (124.43)	55 769 (55 754.57)	55 879
	Total	126	56 456	56 582

Good occurs significantly more frequently in sentences also containing *bad* than in sentences not containing *bad*, and vice versa ($\chi^2 = 135.07, \mathrm{df} = 1, p < 0.001$). Justeson & Katz (1991) apply this procedure to 36 adjectives and get significant results for 25 of them (19 of which remain significant after a Bonferroni correction for multiple tests). They also report that in a larger corpus, the frequency of co-occurrence for all adjective pairs is significantly higher than expected (but do not give any figures). Fellbaum (1995) uses a very similar procedure with words from other word classes, with very similar results.

These studies only look at the co-occurrence of antonyms; they do not apply the same method to word pairs related by other lexical relations (synonymy, taxonomy, etc.). Thus, there is no way of telling whether co-occurrence within the same sentence is something that is typical specifically of antonyms, or whether it is something that characterizes word pairs in other lexical relations, too.

An obvious approach to testing this would be to repeat the study with other types of lexical relations. Alternatively, we can take an exploratory approach that does not start out from specific word pairs at all. Justeson & Katz (1991) investigate the specific grammatical contexts which antonyms tend to co-occur, identifying, among others, coordination of the type [ADJ *and* ADJ] or [ADJ *or* ADJ]. We can use such specific contexts to determine the role of co-occurrence for different types of lexical relations by simply extracting *all* word pairs occurring in the adjective slots of these patterns, calculating their association strength within this pattern as shown in Table 7.14 for the adjectives *good* and *bad* in the BNC, and then categorizing the most strongly associated collocates in terms of the lexical relationships between them.

Table 7.14: Co-occurrence of *good* and *bad* in the first and second slot of [ADJ_1 *and* ADJ_2]

		Second Slot		
		bad	¬bad	Total
First Slot	good	158 (0.89)	476 (633.11)	634
	¬good	35 (192.11)	136 893 (136 735.89)	136 928
	Total	193	137 369	137 562

Note that this is a slightly different procedure from what we have seen before: instead of comparing the frequency of co-occurrence of two words with their individual occurrence in the rest of the corpus, we are comparing it to their individual occurrence *in a given position of a given structure* – in this case [ADJ *and* ADJ] (Stefanowitsch & Gries (2005) call this kind of design *covarying collexeme analysis*).

Table 7.15 shows the thirty most strongly associated adjective pairs coordinated with *and* in the BNC.

Clearly, antonymy is the dominant relation among these word pairs, which are mostly opposites (*black/white, male/female, public/private*, etc.), and sometimes relational antonyms (*primary/secondary, economic/social, economic/political, social/political, lesbian/gay*, etc.). The only cases of non-antonymic pairs are *economic/monetary*, which is more like a synonym than an antonym and the fixed expressions *deaf/dumb* and *hon(ourable)/learned* (as in *honourable and learned gentleman/member/friend*). The pattern does not just hold for the top 30 collocates but continues as we go down the list. There are additional cases of relational antonyms, like *British/American* and *Czech/Slovak* and additional examples of fixed expressions (*alive and well, far and wide, true and fair, null and void, noble and learned*), but most cases are clear antonyms (for example, *syntactic/semantic, spoken/written, mental/physical, right/left, rich/poor, young/old, good/evil*, etc.). The one systematic exceptions are cases like *worse and worse* (a special construction with comparatives indicating incremental change, cf. Stefanowitsch 2007b).

Table 7.15: Co-occurrence of adjectives in the first and second slot of [ADJ_1 *and* ADJ_2] (BNC)

ADJ_1 AND ADJ_2	ADJ_1 with ADJ_2	ADJ_1 with ADJ_{other}	ADJ_{other} with ADJ_2	ADJ_{other} with ADJ_{other}	G
black and white	959	507	667	135 429	7348.90
economic and social	1049	1285	1286	133 942	5920.16
male and female	414	25	26	137 097	5244.75
social and economic	755	1705	862	134 240	4119.00
public and private	369	135	158	136 900	3877.60
deaf and dumb	276	43	8	137 235	3655.01
primary and secondary	262	58	25	137 217	3332.90
lesbian and gay	183	6	22	137 351	2596.57
internal and external	191	28	20	137 323	2595.41
hon. and learned	232	91	118	137 121	2594.96
political and economic	466	1166	1151	134 779	2356.74
social and political	502	1958	1139	133 963	2160.29
national and international	251	443	243	136 625	2075.94
left and right	149	37	33	137 343	1974.66
upper and lower	156	30	105	137 271	1911.70
old and new	214	462	164	136 722	1834.78
economic and monetary	266	2068	89	135 139	1802.61
physical and mental	186	467	54	136 855	1793.37
top and bottom	123	26	6	137 407	1786.23
economic and political	420	1914	1221	134 007	1671.32
local and national	186	309	180	136 887	1667.41
positive and negative	147	179	43	137 193	1653.32
good and bad	158	476	35	136 893	1560.46
private and public	161	236	160	137 005	1514.90
industrial and commercial	174	277	236	136 875	1510.40
past and present	114	60	23	137 365	1497.56
formal and informal	131	116	65	137 250	1494.07
alive and well	111	78	20	137 353	1434.91
central and eastern	155	380	97	136 930	1434.86
present and future	130	95	124	137 213	1412.34

Supplementary Online Material: CWPX

This case study shows how deductive and inductive domains may complement each other: while the deductive studies cited show that antonyms tend to co-occur syntagmatically, the inductive study presented here shows that words that co-occur syntagmatically (at least in certain syntactic contexts) tend to be antonyms. These two findings are not equivalent; the second finding shows that the first finding may indeed be typical for antonymy as opposed to other lexical relations.

The exploratory study was limited to a particular syntactic/semantic context, chosen because it seems semantically and pragmatically neutral enough to allow all kinds of lexical relations to occur in it. There are contexts which might be expected to be particularly suitable to particular kinds of lexical relations and which could be used, given a large enough corpus, to identify word pairs in such relations. For example, the pattern [ADJ *rather than* ADJ] seems semantically predisposed for identifying antonyms, and indeed, it yields pairs like *implicit*/*explicit*, *worse*/*better*, *negative*/*positive*, *qualitative*/*quantitative*, *active*/*passive*, *real*/*apparent*, *local*/*national*, *political*/*economical*, etc. Other patterns are semantically more complex, identifying pairs in more context-dependent oppositions; for example, [ADJ *but not* ADJ] identifies pairs like *desirable*/*essential*, *necessary*/*sufficient*, *similar*/*identical*, *small*/*insignificant*, *useful*/*essential*, *difficult*/*impossible*. The relation between the adjectives in these pairs is best described as pragmatic – the first one conventionally implies the second.

7.2.3 Semantic prosody

Sometimes, the collocates of a node word (or larger expressions) fall into a more or less clearly recognizable semantic class that is difficult to characterize in terms of denotational properties of the node word. Louw (1993: 157) refers to this phenomenon as "semantic prosody", defined, somewhat impressionistically, as the "consistent aura of meaning with which a form is imbued by its collocates".

This definition has been understood by collocation researchers in two different (but related) ways. Much of the subsequent research on semantic prosody is based on the understanding that this "aura" consists of connotational meaning (cf. e.g. Partington 1998: 68), so that words can have a "positive", "neutral" or "negative" semantic prosody. However, Sinclair, who according to Louw invented the term,[7] seems to have in mind "attitudinal or pragmatic" meanings that are much more specific than "positive", "neutral" or "negative". There are insightful terminological discussions concerning this issue (cf. e.g. Hunston 2007), but since

[7]Louw attributes the term to John Sinclair, but Louw (1993) is the earliest appearance of the term in writing. However, Sinclair is clearly the first to discuss the phenomenon itself systematically, without giving it a label (e.g. Sinclair 1991: 74–75).

the term is widely-used in (at least) these two different ways, and since "positive" and "negative" connotations are very general kinds of attitudinal meaning, it seems more realistic to accept a certain vagueness of the term. If necessary, we could differentiate between the general semantic prosody of a word (its "positive" or "negative" connotation as reflected in its collocates) and its specific semantic prosody (the word-specific attitudinal meaning reflected in its collocates).

7.2.3.1 Case study: True feelings

A typical example of Sinclair's approach to semantic prosody, both methodologically and theoretically, is his short case study of the expression *true feelings*. Sinclair (1996b) presents a selection of concordance lines from the COBUILD corpus – Figure 7.1 shows a random sample from the BNC instead, as the COBUILD corpus is not accessible, but Sinclair's findings are well replicated by this sample.

```
 1 f unless you 're absolutely sure of your [true feelings] . I had a similar experience several ye
 2 nces may well not reflect my employer 's [true feelings] on the matter , but once having sustain
 3  and realize it is all right to show our [true feelings] and that it is all right to be rejected
 4 wing right action : acting only from our [true feelings] , not governed by the distortions of em
 5 der , but the problem of ` reading ' the [true feelings] of the individual can be made easier by
 6  other . Having declared to Roderigo his [true feelings] about Othello , Iago later explains why
 7 ell studied in the art of disguising his [true feelings] . Let him not be frightened of me ; let
 8 rised that the TV presenter revealed her [true feelings] towards Nicola so quickly : most people
 9 embers are helpful to show each side the [true feelings] of the other , the need to accept and w
10 good husband , but you like to hide your [true feelings] . ' ` Oh , do n't be so serious , B
11  er , he has n't actually dealt with the [true feelings] that he had towards his father , and wh
12 g as ` friends ' , without revealing her [true feelings] for him . It was still light when he pi
13 t the parents will often not admit their [true feelings] about the child and the incident , acti
14 t a matter of time before she showed her [true feelings] , I was sure of that . Females -- hone
15 m for so long at last gave vent to their [true feelings] . The match had been billed in the Amer
16 eople . And got him plenty sex . Rory 's [true feelings] about the matter were complex but red-b
17 t had finally forced her to confront her [true feelings] for Arnie . Or rather , her lack of fee
18 rage in both hands , and told him of her [true feelings] , they might have had a chance to work
19 andmother finds it difficult to show her [true feelings] . ' said David . ` I think it 's a
20 er heart did more to convince her of her [true feelings] than any rational thinking . She wanted
```

Figure 7.1: Concordance of *true feelings* (BNC, Sample)

On the basis of his concordance, Sinclair then makes a number of observations concerning the use of the phrase *true feelings*, quantifying them informally. He notes three things: first, the phrase is almost always part of a possessive (realized by pronoun, possessive noun phrase or *of*-construction). This is also true of the sample in Figure 7.1, with the exception of line 11 (where there is a possessive relation, but it is realized by the verb *have*).

Second, the expression collocates with verbs of expression (perhaps unsurprising for an expression relating to emotions); this, too, is true for our sample, where such verbs are found in 14 lines: *reflect* (line 2), *show* (lines 3, 9, 14, and 19), *read* (line 5), *declare* (line 6), *disguise* (line 7), *reveal* (line 8), *hide* (line 10), *reveal* (line 12), *admit* (line 13), *give vent to* (line 15), and *tell* (line 18).

Third, and most interesting, Sinclair finds that a majority of his examples express a *reluctance* to express emotions. In our sample, such cases are also noticeably frequent: I would argue that lines 2, 3, 5, 7, 8, 10, 12, 13, 14, 15, and 19 can be interpreted in this way, which would give us a slight majority of 11/20. (Your analysis may differ, as I have made my assessment rather intuitively, instead of coming up with an annotation scheme). In many cases, the reluctance or inability is communicated as part of the verb (like *disguise, conceal* and *hide*), in other cases it is communicated by negation of a verb of expression (like *not admit* in line 13) or by adjectives (like *difficult to show* in line 19).

Sinclair assumes that the denotational meaning of the phrase *true feelings* is "genuine emotions". Based on his observations, he posits that, in addition, it has the semantic prosody "reluctance/inability to express emotions" – an attitudinal meaning much more specific than a general "positive" or "negative" connotation.

The methodological approach taken by Sinclair (and many others in his tradition) can yield interesting observations (at least, if applied very carefully): descriptively, there is little to criticize. However, under the definition of corpus linguistics adopted in this book, Sinclair's observations would be just the first step towards a full analysis. First, note that Sinclair's approach is quantitative only in a very informal sense – he rarely reports exact frequencies for a given semantic feature in his sample, relying instead on general statements about the frequency or rarity of particular phenomena. As we saw above, this is easy to remedy by simply determining the exact number of times that the phenomenon in question occurs in a given sample. However, such exact frequencies do not advance the analysis meaningfully: as long as we do not know how frequent a particular phenomenon is in the corpus as a whole, we cannot determine whether it is a characteristic property of the expression under investigation, or just an accidental one.

Specifically, as long as we do not know how frequent the semantic prosody 'reluctance or inability to express' is in general, we do not know whether it is particularly characteristic of the phrase *true feelings*. It may be characteristic, among other things, (a) of utterances concerning emotions in general, (b) of utterances containing the plural noun *feelings*, (c) of utterances containing the adjective *true*, etc.

In order to determine this, we have to compare our sample of the expression *true feelings* to related expressions that differ with respect to each property potentially responsible for the semantic prosody. For example, we might compare it to the noun *feelings* in order to investigate possibility (b). Figure 7.2 shows a sample of the expression [POSS *feelings*] (the possessive pronoun was included as it, too, may have an influence on the prosody and almost all examples of *true feelings* are preceded by a possessive pronoun).

```
1  by the rest of the board ? Re-programme [your feelings] , in that case . The annual BW accounts
2 the Asian women I spoke to told me about [their feelings] and situations . Here I shall try to d
3 ractive , but I think you might consider [my feelings] as well as your own. , Another pause .
4 o trust her more , dared to feel more of [my feelings] , instead of eating them away . It woul
5 all was in order . It is hard to explain [my feelings] once I did finally set off . For the fi
6 e family and the old person work through [their feelings] about any restrictions . This contract
7  say . ` Nothing is ever going to change [their feelings] towards me . ` I 've tried everything
8 han rights . It is about men reconciling [their feelings] towards their fathers and learning how
9 l family . It is as if to let people see [your feelings] takes away some of your power . But at
10  eyelids defensively lowered to disguise [her feelings] . Crossing her legs discreetly , she du
11 nxiety ? Should n't she just accept that [her feelings] about her mother 's lifestyle were irra
12 o stop things before they went too far . [His feelings] had gone no deeper than the surface . N
13 resentment , because you do n't care for [my feelings] at all . You always think the worst of
14 etence , could n't face having to stifle [her feelings] , her crazy and immature hopes -- hope
15 Remember ? ' ` I thought I could control [my feelings] , have an exciting affair with you and
16  her and kissing her softly , she voiced [her feelings] by saying , ` I love you , Gran . '
17 our lack of understanding with regard to [his feelings] as a father . ' ` Oh , Great-gran ,
18  right , then , the doubts you had about [your feelings] . ' ` You mean my feelings towards
19 y North-West 's Billy Anderson who vents [his feelings] about the lack of North-West representa
20  that is by giving them a copy . That 's [my feelings] erm . I move . Thanks very much indeed
```

Figure 7.2: Concordance of [POSS *feelings*] (BNC, Sample)

The concordance shows that contexts concerning a reluctance or inability to express emotions are not untypical of the expression [POSS *feelings*] – it is found in four out of twenty lines in our sample, i.e. in 20 percent of all cases (lines 5, 10, 14, 15). However, it is nowhere near as frequent as with the expression *true feelings*. We can compare the two samples using the χ^2 test. As Table 7.16 shows, the difference is, indeed, significant ($\chi^2 = 5.23, \mathrm{df} = 1, p < 0.05$).

The semantic prosody is not characteristic of the noun *feelings*, even in possessive contexts. We can thus assume that it is not characteristic of utterances concerned with emotions generally. But is it characteristic of the specific expression *true feelings*, or would we find it in other contexts where a distinction between genuine and non-genuine emotions is made?

Table 7.16: Semantic prosody of *true feelings* and [POSS *feelings*]

		Prosody		
		reluctance	¬reluctance	Total
Expression	true feelings	11 (7.50)	9 (12.50)	20
	[poss *feelings*]	4 (7.50)	16 (12.50)	20
	Total	15	25	40

In order to answer this question, we have to compare the phrase to denotationally synonymous expressions, such as *genuine emotions* (which Sinclair uses to paraphrase the denotational meaning), *genuine feelings*, *real emotions* and *real feelings*. The only one of these expressions that occurs in the BNC more than a handful of times is *real feelings*. A sample concordance is shown in Figure 7.3.

```
 1 r-head wolf-whistles . Real situations , [real feelings] , real people , real love . The album s
 2 onal Checklist : I do my best to hide my [real feelings] from others I always try to please othe
 3  , how to manipulate , how to hide their [real feelings] and how to convince those that love the
 4 f the death of a cousin . Disguising his [real feelins] he wrote cheerfully , telling them that
 5 her words , the counsellor must seek the [real feelings] of the counsellee through careful liste
 6 tant issues are fully discussed and that [real feelings] are expressed rather than avoided . An
 7 at prevented him from ever revealing his [real feelings] to any woman . How she regretted those
 8 ing process of mystification that denies [real feelings] and experiences is a necessary prop to
 9  the play to whom he reveals some of his [real feelings] is Roderigo , but only while using him
10 sked her much sooner if he had known her [real feelings] towards him , but she had been so forma
11  of situation neither can say what their [real feelings] are . A true conversation might be ,
12  clerks are not allowed to express their [real feelings] at work , it is not surprising that the
13 k foolish in public in order to hide his [real feelings] . Men were strange creatures at times .
14 t she could smother the awakening of her [real feelings] for him ? He 'd been important enough t
15 but she hoped she managed to conceal her [real feelings] . Guessing what might greet her in the
16 ight of their honeymoon ? If Ace had any [real feelings] for her he would have taken her prohibi
17  used deliberately as a mask to hide his [real feelings] , she could only guess . ` Let me tak
18 had left him -- but his control over his [real feelings] had remained even then . But what had c
19 ' Relieved that she had not betrayed her [real feelings] , Sophie concentrated on the morning su
20 der has an insight into the Mr. Darcy 's [real feelings] during particular parts of the book . E
```

Figure 7.3: Concordance of *real feelings* (BNC, Sample)

Here, the semantic prosody in question is quite dominant – by my count, it is present in lines 2, 3, 4, 6, 7, 12, 13, 15, 17, 18 and 19, i.e., in 11 of 20 lines. This is the exact proportion also observed with *true feelings*, so even if you disagree with one or two of my categorization decisions, there is no significant difference between the two expressions.

It seems, then, that the semantic prosody Sinclair observes is not attached to the expression *true feelings* in particular, but that it is an epiphenomenon the fact that we typically distinguish between "genuine" (*true*, *real*, etc.) emotions and other emotions in a particular context, namely one where someone is reluctant on unable to express their genuine emotions. Of course, studies of additional expressions with adjectives meaning "genuine" modifying nouns meaning "emotion" might give us a more detailed and differentiated picture, as might studies of other nouns modified by adjectives like *true* (such as *true nature*, *true beliefs*, *true intentions*, etc.). Such studies are left as an exercise to the reader – this case study was mainly meant to demonstrate how informal analyses based on the inspection of concordances can be integrated into a more rigorous research design involving quantification and comparison to a set of control data.

7.2.3.2 Case study: The verb *cause*

A second way in which semantic prosody can be studied quantitatively is implicit in Kennedy's study of collocates of degree adverbs discussed in Section 7.2.1 above. Recall that Kennedy discusses for each degree adverb whether a majority of its collocates has a positive or a negative connotation. This, of course, is a statement about the (broad) semantic prosody of the respective adverb, based not on an inspection and categorization of usage contexts, but on inductively discovered strongly associated collocates.

One of the earliest applications of this procedure is found in Stubbs (1995a). Stubbs studies, among other things, the noun and verb *cause*. He first presents the result of a manual extraction of all nouns (sometimes with adjectives qualifying them, as in the case of *wholesale slaughter*) that occur as subject or object of the verb *cause* or as a prepositional object of the noun *cause* in the LOB. He annotates them in their context of occurrence for their connotation, finding that approximately 80 percent are negative, 18 percent are neutral and 2 percent are positive. This procedure is still very close to Sinclairs approach of inspecting concordances, although is is stricter in terms of categorizing and quantifying the data.

Stubbs then notes that manual inspection and extraction becomes unfeasible as the number of corpus hits grows and suggests that, instead, we should first identify significant collocates of the word or expression we are interested in, and then categorize these significant collocates according to our criteria – note that this is the strategy we also used in Case Study 7.2.2.1 above in order to determine semantic differences between *high* and *tall*.

We will not follow Stubbs' discussion in detail here – his focus is on methodological issues regarding the best way to identify collocates. Since we decided in Section 7.1.3 above to stick with the *G* statistic, this discussion is not central for us. Stubbs does not present the results of his procedure in detail and the corpus he uses is not accessible anyway, so let us use the BNC again and extract our own data.

Table 7.17 shows the result of an attempt to extract direct objects of the verb *cause* from the BNC. I searched for the lemma *cause* where it is tagged as a verb, followed by zero to three words that are not nouns (to take into account the occurrence of determiners, adjectives, etc.) and that are not the word *by* (in order to exclude passives like *caused by negligence, fire, exposure*, etc.), followed by a noun or sequence of nouns, not followed by *to* (in order to exclude causative constructions of the form *caused the glass to break*). This noun, or the last noun in this sequence, is assumed to be the direct object of *cause*. The twenty most frequent nouns are shown in Table 7.17, Column (a).

These collocates clearly corroborate Stubbs' observation about the negative semantic prosody of *cause*. We could now calculate the association strength between the verb and each of these nouns to get a better idea of which of them are significant collocates and which just happen to be frequent in the corpus overall. It should be obvious, however, that the nouns in Table 7.17, Column (a) are not generally frequent in the English language, so we can assume here that they are, for the most part, significant collocates.

But even so, what does this tell us about the semantic prosody of the verb *cause*? It has variously been pointed out (for example, by Louw & Chateau 2010) that other verbs of causation also tend to have a negative semantic prosody – the direct object nouns of *bring about* in Table 7.17, Column (b) and *lead to* in Table 7.17, Column (c) corroborate this. The real question is, again, whether it is the specific expression [*cause* NP] that has the semantic prosody in question, or whether this prosody is found in an entire semantic domain – perhaps speakers of English have a generally negative view of causation.

In order to determine this, it might be useful to compare different expressions of causation to each other rather than to the corpus as a whole – to perform a *differentiating collocate analysis*: just by inspecting the frequencies in Table 7.17, it seems that the negative prosody is much weaker for *bring about* and *lead to* than for *cause*, so, individually or taken together, they could serve as a baseline against which to compare *cause*.

Table 7.17: Noun collocates of three expressions of causation

(a)		(b)		(c)	
[*CAUSE* NP]	Freq.	[*BRING ABOUT* NP]	Freq.	[*LEAD TO* NP]	Freq.
problem	836	*change*	247	*increase*	219
death	358	*improvement*	43	*change*	154
damage	334	*end*	30	*conclusion*	152
concern	284	*death*	22	*development*	133
trouble	269	*downfall*	21	*loss*	123
harm	203	*result*	21	*problem*	122
difficulty	185	*reduction*	19	*death*	114
injury	139	*revolution*	19	*formation*	110
change	128	*increase*	18	*reduction*	105
pain	122	*peace*	17	*improvement*	89
confusion	113	*collapse*	14	*confusion*	80
loss	113	*transformation*	13	*creation*	76
lot	95	*development*	12	*number*	66
increase	93	*shift*	11	*award*	64
delay	90	*decline*	10	*rise*	63
distress	84	*destruction*	10	*discovery*	62
disease	81	*state*	10	*fall*	61
controversy	78	*unity*	10	*result*	61
accident	76	*effect*	9	*decline*	60
cancer	72	*event*	9	*growth*	60
		situation	9		

Supplementary Online Material: BYHW

Table 7.18 shows the results of a differential collocate analysis between *cause* on the one hand and the combined collocates of *bring about* and *lead to* on the other.

Table 7.18: Differential collocates for *cause* compared to *bring about/lead to* in the BNC

Collocate	Collocate with cause	Collocate with other	Other words with cause	Other words with other	*G*
problem	836	126	11 566	15 311	778.63
damage	334	15	12 068	15 422	438.76
concern	284	10	12 118	15 427	387.24
trouble	269	9	12 133	15 428	369.27
harm	203	1	12 199	15 436	318.67
pain	122	4	12 280	15 433	167.17
death	358	136	12 044	15 301	160.75
injury	139	14	12 263	15 423	148.39
difficulty	185	51	12 217	15 386	113.91
stir	70	0	12 332	15 437	113.42
distress	84	5	12 318	15 432	103.52
havoc	62	0	12 340	15 437	100.44
alarm	57	0	12 345	15 437	92.32
delay	90	14	12 312	15 423	80.16
controversy	78	9	12 324	15 428	79.11
sensation	48	0	12 354	15 437	77.73
lot	95	18	12 307	15 419	76.05
cancer	72	9	12 330	15 428	70.73
disease	81	14	12 321	15 423	68.28
offence	55	4	12 347	15 433	64.53

The negative prosody of the verb *cause* is even more pronounced than in the frequency list in Table 7.17: Even the two neutral words *change* and *increase* have disappeared. In contrast, the combined differential collocates of *bring about* and *lead to* as compared to *cause*, shown in Table 7.19 are neutral or even positive.

We can thus conclude, first, that all three verbal expressions of causation are likely to be used to some extent with direct object nouns with a negative connotation. However, it is only the verb *cause* that has a negative semantic prosody. Even the raw frequencies of nouns occurring in the object position of the three expressions suggest this: while *cause* occurs almost exclusively with negatively

Table 7.19: Differential collocates for *bring about/lead to* compared to *cause* in the BNC

Collocate	Collocate with cause	Collocate with other	Other words with cause	Other words with other	G
conclusion	0	155	12 402	15 282	183.49
improvement	4	132	12 398	15 305	126.52
development	11	145	12 391	15 292	109.74
change	128	401	12 274	15 036	96.20
formation	9	111	12 393	15 326	81.82
award	0	64	12 402	15 373	75.60
creation	2	77	12 400	15 360	75.55
discovery	0	62	12 402	15 375	73.23
situation	1	60	12 401	15 377	62.27
understanding	0	52	12 402	15 385	61.40
decision	0	49	12 402	15 388	57.86
qualification	0	49	12 402	15 388	57.86
establishment	1	55	12 401	15 382	56.53
arrest	1	45	12 401	15 392	45.11
speculation	4	55	12 398	15 382	42.15
suggestion	0	34	12 402	15 403	40.13
result	14	82	12 388	15 355	39.71
introduction	0	33	12 402	15 404	38.95
increase	93	237	12 309	15 200	37.85
conviction	0	32	12 402	15 405	37.77

connoted nouns, *bring about* and *lead to* are much more varied. The differential collocate analysis then confirms that within the domain of causation, the verb *cause* specializes in encoding negative caused events, while the other two expressions encode neutral or positive events. Previous research (Louw & Chateau 2010) misses this difference as it is based exclusively on the qualitative inspection of concordances.

Thus, the case study shows, once again, the need for strict quantification and for research designs comparing the occurrence of a linguistic feature under different conditions. There is one caveat of the procedure presented here, however: while it is a very effective strategy to identify collocates first and categorize them according to their connotation afterwards, this categorization is then limited to an assessment of the lexically encoded meaning of the collocates. For example, *problem* and *damage* will be categorized as negative, but a problem does not have to be negative – it can be interesting if it is the right problem and you are in the right mood (e.g. *[O]ne of these excercises caused an interesting problem for several members of the class* [Aiden Thompson, *Who's afraid of the Old Testament God?*]). Even *damage* can be a good thing in particular contexts from particular perspectives (e.g. *[A] high yield of intact PTX [...] caused damage to cancer cells in addition to the immediate effects of PDT* [10.1021/acs.jmedchem.5b01971]). Even more likely, neutral words like *change* will have positive or negative connotations in particular contexts, which are lost in the proces of identifying collocates quantitatively.

Keeping this caveat in mind, however, the method presented in this case study can be applied fruitfully in more complex designs than the one presented here. For example, we have treated the direct object position as a simple category here, but Stefanowitsch & Gries (2003) present data for nominal collocates of the verb *cause* in the object position of different subcategorization patterns. While their results corroborate the negative connotation of *cause* also found by Stubbs (1995a), their results add an interesting dimension: while objects of *cause* in the transitive construction (*cause a problem*) and the prepositional dative (*cause a problem to someone*) refer to negatively perceived external and objective states, the objects of *cause* in the ditransitive refer to negatively experienced internal and/or subjective states. Studies on semantic prosody can also take into account dimensions beyond the immediate structural context – for example, Louw & Chateau (2010) observe that the semantic prosody of *cause* is to some extent specific to particular language varieties, and present interesting data suggesting that in scientific writing it is generally used with a neutral connotation.

7.2.4 Cultural analysis

In collocation research, a word (or other element of linguistic structure) typically stands for itself – the aim of the researcher is to uncover the linguistic properties of a word (or set of words). However, texts are not just manifestations of a language system, but also of the cultural conditions under which they were produced. This allows corpus linguistic methods to be used in uncovering at least some properties of that culture. Specifically, we can take lexical items to represent culturally defined concepts and investigate their distribution in linguistic corpora in order to uncover these cultural definitions. Of course, this adds complexity to the question of operationalization: we must ensure that the words we choose are indeed valid representatives of the cultural concept in question.

7.2.4.1 Case study: Small boys, little girls

Obviously, lexical items used conventionally to refer to some culturally relevant group of people are plausible representatives of the cultural concept of that group. For example, some very general lexical items referring to people (or higher animals) exist in male and female versions – *man/woman, boy/girl, lad/lass, husband/wife, father/mother, king/queen*, etc. If such word pairs differ in their collocates, this could tell us something about the cultural concepts behind them. For example, Stubbs (1995b) cites a finding by Baker & Freebody (1989), that in children's literature, the word *girl* collocates with *little* much more strongly than the word *boy*, and vice versa for *small*. Stubbs shows that this is also true for balanced corpora (see Table 7.20; again, since Stubbs' corpora are not available, I show frequencies from the BNC instead but the proportions are within a few percent points of his). The difference in associations is highly significant ($\chi^2 = 217.66, \text{df} = 1, p < 0.001$).

Table 7.20: *Small* and *little girls* and *boys* (BNC)

		Second Position		
		BOY	GIRL	Total
First Position	LITTLE	791 (927.53)	1148 (1011.47)	1939
	SMALL	336 (199.47)	81 (217.53)	417
	Total	1127	1229	2356

This part of Stubbs' study is clearly deductive: He starts with a hypothesis taken from the literature and tests it against a larger, more representative corpus. The variables involved are, as is typical for collocation studies, nominal variables whose values are words.

Stubbs argues that this difference is due to different connotations of *small* and *little* which he investigates on the basis of the noun collocates to their right and the adjectival and adverbial collocates to the left. Again, instead of Stubbs' original data (which he identifies on the basis of raw frequency of occurrence and only cites selectively), I use data from the BNC and the *G* test statistic. Table 7.21 shows the ten most strongly associated noun collocates to the right of the node word and Table 7.22 shows the ten most strongly associated adjectival collocates to the left.

Table 7.21: Nominal collocates of *little* and *small* at R1 (BNC)

COLLOCATE	Collocate with LITTLE	Collocate with SMALL	Other words with LITTLE	Other words with SMALL	*G*
Most strongly associated with *little*					
bit	2838	30	33 606	31 214	3331.01
girl	1148	70	35 296	31 174	1008.61
doubt	546	3	35 898	31 241	647.25
time	595	23	35 849	31 221	579.93
while	435	0	36 009	31 244	541.06
evidence	324	0	36 120	31 244	402.53
attention	253	1	36 191	31 243	302.56
chance	273	21	36 171	31 223	220.00
money	194	4	36 250	31 240	207.73
interest	213	12	36 231	31 232	189.11
Most strongly associated with *small*					
number	23	1118	36 421	30 126	1553.13
group	123	1089	36 321	30 155	1057.19
amount	7	670	36 437	30 574	974.34
business	36	784	36 408	30 460	971.22
firm	15	456	36 429	30 788	594.11
proportion	0	332	36 444	30 912	515.24
scale	1	265	36 443	30 979	399.02
company	15	316	36 429	30 928	386.62
area	15	302	36 429	30 942	366.16
mammal	0	203	36 444	31 041	314.58

Table 7.22: Adjectival collocates of *little* and *small* at L1 (BNC)

COLLOCATE	Collocate with LITTLE	Collocate with SMALL	Other words with LITTLE	Other words with SMALL	*G*
Most strongly associated with *little*					
nice	356	4	4719	1083	112.25
poor	248	0	4827	1087	98.46
pretty	119	0	4956	1087	46.69
tiny	95	0	4980	1087	37.19
nasty	60	0	5015	1087	23.42
funny	67	1	5008	1086	19.19
dear	47	0	5028	1087	18.32
sweet	42	0	5033	1087	16.36
silly	59	1	5016	1086	16.30
lovely	92	5	4983	1082	13.84
Most strongly associated with *small*					
other	59	141	5016	946	282.80
only	36	119	5039	968	268.74
proximal	0	28	5075	1059	97.76
numerous	4	30	5071	1057	81.67
far	3	19	5072	1068	49.83
wee	2	15	5073	1072	40.67
existing	0	11	5075	1076	38.26
various	6	18	5069	1069	38.01
occasional	1	12	5074	1075	35.08
new	25	28	5050	1059	33.95

This part of the study is more inductive. Stubbs may have expectations about what he will find, but he essentially identifies collocates exploratively and then interprets the findings. The nominal collocates show, according to Stubbs, that *small* tends to mean 'small in physical size' or 'low in quantity', while *little* is more clearly restricted to quantities, including informal quantifying phrases like *little bit*. This is generally true for the BNC data, too (note, however, the one exception among the top ten collocates – *girl*).

The connotational difference between the two adjectives becomes clear when we look at the adjectives they combine with. The word *little* has strong associations to evaluative adjectives that may be positive or negative, and that are often patronizing. *Small*, in contrast, does not collocate with evaluative adjectives.

Stubbs sums up his analysis by pointing out that *small* is a neutral word for describing size, while *little* is sometimes used neutrally, but is more often "non-literal and convey[s] connotative and attitudinal meanings, which are often patronizing, critical, or both." (Stubbs 1995b: 386). The differences in distribution relative to the words *boy* and *girl* are evidence for him that "[c]ulture is encoded not just in words which are obviously ideologically loaded, but also in combinations of very common words" (Stubbs 1995b: 387).

Stubbs remains unspecific as to what that ideology is – presumably, one that treats boys as neutral human beings and girls as targets for patronizing evaluation. In order to be more specific, it would be necessary to turn around the perspective and study all adjectival collocates of *boy* and *girl*. Stubbs does not do this, but Caldas-Coulthard & Moon (2010) look at adjectives collocating with *man*, *woman*, *boy* and *girl* in broadsheet and yellow-press newspapers. In order to keep the results comparable with those reported above, let us stick with the BNC instead. Table 7.23 shows the top ten adjectival collocates of *boy* and *girl*.

The results are broadly similar in kind to those in Caldas-Coulthard & Moon (2010): *boy* collocates mainly with neutral descriptive terms (*small*, *lost*, *big*, *new*), or with terms with which it forms a fixed expression (*old*, *dear*, *toy*, *whipping*). There are the evaluative adjectives *rude* (which in Caldas-Coulthard and Moon's data is often applied to young men of Jamaican descent) and its positively connoted equivalent *naughty*. The collocates of *girl* are overwhelmingly evaluative, related to physical appearance. There are just two neutral adjective (*other* and *dead*, the latter tying in with a general observation that women are more often spoken of as victims of crimes and other activities than men). Finally, there is one adjective signaling marital status. These results also generally reflect Caldas-Coulthard and Moon's findings (in the yellow-press, the evaluations are often heavily sexualized in addition).

Table 7.23: Adjectival collocates of *boy* and *girl* at L1 (BNC)

Collocate	Collocate with boy	Collocate with girl	Other words with boy	Other words with girl	*G*
Most strongly associated with *boy*					
old	634	257	5385	7296	279.98
small	336	81	5683	7472	237.78
dear	126	45	5893	7508	61.30
lost	41	1	5978	7552	58.54
big	167	89	5852	7464	46.02
naughty	71	22	5948	7531	39.75
new	124	69	5895	7484	31.31
rude	19	0	6000	7553	30.93
toy	16	0	6003	7553	26.04
whipping	14	0	6005	7553	22.78
Most strongly associated with *girl*					
young	351	820	5668	6733	111.04
pretty	23	132	5996	7421	62.59
other	194	444	5825	7109	54.56
beautiful	13	87	6006	7466	46.13
attractive	1	35	6018	7518	33.58
blonde	1	29	6018	7524	26.89
single	1	27	6018	7526	24.68
dead	12	57	6007	7496	22.67
unmarried	0	17	6019	7536	19.94
lovely	18	66	6001	7487	19.45

This case study shows how collocation research may uncover facts that go well beyond lexical semantics or semantic prosody. In this case, the collocates of *boy* and *girl* have uncovered a general attitude that sees the latter as up for constant evaluation while the former are mainly seen as a neutral default. That the adjectives *dead* and *unmarried* are among the top ten collocates in a representative, relatively balanced corpus, hints at something darker – a patriarchal world view that sees girls as victims and sexual partners and not much else (other studies investigating gender stereotypes on the basis of collocates of *man* and *woman* are Gesuato (2003) and Pearce (2008)).

8 Grammar

The fact that corpora are most easily accessed via words (or word forms) is also reflected in many corpus studies focusing on various aspects of grammatical structure. Many such studies either take (sets of) words as a starting point for studying various aspects of grammatical structure, or they take easily identifiable aspects of grammatical structure as a starting point for studying the distribution of words. However, as the case studies of the English possessive constructions in Chapters 5 and 6 showed, grammatical structures can be (and are) also studied in their own right, for example with respect to semantic, information-structural and other restrictions they place on particular slots or sequences of slots, or with their distribution across texts, language varieties, demographic groups or varieties.

8.1 Grammar in corpora

There are two major problems to be solved when searching corpora for grammatical structures. We discussed both of them to some extent in Chapter 4, but let us briefly recapitulate and elaborate some aspects of the discussion before turning to the case studies.

First, we must operationally define the structure itself in such a way that we (and other researchers) can reliably categorize potential instances as manifesting the structure or not. This may be relatively straightforward in the case of simple grammatical structures that can be characterized based on tangible and stable characteristics, such as particular configurations of grammatical morphemes and/or categories occurring in sequences that reflect hierarchical relations relatively directly. It becomes difficult, if not impossible, with complex structures, especially in frameworks that characterize such structures with recourse to abstract, non-tangible and theory-dependent constructs (see Sampson 1995 for an attempt at a comprehensive annotation scheme for the grammar of English).

Second, we must define a query that will allow us to retrieve potential candidates from our corpus in the first place (a problem we discussed in some detail in Chapter 4). Again, this is simpler in the case of morphologically marked and relatively simple grammatical structures, for example, the *s*-possessive (as defined above) is typically characterized by the sequence ⟨ `[pos="noun"] [word="'s"%c] [pos="adjective"]* [pos="noun"]` ⟩ in corpora containing texts in standard orthography; it can thus be retrieved from a POS-tagged corpus with a fairly high degree of precision and recall. However, even this simple case is more complex than it seems. The query will produce false hits: in the sequence just given, *'s* may also stand for the verb *be* (*Sam's head of marketing*). The query will also produce false misses: the modified nominal may not always be directly adjacent to the *'s* (for example in *This office is Sam's* or in *Sam's friends and family*), and the *s*-possessive may be represented by an apostrophe alone (for example in *his friends' families*).

Other structures may be difficult to retrieve even though they can be characterized straightforwardly: most linguists would agree, for example, that transitive verbs, are verbs that take a direct object. However, this is of very little help in retrieving transitive verbs even from a POS-tagged corpus, since many noun-phrases following a verb will not be direct objects (*Sam slept the whole day*) and direct objects do not necessarily follow their verb (*Sam, I have not seen*); in addition, noun phrases themselves are not trivial to retrieve.

Yet other structures may be easy to retrieve, but not without retrieving many false hits at the same time. This is the case with ambiguous structures like the *of*-possessive, which can be retrieved by a query along the lines of ⟨ `[pos="noun"] [pos="determiner"]? [pos="adjective"]* [pos="noun"]` ⟩, which will also retrieve, among other things, partitive and quantitative uses of the *of*-construction.

Finally, structures characterized with reference to invisible theoretical constructs ("traces", "zero morphemes", etc.) are so difficult to retrieve that this, in itself, may be a good reason to avoid such invisible constructs whenever possible when characterizing linguistic phenomena that we plan to investigate empirically.

These difficulties do not keep corpus linguists from investigating grammatical structures, including very abstract ones, even though this typically means retrieving the relevant data by mind-numbing and time-consuming manual analysis of the results of very broad searches or even of the corpus itself, if necessary. But they are probably one reason why so much grammatical research in corpus linguistics takes a word-centered approach.

A second reason for a word-centered approach is that it allows us to transfer well-established collocational methods to the study of grammar. In the preceding chapter we saw that while collocation research often takes a sequential approach to co-occurrence, where any word within a given span around a node word is counted as a potential collocate, it is not uncommon to see a structure-sensitive approach that considers only those potential collocates that occur in a particular grammatical position relative to each other – for example, adjectives relative to the nouns they modify or vice versa. In this approach, grammatical structure is already present in the design, even though it remains in the background. We can move these types of grammatical structure into the focus of our investigation, giving us a range of research designs where one variable consists of (part of) the lexicon (with values that are individual words) and one variable consists of some aspect of grammatical structure. In these studies, the retrieval becomes somewhat less of a problem, as we can search for lexical items and identify the grammatical structures in our search results afterwards, though identifying these structures reliably remains non-trivial. We will begin with word-centered case studies and then move towards more genuinely grammatical research designs.

8.2 Case studies

8.2.1 Collocational frameworks and grammar patterns

An early extension of collocation research to the association between words and grammatical structure is Renouf & Sinclair (1991). The authors introduce a novel construct, the *collocational framework*, which they define as "a discontinuous sequence of two words, positioned at one word remove from each other", where the two words in question are always function words – examples are [*a* __ *of*], [*an* __ *of*], [*too* __ *to*] or [*many* __ *of*] (note that *a* and *an* are treated as constituents of different collocational frameworks, indicating a radically word-form-oriented approach to grammar). Renouf and Sinclair are particularly interested in classes of items that fill the position in the middle of collocational frameworks and they see the fact that these items tend to form semantically coherent classes as evidence that collocational frameworks are relevant items of linguistic structure.

The idea behind collocational frameworks was subsequently extended by Hunston & Francis (2000) to more canonical linguistic structures, ranging from very general valency patterns (such as [V NP] or [V NP NP]) to very specific structures like [*there* + Linking Verb + *something* Adjective + *about* NP] (as in *There was something masculine about the dark wood dining room* (Hunston & Francis 2000: 51, 53, 106)). Their essential insight is similar to Renouf and Sinclair's: that such structures (which they call "grammar patterns") are meaningful and that their meaning manifests itself in the collocates of their central slots:

> The patterns of a word can be defined as all the words and structures which are regularly associated with the word and which contribute to its meaning. A pattern can be identified if a combination of words occurs relatively

> frequently, if it is dependent on a particular word choice, and if there is a clear meaning associated with it (Hunston & Francis 2000: 37).

Collocational frameworks and especially grammar patterns have an immediate applied relevance: the COBUILD dictionaries included the most frequently found patterns for each word in their entries from 1995 onward, and there is a two-volume descriptive grammar of the patterns of verbs (Francis et al. 1996) and nouns and adjectives (Francis et al. 1998); there were also attempts to identify grammar patterns automatically (cf. Mason & Hunston 2004). Research on collocational frameworks and grammar patterns is mainly descriptive and takes place in applied contexts, but Hunston & Francis (2000) argue very explicitly for a usage-based theory of grammar on the basis of their descriptions (note that the definition quoted above is strongly reminiscent of the way constructions were later defined in construction grammar (Goldberg 1995: 4), a point I will return to in the Epilogue of this book).

8.2.1.1 Case study: [*a* __ *of*]

As an example of a collocational framework, consider [*a* __ *of*], one of the patterns that Renouf & Sinclair (1991) use to introduce their construct. Renouf and Sinclair use an early version of the *Birmingham Collection of English Text*, which is no longer accessible. To enable us to look at the methodological issues raised by collocational frameworks more closely, I have therefore replicated their study using the BNC. As far as one can tell from the data presented in Renouf & Sinclair (1991), they simply extracted all words occurring in the framework, without paying attention to part-of-speech tagging, so I did the same; it is unclear whether their query was case-sensitive (I used a case insensitive query for the BNC data).

Table 8.1 shows the data from Renouf & Sinclair (1991) and from the BNC. As you can see, the results are roughly comparable, but differ noticeably in some details – two different corpora will never give you quite the same result even with general patterns like the one under investigation.

Renouf and Sinclair first present the twenty items occurring most frequently in the collocational framework, shown in the columns labeled (a). These are, roughly speaking, the words most typical for the collocational framework: when we encounter the framework (in a corpus or in real life), these are the words that are most probable to fill the slot between *a* and *of*. Renouf and Sinclair then point out that the frequency of these items in the collocational framework does not correspond to their frequency in the corpus as a whole, where, for example, *man* is the most frequent of their twenty words, and *lot* is only the ninth-most frequent. The "promotion of *lot* to the top of the list" in the framework [*a* __ *of*],

Table 8.1: The collocational framework [*a* __ *of*] in two corpora

Birmingham Collection of English Text				British National Corpus			
(a)		(b)		(a)		(b)	
Collocate	Frequency	Collocate	Percent	Collocate	Frequency	Collocate	Percent
lot	1322	*couple*	62	*number*	13 766	*couple*	55.72
kind	864	*series*	57	*lot*	13 649	*lot*	48.81
number	762	*pair*	54	*couple*	6620	*variety*	47.54
couple	685	*lot*	53	*series*	5655	*series*	39.76
matter	550	*piece*	36	*result*	5596	*pair*	36.63
sort	451	*quarter*	36	*bit*	4879	*number*	28.21
series	438	*variety*	35	*matter*	4561	*piece*	26.96
piece	414	*member*	34	*variety*	4113	*result*	25.54
bit	379	*number*	30	*member*	3650	*member*	21.00
sense	356	*kind*	21	*range*	3193	*matter*	20.97
pair	320	*sort*	21	*group*	3081	*bit*	18.43
member	302	*matter*	20	*kind*	2522	*range*	15.76
group	293	*result*	20	*piece*	2430	*list*	14.22
result	268	*bit*	19	*sense*	2398	*sense*	11.23
part	222	*bottle*	17	*period*	2350	*kind*	10.71
variety	216	*sense*	13	*set*	2253	*period*	9.75
state	205	*group*	11	*sort*	2243	*sort*	8.33
bottle	175	*state*	7	*pair*	2170	*group*	7.49
man	174	*part*	5	*way*	1942	*set*	5.10
quarter	174	*man*	2	*list*	1770	*way*	2.03

they argue, shows that it is its "tightest collocation". As discussed in Chapter 7, association measures are the best way to asses the difference in frequency of an item under a specific condition (here, the presence of the collocational framework) from its general frequency and I will present the strongest collocates as determined by the *G* statistic below.

Renouf and Sinclair choose a different strategy: for each item, they calculate the percentage of all occurrences of that item within the collocational framework. The results are shown in the columns labeled (b) (for example, *number* occurrs in the BNC a total of 48 806 times, so the 13 799 times that it occurs in the pattern [*a* __ *of*] account for 28.21 percent of its occurrences). As you can see, the order changes slightly, but the basic result appears to remain the same. Broadly speaking, the most strongly associated words in both corpora and by either measure tend to be related to quantities (e.g. *lot, number, couple*), part-whole relations (e.g. *piece, member, group, part*), or types (e.g. *sort* or *variety*). This kind of semantic coherence is presented by Renouf and Sinclair as evidence that collocational frameworks are relevant units of language.

Keeping this in mind, let us discuss the difference between frequency and percentages in some more detail. Note, first, that the reason the results do not change perceptibly is because Renouf and Sinclair do not determine the percentage of occurrences of words inside [*a* __ *of*] for all words in the framework, but only for the twenty nouns that they have already identified as most frequent – the columns labeled (b) thus represent a ranking based on a mixed strategy of preselecting words by their raw frequency and then ranking them by their proportions inside and outside the framework.

If we were to omit the pre-selection stage and calculate the percentages for *all* words occurring in the framework – as we should, if these percentages are relevant – we would find 477 words in the BNC that occur exclusively in the framework, and thus all have an association strength of 100 percent – among them words that fit the proposed semantic preferences of the pattern, like *barrelful*, words that do not fit, like *bomb-burst, hyserisation* or *Jesuitism*, and many misspellings, like *fct* (for *fact*) and *numbe* and *numbr* (for *number*). The problem here is that percentages, like some other association measures, massively overestimate the importance of rare events. In order to increase the quality of the results, let us remove all words that occur five times or less in the BNC. The twenty words in Table 8.2 are then the words with the highest percentages of occurrence in the framework [*a* __ *of*].

Table 8.2: The collocational framework [*a* __ *of*] in the BNC by percentage of occurrences

Collocate	*n*(Framework)	*n*(Corpus)	Percent
headful	6	6	1.00
roomful	19	22	0.86
modicum	63	73	0.86
pocketful	11	13	0.85
fistful	52	64	0.81
founder-member	19	24	0.79
figment	48	62	0.77
gaggle	37	49	0.76
foretaste	48	64	0.75
smattering	44	60	0.73
houseful	10	14	0.71
handful	964	1350	0.71
lorryload	4	6	0.67
truckload	6	9	0.67
lorry-load	8	12	0.67

Supplementary Online Material: QXVR

This list is obviously completely different from the one in Renouf & Sinclair (1991) or our replication. We would not want to call them typical for [*a* __ *of*], in the sense that it is not very probable that we will encounter them in this collocational framework. However, note that they generally represent the same categories as the words in Table 8.1, namely 'quantity' and 'part-whole', indicating a relevant relation to the framework. This relation is, in fact, the counterpart to the one shown in Table 8.1: These are words for which the framework [*a* __ *of*] is typical, in the sense that if we encounter these words, it is very probable that they will be accompanied by this collocational framework.

There are words that are typical for a particular framework, and there are frameworks that are typical for particular words; this difference in perspective may be of interest in particular research designs (cf. Stefanowitsch & Flach 2016 for further discussion). Generally, however, it is best to use an established association measure that will not overestimate rare events. Table 8.3 shows the fifteen most strongly associated words in the framework based on the *G* statistic.

Table 8.3: Top collocates of the collocational framework [*a* __ *of*] (BNC)

Collocate	Collocate in Framework	Collocate outside Framework	Other words in Framework	Other words outside Framework	*G*
lot	14 632	13 329	245 429	98 090 393	135 898.96
number	15 136	32 326	244 925	98 071 396	121 310.72
couple	7042	4694	253 019	98 099 028	68 015.25
series	5985	8237	254 076	98 095 485	51 871.35
result	5610	16 300	254 451	98 087 422	41 874.06
variety	4284	4368	255 777	98 099 354	38 955.58
bit	5026	21 444	255 035	98 082 278	34 141.56
matter	4600	17 145	255 461	98 086 577	32 336.96
member	3950	13 435	256 111	98 090 287	28 388.20
range	3359	16 417	256 702	98 087 305	21 982.09
pair	2331	3593	257 730	98 100 129	19 769.62
piece	2535	6477	257 526	98 097 245	19 442.43
group	3540	37 611	256 521	98 066 111	18 133.73
kind	2599	20 950	257 462	98 082 772	14 632.46
sense	2503	18 846	257 558	98 084 876	14 405.32

Supplementary Online Material: QXVR

This case study has introduced the notion of collocational frameworks as a simple way of studying the relationship between words and their grammatical context and the potential functional nature of this relationship. It is also meant as a reminder that different corpora and especially different measures of collocation strength will yield different results.

8.2.1.2 Case study: [*there* V_{link} *something* ADJ *about* NP]

As an example of a grammar pattern, consider [*there* V_{link} *something* ADJ *about* NP] (Hunston & Francis 2000: 105–106). As is typical of grammar patterns, this pattern constitutes a canonical unit of grammatical structure – unlike Renouf and Sinclair's collocational frameworks.

Hunston and Francis mention this pattern only in passing, noting that it "has the function of evaluating the person or thing indicated in the noun group following *about*". Their usual procedure (which they skip in this case) is to back up such observations concerning the meaning of grammar patterns by listing the most frequent items occurring in this pattern and showing that these form one or more semantic classes (similar to the procedure used by Renouf and Sinclair). In (1), I list all words occurring in the British National Corpus more than twice in the pattern under investigation, with their frequency in parentheses:

(1) *odd* (21), *special* (20), *different* (18), *familiar* (16), *strange* (13), *sinister* (8), *disturbing* (5), *funny* (5), *wrong* (5), *absurd* (4), *appealing* (4), *attractive* (4), *fishy* (4), *paradoxical* (4), *sad* (4), *unusual* (4), *impressive* (3), *shocking* (3), *spooky* (3), *touching* (3), *unique* (3), *unsatisfactory* (3)

The list clearly supports Hunston and Francis's claim about the meaning of this grammar pattern – most of the adjectives are inherently evaluative. There are a few exceptions – *different, special, unusual* and *unique* do not have to be used evaluatively. If they occur in the pattern [*there* V_{link} *something* ADJ *about* NP], however, they are likely to be interpreted evaluatively.

As Hunston & Francis (2000: 105) point out: "Even when potentially neutral words such as nationality words, or words such as *masculine* and *feminine*, are used in this pattern, they take on an evaluative meaning". This is, in fact, a crucial feature of grammar patterns, as it demonstrates that these patterns themselves are meaningful and are able to impart their meaning on words occurring in them. The following examples demonstrate this:

(2) a. There is something horribly cyclical about television advertising. (BNC CBC)

b. It is a big, square box, painted dirty white, and, although he is always knocking through, extending, repapering and spring-cleaning, there is something dead about the place. (BNC HR9)

c. At least it didn't sound now quite like a typewriter, but there was something metallic about it. (BNC J54)

The adjective *cyclical* is neutral, but the adverb *horribly* shows that it is meant evaluatively in (2a); *dead* in its literal sense is purely descriptive, but when applied to things (like a house in 2b), it becomes an evaluation; finally, *metallic* is also neutral, but it is used to evaluate a sound negatively in (2c), as shown by the phrasing *at least ... but.*

Instead of listing frequencies, of course, we could calculate the association strength between the pattern [*there* $\mathrm{V_{link}}$ *something* ADJ *about* NP] and the adjectives occurring in it. I will discuss in more detail how this is done in the next subsection; for now, suffice it to say that it would give us the ranking in Table 8.4.

Table 8.4: Most strongly associated adjectives in the pattern [*there* $\mathrm{V_{link}}$ *something* ADJ *about* NP]

Collocate	Frequency in the pattern	Frequency outside the pattern	Other words in the pattern	Other words outside the pattern	*G*
odd	21	4277	317	7 854 379	158.56
familiar	16	5503	322	7 853 153	104.01
special	20	21 725	318	7 836 931	85.50
strange	13	6026	325	7 852 630	76.77
sinister	8	661	330	7 857 995	74.39
different	18	47 503	320	7 811 153	47.18
fishy	4	104	334	7 858 552	46.27
paradoxical	4	258	334	7 858 398	39.11
disturbing	5	1037	333	7 857 619	37.33
spooky	3	128	335	7 858 528	31.77
absurd	4	922	334	7 857 734	29.02
appealing	4	976	334	7 857 680	28.57
funny	5	4301	333	7 854 355	23.40
shocking	3	541	335	7 858 115	23.21
touching	3	613	335	7 858 043	22.47
creepy	2	63	336	7 858 593	22.37
unsatisfactory	3	757	335	7 857 899	21.22
shifty	2	97	336	7 858 559	20.67
uncatlike	1	0	337	7 858 656	20.11

Supplementary Online Material: K7BC

The ranking does not differ radically from the ranking by frequency in (2) above, but note that the descriptive adjectives *special* and *different* are moved down the list a few ranks and *unique* and *unusual* disappear from the top twenty, sharpening the semantic profile of the pattern.

This case study is meant to introduce the notion of grammar patterns and to show that these patterns often have a relatively stable meaning that can be uncovered by looking at the words that are frequent in (or strongly associated with) them. Like the preceding case study, it also introduced the idea that the relationship between words and units of grammatical structure can be investigated using the logic of association measures. The next sections look at this in more detail.

8.2.2 Collostructional analysis

Under the definition of corpus linguistics used throughout this book, there should be nothing surprising about the idea of investigating the relationship between words and units of grammatical structure based on association measures: a grammatical structure is just another condition under which we can observe the occurrence of lexical items. This is the basic idea of *collostructional analysis*, a methodological perspective first proposed in Stefanowitsch & Gries (2003), who refer to words that are associated with a particular construction a *collexeme* of that construction. Their perspective builds on ideas in collocation analysis, colligation analysis (cf. Section 8.2.4 below) and pattern grammar, but is more rigorously quantitative, and conceptually grounded in construction grammar. It has been applied in all areas of grammar, with a focus on argument structure (see Stefanowitsch & Gries (2009) and Stefanowitsch (2013) for overviews). Like collocation analysis, it is generally inductive, but it can also be used to test certain general hypotheses about the meaning of grammatical constructions.

8.2.2.1 Case study: The ditransitive

Stefanowitsch & Gries (2003) investigate, among other things, which verbs are strongly associated with the ditransitive construction (or ditransitive subcategorization, if you don't like constructions). This is a very direct application of the basic research design for collocates introduced in the preceding chapter.

Their design is broadly deductive, as their hypothesis is that constructions have meaning and specifically, that the ditransitive has a 'transfer' meaning. The design has two nominal variables: ARGUMENT STRUCTURE (with the values DITRANSITIVE and OTHER) and VERB (with values corresponding to all verbs occurring in the construction). The prediction is that the most strongly associated verbs will be verbs of literal or metaphorical transfer. Table 8.5 gives the information needed to calculate the association strength for *give* (although the procedure should be familiar by now), and Table 8.6 shows the ten most strongly associated verbs.[1]

[1]Unlike in the rest of the book, I have to use data from a corpus that is not generally accessible – the British Component of the International Corpus of English. The reason is that analyses like the ones presented here require a treebank (see Section 2.1.4 in Chapter 4), and there is no sufficiently large and generally accessible treebank.

Table 8.5: *Give* and the ditransitive (ICE-GB)

		Argument Structure		
		ditransitive	¬ditransitive	Total
Verb	give	461 (8.63)	574 (1026.37)	1035
	¬give	687 (1139.37)	135 907 (135 454.63)	136 594
	Total	1148	136 481	137 629

Table 8.6: The verbs in the ditransitive construction (ICE-GB, Stefanowitsch & Gries (2003: 229))

Collexeme	Collexeme with Ditransitive	Collexeme with other ASCs	Other verbs with Ditransitive	Other verbs with other ASCs	p_{exact}
give	461	687	574	136 942	0
tell	128	660	907	136 969	1.60×10^{-127}
send	64	280	971	137 349	7.26×10^{-68}
offer	43	152	992	137 477	3.31×10^{-49}
show	49	578	986	137 051	2.23×10^{-33}
cost	20	82	1015	137 547	1.12×10^{-22}
teach	15	76	1020	137 553	4.32×10^{-16}
award	7	9	1028	137 620	1.36×10^{-11}
allow	18	313	1017	137 316	1.12×10^{-10}
lend	7	24	1028	137 605	2.85×10^{-9}

The hypothesis is corroborated: the top ten collexemes (and most of the other significant collexemes not shown here) refer to literal or metaphorical transfer.

However, note that on the basis of lists like that in Table 8.8 we cannot reject a null hypothesis along the lines of "There is no relationship between the ditransitive and the encoding of transfer events", since we did not test this. All we can say is that we can reject null hypotheses stating that there is no relationship between the ditransitive and each individual verb on the list. In practice, this may amount to the same thing, but if we wanted to reject the more general null hypothesis, we would have to code all verbs in the corpus according to whether they are transfer verbs or not, and then show that transfer verbs are significantly more frequent in the ditransitive construction than in the corpus as a whole.

8.2.2.2 Case study: Ditransitive and prepositional dative

Collostructional analysis can also be applied in the direct comparison of two grammatical constructions (or other grammatical features), analogous to the *differential collocate* design discussed in Chapter 7. For example, Gries & Stefanowitsch (2004) compare verbs in the ditransitive and the so-called *to*-dative – both constructions express transfer meanings, but it has been claimed that the ditransitive encodes a spatially and temporally more direct transfer than the *to*-dative (Thompson & Koide 1987). If this is the case, it should be reflected in the verbs most strongly associated to one or the other construction in a direct comparison. Table 8.7 shows the data needed to determine for the verb *give* which of the two constructions it is more strongly attracted to.

Table 8.7: *Give* in the ditransitive and the prepositional dative (ICE-GB)

		Argument Structure		
		ditransitive	¬ditransitive	Total
Verb	give	461 (212.68)	574 (822.32)	1035
	¬give	146 (394.32)	1773 (1524.68)	1919
	Total	607	2347	2954

Give is significantly more frequent than expected in the ditransitive and less frequent than expected in the *to*-dative ($p_{\text{exact}} = 1.8 \times 10^{-120}$). It is therefore said to be a *significant distinctive collexeme* of the ditransitive (again, I will use the term *differential* instead of *distinctive* in the following). Table 8.8 shows the top ten differential collexemes for each construction.

Generally speaking, the list for the ditransitive is very similar to the one we get if we calculate the simple collexemes of the construction; crucially, many of the differential collexemes of the *to*-dative highlight the spatial distance covered by the transfer, which is in line with what the hypothesis predicts.

8.2.2.3 Case study: Negative evidence

Recall from the introductory chapter that one of the arguments routinely made against corpus linguistics is that corpora do not contain negative evidence. Even

Table 8.8: Verbs in the ditransitive and the prepositional dative (ICE-GB, Gries & Stefanowitsch 2004: 106).

Collexeme	Collexeme with Ditransitive	Collexeme with *to*-Dative	Other verbs with Ditransitive	Other verbs with *to*-Dative	p_{exact}
most strongly associated with the ditransitive					
give	461	146	574	1773	1.84×10^{-120}
tell	128	2	907	1917	8.77×10^{-58}
show	49	15	986	1904	8.32×10^{-12}
offer	43	15	992	1904	9.95×10^{-10}
cost	20	1	1015	1918	9.71×10^{-9}
teach	15	1	1020	1918	1.49×10^{-6}
wish	9	1	1026	1918	0.00
ask	12	4	1023	1915	0.00
promise	7	1	1028	1918	0.00
deny	8	3	1027	1916	0.01
most strongly associated with the *to*-dative					
bring	7	82	1028	1837	1.47×10^{-9}
play	1	37	1034	1882	1.46×10^{-6}
take	12	63	1023	1856	0.00
pass	2	29	1033	1890	0.00
make	3	23	1032	1896	0.01
sell	1	14	1034	1905	0.01
do	10	40	1025	1879	0.02
supply	1	12	1034	1907	0.03
read	1	10	1034	1909	0.06
hand	5	21	1030	1898	0.06

corpus linguists occasionally agree with this claim. For example, McEnery & Wilson (2001: 11), in their otherwise excellent introduction to corpus-linguistic thinking, cite the sentence in (3):

(3) * He shines Tony books.

They point out that this sentence will not occur in any given finite corpus, but that this does not allow us to declare it ungrammatical, since it could simply be one of infinitely many sentences that "simply haven't occurred yet". They then offer the same solution Chomsky has repeatedly offered:

> It is only by asking a native or expert speaker of a language for their opinion of the grammaticality of a sentence that we can hope to differentiate unseen but grammatical constructions from those which are simply grammatical but unseen (McEnery & Wilson 2001: 12).

However, as Stefanowitsch (2008; 2006b) points out, zero is just a number, no different in quality from 1, or 461 or any other frequency of occurrence. This means that any statistical test that can be applied to combinations of verbs and grammatical constructions (or any other elements of linguistic structure) that *do* occur together can also be applied to combinations that do *not* occur together. Table 8.9 shows this for the verb *say* and the ditransitive construction in the ICE-GB.

Table 8.9: The non-occurrence of *say* in the ditransitive (ICE-GB)

		Argument Structure		
		ditransitive	¬ditransitive	Total
Verb	say	0 (44.52)	3333 (3288.48)	3333
	¬say	1824 (1779.48)	131 394 (131 438.52)	133 218
	Total	1824	134 727	136 551

Fisher's exact test shows that the observed frequency of zero differs significantly from that expected by chance ($p = 4.3 \times 10^{-165}$) (so does a χ^2 test: $\chi^2 = 46.25, \mathrm{df} = 1, p < 0.001$). In other words, it is very unlikely that sentences like *Alex said Joe the answer* "simply haven't occurred yet" in the corpus. Instead, we can be fairly certain that *say* cannot be used with ditransitive complementation in English. Of course, the corpus data do not tell us *why* this is so, but neither would an acceptability judgment from a native speaker.

Table 8.10 shows the twenty verbs whose non-occurrence in the ditransitive is statistically most significant in the ICE-GB (see Stefanowitsch 2006b: 67). Since the frequency of co-occurrence is always zero and the frequency of other words in the construction is therefore constant, the order of association strength corresponds to the order of the corpus frequency of the words. The point of statistical testing in this case is to determine whether the absence of a particular word is significant or not.

Note that since zero is no different from any other frequency of occurrence, this procedure does not tell us anything about the difference between an intersection of variables that did not occur at all and an intersection that occurred with any other frequency less than the expected one. All the method tells us is whether an occurrence of zero is significantly less than expected.

Table 8.10: Non-occurring verbs in the ditransitive (ICE-GB)

Collexeme	Collexeme with Ditransitive	Collexeme with *to*-Dative	Other verbs with Ditransitive	Other verbs with *to*-Dative	p_{exact}
be	0	25 416	1824	109 311	4.29×10^{-165}
be/have	0	6261	1824	128 466	3.66×10^{-38}
have	0	4303	1824	130 424	2.90×10^{-26}
think	0	3335	1824	131 392	1.90×10^{-20}
say	0	3333	1824	131 394	1.96×10^{-20}
know	0	2120	1824	132 607	3.32×10^{-13}
see	0	1971	1824	132 756	2.54×10^{-12}
go	0	1900	1824	132 827	6.69×10^{-12}
want	0	1256	1824	133 471	4.27×10^{-8}
use	0	1222	1824	133 505	6.77×10^{-8}
come	0	1140	1824	133 587	2.06×10^{-7}
look	0	1099	1824	133 628	3.59×10^{-7}
try	0	749	1824	133 978	4.11×10^{-5}
mean	0	669	1824	134 058	1.21×10^{-4}
work	0	646	1824	134 081	1.65×10^{-4}
like	0	600	1824	134 127	3.08×10^{-4}
feel	0	593	1824	134 134	3.38×10^{-4}
become	0	577	1824	134 150	4.20×10^{-4}
happen	0	523	1824	134 204	8.70×10^{-4}
put	0	513	1824	134 214	9.96×10^{-4}

In other words, the method makes no distinction between zero occurrence and other less-frequent-than-expected occurrences. However, Stefanowitsch (2006b: 70f) argues that this is actually an advantage: if we were to treat an occurrence of zero as special opposed to, say, an occurrence of 1, then a single counterexample to an intersection of variables hypothesized to be impossible will appear to disprove our hypothesis. The knowledge that a particular intersection is significantly less frequent than expected, in contrast, remains relevant even when faced with apparent counterexamples. And, as anyone who has ever elicited acceptability judgments – from someone else or introspectively from themselves – knows, the same is true of such judgments: We may strongly feel that something is unacceptable even though we know of counterexamples (or can even think of such examples ourselves) that seem possible but highly unusual.

Of course, applying significance testing to zero occurrences of some intersection of variables is not always going to provide a significant result: if one (or both) of the values of the intersection are rare in general, an occurrence of zero may not be significantly less than expected. In this case, we still do not know whether the absence of the intersection is due to chance or to its impossibility – but with such rare combinations, acceptability judgments are also going to be variable.

8.2.3 Words and their grammatical properties

Studies that take a collocational perspective on associations between words and grammatical structure tend to start from one or more grammatical structures and inductively identify the words associated with these structures. Moving away from this perspective, we find research designs that begin to resemble more closely the kind illustrated in Chapters 5 and 6, but that nevertheless include lexical items as one of their variables. These designs will typically start from a word (or a small set of words) and identify associated grammatical (structural and semantic) properties. This is of interest for many reasons, for example in the context of how much idiosyncrasy there is in the grammatical behavior of lexical items in general (for example, what are the grammatical differences between near synonyms), or how much of a particular grammatical alternation is lexically determined.

8.2.3.1 Case study: Complementation of *begin* and *start*

There are a number of verbs in English that display variation with respect to their complementation patterns, and the factors influencing this variation have provided (and continue to provide) an interesting area of research for corpus linguists. In an early example of such a study, Schmid (1996) investigates the near-synonyms *begin* and *start*, both of which can occur with *to*-clauses or *ing*-clauses, as shown in (4a–d):

(4) a. It rained almost every day, and she *began to feel* imprisoned. (BNC A7H)
    b. [T]here was a slightly strained period when he first *began working* with the group... (BNC AT1)
    c. The baby wakened and *started to cry.* (BNC CB5)
    d. Then an acquaintance *started talking* to me and diverted my attention. (BNC ABS)

Schmid's study is deductive. He starts by deriving from the literature two hypotheses concerning the choice between the verbs *begin* and *start* on the one hand and *to*- and the *ing*-complements on the other: First, that *begin* signals gradual onsets and *start* signals sudden ones, and second, that *ing*-clauses are typical of dynamic situations while *to*-clauses are typical of stative situations.

His focus is on the second hypothesis, which he tests on the LOB corpus by, first, identifying all occurrences of both verbs with both complementation patterns and, second, categorizing them according to whether the verb in the complement clause refers to an activity, a process or a state. The study involves three nominal variables: MATRIX VERB (with the values BEGIN and START), COMPLEMENTATION (with the values ING-clause and TO-clause) and AKTIONSART (with the values ACTIVITY, PROCESS and STATE). Thus, we are dealing with a multivariate design. The prediction with respect to the complementation pattern is clear – *to*-complements should be associated with activities and *ing*-complements with states, with processes falling somewhere in between. There is no immediate prediction with respect to the choice of verb, but Schmid points out that activities are more likely to have a sudden onset, while states and processes are more likely to have a gradual onset, thus the former might be expected to prefer *start* and the latter *begin*.

Schmid does not provide an annotation scheme for the categories *activity*, *process* and *state*, discussing these crucial constructs in just one short paragraph:

> Essentially, the three possible types of events that must be considered in the context of a beginning are activities, processes and states. Thus, the speaker may want to describe the beginning of a human activity like eating, working or singing; the beginning of a process which is not directly caused by a human being like raining, improving, ripening; or the beginning of a state. Since we seem to show little interest in the beginning of concrete, visible states (cf. e.g. ?*The lamp began to stand on the table.*) the notion of state is in the present context largely confined to bodily, intellectual and emotive states of human beings. Examples of such "private states" (Quirk et al. 1985: 202f) are being ill, understanding, loving.

Quirk et al. (1985: 202–203) mention four types of "private states": intellectual states, like *know, believe, realize*; states of emotion or attitude, like *intend, want, pity*; states of perception, like *see, smell, taste*; and states of bodily sensation, like *hurt, itch, feel cold*. Based on this and Schmid's comments, we might come up with the following rough annotation scheme which thereby becomes our operationalization for AKTIONSART:

(5) A simple annotation scheme for AKTIONSART
   a. ACTIVITY: any externally perceivable event under the control of an animate agent.
   b. PROCESS: any externally perceivable event not under the control of an animate agent, including events involving involuntary animate themes (like *cry, menstruate, shiver*) and events not involving animate entities.
   c. STATE: any externally not perceivable event involving human cognition, as well as unchanging situations not involving animate entities.

Schmid also does not state how he deals with passive sentences like those in (6a, b):

(6) a. [T]he need for correct and definite leadership began to be urgently felt... (LOB G03)

b. Presumably, domestic ritual objects began to be made at much the same time. (LOB J65)

These could be annotated with reference to the grammatical subject; in this case they would always be processes, as passive subjects are never voluntary agents of the event described. Alternatively, they could be annotated with reference to the logical subject, in which case (6a) would be a state ('someone feels something') and (6b) would be an activity ('someone makes domestic ritual objects'). Let us choose the second option here.

Querying (7a, b) yields 348 hits (Schmid reports 372, which corresponds to the total number of hits for these verbs in the corpus, including those with other kinds of complementation):

(7) a. `[lemma="(begin|start)"] [pos="verb`$_{\texttt{pres.part.}}$`"]`

b. `[lemma="(begin|start)"] [word="to"%c] [pos="verb`$_{\texttt{infinitive}}$`"]`

Annotating all 348 hits according to the annotation scheme sketched out above yields the data in Table 8.11 (the complete annotated concordance is part of the Supplementary Online Material). The total frequencies as well as the proportions among the categories differ slightly from the data Schmid reports, but the results are overall very similar.

As always in a configural frequency analysis, we have to correct for multiple testing: there are twelve cells in our table, so our probability of error must be lower than $0.05/12 = 0.0042$. The individual cells (i.e., intersections of variables) have one degree of freedom, which means that our critical χ^2 value is 8.20. This means that there are two types and three antitypes that reach significance: as predicted, activity verbs are positively associated with the verb *start* in combination with *ing*-clauses and state verbs are positively associated with the verb *begin* in combination with *to*-clauses. Process verbs are also associated with *begin* with *to*-clauses, but only marginally significantly so. As for the antitypes, all three verb classes are negatively associated (i.e., less frequent than expected) with the verb *begin* with *ing*-clauses, which suggests that this complementation pattern is generally avoided with the verb *begin*, but this avoidance is particularly pronounced with state and process verbs, where it is statistically significant: the verb *begin* and state/process verbs both avoid *ing*-complementation, and this avoidance seems to add up when they are combined.

Table 8.11: Aktionsart, matrix verb and complementation type (LOB)

	BEGIN			START			
AKTIONSART	ING	TO	Total	ING	TO	Total	Total
ACTIVITY	*Obs.:* 22 *Exp.:* 29.86 χ^2: 2.07	*Obs.:* 93 *Exp.:* 106.86 χ^2: 1.80	115	*Obs.:* 45 *Exp.:* 10.11 χ^2: 120.48	*Obs.:* 23 *Exp.:* 36.17 χ^2: 4.80	68	183
PROCESS	*Obs.:* 1 *Exp.:* 13.22 χ^2: 11.29	*Obs.:* 65 *Exp.:* 47.30 χ^2: 6.62	66	*Obs.:* 5 *Exp.:* 4.47 χ^2: 0.06	*Obs.:* 10 *Exp.:* 16.01 χ^2: 2.26	15	81
STATE	*Obs.:* 1 *Exp.:* 13.71 χ^2: 11.78	*Obs.:* 78 *Exp.:* 49.05 χ^2: 17.08	79	*Obs.:* 2 *Exp.:* 4.64 χ^2: 1.50	*Obs.:* 3 *Exp.:* 16.60 χ^2: 11.14	5	84
Total	24	236	260	52	36	88	348

Supplementary Online Material: 4DYT

Faced with these results, we might ask, first, how they relate to two simpler tests of Schmid's hypothesis – namely two bivariate designs separately testing (a) the relationship between AKTIONSART and COMPLEMENTATION, (b) the relationship between AKTIONSART and MATRIX VERB and (c) the relationship between MATRIX VERB and COMPLEMENTATION TYPE. We have all the data we need to test this in Table 8.11, we just have to sum up appropriately. Table 8.12 shows that AKTIONSART and COMPLEMENTATION TYPE are related: ACTIVITY verbs prefer ING, the other two verb types prefer TO ($\chi^2 = 49.702, \text{df} = 2, p < 0.001$).

Table 8.12: Aktionsart and complementation type (LOB)

		COMPLEMENTATION TYPE		
		ING	TO	Total
AKTIONSART	ACTIVITY	67 (39.97)	116 (143.03)	183
	PROCESS	6 (17.69)	75 (63.31)	81
	STATE	3 (18.34)	81 (65.66)	84
	Total	76	272	348

Table 8.13 shows that AKTIONSART and MATRIX VERB are also related: ACTIVITY verbs prefer TO and STATE verbs prefer ING ($\chi^2 = 32.236, \text{df} = 2, p < 0.001$).

Table 8.13: Aktionsart and matrix verb (LOB)

		MATRIX VERB		
		BEGIN	START	Total
AKTIONSART	ACTIVITY	115 (136.72)	68 (46.28)	183
	PROCESS	66 (60.52)	15 (20.48)	81
	STATE	79 (62.76)	5 (21.24)	84
	Total	260	88	348

Finally, Table 8.14 shows that MATRIX VERB and COMPLEMENTATION TYPE are also related: BEGIN prefers TO and START prefers ING ($\chi^2 = 95.755, \text{df} = 1, p < 0.001$).

Table 8.14: Matrix verb and complementation type

		COMPLEMENTATION TYPE		
		ING	TO	Total
MATRIX VERB	BEGIN	24 (56.78)	236 (203.22)	260
	START	52 (19.22)	36 (68.78)	88
	Total	76	272	348

In other words, every variable in the design is related to every other variable and the multivariate analysis in Table 8.11 shows that the effects observed in the individual bivariate designs simply add up when all three variables are investigated together. Thus, we cannot tell whether any of the three relations between the variables is independent of the other two. In order to determine this, we would have to keep each of the variables constant in turn to see whether the other two still interact in the predicted way (for example, whether *begin* prefers *to*-clauses and *start* prefers *ing*-clauses even if we restrict the analysis to activity verbs, etc.

The second question we could ask faced with Schmid's results is to what extent his second hypothesis – that *begin* is used with gradual beginnings and *start* with sudden ones – is relevant for the results. As mentioned above, it is not tested directly, so how could we remedy this? One possibility is to look at each of the 348 cases in the sample and try to determine the gradualness or suddenness of the beginning they denote. This is sometimes possible, as in (4a) above, where the context suggests that the referent of the subject began to feel imprisoned gradually the longer the rain went on, or in (4c), which suggests that the crying began suddenly as soon as the baby woke up. But in many other cases, it is very difficult to judge, whether a beginning is sudden or gradual – as in (4b, c). To come up with a reliable annotation scheme for this categorization task would be quite a feat.

There is an alternative, however: speakers sometimes use adverbs that explicitly refer to the type of beginning. A query of the BNC for ⟨ `[word=".*ly"%c] [hw="(begin|start)"]` ⟩ yields three relatively frequent adverbs (occurring more than 10 times) indicating suddenness (*immediately*, *suddenly* and *quickly*), and three indicating gradualness (*slowly*, *gradually* and *eventually*). There are more, like *promptly*, *instantly*, *rapidly*. *leisurely*, *reluctantly*, etc., which are much less frequent.

By extracting just these cases, we can directly test the hypothesis that *begin* signals gradual and *start* sudden onsets. The BNC contains 307 cases of [*begin/start to* V_{inf}] and [*begin/start* V*ing*] directly preceded by one of the six adverbs mentioned above. Table 8.15 shows the result of a configural frequency analysis of the variables Onset (sudden vs. gradual, Matrix Verb (begin vs. start and Complementation Type (ing vs. to).

Table 8.15: Adverbs of suddenness and gradualness, matrix verb and complementation type

	begin			start			
Onset	ing	to	Total	ing	to	Total	Total
sudden	*Obs.:* 25	*Obs.:* 85	110	*Obs.:* 58	*Obs.:* 36	94	204
	Exp.: 36.60	*Exp.:* 89.65		*Exp.:* 22.54	*Exp.:* 55.21		
	χ^2: 3.68	χ^2: 0.24		χ^2: 55.79	χ^2: 6.68		
gradual	*Obs.:* 1	*Obs.:* 79	80	*Obs.:* 5	*Obs.:* 18	23	103
	Exp.: 18.48	*Exp.:* 45.27		*Exp.:* 11.38	*Exp.:* 27.87		
	χ^2: 16.53	χ^2: 25.14		χ^2: 3.58	χ^2: 3.50		
Total	26	164	190	63	54	117	307

Supplementary Online Material: DVJ9

Since there are eight cells in the table, the corrected p-value is $0.05/8 = 0.00625$; the individual cells have one degree of freedom, so the critical χ^2 value is 7.48. There are two significant types: SUDDEN ∩ START ∩ ING and GRADUAL ∩ BEGIN ∩ TO. There is one significant and one marginally significant antitype: SUDDEN ∩ START ∩ TO and GRADUAL ∩ BEGIN ∩ ING, respectively. This corroborates the hypothesis that *begin* signals gradual onsets and *start* signals sudden ones, at least when the matrix verbs occur with their preferred complementation pattern.

Summing up the results of both studies, we could posit two "prototype" patterns (in the sense of cognitive linguistics): $[\textit{begin}_{\text{gradual}}\ \text{V}^{\text{stative}}{}_{\text{ing}}]$ and $[\textit{start}_{\text{sudden}}\ \textit{to}\ \text{V}^{\text{activity}}{}_{\text{inf}}]$, and we could hypothesize that speakers will choose the pattern that matches most closely the situation they are describing (something that could then be tested, for example, in a controlled production experiment).

This case study demonstrated a complex design involving grammar, lexis and semantic categories. It also demonstrated that semantic categories can be included in a corpus linguistic design in the form of categorization decisions on the basis of an annotation scheme (in which case, of course, the annotation scheme must be documented in sufficient detail for the study to be replicable), or in the form of lexical items signaling a particular meaning explicitly, such as adverbs of gradualness (in which case we need a corpus large enough to contain a sufficient number of hits including these items). It also demonstrated that such corpus-based studies may result in very specific hypotheses about the function of lexicogrammatical structures that may become the basis for claims about mental representation.

8.2.4 Grammar and context

There is a wide range of contextual factors that are hypothesized or known to influence grammatical variation. These include information status, animacy and length, which we already discussed in the case studies of the possessive constructions in Chapters 5 and 6. Since we have dealt with them in some detail, they will not be discussed further here, but they have been extensively studied for a range of phenomena (e.g. Thompson & Koide 1987 for the dative alternation; Chen 1986 and Gries 2003b for particle placement; Rosenbach 2002 and Stefanowitsch 2003 for the possessives). Instead, we will discuss some less frequently investigated contextual factors here, namely word frequency, phonology, the "horror aequi" and priming.

8.2.4.1 Case study: Adjective order and frequency

In a comprehensive study on adjective order already mentioned in Chapter 4, Wulff (2003) studies (among other things) the hypothesis that in noun phrases with two adjectives, more frequent adjectives precede less frequent ones. There are two straightforward ways of testing this hypothesis. First (as Wulff does), based on mean frequencies: if we assume that the hypothesis is correct, then the mean frequency of the first adjective of two-adjective pairs should be higher than that of the second. Second, based on the number of cases in which the first and second adjective, respectively, are more frequent: if we assume that the hypothesis is correct, there should be more cases where the first adjective is the more frequent one than cases where the second adjective is the more frequent one. Obviously, the two ways of investigating the hypothesis could give us different results.

Let us replicate part of Wulff's study using the spoken part of the BNC (Wulff uses the entire BNC). If we extract all sequences of exactly two adjectives occurring before a noun (excluding comparatives and superlatives), and include only those adjective pairs that (a) occur at least five times, and (b) do not occur more than once in the opposite order, we get the sample in Table 8.16 (the adjective pairs are listed in decreasing order of their frequency of occurrence). The table also lists the frequency of each adjective in the spoken part of the BNC (case insensitive), and, in the final column, states whether the first or the second adjective is more frequent.

Let us first look at just the ten most frequent adjective pairs (Ranks 1–10). The mean frequency of the first adjective is 5493.2, that of the second adjective is 4042.7. Pending significance testing, this would corroborate Wulff's hypothesis. However, in six of these ten cases the second adjective is actually more frequent than the first, which would contradict Wulff's hypothesis. The problem here is that some of the adjectives in first position, like *good* and *right*, are very frequent while some adjectives in second position, like *honourable* and *northern* are very infrequent – this influences the mean frequencies substantially. However, when comparing the frequency of the first and second adjective, we are making a binary choice concerning which of the adjectives is more frequent – we ignore the size of the difference.

If we look at the ten next most frequent adjectives, we find the situation reversed – the mean frequency is 3672.3 for the first adjective and 4072 for the second adjective, contradicting Wulff's hypothesis, but in seven of the ten cases, the first adjective is more frequent, corroborating Wulff's hypothesis.

Table 8.16: Sample of [ADJ_1 ADJ_2] sequences (BNC Spoken)

Rank	ADJ_1	ADJ_2	$n(ADJ_1)$	$n(ADJ_2)$	More Frequent
1.	*great*	*big*	3795	5676	2nd
2.	*nice*	*little*	6246	7715	2nd
3.	*poor*	*old*	1040	5579	2nd
4.	*right*	*honourable*	9205	336	1st
5.	*good*	*old*	16 130	5579	1st
6.	*lovely*	*little*	2394	7715	2nd
7.	*outer*	*northern*	162	307	2nd
8.	*little*	*red*	7715	1133	1st
9.	*little*	*old*	7715	5579	1st
10.	*current*	*financial*	530	808	2nd
11.	*nice*	*old*	6246	5579	1st
12.	*nice*	*big*	6246	5676	1st
13.	*funny*	*old*	1669	5579	2nd
14.	*poor*	*little*	1040	7715	2nd
15.	*big*	*black*	5676	1339	1st
16.	*little*	*black*	7715	1339	1st
17.	*simple*	*harmonic*	835	17	1st
18.	*special*	*educational*	1276	182	1st
19.	*big*	*old*	5676	5579	1st
20.	*pretty*	*little*	344	7715	2nd
21.	*silly*	*little*	684	7715	2nd
22.	*big*	*long*	5676	3759	1st
23.	*silly*	*old*	684	5579	2nd
24.	*bad*	*old*	3051	5579	2nd
25.	*cheeky*	*little*	126	7715	2nd
26.	*compulsory*	*competitive*	80	159	2nd
27.	*nice*	*new*	6246	6337	2nd
28.	*nice*	*young*	6246	1856	1st
29.	*big*	*white*	5676	1241	1st
30.	*beautiful*	*old*	723	5579	2nd
31.	*big*	*heavy*	5676	576	1st
32.	*big*	*red*	5676	1133	1st
33.	*good*	*little*	16 130	7715	1st
34.	*great*	*long*	3795	3759	1st
35.	*grievous*	*bodily*	12	27	2nd
36.	*little*	*blue*	7715	770	1st
37.	*nice*	*fresh*	6246	312	1st
38.	*red*	*hot*	1133	986	1st
39.	*bad*	*little*	3051	7715	2nd
40.	*big*	*open*	5676	1489	1st
41.	*big*	*thick*	5676	346	1st
42.	*good*	*long*	16 130	3759	1st
43.	*little*	*pink*	7715	292	1st
44.	*massive*	*great*	336	3795	2nd
45.	*new*	*little*	6337	7715	2nd
46.	*nice*	*clean*	6246	460	1st
47.	*nice*	*simple*	6246	835	1st
48.	*private*	*rented*	698	30	1st
49.	*common*	*agricultural*	726	328	1st
50.	*domestic*	*political*	209	729	2nd
51.	*grand*	*negative*	254	324	2nd
52.	*grand*	*old*	254	5579	2nd
53.	*little*	*speckled*	7715	15	1st
54.	*little*	*white*	7715	1241	1st
55.	*nice*	*warm*	6246	557	1st
56.	*old*	*wooden*	5579	183	1st
57.	*open*	*agricultural*	1489	328	1st
58.	*outstanding*	*natural*	136	434	2nd
59.	*small*	*local*	2233	3090	2nd

Both ways of looking at the issue have disadvantages. If we go by mean frequency, then individual cases might inflate the mean of either of the two adjectives. In contrast, if we go by number of cases, then cases with very little difference in frequency count just as much as cases with a vast difference in frequency. In cases like this, it may be advantageous to apply both methods and reject the null hypothesis only if both of them give the same result (and of course, our sample should be larger than ten cases).

Let us now apply both perspectives to the entire sample in Table 8.16, beginning with mean frequency. The mean frequency of the first adjective is 4371.14 with a standard deviation of 3954.22, the mean frequency of the second adjective is 3070.98 with a standard deviation of 2882.04. Using the formulas given in Chapter 6, this gives us a *t*-value of 2.04 at 106.06 degrees of freedom, which means that the difference is significant ($p < 0.05$). This would allow us to reject the null hypothesis and thus corroborates Wulff's hypothesis.

Next, let us look at the number of cases that match the prediction. There are 34 cases where the first adjective is more frequent, and 25 cases where the second adjective is more frequent, which seems to corroborate Wulff's hypothesis, but as Table 8.17 shows, the difference is not statistically significant.

Table 8.17: Adjective order and frequency (cf. Table 8.16)

		Observed	Expected	χ^2
More Frequent	ADJ_1	34	29.50	0.69
	ADJ_2	25	29.50	0.69
	Total	59		1.37

Thus, we should be careful to conclude, based on our sample, that there is an influence of word frequency on adjective order. Although the results are encouraging, we would have to study a larger sample (Wulff (2003) does so and shows that, indeed, there is an influence of frequency on order).

This case study was meant to demonstrate that sometimes we can derive different kinds of quantitative predictions from a hypothesis which may give us different results; in such cases, it is a good idea to test all predictions. The case study also shows that word frequency may have effects on grammatical variation, which is interesting from a methodological perspective because not only is corpus linguistics the only way to test for such effects, but corpora are also the only source from which the relevant values for the independent variable can be extracted.

8.2.4.2 Case study: Binomials and sonority

Frozen binomials (i.e. phrases of the type *flesh and blood, day and night, size and shape*) have inspired a substantial body of research attempting to uncover principles determining the order of the constituents. A number of semantic, syntactic and phonological factors have been proposed and investigated using psycholinguistic and corpus-based methods (see Lohmann (2013) for an overview and a comprehensive empirical study). A phonological factor that we will focus on here concerns the sonority of the final consonants of the two constituents: it has been proposed that words with less sonorant final consonants occur before words with more sonorant ones (e.g. Cooper & Ross 1975).

In order to test this hypothesis, we need a sample of binomials. In the literature, such samples are typically taken from dictionaries or similar lists assembled for other purposes, but there are two problems with this procedure. First, these lists contain no information about the frequency (and thus, importance) of the individual examples. Second, these lists do not tell us exactly how "frozen" the phrases are; while there are cases that seem truly non-reversible (like *flesh and blood*), others simply have a strong preference (*day and night* is three times as frequent as *night and day* in the BNC) or even a relatively weak one (*size and shape* is only one-and-a-half times as frequent as *shape and size*). It is possible that the degree of frozenness plays a role – for example, it would be expected that binomials that never (or almost never) occur in the opposite order would display the influence of any factor determining order more strongly than those where the two possible orders are more equally distributed.

We can avoid these problems by drawing our sample from the corpus itself. For this case study, let us select all instances of [NOUN *and* NOUN] that occur at least 30 times in the BNC. Let us further limit our sample to cases where both nouns are monosyllabic, as it is known from the existing research literature that length and stress patterns have a strong influence on the order of binomials. Let us also exclude cases where one or both nouns are in the plural, as we are interested in the influence of the final consonant, and it is unclear whether this refers to the final consonant of the stem or of the word form.

This will give us the 78 expressions in Table 8.18. Next, let us calculate the degree of frozenness by checking for each binomial how often the two nouns occur in the opposite order. The proportion of the more frequent order can then be taken as representing the frozenness of the binomial – it will be 1 for cases where the order never varies and 0.5 for cases where the two orders are equally frequent, with most cases falling somewhere in between.

Table 8.18: Sample of monosyllabic binomials and their sonority

Expression	Order A	Order B	Frozenness	More Sonor.	Expression	Order A	Order B	Frozenness	More Sonor.	Expression	Order A	Order B	Frozenness	More Sonor.
beck and call	40	0	1.00	2nd	(contd.)					(contd.)				
bread and jam	30	0	1.00	2nd	*iron and steel*	127	3	0.98	2nd	*love and care*	33	6	0.85	2nd
bride and groom	94	0	1.00	2nd	*bread and wine*	42	1	0.98	2nd	*boy and girl*	43	8	0.84	1st
cat and mouse	37	0	1.00	2nd	*wife and son*	35	1	0.97	2nd	*food and wine*	74	14	0.84	2nd
day and age	106	0	1.00	1st	*head and tail*	34	1	0.97	2nd	*age and sex*	145	32	0.82	1st
fire and life	31	0	1.00	1st	*rise and fall*	170	5	0.97	2nd	*meat and fish*	30	7	0.81	2nd
life and limb	44	0	1.00	2nd	*song and dance*	68	2	0.97	1st	*war and peace*	71	17	0.81	1st
light and shade	56	0	1.00	2nd	*sight and sound*	33	1	0.97	2nd	*time and place*	187	45	0.81	1st
park and ride	45	0	1.00	2nd	*start and end*	33	1	0.97	2nd	*road and rail*	67	18	0.79	2nd
pay and file	33	0	1.00	1st	*stock and barrel*	30	1	0.97	2nd	*arm and leg*	31	9	0.78	1st
rank and file	159	0	1.00	2nd	*bread and cheese*	81	3	0.96	2nd	*land and sea*	51	15	0.77	2nd
right and wrong	126	0	1.00	2nd	*wife and child*	54	2	0.96	1st	*north and west*	112	36	0.76	1st
rock and roll	106	0	1.00	2nd	*hand and foot*	52	2	0.96	1st	*day and night*	310	101	0.75	1st
tooth and nail	38	0	1.00	2nd	*church and state*	102	4	0.96	1st	*date and time*	74	25	0.75	2nd
touch and go	43	0	1.00	2nd	*knife and fork*	87	4	0.96	1st	*date and place*	28	10	0.74	2nd
track and field	47	0	1.00	2nd	*oil and gas*	392	26	0.94	1st	*mind and body*	138	51	0.73	2nd
life and work	147	1	0.99	1st	*front and rear*	30	2	0.94	2nd	*south and east*	119	44	0.73	1st
flesh and blood	109	1	0.99	1st	*fruit and veg*	36	3	0.92	2nd	*home and school*	43	16	0.73	2nd
fish and chip	103	1	0.99	1st	*pride and joy*	66	6	0.92	2nd	*north and east*	68	27	0.72	1st
mum and dad	490	5	0.99	1st	*food and fuel*	30	4	0.88	2nd	*snow and ice*	53	22	0.71	1st
food and drink	333	4	0.99	1st	*stress and strain*	37	5	0.88	2nd	*size and shape*	116	53	0.69	1st
horse and cart	74	1	0.99	1st	*face and neck*	59	9	0.87	1st	*south and west*	73	37	0.66	1st
ebb and flow	68	1	0.99	2nd	*wind and rain*	94	15	0.86	2nd	*science and art*	30	16	0.65	1st
man and wife	63	1	0.98	1st	*size and weight*	31	5	0.86	1st	*time and cost*	30	21	0.59	1st
heart and soul	57	1	0.98	2nd	*heart and lung*	30	5	0.86	2nd	*nose and mouth*	35	26	0.57	1st
hip and thigh	50	1	0.98	2nd	*league and cup*	41	7	0.85	1st	*care and skill*	36	30	0.55	1st
lock and key	44	1	0.98	2nd	*head and neck*	79	14	0.85	1st					

Supplementary Online Material: NFHY

Finally, we need to code the final consonants of all nouns for sonority and determine which of the two final consonants is more sonorant – that of the first noun, or that of the second. For this, let us use the following (hopefully uncontroversial) sonority hierarchy:

(8) [vowels] > [semivowels] > [liquids] > [h] > [nasals] > [voiced fricatives] > [voiceless fricatives] > [voiced affricates] > [voiceless affricates] > [voiced stops] > [voiceless stops]

The result of all these steps is shown in Table 8.18. The first column shows the binomial in its most frequent order, the second column gives the frequency of the phrase in this order, the third column gives the frequency of the less frequent order (the reversal of the one shown), the fourth column gives the degree of frozenness (i.e., the percentage of the more frequent order), and the fifth column records whether the final consonant of the first or of the second noun is less sonorant.

Let us first simply look at the number of cases for which the claim is true or false. There are 42 cases where the second word's final consonant is more sonorant than that of the second word (as predicted), and 36 cases where the second word's final consonant is less sonorant than that of the first (counter to the prediction). As Table 8.19 shows, this difference is nowhere near significant.

Table 8.19: Sonority of the final consonant and word order in binomials (counts)

		Observed	Expected	χ^2
More Sonorant	First Word	36	39	0.23
	Second Word	42	39	0.23
	Total	78		0.46

However, note that we are including both cases with a very high degree of frozenness (like *beck and call*, *flesh and blood*, or *lock and key*) and cases with a relatively low degree of frozenness (like *nose and mouth*, *day and night*, or *snow and ice*: this will dilute our results, as the cases with low frozenness are not predicted to adhere very strongly to the *less-before-more-sonorant* principle.

We could, of course, limit our analysis to cases with a high degree of frozenness, say, above 90 percent (the data is available, so you might want to try). However, it would be even better to keep all our data and make use of the rank order that the frozenness measure provides: the prediction is that cases with a high frozenness rank will adhere to the sonority constraint with a higher probability than those with a low frozenness rank. Table 8.18 contains all the data we need to determine the median of words adhering or not adhering to the constraint, as well as the rank sums and number of cases, which we need to calculate a U-test. We will not go through the test step by step (but you can try for yourself if you want to). Table 8.20 provides the necessary values derived from Table 8.18.

Table 8.20: Sonority of the final consonant and word order in binomials (ranks)

	Final Consonant less sonorous	
	first word	second word
Median	32	51
Rank Sum	1393	1688
No. of Data Points	42	36

The binomials adhering to the *less-before-more-sonorant* principle have a much higher median frozenness rank than those not adhering to the constraint – in other words, binomials with a high degree of frozenness tend to adhere to the constraint, binomials with a low degree of frozenness do not. The U-test shows that the difference is highly significant ($U = 490, N_1 = 36, N_2 = 42, p < 0.001$).

Like the case study in Section 8.2.4.1, this case study was intended to show that sometimes we can derive different kinds of quantitative predictions from a hypothesis; however, in this case one of the possibilities more accurately reflects the hypothesis and is thus the one we should base our conclusions on. The case study was also meant to provide an example of a corpus-based design where it is more useful to operationalize one of the constructs (Frozenness) as an ordinal, rather than a nominal variable. In terms of content, it was meant to demonstrate how phonology can interact with grammatical variation (or, in this case, the absence of variation) and how this can be studied on the basis of corpus data; cf. Schlüter (2003) for another example of phonology interacting with grammar, and cf. Lohmann (2013) for a comprehensive study of binomials.

8.2.4.3 Case study: Horror aequi

In a number of studies, Günter Rohdenburg and colleagues have studied the influence of contextual (and, consequently, conceptual) complexity on grammatical variation (e.g. Rohdenburg 1995; 2003). The general idea is that in contexts that are already complex, speakers will try to choose a variant that reduces (or at least does not contribute further to) this complexity. A particularly striking example of this is what Rohdenburg (adapting a term from Karl Brugmann) calls the *horror aequi* principle: "the widespread (and presumably universal) tendency to avoid the repetition of identical and adjacent grammatical elements or structures" (Rohdenburg 2003: 206).

Take the example of matrix verbs that normally occur alternatively with a *to*-clause or an *ing*-clause (like *begin* and *start* in Case Study 8.2.3.1 above). Rohdenburg (1995: 380) shows, on the basis of the text of an 18th century novel, that where such matrix verbs occur as *to*-infinitives, they display a strong preference for *ing*-complements. For example, in the past tense, *start* freely occurs either with a *to*-complement, as in (9a) or with an *ing*-complement, as in (9b). However, as a *to*-infinitive it would avoid the *to*-complement, although not completely, as (9c) shows, and strongly prefer the *ing*-form, as in (9d):

(9) a. I started to think about my childhood again... (BNC A0F)
   b. So I started thinking about alternative ways to earn a living... (BNC C9H)
   c. ... in the future they will actually have to start to think about a fairer electoral system... (BNC JSG)
   d. He will also have to start thinking about a partnership with Skoda before (BNC A6W)

Impressionistically, this seems to be true: in the BNC there are 11 cases of *started to think about*, 18 of *started thinking about*, only one of *to start to think about* but 35 of *to start thinking about.*

Let us attempt a more comprehensive analysis and look at all cases of the verb *start* with a clausal complement in the BNC. Since we are interested in the influence of the tense/aspect form of the verb *start* on complementation choice, let us distinguish the inflectional forms *start* (base form), *starts* (3rd person), *started* (past tense/past participle) and *starting* (present participle); let us further distinguish cases of the base form *start* with and without the infinitive marker *to* (we can derive the last two figures by first searching for (10a) and (10b) and then for (10c) and (10d), and then subtracting the frequencies of the latter two from those of the former two, respectively:

(10) a. `[word="start"%c] [word="to"%c]`
   b. `[word="start"%c] [word=".*ing"%c]`

c. `[word="to"%c] [word="start"%c] [word="to"%c]`

d. `[word="to"%c] [word="start"%c] [word=".*ing"%c]`

Table 8.21 shows the observed and expected frequencies of *to-* and *ing*-complements for each of these forms, together with the expected frequencies and the χ^2 components.

Table 8.21: Complementation of *start* and the horror aequi principle

	Complementation Type		
Noun Category	ing	to	Total
∅ start	*Obs.:* 2706 *Exp.:* 2249.15 χ^2: 92.80	*Obs.:* 1434 *Exp.:* 1890.85 χ^2: 110.38	4140
to start	*Obs.:* 1108 *Exp.:* 642.15 χ^2: 337.96	*Obs.:* 74 *Exp.:* 539.85 χ^2: 402.00	1182
starts	*Obs.:* 496 *Exp.:* 585.65 χ^2: 13.72	*Obs.:* 582 *Exp.:* 492.35 χ^2: 16.32	1078
started	*Obs.:* 3346 *Exp.:* 3673.61 χ^2: 29.22	*Obs.:* 3416 *Exp.:* 3088.39 χ^2: 34.75	6762
starting	*Obs.:* 40 *Exp.:* 545.45 χ^2: 468.38	*Obs.:* 964 *Exp.:* 458.55 χ^2: 557.13	1004
Total	7696	6470	14 166

The most obvious and, in terms of their χ^2 components, most significant deviations from the expected frequencies are indeed those cases where the matrix verb *start* has the same form as the complement clause: there are far fewer cases of [*to start to* V_{inf}] and [*starting* $V_{pres.part.}$] and, conversely, far more cases of [*to start* $V_{pres.part.}$] and [*starting to* V_{inf}] than expected. Interestingly, if the base form of *start* does not occur with an infinitive particle, the *to*-complement is still strongly avoided in favor of the *ing*-complement, though not as strongly as in the case of the base form with the infinitive particle. It may be that *horror aequi* is a graded principle – the stronger the similarity, the stronger the avoidance.

This case study is intended to introduce the notion of *horror aequi*, which has been shown to influence a number of grammatical and morphological variation phenomena (cf. e.g. Rohdenburg 2003, Vosberg 2003, Rudanko 2003, Gries & Hilpert 2010). Methodologically, it is a straightforward application of the χ^2 test, but one where the individual cells of the contingency table and their χ^2 values are more interesting than the question whether the observed distribution as a whole differs significantly from the expected one.

8.2.4.4 Case study: Synthetic and analytic comparatives and persistence

The *horror aequi* principle has been shown to have an effect on certain kinds of variation and it can plausibly be explained as a way of reducing complexity (if the same structure occurs twice in a row, this might cause problems for language processing). However, there is another well-known principle that is, in a way, the opposite of *horror aequi*: structural priming. The idea of priming comes from psychology, where it refers to the fact that the response to a particular stimulus (the *target*) can be influenced by a preceding stimulus (the *prime*). For example, if subjects are exposed to a sequence of two pictures, they will identify an object on the second picture (say, a loaf of bread) faster and more accurately if it is related to the the scene in the first picture (say, a kitchen counter) (cf. Palmer 1975). Likewise, they will be faster to recognize a string of letters (say, *BUTTER*) as a word if it is preceded by a related word (say, *BREAD*) (cf. Meyer & Schvaneveldt 1971).

Bock (1986) shows that priming can also be observed in the production of grammatical structures. For example, if people read a sentence in the passive and are then asked to describe a picture showing an unrelated scene, they will use passives in their description more frequently than expected. She calls this *structural priming*. Interestingly, such priming effects can also be observed in naturally occurring language, i.e. in corpora (see Gries 2005 and Szmrecsanyi 2005; 2006) – if speakers use a particular syntactic structure, this increases the probability that they will use it again within a relatively short span.

For example, Szmrecsanyi (2005) argues that persistence is one of the factors influencing the choice of adjectival comparison. While most adjectives require either synthetic comparison (*further*, but not **more far*) or analytic comparison (*more distant*, but not **distanter*), some vary quite freely between the two (*friendlier/more friendly*). Szmrecsanyi hypothesizes that one of many factors influencing the choice is the presence of an analytic comparative in the directly preceding context: if speakers have used an analytic comparative (for example, with an adjective that does not allow anything else), this increases the probability that they will use it within a certain span with an adjective that would theoretically also allow a synthetic comparison. Szmrecsanyi shows that this is the case, but that it depends crucially on the distance between the two instances of comparison: the persistence is rather short-lived.

Let us attempt to replicate his findings in a small analysis focusing only on persistence and disregarding other factors. Studies of structural priming have two nominal variables: the Prime, a particular grammatical structure occurring in a discourse, and the Target, the same (or a similar) grammatical structure occurring in the subsequent discourse. In our case, the grammatical structure is Comparative with the two values analytic and synthetic. In order to determine whether priming occurs and under what conditions, we have to extract a set of potential targets and the directly preceding discourse from a corpus. The hypothesis is always that the value of the prime will correlate with the value of the target – in our case, that analytic comparatives have a higher probability of occurrence after analytic comparatives and synthetic comparatives have a higher probability of occurrence after synthetic comparatives.

For our purposes, let us include only adjectives with exactly two syllables, as length and stress pattern are known to have an influence on the choice between the two strategies and must be held constant in our design. Let us further focus on adjectives with a relatively even distribution of the two strategies and include only cases where the less frequent comparative form accounts for at least forty percent of all comparative forms. Finally, let us discard all adjectives that occur as comparatives less than 20 times in the BNC. This will leave just six adjectives: *angry*, *empty*, *friendly*, *lively*, *risky* and *sorry*.

Let us extract all synthetic and analytic forms of these adjectives from the BNC. This will yield 452 hits, of which two are double comparatives (*more livelier*), which are irrelevant to our design and must be discarded. This leaves 450 potential targets – 241 analytic and 209 synthetic. Of these, 381 do not have an additional comparative form in a span of 20 tokens preceding the comparative – whatever determined the choice between analytic and synthetic comparatives in these cases, it is not priming. These non-primed comparatives are fairly evenly distributed – 194 are analytic comparatives and 187 are synthetic, which is not significantly different from a chance distribution ($\chi^2 = 0.13, \text{df} = 1, p = 0.7199$), suggesting that our sample of adjectives does indeed consist of cases that are fairly evenly distributed across the two comparative strategies (see Supplementary Online Material for the complete annotated concordance).

This leaves 69 targets that are preceded by a comparative prime in the preceding span of 20 tokens. Table 8.22 shows the distribution of analytic and synthetic primes and targets (if there was more than one comparative in the preceding context, only the one closer to the comparative in question was counted).

Table 8.22: Comparatives preceding comparatives in a context of 20 tokens (BNC)

		TARGET		
		SYNTHETIC	ANALYTIC	Total
PRIME	SYNTHETIC	34 (27.93)	13 (19.07)	47
	ANALYTIC	7 (13.07)	15 (8.93)	22
	Total	28	41	69

Supplementary Online Material: H4BM

There is a significant influence of PRIME on TARGET: synthetic comparatives are more frequent than expected following synthetic comparatives, and analytic comparatives are more frequent than expected following analytic comparatives ($\chi^2 = 10.205, \text{df} = 1, p < 0.01$). The effect is only moderate ($\phi = 0.3846$), but note that the context within which we looked for potential primes is quite large – in some cases, the prime will be quite far away from the target, as in (11a), in other cases it is very close, as in (11b):

(11) a. But the statistics for the second quarter, announced just before the October Conference of the Conservative Party, were even more damaging to the Government showing a rise of 17 percent on 1989. Indeed these figures made even sorrier reading for the Conservatives when one realised... (BNC G1J)

b. Over the next ten years, China will become economically more liberal, internationally more friendly... (BNC ABD)

Obviously, we would expect a much stronger priming effect in a situation like that in (11b), where one word intervenes between the two comparatives, than in a situation like (11a), where 17 words (and a sentence boundary) intervene. Let us therefore restrict the context in which we count analytic comparatives to a size more likely to lead to a priming effect – say, seven words (based on the factoid that short term memory can hold up to seven units). Table 8.23 shows the distribution of primes and targets in this smaller window.

Table 8.23: Comparatives preceding comparatives in a context of 7 tokens (BNC)

		PRIME		
		SYNTHETIC	ANALYTIC	Total
TARGET	SYNTHETIC	21 (15.40)	7 (12.60)	28
	ANALYTIC	1 (6.60)	11 (5.40)	12
	Total	22	18	40

Supplementary Online Material: H4BM

Again, the effect is significant ($\chi^2 = 15.08, \text{df} = 1, p < 0.001$), but crucially, the effect size has increased noticeably to $\phi = 0.6141$. This suggests that the structural priming effect depends quite strongly on the distance between prime and target.

This case study demonstrates structural priming (cf. Szmrecsanyi (2005) for additional examples) and shows how it can be studied on the basis of corpora. It also demonstrates that slight adjustments in the research design can have quite substantial effects on the results.

8.2.5 Variation and change

8.2.5.1 Case study: Sex differences in the use of tag questions

Grammatical differences may also exist between varieties spoken by subgroups of speakers defined by demographic variables, for example, when the speech of younger speakers reflects recent changes in the language, or when speakers from different educational or economic backgrounds speak different established sociolects. Even more likely are differences in usage preference. For example, Lakoff (1973) claims that women make more intensive use of tag questions than men. Mondorf (2004b) investigates this claim in detail on the basis of the London-Lund Corpus, which is annotated for intonation among other things. Mondorf's analysis not only corroborates the claim that women use tag questions more frequently than men, but also shows qualitative differences in terms of their form and function.

This kind of analysis requires very careful, largely manual data extraction and annotation so it is limited to relatively small corpora, but let us see what we can do in terms of a larger-scale analysis. Let us focus on tag questions with negative polarity containing the auxiliary *be* (e.g. *isn't it*, *wasn't she*, *am I not*, *was it not*). These can be extracted relatively straightforwardly even from an untagged corpus using the following queries:

(12) a. `[word="(am|are|is|was|were)"%c] [word="n't"%c] [word="(I|you|he|she|it|we|they)"%c] [word="[.,!?]"]`
b. `[word="(am|are|is|was|were)"%c] [word="(I|you|he|she|it|we|they)"%c] [word="not"%c] [word="[.,!?]"]`

The query in (12a) will find all finite forms of the verb *be* (as non-finite forms cannot occur in tag questions), followed by the negative clitic *n't*, followed by a pronoun; the query in (12b) will do the same thing for the full form of the particle *not*, which then follows rather than precedes the pronoun. Both queries will only find those cases that occur before a punctuation mark signaling a clause boundary (what to include here will depend on the transcription conventions of the corpus, if it is a spoken one).

The queries are meant to work for the spoken portion of the BNC, which uses the comma for all kinds of things, including hesitation or incomplete phrases, so we have to make a choice whether to exclude it and increase the precision or to include it and increase the recall (I will choose the latter option). The queries are not perfect yet: British English also has the form *ain't it*, so we might want to include the query in (13a). However, *ain't* can stand for *be* or for *have*, which lowers the precision somewhat. Finally, there is also the form *innit* in (some varieties of) British English, so we might want to include the query in (13b). However, this is an invariant form that can occur with any verb or auxiliary in the main clause, so it will decrease the precision even further. We will ignore *ain't* and *innit* here (they are not particularly frequent and hardly change the results reported below):

(13) a. `[word="ai"%c] [word="n't"%c] [word="(I|you|he|she|it|we|they)"%c] [word="[.,!?]"]`
b. `[word="in"%c] [word="n"%c] [word="it"%c] [word="[.,!?]"]`

In the part of the spoken BNC annotated for speaker sex, there are 3751 hits for the patterns in (12a,b) for female speakers (only 20 of which are for 12b), and 3050 hits for male speakers (only 42 of which are for 12b). Of course, we cannot assume that there is an equal amount of male and female speech in the corpus, so the question is what to compare these frequencies against. Obviously, such tag questions will normally occur in declarative sentences with positive polarity containing a finite form of *be*. Such sentences cannot be retrieved easily, so it is difficult to determine their precise frequency, but we can estimate it. Let us search for finite forms of *be* that are not followed by a negative clitic (*isn't*) or particle (*is not*) within the next three tokens (to exclude cases where the particle is preceded by an adverb, as in *is just/obviously/... not*). There are 146 493 such occurrences for female speakers and 215 219 for male speakers. The query will capture interrogatives, imperatives, subordinate clauses and other contexts that cannot contain tag questions, so let us draw a sample of 100 hits from both samples and determine how many of the hits are in fact declarative sentences with positive polarity that could (or do) contain a tag question. Let us assume that we find 67 hits in the female-speaker sample and 71 hits in the male-speaker sample to be such sentences. We can now adjust the total results of our queries by multiplying them with 0.67 and 0.71 respectively, giving us 98 150 sentences for female and 152 806 sentences for male speakers. In other words, male speakers produce 60.89 percent of the contexts in which a negative polarity tag question with *be* could occur. We can cross-check this by counting the total number of words uttered by male and female speakers in the spoken part of the BNC: there are 5 654 348 words produced by men and 3 825 804 words produced by women, which means that men produce 59.64 percent of the words, which fits our estimate very well.

These numbers can now be used to compare the number of tag questions against, as shown in Table 8.24. Since the tag questions that we found using our queries have negative polarity, they are not included in the sample, but must occur as tags to a subset of the sentences. This means that by subtracting the number of tag questions from the total for each group of speakers, we get the number of sentences without tag questions.

The difference between male and female speakers is highly significant, with female speakers using substantially more tag questions than expected, and male speakers using substantially fewer ($\chi^2 = 743.07, \mathrm{df} = 1, p < 0.001$).

This case study was intended to introduce the study of sex-related differences in grammar (or grammatical usage); cf. Mondorf (2004a) for additional studies and an overview of the literature. It was also intended to demonstrate the kinds of steps necessary to extract the required frequencies for a grammatical research question from an untagged corpus, and the ways in which they might be estimated if they cannot be determined precisely. Of course, these steps and considerations depend to a large extent on the specific phenomenon under investigation;

Table 8.24: Negative polarity tag questions in male and female speech in the spoken BNC

		Speaker Sex		
		female	male	Total
Tag Question	with	3771 (2684.15)	3092 (4178.85)	6863
	without	94 379 (95 465.85)	149 714 (148 627.15)	244 093
	Total	98 150	152 806	250 956

one reason for choosing tag questions with *be* is that they, and the sentences against which to compare their frequency, are much easier to extract from an untagged corpus than is the case for tag questions with *have*, or, worst of all, *do* (think about all the challenges these would confront us with).

8.2.5.2 Case study: Language change

Grammatical differences between varieties of a language will generally change over time – they may increase, as speech communities develop separate linguistic identities or even lose contact with each other, or they may decrease, e.g. through mutual influence. For example, Berlage (2009) studies word-order differences in the placement of adpositions in British and American English, focusing on *notwithstanding* as a salient member of a group of adpositions that can occur as both pre- and postpositions in both varieties. Two larger questions that she attempts to answer are, first, the diachronic development and, second, the interaction of word order and grammatical complexity. She finds that the prepositional use is preferred in British English (around two thirds of all uses are prepositions in present-day British newspapers) while American English favors the postpositional use (more than two thirds of occurrences in American English are postpositions). She shows that the postpositional use initially accounted for around a quarter of all uses but then almost disappeared in both varieties; its re-emergence in American English is a recent development (the convergence and/or divergence of British and American English has been intensively studied, cf. e.g. Hundt 1997 and Hundt 2009).

The basic design with which to test the convergence or divergence of two varieties with respect to a particular feature is a multivariate one with Variety and

Period as independent variables and the frequency of the feature as a dependent one. Let us try to apply such a design to *notwithstanding* using the LOB, BROWN, FLOB and FROWN corpora (two British and two American corpora each from the 1960s and the 1990s). Note that these corpora are rather small and 30 years is not a long period of time, so we would not necessarily expect results even if the hypothesis were correct that American English reintroduced postpositional *notwithstanding* in the 20th century (it is likely to be correct, as Berlage shows on a much larger data sample from different sources).

Notwithstanding is a relatively infrequent adposition: there are only 36 hits in the four corpora combined. Table 8.25 shows their distribution across the eight conditions.

Table 8.25: *Notwithstanding* as a preposition and postposition in British and American English

	1961					1991					
	BrE		AmE		Total	BrE		AmE		Total	Total
preposition	*Obs.:*	12	*Obs.:*	3	15	*Obs.:*	7	*Obs.:*	5	12	27
	Exp.:	6.63	*Exp.:*	5.05		*Exp.:*	8.70	*Exp.:*	6.63		
	χ^2:	4.36	χ^2:	0.83		χ^2:	0.33	χ^2:	0.40		
tablevspace postposition	*Obs.:*	0	*Obs.:*	1	1	*Obs.:*	2	*Obs.:*	7	9	10
	Exp.:	2.45	*Exp.:*	1.87		*Exp.:*	3.22	*Exp.:*	2.45		
	χ^2:	2.45	χ^2:	0.40		χ^2:	0.46	χ^2:	8.42		
Total	12		4		16	9		12		21	37

While the prepositional use is more frequent in both corpora from 1961, the postpositional use is the more frequent one in the American English corpus from 1991. A CFA shows that the intersection 1991 ∩ am.engl ∩ postposition is the only one whose observed frequencies differ significantly from the expected.

Due to the small number of cases, we would be well advised not to place too much confidence in our results, but as it stands they fully corroborate Berlage's claims that British English prefers the prepositional use and American English has recently begun to prefer the postpositional use.

This case study is intended to provide a further example of a multivariate design and to show that even small data sets may provide evidence for or against a hypothesis. It is also intended to introduce the study of the convergence and/ or divergence of varieties and the basic design required. This field of studies is of interest especially in the case of pluricentric languages like, for example, English, Spanish or Arabic (see Rohdenburg & Schlüter (2009), from which Berlage's study is taken, for a broad, empirically founded introduction to the contrastive study of British and American English grammar; cf. also Leech & Kehoe (2006)).

8.2.5.3 Case study: Grammaticalization

One of the central issues in grammaticalization theory is the relationship between grammaticalization and discourse frequency. Very broadly, the question is whether a rise in discourse frequency is a precondition for (or at least a crucial driving force in) the grammaticalization of a structure, or whether it is a consequence.

Since corpora are the only source for the identification of changes in discourse frequency, this is a question that can only be answered using corpus-linguistic methodology. An excellent example is Mair (2004), which looks at a number of grammaticalization phenomena to answer this and other questions.

He uses the OED's citation database as a corpus (not just the citations given in the OED's entry for the specific phenomena he is interested in, but all citations used in the entire OED). It is an interesting question to what extent such a citation database can be treated as a corpus (cf. the extensive discussion in Hoffmann 2004). One argument against doing so is that it is an intentional selection of certain examples over others and thus may not yield an authentic picture of any given phenomenon. However, as Mair points out, the vast majority of examples of a given phenomenon X will occur in citations that were collected to illustrate other phenomena, so they should constitute random samples with respect to X. The advantage of citation databases for historical research is that the sources for citations will have been carefully checked and very precise information will be available as to their year of publication and their author.

Let us look at one of Mair's examples and compare his results to those derived from more traditional corpora, namely the Corpus of Late Modern English Texts (CLMET), LOB and FLOB. The example is that of the *going-to* future. It is relatively easy to determine at what point at the latest the sequence [*going to* $\mathrm{V}_{\mathrm{inf}}$] was established as a future marker. In the literature on *going to*, the following example from the 1482 *Revelation to the Monk of Evesham* is considered the first documented use with a future meaning (it is also the first citation in the OED):

(14) Therefore while thys onhappy sowle by the vyctoryse pompys of her enmyes was goyng to be broughte into helle for the synne and onleful lustys of her body.

Mair also notes that the *going-to* future is mentioned in grammars from 1646 onward; at the very latest, then, it was established at the end of the 17th century. If a rise in discourse frequency is a precondition for grammaticalization, we should see such a rise in the period leading up to the end of the 17th century; if not, we should see such a rise only after this point.

Figure 8.1 shows Mair's results based on the OED citations, redrawn as closely as possible from the plot he presents (he does not report the actual frequencies). It also shows frequency data for the query ⟨ `[word="going"%c] [word="to"%c] [pos="V.*"]` ⟩ from the periods covered by the CLMET, LOB and FLOB. Note that Mair categorizes his data in quarter centuries, so the same has to be done for the CLMET. Most texts in the CLMET are annotated for a precise year of publication, but sometimes a time span is given instead. In these cases, let us put the texts into the quarter century that the larger part of this time span falls into. LOB and FLOB represent the quarter-centuries in which they were published. One quarter century is missing: there is no accessible corpus of British English covering the period 1926–1950. Let us extrapolate a value by taking the mean of the period preceding and following it. To make the corpus data comparable to Mair's, there is one additional step that is necessary: Mair plots frequencies per 10 000 citations; citations in the relevant period have a mean length of 12 words (see Hoffmann 2004: 25) – in other words, Mair's frequencies are per 120 000 words, so we have to convert our raw frequencies into frequencies per 120 000 words too. Table 8.26 shows the raw frequencies, normalized frequencies and data sources.

Table 8.26: Discourse frequency of *going to*

Period starting	Raw Freq.	No. of words	Freq. p. 120t words	Data Source
1701	14	168 799	9.95	CLMET
1726	242	4 623 107	6.28	CLMET
1751	591	5 446 006	13.02	CLMET
1776	258	4 308 242	7.19	CLMET
1801	231	3 087 842	8.98	CLMET
1826	552	8 024 490	8.25	CLMET
1851	442	5 335 906	9.94	CLMET
1876	816	5 349 213	18.31	CLMET
1901	722	3 997 155	21.68	CLMET
1926			21.50	(Extrapolated)
1951	180	1 012 985	21.32	LOB
1976	236	1 009 304	28.06	FLOB

The grey line in Figure 8.1 shows Mair's conservative estimate for the point at which the construction was firmly established as a way to express future tense.

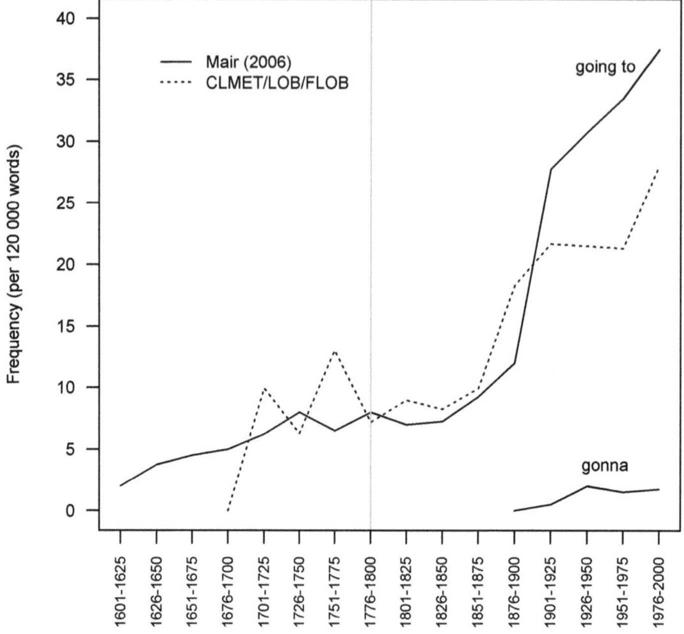

Figure 8.1: Grammaticalization and discourse frequency of *going to*

As the results from the OED citations and from the corpora show, there was only a small rise in frequency during the time that the construction became established, but a substantial jump in frequency afterwards. Interestingly, around the time of that jump, we also find the first documented instances of the contracted form *gonna* (from Mair's data – the contracted form is not frequent enough in the corpora used here to be shown). These results suggest that semantic reanalysis is the first step in grammaticalization, followed by a rise in discourse frequency accompanied by phonological reduction.

This case study demonstrates that very large collections of citations can indeed be used as a corpus, as long as we are investigating phenomena that are likely to occur in citations collected to illustrate other phenomena; the results are very similar to those we get from well-constructed linguistic corpora. The case study also demonstrates the importance of corpora in diachronic research, a field of study which, as mentioned in Chapter 1 has always relied on citations drawn from authentic texts, but which can profit from querying large collections of such texts and quantifying the results.

8.2.6 Grammar and cultural analysis

Like words, grammatical structures usually represent themselves in corpus linguistic studies – they are either investigated as part of a description of the syntactic behavior of lexical items or they are investigated in their own right in order to learn something about their semantic, formal or functional restrictions. However, like words, they can also be used as representatives of some aspect of the speech community's culture, specifically, a particular culturally defined scenario. To take a simple example: if we want to know what kinds of things are transferred between people in a given culture, we may look at the theme arguments of ditransitive constructions in a large corpus; we may look for collocates in the verb and theme positions of the ditransitive if we want to know *how* particular things are transferred (cf. Stefanowitsch & Gries 2009). In this way, grammatical structures can become diagnostics of culture. Again, care must be taken to ensure that the link between a grammatical structure and a putative scenario is plausible.

8.2.6.1 Case study: He said, she said

In a paper on the medial representation of men and women, Caldas-Coulthard (1993) finds that men are quoted vastly more frequently than women in the COBUILD corpus (cf. also Chapter 9). She also notes in passing that the verbs of communication used to introduce or attribute the quotes differ – both men's and women's speech is introduced using general verbs of communication, such as *say* or *tell*, but with respect to more descriptive verbs, there are differences: "Men *shout* and *groan*, while women (and children) *scream* and *yell*" (Caldas-Coulthard 1993: 204).

The construction [QUOTE + Subj + V] is a perfect example of a diagnostic for a cultural frame: it is routinely used (in written language) to describe a speech event. Crucially, the verb slot offers an opportunity to introduce additional information (such as the manner of speaking, as in the examples of manner verbs verbs just mentioned (that often contain evaluations), but also the type of speech act being performed (*ask*, *order*, etc.). It is also easy to find even in an untagged corpus, since it includes (by definition) a passage of direct speech surrounded by quotation marks, a subject that is, in an overwhelming number of cases, a pronoun, and a verb (or verb group) – typically in that order. In a written corpus, we can thus query the sequence ⟨`[word="'''"] [pos="pronoun"] [pos="verb"]`⟩ to find the majority of examples of the construction. In order to study differences in the representation of men and women, we can query the pronouns *he* and *she* separately to obtain representative samples of male and female speech act events without any annotation.

Table 8.27: Verbal collexemes of [QUOTE + Pron + V] (BNC)

VERB	Frequency with MALE SUBJECTS	Frequency with FEMALE SUBJECTS	Other words w. MALE SUBJECTS	Other words w. FEMALE SUBJECTS	*G*
Most strongly associated with MALE SUBJECTS					
say	19 301	11 710	34 916	26 180	221.11
growl	158	5	54 059	37 885	131.83
drawl	172	10	54 045	37 880	122.79
write	239	56	53 978	37 834	66.27
grate	80	4	54 137	37 886	59.78
grin	301	89	53 916	37 801	58.44
add	1526	771	52 691	37 119	57.04
rasp	78	7	54 139	37 883	46.78
continue	368	140	53 849	37 750	40.82
snarl	82	13	54 135	37 877	34.19
roar	54	5	54 163	37 885	31.89
chuckle	113	28	54 104	37 862	29.00
murmur	633	311	53 584	37 579	27.10
comment	117	34	54 100	37 856	23.37
shout	349	155	53 868	37 735	23.34
gesture	93	24	54 124	37 866	22.50
grunt	51	8	54 166	37 882	21.45
boom	26	1	54 191	37 889	20.78
wink	34	3	54 183	37 887	20.55
claim	69	16	54 148	37 874	19.35
Most strongly associated with FEMALE SUBJECTS					
whisper	393	666	53 824	37 224	205.21
cry	216	395	54 001	37 495	137.79
feel	94	206	54 123	37 684	92.86
manage	32	116	54 185	37 774	85.60
snap	174	275	54 043	37 615	73.81
retort	75	155	54 142	37 735	64.59
protest	60	136	54 157	37 754	63.88
giggle	13	61	54 204	37 829	53.40
try	85	152	54 132	37 738	50.91
ask	2136	1860	52 081	36 030	49.95
flush	5	41	54 212	37 849	46.53
wail	8	46	54 209	37 844	44.92
swallow	24	71	54 193	37 819	44.23
gasp	69	125	54 148	37 765	42.75
exclaim	137	196	54 080	37 694	42.44
force	9	45	54 208	37 845	40.85
flare	1	27	54 216	37 863	40.41
hear	82	130	54 135	37 760	35.01
sob	13	45	54 204	37 845	32.02
blush	3	27	54 214	37 863	31.65

Supplementary Online Material: RLW8

This design can be applied deductively, if we have hypotheses about the gender-specific usage of particular (sets of) verbs, or inductively, if we simply calculate the association strength of all verbs to one pronoun as compared to the other. In either case we have two nominal variables, SUBJECT OF QUOTED SPEECH, with the variables MALE (*he*) and FEMALE (*she*), and SPEECH ACTIVITY VERB with all occurring verbs as its values. Table 8.27 shows the results of an inductive application of the design to the BNC.

There is a clear difference that corroborates Caldas-Coulthard's casual observation: the top ten verbs of communication associated with men contain five verbs conveying a rough, unpleasant and/or aggressive manner of speaking (*growl, grate, rasp, snarl, roar*), while those for women only include one (*snap*, related to irritability rather than outright aggression). Interestingly, two very general communication verbs, *say* and *write*, are also typical for men's reported speech. Women's speech is introduced by verbs conveying weakness or communicative subordination (*whisper, cry, manage, protest, wail* and *deny*).

8.2.7 Grammar and counterexamples

While this book focuses on quantitative designs, non-quantitative designs are possible within the general framework adopted. Chapter 3 included a discussion of counterexamples and their place in a scientific framework for corpus linguistics. Let us conclude this chapter with a case study making use of them.

8.2.7.1 Case study: *To*- vs. *that*-complements

A good case study for English that is based largely on counterexamples is Noël (2003), who looks at a number of claims made about the semantics of infinitival complements as compared to *that*-clauses. He takes claims made by other authors based on their intuition and treats them like Popperian hypotheses, searching the BNC for counterexamples. He mentions more or less informal impressions about frequencies, but only to clarify that the counterexamples are not just isolated occurrences that could be explained away.

For example, he takes the well-known claim that with verbs of knowing, infinitival complements present knowledge as subjective/personal, while *that*-clauses present knowledge as objective/impersonal/public. This is supposed to explain acceptability judgments like the following (Borkin 1973: 45–46, Wierzbicka 1988: 50, 136):

(15) a. He found her to be intelligent.
b. * I bet that if you look in the files, you'll find her to be Mexican.
c. I bet that if you look in the files, you'll find that she is Mexican.

The crucial counterexample here would be one like (15b), with an infinitival complement that expresses knowledge that is "public" rather than "personal/experiential"; also of interest would be examples with *that*-clauses that express personal/experiential knowledge. The corresponding queries are easy enough to define:

(16) a. `[word="(find|finds|finding|found)"%c] [word="(me|you|him|her|it|us|them)"%c] [word="to"%c] [word="be"%c]`
b. `[word="(find|finds|finding|found)"%c] [word="that"%c] [word="(I|you|he|she|it|we|they)"%c] [word="(is|are|was|were)"%c]`

This query follows the specific example in (15b) very narrowly – we could, of course, define a broader one that would capture, for example, proper names and noun phrases in addition to pronouns. But remember that we are looking for counterexamples, and if we can find these with a query following the structure of supposedly non-acceptable sentences very closely, they will be all the more convincing.

The BNC contains not just one, but many counterexamples. Here are some examples with *that*-complements expressing subjective, personal knowledge:

(17) a. Erika was surprised to find that she was beginning to like Bach (BNC A7A)
b. [A]che of loneliness apart, I found that I was stimulated by the challenge of finding my way about this great and beautiful city. (BNC AMC)

And here are some with *to*-complements expressing objective, impersonal knowledge:

(18) a. Li and her coworkers have been able to locate these sequence variations ... in the three-dimensional structure of the toxin, and found them to be concentrated in the β sheets of domain II. (BNC ALV)
b. The visiting party, who were the first and last ever to get a good look at the crater of Perboewetan, found it to be about 1000 metres in diameter and about fifty metres deep. (BNC ASR)

These counterexamples (and others not cited here) in fact give us a new hypothesis as to what the specific semantic contribution of the *to*-complement may be: if used to refer to objective knowledge, it overwhelmingly refers to situations where this objective knowledge was not previously known to the participants of the situation described. In fact, if we extend our search for counterexamples beyond the BNC to the world-wide web, we find examples that are even more parallel to (15b), such as (19), all produced by native speakers of English:

(19) a. Afterwards found that French had stopped ship and found her to be German masquerading as Greek. (www.hmsneptune.com)
   b. I was able to trace back my Grandfathers name ... to Scotland and then into Sussex and Surrey, England. Very exciting! Reason being is because we were told that the ancestors were Irish and we found them to be Scottish! (www.gettheeblowdryer.com)
   c. Eishaus – This place is an Erlangen institution, should you ever get to meet the owner you'll find him to be American, he runs this wonderful ice cream shop as his summer job away from his 'proper' job in the states. (theerlangenexpat.wordpress.com)

Again, what is different in these examples from the (supposedly unacceptable) example (15b) is that the knowledge in question is new (and surprising) to the participants of the situation – a seemingly Greek ship turning out to be German, a supposedly Irish ancestor turning out to be Scottish, and the proprietor of an ice-cream shop in the small Bavarian town of Erlangen turning out to be American.

This observation could now be used as the basis for a new hypothesis concerning the difference between the two constructions, but even if it is not or if this hypothesis turned out to be false, the counterexamples clearly disprove the claim by Wierzbicka and others concerning the subjective/objective distinction (Noël 2003 actually goes on to propose an information-structural account of the difference between the *to*- and the *that*-complement).

This case study was intended to show how counterexamples may play a role in disproving hypotheses based on introspection and constructed examples (see Meurers 2005 and Meurers & Müller 2009 as good examples for the theoretically informed search for counterexamples).

9 Morphology

We saw in Chapter 8 that the wordform-centeredness of most corpora and corpus-access tools requires a certain degree of ingenuity when studying structures larger than the word. It does not pose particular problems for corpus-based morphology, which studies structures smaller than the word. Corpus morphology is mostly concerned with the distribution of affixes, and retrieving all occurrences of an affix plausibly starts with the retrieval of all strings potentially containing this affix. We could retrieve all occurrences of *-ness*, for example, with a query like ⟨`[word=".+ness(es)?"%c]`⟩. The recall of this query will be close to 100 percent, as all words containing the suffix *-ness* end in the string `ness`, optionally followed by the string `es` in the case of plurals. Depending on the tokenization of the corpus, this query might miss cases where the word containing the suffix *-ness* is the first part of a hyphenated compound, such as *usefulness-rating* or *consciousness-altering*; we could alter the query to something like ⟨`[word=".+ness(es)?(--.+=)?"%c]`⟩ if we believe that including these cases in our sample is crucial. The precision of such a query will not usually be 100 percent, as it will also retrieve words that accidentally happen to end with the string specified in our query – in the case of *-ness*, these would be words like *witness*, *governess* or place names like *Inverness*. The degree of precision will depend on how unique the string in our query is for the affix in question; for *-ness* and *-ity* it is fairly high, as there are only a few words that share the same string accidentally (examples like those just mentioned for *-ness* and words like *city* and *pity* for *-ity*), for a suffix like *-ess* ('female animate entity') it is quite low, as a query like ⟨`[word=".+ess(es)?"%c]`⟩ will also retrieve all words with the suffixes *-ness* and *-less*, as well as many words whose stem ends in *ess*, like *process*, *success*, *press*, *access*, *address*, *dress*, *guess* and many more.

However, once we have extracted and – if necessary – manually cleaned up our data set, we are faced with a problem that does not present itself when studying lexis or grammar: the very fact that affixes do not occur independently but always as parts of words, some of which (like *wordform-centeredness* in the first sentence of this chapter) have been created productively on the fly for a specific purpose, while others (like *ingenuity* in the same sentence) are conventionalized lexical items that are listed in dictionaries, even though they are theoretically the result of attaching an affix to a known stem (like *ingen-*, also found in *ingenious* and, confusingly, its almost-antonym *ingenuous*). We have to keep the difference between these two kinds of words in mind when constructing morphological research designs; since the two kinds are not always clearly distinguishable, this is more difficult than it sounds. Also, the fact that affixes always occur as parts of words has consequences for the way we can, and should, count them; in quantitative corpus-linguistics, this is a crucial point, so I will discuss it in quite some detail before we turn to our case studies.

9.1 Quantifying morphological phenomena

9.1.1 Counting morphemes: Types, tokens and hapax legomena

Determining the frequency of a linguistic phenomenon in a corpus or under a particular condition seems a straightforward task: we simply count the number of instances of this phenomenon in the corpus or under that condition. However, this sounds straightforward (in fact, tautological) only because we have made tacit assumptions about what it means to be an "instance" of a particular phenomenon.

When we are interested in the frequency of occurrence of a particular word, it seems obvious that every occurrence of the word counts as an instance. In other words, if we know how often the word occurs in our data, we know how many instances there are in our data. For example, in order to determine the number of instances of the definite article in the BNC, we construct a query that will retrieve the string `the` in all combinations of upper and lower case letters, i.e. at least *the*, *The*, and *THE*, but perhaps also *tHe*, *ThE*, *THe*, *tHE* and *thE*, just to be sure). We then count the hits (since this string corresponds uniquely to the word *the*, we don't even have to clean up the results manually). The query will yield 6 041 234 hits, so there are 6 041 234 instances of the word *the* in the BNC.

When searching for grammatical structures (for example in Chapters 5 and 6), simply transferred this way of counting occurrences. For example, in order to determine the frequency of the *s*-possessive in the BNC, we would define a reasonable query or set of queries (which, as discussed in various places in this book, can be tricky) and again simply count the hits. Let us assume that the query ⟨`[pos="(POS|DPS)"] [pos=".*AJ.*"]? [pos=".*NN.*"]`⟩ is a reasonable approximation: it retrieves all instances of the possessive clitic (tagged `POS` in the BNC) or a possessive determiner (`DPS`), optionally followed by a word tagged as an adjective (`AJ0`, `AJC` or `AJS`, even if it is part of an ambiguity tag), followed by a word tagged as a noun (`NN0`, `NN1` or `NN2`, even if it is part of an ambiguity tag). This query will retrieve 1 651 908 hits, so it seems that there are 1 651 908 instances of the *s*-possessive in the BNC.

However, there is a crucial difference between the two situations: in the case of the word *the*, every instance is identical to all others (if we ignore upper and lower case). This is not the case for the *s*-possessive. Of course, here, too, many instances are identical to other instances: there are exact repetitions of proper names, like *King's Cross* (322 hits) or *People's revolutionary party* (47), of (parts of) idiomatic expressions, like *arm's length* (216) or *heaven's sake* (187) or non-idiomatic but nevertheless fixed phrases like *its present form* (107) or *child's best interest* (26), and also of many free combinations of words that recur because they are simply communicatively useful in many situations, like *her head* (5105), *his younger brother* (112), *people's lives* (224) and *body's immune system* (29).

This means that there are two different ways to count occurrences of the *s*-possessive. First, we could simply count all instances without paying any attention to whether they recur in identical form or not. When looking at occurrences of a linguistic item or structure in this way, they are referred to as *tokens*, so 1 651 908 is the *token frequency* of the possessive. Second, we could exclude repetitions and count only the number of instances that are different from each other, for example, we would count *King's Cross* only the first time we encounter it, disregarding the other 321 occurrences. When looking at occurrences of linguistic items in this way, they are referred to as *types*; the type frequency of the *s*-possessive in the BNC is 268 450 (again, ignoring upper and lower case). The type frequency of *the*, of course, is 1.

Let us look at one more example of the type/token distinction before we move on. Consider the following famous line from the theme song of the classic television series "Mister Ed":

(1) A horse is a horse, of course, of course...

At the word level, it consists of nine tokens (if we ignore punctuation): *a*, *horse*, *is*, *a*, *horse*, *of*, *course*, *of*, and *course*, but only of five types: *a*, *horse*, *is*, *of*, and *course*. Four of these types occur twice, one (*is*) occurs only once. At the level of phrase structure, it consists of seven tokens: the NPs *a horse*, *a horse*, *course*, and *course*, the PPs *of course* and *of course*, and the VP *is a horse*, but only of three types: VP, NP and PP.

In other words, we can count *instances* at the level of types or at the level of tokens. Which of the two levels is relevant in the context of a particular research design depends both on the kind of phenomenon we are counting and on our research question. When studying words, we will normally be interested in how often they are used under a particular condition, so it is their token frequency that is relevant to us; but we could imagine designs where we are mainly interested in whether a word occurs at all, in which case all that is relevant is whether its type frequency is one or zero. When studying grammatical structures, we will also mainly be interested in how frequently a particular grammatical structure is used under a certain condition, regardless of the words that fill this structure. Again, it is the token frequency that is relevant to us. However, note that we can (to some extent) ignore the specific words filling our structure only because we are assuming that the structure and the words are, in some meaningful sense, independent of each other; i.e., that the same words could have been used in a different structure (say, an *of*-possessive instead of an *s*-possessive) or that the same structure could have been used with different words (e.g. *John's spouse* instead of *his wife*). Recall that in our case studies in Chapter 6 we excluded all instances where this assumption does not hold (such as proper names and fixed expressions); since there is no (or very little) choice with these cases, including them, let alone counting repeated occurrences of them, would have added nothing (we did, of course, include repetitions of free combinations, of which there were four in our sample: *his staff, his mouth, his work* and *his head* occurred twice each).

Obviously, instances of morphemes (whether inflectional or derivational) can be counted in the same two ways. Take the following passage from William Shakespeare's play Julius Cesar:

(2) CINNA: ... Am I a married man, or a bachelor? Then, to answer every man directly and briefly, wisely and truly: wisely I say, I am a bachelor.

Let us count the occurrences of the adverbial suffix *-ly*. There are five word tokens that contain this suffix (*directly, briefly, wisely, truly*, and *wisely*), so its token frequency is five; however, there are only four types, since *wisely* occurs twice, so its type frequency in this passage is four.

Again, whether type or token frequency is the more relevant or useful measure depends on the research design, but the issue is more complicated than in the case of words and grammatical structures. Let us begin to address this problem by looking at the diminutive affixes *-icle* (as in *cubicle, icicle*) and *mini-* (as in *minivan, mini-cassette*).

9.1.1.1 Token frequency

First, let us count the tokens of both affixes in the BNC. This is relatively easy in the case of *-icle*, since the string `icle` is relatively unique to this morpheme (the name *Pericles* is one of the few false hits that the query ⟨`[word=".+icles?"%c]`⟩ will retrieve). It is more difficult in the case of *mini-*, since there are words like *minimal, minister, ministry, miniature* and others that start with the string `mini` but do not contain the prefix *mini-*. Once we have cleaned up our concordances (available in the Supplementary Online Material, file LMY7), we will find that *-icle* has a token frequency of 20 772 – more than ten times that of *mini-*, which occurs only 1702 times. We might thus be tempted to conclude that *-icle* is much more important in the English language than *mini-*, and that, if we are interested in English diminutives, we should focus on *-icle*. However, this conclusion would be misleading, or at least premature, for reasons related to the problems introduced above.

Recall that affixes do not occur by themselves, but always as parts of words (this is what makes them affixes in the first place). This means that their token frequency can reflect situations that are both quantitatively and qualitatively very different. Specifically, a high token frequency of an affix may be due to the fact that it is used in a small number of very frequent words, or in a large number of very infrequent words (or something in between). The first case holds for *-icle*: the three most frequent words it occurs in (*article, vehicle* and *particle*) account for 19 195 hits (i.e., 92.41 percent of all occurrences). In contrast, the three most frequent words with *mini-* (*mini-bus, mini-bar* and *mini-computer*) account for only 557 hits, i.e. 32.73 percent of all occurrences. To get to 92.4 percent, we would have to include the 253 most frequent words (roughly two thirds of all types).

In other words, the high token frequency of *-icle* tells us nothing (or at least very little) about the importance of the affix; if anything, it tells us something about the importance of some of the words containing it. This is true regardless of whether we look at its token frequency in the corpus as a whole or under specific conditions; if its token frequency turned out to be higher under one condition than under the other, this would point to the association between that condition and one or more of the words containing the affix, rather than between the condition and the affix itself.

For example, the token frequency of the suffix *-icle* is higher in the BROWN corpus (269 tokens) than in the LOB corpus (225 tokens). However, as Table 9.1 shows, this is simply due to differences in the frequency of individual words – the words *particle* and *vehicle* are substantially more frequent in the BROWN corpus, and while, conversely, *article* is more frequent in the LOB corpus, it cannot make up for the difference. As the χ^2 components show, the difference in frequency of some of the individual words is even statistically significant, but nothing follows from this with respect to the suffix *-icle*.

Table 9.1: Words containing *-icle* in two corpora

Word	Corpus: LOB		Corpus: BROWN		Total
article	*Obs.:*	126	*Obs.:*	99	225
	Exp.:	102.48	*Exp.:*	122.52	
	χ^2:	5.40	χ^2:	4.52	
particle	*Obs.:*	38	*Obs.:*	64	102
	Exp.:	46.46	*Exp.:*	55.54	
	χ^2:	1.54	χ^2:	1.29	
vehicle	*Obs.:*	39	*Obs.:*	88	127
	Exp.:	57.84	*Exp.:*	69.16	
	χ^2:	6.14	χ^2:	5.13	
chronicle	*Obs.:*	7	*Obs.:*	7	14
	Exp.:	6.38	*Exp.:*	7.62	
	χ^2:	0.06	χ^2:	0.05	
ventricle	*Obs.:*	8	*Obs.:*	4	12
	Exp.:	5.47	*Exp.:*	6.53	
	χ^2:	1.18	χ^2:	0.98	
auricle	*Obs.:*	5	*Obs.:*	0	5
	Exp.:	2.28	*Exp.:*	2.72	
	χ^2:	3.26	χ^2:	2.72	
fascicle	*Obs.:*	0	*Obs.:*	3	3
	Exp.:	1.37	*Exp.:*	1.63	
	χ^2:	1.37	χ^2:	1.14	
testicle	*Obs.:*	0	*Obs.:*	2	2
	Exp.:	0.91	*Exp.:*	1.09	
	χ^2:	0.91	χ^2:	0.76	
conventicle	*Obs.:*	1	*Obs.:*	0	1
	Exp.:	0.46	*Exp.:*	0.54	
	χ^2:	0.65	χ^2:	0.54	
cuticle	*Obs.:*	1	*Obs.:*	0	1
	Exp.:	0.46	*Exp.:*	0.54	
	χ^2:	0.65	χ^2:	0.54	
canticle	*Obs.:*	0	*Obs.:*	1	1
	Exp.:	0.46	*Exp.:*	0.54	
	χ^2:	0.46	χ^2:	0.38	
icicle	*Obs.:*	0	*Obs.:*	1	1
	Exp.:	0.46	*Exp.:*	0.54	
	χ^2:	0.46	χ^2:	0.38	
Total		225		269	494

Even if all words containing a particular affix were more frequent under one condition (e.g. in one variety) than under another, this would tell us nothing certain about the affix itself: while such a difference in frequency could be due to the affix itself (as in the case of the adverbial suffix *-ly*, which is disappearing from American English, but not from British English), it could also be due exclusively to the words containing the affix.

This is not to say that the token frequencies of affixes can never play a useful role; they may be of interest, for example, in cases of morphological alternation (i.e. two suffixes competing for the same stems, such as *-ic* and *-ical* in words like *electric/al*); here, we may be interested in the quantitative association between particular stems and one or the other of the affix variants, essentially giving us a collocation-like research design based on token frequencies. But for most research questions, the distribution of token frequencies under different conditions is meaningless.

9.1.1.2 Type frequency

In contrast, the type frequency of an affix is a fairly direct reflection of the importance of the affix for the lexicon of a language: obviously an affix that occurs in many different words is more important than one that occurs only in a few words. Note that in order to compare type frequencies, we have to correct for the size of the sample: all else being equal, a larger sample will contain more types than a smaller one simply because it offers more opportunities for different types to occur (a point we will return to in more detail in the next subsection). A simple way of doing this is to divide the number of types by the number of tokens; the resulting measure is referred to very transparently as the *type/token ratio* (or TTR):

(3) $$\text{TTR} = \frac{n\,(\text{types})}{n\,(\text{tokens})}$$

The TTR is the percentage of types in a sample are different from each other; or, put differently, it is the mean probability that we will encounter a new type if we go through the sample item by item.

For example, the affix *-icle* occurs in just 31 different words in the BNC, so its TTR is $31/20772 = 0.0015$. In other words, 0.15 percent of its tokens in the BNC are different from each other, the vast remainder consists of repetitions. Put differently, if we go through the occurrences of *-icle* in the BNC item by item, the probability that the next item instantiating this suffix will be a type we have not seen before is 0.15 percent, so we will encounter a new type on average once every 670 words. For *mini-*, the type-token ratio is much higher: it occurs in 382 different words, so its TTR is $382/1702 = 0.2244$. In other words, almost a quarter of all occurrences of *mini-* are different from each other. Put differently, if we go through the occurrences of *mini-* in the BNC word by word, the probability that the next instance is a new type would be 22.4 percent, so we will encounter a new type about every four to five hits. The differences in their TTRs suggests that *mini-*, in its own right, is much more central in the English lexicon than *-icle*, even though the latter has a much higher token frequency. Note that this is a statement only about the affixes; it does not mean that the *words* containing *mini-* are individually or collectively more important than those containing *-icle* (on the contrary: words like *vehicle, article* and *particle* are arguably much more important than words like *minibus, minicomputer* and *minibar*).

Likewise, observing the type frequency (i.e. the TTR) of an affix under different conditions provides information about the relationship between these conditions and the affix itself, albeit one that is mediated by the lexicon: it tells us how important the suffix in question is for the subparts of the lexicon that are relevant under those conditions. For example, there are 7 types and 9 tokens for *mini-* in the 1991 British FLOB corpus (two tokens each for *mini-bus* and *mini-series* and one each for *mini-charter, mini-disc, mini-maestro, mini-roll* and *mini-submarine*), so the TTR is $7/9 = 0.7779$. In contrast, in the 1991 US-American FROWN corpus, there are 11 types and 12 tokens (two tokens for *mini-jack*, and one token each for *mini-cavalry, mini-cooper, mini-major, mini-retrospective, mini-version, mini-boom, mini-camp, mini-grinder, mini-series*, and *mini-skirt*), so the TTR is $11/12 = 0.9167$. This suggests that the prefix *mini-* was more important to the US-English lexicon than to the British English lexicon in the 1990s, although, of course, the samples and the difference between them are both rather small, so we would not want to draw that conclusion without consulting larger corpora and, possibly, testing for significance first (a point I will return to in the next subsection).

9.1.1.3 Hapax legomena

While type frequency is a useful way of measuring the importance of affixes in general or under specific conditions, it has one drawback: it does not tell us whether the affix plays a productive role in a language at the time from which we take our samples (i.e. whether speakers at that time made use of it when coining new words). An affix may have a high TTR because it was productively used at the time of the sample, or because it was productively used at some earlier period in the history of the language in question. In fact, an affix can have a high TTR even if it was never productively used, for example, because speakers at some point borrowed a large number of words containing it; this is the case for a number of Romance affixes in English, occurring in words borrowed from Norman French but never (or very rarely) used to coin new words. An example is the suffix *-ence/-ance* occurring in many Latin and French loanwords (such as *appearance, difference, existence, influence, nuisance, providence, resistance, significance, vigilance,* etc.), but only in a handful of words formed in English (e.g. *abidance, forbearance, furtherance, hinderance,* and *riddance*).

In order to determine the productivity (and thus the current importance) of affixes at a particular point in time, Harald Baayen (cf. e.g. Baayen 2009 for an overview) has suggested that we should focus on types that only occur once in the corpus, so-called *hapax legomena* (Greek for 'said once'). The assumption is that productive uses of an affix (or other linguistic rule) should result in one-off coinages (some of which may subsequently spread through the speech community while others will not).

Of course, not all hapax legomena are the result of productive rule-application: the words *wordform-centeredness* and *ingenuity* that I used in the first sentence of this chapter are both hapax legomena in this book (or would be, if I did not keep mentioning them). However, *wordform-centeredness* is a word I coined productively and which is (at the time of writing) not documented anywhere outside of this book; in fact, the sole reason I coined it was in order to use it as an example of a hapax legomenon later). In contrast, *ingenuity* has been part of the English language for more than four-hundred years (the OED first records it in 1598); it occurs only once in this book for the simple reason that I only needed it once (or pretended to need it, to have another example of a hapax legomenon). So a word may be a hapax legomenon because it is a productive coinage, or because it is infrequently needed (in larger corpora, the category of hapaxes typically also contains misspelled or incorrectly tokenized words which will have to be cleaned up manualy – for example, the token *manualy* is a hapax legomenon in this book because I just misspelled it intentionally, but the word *manually* occurs dozens of times in this book).

Baayen's idea is quite straightforwardly to use the phenomenon of *hapax legomenon* as an operationalization of the construct "productive application of a rule" in the hope that the correlation between the two notions (in a large enough corpus) will be substantial enough for this operationalization to make sense.[1]

[1]Note also that the productive application of a suffix does not necessarily result in a hapax legomenon: two or more speakers may arrive at the same coinage, or a single speaker may like their own coinage so much that they use it again; some researchers therefore suggest that we should also pay attention to "dis legomena" (words occurring twice) or even "tris legomena" (words occurring three times). We will stick with the mainstream here and use only hapax legomena.

Like the number of types, the number of hapax legomena is dependent on sample size (although the relationship is not as straightforward as in the case of types, see next subsection); it is useful, therefore, to divide the number of hapax legomena by the number of tokens to correct for sample size:

(4) $$\text{HTR} = \frac{n\,(\text{hapax legomena})}{n\,(\text{tokens})}$$

We will refer to this measure as the hapax-token ratio (or HTR) by analogy with the term *type-token ratio*. Note, however, that in the literature this measure is referred to as *P* for "Productivity" (following Baayen, who first suggested the measure); I depart from this nomenclature here to avoid confusion with *p* for "probability (of error)".

Let us apply this measure to our two diminutive affixes. The suffix *-icle* has just five hapax legomena in the BNC (*auricle, denticle, pedicle, pellicle* and *tunicle*). This means that its HTR is $5/20772 = 0.0002$, so 0.02 percent of its tokens are hapax legomena. In contrast, there are 247 hapax legomena for *mini-* in the BNC (including, for example, *mini-earthquake, mini-daffodil, mini-gasometer, mini-cow* and *mini-wurlitzer*). This means that its HTR is $247/1702 = 0.1451$, so 14.5 percent of its tokens are hapax legomena. Thus, we can assume that *mini-* is much more productive than *-icle*, which presumably matches the intuition of most speakers of English.

9.1.2 Statistical evaluation

As pointed out in connection with the comparison of the TTRs for *mini-* in the FLOB and the FROWN corpus, we would like to be able to test differences between two (or more) TTRs (and, of course, also two or more HTRs) for statistical significance. Theoretically, this could be done very easily. Take the TTR: if we interpret it as the probability of encountering a new type as we move through our samples, we are treating it like a nominal variable TYPE, with the values NEW and SEEN BEFORE. One appropriate statistical test for distributions of nominal values under different conditions is the χ^2 test, which we are already more than familiar with. For example, if we wanted to test whether the TTRs of *-icle* and *mini-* in the BNC differ significantly, we might construct a table like Table 9.2.

The χ^2 test would tell us that the difference is highly significant with a respectable effect size ($\chi^2 = 4334.67, \text{df} = 1, p < 0.001, \phi = 0.4392$). For HTRs, we could follow a similar procedure: in this case we are dealing with a nominal variable TYPE with the variables OCCURS ONLY ONCE and OCCURS MORE THAN ONCE, so we could construct the corresponding table and perform the χ^2 test.

Table 9.2: Type/token ratios of *-icle* and *mini-* in the BNC

		Affix		
		-icle	mini-	Total
Type	new	31 (381.72)	382 (31.28)	413
	seen before	20 741 (20 390.28)	1320 (1670.72)	22 061
	Total	20 772	1702	22 474

However, while the logic behind this procedure may seem plausible in theory both for HTRs and for TTRs, in practice, matters are much more complicated. The reason for this is that, as mentioned above, type-token ratios and hapax-token ratios are dependent on sample size.

In order to understand why and how this is the case and how to deal with it, let us leave the domain of morphology for a moment and look at the relationship between tokens and types or hapax legomena in texts. Consider the opening sentences of Jane Austen's novel *Pride and Prejudice* (the novel is freely available from Project Gutenberg and in the Supplementary Online Material, file TXQP):

(5) It is a truth universally acknowledged, that $a_{2/-1}$ single man in possession of a_3 good fortune, must be $in_{2/-1}$ want $of_{2/-1}$ a_4 wife. However little known the feelings or views of_3 such a_5 $man_{2/-1}$ may $be_{2/-1}$ on his first entering a_6 neighbourhood, this $truth_{2/-1}$ $is_{2/-1}$ so well fixed in_3 $the_{2/-1}$ minds of_4 the surrounding families, $that_{2/-1}$ he is_3 considered the rightful property of_5 some one $or_{2/-1}$ other of_6 their daughters.

All words without a subscript are new types and hapax legomena at the point at which they appear in the text; if a word has a subscript, it means that it is a repetition of a previously mentioned word, the subscript is its token frequency at this point in the text. The first repetition of a word is additionally marked by a subscript reading -1, indicating that it ceases to be hapax legomenon at this point, decreasing the overall count of hapaxes by one.

As we move through the text word by word, initially all words are new types and hapaxes, so the type- and hapax-counts rise at the same rate as the token counts. However, it only takes eight token before we reach the first repetition (the word *a*), so while the token frequency rises to 8, the type count remains constant at seven and the hapax count falls to six. Six words later, there is another occurrence of *a*, so type and hapax counts remain, respectively, at 12 and 11 as the token count rises to 14, and so on. In other words, while the number of types and the number of hapaxes generally increase as the number of tokens in a sample increases, they do not increase at a steady rate. The more types have already occurred, the more types there are to be reused (put simply, speakers will encounter fewer and fewer communicative situations that require a new type), which makes it less and less probable that new types (including new hapaxes) will occur. Figure 9.1 shows how type and hapax counts develop in the first 100 words of *Pride and Prejudice* (on the left) and in the whole novel (on the right).

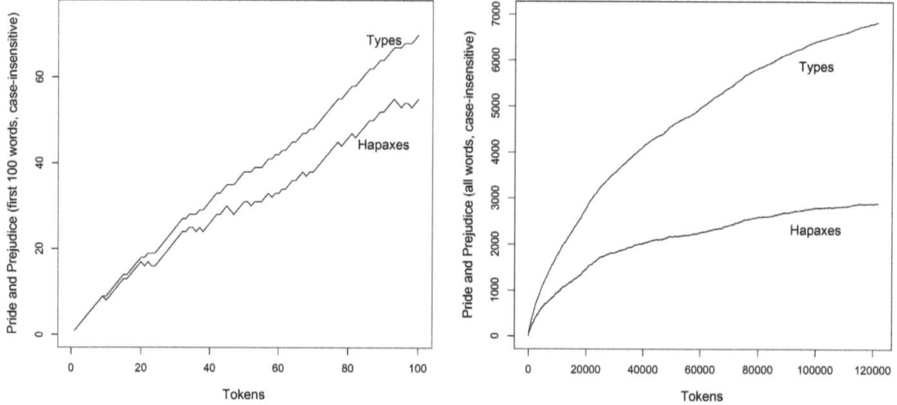

Figure 9.1: TTR and HTR in Jane Austen's *Pride and Prejudice*

As we can see by looking at the first 100 words, type and hapax counts fall below the token counts fairly quickly: after 20 tokens, the TTR is $18/20 = 0.9$ and the HTR is $17/20 = 0.85$, after 40 tokens the TTR is $31/40 = 0.775$ and the HTR is $26/40 = 0.65$, after 60 tokens the HTR is $42/60 = 0.7$ and the TTR is $33/60 = 0.55$, and so on (note also how the hapax-token ratio sometimes drops before it rises again, as words that were hapaxes up to a particular point in the text reoccur and cease to be counted as hapaxes). If we zoom out and look at the entire novel, we see that the growth in hapaxes slows considerably, to the extent that it has almost stopped by the time we reach the end of the novel. The growth in types also slows, although not as much as in the case of the hapaxes. In both cases this means that the ratios will continue to fall as the number of tokens increases.

Now imagine we wanted to use the TTR and the HTR as measures of Jane Austen's overall lexical productivity (referred to as "lexical richness" in computational stylistics and in second-language teaching): if we chose a small sample of her writing, the TTR and the HTR would be larger than if we chose a large sample, to the extent that the scores derived from the two samples would differ significantly. Table 9.3 shows what would happen if we compared the TTR of the first chapter with the TTR of the entire rest of the novel.

Table 9.3: Type/token ratios in the novel *Pride and Prejudice*

		Type		
		NEW	¬NEW	Total
Text Sample	FIRST CHAPTER	321	6829	7150
		(47.29)	(7102.71)	
	¬FIRST CHAPTER	528	120 679	121 207
		(801.71)	(120 405.29)	
	Total	849	127 508	128 357

The TTR for the first chapter is an impressive 0.3781, that for the rest of the novel is a measly 0.0566, and the difference is highly significant ($\chi^2 = 1688.7$, df = 1, $p < 0.001$, $\phi = 0.1147$). But this is not because there is anything special about the first chapter; the TTR for the second chapter is 0.3910, that for the third is 0.3457, that for chapter 4 is 0.3943, and so on. The reason why the first chapter (or any chapter) looks as though it has a significantly higher TTR than the novel as a whole is simply because the TTR will drop as the size of the text increases.

Therefore, comparing TTRs derived from samples of different sizes will always make the smaller sample look more productive. In other words, we cannot compare such TTRs, let alone evaluate the differences statistically – the result will simply be meaningless. The same is true for HTRs, with the added problem that, under certain circumstances, it will decrease at some point as we keep increasing the sample size: at some point, all possible words will have been used, so unless new words are added to the language, the number of hapaxes will shrink again and finally drop to zero when all existing types have been used at least twice.

We will encounter the same problem when we compare the TTR or HTR of particular affixes or other linguistic phenomena, rather than that of a text. Consider Figures 9.2a and 9.2b, which show the TTR and the HTR of the verb suffixes *-ise/-ize* (occurring in words like *realize, maximize* or *liquidize*) and *-ify* (occurring in words like *identify, intensify* or *liquify*).

As we can see, the TTR and HTR of both affixes behave roughly like that of Jane Austen's vocabulary as a whole as we increase sample size: both of them

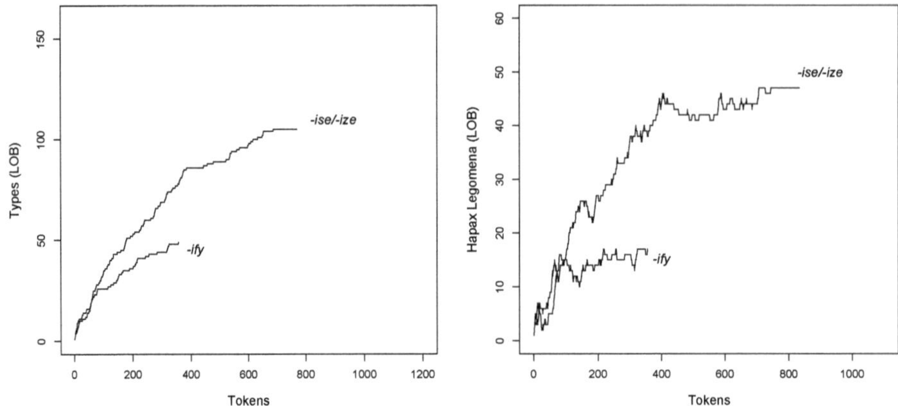

Figure 9.2: (a) TTRs and (b) HTRs for *-ise/-ize* and *-ify* in the LOB corpus

grow fairly quickly at first before their growth slows down; the latter happens more quickly in the case of the HTR than in the case of the TTR, and, again, we observe that the HTR sometimes decreases as types that were hapaxes up to a particular point in the sample reoccur and cease to be hapaxes.

Taking into account the entire sample, the TTR for *-ise/-ize* is 105/834 = 0.1259 and that for *-ify* is 49/356 = 0.1376; it seems that *-ise/-ize* is slightly more important to the lexicon of English than *-ify*. A χ^2 test suggests that the difference is not significant (cf. Table 9.4; $\chi^2 = 0.3053$, df = 1, $p > 0.05$).

Table 9.4: Type/token ratios of *-ise/-ize* and *-ify* (LOB)

		Type		
		new	seen before	Total
Affix	-ise/-ize	105 (107.93)	729 (726.07)	834
	-ify	49 (46.07)	307 (309.93)	356
	Total	154	1036	1190

Supplementary Online Material: EWTN

Likewise, taking into account the entire sample, the HTR for *-ise/-ize* is 47/834 = 0.0563 and that for *-ify* is 17/365 = 0.0477; it seems that *-ise/-ize* is slightly more productive than *-ify*. However, again, the difference is not significant (cf. Table 9.5; $\chi^2 = 0.3628$, df = 1, $p > 0.05$).

Table 9.5: Hapax/token ratios of *-ise/-ize* and *-ify* (LOB)

		TYPE		
		HAPAX	¬HAPAX	Total
AFFIX	-ISE/-IZE	47 (44.85)	787 (789.15)	834
	-IFY	17 (19.15)	339 (336.85)	356
	Total	64	1126	1190

However, note that *-ify* has a token frequency that is less than half of that of *-ise/-ize*, so the sample is much smaller: as in the example of lexical richness in *Pride and Prejudice*, this means that the TTR and the HTR of this smaller sample are exaggerated and our comparisons in Tables 9.4 and 9.5 as well as the accompanying statistics are, in fact, completely meaningless.

The simplest way of solving the problem of different sample sizes is to create samples of equal size for the purposes of comparison. We simply take the size of the smaller of our two samples and draw a random sample of the same size from the larger of the two samples (if our data sets are large enough, it would be even better to draw random samples for both affixes). This means that we lose some data, but there is nothing we can do about this (note that we can still include the discarded data in a qualitative description of the affix in question).[2]

Figures 9.3a and 9.3b show the growth rates of the TTR and the HTR of a sub-sample of 356 tokens of *-ise/-ize* in comparison with the total sample of the same size for *-ify* (the sample was derived by first deleting every second hit, then every seventh hit and finally every ninetieth hit, making sure that the remaining hits are spread throughout the corpus).

The TTR of *-ise/-ize* based on the random sub-sample is $^{78}/_{356} = 0.2191$, that of *-ify* is still $^{49}/_{356} = 0.1376$; the difference between the two suffixes is much clearer now, and a χ^2 test shows that it is very significant, although the effect size is weak (cf. Table 9.6; $\chi^2 = 8.06, \text{df} = 1, p < 0.01, \phi = 0.1064$).

[2]In studies of lexical richness, a measure called *Mean Segmental Type-Token Ratio* (MSTTR) is sometimes used (cf. Johnson 1944). This measure is derived by dividing the texts under investigation into segments of equal size (often segments of 100 words), determining the TTR for each segment, and then calculating an average TTR. This allows us to compare the TTR of texts of different sizes without discarding any data. However, this method is not applicable to the investigation of morphological productivity, as most samples of 100 words (or even 1000 or 10 000 words) will typically not contain enough cases of a given morpheme to determine a meaningful TTR.

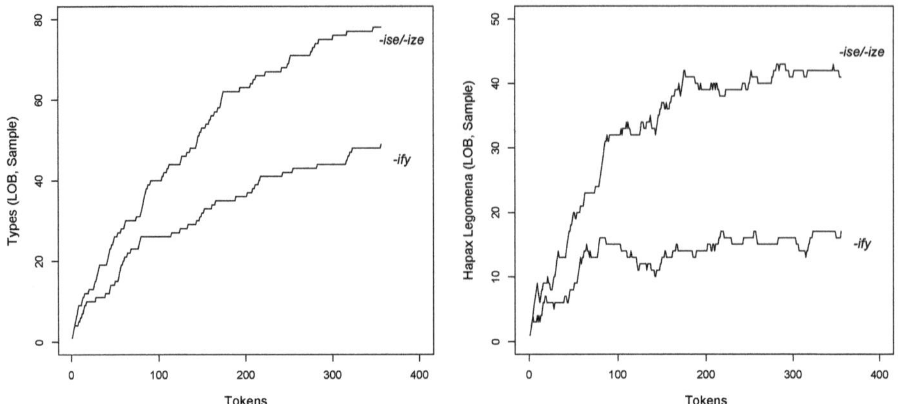

Figure 9.3: (a) TTRs and (b) HTRs for *-ise/-ize* and *-ify* in the LOB corpus

Table 9.6: Type/token ratios of *-ise/-ize*/ *-ise/-ize* (sample) and *-ify* (LOB)

		Type		
		new	seen before	Total
Affix	-ise/-ize	78 (63.50)	278 (292.50)	356
	-ify	49 (63.50)	307 (292.50)	356
	Total	127	585	712

Table 9.7: Hapax/token ratios of *-ise/-ize* (sample) and *-ify* (LOB)

		Type		
		hapax	¬hapax	Total
Affix	-ise/-ize	41 (29.00)	315 (327.00)	356
	-ify	17 (29.00)	339 (327.00)	356
	Total	58	654	712

Likewise, the HTR of *-ise/-ize* based on our sub-sample is 41/356 = 0.1152, the HTR of *-ify* remains 17/365 = 0.0477. Again, the difference is much clearer, and it, too, is now very significant, again with a weak effect size (cf. Table 9.7; $\chi^2 = 10.81, \mathrm{df} = 1, p < 0.01, \phi = 0.1232$).

In the case of the HTR, decreasing the sample size is slightly more problematic than in the case of the TTR. The proportion of hapax legomena actually resulting from productive rule application becomes smaller as sample size decreases. Take example (2) from Shakespeare's *Julius Caesar* above: the words *directly, briefly* and *truly* are all hapaxes in the passage cited, but they are clearly not the result of a productively applied rule-application (all of them have their own entries in the OALD, for example). As we increase the sample, they cease to be hapaxes (*directly* occurs 9 times in the entire play, *briefly* occurs 4 times and *truly* 8 times). This means that while we must draw random samples of equal size in order to compare HTRs, we should make sure that these samples are as large as possible.

9.2 Case studies

9.2.1 Morphemes and stems

One general question in (derivational) morphology concerns the category of the stem which an affix may be attached to. This is obviously a descriptive issue that can be investigated on the basis of corpora very straightforwardly simply by identifying all types containing the affix in question and describing their internal structure. In the case of affixes with low productivity, this will typically add little insight over studies based on dictionaries, but for productive affixes, a corpus analysis will yield more detailed and comprehensive results since corpora will contain spontaneously produced or at least recently created items not (yet) found in dictionaries. Such newly created words will often offer particularly clear insights into constraints that an affix places on its stems. Finally, corpus-based approaches are without an alternative in diachronic studies and yield particularly interesting results when used to study changes in the quality or degree of productivity, (cf. for example Dalton-Puffer 1996).

In the study of constraints placed by derivational affixes on the stems that they combine with, the combinability of derivational morphemes (in an absolute sense or in terms of preferences) is of particular interest. Again, corpus linguistics is a uniquely useful tool to investigate this.

Finally, there are cases where two derivational morphemes are in direct competition because they are functionally roughly equivalent (e.g. *-ness* and *-ity*, both of which form abstract nouns from typically adjectival bases, *-ise/-ize* and *-ify*, which form process verbs from nominal and adjectival bases, or *-ic* and *-ical*, which form adjectives from typically nominal bases). Here, too, corpus linguistics provides useful tools, for example to determine whether the choice between affixes is influenced by syntactic, semantic or phonological properties of stems.

9.2.1.1 Case study: Phonological constraints on *-ify*

As part of a larger argument that *-ise/-ize* and *-ify* should be considered phonologically conditioned allomorphs, Plag (1999) investigates the phonological constraints that *-ify* places on its stems. First, he summarizes the properties of stems in established words with *-ify* as observed in the literature. Second, he checks these observations against a sample of twenty-three recent (20th century) coinages from a corpus of neologisms to ensure that the constraints also apply to productive uses of the affix. This is a reasonable approach. The affix was first borrowed into English as part of a large number of French loanwords beginning in the late 13th century; two thirds of all non-hapax types and 19 of the 20 most frequent types found in the BNC are older than the 19th century. Thus, it is possible that the constraints observed in the literature are historical remnants not relevant to new coinages.

The most obvious constraint is that the syllable directly preceding *-ify* must carry the main stress of the word. This has a number of consequences, of which we will focus on two: First, monosyllabic stems (as in *falsify*) are preferred, since they always meet this criterion. Second, if a polysyllabic stem ends in an unstressed syllable, the stress must be shifted to that syllable (as in *perSONify* from *PERson*);[3] since this reduces the transparency of the stem, there should be a preference for those polysyllabic stems which already have the stress on the final syllable.

Plag simply checks his neologisms against the literature, but we will evaluate the claims from the literature quantitatively. Our main hypothesis will be that neologisms with *-ify* do not differ from established types with respect to the fact that the syllable directly preceding the suffix must carry primary stress, with the consequences that (i) they prefer monosyllabic stems, and (ii) if the stem is polysyllabic, they prefer stems that already have the primary stress on the last syllable. Our independent variable is therefore LEXICAL STATUS with the values ESTABLISHED WORD vs. NEOLOGISM (which will be operationalized presently). Our

[3]This is a simplification: stress-shift only occurs with unstressed closed syllables or sequence of two unstressed syllables (*SYLlable* – *sylLAbify*). Occasionally, stem-final consonants are deleted (as in *liquid* – *liquify*); cf. Plag (1999) for a more detailed discussion.

dependent variables are Syllabicity with the values monosyllabic and polysyllabic, and Stress Shift with the values required vs. not required (both of which should be self-explanatory).

Our design compares two predefined groups of types with respect to the distribution that particular properties have in these groups; this means that we do not need to calculate TTRs or HTRs, but that we need operational definitions of the values established word and neologism. Following Plag, let us define neologism as "coined in the 20th century", but let us use a large historical dictionary (the Oxford English Dictionary, 3rd edition) and a large corpus (the BNC) in order to identify words matching this definition; this will give us the opportunity to evaluate the idea that hapax legomena are a good way of operationalizing productivity.

Excluding cases with prefixed stems, the OED contains 456 entries or sub-entries for verbs with *-ify*, 31 of which are first documented in the 20th century. Of the latter, 21 do not occur in the BNC at all, and 10 do occur in the BNC, but are not hapaxes (see Table 9.8 below). The BNC contains 30 hapaxes, of which 13 are spelling errors and 7 are first documented in the OED before the 20th century (*carbonify, churchify, hornify, preachify, saponify, solemnify, townify*). This leaves 10 hapaxes that are plausibly regarded as neologisms, none of which are listed in the OED (again, see Table 9.8). In addition, there are four types in the BNC that are not hapax legomena, but that are not listed in the OED; careful cross-checks show that these are also neologisms. Combining all sources, this gives us 45 neologisms.

Before we turn to the definition and sampling of established types, let us determine the precision and recall of the operational definition of neologism as "hapax legomenon in the BNC", using the formulas introduced in Chapter 4. Precision is defined as the number of true positives (items that were found and that actually are what they are supposed to be) divided by the number of all positives (all items found); 10 of the 30 hapaxes in the BNC are actually neologisms, so the precision is $10/30 = 0.3333$. Recall is defined as the number of true positives divided by the number of true positives and false negatives (i.e. all items that should have been found); 10 of the 45 neologisms were actually found by using the hapax definition, so the recall is $10/45 = 0.2222$. In other words, neither precision nor recall of the method are very good, at least for moderately productive affixes like *-ify* (the method will presumably give better results with highly productive affixes). Let us also determine the recall of neologisms from the OED (using the definition "first documented in the 20th century according to the OED"): the OED lists 31 of the 45 neologisms, so the recall is $31/45 = 0.6889$; this is much better than the recall of the corpus-based hapax definition, but it also shows that if we combine

Table 9.8: Twentieth century neologisms with *-ify*

First documented in the OED in the 20th century	
(i)	also occur in the BNC, but not as hapaxes: *bourgeoisify, esterify, gentrify, karstify, massify, Nazify, syllabify, vinify, yuppify, zombify*
(ii)	do not occur in the BNC: *ammonify, aridify, electronify, glassify, humify, iconify, jazzify, mattify, metrify, mucify, nannify, passivify, plastify, probabilify, Prussify, rancidify, sinify, trendify, trustify, tubify, youthify*
Not documented in the OED at all	
(iii)	occur in the BNC as hapaxes: *faintify, fuzzify, lewisify, rawify, rockify, sickify, sonify, validify, yankify, yukkify*
(iv)	occur in the BNC, but not as hapaxes: *commodify, desertify, extensify, geriatrify*

corpus data and dictionary data, we can increase coverage substantially even for moderately productive affixes.

Let us now turn to the definition of ESTABLISHED TYPES. Given our definition of NEOLOGISMS, established types would first have to be documented before the 20th century, so we could use the 420 types in the OED that meet this criterion (again, excluding prefixed forms). However, these 420 types contain many very rare or even obsolete forms, like *duplify* 'to make double', *eaglify* 'to make into an eagle' or *naucify* 'to hold in low esteem'. Clearly, these are not "established" in any meaningful sense, so let us add the requirement that a type must occur in the BNC at least twice to count as established. Let us further limit the category to verbs first documented before the 19th century, in order to leave a clear diachronic gap between the established types and the productive types. This leaves the words in Table 9.9.[4]

Let us now evaluate the hypotheses. Table 9.10 shows the type frequencies for monosyllabic and polysyllabic stems in the two samples. In both cases, there is

[4]Interestingly, leaving out words coined in the 19th century does not make much of a difference: although the 19th century saw a large number of coinages (with 138 new types it was the most productive century in the history of the suffix), few of these are frequent enough today to occur in the BNC; if anything, we should actually extend our definition of neologisms to include the 19th century.

a preference for monosyllabic stems (as expected), but interestingly, this preference is less strong among the neologisms than among the established types and this difference is very significant ($\chi^2 = 7.37, \text{df} = 1, p < 0.01, \phi = 0.2577$).

Table 9.9: Control sample of established types with the suffix *-ify*.

acidify, amplify, beatify, beautify, certify, clarify, classify, crucify, damnify, deify, dignify, diversify, edify, electrify, exemplify, falsify, fortify, Frenchify, fructify, glorify, gratify, identify, indemnify, justify, liquify/liquefy, magnify, modify, mollify, mortify, mummify, notify, nullify, ossify, pacify, personify, petrify, prettify, purify, qualify, quantify, ramify, rarify, ratify, rectify, sacrify, sanctify, satisfy, scarify, signify, simplify, solidify, specify, stratify, stultify, terrify, testify, transmogrify, typify, uglify, unify, verify, versify, vilify, vitrify, vivify

Table 9.10: Monosyllabic and bisyllabic stems with *-ify*

		Number of Syllables		
		monosyllabic	polysyllabic	Total
Status	established	57 (51.14)	9 (14.86)	66
	neologism	29 (34.86)	16 (10.14)	45
	Total	86	25	111

Given the fact that there is a significantly higher number of neologisms with polysyllabic stems than expected on the basis of established types, the second hypothesis becomes more interesting: does this higher number of polysyllabic stems correspond with a greater willingness to apply it to stems that then have to undergo stress shift (which would be contrary to our hypothesis, which assumes that there will be no difference between established types and neologisms)?

Table 9.11 shows the relevant data: it seems that there might indeed be such a greater willingness, as the number of neologisms with polysyllabic stems requiring stress shift is higher than expected; however, the difference is not statistically significant ($\chi^2 = 1.96, \mathrm{df} = 1, p > 0.05, \phi = 0.28$) (strictly speaking, we cannot use the χ^2 test here, since half of the expected frequencies are below 5, but Fisher's exact test confirms that the difference is not significant).

Table 9.11: Stress shift with polysyllabic stems with *-ify*

		Shift		
		not required	required	Total
Status	established	3	6	9
		(4.68)	(4.32)	
	neologism	10	6	16
		(8.32)	(7.68)	
	Total	13	12	25

This case study demonstrates some of the problems and advantages of using corpora to identify neologisms in addition to existing dictionaries. It also constitutes an example of a purely type-based research design; note, again, that such a design is possible here because we are not interested in the type frequency of a particular affix under different conditions (in which case we would have to calculate a TTR to adjust for different sample sizes), but in the distribution of the variables Syllable Length and Stress Shift in two qualitatively different categories of types. Finally, note that the study comes to different conclusions than the impressionistic analysis in Plag (1999), so it demonstrates the advantages of strictly quantified designs.

9.2.1.2 Case study: Semantic differences between *-ic* and *-ical*

Affixes, like words, can be related to other affixes by lexical relations like synonymy, antonymy, etc. In the case of (roughly) synonymous affixes, an obvious research question is what determines the choice between them – for example, whether there are more fine-grained semantic differences that are not immediately apparent.

One way of approaching this question is to focus on stems that occur with both affixes (such as *liqui(d)* in *liquidize* and *liquify*/*liquefy*, *scarce* in *scarceness* and *scarcity* or *electr-* in *electric* and *electrical*) and to investigate the semantic contexts in which they occur – for example, by categorizing their collocates, analogous to the way Taylor (2003) categorizes collocates of *high* and *tall* (cf. Chapter 7, Section 7.2.2.1).

A good example of this approach is found in Kaunisto (1999), who investigates the pairs *electric*/*electrical* and *classic*/*classical* on the basis of the British Newspaper *Daily Telegraph*. Since his corpus is not accessible, let us use the LOB corpus instead to replicate his study for *electric*/*electrical*. It is a study with two nominal variables: Affix Variant (with the values -ic and -ical), and Semantic Category (with a set of values to be discussed presently). Note that this design can be based straightforwardly on token frequency, as we are not concerned with the relationship between the stem and the affix, but with the relationship between the stem-affix combination and the nouns modified by it. Put differently, we are not using the token frequency of a stem-affix combination, but of the collocates of words derived by a particular affix.

Kaunisto uses a mixture of dictionaries and existing literature to identify potentially interesting values for the variable Semantic Category; we will restrict ourselves to dictionaries here. Consider the definitions from six major dictionaries in (6) and (7):

(6) *electric*
   a. connected with electricity; using, produced by or producing electricity (OALD)
   b. of or relating to electricity; operated by electricity (MW)
   c. working by electricity; used for carrying electricity; relating to electricity (MD)
   d. of, produced by, or worked by electricity (CALD)
   e. needing electricity to work, produced by electricity, or used for carrying electricity (LDCE)
   f. work[ing] by means of electricity; produced by electricity; designed to carry electricity; refer[ring] to the supply of electricity (Cobuild)

(7) *electrical*
   a. connected with electricity; using or producing electricity (OALD)
   b. of or relating to electricity; operated by electricity (MW) [mentioned as a synonym under corresp. sense of *electric*]
   c. working by electricity; relating to electricity (MD)
   d. related to electricity (CALD, LDCE)
   e. work[ing] by means of electricity; supply[ing] or us[ing] electricity; energy ... in the form of electricity; involved in the production and supply of electricity or electrical goods (Cobuild)

MW treats the two words as largely synonymous and OALD distinguishes them only insofar as mentioning for *electric*, but not *electrical*, that it may refer to phenomena 'produced by electricity' (this is meant to cover cases like *electric current/charge*); however, since both words are also defined as referring to anything 'connected with electricity', this is not much of a differentiation (the entry for *electrical* also mentions *electrical power/energy*). Macmillan's dictionary also treats them as largely synonymous, although it is pointed out specifically that *electric* refers to entities 'carrying electricity' (citing *electric outlet/plug/cord*). CALD and LDCE present *electrical* as a more general word for anything 'related to electricity', whereas they mention specifically that *electric* is used for things 'worked by electricity' (e.g. *electric light/appliance*) or 'carrying electricity' (presumably *cords, outlets*, etc.) and phenomena produced by electricity (presumably *current, charge*, etc.). Collins presents both words as referring to electric(al) appliances, with *electric* additionally referring to things 'produced by electricity', 'designed to carry electricity' or being related to the 'supply of electricity' and *electrical* additionally referring to 'energy' or entities 'involved in the production and supply of electricity' (presumably energy companies, engineers, etc.).

Summarizing, we can posit the following four broad values for our variable Semantic Category, with definitions that are hopefully specific enough to serve as an annotation scheme:

- devices and appliances working by electricity (*light, appliance*, etc.)
- energy in the form of electricity (*power, current, charge, energy*, etc.)
- the industry researching, producing or supplying energy, i.e. companies and the people working there (*company, engineer*, etc.)
- circuits, broadly defined as entities producing or carrying electricity, including (*cord, outlet, plug*, but also *power plant*, etc.)

The definitions are too heterogeneous to base a specific hypothesis on them, but we might broadly expect *electric* to be more typical for the categories device and circuit and *electrical* for the category industry.

Table 9.12 shows the token frequency with which nouns from these categories are referred to as *electric* or *electrical* in the LOB corpus; in order to understand how these nouns were categorized, it also lists all types found for each category (one example was discarded because it was metaphorical).

The difference between *electric* and *electrical* is significant overall ($\chi^2 = 12.68$, df $= 3, p < 0.01, \phi = 0.2869$), suggesting that the two words somehow differ with

Table 9.12: Entities described as *electric* or *electrical* in the LOB corpus

Noun	Adjective: electric		Adjective: electrical		Total
device	*Obs.:*	17	*Obs.:*	13	30
	Exp.:	12.08	*Exp.:*	17.92	
	χ^2:	2.01	χ^2:	1.35	
	bulb, calculating machine, chair, cooker, dog, drill, fence, fire, heating element, light switch, motor, mowing, stove, torch, tricycle		*amplifier, apparatus, fire, goods, machine, machinery, power unit, sign, supply, system, system, transmission*		
energy	*Obs.:*	11	*Obs.:*	13	24
	Exp.:	9.66	*Exp.:*	14.34	
	χ^2:	0.19	χ^2:	0.12	
	attraction, bill, blue, current, effect, field, force, light, space constant		*accident, activity, condition, load, output, phenomenon, property, resistance*		
circuit	*Obs.:*	2	*Obs.:*	3	5
	Exp.:	2.01	*Exp.:*	2.99	
	χ^2:	0.00	χ^2:	0.56	
	battery, line		*circuit, conductivity*		
industry	*Obs.:*	1	*Obs.:*	17	18
	Exp.:	7.25	*Exp.:*	10.75	
	χ^2:	5.38	χ^2:	3.63	
	company		*communication theory, counterpart, development, engineer, industry, trade, work*		
Total		31		46	77

Supplementary Online Material: KVCF

respect to their preferences for these categories. Since we are interested in the nature of this difference, it is much more insightful to look at the χ^2 components individually. This gives us a better idea where the overall significant difference comes from. In this case, it comes almost exclusively from the fact that *electrical* is indeed associated with the research and supply of electricity (INDUSTRY), although there is a slight preference for *electric* with nouns referring to devices. Generally, the two words seem to be relatively synonymous, at least in 1960s British English.

Let us repeat the study with the BROWN corpus. Table 9.13 lists the token frequencies for the individual categories and, again, all types found for each category.

Again, the overall difference between the two words is significant and the effect is slightly stronger than in the LOB corpus ($\chi^2 = 22.83, \text{df} = 3, p < 0.001, \phi = 0.3413$), suggesting a stronger differentiation between them. Again, the most interesting question is where the effect comes from. In this case, devices are much more frequently referred to as *electric* and less frequently as *electrical* than expected, and, as in the LOB corpus, the nouns in the category *industry* are more frequently referred to as *electrical* and less frequently as *electric* than expected (although not significantly so). Again, there is no clear difference with respect to the remaining two categories.

Broadly speaking, then, one of our expectations is borne out by the British English data and one by the American English data. We would now have to look at larger corpora to see whether this is an actual difference between the two varieties or whether it is an accidental feature of the corpora used here. We might also want to look at more modern corpora – the importance of electricity in our daily lives has changed quite drastically even since the 1960s, so the words may have specialized semantically more clearly in the meantime. Finally, we would look more closely at the categories we have used, to see whether a different or a more fine-grained categorization might reveal additional insights (Kaunisto (1999) goes on to look at his categories in more detail, revealing more fine-grained differences between the words).

Of course, this kind of investigation can also be designed as an inductive study of differential collocates (again, like the study of synonyms such as *high* and *tall*). Let us look at the nominal collocates of *electric* and *electrical* in the BNC. Table 9.14 shows the results of a differential-collocate analysis, calculated on the basis of all occurrences of *electric/al* in the BNC that are directly followed by a noun.

Table 9.13: Entities described as *electric* or *electrical* in the BROWN corpus

NOUN	ADJECTIVE				Total
	ELECTRIC		ELECTRICAL		
DEVICE	*Obs.:*	29	*Obs.:*	3	32
	Exp.:	18.29	*Exp.:*	13.71	
	χ^2:	6.28	χ^2:	8.37	
	amplifier, blanket, bug, chair computer, drive, gadget, hand tool, hand-blower, heater, heater, horn, icebox, lantern, model, range, razor, refrigerator, signs, spit, toothbrush		*control, display, torquers*		
ENERGY	*Obs.:*	15	*Obs.:*	17	32
	Exp.:	18.29	*Exp.:*	13.71	
	χ^2:	0.59	χ^2:	0.79	
	arc, current, discharge, power, rate, shock, universe, utility rate		*body, characteristic, charges, distribution, conditional, energy, force, form, power, shock, signal, stimulation*		
CIRCUIT	*Obs.:*	4	*Obs.:*	9	13
	Exp.:	7.43	*Exp.:*	5.57	
	χ^2:	1.58	χ^2:	2.11	
	circuit, light plant, power plant		*contact line, outlet, pickoff, wire, wiring*		
INDUSTRY	*Obs.:*	8	*Obs.:*	13	21
	Exp.:	12.00	*Exp.:*	9.00	
	χ^2:	1.33	χ^2:	1.78	
	company, corporation, Inc. utility business, utility company		*case, company, discovery, engineer, equipment, literature, manufacturer, work*		
Total		56		42	98

Supplementary Online Material: KVCF

The results largely agree with the preferences also uncovered by the more careful (and more time-consuming) categorization of a complete data set, with one crucial difference: there are members of the category DEVICE among the significant differential collocates of both variants. A closer look reveals a systematic difference within this category: the DEVICE collocates of *electric* refer to specific devices (such as *light, guitar, light, kettle,* etc.); in contrast, the DEVICE collocates of *electrical* refer to general classes of devices (*equipment, appliance, system*). This difference was not discernible in the LOB and BROWN datasets (presumably because they were too small), but it is discernible in the data set used by Kaunisto (1999), who posits corresponding subcategories. Of course, the BNC is a much more recent corpus than LOB and BROWN, so, again, a diachronic comparison would be interesting.

There is an additional pattern that would warrant further investigation: there are collocates for both variants that correspond to what some of the dictionaries we consulted refer to as 'produced by energy': *shock, field* and *fire* for *electric* and *signal, energy, impulse* for *electrical.* It is possible that *electric* more specifically characterizes phenomena that are *caused* by electricity, while *electrical* characterizes phenomena that *manifest* electricity.

The case study demonstrates, then, that a differential-collocate analysis is a good alternative to the manual categorization and category-wise comparison of all collocates: it allows us to process very large data sets very quickly and then focus on the semantic properties of those collocates that are shown by the statistical analysis to differentiate between the variants.

We must keep in mind, however, that this kind of study does not primarily uncover differences between affixes, but differences between specific word pairs containing these affixes. They are, as pointed out above, essentially lexical studies of near-synonymy. Of course, it is possible that by performing such analyses for a large number of word pairs containing a particular affix pair, general semantic differences may emerge, but since we are frequently dealing with highly lexicalized forms, there is no guarantee for this. Gries (2001; 2003b) has shown that *-ic*/*-ical* pairs differ substantially in the extent to which they are synonymous; for example, he finds substantial difference in meaning for *politic*/*political* or *poetic*/*poetical,* but much smaller differences, for example, for *bibliographic*/*bibliographical,* with *electric*/*electrical* somewhere in the middle. Obviously, the two variants have lexicalized independently in many cases, and the specific differences in meaning resulting from this lexicalization process are unlikely to fall into clear general categories.

Table 9.14: Differential nominal collocates of *electric* and *electrical* in the BNC

COLLOCATE	Frequency with *electric*	Frequency with *electrical*	Other words with *electric*	Other words with *electrical*	*G*
Most strongly associated with ELECTRIC					
shock	140	2	2692	2027	136.60
light	122	2	2710	2027	116.99
field	191	23	2641	2006	104.41
guitar	81	0	2751	2029	88.50
fire	109	7	2723	2022	78.62
car	59	2	2773	2027	50.11
motor	63	3	2769	2026	49.42
blanket	46	1	2786	2028	42.07
window	38	0	2794	2029	41.27
kettle	37	0	2795	2029	40.18
cooker	34	0	2798	2029	36.91
drill	39	1	2793	2028	34.75
train	32	0	2800	2029	34.73
co	27	0	2805	2029	29.28
vehicle	24	0	2808	2029	26.02
fan	21	0	2811	2029	22.76
lighting	21	0	2811	2029	22.76
fence	20	0	2812	2029	21.67
tramway	20	0	2812	2029	21.67
traction	19	0	2813	2029	20.58
Most strongly associated with ELECTRICAL					
engineering	0	108	2832	1921	192.16
engineer	0	89	2832	1940	157.84
equipment	6	106	2826	1923	147.96
goods	1	88	2831	1941	146.12
activity	1	85	2831	1944	140.79
appliance	3	69	2829	1960	100.18
conductivity	0	35	2832	1994	61.51
fault	0	34	2832	1995	59.75
signal	8	53	2824	1976	54.50
stimulation	0	26	2832	2003	45.63
union	0	26	2832	2003	45.63
energy	2	33	2830	1996	44.78
impulse	2	32	2830	1997	43.14
retailer	0	21	2832	2008	36.82
property	0	20	2832	2009	35.06
work	0	19	2832	2010	33.30
control	1	23	2831	2006	33.10
system	6	31	2826	1998	28.06
circuit	10	37	2822	1992	27.06
recording	1	19	2831	2010	26.44

Supplementary Online Material: Y7JC

9.2.1.3 Case study: Phonological differences between *-ic* and *-ical*

In an interesting but rarely-cited paper, Or (1994) collects a number of hypotheses about semantic and, in particular, phonological factors influencing the distribution of *-ic* and *-ical* that she provides impressionistic corpus evidence for but does not investigate systematically. A simple example is the factor Length: Or hypothesizes that speakers will tend to avoid long words and choose the shorter variant *-ic* for long stems (in terms of number of syllables). She reports that "a survey of a general vocabulary list" corroborates this hypothesis but does not present any systematic data.

Let us test this hypothesis using the LOB corpus. Since this is a written corpus, let us define Length in terms of letters and assume that this is a sufficiently close approximation to phonological length. Tables 9.15 and 9.16 lists all types with the two suffixes from LOB in decreasing order of length; note that since the point here is to show the influence of length on suffix choice, prefixed stems, compound stems, etc. are included in their full form (the lists are included in a more readable format in the Supplementary Online Materials, file U7BR).

We can test the hypothesis based on the mean length of the two samples using a t-test, or by ranking them by length using the U test. As mentioned in Chapter 6, word length (however we measure it) rarely follows a normal distribution, so the U test would probably be the better choice in this case, but let us use the t-test for the sake of practice (the data are there in full, if you want to calculate a U test).

There are 373 stem types occurring with *-ic* in the LOB corpus, with a mean length of 7.32 and a sample variance of 5.72; there are 153 stem types occurring with *-ical*, with a mean length of 6.60 and a sample variance of 4.57. Applying the formula in (15) from Chapter 6, we get a t-value of 2.97. There are 314.31 degrees of freedom in our sample (as calculated using the formula in 16), which means that $p < 0.001$. In other words, length (as measured in letters) seems to have an influence on the choice between the two affixes, with longer stems favoring *-ic*.

This case study has demonstrated the use of a relatively simple operationalization to test a hypothesis about phonological length. We have used samples of types rather than samples of tokens, as we wanted to determine the influence of stem length on affix choice – in this context, the crucial question is how many stems of a given length occur with a particular affix variant, but it does not matter how *often* a particular stem does so. However, if there was more variation between the two suffixes, the frequency with which a particular stem is used with a particular affix might be interesting, as it would allow us to approach the question by ranking stems in terms of their preference and then correlating this ranking with their length.

Table 9.15: Adjectives with *-ic* by length (LOB)

function-theoretic, non-stoichiometric (15), *crystallographic, politico-economic, pseudo-scientific, uncharacteristic* (14), *antihaemophilic, electro(-)magnetic, non-pornographic, semi-logarithmic* (13), *characteristic, claustrophobic, electrographic, metallographic, non-diastematic, part-apologetic, potentiometric, quasi-acrobatic, spectrographic, thermoelectric* (12), *architectonic, choreographic, deterministic, electrostatic, ferromagnetic, hypereutectic, idiosyncratic, materialistic, nationalistic, non-parametric, philanthropic, probabilistic, pseudomorphic, thermodynamic, trans-economic, unsympathetic* (11), *aristocratic, bureaucratic, catastrophic, electrolytic, enthusiastic, evangelistic, haemorrhagic, hieroglyphic, homoeopathic, hydrochloric, hydrofluoric, journalistic, kinaesthetic, melodramatic, meritocratic, monosyllabic, naturalistic, neurasthenic, non-alcoholic, orthographic, paramagnetic, philharmonic, photographic, phylogenetic, polysyllabic, pornographic, positivistic, programmatic, prophylactic, thermometric, unscientific* (10), *aerodynamic, anaesthetic, apocalyptic, atmospheric, demographic, endocentric, gastronomic, geostrophic, gravimetric, haemophilic, logarithmic, macroscopic, mechanistic, meromorphic, microscopic, modernistic, monotechnic, non-catholic, non-dogmatic, non-dramatic, ontogenetic, orthopaedic, over-drastic, pessimistic, philosophic, phototactic, plutocratic, prehistoric, psychiatric, ritualistic, socialistic, sycophantic, syllogistic, sympathetic, symptomatic, syntagmatic, telegraphic, tetra-acetic, therapeutic, unaesthetic, unpatriotic, unrealistic* (9), *aldermanic, altruistic, antiseptic, apologetic, asymmetric, asymptotic, autocratic, barometric, bimetallic, cabalistic, concentric, corybantic, democratic, dielectric, diplomatic, egocentric, electronic, eulogistic, exocentric, fatalistic, geocentric, haemolytic, histrionic, humanistic, hyperbolic, hypodermic, idealistic, legalistic, linguistic, megalithic, monolithic, nihilistic, novelistic, optimistic, pentatonic, philatelic, phosphoric, polyphonic, scholastic, scientific, stochastic, supersonic, systematic, telepathic, telephonic, telescopic, theocratic, ultrasonic, undogmatic, undramatic, uneconomic, volumetric* (8), *acrobatic, aesthetic, alcoholic, algebraic, analgesic, antigenic, apathetic, apostolic, authentic, automatic, axiomatic, ballistic, catalytic, chromatic, cinematic, dualistic, eccentric, energetic, enigmatic, fantastic, geometric, geotactic, heuristic, homonymic, hydraulic, inorganic, intrinsic, kinematic, lethargic, messianic, morphemic, neolithic, nicotinic, nostalgic, nucleonic, panoramic, parabolic, paralytic, parasitic, patriotic, pneumatic, pragmatic, prophetic, quadratic, realistic, sarcastic, schematic, spasmodic, strategic, stylistic, sub-atomic, sulphuric, symphonic, syntactic, synthetic, telegenic, traumatic* (7), *academic, acoustic, allergic, anarchic, aromatic, artistic, asthenic, athletic, barbaric, carbolic, cathodic, catholic, cherubic, climatic, cyclonic, diabetic, dietetic, dogmatic, domestic, dramatic, dynastic, eclectic, economic, egoistic, electric, elliptic, emphatic, epigonic, esoteric, forensic, galvanic, gigantic, heraldic, historic, horrific, hygienic, hypnotic, isotopic, magnetic, majestic, metallic, monastic, narcotic, neurotic, operatic, pathetic, pedantic, periodic, phonetic, platonic, podzolic, potassic, prolific, quixotic, rhythmic, romantic, sadistic, sardonic, semantic, specific, sporadic, syllabic, symbolic, synaptic, synoptic, tectonic, terrific, theistic, thematic, volcanic* (6), *amoebic, angelic, anionic, aquatic, archaic, botanic, bucolic, caustic, ceramic, chaotic, chronic, classic, cryptic, delphic, demonic, drastic, dynamic, elastic, endemic, enteric, erratic, frantic, gastric, generic, genetic, glottic, graphic, idyllic, kinetic, laconic, lunatic, melodic, motivic, nomadic, numeric, oceanic, oolitic, organic, pacific, phallic, politic, prosaic, psychic, spastic* (5), *acetic, arctic, atomic, bardic, cosmic, cyclic, cystic, erotic, exotic, ferric, gnomic, gothic, hectic, heroic, ironic, italic, mosaic, myopic, mystic, mythic, niobic, nitric, oxalic, photic, poetic, public, rustic, scenic, static, tannic, tragic* (4), *basic, civic, comic, cubic, ionic, lyric, magic, tonic, toxic* (3), *epic* (2)

Table 9.16: Adjectives with *-ical* by length (LOB)

autobiographical, palaeontological (12), *anthropological, pharmacological, physiographical, trigonometrical* (11), *archaeological, ecclesiastical, eschatological, haematological, iconographical, meteorological, methodological, pharmaceutical, quasi-classical* (10), *chronological, entomological, metallurgical, morphological, philosophical, photochemical, physiological, psychological, radiochemical, technological, theorematical, toxicological, unsymmetrical, untheological* (9), *aeronautical, aetiological, alphabetical, anti-clerical, arithmetical, astronomical, biographical, cosmological, etymological, genealogical, geographical, hypocritical, hypothetical, mathematical, metaphorical, metaphysical, non-technical, pathological, pre-classical, radiological, schismatical, self-critical, sociological, systematical, uneconomical, unrhythmical* (8), *allegorical, biochemical, categorical, cylindrical, dialectical, egotistical, evangelical, geometrical, grammatical, ideological, monarchical, mycological, nonsensical, obstetrical, paradisical, paradoxical, pedagogical, pedological, puranitical, purinatical, puritanical, serological, statistical, sub(-)tropical, subtropical, symmetrical, synagogical, theological, theoretical, unpractical* (7), *a-political, acoustical, analytical, anatomical, biological, diabolical, economical, ecumenical, electrical, elliptical, geological, historical, hysterical, liturgical, mechanical, methodical, oratorical, rhetorical, symbolical, theatrical, unbiblical, uncritical* (6), *classical, empirical, fanatical, graphical, identical, juridical, numerical, political, satirical, sceptical, spherical, technical, unethical, unmusical, untypical, whimsical* (5), *atypical, biblical, cervical, chemical, clerical, clinical, critical, cyclical, inimical, ironical, metrical, mystical, mythical, physical, poetical, surgical, tactical, tropical, vertical* (4), *comical, conical, cynical, ethical, lexical, lyrical, magical, medical, optical, topical, typical* (3)

9.2.1.4 Case study: Affix combinations

It has sometimes been observed that certain derivational affixes show a preference for stems that are already derived by a particular affix. For example, Lindsay (2011) and Lindsay & Aronoff (2013) show that while *-ic* is more productive in general than *-ical*, *-ical* is more productive with stems that contain the affix *-olog-* (for example, *morphological* or *methodological*). Such observations are interesting from a descriptive viewpoint, as such preferences need to be taken into account, for example, in dictionaries, in teaching word-formation to non-native speakers or when making or assessing stylistic choices. They are also interesting from a theoretical perspective, first, because they need to be modeled and explained within any morphological theory, and second, because they may interact with other factors in a number of different ways.

For example, Case Study 9.2.1.3 demonstrates that longer stems generally seem to prefer the variant *-ic*; however, the mean length of derived stems is necessarily longer than that of non-derived stems, so it is puzzling, at first glance, that stems with the affix *-olog-* should prefer *-ical*. Of course, *-olog-* may be an exception, with derived stems in general preferring the shorter *-ic*; however, we would still need to account for this exceptional behavior.

But let us start more humbly by laying the empirical foundations for such discussions and test the observation by Lindsay (2011) and Lindsay & Aronoff (2013). The authors themselves do so by comparing the ratio of the two suffixes for stems that occur with both suffixes. Let us return to their approach later, and start by looking at the overall distribution of stems with *-ic* and *-ical.*

First, though, let us see what we can find out by looking at the overall distribution of types, using the four-million-word BNC Baby. Once we remove all prefixes and standardize the spelling, there are 846 types for the two suffixes. There is a clear overall preference for *-ic* (659 types) over *-ical* (187 types) (incidentally, there are only 54 stems that occur with both suffixes). For stems with *-(o)log-*, the picture is drastically different: there is an overwhelming preference for *-ical* (55 types) over *-ic* (3 types). We can evaluate this difference statistically, as shown in Table 9.17.

Table 9.17: Preference of stems with *-olog-* for *-ic* and *-ical*

		Suffix Variant		
		-ic	-ical	Total
Stem Type	with -olog-	3 (45.18)	55 (12.82)	58
	without -olog-	656 (613.82)	132 (174.18)	788
	Total	659	187	846

Unsurprisingly, the difference between stems with and without the affix *-olog-* is highly significant ($\chi^2 = 191.27, \text{df} = 1, p < 0.001$) – stems with *-olog-* clearly favor the variant *-ical* against the general trend.

As mentioned above, this could be due specifically to the affix *-olog-*, but it could also be a general preference of derived stems for *-ical.* In order to determine this, we have to look at derived stems with other affixes. There are a number of other affixes that occur frequently enough to make them potentially interesting, such as *-ist-*, as in *statistic(al)* (*-ic* vs. *-ical*: 74/2), *-graph-*, as in *geographic(al)* (19/8), or *-et-*, as in *arithmetic(al)* (32/9). Note that all of them have more types with *-ic*, which suggests that derived stems in general, possibly due to their length, prefer *-ic* and that *-olog-* really is an exception.

But there is a methodological issue that we have to address before we can really conclude this. Note that we have been talking of a "preference" of particular stems for one or the other suffix, but this is somewhat imprecise: we looked at the total number of stem types with *-ic* and *-ical* with and without additional suffixes. While differences in number are plausibly attributed to preferences, they may also be purely historical leftovers due to the specific history of the two suffixes (which is rather complex, involving borrowing from Latin, Greek and, in the case of *-ical*, French). More convincing evidence for a productive difference in preferences would come from stems that take both *-ic* and *-ical* (such as *electric/al*, *symmetric/al* or *numeric/al*, to take three examples that display a relatively even distribution between the two): for these stems, there is obviously a choice, and we can investigate the influence of additional affixes on that choice.

Lindsay (2011) and Lindsay & Aronoff (2013) focus on precisely these stems, checking for each one whether it occurs more frequently with *-ic* or with *-ical* and calculating the preference ratio mentioned above. They then compare the ratio of all stems to that of stems with *-olog-* (see Table 9.18).

Table 9.18: Stems favoring *-ic* or *-ical* in the COCA (Lindsay 2011: 194)

	Total Stems	Ratio	*-olog-* stems	Ratio
favoring *-ic*	1197	$\frac{4.5}{1}$	13	$\frac{1}{5.6}$
favoring *-ical*	268		73	
Total	1465		86	

The ratios themselves are difficult to compare statistically, but they are clearly the right way of measuring the preference of stems for a particular suffix. So let us take Lindsay and Aronoff's approach one step further: Instead of calculating the overall preference of a particular type of stem and comparing it to the overall preference of all stems, let us calculate the preference for each stem individually. This will give us a preference measure for each stem that is, at the very least, ordinal.[5] We can then rank stems containing a particular affix and stems not containing that affix (or containing a specific different affix) by their preference for one or the other of the suffix variants and use the Mann-Whitney *U*-test to determine whether the stems with *-olog-* tend to occur towards the *-ical* end of

[5] In fact, measures derived in this way are cardinal data, as the value can range from 0 to 1 with every possible value in between; it is safer to treat them as ordinal data, however, because we don't know whether such preference values are normally distributed. In fact, since they are based on word frequency data, which we know *not* to be normally distributed, it is a fair guess that the preference data are not normally distributed.

the ranking. That way we can treat preference as the matter of degree that it actually is, rather than as an absolute property of stems.

The BNC Baby does not contain enough derived stems that occur with both suffix variants, so let us focus on two specific suffixes and extract the relevant data from the full BNC. Since *-ist* is roughly equal to *-olog-* in terms of type frequency, let us choose this suffix for comparison. Table 9.19 shows the 34 stems containing either of these suffixes, their frequency of occurrence with the variants *-ic* and *-ical*, the preference ratio for *-ic*, and the rank.

The different preferences of stems with *-ist* and *-olog-* are very obvious even from a purely visual inspection of the table: stems with the former occur at the top of the ranking, stems with the latter occur at the bottom and there is almost no overlap. This is reflected clearly in the median ranks of the two stem types: the median for *-ist* is 4.5 ($N = 8$, rank sum $= 38$), the median for *-olog-* is 21.5 ($N = 26$, rank sum $= 557$). A Mann-Whitney U test shows that this difference is highly significant ($U = 2, N_1 = 8, N_2 = 26, p < 0.001$).

Now that we have established that different suffixes may, indeed, display different preferences for other suffixes (or suffix variants), we could begin to answer the question why this might be the case. In this instance, the explanation is likely found in the complicated history of borrowings containing the suffixes in question. The point of this case study was not to provide such an explanation but to show how an empirical basis can be provided using token frequencies derived from linguistic corpora.

9.2.2 Morphemes and demographic variables

There are a few studies investigating the productivity of derivational morphemes across language varieties (e.g., medium or genre), across groups defined by sex, education and/or class, or across varieties. This is an extremely interesting area of research that may offer valuable insights into the very nature of morphological richness and productivity, allowing us, for example, to study potential differences between regular, presumably subconscious applications of derivational rules and the deliberate coining of words. Despite this, it is an area that has not been studied too intensively, so there is much that remains to be discovered.

9.2.2.1 Case study: Productivity and genre

Guz (2009) studies the prevalence of different kinds of nominalization across genres. The question whether the productivity of derivational morphemes differs across genres is a very interesting one, and Guz presents a potentially more

Table 9.19: Preferences of stems containing *-ist* and *-olog-* for the suffix variants *-ic* and *-ical* (BNC)

Stem	Suffix	*n*(-ic)	*n*(-ical)	*p*(-ic)	Rank
realist-	*-ist*	2435	1	0.9996	1
atomist-	*-ist*	54	1	0.9818	2
egoist-	*-ist*	50	1	0.9804	3
syllogist-	*-ist*	8	1	0.8889	4
atheist-	*-ist*	25	9	0.7353	5
casuist-	*-ist*	2	1	0.6667	6
logist-	*-ist*	148	94	0.6116	7
pedolog-	*-olog-*	2	8	0.2000	8
hydrolog-	*-olog-*	7	56	0.1111	9
egotist-	*-ist*	4	54	0.0690	10
pharmacolog-	*-olog-*	5	72	0.0649	11
serolog-	*-olog-*	3	54	0.0526	12
haematolog-	*-olog-*	2	40	0.0476	13
litholog-	*-olog-*	1	24	0.0400	14
petrolog-	*-olog-*	1	28	0.0345	15
etymolog-	*-olog-*	1	29	0.0333	16
morpholog-	*-olog-*	11	347	0.0307	17
immunolog-	*-olog-*	3	107	0.0273	18
philolog-	*-olog-*	1	39	0.0250	19
aetiolog-	*-olog-*	1	40	0.0244	20
mineralogic	*-olog-*	1	41	0.0238	21
patholog-	*-olog-*	4	319	0.0124	22
histolog-	*-olog-*	5	404	0.0122	23
radiolog-	*-olog-*	2	171	0.0116	24
epidemiolog-	*-olog-*	2	186	0.0106	25
epistemolog-	*-olog-*	2	206	0.0096	26
physiolog-	*-olog-*	7	778	0.0089	27
ontolog-	*-olog-*	2	279	0.0071	28
geolog-	*-olog-*	7	999	0.0070	29
biolog-	*-olog-*	6	2093	0.0029	30
ecolog-	*-olog-*	2	746	0.0027	31
sociolog-	*-olog-*	1	808	0.0012	32
technolog-	*-olog-*	2	1666	0.0012	33
ideolog-	*-olog-*	1	1696	0.0006	34

Supplementary Online Material: VQTL

detailed analysis than previous studies in that he looks at the prevalence of different stem types for each affix, so that qualitative as well as quantitative differences in productivity could, in theory, be studied. In practice, unfortunately, the study offers preliminary insights at best, as it is based entirely on token frequencies, which, as discussed in Section 9.1 above, do not tell us anything at all about productivity.

We will therefore look at a question inspired by Guz's study, and use the TTR and the HTR to study the relative importance and productivity of the nominalizing suffix *-ship* (as in *friendship*, *lordship*, etc.) in newspaper language and in prose fiction. The suffix *-ship* is known to have a very limited productivity, and our hypothesis (for the sake of the argument) will be that it is more productive in prose fiction, since authors of fiction are under pressure to use language creatively (this is not Guz's hypothesis; his study is entirely explorative).

The suffix has a relatively high token frequency: there are 2862 tokens in the fiction section of the BNC, and 7189 tokens in the newspaper section (including all sub-genres of newspaper language, such as reportage, editorial, etc.) (the data are provided in the Supplementary Online Material, file LAF3). This difference is not due to the respective sample sizes: the fiction section in the BNC is much larger than the newspaper section; thus, the difference token frequency would suggest that the suffix is more important in newspaper language than in fiction. However, as extensively discussed in Section 9.1.1, token frequency cannot be used to base such statements on. Instead, we need to look at the type-token ratio and the hapax-token ratio.

To get a first impression, consider Figure 9.4, which shows the growth of the TTR (left) and HTR (right) in the full FICTION and NEWSPAPER sections of the BNC.

Both the TTR and the HTR suggest that the suffix is more productive in fiction: the ratios rise faster in FICTION than in NEWSPAPERS and remain consistently higher as we go through the two sub-corpora. It is only when the tokens have been exhausted in the fiction subcorpus but not in the newspaper subcorpus, that the ratios in the latter slowly catch up. This broadly supports our hypothesis, but let us look at the genre differences more closely both qualitatively and quantitatively.

In order to compare the two genres in terms of the type-token and hapax-token ratios, they need to have the same size. The following discussion is based on the full data from the fiction subcorpus and a subsample of the newspaper corpus that was arrived at by deleting every second, then every third and finally every 192nd example, ensuring that the hits in the sample are spread through the entire newspaper subcorpus.

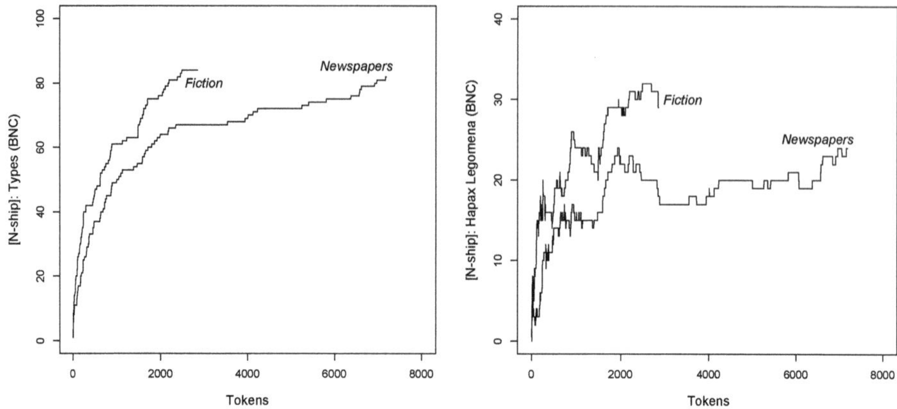

Figure 9.4: Nouns with the suffix *-ship* in the GENRE categories FICTION and NEWSPAPERS (BNC)

Let us begin by looking at the types. Overall, there are 96 different types, 48 of which occur in both samples (some examples of types that frequent in both samples are *relationship* (the most frequent word in the fiction sample), *championship* (the most frequent word in the news sample), *friendship, partnership, lordship, ownership* and *membership.* In addition, there are 36 types that occur only in the prose sample (for example, *churchmanship, dreamership, librarianship* and *swordsmanship*) and 12 that occur only in the newspaper sample (for example, *associateship, draughtsmanship, trusteeship* and *sportsmanship*). The number of types exclusive to each genre suggests that the suffix is more important in FICTION than in NEWSPAPERS.

The TTR of the suffix in newspaper language is $60/2862 = 0.021$, and the HTR is $20/2862 = 0.007$. In contrast, the TTR in fiction is $84/2862 = 0.0294$, and the HTR is $29/2862 = 0.0101$. Although the suffix, as expected, is generally not very productive, it is more productive in fiction than in newspapers. As Table 9.20 shows, this difference is statistically significant in the sample ($\chi^2 = 4.1, \text{df} = 1, p < 0.005$). This corroborates our hypothesis, but note that it does not tell us whether the higher productivity of *-ship* is something unique about this particular morpheme, or whether fiction generally has more derived words due to a higher overall lexical richness. To determine this, we would have to look at more than one affix.

Let us now turn to the hapax legomena. These are so rare in both genres that the difference in TTR is not statistically significant, as Table 9.21 shows ($\chi^2 = 1.67, \text{df} = 1, p = 0.1966$). We would need a larger corpus to see whether the difference would at some point become significant.

Table 9.20: Types with *-ship* in prose fiction and newspapers

		Type		
		new	¬new	Total
Genre	fiction	84 (72.00)	2778 (2790.00)	2862
	newspaper	60 (72.00)	2802 (2790.00)	2862
	Total	144	5580	5724

Table 9.21: Hapaxes with *-ship* in prose fiction and newspapers

		Type		
		hapax	¬hapax	Total
Genre	fiction	29 (24.50)	2833 (2837.50)	2862
	newspaper	20 (24.50)	2842 (2837.50)	2862
	Total	49	5675	5724

To conclude this case study, let us look at a particular problem posed by the comparison of the same suffix in two genres with respect to the HTR. At first glance – and this is what is shown in Table 9.21 – there seem to be 29 hapaxes in fiction and 20 in prose. However, there is some overlap: the words *generalship*, *headship*, *managership*, *ministership* and *professorship* occur as hapax legomena in both samples; other words that are hapaxes in one subsample occur several times in the other, such as *brinkmanship*, which is a hapax in fiction but occurs twice in the newspaper sample, or *acquaintanceship*, which is a hapax in the newspaper sample but occurs 15 times in fiction.

It is not straightforwardly clear whether such cases should be treated as hapaxes. If we think of the two samples as subsamples of the same corpus, it is very counterintuitive to do so. It might be more reasonable to count only those words as hapaxes whose frequency in the combined subsamples is still one. However, the notion "hapax" is only an operational definition for neologisms, based on the hope that the number of hapaxes in a corpus (or sub-corpus) is somehow indicative of the number of productive coinages. We saw in Case Study 9.2.1.1 that this is a somewhat vain hope, as the correlation between neologisms and hapaxes is not very impressive.

Still, if we want to use this operational definition, we have to stick with it and define hapaxes strictly relative to whatever (sub-)corpus we are dealing with. If we extend the criterion for hapax-ship beyond one subsample to the other, why stop there? We might be even stricter and count only those words as hapaxes that are still hapaxes when we take the entire BNC into account. And if we take the entire BNC into account, we might as well count as hapaxes only those words that occur only once in all accessible archives of the language under investigation. This would mean that the hapaxes in any sample would overwhelmingly cease to be hapaxes – the larger our corpus, the fewer hapaxes there will be. To illustrate this: just two words from the fiction sample retain their status as hapax legomena if we search the Google Books collection: *impress-ship*, which does not occur at all (if we discount linguistic accounts which mention it, such as Trips (2009), or this book, once it becomes part of the Google Books archive), and *cloudship*, which does occur, but only referring to water- or airborne vehicles. At the same time, the Google Books archive contains hundreds (if not thousands) of hapax legomena that we never even notice (such as *Johnship* 'the state of being the individual referred to as *John*'). The idea of using hapax legomena is, essentially, that a word like *mageship*, which is a hapax in the fiction sample, but not in the Google Books archive, somehow stands for a word like *Johnship*, which is a true hapax in the English language.

This case study has demonstrated the potential of using the TTR and the HTR not as a means of assessing morphological richness and productivity as such, but as a means of assessing genres with respect to their richness and productivity. It has also demonstrated some of the problems of identifying hapax legomena in the context of such cross-variety comparisons. As mentioned initially, there are not too many studies of this kind, but Plag (1999) presents a study of productivity across written and spoken language that is a good starting point for anyone wanting to fill this gap.

9.2.2.2 Case study: Productivity and speaker sex

Morphological productivity has not traditionally been investigated from a sociolinguistic perspective, but a study by Säily (2011) suggests that this may be a promising field of research. Säily investigates differences in the productivity of the suffixes *-ness* and *-ity* in the language produced by men and women in the

BNC. She finds no difference in productivity for *-ness*, but a higher productivity of *-ity* in the language produced by men (cf. also Säily & Suomela 2009 for a diachronic study with very similar results). She uses a sophisticated method involving the comparison of the suffixes' type and hapax growth rates, but let us replicate her study using the simple method used in the preceding case study, beginning with a comparison of type-token ratios.

The BNC contains substantially more speech and writing by male speakers than by female speakers, which is reflected in differences in the number of affix tokens produced by men and women: for *-ity*, there are 2562 tokens produced by women and 8916 tokens produced by men; for *-ness*, there are 616 tokens produced by women and 1154 tokens produced by men (note that unlike Säily, I excluded the words *business* and *witness*, since they did not seem to me to be synchronically transparent instances of the affix). To get samples of equal size for each affix, random subsamples were drawn from the tokens produced by men.

Based on these subsamples, the type-token ratios for *-ity* are 0.0652 for men and 0.0777 for women; as Table 9.22 shows, this difference is not statistically significant ($\chi^2 = 3.01, \text{df} = 1, p < 0.05, \phi = 0.0242$).

Table 9.22: Types with *-ity* in male and female speech (BNC)

		Type		
		new	seen before	Total
Speaker Sex	female	167 (183.00)	2395 (2379.00)	2562
	male	199 (183.00)	2363 (2379.00)	2562
	Total	366	4758	5124

The type-token ratios for *-ness* are much higher, namely 0.1981 for women and 0.2597 for men. As Table 9.23 shows, the difference is statistically significant, although the effect size is weak ($\chi^2 = 5.37, \text{df} = 1, p < 0.05, \phi = 0.066$).

Note that Säily investigates spoken and written language separately and she also includes social class in her analysis, so her results differ from the ones presented here; she finds a significantly lower HTR for *-ness* in lower-class women's speech in the spoken subcorpus, but not in the written one, and a significantly lower HTR for *-ity* in both subcorpora. This might be due to the different methods used, or to the fact that I excluded *business*, which is disproportionally fre-

Table 9.23: Types with *-ness* in male and female speech (BNC)

		Type		
		NEW	SEEN BEFORE	Total
Speaker Sex	FEMALE	122 (139.00)	494 (477.00)	616
	MALE	156 (139.00)	460 (477.00)	616
	Total	278	954	1232

quent in male speech and writing in the BNC and would thus reduce the diversity in the male sample substantially. However, the type-based differences do not have a very impressive effect size in our design and they are unstable across conditions in Säily's, so perhaps they are simply not very substantial.

Let us turn to the HTR next. As before, we are defining what counts as a hapax legomenon not with reference to the individual subsamples of male and female speech, but with respect to the combined sample. Table 9.24 shows the hapaxes for *-ity* in the male and female samples. The HTRs are very low, suggesting that *-ity* is not a very productive suffix: 0.0099 in female speech and 0.016 in male speech.

Table 9.24: Hapaxes with *-ity* in sampes of male and female speech (BNC)

MALE SPEECH
abnormality, antiquity, applicability, brutality, civility, criminality, deliverability, divinity, duplicity, eccentricity, eventuality, falsity, femininity, fixity, frivolity, illegality, impurity, inexorability, infallibility, infirmity, levity, longevity, mediocrity, obesity, perversity, predictability, rationality, regularity, reliability, scarcity, seniority, serendipity, solidity, subsidiarity, susceptibility, tangibility, verity, versatility, virtuality, vitality, voracity
FEMALE SPEECH
absurdity, adjustability, admissibility, centrality, complicity, effemininity, enormity, exclusivity, gratuity, hilarity, humility, impunity, inquisity, morbidity, municipality, originality, progility, respectability, sanity, scaleability, sincerity, spontaneity, sterility, totality, virginity

Although the difference in HTR is relatively small, Table 9.25 shows that it is statistically significant, albeit again with a very weak effect size ($\chi^2 = 3.93, \text{df} = 1, p < 0.05, \phi = 0.0277$).

Table 9.25: Hapax legomena with *-ity* in male and female speech (BNC)

		Type		
		hapax	¬hapax	Total
Speaker Sex	female	25 (33.00)	2537 (2529.00)	2562
	male	41 (33.00)	2521 (2529.00)	2562
	Total	66	5058	5124

Table 9.26 shows the hapaxes for *-ness* in the male and female samples. The HTRs are low, but much higher than for *-ity*, 0.0795 for women and 0.1023 for men.

As Table 9.27 shows, the difference in HTRs is not statistically significant, and the effect size would be very weak anyway ($\chi^2 = 1.93, \text{df} = 1, p > 0.05, \phi = 0.0395$).

In this case, the results correspond to Säily's, who also finds a significant difference in productivity for *-ity*, but not for *-ness*.

This case study was meant to demonstrate, once again, the method of comparing TTRs and HTRs based on samples of equal size. It was also meant to draw attention to the fact that morphological productivity may be an interesting area of research for variationist sociolinguistics; however, it must be pointed out that it would be premature to conclude that men and women differ in their productive use of particular affixes; as Säily herself points out, men and women are not only represented unevenly in quantitative terms (with a much larger proportion of male language included in the BNC), but also in qualitative terms (the language varieties with which they are represented differ quite strikingly). Thus, this may actually be another case of different degrees of productivity in different language varieties (which we investigated in the preceding case study).

Table 9.26: Hapaxes with *-ness* in samples of male and female speech (BNC)

MALE SPEECH
abjectness, adroitness, aloneness, anxiousness, awfulness, barrenness, blackness, blandness, bluntness, carefulness, centredness, cleansiness, clearness, cowardliness, crispness, delightfulness, differentness, dizziness, drowsiness, dullness, eyewitnesses, fondness, fulfilness, genuineness, godliness, graciousness, headedness, heartlessness, heinousness, keenness, lateness, likeliness, limitedness, loudness, mentalness, messiness, narrowness, nearness, neighbourliness, niceness, numbness, pettiness, pleasantness, plumpness, positiveness, quickness, reasonableness, rightness, riseness, rudeness, sameness, sameyness, separateness, shortness, smugness, softness, soreness, springiness, steadiness, stubbornness, timorousness, toughness, uxoriousness
FEMALE SPEECH
ancientness, appropriateness, badness, bolshiness, chasifness, childishness, chubbiness, clumsiness, conciseness, eagerness, easiness, faithfulness, falseness, feverishness, fizziness, freshness, ghostliness, greyness, grossness, grotesqueness, heaviness, laziness, likeness, mysteriousness, nastiness, outspokenness, pinkness, plainness, politeness, prettiness, priggishness, primness, randomness, responsiveness, scratchiness, sloppiness, smoothness, stiffness, stretchiness, tenderness, tightness, timelessness, timidness, ugliness, uncomfortableness, unpredictableness, untidiness, wetness, zombieness

Table 9.27: Hapax legomena with *-ness* in male and female speech (BNC)

		Type		
		HAPAX	¬HAPAX	Total
Speaker Sex	FEMALE	49 (56.00)	567 (560.00)	616
	MALE	63 (56.00)	553 (560.00)	616
	Total	112	1120	1232

10 Text

As mentioned repeatedly, linguistic corpora, by their nature, consist of word forms, while other levels of linguistic representation are not represented unless the corresponding annotations are added. In written corpora, there is one level other than the lexical that is (or can be) directly represented: the text. Well-constructed linguistic corpora typically consist of (samples from) individual texts, whose meta-information (author, title, original place and context of publication, etc.) are known. There is a substantial body of corpus-linguistic research based on designs that combine the two inherently represented variables Word (Form) and Text; such designs may be concerned with the occurrence of words in individual texts, or, more typically, with the occurrence of words in clusters of texts belonging to the same language variety (defined by topic, genre, function, etc.).

Texts are, of course, produced by speakers, and depending on how much and what kind of information about these speakers is available, we can also cluster texts according to demographic variables such as dialect, socioeconomic status, gender, age, political or religious affiliation, etc. (as we have done in many of the examples in earlier chapters). In these cases, quantitative corpus linguistics is essentially a variant of sociolinguistics, differing mainly in that the linguistic phenomena it pays most attention to are not necessarily those most central to sociolinguistic research in general.

10.1 Keyword analysis

In the investigation of relationships between words (or other units of language structure) and texts (or clusters of texts), researchers frequently use a method referred to as *keyword analysis*.[1] The term was originally used in contexts where cultural values and practices were studied through particular lexical items (cf. Williams 1976, Wierzbicka 2003); in corpus linguistics, it is used in a related but

[1]The term *keyword* is frequently spelled as two words (*key word*) or with a hyphen (*key-word*). I have chosen the spelling as a single word here because it seems simplest (at least to me, as a native writer of German, where compounds are always spelled as single words).

slightly broader sense of words that are characteristic of a particular text, language variety or demographic in the sense that they occur with "unusual frequency in a given text" or set of texts, where "unusual" means high "by comparison with a reference corpus of some kind" (Scott 1997: 236).

In other words, the corpus-linguistic identification of keywords is analogous to the identification of differential collocates, except that it analyses the association of a word W to a particular text (or collection of texts) T in comparison to the language as a whole (as represented by the reference corpus, which is typically a large, balanced corpus). Table 10.1 shows this schematically.

Table 10.1: A generic 2-by-2 table for keyword analysis

		Text		
		TEXT/CORPUS T	REFERENCE CORPUS	Total
Word	WORD W	O_{11}	O_{12}	R_1
	OTHER WORDS	O_{21}	O_{22}	R_2
	Total	C_1	C_2	N

Just like collocation analysis, keyword analysis is most often applied inductively, but there is nothing that precludes a deductive design if we have hypotheses about the over- or underrepresentation of particular lexical items in a particular text or collection of texts. In either case, we have two nominal variables: Keyword (with the individual words as values) and Text (with the values text and reference corpus).

If keyword analysis is applied to a single text, the aim is typically to identify either the topic area or some stylistic property of that text. When applied to text categories, the aim is typically to identify general lexical and/or grammatical properties of the language variety represented by the text categories.

As a first example of the kind of results that keyword analysis yields, consider Table 10.2, which shows the 20 most frequent tokens (including punctuation marks) in the LOB corpus and two individual texts (all words were converted to lower case).

As we can see, the differences are relatively small, as all lists are dominated by frequent function words and punctuation marks. Ten of these occur on all three lists (*a*, *and*, *in*, *of*, *that*, *the*, *to*, *was*, the comma and the period), and another six occur on two of them (*as*, *he*, *it*, *on*, and opening and closing quotation marks – although the latter are single quotation marks in the case of LOB and double quotation marks in the case of Text B). Even the types that occur only

Table 10.2: Most frequent words in three texts (relative frequencies)

LOB		Text A		Text B	
the	0.059 000	*the*	0.061 000	*the*	0.058 500
,	0.047 100	,	0.058 400	.	0.056 000
.	0.043 500	.	0.044 900	,	0.045 200
of	0.030 900	*in*	0.038 300	*of*	0.025 800
and	0.024 100	*of*	0.034 000	*a*	0.023 100
to	0.023 100	*and*	0.025 600	*to*	0.020 800
a	0.019 700	(	0.013 700	*he*	0.019 200
in	0.018 400	)	0.013 700	“	0.015 000
that	0.009 800	*at*	0.012 300	”	0.014 900
is	0.009 600	*a*	0.011 900	*and*	0.014 800
was	0.009 200	*to*	0.011 700	*his*	0.014 000
it	0.009 100	*was*	0.011 600	*was*	0.013 800
‘	0.008 700	*neosho*	0.011 200	*in*	0.011 200
’	0.008 500	*were*	0.011 000	*that*	0.011 000
for	0.008 000	*species*	0.007 800	*had*	0.009 900
he	0.007 800	*station*	0.007 100	*hume*	0.008 100
i	0.006 600	*river*	0.006 700	*on*	0.007 800
as	0.006 300	*that*	0.006 500	*it*	0.006 800
with	0.006 200	*by*	0.006 400	–	0.006 300
be	0.006 200	*1959*	0.006 200	*as*	0.006 300

once are mostly uninformative with respect to the language variety (or text category) we may be dealing with (*1959*, *at*, *by*, *for*, *had*, *is*, *with*, the hyphen and opening and closing parentheses). The only exceptions are four content words in Text A: *Neosho*, *river*, *species*, *station* – these suggest that the text is about the *Neosho* river and perhaps that it deals with biology (as suggested by the word *species*).

Applying keyword analysis to each text or collection of texts allows us to identify the words that differ most significantly in frequency from the reference corpus, telling us how the text in question differs lexically from the (written) language of its time as a whole. Table 10.3 lists the keywords for Text A.

The keywords now convey a very specific idea of what the text is about: there are two proper names of rivers (the *Neosho* already seen on the frequency list and the *Marais des Cygnes*, represented by its constituents *Cygnes*, *Marais* and *des*), and there are a number of words for specific species of fish as well as the words *river* and *channel*.

Table 10.3: Keywords in a report on fish populations

KEYWORD	Frequency in REPORT	Frequency in LOB	Other words in REPORT	Other words in LOB	G
neosho	277	0	24 525	1 157 496	2143.86
species	194	25	24 608	1 157 471	1346.35
station	177	119	24 625	1 157 377	975.30
river	165	104	24 637	1 157 392	921.71
1957	137	57	24 665	1 157 439	827.02
1959	153	124	24 649	1 157 372	807.66
kansas	107	2	24 695	1 157 494	807.54
cygnes	94	0	24 708	1 157 496	726.84
marais	94	1	24 708	1 157 495	715.78
catfish	90	0	24 712	1 157 496	695.89
des	97	29	24 705	1 157 467	615.32
fish	121	121	24 681	1 157 375	605.36
upper	103	61	24 699	1 157 435	582.56
abundance	81	7	24 721	1 157 489	577.70
(	340	2902	24 462	1 154 594	577.41
)	340	2926	24 462	1 154 570	573.12
channel	88	22	24 714	1 157 474	571.26
shiner	75	3	24 727	1 157 493	554.56
lower	103	120	24 699	1 157 376	493.68
minnow	63	1	24 739	1 157 495	476.80

The text is clearly about fish in the two rivers. The occurrence of the words *station* and *abundance* suggests a research context, which is supported by the occurrence of two dates and opening and closing parentheses (which are often used in scientific texts to introduce references). The text in question is indeed a scientific report on fish populations: *Fish Populations, Following a Drought, In the Neosho and Marais des Cygnes Rivers of Kansas* (available via Project Gutenberg and in the Supplementary Online Material, file TXQP). Note that the occurrence of some tokens (such as the dates and the parentheses) may be characteristic of a language variety rather than an individual text, a point we will return to below.

Next, consider Table 10.4, which lists the keywords for Text B. Three things are noticeable: the keyness of a number of words that are most likely proper names

Table 10.4: Keywords in a science fiction novel

Keyword	Frequency in novel	Frequency in LOB	Other words in novel	Other words in LOB	*G*
"	604	77	24 198	1 157 419	4205.14
"	601	121	24 201	1 157 375	4011.51
hume	325	2	24 477	1 157 494	2491.69
–	254	0	24 548	1 157 496	1965.62
vye	228	0	24 574	1 157 496	1764.18
rynch	134	0	24 668	1 157 496	1036.34
.	2252	50 324	22 550	1 107 172	1000.71
he	772	9068	24 030	1 148 428	952.74
wass	100	0	24 702	1 157 496	773.25
his	565	6272	24 237	1 151 224	740.62
's	214	1177	24 588	1 156 319	510.86
the	2352	68 350	22 450	1 089 146	475.70
had	397	5473	24 405	1 152 023	398.13
brodie	44	0	24 758	1 157 496	340.13
was	556	10 685	24 246	1 146 811	327.11
,	1820	54 548	22 982	1 102 948	319.74
flitter	41	0	24 761	1 157 496	316.94
a	931	22 857	23 871	1 134 639	313.16
hunter	43	12	24 759	1 157 484	275.20
could	171	1741	24 631	1 155 755	244.22

(*Hume, Vye, Rynch, Wass, Brodie* and *Jumala*), pronouns (*he, his*) and punctuation marks indicative of direct speech (the quotation marks and the exclamation mark).

This does not tell us anything about this particular text, but taken together, these pieces of evidence point to a particular genre: narrative text (novels, short stories, etc.). The few potential content words suggest a particular sub-genre: the archaic *hunter* in combination with the unusual word *flitter* is suggestive of fantasy or science fiction. If we were to include the next twenty most strongly associated nouns, we would find *patrol, camp, needler, safari, guild, tube, planet* and *out-hunter*, which corroborate the impression that we are dealing with a science-fiction novel. And indeed, the text in question is the science-fiction novel

Starhunter by Andre Alice Norton (available via Project Gutenberg in the Supplementary Online Material, file TXQP).

Again, the keywords identified are a mixture of topical markers and markers for the language variety (in this case, the genre) of the text, so even a study of the keywords of single texts provides information about more general linguistic properties of the text in question as well as its specific topic. But keyword analysis reveals its true potential when we apply it to clusters of texts, as in the case studies in the next section.

10.2 Case studies

10.2.1 Language variety

Keyword analysis has been applied to a wide range of language varieties defined by topic area (e.g. travel writing), genre (e.g. news reportage) or both (e.g. history textbooks) (see the contributions in Bondi & Scott 2010 for recent examples). Here, we will look at two case studies of scientific language.

10.2.1.1 Case study: Keywords in scientific writing

There are a number of keyword-based analyses of academic writing (cf., for example, Scott & Tribble 2006 on literary criticism, Römer & Wulff 2010 on academic student essays). Instead of replicating one of these studies in detail, let us look more generally at the Learned and Scientific Writing section of the LOB (Section J), using the rest of the corpus (all sections except Section J) as a reference corpus. Table 10.5 shows the keywords for this section.

It is immediately obvious from the preponderance of scientific terminology that we are dealing with Scientific English – there are general scientific terms like *fig(ure), data experiment* or *model*, mathematical terms and symbols (*equation, values*, the equals and percent signs), and a few words from chemistry (*oxygen, sodium*) (the reason the @ sign appears on this list is because it is used to mark places in the corpus where material such as mathematical formulae and operators have been deleted).

It may not be surprising that scientific terminology dominates in a corpus of Scientific English, but it demonstrates that keyword analysis works. Given this, we can make some more profound observations on the basis of the list in Table 10.5. For example, we observe that certain kinds of punctuation are typical of academic writing in general (such as the parentheses, which we already suspected based on the analysis of the fish population report in Section 10.1 above).

Table 10.5: Key words in the Learned and Scientific Writing section of LOB

Keyword	Frequency in LOB J	Frequency in other sections	Other words in LOB J	Other words in other sections	G
of	7899	27 846	173 017	948 734	1065.05
@	313	36	180 603	976 544	942.82
(	1099	1803	179 817	974 777	844.53
)	1101	1825	179 815	974 755	834.66
the	13 125	55 225	167 791	921 355	666.50
=	102	3	180 814	976 577	352.44
is	2482	8619	178 434	967 961	348.24
in	4332	16 917	176 584	959 663	345.37
fig	113	31	180 803	976 549	280.03
data	88	8	180 828	976 572	274.33
equation	72	0	180 844	976 580	267.29
values	111	47	180 805	976 533	235.70
oxygen	63	2	180 853	976 578	216.69
sodium	60	2	180 856	976 578	205.74
results	121	81	180 795	976 499	204.67
obtained	98	49	180 818	976 531	193.33
experiments	72	15	180 844	976 565	192.40
%	77	22	180 839	976 558	188.44
model	83	33	180 833	976 547	180.80
solution	96	53	180 820	976 527	180.43

Even more interestingly, keyword analysis can reveal function words that are characteristic for a particular language variety and thus give us potential insights into grammatical structures that may be typical for it; for example, *is*, *the* and *of* are among the most significant keywords of Scientific English. The last two are presumably related to the *nominal style* that is known to characterize academic texts, while the higher-than-normal frequency of *is* may be due to the prevalence of definitions, statements of equivalence, etc. This (and other observations made on the basis of keyword analysis) would of course have to be followed up by more detailed analyses of the function these words serve – but keyword analysis tells us what words are likely to be interesting to investigate.

10.2.1.2 Case study: [a + __ + of] in Scientific English

Of course, keyword analysis is not the only way to study lexical characteristics of language varieties. In principle, any design studying the interaction of lexical items with other units of linguistic structure can also be applied to specific language varieties.

For example, Marco (2000) investigates collocational frameworks (see Chapter 8, Section 8.2.1) in medical research papers. While this may not sound particularly interesting at first glance, it turns out that even highly frequent frameworks like [*a* __ *of*] are filled by completely different items from those found in the language as a whole, which is important for many applied purposes (such as language teaching or machine processing of language), but which also shows just how different language varieties can actually be. Since Marco's corpus is not publicly available and the Learned and Scientific Writing section of LOB is too small for this kind of analysis, let us use the Written Academic subsection of the BNC Baby. Table 10.6 shows the 15 most strongly associated collocates in the framework [*a* __ *of*], i.e. the words whose frequency of occurrence inside this framework differs most significantly from their frequency of occurrence outside of this framework in the same corpus section.

If we compare the result in Table 10.6 to that in Table 8.3 in Chapter 8, we notice clear differences between the use of this framework in academic texts and the language as a whole; for example, *lot*, which is most strongly associated with the framework in the general language occurs in 9th position, while the top collocates of the framework are more precise quantification terms like *number* or *series*, and general scientific terms like *result* and *function*.

However, the two lists – that in Table 8.3 and that presented here – were derived independently from different corpora, making it difficult to determine the true extent of the differences. In particular, in each of the two corpora the words in the pattern compete with the words outside of the pattern, which are obviously from the same discourse domains. To get a clearer idea of the different function(s) that a pattern might play in two different language varieties, we can combine collocational framework analysis and keyword analysis: we extract all words occurring in a collocational framework (or grammar pattern, construction, etc.) in a particular language variety, and compare them to the words occurring in the same pattern in a reference corpus (Stefanowitsch 2017 refers to this mix of keyword and collostructional analysis as "textually-distinctive [i.e., differential] collexeme analysis").

Table 10.7 shows the result of such an analysis in the BNC Baby, comparing words occurring in the framework [*a(n)* _ *of*] in the Written Academic section to the words occurring in the same pattern in the rest of the corpus (all sections other than Written Academic).

The scientific vocabulary now dominates the collocates of the framework even more clearly than in the simple collocational framework analysis above: the in-

Table 10.6: Collocates of the framework [*a* __ *of*] in the Written Academic subsection of BNC Baby

COLLOCATE	Frequency in [*a* __ *of*]	Frequency in other contexts	Other words in [*a* __ *of*]	Other words in other contexts	*G*
number	272	805	2965	1 138 862	2001.84
series	99	203	3138	1 139 464	783.67
variety	82	163	3155	1 139 504	652.77
result	98	425	3139	1 139 242	650.60
matter	61	190	3176	1 139 477	439.56
function	65	319	3172	1 139 348	416.52
range	66	388	3171	1 139 279	401.45
set	59	442	3178	1 139 225	332.64
lot	36	61	3201	1 139 606	295.19
form	65	933	3172	1 138 734	288.42
combination	34	115	3203	1 139 552	239.89
measure	35	139	3202	1 139 528	237.13
consequence	33	109	3204	1 139 558	234.18
piece	29	73	3208	1 139 594	219.15
group	43	605	3194	1 139 062	192.12
list	28	125	3209	1 139 542	183.85
source	26	161	3211	1 139 506	155.38
way	41	870	3196	1 138 797	152.06
study	36	594	3201	1 139 073	150.15
sense	29	294	3208	1 139 373	147.07

Supplementary Online Material: FXHV

formal *a lot of* and other colloquial words are now completely absent. This case study shows the variability that even seemingly simple grammatical patterns may display across language varieties. It is also meant to demonstrate how simple techniques like collocational-framework analysis can be combined with more sophisticated techniques to yield more insightful results.

10.2.2 Comparing speech communities

As pointed out at the beginning of this chapter, a keyword analysis of corpora that are defined by demographic variables is essentially a variant of variationist sociolinguistics. The basic method remains the same, the only difference being that the corpora under investigation have to be constructed based on the variables in question, or, more typically, that existing corpora have to be separated into subcorpora accordingly. This is true for inductive keyword analyses as well

Table 10.7: Textually differential collexemes in the framework [*a* + _- + *of*] in the Written Academic section of BNC Baby compared to all other sections

Keyword	Frequency in [*a* + _ + *of*] in Wrt. Acad.	Frequency in [*a* + _ + *of*] in other sections	Frequency in other contexts in Wrt. Acad.	Frequency in other contexts in other sections	*G*
number	272	151	1 139 395	3 505 016	298.08
function	65	0	1 139 602	3 505 167	182.66
form	65	17	1 139 602	3 505 150	108.52
variety	82	35	1 139 585	3 505 132	107.36
range	66	20	1 139 601	3 505 147	103.44
result	98	64	1 139 569	3 505 103	94.03
series	99	81	1 139 568	3 505 086	76.07
study	36	6	1 139 631	3 505 161	70.09
measure	35	6	1 139 632	3 505 161	67.59
consequence	33	5	1 139 634	3 505 162	65.95
set	59	32	1 139 608	3 505 135	65.79
solution	23	0	1 139 644	3 505 167	64.63
critique	23	1	1 139 644	3 505 166	56.88
theory	20	0	1 139 647	3 505 167	56.20
process	26	5	1 139 641	3 505 162	48.48
matrix	17	0	1 139 650	3 505 167	47.77
feature	15	0	1 139 652	3 505 167	42.15
breach	19	2	1 139 648	3 505 165	41.31
combination	34	16	1 139 633	3 505 151	41.86
consideration	14	0	1 139 653	3 505 167	39.34

Supplementary Online Material: MPXF

as for the kind of deductive analysis of individual words or constructions that we used in some of the examples in earlier chapters. The dependent variable will, as in all examples in this and the preceding chapter, always be nominal, consisting of (some part of) the lexicon (with words as values).

Lectal variety (dialect, sociolect, etc.) is an obvious demographic category to investigate using corpus-linguistic methods. Language varieties differ from each other along a number of dimensions, one of which is the lexicon. While lexical differences have not tended to play a major role in mainstream sociolinguistics, they do play a role in corpus-based sociolinguistics – presumably, because they are relatively easy to extract from appropriately constructed corpora, but also because they have traditionally been an important defining criterion of dialects (and continue to be so, especially in applied contexts).

Many of the examples in the early chapters of this book demonstrate how, in principle, lexical differences between varieties can be investigated – take two sufficiently large corpora representing two different varieties, and study the distribution of a particular word across these two corpora. Alternatively, we can study the distribution of *all* words across the two corpora in the same way as we studied their distribution across texts or language varieties in the preceding section.

This was actually done fairly early, long before the invention of keyword analysis, by Johansson & Hofland (1989). They compare all word forms in the LOB and BROWN corpora using a "coefficient of difference", essentially the percentage of the word in the two corpora.[2] In addition, they test each difference for significance using the χ^2 test. As discussed in Chapter 7, it is more recommendable – and, in fact, simpler – to use an association measure like *G* right away, as percentages will massively overestimate infrequent events (a word that occurs only a single time will be seen as 100 percent typical of whichever corpus it happens to occur in); also, the χ^2 test cannot be applied to infrequent words. Still, Johansson and Hofland's basic idea is highly innovative and their work constitutes the first example of a keyword analysis that I am aware of.

Comparing two (large) corpora representing two varieties will not, however, straightforwardly result in a list of dialect differences. Instead, there are at least five types of differences that such a comparison will uncover. Not all of them will be relevant to a particular research design, and some of them are fundamental problems for any research design and must be dealt with before we can proceed.

Table 10.8 shows the ten most strongly differential keywords for the LOB and BROWN corpora. The analysis is based on the tagged versions of the two corpora as originally distributed by ICAME.

For someone hoping to uncover dialectal differences between British and American English, these lists are likely to be confusing, to say the least. The hyphen is the strongest American keyword? Quotation marks are typical for British English? The word *The* is typically American? Clitics like *n't*, *'s* and *'m* are British, while words containing these clitics, like *didn't*, *it's* and *I'm* are American? Of

[2]More precisely, in its generalized form, this coefficient is calculated by the following formula, given two corpora A and B:

$$\frac{\frac{f(\text{word}_A)}{\text{size}_A} - \frac{f(\text{word}_B)}{\text{size}_B}}{\frac{f(\text{word}_A)}{\text{size}_A} + \frac{f(\text{word}_B)}{\text{size}_B}}$$

This formula will give us the percentage of uses of the word in Corpus A or Corpus B (whichever is larger), with a negative sign if it occurs in Corpus B.

Table 10.8: Key words of British and American English based on a comparison of LOB and BROWN

KEYWORD	Frequency in BROWN	Frequency in LOB	Other words in BROWN	Other words in LOB	*G*
Most strongly associated with AMERICAN ENGLISH					
–	3385	0	1 134 081	1 157 496	4757.04
J	1776	128	1 135 690	1 157 368	1731.31
Mr.	851	0	1 136 615	1 157 496	1194.98
]	798	0	1 136 668	1 157 496	1120.54
F	1017	102	1 136 449	1 157 394	884.66
Mrs.	534	0	1 136 932	1 157 496	749.77
don't	489	0	1 136 977	1 157 496	686.58
The	455	0	1 137 011	1 157 496	638.83
didn't	402	0	1 137 064	1 157 496	564.41
program	376	0	1 137 090	1 157 496	527.90
toward	386	14	1 137 080	1 157 482	439.73
it's	302	0	1 137 164	1 157 496	424.00
I'm	269	0	1 137 197	1 157 496	377.66
New	548	91	1 136 918	1 157 405	370.86
cannot	258	0	1 137 208	1 157 496	362.22
State	254	1	1 137 212	1 157 495	344.89
States	443	69	1 137 023	1 157 427	311.58
Dr.	192	0	1 137 274	1 157 496	269.55
center	188	0	1 137 278	1 157 496	263.94
that's	187	0	1 137 279	1 157 496	262.53
Most strongly associated with BRITISH ENGLISH					
‘	0	10 114	1 137 466	1 147 382	13 889.20
’	0	9860	1 137 466	1 147 636	13 539.30
-	72	3942	1 137 394	1 153 554	4782.05
n't	0	1952	1 137 466	1 155 544	2673.75
Mr	0	1508	1 137 466	1 155 988	2065.30
's	0	1177	1 137 466	1 156 319	1611.81
!	0	1030	1 137 466	1 156 466	1410.44
...	0	665	1 137 466	1 156 831	910.52
'd	0	535	1 137 466	1 156 961	732.49
'll	0	505	1 137 466	1 156 991	691.41
@	0	349	1 137 466	1 157 147	477.80
s	0	339	1 137 466	1 157 157	464.11
'm	0	339	1 137 466	1 157 157	464.11
've	0	335	1 137 466	1 157 161	458.63
I	5159	7628	1 132 307	1 149 868	440.05
Mrs	0	292	1 137 466	1 157 204	399.76
're	0	276	1 137 466	1 157 220	377.85
d	0	260	1 137 466	1 157 236	355.95
labour	3	276	1 137 463	1 157 220	348.90
	0	247	1 137 466	1 157 249	338.15

course not – all of these apparent differences between American and British English are actually differences in the way the two corpora were prepared. The tagged version of the BROWN corpus does not contain quotation marks because they have intentionally been stripped from the text. *The* with an uppercase *T* does not occur in the tagged LOB corpus, because case is normalized such that only proper names are capitalized. And clitics are separate tokens in LOB but not in BROWN.

In other words, the two corpora have to be made comparable before they can be compared. Table 10.9 shows the 10 most strongly differential keywords for the LOB and BROWN corpora respectively, after all words in both corpora have been put into lowercase, all clitics in BROWN have been separated from their stems, and all tokens consisting exclusively of punctuation marks have been removed, as have periods at the end of abbreviations like *mr.* and *st.*

This list is much more insightful. There are still some artifacts of corpus construction: the codes F and J are used in BROWN to indicate that letter combinations and formulae have been removed. But the remainder of the keywords is now representative of the kinds of differences a dialectal keyword analysis will typically uncover.

First, there are differences in spelling. For example, *labour* and *behaviour* are spelled with *ou* in Britain, but with *o* in the USA, the US-American *defense* is spelled *defence* in Britain, and the British *programme* is spelled *program* in the USA. These differences are dialectal and may be of interest in applied contexts, but they are not likely to be of primary interest to most linguists. In fact, they are often irritating, since of course we would like to know whether words like *labo(u)r* or *behavio(u)r* are more typical for British or for American English aside from the spelling differences. To find out, we have to normalize spellings in the corpora before comparing them (which is possible, but labo(u)r-intensive).

Second, there are proper nouns that differ in frequency across corpora: for example, geographical names like *London*, *Britain*, *Commonwealth*, and *(New) York* will differ in frequency because their referents are of different degrees of interest to the speakers of the two varieties. There are also personal names that differ across corpora; for example, the name *Macmillan* occurs 63 times in the LOB corpus but only once in BROWN; this is because in 1961, Harold Macmillan was the British Prime Minister and thus Brits had more reason to mention the name. But there are also names that differ in frequency because they differ in popularity in the speech communities: for example, *Mike* is a keyword for BROWN, *Michael* for LOB. Thus, proper names may differ in frequency for purely cultural or for linguistic reasons; the same is true of common nouns.

Table 10.9: Key words of British and American English based on a comparison of LOB and BROWN

KEYWORD	Frequency in BROWN	Frequency in LOB	Other words in BROWN	Other words in LOB	*G*
Most strongly associated with AMERICAN ENGLISH					
j	1897	134	1 012 415	1 012 851	1827.29
f	1077	131	1 013 235	1 012 854	844.56
program	393	0	1 013 919	1 012 985	544.38
toward	386	14	1 013 926	1 012 971	432.73
states	603	123	1 013 709	1 012 862	345.32
center	224	0	1 014 088	1 012 985	310.26
state	807	271	1 013 505	1 012 714	278.19
defense	167	0	1 014 145	1 012 985	231.31
u.s.	162	0	1 014 150	1 012 985	224.38
ca	171	2	1 014 141	1 012 983	217.80
labor	149	0	1 014 163	1 012 985	206.37
color	140	0	1 014 172	1 012 985	193.91
programs	139	0	1 014 173	1 012 985	192.52
federal	246	33	1 014 066	1 012 952	183.70
york	302	65	1 014 010	1 012 920	165.72
fiscal	120	1	1 014 192	1 012 984	156.01
american	569	226	1 013 743	1 012 759	152.57
rhode	105	1	1 014 207	1 012 984	135.50
wo	105	1	1 014 207	1 012 984	135.50
washington	206	36	1 014 106	1 012 949	131.73
Most strongly associated with BRITISH ENGLISH					
labour	4	276	1 014 308	1 012 709	346.62
london	89	492	1 014 223	1 012 493	308.49
sir	95	456	1 014 217	1 012 529	257.80
i	5854	7635	1 008 458	1 005 350	239.77
colour	0	140	1 014 312	1 012 845	194.27
mr	851	1508	1 013 461	1 011 477	186.50
towards	64	318	1 014 248	1 012 667	184.63
centre	2	144	1 014 310	1 012 841	181.46
round	75	336	1 014 237	1 012 649	179.58
she	2995	4090	1 011 317	1 008 895	171.95
defence	1	129	1 014 311	1 012 856	168.67
commonwealth	7	156	1 014 305	1 012 829	168.41
programme	0	117	1 014 312	1 012 868	162.36
british	118	397	1 014 194	1 012 588	159.98
s	129	397	1 014 183	1 012 588	143.56
her	3040	4034	1 011 272	1 008 951	141.93
behaviour	3	119	1 014 309	1 012 866	141.13
council	103	343	1 014 209	1 012 642	136.58
britain	55	249	1 014 257	1 012 736	134.25
d	105	340	1 014 207	1 012 645	130.96

Third, nouns may differ in frequency not because they are dialectal, but because the things they refer to play a different role in the respective cultures. *State*, for example, is a word found in both varieties, but it is more frequent in US-American English because the USA is organized into 50 states that play an important cultural and political role.

Fourth, nouns may differ in frequency due to dialectal differences (as we saw in many of the examples in previous chapters). Take *toward* and *towards*, which mean the same thing, but for which the first variant is preferred in US-American and the second in British English. Or take *round*, which is an adjective meaning 'shaped like a circle or a ball' in both varieties, but also an adverb with a range of related meanings that corresponds to American English *around*.

This case study was mainly intended to demonstrate the difficulty of comparing corpora that are not really comparable in terms of the way they have been constructed. It was also meant to demonstrate how large-scale comparisons of varieties of a language can be done and what kind of results they yield. From a theoretical perspective, these results may seem to be of secondary interest, at least in the domain of lexis, since lexical differences between the major varieties of English are well documented. But from a lexicographical perspective, large-scale comparisons of varieties are useful, especially because dialectal differences are constantly evolving.

10.2.2.1 Case study: British vs. American culture

Keyword analysis of language varieties is often done not to uncover dialectal variation, but to identify cultural differences between speech communities. Such studies have two nominal variables: Culture (operationalized as "corpus containing language produced by members of the culture") and Area of Life (operationalized as "semantic field"). They then investigate the importance of different areas of life for the cultures involved (where the importance of an area is operationalized as "having a large number of words from the corresponding semantic field among the differential keywords"). The earliest study of this kind is Leech & Fallon (1992), which is based on the keyword list of British and American English in Johansson & Hofland (1989).

The authors inductively identify words pointing to cultural contrasts by discarding all words whose distribution across the two corpora is not significant, all proper names, and all words whose significant differences in distribution are due to dialectal variation (including spelling variation). Next, they look at concordances of the remaining words to determine first, which senses are most frequent and thus most relevant for the observed differences, and second, whether the words are actually distributed across the respective corpus, discarding those whose overall frequency is simply due to their frequent occurrence in a single file (since those words would not tell us anything about cultural differences). Finally, they sort the words into semantic fields such as *sport, travel and transport, business, mass media, military*, etc., discussing the quantitative and qualitative differences for each semantic field.

For example, they note that there are obvious differences between the types of sports whose vocabulary differentiates between the two corpora (*baseball* is associated with the BROWN corpus, *cricket* and *rugby* with the LOB corpus), reflecting the importance of these sports in the two cultures, but also that general sports vocabulary (*athletic, ball, playing, victory*) is more often associated with the BROWN corpus, suggesting a greater overall importance of sports in 1961 US-American culture. Except for one case, they do not present the results systematically. They list lexical items they found to differentiate between the corpora, but it is unclear whether these lists are exhaustive or merely illustrative (the only drawback of this otherwise methodologically excellent study).

The one case where they do present a table is the semantic field MILITARY. Their results are shown in Table 10.10 (I have recalculated them using the *G* value we have used throughout this and the preceding section).

There are two things to note about this list. First, as Leech & Fallon (1992) point out, many of these words do not occur exclusively, or even just most frequently, in the military domain. For a principled study of the different role that the military may play in British and American culture, it would be necessary to limit the study to unambiguously military words like *militia*, or to check all instances of ambiguous words individually and only include those used in military contexts. For example, (1a) would have to be included, while (1b) is clearly about hunting and would have to be excluded:

(1) a. These remarkable ships and weapons, ranging the oceans, will be capable of accurate fire on *targets* virtually anywhere on earth. (BROWN G35)

b. A trap for throwing these miniature clays fastens to the barrel so that the shooter can throw his own *targets*. (BROWN E10)

Second, the list is not exhaustive, listing only words which show a significant difference across the two varieties. For example, the obvious items *soldier* and *soldiers* are missing because they are roughly equally frequent in the two varieties. However, if we want to make strong claims about the role of a particular domain of life (i.e., semantic field) in a culture, we need to take into consideration not just the words that show significant differences but also the ones that do not. If there are many of the latter, this would weaken the results.

Table 10.10: Military keywords in BROWN and LOB (cf. Leech & Fallon 1992: 49–50)

Word	f_W(BROWN)	f_W(LOB)	f_{OTH}(BROWN)	f_{OTH}(LOB)	G	Word	f_W(BROWN)	f_W(LOB)	f_{OTH}(BROWN)	f_{OTH}(LOB)	G	Word	f_W(BROWN)	f_W(LOB)	f_{OTH}(BROWN)	f_{OTH}(LOB)	G
Keywords for American English						(AmE contd.)						(AmE contd.)					
corps	110	10	1 014 202	1 012 975	97.39	*patrol*	25	6	1 014 287	1 012 979	12.49	*strategic*	23	9	1 014 289	1 012 976	6.32
missile	48	5	1 014 264	1 012 980	40.30	*fire*	187	125	1 014 125	1 012 860	12.32	*battery*	18	6	1 014 294	1 012 979	6.26
sherman	29	0	1 014 283	1 012 985	40.16	*code*	39	14	1 014 273	1 012 971	12.24	*arms*	121	85	1 014 191	1 012 900	6.28
fallout	31	1	1 014 281	1 012 984	35.42	*volunteers*	29	8	1 014 283	1 012 977	12.63	*march*	121	85	1 014 191	1 012 900	6.28
mobile	44	6	1 014 268	1 012 979	32.57	*submarine*	26	7	1 014 286	1 012 978	11.62	*bullet*	28	12	1 014 284	1 012 973	6.56
fort	55	11	1 014 257	1 012 974	31.96	*division*	107	64	1 014 205	1 012 921	10.87	*pirates*	12	3	1 014 300	1 012 982	5.77
marine	55	12	1 014 257	1 012 973	29.84	*combat*	27	8	1 014 285	1 012 977	10.87	*targets*	22	9	1 014 290	1 012 976	5.61
major	247	142	1 014 065	1 012 843	28.56	*missiles*	32	11	1 014 280	1 012 974	10.68	*tactics*	20	8	1 014 292	1 012 977	5.30
plane	114	49	1 014 198	1 012 936	26.57	*rifles*	23	6	1 014 289	1 012 979	10.61	*war*	464	396	1 013 848	1 012 589	5.30
guns	42	8	1 014 270	1 012 977	25.30	*troop*	16	3	1 014 296	1 012 982	9.75	*armies*	15	5	1 014 297	1 012 980	5.22
column	71	24	1 014 241	1 012 961	24.25	*missions*	16	3	1 014 296	1 012 982	9.75	*marching*	15	5	1 014 297	1 012 980	5.22
rifle	63	20	1 014 249	1 012 965	23.34	*viet*	16	3	1 014 296	1 012 982	9.75	*commands*	15	5	1 014 297	1 012 980	5.22
losses	46	11	1 014 266	1 012 974	23.05	*force*	230	168	1 014 082	1 012 817	9.62	*signal*	63	40	1 014 249	1 012 945	5.15
gun	118	56	1 014 194	1 012 929	22.51	*victory*	61	32	1 014 251	1 012 953	9.16	*weapon*	42	24	1 014 270	1 012 961	4.95
enemy	88	36	1 014 224	1 012 949	22.43	*codes*	17	4	1 014 295	1 012 981	8.64	*civilian*	24	11	1 014 288	1 012 974	4.93
cavalry	26	3	1 014 286	1 012 982	20.88	*slug*	10	1	1 014 302	1 012 984	8.54	*enlisted*	11	3	1 014 301	1 012 982	4.85
military	212	133	1 014 100	1 012 852	18.15	*bombers*	22	7	1 014 290	1 012 978	8.13	*infantry*	16	6	1 014 296	1 012 979	4.70
armed	60	22	1 014 252	1 012 963	18.25	*signals*	29	11	1 014 283	1 012 974	8.37	*territorial*	14	5	1 014 298	1 012 980	4.43
ballistic	17	1	1 014 295	1 012 984	17.21	*manned*	12	2	1 014 300	1 012 983	7.91	*fought*	46	28	1 014 266	1 012 957	4.40
mercenaries	12	0	1 014 300	1 012 985	16.62	*battle*	87	54	1 014 225	1 012 931	7.75	*command*	72	49	1 014 240	1 012 936	4.37
veterans	16	1	1 014 296	1 012 984	15.94	*fighters*	16	4	1 014 296	1 012 981	7.69	*peace*	198	159	1 014 114	1 012 826	4.22
warfare	43	14	1 014 269	1 012 971	15.43	*victor*	23	8	1 014 289	1 012 977	7.55	*winchester*	12	4	1 014 300	1 012 981	4.18
aircraft	70	31	1 014 242	1 012 954	15.41	*lieutenant*	29	12	1 014 283	1 012 973	7.24						
headquarters	65	28	1 014 247	1 012 957	15.09	*bombs*	35	16	1 014 277	1 012 969	7.23	Key words for British English					
militia	11	0	1 014 301	1 012 985	15.23	*destroy*	48	25	1 014 264	1 012 960	7.34	*medal*	7	37	1 014 305	1 012 948	22.48
squad	18	2	1 014 294	1 012 983	14.70	*veteran*	27	11	1 014 285	1 012 974	6.93	*trench*	2	15	1 014 310	1 012 970	11.27
patriot	10	0	1 014 302	1 012 985	13.85	*campaigns*	17	5	1 014 295	1 012 980	6.90	*disarmament*	11	27	1 014 301	1 012 958	6.97
strategy	22	4	1 014 290	1 012 981	13.70	*assault*	15	4	1 014 297	1 012 981	6.77	*tanks*	18	35	1 014 294	1 012 950	5.57
shot	113	65	1 014 199	1 012 920	13.04	*pentagon*	13	3	1 014 299	1 012 982	6.73	*rank*	24	43	1 014 288	1 012 942	5.49
bullets	21	4	1 014 291	1 012 981	12.65	*mission*	78	49	1 014 234	1 012 936	6.64	*conquest*	9	20	1 014 303	1 012 965	4.29

Supplementary Online Material: 847K

Third, the study of cultural importance cannot be separated entirely from the study of dialectal preferences. For example, the word *armistice* occurs 15 times in the LOB corpus but only 4 times in BROWN, making it a significant keyword for British English (G^2 = 6.80). However, before we conclude that British culture is more peaceful than American culture, we should check synonyms. We find that *truce* occurs 5 times in BROWN and not at all in LOB, making it an equally significant keyword for American English (G^2 = 6.92). Finally, *cease-fire* occurs 7 times in each corpus. In other words, the two cultures differ not in the importance of cease-fires, but in the words they use to denote them – similar dialectal preferences may well underlie other items on Leech and Fallon's list.

Overall, however, Leech & Fallon (1992) were careful to include words that occur in military contexts in a substantial number of instances and to cover the semantic field broadly (*armistice* and *truce* were two of the few words I was able to think of that turned out to have significant associations). Thus, their conclusion that the concept WAR played a more central role in US culture in 1961 than it did in British culture seems reliable.

This case study is an example of a very carefully constructed and executed contrastive cultural analysis based on keywords. Note, especially, that Leech and Fallon do not just look for semantic fields that are strongly represented among the statistically significant keywords of one corpus, but that they check the entire semantic field (or a large portion of it) with respect to its associations in both corpora. In other words, they do not look only for evidence, but also for counter-evidence, something that is often lacking in cultural keyword studies.

10.2.2.2 Case study: "African" keywords

Another study that involves keyword analyses aimed at identifying significant cultural concepts is Wolf & Polzenhagen (2007). The authors present (among other things) an analysis of "African" keywords arrived at by comparing a corpus of Cameroon English to the combined FLOB/FROWN corpora (jointly meant to present "Western culture"). Their study is partially deductive, in that they start out from a pre-conceived "African model of community" which, so they claim, holds for all of sub-Saharan Africa and accords the extended family and community a central role in a "holistic cosmology" involving hierarchical structures of authority and respect within the community, extending into the "spiritual world of the ancestors", and also involving a focus on gods and witchcraft.

The model seems somewhat stereotypical, to say the least, but a judgment of its accuracy is beyond the scope of this book. What matters here is that it guides the authors in their search for keywords that might differentiate between their two corpora. Unlike Leech and Fallon in the study described above, it seems that they did not create a complete list of differential keywords and then categorized them into semantic fields, but instead focused on words for kinship relations, spiritual entities and witchcraft straight away.

This procedure yields seemingly convincing word lists like that in Table 10.11, which the authors claim shows "the salience of authority and respect and the figures that can be associated with them" Wolf & Polzenhagen (2007: 420).

Table 10.11: Keywords relating to authority and respect in a corpus of Cameroon English (from Wolf & Polzenhagen 2007: 421).

Keyword	CEC	FLOB/FROWN	G	p-value
authority	301	556	9.10	0.0026
respect	232	226	82.20	0.0000
obedience	23	8	25.30	0.0000
obey	80	24	95.90	0.0000
disobedience	30	4	49.90	0.0000
chief	373	219	267.90	0.0000
chiefdom	28	2	53.50	0.0000
dignitaries	11	4	11.70	0.0006
leader	312	402	56.70	0.0000
leadership	86	128	9.40	0.0022
ruler	59	28	51.70	0.0000
father	365	793	22.50	0.0000
elder	59	68	22.50	0.0000
teacher	293	254	127.90	0.0000
priest	82	132	6.20	0.0128

However, it is very difficult to tell whether this is a real result or whether it is simply due to the specific selection of words they look at. Some obvious items from the semantic field AUTHORITY are missing from their list – for example, *command, rule, disobey, disrespect*, and *power*. As long as we do not know whether they failed to check the keyness of these (and other) AUTHORITY words, or whether they did check them but found them not to be significant, we cannot claim that authority and respect play a special role in African culture(s) for the simple reason that we cannot exclude the possibility that these words may actually be significant keywords for the combined FROWN/FLOB corpus.

With respect to the latter, note that it is also questionable whether one can simply combine a British and an American corpus to represent "Western" culture. First, it assumes that the two cultures individually belong to such a larger culture and can jointly represent it. Second, it assumes that these two cultures do not accord any specific importance to whatever domain we are looking at. However, especially if we choose our keywords selectively, we could easily show that *Authority* has a central place in British or American culture. Table 10.12 lists ten significantly associated keywords from each corpus, resulting from the direct comparison discussed in 10.2.2. By presenting just one or the other list, we could make any argument about Britain, the USA and authority that suits our purposes.

This case study demonstrates some of the potential pitfalls of cultural keyword analysis. This is not to suggest that Wolf & Polzenhagen (2007) is methodologically flawed, but that the way they present the results does not allow us to determine the methodological soundness of their approach. Generally, semantic domains should be extracted from corpora as exhaustively as possible in such analyses, and all results should be reported. Also, instead of focusing on one culture and using another culture as the reference corpus, it seems more straightforward to compare specific cultures (for example in the sense of "speech communities within a nation state") directly, as Leech & Fallon (1992) do (cf. also Oakes & Farrow 2007 for a method than can be used to compare more than two varieties against each other in a single analysis).

10.2.3 Co-occurrence of lexical items and demographic categories

The potential overlap between keyword analysis and sociolinguistics becomes most obvious when using individual demographic variables such as sex, age, education, income, etc. as individual variables. Note that such variables may be nominal (sex), or ordinal (age, income, education); however, even potentially ordinal variables are treated as nominal in keyword-based studies, since keyword analysis cannot straightforwardly deal with ordinal data (although it could, in principle, be adapted to do so).

10.2.3.1 Case study: A deductive approach to sex differences

A thorough study of lexical differences between male and female speech is Schmid (2003) (inspired by an earlier, less detailed study by Rayson et al. 1997). Schmid uses the parts of the BNC that contain information about speaker sex (which means that he simply follows the definition of Sex used by the corpus creators); he uses the difference coefficient from Johansson & Hofland (1989) discussed in Section 10.2.2 above. His procedure is at least partially deductive in

Table 10.12: Key words from the domain AUTHORITY in British and American English

KEYWORD	Frequency in BROWN	Frequency in LOB	Other words in BROWN	Other words in LOB	*G*
AUTHORITY key words in American English					
law	299	159	1 137 167	1 157 337	45.98
leadership	92	36	1 137 374	1 157 460	26.34
boss	20	6	1 137 446	1 157 490	8.20
elders	9	1	1 137 457	1 157 495	7.50
leaders	107	77	1 137 359	1 157 419	5.45
preacher	11	3	1 137 455	1 157 493	5.00
respect	125	94	1 137 341	1 157 402	4.96
teacher	80	57	1 137 386	1 157 439	4.29
dignitaries	3	0	1 137 463	1 157 496	4.21
obedience	9	3	1 137 457	1 157 493	3.25
AUTHORITY key words in British English					
lord	93	272	1 137 373	1 157 224	88.61
ruler	3	30	1 137 463	1 157 466	25.17
monarchy	0	18	1 137 466	1 157 478	24.64
authority	93	160	1 137 373	1 157 336	16.81
father	184	274	1 137 282	1 157 222	16.27
monarch	3	19	1 137 463	1 157 477	12.70
bishop	18	44	1 137 448	1 157 452	10.80
lordship	3	15	1 137 463	1 157 481	8.53
archbishop	8	23	1 137 458	1 157 473	7.31
schoolteacher	0	4	1 137 466	1 157 492	5.48

that he focuses on particular Semantic Domains in which differences between male and female language are expected according to authors like Lakoff (1973), for example, color, clothing, body and health, car and traffic and public affairs. As far as one can tell from his description of his methodology, he only looks at selected words from each category, so the reliability of the results depends on the plausibility of his selection.

One area in which this is unproblematic is color: Schmid finds that all basic color terms (*black, white, red, yellow, blue, green, orange, pink, purple, grey*) are more frequent in women's language than in men's language. Since basic color terms are (synchronically) a closed set and Schmid looks at the entire set, the results may be taken to suggest that women talk about color more often than men do. Similarly, for the domain temporal deixis Schmid looks at the expressions *yesterday, tomorrow, last week, tonight, this morning, today, next week, last year* and *next year* and finds that all but the last three are significantly more frequently used by women. While this is not a complete list of temporal deictic expressions, it seems representative enough to suggest that the results reflect a real difference.

The semantic domain personal reference is slightly more difficult – it is large, lexically diverse and has no clear boundaries. Schmid operationalizes it in terms of the pronouns *I, you, he, she, we, they* and the relatively generic human nouns *boy, girl, man, men, people, person, persons, woman, women* (it is unclear why the sex-neutral *child(ren)* and the plurals *boys* and *girls* are missing). This is not a bad selection, but it is clear that there are many other ways of referring to persons – proper names, kinship terms, professions, to name just a few. There may be good reasons for excluding these, but doing so means that we are studying not the semantic field of personal reference as a whole, but a particular aspect of it.

Table 10.13 shows the distribution of these nouns across the parts of the BNC annotated for speaker sex, both written and spoken (I have added the missing plurals *boys* and *girls* and the words *child* and *children*).

Within the limitations just mentioned, it seems that a good case can be made that women's speech is characterized by a higher proportion of personal reference terms (at least if the corpus is well constructed, a point I will return to in the next subsection). The words selected to represent this domain form a well-delineated set – stylistically neutral English nouns referring to people with no additional semantic content other than sex (the pronouns are even a closed set). The only potential caveat is just that the words are stylistically neutral and that the results may thus reflect a tendency of women to use a more standard variety of the language. Thus, we might want to look at synonyms for *man, woman, boy, girl* and *child.* Table 10.14 shows the results.

Table 10.13: Differential collocates for men and women in the domain PERSONAL REFERENCE

KEYWORD	Frequency in MEN'S SPEECH	Frequency in WOMEN'S SPEECH	Other words in MEN'S SPEECH	Other words in WOMEN'S SPEECH	*G*
More strongly associated with WOMEN'S SPEECH					
she	84 269	207 627	40 572 767	20 706 318	168 337.07
you	248 964	245 315	40 408 072	20 668 630	51 667.80
i	327 062	299 568	40 329 974	20 614 377	51 469.11
he	257 229	198 292	40 399 807	20 715 653	18 030.23
women	7196	11 889	40 649 840	20 902 056	6358.45
woman	6295	8445	40 650 741	20 905 500	3344.08
girl	4428	6342	40 652 608	20 907 603	2783.36
child	6741	6933	40 650 295	20 907 012	1614.32
girls	2494	3568	40 654 542	20 910 377	1563.12
they	165 574	96 343	40 491 462	20 817 602	918.67
children	12 558	9110	40 644 478	20 904 835	610.11
boy	4888	3936	40 652 148	20 910 009	427.52
man	25 518	15 150	40 631 518	20 898 795	193.02
boys	2850	1876	40 654 186	20 912 069	67.48
people	39 178	20 907	40 617 858	20 893 038	18.33
men	15 003	8046	40 642 033	20 905 899	9.06
person	9726	5262	40 647 310	20 908 683	8.65
More strongly associated with MEN'S SPEECH					
persons	1982	397	40 655 054	20 913 548	357.11
we	142 180	67 749	40 514 856	20 846 196	272.04

We see the same general difference as before, so the result is not due to different style preferences of men and women, but to the semantic field under investigation.

Many other fields that Schmid investigates make it much more difficult to come up with a plausibly representative sample of words. For example, for the domain HEALTH AND BODY, Schmid looks at *breast, hair, headache, legs, sore throat, doctor, sick, ill, leg, eyes, finger, fingers, eye, body, hands,* and *hand* and finds that with the exception of *hand* they are all more frequently used by women. The selection seems small and rather eclectic, however, so let us enlarge the set with the words *ache, aching, flu, health, healthy, influenza, medicine, nurse, pain* and *unwell* from the domain HEALTH and *arms, ear, ears, feet, foot, kidneys, liver, mouth, muscles, nose, penis, stomach, teeth, thumb, thumbs, tooth, vagina* and *vulva* from the domain BODY. Table 10.15 shows the results.

Table 10.14: More differential collocates for men and women in the domain PERSONAL REFERENCE

KEYWORD	Frequency in MEN'S SPEECH	Frequency in WOMEN'S SPEECH	Other words in MEN'S SPEECH	Other words in WOMEN'S SPEECH	*G*
More strongly associated with WOMEN'S SPEECH					
lady	2893	3482	40 654 143	20 910 463	1137.84
lass	75	291	40 656 961	20 913 654	319.45
guy	1298	1120	40 655 738	20 912 825	157.15
kids	1288	1103	40 655 748	20 912 842	150.78
ladies	937	864	40 656 099	20 913 081	149.84
gentleman	793	671	40 656 243	20 913 274	87.92
lad	744	607	40 656 292	20 913 338	69.43
lasses	11	54	40 657 025	20 913 891	66.64
bairns	14	49	40 657 022	20 913 896	50.70
bairn	11	38	40 657 025	20 913 907	39.01
kid	631	469	40 656 405	20 913 476	35.60
bloke	521	378	40 656 515	20 913 567	25.32
lassie	22	38	40 657 014	20 913 907	21.46
toddler	64	70	40 656 972	20 913 875	18.80
toddlers	30	38	40 657 006	20 913 907	13.64
fellows	252	173	40 656 784	20 913 772	8.37
wean	17	21	40 657 019	20 913 924	7.20
blokes	111	86	40 656 925	20 913 859	7.94
lassies	4	9	40 657 032	20 913 936	6.71
Non-significant:					
laddie	48	37	40 656 988	20 913 908	3.34
tots	11	12	40 657 025	20 913 933	3.20
nipper	4	6	40 657 032	20 913 939	2.82
chaps	174	107	40 656 862	20 913 838	2.08
brat	41	29	40 656 995	20 913 916	1.69
chit	27	14	40 657 009	20 913 931	0.00
geezer	33	21	40 657 003	20 913 924	0.57
fellow	1602	849	40 655 434	20 913 096	0.49
laddies	2	2	40 657 034	20 913 943	0.43
brats	17	11	40 657 019	20 913 934	0.35
geezers	7	5	40 657 029	20 913 940	0.31
tot	35	21	40 657 001	20 913 924	0.31
chits	6	4	40 657 030	20 913 941	0.16
weans	8	5	40 657 028	20 913 940	0.11
More strongly associated with MEN'S SPEECH					
guys	464	135	40 656 572	20 913 810	37.39
infants	269	63	40 656 767	20 913 882	36.71
gentlemen	736	268	40 656 300	20 913 677	24.66
infant	718	268	40 656 318	20 913 677	21.02
lads	599	244	40 656 437	20 913 701	9.74
Non-significant:					
chap	782	370	40 656 254	20 913 575	1.77
nippers	7	2	40 657 029	20 913 943	0.59

Table 10.15: Differential collocates for men and women in the domain BODY AND HEALTH

KEYWORD	Frequency in MEN'S SPEECH	Frequency in WOMEN'S SPEECH	Other words in MEN'S SPEECH	Other words in WOMEN'S SPEECH	*G*
More strongly associated with WOMEN'S SPEECH					
eyes	9777	14 158	40 647 259	20 899 787	6318.27
hair	3585	5890	40 653 451	20 908 055	3127.21
mouth	3176	4202	40 653 860	20 909 743	1625.89
nurse	546	1421	40 656 490	20 912 524	1198.33
arms	3473	3896	40 653 563	20 910 049	1105.16
hands	6817	6289	40 650 219	20 907 656	1092.52
fingers	1891	2535	40 655 145	20 911 410	1002.43
hand	14 128	9927	40 642 908	20 904 018	554.97
throat	1052	1377	40 655 984	20 912 568	523.23
legs	2306	2164	40 654 730	20 911 781	395.14
ill	1380	1465	40 655 656	20 912 480	367.74
health	4467	3501	40 652 569	20 910 444	339.81
feet	5672	4178	40 651 364	20 909 767	303.10
sick	1394	1384	40 655 642	20 912 561	294.81
stomach	933	1022	40 656 103	20 912 923	275.34
pain	2495	2085	40 654 541	20 911 860	261.15
leg	1583	1370	40 655 453	20 912 575	194.19
breast	405	517	40 656 631	20 913 428	188.13
ears	1104	1002	40 655 932	20 912 943	165.64
aching	123	231	40 656 913	20 913 714	143.68
ache	113	217	40 656 923	20 913 728	138.28
nose	1674	1331	40 655 362	20 912 614	137.27
finger	1249	1037	40 655 787	20 912 908	126.79
body	9066	5478	40 647 970	20 908 467	87.25
flu	91	153	40 656 945	20 913 792	83.62
headache	243	277	40 656 793	20 913 668	81.25
teeth	2015	1415	40 655 021	20 912 530	78.80
thumb	422	343	40 656 614	20 913 602	38.66
eye	3716	2254	40 653 320	20 911 691	37.57
sore	329	280	40 656 707	20 913 665	37.45
kidneys	70	91	40 656 966	20 913 854	34.18
medicine	733	525	40 656 303	20 913 420	32.77
doctor	4329	2546	40 652 707	20 911 399	28.42
ear	1207	788	40 655 829	20 913 157	26.58
healthy	788	516	40 656 248	20 913 429	17.82
thumbs	84	82	40 656 952	20 913 863	16.71
unwell	63	59	40 656 973	20 913 886	10.71
foot	3043	1700	40 653 993	20 912 245	7.37
liver	212	136	40 656 824	20 913 809	3.97
Non-significant:					
muscles	900	512	40 656 136	20 913 433	3.28
influenza	39	29	40 656 997	20 913 916	2.21
More strongly associated with MEN'S SPEECH					
penis	264	68	40 656 772	20 913 877	29.32
vagina	140	39	40 656 896	20 913 906	12.76
vulva	27	3	40 657 009	20 913 942	9.38
Non-significant:					
tooth	252	126	40 656 784	20 913 819	0.07

The larger sample supports Schmid's initial conclusion, but even the larger sample is far from exhaustive. Still this case study has demonstrated that if we manage to come up with a justifiable selection of lexical items, a deductive keyword analysis can be used to test a particular hypothesis in an efficient and principled way.

10.2.3.2 Case study: An inductive approach to sex differences

An inductive design will give us a more complete and less biased picture, but also one that is much less focused. For example, Rayson et al. (1997), whose study inspired the one by Schmid discussed in the preceding section, apply inductive keyword analysis to the utterances with FEMALE VS. MALE speaker information in the spoken-conversation subcorpus of the BNC (like Schmid, they simply follow the corpus creators' implicit definition of SEX). Table 10.16 shows the 15 most significant keywords im women's speech and men's speech (the results differ minimally from those in Rayson et al. (1997: 136–137), since they use the χ^2 statistic while we will use the *G* statistic again.

Two differences are obvious immediately. First, there are pronouns among the most significant keywords of women's speech, but not of men's speech, corroborating Schmid's finding concerning personal reference. This is further supported if we include the next thirty-five most significant keywords, which contain three additional pronouns (*him*, *he*, and *me*) and eight proper names for women's speech, but no pronouns and only a single proper name for men's speech (although there are two terms of address, *mate* and *sir*). Second, there are three instances of cursing/taboo language among the most significant male keywords (*fucking*, *fuck* and *Jesus*), but not among female keywords, corroborating findings of a number of studies focusing on cursing (cf. Murphy 2009).

In order to find significant differences in other domains, we would now have to sort the entire list into semantic categories (as Leech & Fallon did for British and American English). This is clearly much more time-consuming than Schmid's analysis of preselected items – for example, looking at the first fifty keywords in male and female speech will reveal no clear additional differences, although they point to a number of potentially interesting semantic fields (for example, the occurrence of *lovely* and *nice* as female keywords points to the possibility that there might be differences in the use of evaluative adverbs).

This case study, as well as the preceding one, demonstrates the use of keyword analyses with demographic variables traditionally of interest to sociolinguistics (see Rayson et al. 1997 for additional case studies involving age and social class, as well as interactions between sex, age and class). Taken together, they are also intended to show the respective advantages and disadvantages of deductive and inductive approaches in this area.

Table 10.16: Keywords im women's speech and men's speech in the BNC conversation subcorpus

Keyword	Frequency in men's speech	Frequency in women's speech	Other words in men's speech	Other words in women's speech	G
Most strongly associated with men					
fucking	1383	326	1 485 136	2 307 603	1251.11
er	9415	9337	1 477 104	2 298 592	939.41
the	43 385	57 367	1 443 134	2 250 562	648.86
yeah	21 888	28 793	1 464 631	2 279 136	343.21
[unclear]	30 659	41 710	1 455 860	2 266 219	312.08
minus	257	35	1 486 262	2 307 894	302.37
right	6081	7092	1 480 438	2 300 837	266.10
aye	1164	876	1 485 355	2 307 053	265.55
hundred	1473	1233	1 485 046	2 306 696	256.96
fuck	331	106	1 486 188	2 307 823	241.58
is	13 277	17 337	1 473 242	2 290 592	225.16
two	4282	5019	1 482 237	2 302 910	181.10
a	28 415	39 787	1 458 104	2 268 142	179.01
jesus	177	36	1 486 342	2 307 893	174.00
three	2707	2960	1 483 812	2 304 969	172.26
no	14 836	19 976	1 471 683	2 287 953	172.98
ah	2374	2606	1 484 145	2 305 323	147.97
four	2116	2284	1 484 403	2 305 645	143.86
doo	258	111	1 486 261	2 307 818	142.61
c	515	358	1 486 004	2 307 571	139.39
Most strongly associated with women					
she	7037	22 807	1 479 482	2 285 122	3291.17
her	2313	7306	1 484 206	2 300 623	990.40
said	4911	12 375	1 481 608	2 295 554	881.37
n't	24 221	44 380	1 462 298	2 263 549	444.52
i	54 825	93 330	1 431 694	2 214 599	307.00
and	29 109	50 467	1 457 410	2 257 462	231.78
cos	3314	6864	1 483 205	2 301 065	191.93
to	23 693	40 934	1 462 826	2 266 995	175.92
christmas	285	1005	1 486 234	2 306 924	171.10
charlotte	24	298	1 486 495	2 307 631	170.52
thought	1545	3523	1 484 974	2 304 406	166.21
oh	13 236	23 472	1 473 283	2 284 457	152.83
lovely	406	1217	1 486 113	2 306 712	145.25
mm	7067	13 039	1 479 452	2 294 890	139.46
because	1830	3901	1 484 689	2 304 028	129.79
nice	1275	2874	1 485 244	2 305 055	128.33
had	3975	7601	1 482 544	2 300 328	115.95
jonathan	31	250	1 486 488	2 307 679	111.58
going	3058	5981	1 483 461	2 301 948	110.66
did	6323	11 556	1 480 196	2 296 373	110.87

Note that one difficulty with sociolinguistic research focusing on lexical items is that topical differences in the corpora may distort the picture. For example, among the female keywords we find words like *kitchen, baby, biscuits, husband, bedroom,* and *cooking* which could be used to construct a stereotype of women's language as being home- and family-oriented. In contrast, among the male keywords we find words like *minus, plus, percent, equals, squared, decimal* as well as many number words, which could be used to construct a stereotype of male language as being concerned with abstract domains like mathematics. However, these differences very obviously depend on the topics of the conversations included in the corpus. It is not inconceivable, for example, that male linguists constructing a spoken corpus will record their male colleagues in a university setting and their female spouses in a home setting. Thus, we must take care to distinguish stable, topic-independent differences from those that are due to the content of the corpora investigated. This should be no surprise, of course, since keyword analysis was originally invented to uncover precisely such differences in content.

10.2.4 Ideology

Just as we can choose texts to stand for demographic variables, we can choose them to stand for the world views or ideologies of the speakers who produced them. Note that in this case, the texts serve as an operational definition of the corresponding ideology, an operationalization that must be plausibly justified.

10.2.4.1 Case study: Political ideologies

As an example, consider Rayson (2008), who compares the election manifestos of the Labour Party and the Liberal Democrats for the 2001 general election in Great Britain in order to identify differences in the underlying ideologies.

Table 10.17 shows the result of this direct comparison, derived from an analysis of the two party manifestos, which can be found online and which were converted into corpora with comparable tokenization for this case study (the tokenized versions are available in the Supplementary Online Material, file TXQP). The results differ from Rayson's in a few details, due to slightly different decisions about tokenization, but they are identical with respect to all major observations.

Obviously, the names of each party are overrepresented in the respective manifestos as compared to that of the other party. More interesting is the fact that *would* is a keyword for the Liberal Democrats; this is because their manifesto

Table 10.17: Differential collocates for the Labour and Liberal Democrat manifestos (2001)

Keyword	Frequency in labour	Frequency in Lib. Dem.	Other words in labour	Other words in Lib. Dem.	*G*
Most strongly associated with labour					
cent	92	1	33 817	21 472	81.20
per	114	9	33 795	21 464	64.63
–	114	12	33 795	21 461	55.44
our	284	75	33 625	21 398	53.10
labour	172	36	33 737	21 437	45.46
£	133	26	33 776	21 447	38.20
now	77	8	33 832	21 465	37.72
1997	60	4	33 849	21 469	36.56
million	68	6	33 841	21 467	36.48
next	55	4	33 854	21 469	32.32
is	335	119	33 574	21 354	32.10
since	39	2	33 870	21 471	26.09
ten-year	26	0	33 883	21 473	25.52
;	79	14	33 830	21 459	25.28
billion	43	4	33 866	21 469	22.42
Most strongly associated with liberal democrats					
•	146	300	33 763	21 173	148.96
liberal	0	47	33 909	21 426	89.12
would	11	68	33 898	21 405	75.99
democrats	0	40	33 909	21 433	75.84
which	37	92	33 872	21 381	56.15
also	50	88	33 859	21 385	35.19
of	770	665	33 139	20 808	34.88
environmental	15	46	33 894	21 427	33.87
green	3	26	33 906	21 447	32.94
establish	7	33	33 902	21 440	32.33
powers	6	29	33 903	21 444	28.79
will	517	460	33 392	21 013	28.34
taxation	0	14	33 909	21 459	26.53
the	1559	1194	32 350	20 279	25.49
energy	9	31	33 900	21 442	24.94

Supplementary Online Material: PYX4

mentions hypothetical events more frequently, which Rayson takes to mean that they did not expect to win the election.

Going beyond Rayson's discussion of individual words, note that the Labour manifesto does not have any words relating to specific policies among the ten strongest keywords, while the Liberal Democrats have *green* and *environmental*, pointing to their strong environmental focus, as well as *powers*, which, when we look at the actual manifesto, turns out to be due to the fact that they are very concerned with the distribution of decision-making powers. Why might this be the case? We could hypothesize that since the Labour Party was already in power in 2001, they might have felt less of a need than the Liberal Democrats to mention specific policies that they were planning to implement. Support for this hypothesis comes from the fact that the Liberal Democrats not only use the word *would* more frequently than Labour, but also the word *will*.

In order to test this hypothesis, we would have to look at a Labour election manifesto during an election in which they were not in power: the prediction would be that in such a situation, we would find words relating to specific policies. Let us take the 2017 election as a test case. There are two ways in which we could now proceed: We could compare the Labour 2017 manifesto to the 2001 manifesto, or we could simply repeat Rayson's analysis and compare the 2017 manifestos of Labor and the Liberal Democrats. To be safe, let us do both (again, the 2017 manifestos, converted into comparable form, are found in the Supplementary Online Material, file TXQP).

Table 10.18 shows the results of a comparison between the 2017 Labour and Liberal Democrat manifestos and Table 10.19 shows the results of the comparison between the 2001 and 2017 Labour manifestos. In both cases, only the keywords for the Labour 2017 manifesto are shown, since these are what our hypothesis relates to.

The results of both comparisons bear out the prediction: most of the significant keywords in the 2017 manifesto relate to specific policies. The comparison with the Liberal Democrat manifesto highlights core Labour policies, with words like *workers*, *unions*, *women* and *workplace*. The comparison with 2001 partially highlights the same areas, suggesting a return to such core policies between the 2001 "New Labour" era of Tony Blair and the 2017 "radical left" era of Jeremy Corbyn. The comparison also highlights the topical dominance of the so-called *Brexit* (a plan for the UK to leave the European Union): this is reflected in the word *Brexit* itself, but likely also in words like *ensure*, *protect* and *protections*, and *businesses*, which refer to the economic consequences of the so-called Brexit. Of course, the fact that our prediction is borne out does not mean that the hypothesis about

Table 10.18: Differential collocates for the 2017 Labour manifesto (comparison to Liberal Democrats)

Keyword	Frequency in labour	Frequency in Lib. Dem.	Other words in labour	Other words in Lib. Dem.	*G*
labour	338	9	25 702	23 578	367.82
will	666	211	25 374	23 376	208.60
our	261	102	25 779	23 485	57.62
workers	61	8	25 979	23 579	41.12
we	422	233	25 618	23 354	38.72
cent	20	0	26 020	23 587	25.80
trade	47	11	25 993	23 576	20.66
unions	15	0	26 025	23 587	19.35
few	14	0	26 026	23 587	18.06
women	34	7	26 006	23 580	16.80
potential	12	0	26 028	23 587	15.48
back	34	8	26 006	23 579	14.87
workplace	11	0	26 029	23 587	14.19
trading	11	0	26 029	23 587	14.19
south	11	0	26 029	23 587	14.19

Supplementary Online Material: KVMN

being or not being in power is correct. It could simply be that Labour was not particularly political in 2001 and has generally regained a focus on issues.

This case study has demonstrated that keyword analysis can be used to investigate ideological differences through linguistic differences. In such investigations, of course, identifying keywords is only the first step, to be followed by a closer analysis of how these keywords are used in context (cf. Rayson 2008, who presents KWIC concordances of some important keywords, and Scott 1997, who identifies collocates of the keywords in a sophisticated procedure that leads to highly insightful clusters of keywords).

One issue that needs consideration is whether in the context of a specific research design it is more appropriate to compare two texts potentially representing different ideologies directly to each other, as Rayson does, or whether it is more appropriate to compare each of the two texts to a large reference corpus, as the usual procedure in keyword analysis would be. In the first case, the focus will necessarily be on differences, as similarities are removed from the analysis by virtue of the fact that they will not be statistically significant – we could call

Table 10.19: Differential collocates for the 2017 Labour manifesto (comparison to 2001)

KEYWORD	Frequency in 2001	Frequency in 2017	Other words in 2001	Other words in 2017	*G*
labour	172	338	33 737	25 702	108.65
will	517	666	33 392	25 374	80.32
workers	11	61	33 898	25 979	52.77
end	6	43	33 903	25 997	42.15
that	171	247	33 738	25 793	41.52
homes	5	37	33 904	26 003	36.77
brexit	0	21	33 909	26 019	35.03
ensure	52	104	33 857	25 936	34.20
businesses	7	36	33 902	26 004	29.83
government	64	110	33 845	25 930	27.56
protect	8	34	33 901	26 006	24.94
women	8	34	33 901	26 006	24.94
mental	3	24	33 906	26 016	24.62
trade	17	47	33 892	25 993	23.69
protections	0	14	33 909	26 026	23.35

Supplementary Online Material: VU79

this procedure *differential keyword analysis*. In the second case, both similarities and differences could emerge; however, so would any vocabulary that is associated with the domain of politics in general. Which strategy is more appropriate depends on the aims of our study.

10.2.4.2 Case study: The importance of men and women

Just as text may stand for something other than a text, words may stand for something other than words in a given research design. Perhaps most obviously, they may stand for their referents (or classes of referents). If we are careful with our operational definitions, then, we may actually use corpus-linguistic methods to investigate not (only) the role of words in texts, but the role of their referents in a particular community.

In perhaps the first study attempting this, Kjellmer (1986) uses the frequency of masculine and feminine pronouns in the topically defined subcorpora of the LOB and BROWN corpora as an indicator of the importance accorded to women in the respective discourse domain. His research design is essentially deductive, since he starts from the hypothesis that women will be mentioned less frequently than men. The design has two nominal variables: Sex (with the values man and woman, operationalized as "male pronoun" and "female pronoun") and Text Category (with the values provided by the text categories of the LOB/BROWN corpora).

First, Kjellmer notes that overall, men are referred to much more frequently than women: There are 18 116 male pronouns in the LOB corpus compared to only 8366 female ones (Kjellmer's figures differ very slightly from the ones given here and below, perhaps because he used an earlier version of the corpus). This difference between male and female pronouns is significant: using the single-variable version of the χ^2 test introduced in Chapter 6, and assuming that the population in 1961 consisted of 50 percent men and 50 percent women, we get the expected frequencies shown in Table 10.20 ($\chi^2 = 3589.70$, (df = 1), $p < 0.001$).

Table 10.20: Observed and expected frequencies of male and female pronouns in the LOB corpus (based on the assumption of equal proportions)

		Observed	Expected	χ^2
Pronoun	male	18 116	13 241	1794.85
	female	8366	13 241	1794.85
	Total	26 482		3589.70

In other words, women are drastically underrepresented among the people mentioned in the LOB corpus (in the BROWN corpus, Kjellmer finds, things are even worse). We might want to blame this either on the fact that the corpus is from 1961, or on the possibility that many of the occurrences of male pronouns might actually be "generic" uses, referring to mixed groups or abstract (categories of) people of any sex. However, Kjellmer shows that only 4 percent of the male pronouns are used generically, which does not change the imbalance perceptibly; also, the FLOB corpus from 1991 shows almost the same distribution of male and female pronouns, so at least up to 1991, nothing much changed in with respect to the underrepresentation of women.

Kjellmer's main question is whether, given this overall imbalance, there are differences in the individual text categories, and as Table 10.21 shows, this is indeed the case.

Even taking into consideration the general overrepresentation of men in the corpus, they are overrepresented strongly in reportage and editorials, religious

Table 10.21: Male and female pronouns in the different text categories of the LOB corpus

Text Category	Pronoun: male	Pronoun: female	Total
A. Press: Reportage	*Obs.*: 1615 *Exp.*: 1315.50 χ^2: 68.19	*Obs.*: 308 *Exp.*: 607.50 χ^2: 147.65	1923
B. Press: Editorial	*Obs.*: 576 *Exp.*: 465.18 χ^2: 26.40	*Obs.*: 104 *Exp.*: 214.82 χ^2: 57.17	680
C. Press: Reviews	*Obs.*: 686 *Exp.*: 617.73 χ^2: 7.54	*Obs.*: 217 *Exp.*: 285.27 χ^2: 16.34	903
D. Religion	*Obs.*: 462 *Exp.*: 337.94 χ^2: 45.54	*Obs.*: 32 *Exp.*: 156.06 χ^2: 98.62	494
E. Skills and Hobbies	*Obs.*: 325 *Exp.*: 288.68 χ^2: 4.57	*Obs.*: 97 *Exp.*: 133.32 χ^2: 9.89	422
F. Popular Lore	*Obs.*: 1157 *Exp.*: 1255.30 χ^2: 7.70	*Obs.*: 678 *Exp.*: 579.70 χ^2: 16.67	1835
G. Belles Lettres, Biography, Memoirs	*Obs.*: 2876 *Exp.*: 2505.81 χ^2: 54.69	*Obs.*: 787 *Exp.*: 1157.19 χ^2: 118.42	3663
H. Miscellaneous	*Obs.*: 227 *Exp.*: 203.17 χ^2: 2.79	*Obs.*: 70 *Exp.*: 93.83 χ^2: 6.05	297
J. Learned	*Obs.*: 1079 *Exp.*: 807.22 χ^2: 91.50	*Obs.*: 101 *Exp.*: 372.78 χ^2: 198.14	1180
K. General Fiction	*Obs.*: 2058 *Exp.*: 2399.09 χ^2: 48.50	*Obs.*: 1449 *Exp.*: 1107.91 χ^2: 105.01	3507
L. Mystery and Detective Fiction	*Obs.*: 1900 *Exp.*: 1870.29 χ^2: 0.47	*Obs.*: 834 *Exp.*: 863.71 χ^2: 1.02	2734
M. Science Fiction	*Obs.*: 336 *Exp.*: 283.90 χ^2: 9.56	*Obs.*: 79 *Exp.*: 131.10 χ^2: 20.71	415
N. Adventure and Western Fiction	*Obs.*: 2373 *Exp.*: 2489.39 χ^2: 5.44	*Obs.*: 1266 *Exp.*: 1149.61 χ^2: 11.78	3639
P. Romance and Love Story	*Obs.*: 2112 *Exp.*: 2958.68 χ^2: 242.29	*Obs.*: 2213 *Exp.*: 1366.32 χ^2: 524.67	4325
R. Humor	*Obs.*: 334 *Exp.*: 318.10 χ^2: 0.79	*Obs.*: 131 *Exp.*: 146.90 χ^2: 1.72	465
Total	18116	8366	26482

writing and belles-lettres/biographies – all "factual" language varieties, suggesting that actual, existing men are simply thought of as more worthy topics of discussion than actual, existing women. Women, in contrast, are overrepresented in popular lore, general fiction, adventure and western, and romance and love stories (overrepresented, that is, compared to their general underrepresentation; in absolute numbers, they are mentioned less frequently in every single category except romance and love stories). In other words, fictive women are slightly less strongly discriminated against in terms of their worthiness for discussion than are real women.

Other researchers have taken up and expanded Kjellmer's method of using the distribution of male and female pronouns (and other gendered words) in corpora to assess the role of women in society (see, e.g. Romaine 2001, Baker 2010b; Twenge et al. 2012 and the discussion of their method by Liberman 2012, and Subtirelu 2014).

10.2.5 Time periods

10.2.5.1 Case study: Verbs in the *going-to* future

Just as we can treat speech communities, demographic groups or ideologies as subcorpora which we can compare using keyword analysis or textually differential collexeme analysis, we can treat time periods as such subcorpora. This allows us to track changes in vocabulary or in lexico-grammatical associations. This procedure was first proposed by Martin Hilpert and applied comprehensively in Hilpert (2008) to investigate future tense constructions in a range of Germanic languages.

Let us take the English *going-to* future as an example and study potential changes in the verbs that it occurs with during the 18th and 19th centuries, i.e. in the centuries when, as shown in Case Study 8.2.5.3 in Chapter 8, it first grammaticalized and then rose drastically in terms of discourse frequency.

For Present-Day English, Gries & Stefanowitsch (2004) confirm in a differential collexeme analysis the long-standing observation that in a direct comparison of the *going-to* future and the *will* future, the former tends to be associated with verbs describing intentional, dynamic and often very specific activities, while the latter is preferred for non-agentive, low-dynamicity processes and states. This makes sense given that the *going-to* future probably derived from phrases describing people literally going to some location in order to do something. Since despite these preferences, the *going-to* future can be used with processes and states in Present-Day English, we might expect to see a development, with the construction being more strongly restricted to activities in earlier periods and then relaxing these restrictions somewhat over time.

Let us first compare the newly emerged *going-to* future against the established *will* future for each period individually, i.e. by applying a standard differential collexeme analysis. Let us use the Corpus of Late Modern English Texts (CLMET) already used in Case Study 8.2.5.3. In addition to providing the year of publication for most texts, this corpus also provides a categorization into three periods that cover precisely the time span we are interested in: 1710–1780, 1780–1850 and 1850–1920 (note that the periods overlap, but this is presumably just an error in the metadata for the corpus).

Table 10.22 shows the top ten differential collexemes for the *going-to* future (some collexemes were removed since they were clearly mistagged nouns, namely *bed* (5:0, G = 34.38) in Period 1, *bed* (12:0, G = 80.00), *sleep* (11:11, G = 43.62), *work* (10:32, G = 22.86) and *supper* (4:0, G = 27.5) in Period 2, and *sleep* (27:9, G = 100.52) and *bed* (15:0, G = 77.31) in Period 3 (the raw data for the studies in this section are available in the Supplementary Online Material: Q8DT).

In all three periods, there is a clear preference for activities. In Period 1, all of the top ten verbs fall into this category (*relate* here being used exclusively in the sense of 'tell', as in *...when my Tranquillity was all at once interrupted by an Accident which I am going to relate to you* (CLMET 86)). In Period 2, we see a few cases of process and state verbs, namely *faint, reside,* and possibly *begin.* This trend continues in Period 3, with the process and state verbs *happen, live* and *cry.* This generally corroborates our expectation about the development of the construction (see also Hilpert (2008: 119) for very similar results).

Let us now turn to the direct comparison of diachronic periods proposed and pioneered by Hilpert. As mentioned above, Hilpert (2008) uses the multinomial test to compare three (or more) periods directly against each other. Let us instead compare the three periods pairwise (Period 1 and Period 2, and Period 2 and Period 3). This allows us to use the standard keyword analysis introduced in Section 10.2.1.2 above.

Table 10.23 shows the result of the comparison of the first two periods. The top 15 texually differential collexemes are shown for both periods, because in both cases there are significant collexemes that share the same rank so that there is no natural cutoff point before rank 15 (again, two words were removed because they were mistagged nouns, namely *ruin* (6:1, G = 4.55) and *decay* (3:0, G = 4.5), both from Period 1).

The results are less clear than for the individual differential collexeme analyses presented in Table 10.22: both periods have process and state verbs among the top textually differential collexemes (*cry, decay* and arguably *wait* in the first

Table 10.22: Differential collexemes of the *going-to* future compared to the *will*-future in three time periods of English

COLLEXEME	Frequency in GOING TO V	Frequency in WILL V	Other words in GOING TO V	Other words in WILL V	*G*
Period 1: 1710–1780					
say	59	234	827	26 371	129.26
marry	27	35	859	26 570	103.60
speak	28	54	858	26 551	91.36
fight	14	19	872	26 586	52.63
visit	11	12	875	26 593	44.64
relate	11	20	875	26 585	36.67
reply	6	3	880	26 602	30.00
tell	33	315	853	26 290	29.66
write	18	113	868	26 492	26.42
express	5	4	881	26 601	22.27
Period 2: 1780–1850					
say	61	308	928	26 266	100.03
marry	23	46	966	26 528	69.04
leave	29	157	960	26 417	43.99
faint	6	0	983	26 574	39.97
begin	14	39	975	26 535	34.98
reside	4	0	985	26 574	26.64
dine	7	9	982	26 565	25.36
propose	6	5	983	26 569	25.17
visit	6	11	983	26 563	18.69
speak	16	112	973	26 462	18.35
Period 3: 1850–1920					
marry	47	56	1899	23 848	110.76
do	137	636	1719	22 688	93.54
say	80	303	1833	23 354	70.94
happen	32	57	1929	23 846	58.16
leave	42	140	1909	23 680	42.65
ask	29	76	1935	23 808	37.98
live	27	67	1939	23 826	37.22
play	17	25	1959	23 910	34.88
cry	9	7	1975	23 946	25.49
wash	9	8	1975	23 944	24.07

Table 10.23: Textually differential collexemes of the *going-to* future in 1710–1780 vs. 1780–1850

COLLEXEME	Frequency in PERIOD 1	Frequency in PERIOD 2	Other words in PERIOD 1	Other words in PERIOD 2	*G*
Most strongly associated with Period 1 (1710–1780)					
answer	12	2	874	987	9.13
speak	28	16	858	973	4.88
abuse	3	0	883	989	4.50
acquaint	3	0	883	989	4.50
bid	3	0	883	989	4.50
cry	3	0	883	989	4.50
cut	3	0	883	989	4.50
decay	3	0	883	989	4.50
interrupt	3	0	883	989	4.50
rise	3	0	883	989	4.50
rush	3	0	883	989	4.50
sup	3	0	883	989	4.50
transcribe	3	0	883	989	4.50
undertake	3	0	883	989	4.50
wait	3	0	883	989	4.50
Most strongly associated with Period 2 (1780–1850)					
leave	9	29	877	960	9.17
sleep	1	11	885	978	8.73
faint	0	6	886	983	7.69
call	1	9	885	980	6.54
stop	0	5	886	984	6.41
show	0	5	886	984	6.41
stand	0	4	886	985	5.13
turn	1	7	885	982	4.44
be	82	120	804	869	4.06
tie	0	3	886	986	3.84
sell	0	3	886	986	3.84
sail	0	3	886	986	3.84
prove	0	3	886	986	3.84
dance	0	3	886	986	3.84
buy	0	3	886	986	3.84

period and *sleep*, *faint*, *be* and arguably *stand* in the second period). Still, it might be seen as corroboration of our expectation that the very non-agentive *be* is a significant collexeme for the second period.

Table 10.24 shows the results for a direct comparison of the second against the third period.

Table 10.24: Textually differential collexemes of the *going-to* future in 1780–1850 vs. 1850–1920

Collexeme	Frequency in Period 1	Frequency in Period 2	Other words in Period 1	Other words in Period 2	*G*
Most strongly associated with Period 2 (1780–1850)					
relate	5	0	984	1993	11.05
fight	7	1	982	1992	10.26
speak	16	9	973	1984	9.99
commence	4	0	985	1993	8.84
mention	4	0	985	1993	8.84
reside	4	0	985	1993	8.84
write	18	14	971	1979	7.24
encounter	3	0	986	1993	6.63
reply	3	0	986	1993	6.63
tie	3	0	986	1993	6.63
Most strongly associated with Period 3 (1850–1920)					
do	24	137	965	1856	29.17
get	3	33	986	1960	12.69
stay	1	16	988	1977	7.53
wash	0	9	989	1984	7.27
cry	0	9	989	1984	7.27
happen	6	32	983	1961	5.95
find	0	7	989	1986	5.65
live	5	27	984	1966	5.11
sing	0	6	989	1987	4.84
end	0	6	989	1987	4.84

Here, the results are somewhat clearer: While the second period now has just one potential non-agentive verb (*reside*), the third period has five (*cry*, *happen*, *live*, *end* and arguably *stay*).

This case study is meant to demonstrate the use of collostructional analysis and keyword analysis, specifically, textual differential collexeme analysis, as a method for diachronic linguistics. Both approaches – separate analyses of successive periods or direct (pairwise or multinomial) comparisons of successive periods – can uncover changes in the association between grammatical constructions and lexical items, and thereby in the semantics of constructions. The separate analysis of successive periods seems conceptually more straightforward (cf. Stefanowitsch 2006a for criticism of the direct comparison of historical periods), but the direct comparison can be useful in that it automatically discards similarities between periods and puts differences in sharp focus.

10.2.5.2 Case study: Culture across time

As has become clear, a comparison of speech communities often results in a comparison of cultures, but of course culture can also be studied on the basis of a corpus without such a comparison. Referents that are important in a culture are more likely to be talked and written about than those that are not; thus, in a sufficiently large and representative corpus, the frequency of a linguistic item may be taken to represent the importance of its referent in the culture. This is the basic logic behind a research tradition referred to as "culturomics", a word that is intended to mean something like "rigorous quantitative inquiry to a wide array of new phenomena spanning the social sciences and the humanities" (Michel et al. 2011: 176). In practice, culturomics is simply the application of standard corpus-linguistic techniques (word frequencies, tracked across time), and it has yielded some interesting results (if applied carefully, which is not always the case).

Michel et al. (2011) present a number of small case studies intended to demonstrate the potential of culturomics. They use the Google Books corpus, a large collection of *n*-grams ranging from single words to 5-grams, derived from the Google Books archive and freely available for download to anyone with enough patience and a large enough hard disk (see Study Notes).

The use of the Google Books archive may be criticized because it is not a balanced corpus, but the authors point out that first, it is the largest corpus available and second, books constitute cultural products and thus may not be such a bad choice for studying culture after all. These are reasonable arguments, but if possible, it seems a good idea to complement any analysis done with Google Books with an analysis of a more rigorously constructed balanced corpus.

As a simple example, consider the search for the word *God* in the English part of the Google Books archive, covering the 19th and 20th centuries. I used the 2012 version of the corpus, so the result differs very slightly from theirs. I also repeated the analysis using the Corpus of Historical American English (COHA), which spans more or less the same period.

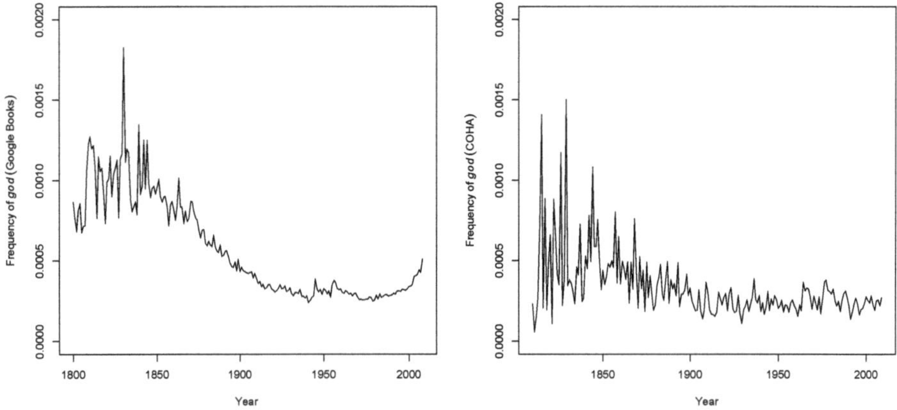

Figure 10.1: *God* in English Books and in COHA

Clearly, the word *God* has decreased in frequency – dramatically so in the Google Books archive, slightly less dramatically so in COHA. The question is what conclusions to draw from this. The authors present it as an example of the "history of religion", concluding from their result somewhat flippantly that "'God' is not dead but needs a new publicist". This flippancy, incidentally, signals an unwillingness to engage with their own results in any depth that is not entirely untypical of researchers in culturomics.

Broadly speaking the result certainly suggests a waning dominance of religion on topic selection in book publishing (Google Books), and slightly less so in published texts in general (COHA). This is not surprising to anyone who has paid attention for the last 200 years; more generally, it is not surprising that the rise and fall in importance of particular topics is reflected in the frequency of the vocabulary used to talk and write about these topics, but the point of this case study was mainly to demonstrate that the method works.

While it is not implausible to analyze culture in general on the basis of a literary corpus, any analysis that involves the area of publishing itself will be particularly convincing. One such example is the use of frequencies to identify periods of censorship in Michel et al. (2011). For example, they search for the name of the Jewish artist *Marc Chagall* in the German and the US-English corpora. As Figure 10.2 shows, there is a first peak in the German corpus around 1920, but during the time of the Nazi government, the name drops to almost zero while it continues to rise in the US-English corpus.

The authors plausibly take this drastic drop in frequency as evidence of political censorship – Chagall's works, like those of other Jewish artists, were declared

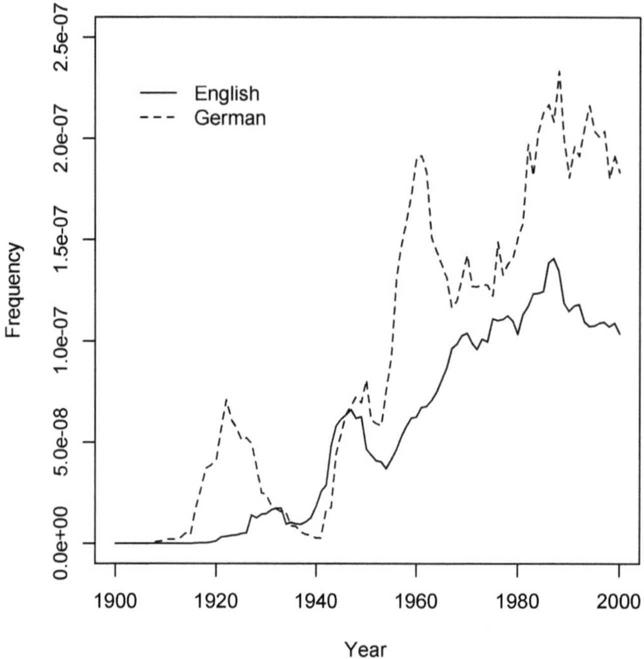

Figure 10.2: The name *Marc Chagall* in the US-English and the German parts of the Google Books corpus

to be "degenerate" and confiscated from museums, and it makes sense that his name would not be mentioned in books written in Nazi Germany. However, the question is, again, what conclusions to draw from such an analysis. Specifically, we know how to interpret the drop in frequency of the name *Marc Chagall* during the Nazi era in Germany because we know that Marc Chagall's works were banned. But if we did not know this, we would not know how to interpret the change in frequency, since words, especially names, may rise or fall in frequency for all kinds of reasons.

Consider the following figure, which shows the development of the frequency of the name *Karl Marx* in the German and English Google Books archive (extracted from the bigram files downloaded from the Google Books site, see Supplementary Online Material, file CUBF). Note the different frequency scales – the name is generally much more frequent in German than in English, but what interests us are changes in frequency.

Again, we see a rise in frequency in the 1920s, and then a visible decrease during the Nazi era from 1933 to 1945. Again, this can plausibly be seen as evidence

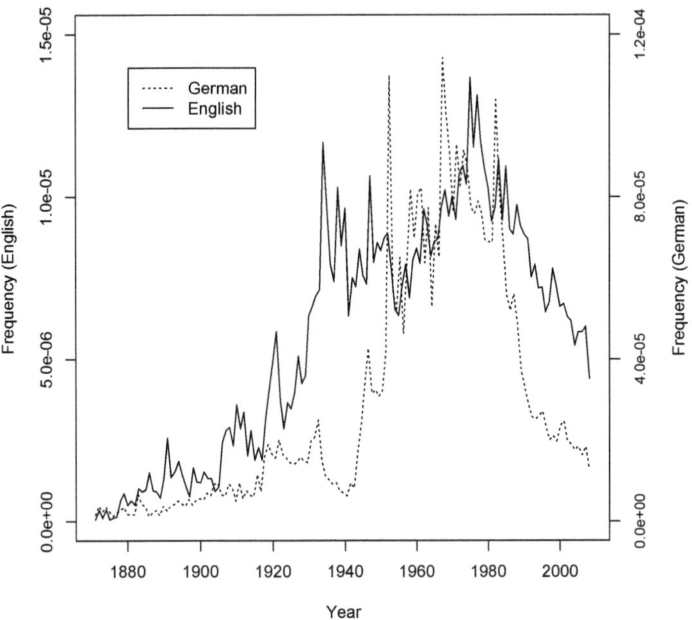

Figure 10.3: The name *Karl Marx* in the English and the German parts of the Google Books corpus

for censorship in Nazi Germany. Plausibly, because we know that the Nazis censored Karl Marx's writings – they were among the first books to be burned in the Nazi book burnings of 1933. But what about other drops in frequency, both in English and in German? There are some noticeable drops in frequency in English: after 1920, between 1930 and 1940 (with some ups and downs), and at the beginning of the 1950s. Only the latter could plausibly be explained as the result of (implicit) censorship during the McCarthy era. Finally, the frequency drops massively in both languages after 1980, but there was no censorship in either speech community. A more plausible explanation is that in the 1980s, neoliberal capitalism became a very dominant ideology, and Marx's communist ideas simply ceased to be of interest to many people (if this explanation is correct, we might see the frequency of the name rise again, given the current wide-spread disillusionment with neoliberalism).

Thus, the rise and fall in frequency cannot be attributed to a particular cause without an investigation of the social, economic and political developments during the relevant period. As such, culturomics can at best point us towards potentially interesting cultural changes that then need to be investigated in other disciplines. At worst, it will simply tell us what we already know from those other disciplines. In order to unfold their potential, such analyses would have to be done at a much larger scale – the technology and the resources are there, and with the rising interest in *digital humanities* we might see such large-scale analyses at some point.

11 Metaphor

The ease with which corpora are accessed via word forms is an advantage as long as it is our aim to investigate words, for example with respect to their relationship to other words, to their internal structure or to their distribution across grammatical structures and across texts and language varieties. As we saw in Chapter 8, the difficulty of accessing corpora at levels of linguistic representation other than the word form is problematic where our aim is to investigate grammar in its own right, but since grammatical structures tend to be associated with particular words and/or morphemes, these difficulties can be overcome to some extent.

When it comes to investigating phenomena that are not lexical in nature, the word-based nature of corpora is clearly a disadvantage and it may seem as though there is no alternative to a careful manual search and/or a sophisticated annotation (manual, semi-manual or based on advanced natural-language technology). However, corpus linguists have actually uncovered a number of relationships between words and linguistic phenomena beyond lexicon and grammar without making use of such annotations. In the final chapter of this book, we will discuss a number of case studies of one such phenomenon: metaphor.

11.1 Studying metaphor in corpora

Metaphor is traditionally defined as the transfer of a word from one referent (variously called vehicle, figure or source) to another (the tenor, ground or target) (cf. e.g. Aristotle, *Poetics*, XXI). If metaphor were indeed located at the word level, it should be straightforwardly amenable to corpus-linguistic analysis. Unfortunately, things are slightly more complicated. First, the transfer does not typically concern individual words but entire semantic fields (or even conceptual domains, according to some theories). Second, as discussed in some detail in Chapter 4, there is nothing in the word itself that distinguishes its literal and metaphorical uses. One way around this problem is manual annotation, and there are very detailed and sophisticated proposals for annotation procedures (most notably the Pragglejaz Metaphor Identification Procedure, cf., for example, Steen et al. 2010).

However, as stressed in various places throughout this book, the manual annotation of corpora severely limits the amount of data that can be included in a research design; this does not invalidate manual annotation, but it makes alternatives highly desirable. Two broad alternatives have been proposed in corpus linguistics. Since these were discussed in some detail in Chapter 4, we will only repeat them briefly here before illustrating them in more detail in the case studies.

11.2 Case studies

The first approach to extracting metaphors from corpora starts from a source domain, searching for individual words or sets of words (synonym sets, semantic fields, discourse domains) and then identifying the metaphorical uses and the respective targets and underlying metaphors manually. This approach is extensively demonstrated, for example, in Deignan (1999a,b; 2005). The three case studies in Section 11.2.1 use this approach. The second approach starts from a target domain, searching for abstract words describing (parts of) the target domain and then identifying those that occur in a grammatical pattern together with items from a different semantic domain (which will normally be a source domain). This approach has been taken by Stefanowitsch (2004; 2006c) and others. The case studies in Section 11.2.2 use this approach. A third approach has been suggested by Wallington et al. (2003): they attempt to identify words that are not themselves part of a metaphorical transfer but that point to a metaphorical transfer in the immediate context (the expression *figuratively speaking* would be an obvious candidate). This approach has not been taken up widely, but it is very promising at least for the identification of certain types of metaphor, and of course the expressions in question are worthy of study in their own right, so one of the case studies in Section 11.2.3 takes a closer look at it.

11.2.1 Source domains

Among other things, the corpus-based study of (small set of) source domain words may provide insights into the systematicity of metaphor (cf. esp. Deignan 1999b). In cognitive linguistics, it is claimed that metaphor is fundamentally a mapping from one conceptual domain to another, and that metaphorical expressions are essentially a reflex of such mappings. This suggests a high degree of isomorphism between literal and metaphorical language: words should essentially display the same systemic and usage-based behavior when they are used as the source domain of a metaphor as when they are used in their literal sense unless there is a specific reason in the semantics of the target domain that precludes this (Lakoff 1993).

11.2.1.1 Case study: Lexical relations and metaphorical mapping

Deignan (1999b) tests the isomorphism between literal and metaphorical uses of source-domain vocabulary very straightforwardly by looking at synonymy and antonymy. Deignan argues that these lexical relations should be transferred to the target domain, such that, for example, metaphorical meanings of *cold* and *hot* should also be found for *cool* and *warm* respectively, since their literal meanings are very similar. Likewise, metaphorical *hot* and *cold* should encode opposites in the same way they do in their literal uses.

Let us replicate Deignans study using the BNC Baby. To keep other factors equal, let us focus on attributive uses of adjectives that modify target domain nouns (as in *cold facts*), or nouns that are themselves used metaphorically (as in "The project went into *cold storage*" meaning work on it ceased). Deignan focuses on the base forms of these adjectives, let us do the same. She also excludes "highly fixed collocations and idioms" because their potential metaphorical origin may no longer be transparent – let us not follow her here, as we can always identify and discuss such cases after we have extracted and tabulated our data.

Deignan does not explicitly present an annotation scheme, but she presents dictionary-like definitions of her categories and extensive examples of her categorization decisions that, taken together, serve the same function. Her categories differ in number (between four and ten) and semantic granularity across the four words, let us design a stricter annotation scheme with a minimal number of categories.

Let us assume that survey of the dictionaries already used in Case Study 9.2.1.2 yields the following major metaphor categories:

1. ACTIVITY, with the metaphors HIGH ACTIVITY IS HEAT and LOW ACTIVITY IS COLDNESS, as in *cold/hot war, hot pursuit, hot topic*, etc.). This sense is not recognized by the dictionaries, except insofar as it is implicit in the definitions of *cold war, hot pursuit, cold trail*, etc. It is understood here to include a sense of *hot* described in dictionaries as "currently popular" or "of immediate interest" (e.g. *hot topic*).

2. AFFECTION, with the metaphors AFFECTION IS HEAT and INDIFFERENCE IS COLDNESS, as in *cold stare, warm welcome*, etc. This sense is recognized by all dictionaries, but we will interpret it to include sense connected with sexual attraction and (un)responsiveness, e.g. *hot date*.

3. TEMPERAMENT, with the metaphors EMOTIONAL BEHAVIOR IS HEAT and RATIONAL BEHAVIOR IS COLDNESS, as in *cool head, cold facts, hot temper*, etc. Most dictionaries recognize this sense as distinct from the previous one – both are concerned with emotion or its absence, but in case of the AFFECTION, the distinction is one between affectionate feelings and their absense, in the case of TEMPERAMENT the distinction is one between behavior based on any emotion and behavior unaffected by emotion.

4. SYNESTHESIA, a category covering uses described in dictionaries as "conveying or producing the impression of being hot, cold, etc." in some sensory domain other than temperature, i.e. *warm color, cold light, cool voice*, etc.

5. EVALUATION, with the (potential) metaphor POSITIVE THINGS HAVE A TEMPERATURE, as in *a really cool movie, a cool person, a hot new idea*, etc. This may not be a metaphor at all, as both uses are very idiomatic; in fact, *hot* in this sense could be included under *activity* or *affection*, and *cool* in this sense is presumably derived from *temperament*.

Table 11.1 lists the token frequencies of the four adjectives with each of these broad metaphorical categories as well as all types instantiating the respective category. There is one category that does not show any significant deviations from the expected frequencies, namely the infrequently instantiated category SYNESTHESIA. For all other categories, there are clear differences that are unexpected from the perspective of conceptual metaphor theory.

The category *activity* is instantiated only for the words *cold* and *hot* and its absence for the other two words is significant. We can imagine (and, in a sufficiently large data set, find) uses for *cool* and *warm* that would fall into this category. For example, Frederick Pohl's 1981 novel *The Cool War* describes a geopolitical situation in which political allies sabotage each other's economies, and it is occasionally used to refer to real-life situations as well. But this seems to be a deliberate analogy rather than a systematic use, leaving us with an unexpected gap in the middle of the linguistic scale between hot and cold.

The category *affection* is found with three of the four words, but its absence for the word *cool* is statistically significant, as is its clear overrepresentation with *warm*. This lack of systematicity is even more unexpected than the one observed with *activity*: for the latter, we could argue that it reflects a binary distinction that uses only the extremes of the scale, for example because there is not enough of a potential conceptual difference between a *cold war* and a *cool war*. With

Table 11.1: TEMPERATURE metaphors (BNC Baby)

Noun	Adjective								Total
	COLD		COOL		WARM		HOT		
ACTIVITY	*Obs.:*	13	*Obs.:*	0	*Obs.:*	0	*Obs.:*	9	22
	Exp.:	8.36	*Exp.:*	4.62	*Exp.:*	3.96	*Exp.:*	5.06	
	χ^2:	2.58	χ^2:	4.62	χ^2:	3.96	χ^2:	3.07	
	storage, turkey, war		–		–		*pursuit, seat, spot, time, war*		
AFFECTION	*Obs.:*	9	*Obs.:*	0	*Obs.:*	16	*Obs.:*	2	27
	Exp.:	10.26	*Exp.:*	5.67	*Exp.:*	4.86	*Exp.:*	6.21	
	χ^2:	0.15	χ^2:	5.67	χ^2:	25.53	χ^2:	2.85	
	atmosphere, disapproval, eyes, note, person, response, sarcasm, savagery, shoulder		–		*affinities, approval, embrace, feeling, glow, kiss, liking, nest, presence, relief, smile, welcome*		*date, pants*		
TEMPERAMENT	*Obs.:*	14	*Obs.:*	13	*Obs.:*	0	*Obs.:*	1	28
	Exp.:	10.64	*Exp.:*	5.88	*Exp.:*	5.04	*Exp.:*	6.44	
	χ^2:	1.06	χ^2:	8.62	χ^2:	5.04	χ^2:	4.60	
	approach, blood, calculation, clarity, facts, reality, reminder		*analysis, composure, customer, firmness, head, look, response, restraint, Rose (prop. name), silence, temper*		–		*spirits*		
SYNESTHESIA	*Obs.:*	2	*Obs.:*	1	*Obs.:*	2	*Obs.:*	0	5
	Exp.:	1.90	*Exp.:*	1.05	*Exp.:*	0.90	*Exp.:*	1.15	
	χ^2:	0.01	χ^2:	0.00	χ^2:	1.34	χ^2:	1.15	
	fire, grey		*voice*		*colour, glow*		–		
EVALUATION	*Obs.:*	0	*Obs.:*	7	*Obs.:*	0	*Obs.:*	11	18
	Exp.:	6.84	*Exp.:*	3.78	*Exp.:*	3.24	*Exp.:*	4.14	
	χ^2:	6.84	χ^2:	2.74	χ^2:	3.24	χ^2:	11.37	
	–		*countess, dude, million, thing*		–		*favourite, gunner, handicap, multimedia system, shot, stuff, tips*		
Total	38		21		23		18		100

Supplementary Online Material: WLVF

AFFECTION, in contrast, this explanation is not adequate, as the entire scale is used. It remains unclear, therefore, why *warm* should be so prominently used here, and why *cool* is so rare (it is possible: the dictionaries list examples like *a cool manner, a cool reply*).

With *temperament*, we find a partially complementary situation: again, three of the four words occur with this metaphor, including, again, the extreme points. However, in this case it is *cool* that is significantly overrepresented and *warm* that is significantly absent. A possible explanation would be that there is a potential for confusion between the metaphors *affection is temperature* and *temperament is temperature*, and so speakers divide up the continuum from cold to hot between them. However, this does not explain why *cold* is frequently used in both metaphorical senses.

The gaps in the last category, EVALUATION, are less confusing. As mentioned above, this is probably not a single coherent category and we would not expect uses to be equally disributed across the four words.

This case study demonstrates the use of corpus data to evaluate claims about conceptual structure. Specifically, it shows how a central claim of conceptual metaphor theory can be investigated (see the much more detailed discussion in Deignan (1999b).

11.2.1.2 Case study: Word forms in metaphorical mappings

Another area in which we might expect a large degree of isomorphism between literal and metaphorical uses of a word is the quantitative and qualitative distribution of word forms. In a highly intriguing study, Deignan (2006) investigate the metaphors associated with the source domain words *flame* and *flames* in terms of whether they occur in positively or negatively connoted contexts.

Her study is generally deductive in that she starts with an expectation (if not quite a full-fledged hypothesis) that there are frequently differences between the singular and the plural forms of a metaphorically used word with respect to connotation.

A cursory look at a few relatively randomly selected examples appears to corroborate this expression. More precisely, it seems that the singular form *flame* has positive connotations more frequently than expected (cf. 1), while the plural form *flames* has negative connotations more frequently than expected (cf. 2):

(1) a. [T]he flame of hope burns brightly here. (BNC AJD)
    b. Emilio Estevez, sitting on the sofa next to old flame Demi Moore... (BNC CH1)

(2) a. ...the flames of civil war engulfed the central Yugoslav republic. (BNC AHX)

b. The game was going OK and then it went up in flames. (BNC CBG)

Deignan studies this potential difference systematically based on a sample of more than 1500 hits for *flame/s* in the Bank of English (a proprietary, non-accessible corpus owned by HarperCollins), from which she manually extracts all 153 metaphorical uses. These are then categorized according to their connotation. Deignan's design thus has two nominal variables: Word Form of Flame (with the variables singular and plural) and Connotation of Metaphor (with the values positive and negative. She does not provide an annotation scheme for categorizing the metaphorical expressions, but she provides a set of examples that are intuitively quite plausible. Table 11.2 shows her results ($\chi^2 = 53.98$, df = 1, $p < 0.001$).

Table 11.2: Positive and negative metaphors with singular and plural forms of *flame* (Deignan 2006: 117)

		Word Form of Flame		
		singular	plural	Total
Connotation	positive	90 (70.78)	24 (43.22)	114
	negative	5 (24.22)	34 (14.78)	39
	Total	95	58	153

Clearly, metaphorical singular *flame* is used in positive metaphorical contexts much more frequently than metaphorical plural *flames*. Deignan tentatively explains this in relation to the literal uses of *flame(s)*: a single flame is "usually under control", and it may "be if use, as a candle or a burning match". If there is more than one flame, we are essentially dealing with a fire – "flames are often undesired, out of control and very dangerous" (Deignan 2006: 117).

This explanation itself is of course a hypothesis about the literal use of singular and plural *flame* that must be tested separately. Deignan does not provide such a test, so let us do it here. Let us select a sample of 20 hits each for literal uses the singular and plural of *flame(s)* from the BNC (as mentioned above, Deignan's corpus is not accessible, so we must hope that the BNC is roughly comparable). Figure 11.1 shows the sample for singular (lines 1–20) and plural (21–40).

```
1 ford base . The jet crashed in a ball of [flame] , destroying 15 cars and damaging 10 mo
2  face down , applying the cheroot to the [flame] . But his eyes never left the four men
3 ls of a child 's that had passed through [flame] and were partially melted . They would
4 ontainer next to him . An orange ball of [flame] ripped up into the sky , bathing the de
5 went out of one door but then a sheet of [flame] came down and blocked me , so I had to
6  . The fire burns evenly with a thin hot [flame] , as though there are no oils or resins
7 ill-smouldering logs , fanning them into [flame] . He places some more logs from a pile
8  of sherry to the momentary blue veil of [flame] on the pudding , been what she would ha
9 truck one and cupped his hand around the [flame] . ` Cheers , ' said the man and dis
10 ed with the element , burning circles of [flame] round creatures she had demanded Ariel
11 the soft promise of the light burst into [flame] ; the vanguard of the islanders fell ba
12 arched for his lighter , and touched the [flame] to the tip to make contact with him . I
13  again , tighter this time , guiding the [flame] . She sucked , and the cigarette end gl
14   There , ' she shouted , pluming liquid [flame] from one claw , ` you 're not the onl
15 and steady to bring the cigarette to the [flame] and kept it for a few seconds longer th
16 ern horns outside their house , the weak [flame] of the candles fluttering in their prot
17 the upstairs windows , a sudden spurt of [flame] , and a part of the roof begin to sag o
18  however , disappear in a white sheet of [flame] . He just kept right on kicking Pikey ,
19 ue to finish . Do n't cook over a fierce [flame] . The outside of the food will cook bef
20 no cushion . Candle erm Church , steeple [Flame] . Steeple . Got it got it got it got it

21 it was winning its battle to put out the [flames] . He had to do it now , while it was s
22 ner , arm raised . Its back was to him , [flames] still glowing deep in its side . He ra
23  how the roof caved in before a sheet of [flames] spread across the fuselage , cutting h
24 control down a steep hill and burst into [flames] . The fully-laden truck careered throu
25 s spent more than two hours fighting the [flames] , police said . Bowbazaar , in the cen
26 h a shining chair by a fire with fragile [flames] . These images had what Alexander desi
27 lood rejected -- racks of fragile spiked [flames] of votive candles , elaborate china an
28 ce , looking into the authentic fake gas [flames] as he sipped his drink . He touched hi
29 ross to the fireplace , staring into the [flames] . ` There 's no reason why he should
30 the ground and died , no explosions , no [flames] reaching to the sky . It simply flippe
31 ack of her head , protected her from the [flames] and blocked out any further damage to
32 W went first , its roof torn open by the [flames] and blast as if by a giant unseen can
33 stunned and wearied by the water and the [flames] , the howling and frantic clangour of
34 annonballs , and caught the smell of the [flames] , of split flesh , and heard the howls
35  . And the best is yet to come . ' ` The [flames] of hell ? ' ` Exactly . Operatic
36 ds , then night crept back in around the [flames] . Trails of burning liquid spiderwebbe
37 e properly . Susan reeled away from us , [flames] springing up where she had been touche
38  , and his leg broke in two places . The [flames] were dying down . I could see his blac
39 mes and lower temperatures to reduce the [flames] . ` Eventually all the cooking was do
40 s . This is Crystal Palace going up in f [flames] . November the thirtieth nineteen thir
```

Figure 11.1: Concordance of *flame(s)* (BNC, Sample)

It is difficult to determine which hits should be categorized as positive and which as negative. Let us assume that any unwanted and/or destructive fire should be characterized as negative, and, on this basis, categorize lines 1, 3, 4, 5, 11, 14, 17, 18, 21, 22, 23, 24, 25, 30, 31, 33, 34, 35, 36, 37, 38 and 40 as NEGATIVE and the rest as POSITIVE. This would give us the result in Table 11.3 (if you disagree with the categorization, come up with your own and do the corresponding calculations).

Table 11.3: Positive and negative contexts for literal uses of singular and plural forms of *flame/s*

		WORD FORM OF FLAME		
		POSITIVE	NEGATIVE	Total
CONNOTATION	SINGULAR	12 (9.00)	8 (11.00)	20
	PLURAL	6 (9.00)	14 (11.00)	20
	Total	18	22	40

It does seem that negative connotations are found more frequently with literal uses of the plural form *flames* than with literal uses of the singular form *flame*. Despite the small size of the sample used here, this difference only just fails to reach statistical significance ($\chi^2 = 3.64$, df $= 1$, $p = 0.0565$). The difference would likely become significant if we used a larger sample. However, it is nowhere near as pronounced as in the metaphorical uses presented by Deignan. A crucial difference between literal and metaphorical uses may be that fire is inherently dangerous and so literal references to fire are more likely to be negative than metaphorical ones, that allow us to focus on other aspects of fire. Interestingly, however, most of the negative uses of singular *flame* occur in constructions like *ball of flame*, *sheet of flame* and *spurt of flame*, where *flame* could be argued to be a mass noun rather than a true singular form. If we remove these five uses, then the difference between singular and plural becomes very significant even in the now further reduced sample ($\chi^2 = 8.58$, df $= 1$, $p < 0.01$).

Thus, Deignan's explanation appears to be generally correct, providing evidence for a substantial degree of isomorphism between literal and figurative uses of (at least some) words. An analysis of more such cases could show whether this isomorphism between literal and metaphorical uses is a general principle (as the conceptual theory of metaphor as Lakoff (1993) suggests it should be.

This case study demonstrates first, how to approach the study of metaphor starting from source-domain words, and, second, that such an approach may be applied not just descriptively, but in the context of answering fundamental questions about the nature of metaphor.

11.2.1.3 Case study: The impact of metaphorical expressions

A slightly different example of a source-domain oriented study is found in Stefanowitsch (2005), which investigates the relationship between metaphorical and literal expressions hinted at at the end of the preceding case study. The aim of the study is to uncover evidence for the function of metaphorical expressions that have literal paraphrases, such as [*dawn of* NP] in examples like (3a), which is seemingly equivalent to the literal [*beginning of* NP] in (3b):

(3) a. [I]t has taken until the dawn of the 21st century to realise that the best methods of utilising . . . our woodlands are those employed a millennium ago. (BNC AHD)

b. Communal life survived until the beginning of the nineteenth century and traditions peculiar to that way of life had lingered into the present. (BNC AEA)

Other examples studied in Stefanowitsch (2005) are *in the center/heart of*, *at the center/heart of* and *a(n) increase/growth/rise in*. The studies have two nominal variables: the independent variable is Metaphoricity of Pattern (whose values are pairs of patterns like the one illustrated in examples (3a, b)), the dependent variable is Noun (whose values are the nouns in the NP slot provided by these patterns. Methodologically, this corresponds to a differential collexeme analysis (Chapter 8, Case Study 8.2.2.2).

The studies are deductive in that they aim to test the hypothesis that metaphorical language serves a cognitive function and that for each pair of patterns investigated, the metaphorical variant should be used with nouns referring to more complex entities. The construct complexity is operationalized in the form of axioms derived from gestalt psychology, such as the following:

> Concepts representing entities that have a simple shape and/or have a clear boundary are less complex than those representing entities with complex shapes or fuzzy boundaries (because they are more easily delineable). This follows from the gestalt principles of closure and simplicity (Stefanowitsch 2005: 170).

For each pair of expressions, the differential collexemes are identified and the resulting lists are compared against these axiomatic assumptions. Let us illustrate this using the pattern *the dawn/beginning of NP*. A case insensitive query for the string `dawn` or `beginning`, followed by *of*, followed by up to three words that are not a noun, followed by a noun yields the results shown in Table 11.4 (they are very similar to those based on a more careful manual extraction in Stefanowitsch 2005).

Table 11.4: Differential collexemes of *beginning of NP* and *dawn of NP* (BNC)

COLLEXEME	Frequency with DAWN	Frequency with BEGINNING	Other words with DAWN	Other words with BEGINNING	*G*
Most strongly associated with DAWN					
civilisation	25	1	112	3584	161.39
history	9	12	128	3573	32.18
time	13	39	124	3546	31.27
era	10	30	127	3555	23.87
dream	4	1	133	3584	21.60
mankind	3	0	134	3585	19.88
day	9	33	128	3552	18.70
age	5	8	132	3577	16.45
...					
Most strongly associated with BEGINNING					
year	1	317	136	3268	17.78
century	4	382	133	3203	11.41
chapter	0	100	137	3485	7.61
end	0	94	137	3491	7.14
war	0	75	137	3510	5.68
week	0	61	137	3524	4.61
month	0	60	137	3525	4.54
period	0	55	137	3530	4.16
term	0	51	137	3534	3.85

Unsurprisingly, both expressions are associated almost exclusively with words referring to events and time spans (or, in some cases, with entities that exist through time, like *mankind*, or that we interact with through time, like *chapter*). Crucially, most of the nouns associated with the literal *beginning of* refer to time spans with clear boundaries and a clearly defined duration (*year*, *century*, etc.), while those associated with the metaphorical *dawn of* refer to events and time spans without clear boundaries or a clear duration (*civilization*, *time*, *history*, *age*, *era, culture*). The one apparent exception is *day*, but this occurs exclusively in literal uses of *dawn of*, such as *It was the dawn of the fourth day since the murder* (BNC CAM). This (and similar results for other pairs of expressions) are presented in Stefanowitsch (2005) as evidence for a cognitive function of metaphor.

In a short discussion of this study, Liberman (2005) notes in passing that even individual decades and centuries may differ in the degree to which they prefer *beginning of* or *dawn of*: using internet search engines, he shows that *dawn of the 1960s* is more probable than *dawn of the 1980s* compared to *beginning of the 1960s/1980s*, and that *dawn of the 21st century* is more probable than *dawn of the 18th century* compared to *beginning of the 18th/21st century.* He rightly points out that this seems to call into question the properties of boundedness and well-defined length that Stefanowitsch (2005) appeals to, since obviously all decades/centuries are equally bounded.

Since search engine frequency data are notoriously unreliable, let us replicate this observation in a large corpus, the 400+ million word Corpus of Contemporary American English (COCA). The names of decades (such as *1960s* or *sixties*) occur too infrequently with *dawn of* in this corpus to say anything useful about them, but the names of centuries are frequent enough for a differential collexeme analysis.

Table 11.5 shows the percentage of *dawn of* for the past ten centuries (spelling) variants of the respective centuries, such as *19th century, nineteenth century*, etc.) as well as spelling errors were normalized to the spelling shown in this table.

There are clear differences between the centuries associated with DAWN and those associated with BEGINNING: the literal expression is associated with the past (*nineteenth, seventeenth* (just below significance)), while the metaphorical expression, as already observed by Liberman, is associated with the twenty-first century, i.e., the future (the expressions *a new, our new* and *the incoming* also support this). I would argue that this does point to a difference in boundedness and duration. While all centuries are objectively speaking, of the same length and have the same clear boundaries, it seems reasonable to assume that the past feels more bounded than the future because it is actually over, and we can imagine it in its entirety. In contrast, none of the speakers in the COCA will live to see the end of the 21st century, making it conceptually less bounded to them.

If this is true, then we should be able to observe the same effect in the past: When the twentieth century was still the future, it, too, should have been associated with the metaphorical *dawn of.* Let us test this hypothesis using the Corpus of Historical American English, which includes language from the early nineteenth to the very early twenty-first century – in a large part of the corpus, the twentieth century was thus entirely or partly in the future. Table 11.6 shows the differential collexemes of the two expressions in this corpus.

Table 11.5: Differential collexemes of *dawn/beginning of* __ *century* (COCA)

Collexeme	Frequency with dawn	Frequency with beginning	Other words with dawn	Other words with beginning	*G*
Most strongly associated with dawn of __ century					
the twenty-first	32	90	52	623	29.93
a new	7	6	77	707	15.33
a	1	0	83	713	4.51
America's	1	0	83	713	4.51
an American	1	0	83	713	4.51
an Asian	1	0	83	713	4.51
our new	1	0	83	713	4.51
that ancient	1	0	83	713	4.51
the eleventh	1	0	83	713	4.51
the incoming	1	0	83	713	4.51
Most strongly associated with beginning of __ century					
the	2	94	82	619	11.46
the nineteenth	2	68	82	645	6.40
this	5	97	79	616	4.69
the seventeenth	0	14	84	699	3.15

Table 11.6: Differential collexemes of *dawn/beginning of* __ *century* (COHA)

Collexeme	Frequency with dawn	Frequency with beginning	Other words with dawn	Other words with beginning	*G*
Most strongly associated with dawn of __ century					
the twenty-first	7	14	23	908	24.09
another	2	0	28	922	13.96
america's	1	0	29	922	6.95
that	1	0	29	922	6.95
the twentieth	7	72	23	850	6.53
Most strongly associated with beginning of __ century					
this	0	108	30	814	7.35

As predicted, the twentieth century is now associated with the metaphorical expression (as is the twenty-first). In addition, there is the expression *America's century* in both corpora, and *an American* and *an Asian* in COCA. These, I would argue, do not refer to precise centuries but are to be understood as labels for eras. In sum, I would conclude that the idea of boundedness accounts for the apparent exceptions too, at least in the case of centuries, supporting a cognitive function of metaphor.

Even if we agree with this conclusion in general, however, it does not preclude a more literary, rhetorical function for metaphor in addition: while some of the expression pairs investigated in Stefanowitsch (2005) are fairly neutral with respect to genre or register, metaphorical *dawn of* intuitively has a distinctly literary flavor. To conclude this section, let us check the distribution of the hits for the query outlined above across the text categories defined in the BNC. Table 11.7 shows the results (note that the categories Spoken Conversation and Spoken Other from the BNC have been collapsed into a single category here).

It is very obvious that the metaphorical expression *the dawn of* is significantly overrepresented in the text category FICTION and underrepresented in the text categories ACADEMIC and SPOKEN, corroborating the intuition about the literaryness of the expression. Within this text category, of course, it may well have the cognitive function attributed to it in Stefanowitsch (2005).

This case study demonstrates use of the differential collexeme analysis (and thus of collocational methods in general) that goes beyond associations between words and other elements of structure and instead uses words and grammatical patterns as ways of investigating semantic associations. Direct comparisons of literal and metaphorical language are rare in the research literature, so this remains a potentially interesting field of research. The study also demonstrates that the distribution of particular metaphorical expressions across varieties, which can easily be determined in corpora that contain the relevant metadata, may shed light on the function of those expressions (and of metaphor in general).

11.2.2 Target domains

As discussed in Chapter 4, there are two types of metaphorical utterances: those that could be interpreted literally in their entirety (like the example *I am burned up* from Lakoff & Kövecses 1987: 203), and those that contain vocabulary from both the source and the target domain (like *He was filled with anger*). Stefanowitsch (2004; 2006c) refers to the latter as *metaphorical patterns*, defined as follows:

> A metaphorical pattern is a multi-word expression from a given source domain (SD) into which one or more specific lexical item from a given target domain (TD) have been inserted (Stefanowitsch 2006c: 66).

Table 11.7: The expressions *dawn of* and *beginning of* by text category (BNC)

Text Category	Expression: dawn of		Expression: beginning of		Total
prose	*Obs.:*	54	*Obs.:*	1324	1378
	Exp.:	50.72	*Exp.:*	1327.28	
	χ^2:	0.21	χ^2:	0.01	
miscellaneous published	*Obs.:*	30	*Obs.:*	653	683
	Exp.:	25.14	*Exp.:*	657.86	
	χ^2:	0.94	χ^2:	0.04	
fiction	*Obs.:*	28	*Obs.:*	230	258
	Exp.:	9.50	*Exp.:*	248.50	
	χ^2:	36.05	χ^2:	1.38	
newspaper	*Obs.:*	13	*Obs.:*	220	233
	Exp.:	8.58	*Exp.:*	224.42	
	χ^2:	2.28	χ^2:	0.09	
academic	*Obs.:*	11	*Obs.:*	731	742
	Exp.:	27.31	*Exp.:*	714.69	
	χ^2:	9.74	χ^2:	0.37	
unpublished	*Obs.:*	1	*Obs.:*	162	163
	Exp.:	6.00	*Exp.:*	157.00	
	χ^2:	4.17	χ^2:	0.16	
spoken (all)	*Obs.:*	0	*Obs.:*	265	265
	Exp.:	9.75	*Exp.:*	255.24	
	χ^2:	9.75	χ^2:	0.37	
Total		137		3585	3722

In the example just cited, the multi-word source-domain expression would be [$\text{NP}_{\text{container}}$ *be filled with* $\text{NP}_{\text{substance}}$], the source domain would be that of substances in containers. The target domain word that has been inserted in this expression is *anger*, yielding the metaphorical pattern [$\text{NP}_{\text{container}}$ *be filled with* $\text{NP}_{\text{emotion}}$]. The metaphors instantiated by this pattern include "an emotion is a substance" and "experiencing an emotion is being filled with a substance".

A metaphorical pattern analysis of a given target domain (like 'anger') thus proceeds by selecting one or more words that refer to (or are inherently connected with) this domain (for example, the word *anger*, or the set *irritation, annoyance, anger, rage, fury,* etc.) and retrieve all instances of this word or set of words from a corpus. The next step consists in identifying all cases where the search term(s) occur in a multi-word expression referring to some domain other than emotions. Finally, the source domains of these expressions are identified, giving us the metaphor instantiated by each metaphorical pattern. The patterns can then be grouped into larger sets corresponding to metaphors like "emotions are substances".

11.2.2.1 Case study: Happiness across cultures

Stefanowitsch (2004) investigates differences in metaphorical patterns associated with *happiness* in American English and its translation equivalent *Glück* in German. The study finds, among other things, that the metaphors THE ATTEMPT TO ACHIEVE HAPPINESS IS A SEARCH/PURSUIT and CAUSING HAPPINESS IS A TRANSACTION are instantiated more frequently in American English than in German. The question, raised but not addressed in Stefanowitsch (2004), is whether this is a linguistic difference or a cultural difference. The word *Glück* is a close translation equivalent of *happiness*, but the meaning of these two words is not identical. For example, as Goddard (1998) argues and Stefanowitsch (2004) shows empirically (cf. Case Study 11.2.2.2), the German word describes a more intense emotion than the English one. This may have consequences for the metaphors a word is associated with. Alternatively, the emotional state described by both *Glück* and *happiness* may play a different role in German vs. American culture, for example, in regard to beliefs about whether and how one can actively try to cause or achieve it. In order to answer this question, we need to compare metaphorical patterns associated with *happiness* in different English-speaking cultures (or patterns associated with *Glück* in different German-speaking ones).

Let us attempt to do this, focusing on the two metaphors just mentioned but discussing others in passing. In order to introduce the method of metaphorical pattern analysis, let us limit the study to small samples of language, which will allow us to study the relevant concordances in detail. This will make it less probable that we will find statistically significant differences, so let us treat the following as an exploratory pilot study. Given how frequently we have compared British and American English in this book, these two varieties may seem an obvious place to start, but the two cultures may be too similar, and the word *happiness* happens to be too infrequent in the BROWN corpus anyway. Let us compare British English (the LOB corpus) and Indian English (the Kolhapur corpus constructed along the same categories) instead. Figure 11.2 shows all hits of the query ⟨ `[word="happiness"%c]` ⟩.

The very first line contains an example of one of the SEARCH/PURSUIT metaphor, namely the metaphorical pattern [*pursuit of* NP_{EMOT}]. If we go through the entire concordance, we find three additional patterns instantiating this metaphor, namely [*seek* NP_{EMOT}] (line 14), [NP_{EMOT} *be found in* V_{ing}] (line 17) and [NP_{EXP}

```
 1 rences in the way of life and pursuit of [happiness] , differences in our social system and
 2  and laughter , he feels , engender more [happiness] than politics or philanthropy . at a me
 3 experiences the true meaning of love and [happiness] . ' X-certificate . Phillipe Lemarre ha
 4  used of experiences of life and death , [happiness] and sorrow ( cf Job 9.25 ; Ps 16.10 ; I
 5 or an ultimate goal to the merriment and [happiness] that life does contain in some of its s
 6  says about the relation of goodness and [happiness] . most people know Heine's brilliant je
 7 duty is not concerned with consequence : [happiness] is concerned with nothing else . here w
 8  about the supreme good - which includes [happiness] . A E Taylor has said that what disting
 9 ending improvement need not mean perfect [happiness] there any more than here . but after se
10 ew moral intuition . ` that goodness and [happiness] ought to go together , and the existenc
11 he seems to have overcome the dualism of [happiness] and duty but at a cost . he has been vi
12 dly meets the problem ` does Kant regard [happiness] as a good thing or not ? ' the answer w
13 we prove ourselves worthy or unworthy of [happiness] in the next . but in this life is it no
14 n this life is it not lawful to seek the [happiness] of others ? on stern Kantian grounds ,
15 ng attitudes , to a life of fulfilment , [happiness] and success . as each year passes the s
16 e and the car , will not bring increased [happiness] to our increased leisure . nor will the
17 ge of this fundamental truth - that real [happiness] and satisfaction is found in doing for
18 hich no one will read . '' sign here for [happiness] . Judith Simons meets a woman who share
19 hrough it - that moment when all hope of [happiness] seems lost for ever . they said they 'd
20 nts are able to provide tranquillity and [happiness] within the home itself , and in their d
21  not only in money but in the health and [happiness] of its people and the enhanced prestige
22 hey studied Richard Lucas' enquiry after [happiness] , Norris' sermons , Stephen's letters a
23 ctively in the sacrifice of her sister's [happiness] , or in consolidating her own usurpatio
24 he summertime , sent her into shrieks of [happiness] . she loved bright objects and pleasant
25 us beauty of the Latin liturgy ` a vital [happiness] ' . it was to him a means of mediation
26 ture . to all who have retired , we wish [happiness] and long life . research leaders honour
27 her told stories about the war a curious [happiness] came over him which the stories themsel
28 tomorrow afternoon ? ' he felt a glow of [happiness] steal over him . everything was all rig
29 ee you happy . ' ` there will n't be any [happiness] for me until I can prove him guilty . '
30 ith an undescribable expression of utter [happiness] . seeing Heather he came to her and dan
31  in turn with an expression of ineffable [happiness] on his flat face . quickly taking his c
32 ommand . Sirisec . '' he looked up , all [happiness] gone from his leathery features . ` oh
33 . though he never expected to attain the [happiness] he yearned for in a daughter-in-law and
34  West again . Barry had brought her more [happiness] than she had ever known was possible ,
35 ut there 'll be sons for you - aye , and [happiness] , too - when Helen 's gone from your si
36 y known before that there was no hope of [happiness] in the future for her and Gavin . if he
37 is own love for her , his desire for her [happiness] . far better that she should believe hi
38 e word . Nicholas , Philip ... where was [happiness] , or peace of mind ? Philip put out a h
39 ved Sandra too deeply to ruin her future [happiness] . had ever circumstances conspired so c
40 tood there staring at Julia with all the [happiness] draining out of her pretty little face
41 a burden to be endured and never never a [happiness] to be anticipated . now , her young mou
42 wards he had believed that she had found [happiness] with the bluff sailor and he 'd been ge
43 y nothing of this . it concerns Missie's [happiness] . '' so that was it ! someone was anxio
44 k . ' Mollie followed him , bemused with [happiness] . she moved on a cloud , floating effor
45  they sat for an hour , bemused by their [happiness] , feeling that all things were possible
46 on of Dorcas and Adrian Mallory , of the [happiness] of that girl on the eve of her marriage
47 change , even for a fortnight , the warm [happiness] of being with Neil , of sharing with hi
48 mented minute had been a tiny stretch of [happiness] . he leaned from the carriage window an
49 ery on a fast vanishing hope of ultimate [happiness] . Betty was right . Kay must not be for
50 ' ` yes , and we 'll drink to our future [happiness] , Bill ! ' she answered , raising her f
51 s of golden sunshine and music and utter [happiness] . the knowledge that she might never se
52 em , Tandy felt a private little glow of [happiness] . for so long , now , she 'd felt respo
53 re so selfish . " " The whole concept of [happiness] , mother dearest , is outdated . Your ph
```

Figure 11.2: Concordance of *happiness* (LOB)

find NP_{EMOT}] (line 42), with NP_{EXP} indicating the slot for the noun referring to the experiencer of the emotion. Note that, as is typical in metaphorical pattern analysis, the patterns are generalized with respect to the slot of the emotion noun (we could find the same patterns with other emotions), and they are relatively close in form to the actual citation. We could subsume the passive in line 17 under the same pattern as the active in line 42, of course, but there might be differences across emotion terms, varieties, etc. concerning voice (and other formal aspects of the pattern), and there is little gained by discarding this information.

The TRANSFER metaphor is also instantiated a number of times in the concordance, namely as [NP_{STIM} *bring* NP_{EMOT}] (lines 16 and 42), and [NP_{STIM} *provide* NP_{EMOT}] (line 20).

Additional clear cases of metaphorical patterns are [*glow of* NP_{EMOT}] (lines 28 and 53) and [*warm* NP_{EMOT}] (line 47), which instantiate the metaphor HAPPINESS IS WARMTH, and [NP_{EMOT} *drain out of* NP_{EXP}*'s face*] (line 40), which instantiates HAPPINESS IS A LIQUID FILLING THE EXPERIENCER. In other cases, it depends on our judgment (which we have to defend within a given research design) whether a hit constitutes a metaphorical pattern. For example, do we want to analyze [NP_{STIM} *'s* NP_{EMOT}] (lines 23 and 43) and [PRON.POSS.$_{STIM}$ NP_{EMOT}] (lines 37, 39, 45, 50) as HAPPINESS IS A POSSESSED OBJECT, or do we consider the possessive construction to be too abstract semantically to be analyzed as metaphorical? Similarly, do we analyze [NP_{STIM} *engender* NP_{EMOT}] (line 2) as an instance of HAPPINESS IS AN ORGANISM, based on the etymology of *engender*, which comes from Latin *generare beget* and was still used for organisms in Middle English (cf. Chaucer's *...swich licour, / Of which vertu engendred is the flour*)? You might want to think about these and other cases in the concordance, to get a sense of the kind of annotation scheme you would need to make such decisions on a principled, replicable basis.

For now, let us turn to Indian English. Table 11.3 shows the hits for the query ⟨ `[word="happiness"%c]` ⟩ in the Kolhapur corpus. Here, 35 hits for the phrase *harmonious happiness* have been removed, because they all came from one text extolling the virtues of the *principle of harmonious happiness* (17 hits), *(moral) standard of harmonious happiness* (15 hits), *(moral) good of harmonious happiness)* (2 hits) or *nor of harmonious happiness* (1 hit). This text is obviously very much an outlier, as it contains almost as many hits as the entire rest of the corpus combined, and as the hits are extremely restricted in their linguistic behavior. To discard them might not seem ideal, but to include them would be even less so.

Again, the SEARCH metaphor is instantiated several times in the concordance: we find [*search for* NP_{EMOT}] (lines 2 and 4) and [NP_{EXP} *seek* NP_{EMOT}] (lines 3 and 5). They all seem to be from the same text, so similar considerations apply

```
 1 ove . Dr . Patwardhan expresses both her [happiness] at seeing the growth of Anandgram and he
 2 with mature understanding the search for [happiness] of an actress . The Shyam Benegal and Bl
 3 nd lives on her earnings makes Usha seek [happiness] elsewhere . The search for happiness of
 4 eek happiness elsewhere . The search for [happiness] of this intensely sensitive girl leads h
 5  are seeking something , seeking peace , [happiness] , seeking a nobler way of life , seeking
 6 e occasion , the Buddha himself bringing [happiness] to a doomed city , and accordingly , the
 7  their suffering and obtain security and [happiness] is by seeking to change and transform so
 8 e and notoriety , censure and praise and [happiness] and misery . Just as the stalk gives bir
 9 tute , consoled the stricken and brought [happiness] to the miserable . He did not run away f
10 th the physical body is another name for [happiness] . Finally , when the mind is stilled ( i
11 d through such purity of mind to achieve [happiness] . It also says that if one acts or speak
12 or control of mind which is conducive to [happiness] because it flits and floats all over and
13 ual cooperation , the key to success and [happiness] , are at a discount . Even people who ar
14 edas there are many prayers for wealth , [happiness] and glory . " We call on Thee for prospe
15 from sin and full of wealth , leading to [happiness] day by day . " ( Rig ) " May I be glorio
16  I am confident that I can sing to bring [happiness] to my listeners and fulfilment to myself
17 se wanderers together again and there is [happiness] . When they all return to Jaipur they di
18  his old position . Thus there is double [happiness] for all . This plot will give an idea of
19 s possible at the cost of the people ' s [happiness] . The freedom fighter for India against
20 is this ennobling vision of the world of [happiness] and contentment which I have always born
21 eace alone there is human fulfilment and [happiness] . But even if the goal appears distant ,
22 with the peace and prosperity , life and [happiness] of the society ? The only answer to this
23 of you . I wish you every prosperity and [happiness] in the coming years . I have served you
24 ull of vegetation , trees , orchards and [happiness] . But she could not do that for she was
25 ould make her if you did . Learn to give [happiness] to people , all you modern children are
26  didn ' t wish to come in the way of our [happiness] , at which she , my wife , pretended to
27 hree children . They did not know of the [happiness] we shared -- the exciting excursions , t
28 for breakfast with us . It gave us great [happiness] , though he was not his cheerful old sel
29 t more could she desire ? The goddess of [happiness] and mirth had visited her . Forty-five m
30 ure of health . Nobody was bursting with [happiness] ; there was no expectation of sharing in
31  pronounced my son as completely cured . [Happiness] flooded my heart . Silently I held my wi
32 l . He was filled with a kind of childsh [happiness] . He wanted to scamper over the rocks ,
33  said Joan . Janaki ' s face beamed with [happiness] at the comparison . From that day , Joan
34  had a warm sniff of its steam . But his [happiness] drove him into one of those sudden snooz
35 on ' s ? Have I always placed Dinesh ' s [happiness] above mine ? Am I not selfish and posses
36 me in ample measure for the pleasure and [happiness] my stories and novels have brought into
37 tting together , bit by bit . Moments of [happiness] are such fleeting things . Maybe they al
38 leeting things . Maybe they always are . [Happiness] - - maybe it ' s just the burden of a bi
39 is door had played a stellar role in his [happiness] . Day after day , he had sat there like
40 rtainly put me on the highway to eternal [happiness] but it could do nothing about my immedia
41 rs will travel through life in peace and [happiness] in spite of delays , discomfort and suff
```

Figure 11.3: Concordance of *happiness* (Kolhapur)

as in the case of the *principle/standard of harmonious happiness*. We also find the transfer metaphor quite strongly represented: [$\mathrm{NP}_{\mathrm{STIM}}$ *bring* $\mathrm{NP}_{\mathrm{EMOT}}$] (lines 6, 9, 16), [$\mathrm{NP}_{\mathrm{EXP}}$ *obtain* $\mathrm{NP}_{\mathrm{EMOT}}$] (line 7), [$\mathrm{NP}_{\mathrm{STIM}}$ *give* $\mathrm{NP}_{\mathrm{EMOT}}$] (lines 25, 28) and [$\mathrm{NP}_{\mathrm{EXP}}$ *share* $\mathrm{NP}_{\mathrm{EMOT}}$] (line 27).

Again, there are other clear cases of metaphor, such as [$\mathrm{NP}_{\mathrm{EXP}}$ *burst with* $\mathrm{NP}_{\mathrm{EMOT}}$] (line 30), [$\mathrm{NP}_{\mathrm{EMOT}}$ *flood* $\mathrm{NP}_{\mathrm{EXP}}$*'s heart*] (line 31), and [$\mathrm{NP}_{\mathrm{EXP}}$ *be filled with* $\mathrm{NP}_{\mathrm{EMOT}}$] (line 32) (again, they seem to be from the same text).

Comparing the metaphors we set out to investigate, we see that the PURSUIT and SEARCH metaphors are fairly evenly distributed across the two varieties, with no significant difference even on the horizon. The TRANSFER metaphor, in contrast, shows clear differences, and as Table 11.8 shows, this difference is almost significant even in our small sample ($\chi^2 = 3.17$, df $= 1$, $p = 0.075$). This would be an interesting difference to look at in a larger study, especially since the two varieties differ not only in the token frequency of this metaphor, but also in the type frequency – the LOB corpus contains only two different patterns instantiating this metaphor, the Kolhapur corpus contains four.

Table 11.8: CAUSING HAPPINESS IS A TRANSFER in two corpora (LOB, Kolhapur)

		CORPUS		
		LOB	KOLHAPUR	Total
TYPE	TRANSFER	3 (5.64)	7 (4.36)	10
	¬TRANSFER	50 (47.36)	34 (36.64)	84
	Total	53	41	94

This case study demonstrates the basic procedure of Metaphorical Pattern Analysis and some of the questions raised by the need to categorize corpus hits. It also shows that even a small-scale study of such patterns may provide interesting results on which we can build hypotheses to be tested on larger data sets. Finally, it shows that there may well be differences between cultures in the metaphorical patterns and the overarching metaphors they instantiate (cf. e.g. Rojo López & Orts Llopis 2010, Rojo López 2013 and Ogarkova & Soriano Salinas 2014 for cross-linguistic comparisons and Díaz-Vera & Caballero 2013, Díaz-Vera 2015 and Güldenring 2017 for comparisons across different varieties of English; cf. also Tissari 2003; 2010 for comparisons across time periods within one language).

11.2.2.2 Case study: Intensity of emotions

Whether we start from the source domain or from the target domain, the extraction of metaphorical patterns from large corpora typically requires time-consuming manual annotation. However, if we are interested in specific metaphors, we can speed up the extraction significantly, by looking for utterances containing vocabulary from the source and target domains we are interested in. For example, Martin (2006) compiles lists of words from two domains (such as WAR and COMMERCIAL ACTIVITY and then searches a large corpus for instances where items from both lists co-occur in a particular span.

We can take this basic idea and apply it in a linguistically slightly more conservative way to target-item oriented versions of metaphorical pattern analysis. Instead of searching for co-occurrence in a span, let us construct a set of structured queries that would find metaphorical patterns instantiating a given metaphor. As mentioned in Case Study 11.2.2.1, the word *happiness* and its German translation equivalent *Glück* may differ in the intensity of the emotion they refer to. In Stefanowitsch (2004), this hypothesis is tested by investigating metaphors that plausibly reflect such a difference in intensity. Specifically, it is shown that while both *happiness* and *Glück* are found with metaphors describing an emotion as a substance in a container (the experiencer), *Glück* is found significantly more frequently with metaphors describing the experiencer as a container that disintegrates because it cannot withstand the pressure of the substance. The same difference is found within English between the words *happiness* and *joy.*

Let us investigate these metaphors with respect to frequent basic emotion terms in English, to see whether there are general differences between emotions with respect to metaphorical intensity. Stefanowitsch (2006c) lists the metaphorical patterns for five English emotion terms, categorized into general metaphors. Combining all patterns occurring with at least one emotion noun, the patterns in (4) are identified or the metaphor EMOTIONS ARE A SUBSTANCE IN A CONTAINER with *an experiencer is a container* (instead of the experiencer themselves, the patterns may also refer to their *heart, face, eyes, mind, voice,* etc.):

(4) a. NP_{EMOT} *fill* NP_{EXP}
b. NP_{STIM} *fill* NP_{EXP} with NP_{EMOT}
c. NP_{EXP} *fill* (up) with NP_{EMOT}
d. NP_{EXP} *be filled with* NP_{EMOT}
e. NP_{EXP} *be full of* NP_{EMOT}
f. NP_{EXP} *be(come)* filled with NP_{EMOT}

g. NP_{EMOT} *seep into* NP_{EXP}
h. NP_{EMOT} *spill into* NP_{EXP}
i. NP_{EMOT} *flood through* NP_{EXP}

Let us ignore the patterns in (4g–i), which occurred only once each in Stefanowitsch (2006c). The rest then form a set of expressions with relatively simple structures that we can extract using the following queries (shown here for the noun *happiness*):

(5) a. `[hw="full"] [hw="of"] []{0,2} [word="happiness"%c]`
b. `[hw="(fill|filled)"] [hw="with"] []{0,2} [word="happiness"%c]`
c. `[word="happiness"%c] [pos=".*(VB|VD|VH|VM).*"] [pos=".*AV0.*"] [hw="fill" & pos=".*VV.*"]`

The paper also lists a number of metaphorical patterns that describe an increasing pressure, e.g. [NP_{EMOT} *build inside* NP_{EXP}] or an overflowing, e.g. [NP_{EXP} *brim over with* NP_{EMOT}], but let us focus on those patterns that describe a sudden failure to contain the substance. These are listed in (6):

(6) a. *burst/outburst/explosion of* NP_{EMOT}
b. NP_{EMOT} *burst in/through* NP_{EXP}
c. NP_{EMOT} *burst (out)*
d. NP_{EMOT} *erupt/explode*
e. NP_{EMOT} *blow up*
f. NP_{EXP} *burst/erupt/explode with* NP_{EMOT}
g. *explosive* NP_{EMOT}
h. *volcanic* NP_{EMOT}

We can extract these patterns using the following queries (shown, again, for *happiness*):

(7) a. `[word="happiness"%c & pos=".*NN.*"] [hw="(burst|erupt|explode)" & pos=".*VV.*"]`
b. `[word="happiness"%c & pos=".*NN.*"] [hw="(blow)" & pos=".*VV.*"][word="up"%c]`
c. `[hw="(explosive|eruptive|volcanic)"] [word="happiness"%c & pos=".*NN.*"]`
d. `[hw="(burst|erupt|explode)" & pos=".*VV.*"] [word="(in|with)"%c] [word="happiness"%c & pos=".*NN.*"]`

e. `[hw="(outburst|burst|eruption|explosion)"] [word="of"%c] [word="happiness"%c & pos=".*NN.*"]`

We are now searching for combinations of a target-domain item with specific source domain items in specific structural configurations. In doing so, we will reduce recall compared to a manual extraction, but the precision is very high, allowing us to query large corpora and to work with the results without annotating them manually.

Let us apply both sets of queries to the basic emotion nouns *anger, desire, disgust, fear, happiness, pride, sadness, shame.* Table 11.9 shows the tabulated results for the queries in (5) compared against the overall frequency of the respective nouns in the BNC.

There are two emotion nouns whose frequency in these metaphorical patterns deviates from the expected frequency: *desire* is described as a substance in a container less frequently than expected, and *sadness* is more frequently than expected. It is an interesting question why this should be the case, but it is not plausibly related to the intensity of the respective emotions.

Table 11.10 shows the tabulated results for the queries in (7) compared against the overall frequency of the respective nouns in the BNC.

Two emotion nouns occur with the BURSTING metaphors noticeably more frequently than expected, namely *anger* and *pride* (the latter marginally significantly); three occur noticeably less frequently, *desire, fear* and *shame.* Again, this does not seem to be related to the intensity of the emotion – fear or desire can be just as intense as anger or pride. Instead, it seems to be related to the likelihood that the emotion will be outwardly visible, for example, by resulting in a particular kind of behavior toward others. Again, *desire* is an exception, it may be that it does not participate in *container* metaphors at all.

This case study demonstrates how central metaphors for a given target domain can be identified by searching for combinations of words describing (aspects of) the source and the target domain in question. It also shows that these metaphors can be associated to different degrees with different words within a given target domain (cf. e.g. Stefanowitsch 2006c, Turkkila 2014). It is unclear to what extent this lexeme specificity of metaphorical mappings supports or contradicts current cognitive theories of metaphor, so it is potentially a very interesting area of research.

Table 11.9: The metaphor EMOTIONS ARE A SUBSTANCE FILLING THE EXPERIENCER (BNC)

	FILLING/FULLNESS metaphors				
EMOTION	YES		NO		Total
ANGER	*Obs.:*	29	*Obs.:*	3512	3541
	Exp.:	21.07	*Exp.:*	3519.93	
	χ^2:	2.99	χ^2:	0.02	
DESIRE	*Obs.:*	7	*Obs.:*	5055	5062
	Exp.:	30.12	*Exp.:*	5031.88	
	χ^2:	17.74	χ^2:	0.11	
DISGUST	*Obs.:*	6	*Obs.:*	604	610
	Exp.:	3.63	*Exp.:*	606.37	
	χ^2:	1.55	χ^2:	0.01	
FEAR	*Obs.:*	47	*Obs.:*	7117	7164
	Exp.:	42.62	*Exp.:*	7121.38	
	χ^2:	0.45	χ^2:	0.00	
HAPPINESS	*Obs.:*	15	*Obs.:*	1601	1616
	Exp.:	9.61	*Exp.:*	1606.39	
	χ^2:	3.02	χ^2:	0.02	
PRIDE	*Obs.:*	11	*Obs.:*	2714	2725
	Exp.:	16.21	*Exp.:*	2708.79	
	χ^2:	1.68	χ^2:	0.01	
SADNESS	*Obs.:*	13	*Obs.:*	738	751
	Exp.:	4.47	*Exp.:*	746.53	
	χ^2:	16.29	χ^2:	0.10	
SHAME	*Obs.:*	11	*Obs.:*	1883	1894
	Exp.:	11.27	*Exp.:*	1882.73	
	χ^2:	0.01	χ^2:	0.00	
Total	139		23224		23 363

Table 11.10: The metaphor EMOTIONS ARE A SUBSTANCE BURSTING THE EXPERIENCER (BNC)

	BURSTING/EXPLODING metaphors				
EMOTION	YES		NO		Total
ANGER	*Obs.:*	42	*Obs.:*	3499	3541
	Exp.:	9.40	*Exp.:*	3531.60	
	χ^2:	113.12	χ^2:	0.30	
DESIRE	*Obs.:*	4	*Obs.:*	5058	5062
	Exp.:	13.43	*Exp.:*	5048.57	
	χ^2:	6.62	χ^2:	0.02	
DISGUST	*Obs.:*	1	*Obs.:*	609	610
	Exp.:	1.62	*Exp.:*	608.38	
	χ^2:	0.24	χ^2:	0.00	
FEAR	*Obs.:*	1	*Obs.:*	7163	7164
	Exp.:	19.01	*Exp.:*	7144.99	
	χ^2:	17.06	χ^2:	0.05	
HAPPINESS	*Obs.:*	2	*Obs.:*	1614	1616
	Exp.:	4.29	*Exp.:*	1611.71	
	χ^2:	1.22	χ^2:	0.00	
PRIDE	*Obs.:*	12	*Obs.:*	2713	2725
	Exp.:	7.23	*Exp.:*	2717.77	
	χ^2:	3.14	χ^2:	0.01	
SADNESS	*Obs.:*	0	*Obs.:*	751	751
	Exp.:	1.99	*Exp.:*	749.01	
	χ^2:	1.99	χ^2:	0.01	
SHAME	*Obs.:*	0	*Obs.:*	1894	1894
	Exp.:	5.03	*Exp.:*	1888.97	
	χ^2:	5.03	χ^2:	0.01	
Total	62		23301		23 363

11.2.3 Metaphor and text

11.2.3.1 Case study: Identifying potential source domains

If we are interested in questions relating to a particular source domain, as in Section 11.2.1, or to a particular target domain, as in Section 11.2.2, our first task is to define a representative set of lexical items to query. This set may be dictated by the hypothesis we are planning to test, or we may, in more exploratory studies, assemble it on the basis of thesauri or words and patterns identified in previous studies. If, on the other hand, we are interested in source domains associated with a particular target domain, matters are more complicated. We can start by selecting a set of target-domain items and then identify all source domains in the metaphorical patterns of these items, but while this will tell us something about these items, it does not tell us much about the target domain as a whole. Or we can identify the source domains manually, which restricts the amount of data we can reasonably process.

Partington (1998) suggests a promising solution to this problem: If we apply a keyword analysis (cf. Chapter 10) to a thematic corpus dealing with the target domain in question, then the dominant source domains in that target domain should be visibly represented among the keywords. Thus, searching the results for items that do not, in their literal meaning, belong to the target domain should identify items that ar used metaphorically in the target domain.

To demonstrate this method, let us define a subcorpus for the domain ECONOMY in the BNC Baby. This is easiest done by using the meta-information supplied by the corpus makers, which includes the category "commerce" as a subcategory of "newspaper" (cf. Table 2.2 in Chapter 2). Let us determine the keywords in this subcorpus compared to the rest of the NEWSPAPER subcorpus (excluding the SPOKEN, FICTION and ACADEMIC subcorpora, in order to reduce the number of keywords that are typical for newspaper language in general). Table 11.11 shows selected results of a keyword analysis of these files.

As expected, most of the strongest keywords for the subcorpus are directly related to the domain of economics. Among the Top 15 (shown in the first part of the table), only two are not directly related to this domain: the proper name *Middlesbrough* and the word *rise*. The keyness of the former is due to the fact that one of the files in the BNC Baby COMMERCIAL subcorpus is from the Northern Echo, a regional newspaper covering County Durham and Teesside – Middlesbrough is the largest town in this region and is thus mentioned frequently, but it is not generally an important town, so it is hardly mentioned outside of this text. The keyness of the latter is more interesting, as it is the kind of word we are looking for: its literal meaning, 'motion from a lower to a higher position', would

Table 11.11: Selected keywords from the newspaper subcategory COMMERCE (BNC Baby)

Rank	KEYWORD	Frequency in *commerce*	Frequency in *other*	Other words in *commerce*	Other words in *other*	*G*
Top 15						
1	*share*	576	173	170 065	913 288	1381.11
2	*profit*	443	54	170 198	913 407	1315.96
3	*company*	561	409	170 080	913 052	894.99
4	*market*	403	246	170 238	913 215	713.80
5	*p.c.*	175	0	170 466	913 461	647.28
6	*group*	434	394	170 207	913 067	594.57
7	*business*	372	287	170 269	913 174	571.85
8	*Middlesbrough*	203	39	170 438	913 422	550.49
9	*investor*	161	6	170 480	913 455	545.85
10	*rate*	245	154	170 396	913 307	426.77
11	*dividend*	115	3	170 526	913 458	398.39
12	*price*	262	211	170 379	913 250	391.16
13	*investment*	164	52	170 477	913 409	385.95
14	*rise*	221	146	170 420	913 315	374.09
15	*property*	168	66	170 473	913 395	365.57
Additional words relating to VERTICALITY in Top 200						
31	*fall*	191	238	170 450	913 223	198.37
48	*jump*	80	42	170 561	913 419	153.15
61	*up*	548	1630	170 093	911 831	127.87
96	*low*	111	167	170 530	913 294	93.67
123	*slump*	42	22	170 599	913 439	80.49
156	*plunge*	36	20	170 605	913 441	66.98
174	*below*	47	46	170 594	913 415	60.65
186	*high*	179	474	170 462	912 987	57.29
188	*leap*	33	21	170 608	913 440	57.06
192	*surge*	29	15	170 612	913 446	55.92
200	*soar*	27	13	170 614	913 448	53.85
Other potential metaphors in Top 200						
81	*cut*	146	246	170 495	913 215	106.57
82	*inflation*	51	23	170 590	913 438	104.76
84	*stake*	80	78	170 561	913 383	103.56
89	*growth*	63	47	170 578	913 414	98.92
105	*chain*	45	22	170 596	913 439	89.13
133	*expansion*	30	8	170 611	913 453	74.57
138	*fixed*	27	5	170 614	913 456	73.82
157	*recovery*	51	49	170 590	913 412	66.80
181	*close*	136	316	170 505	913 145	58.29
183	*float*	27	11	170 614	913 450	57.89
184	*flotation*	19	2	170 622	913 459	57.74
193	*outlet*	24	8	170 617	913 453	55.50

Supplementary Online Material: UH9B

not be expected to be particularly central to the domain of economics. More interestingly, there are 11 additional words from the domain of 'vertical motion' among the Top 200 keywords, making it the largest single semantic field other than 'economy' (see second part of the table). There are only 12 other words whose literal meaning is not directly related to economy, listed in the third part of the table, from source domains such as 'increase in size' (*inflation*, *growth*, *expansion*), 'health' (*recovery*) and 'bodies of water' (*float(ation)*, *outlet*).

This suggests that 'vertical motion' is a central source domain in the domain of economics, which we can now study by querying the respective keywords as well as other words from this domain (which we could get from a thesaurus). As an example, consider the concordance of the lemma *rise* in Figure 11.4 (a random sample of 20 hits from the 221 hits in the COMMERCE section in the BNC Baby).

```
 1 ts for the year to March . The price has [risen] by 119p since Caradon announced a possi
 2  was more than accounted for by a £1.6m [rise] in its Channel 4 subscription and by £
 3 aid that the top rate of income tax will [rise] to 50 p.c. on income , after allowances
 4 ay . The Pearl Investor Confidence Index [rose] by 1.2 p.c. last month -- its largest
 5  December , this figure was said to have [risen] to 17,000 a month at $25,000 ( £14,200
 6 by shoppers APPLICATIONS for credit have [risen] sharply in the wake of the Tory 's elec
 7  quarter of the year , despite a 15 p.c. [rise] in sales to $373m ( £214m ) . City : Q
 8 rman of United Biscuits , saw his salary [rise] from £233,000 to £425,000 last year .
 9 nce of the quality food retailers with a [rise] of almost 25% . Liz Dolan 's Surrey bui
10 s . They gave themselves an average 1992 [rise] of 5% , says the IoD , and a lot got ev
11  75p , while Fuller Smith , with profits [rising] to £3.75m ( £3.6m ) at midway , climb
12 LJ from SmithKline Beecham helped shares [rise] 23p to 248p . Merrydown is financing th
13 op up at Wessex WESSEX Water saw profits [rise] 11.3% to £44.3m in the first half help
14 s interims tomorrow , with a 10% profits [rise] to £101m expected . Northumbrian Water
15 es added 2p to 270p after a 10% dividend [rise] to 3.3p . Property divi slide GREAT Por
16 es on the dairy industry . Welcoming the [rise] in retail sales figures for October , C
17 isation of Petroleum Exporting Countries [rose] 100,000 barrels per day to 24.2 million
18  £13 barrier but Glaxo failed to hold a [rise] above £8 . To a degree some of the ris
19 he jobs queue since unemployment started [rising] in April 1990 . Employment Secretary Gi
20  parts of the country , with the biggest [rises] again in London and the SouthEast , fol
```

Figure 11.4: A concordance of the wordform *rise* in COMMERCE texts (BNC Baby, sample)

First, the concordance corroborates our suspicion that *rise* is not used literally in the domain of economics. All 20 hits refer not to vertical motion, but to an increase in quantity, i.e., they instantiate the metaphor MORE IS UP. This is true both of verbal uses (in lines 1, 3, 4, 5, 6, 8, 11, 12, 13, 17, and 19) and to the nominal uses in the remaining lines. Second, the nouns in the surrounding context show where this metaphor is applied, namely overwhelmingly to genuinely economic concepts like *prices, tax rates, salaries, sales, dividends, profits, shares,* etc.

The results of such a keyword analysis can now be used as a basis for all kinds of studies. For example, we may simply be interested in describing frequent metaphorical patterns in the data (say, in the context of teaching English for Special Purposes); some very noticeable examples are [$rise_N$ *in* NP] (lines 2, 7, 16) and [*see* NP $rise_V$] (lines 8, 13), or [*hold a* $rise_N$] (line 18).

Or we may be interested in the kind of research question discussed in Case Study 11.2.1.1, i.e. in whether literal synonyms and antonyms of *rise* are mapped isomorphically onto the domain of economics (the fact that *jump, surge* and *soar* as well as *fall, slump* and *plunge* are among the top 200 keywords certainly suggests they are.

Or we may be interested in the kind of research question discussed in Case Study 11.2.1.3, i.e. in what, if any, differences there are between the metaphorical pattern [*rise in* NP] and its literal equivalent [*increase in* NP]. For example, a query of the BNC for (8) results in 84 hits for *rising cost(s)* as opposed to 34 hits for *increasing cost(s)* and 7 hits for *rising profit(s)* as opposed to 12 hits for *increasing profit(s)*:

(8) `[word="(rising|increasing)"%c] [word="(cost|profit)s?"%c]`

It is left as an exercise for the reader to test this distribution for significance using the χ^2 test or a similar test (but use a separate sheet of paper, as the margin of this page will be too small to contain your calculations). If more such differences can be found, this might suggest that the metaphor "increase in quantity is upward motion" is associated more strongly with spending money than with making money.

This case study demonstrates that central metaphors for a given target domain can be identified by applying a keyword analysis to a specialized corpus of texts from that domain. The case study does not discuss a particular research question, but obviously, the method is useful in the context of many different research designs. Of course, it requires specialized corpora for the target domain under investigation. Such corpora are not available (and in some cases not imaginable) for all target domains, so the method works better for some target domains (such as ECONOMICS) than for others (like *emotions*).

11.2.3.2 Case study: Metaphoricity signals

Although metaphorical expressions are pervasive in all language varieties and speakers do not generally seem to draw special attention to their occurrence, there is a wide range of devices that mark non-literal language more or less explicitly (as in *metaphorically/figuratively speaking*, *picture* NP *as* NP, *so to speak/ say*):

(9) a. ...the princess held a gun to Charles's head, figuratively speaking... (BNC CBF)
   b. He pictures eternity as a filthy Russian bathhouse... (BNC A18)
   c. ...the only way they can deal with crime is to fight fire, so to speak, with fire. (BNC ABJ)

Wallington et al. (2003) investigate the extent to which these devices, which they call *metaphoricity signals*, correlate systematically with the occurrence of metaphorical expressions in language use. They find no strong correlation, but as they note, this may well be due to various aspects of their design. First, they adopt a very broad view of what constitutes a metaphoricity signal, including expressions like *a kind/type/sort of*, *not so much* NP *as* NP and even prefixes like *super-*, *mini-*, etc. While some or all of these signals may have an affinity to certain kinds of non-literal language, one would not really consider them to be *metaphoricity* signals in the same way as those in (9a–c). Second, they investigate a carefully annotated, but very small corpus. Third, they do not distinguish between strongly conventionalized metaphors, which are found in almost every utterance and are thus unlikely to be explicitly signaled, and weakly conventionalized metaphors, which seems more likely to be signaled explicitly *a priori*).

More restricted case studies are needed to determine whether the idea of metaphoricity signals is, in principle, plausible. Let us look at what is intuitively the clearest case of such a signal on Wallington et al.'s list: the sentence adverbials *metaphorically speaking* and *figuratively speaking*. As a control, let us use the roughly equally frequent sentence adverbial *technically speaking*, which does not signal metaphoricity but which can, of course, co-occur with (conventionalized) metaphors and which can thus serve as a baseline.

There are 22 cases of *technically speaking* in the BNC:

(10) a. Do you mind if, *technically speaking*, I resign rather than you sack me? (BNC A0F)
   b. *Technically speaking* as long as nobody was hurt, no injuries, no damage to the other vehicle, this is not an accident. (BNC A5Y)
   c. [*T*]*echnically speaking*, [...] if you put her out into the road she would have no roof over her head and we should have to take her in. (BNC AC7)

d. You will have to be the builder, *technically speaking*. (BNC AM5)
e. *Technically speaking*, the only difference between VHS and VHS-C is in the length of the tape in the cassette [...]. (BNC CBP)
f. [U]nlike financial controllers, directors can, *technically speaking*, be held liable for negligence and consequently sued. (BNC CBU)
g. *Technically speaking* [...], the unique formula penetrates the hair, enters the cortex and strengthens the hair bonds. (BNC CFS)
h. As novelists, however, Orwell and Waugh evolve not towards each other but, *technically speaking*, in opposite directions. (BNC CKN)
i. Under the Net [...] is *technically speaking* a memoir-novel [...], being composed as autobiography in the first person [...]. (BNC CKN)
j. [T]he greater part of the works of art in the trade are *technically speaking* 'second-hand goods'. (BNC EBU)
k. [T]he listener feels uncomfortably voyeuristic at times (yes, yes, I know that *technically speaking*, a listener can't be voyeuristic. (BNC ED7)
l. Adulterers. That's what they both were, *technically speaking*. (BNC F9C)
m. *Technically speaking*, this [walk] will certainly lead to the semi-recumbent stone circle of Strichen in the district of Banff and Buchan [...]. (BNC G1Y)
n. Richard was quite correct, as *technically speaking* they were all in harbour, in addressing them by the names of their craft. (BNC H0R)
o. 'What's to stop you simply saying that my designs aren't suitable [...]' 'Nothing, I suppose, *technically speaking*.' (BNC H97)
p. At least I was still a virgin, *technically speaking*. (BNC HJC)
q. The mike concealed in the head of the figure is only medium-quality, *technically speaking* [...]. (BNC HTT)
r. 'Well, *technically speaking* [...] you are no longer in a position to provide him with employment.' (BNC HWN)
s. Getting it right – *technically speaking* (BNC HX4)
t. *Technically speaking*, of course, she was off duty now and one of the night sisters had responsibility for the unit [...]. (BNC JYB)
u. [*T*]*echnically speaking* I suppose it is burnt but well done [...] (BNC KBP)
v. [Speaker A:] And they class it as the south. Bloody ridiculous. [Speaker B:] Well it is, *technically speaking*, south of a ...(BNC KDD)

Taking a generous view, four of these are part of a clause that arguably contains a metaphor: (10f) uses *hold* as part of the phrase *hold liable*, instantiating a metaphor like “believing something about someone is holding them” (cf. also *hold s.o. responsible/accountable, hold in high esteem*); (10h) uses the verb *evolve* metaphorically to refer to a non-evolutionary development and then uses the spatial expressions *towards* and *opposite direction* metaphorically to describe the quality of the development; (10r) uses *provide* as part of the phrase *provide employment*, which instantiates a metaphor like “causing someone to be in a state is transferring an object to them” (cf. also *provide s.o. with an opportunity/insight/power...*); (10t) contains the spatial preposition *off* as part of the phrase *off duty*, which could be said to instantiate the metaphor “a situation is a location”. Note that all four expressions involve highly conventionalized metaphors, that would hardly be noticed as such by speakers.

There are 7 hits for the sentence adverbial *metaphorically speaking* in the BNC:

(11) a. A convicted mass murderer has, for the second time, bloodied the nose, *metaphorically speaking*, of Malcolm Rifkind, the Secretary of State for Scotland, by successfully pursuing a claim for damages. (BNC A3G)

b. Yet, when I was seven years old, I should have thought him a very silly little boy indeed not to have understood about *metaphorically speaking*, even if he had never heard of it, and it does seem that what he possessed in the way of scientific approach he lacked in common sense. (BNC AC7)

c. Good caddies have good temperaments. Just watch Ian Wright getting a lambasting from Seve Ballesteros and see if Ian ever answers back, or, indeed, reacts in any way other than to quietly stand and take it on the chin, *metaphorically speaking* of course. (BNC ASA)

d. Family [are] a safe investment, but in love you can make a killing overnight. *Metaphorically speaking*, I hasten to add. (BNC BMR)

e. *Metaphorically speaking*, the research front is a frozen moment in time [...]. (BNC HPN)

f. Gregory put the boot in... *metaphorically speaking*! (BNC K25)

g. Mr Allenby are you ready to burst into song? *Metaphorically speaking*. (BNC KM7)

In clear contrast to *technically speaking*, six of these seven hits occur in clauses that contain a metaphor: *bloody the nose of sb* in (11a) means ‘be successful in court against sb’, instantiating the metaphor LEGAL FIGHT IS PHYSICAL FIGHT; *take it on the chin* in (11c) means 'endure being criticized', instantiating the metaphor ARGUMENT IS PHYSICAL FIGHT; *make a killing* in (11d) means 'be financially successful', instantiating the metaphor COMMERCIAL ACTIVITY IS A HUNT; *a frozen moment in time* in (11e) means 'documentation of a particular state', instantiating the metaphor TIME IS A FLOWING BODY OF WATER; *put the boot in* in (11f) means 'treat sb cruelly', instantiating the metaphor LIFE (OR SPORTS) IS PHYSICAL FIGHT; *burst into song* in (11g) means "take one's turn speaking", instantiating the metaphor SPEAKING IS SINGING. The only exception is (11b); this is a metalinguistic use, indicating that someone did not understand that an utterance was meant metaphorically, rather than marking an utterance as metaphorical.

There are 13 hits for *figuratively speaking* in the BNC:

(12) a. The darts, the lumps of poison and the raw materials from which it is extracted all provide a challenge for others with a taste (*figuratively speaking*) for excitement. (BNC AC9)

b. Alternatively, you could select spiky, upright plants like agaves or yuccas to transport you across the world, *figuratively speaking*, to the great deserts of North America. (BNC ACX)

c. Palladium, statue of the goddess Pallas (Minerva) at Troy on which the city's safety was said to depend, hence, *figuratively speaking*, the Bar seen as a bulwark of society. (BNC B0Y)

d. *Figuratively speaking*, who would not give their right arm to find such a love? (BNC B21)

e. [I]t is surprising to me that this process was ever permitted on this site at all (being *figuratively speaking* within arms length of the dwellings). (BNC B2D)

f. *Figuratively speaking*, we also make the law of value serve our aims. (BNC BMA)

g. This schlocky international movie, photographed in eye-straining colour, cashing in (*figuratively speaking*) on the craze for James Bond pictures [...]. (BNC C9U)

h. He said: 'I'm not sure if the princess held a gun to Charles's head, *figuratively speaking*, but it seems if she wanted something said.' (BNC CBF)

i. Let's pick someone completely at random, now we've had Tracey *figuratively speaking*! (BNC F7U)

j. '*Figuratively speaking*', he declared, 'in case of need, Soviet artillerymen can support the Cuban people with their rocket fire [...]'. (BNC G1R)
k. [Customer talking to a clerk about a coat.] 'You told me it it was guaranteed waterproof.' 'I didn't! I've never seen you before in my life!' [...] '*Figuratively speaking*, I meant. I bought it a few months ago and I was assured they were waterproof.' (BNC HGY)
l. [T]he superego [...] possesses the notable psychological property of being – *figuratively speaking* – partly soluble in alcohol! (BNC HTP)
m. Joan Daniels has now been appointed Honorary Treasurer of the Medau Society and we wish her the best of luck in balancing the books – *figuratively speaking*! (BNC KAE)

Here, we would expect to find not just metaphors but also other kinds of nonliteral language – which we do in almost all cases. The one exception is (12i), where the context (even enlarged beyond what is shown here) does not contain anything that could be a metaphor (it might be a metalinguistic use, indicating that the person called Tracey has been speaking figuratively). All other cases are clearly figurative: *a taste for excitement* in (12a) means 'an experience', instantiating the metaphor EXPERIENCE IS TASTE; *transport sb. across the world* in (12b) means 'make sb think of a distant location', instantiating the metaphor IMAGINARY DISTANCE IS PHYSICAL DISTANCE, *bulwark of society* in (12c) means 'defender of society', instantiating the metaphor DEFENSE IS A WALL, *give one's right arm to do sth* in (12d) means 'want sth very much', instantiating the metonymy BODY PART FOR PERSONAL VALUE; *be within arm's length* in (12e) means 'be in close proximity', instantiating the metonymy ARM'S LENGTH FOR SHORT DISTANCE; *make sth serve one's aims* in (12f) means 'put sth to use in achieving sth', instantiating the metaphor TO BE USED IS TO SERVE; *cash in* in (12g) means 'be successful', instantiating the metaphor LIFE IS COMMERCIAL TRANSACTION; *hold gun to sb's head* in (12h) means 'coerce sb to act', instantiating the metaphor POWER IS PHYSICAL FORCE; (12j) is from a speech by the Soviet head of state Nikita Khrushchev in which he uses *artillery* to refer metonymically about nuclear missiles; *you told me* in (12k) means 'your co-employee told me', instantiating the metonymy EMPLOYEE FOR COMPANY; *the superego is soluble in alcohol* in (12l) means 'self-control disappears when drunk ', instantiating the metaphor CHARACTER IS A PHYSICAL SUBSTANCE; *balance the books* in (12m) means 'make sure debits and credits match', instantiating the metaphor ABSTRACT ENTITIES ARE PHYSICAL ENTITIES.

We can now compare the literal and metaphorical contexts in which the expressions *technically speaking* and *metaphorically/figuraltively speaking* occur. If the latter are a metaphoricity signal, they should occur significantly more frequently in metaphorical contexts than the former. Table 11.12 shows the tabulated results from the discussion above, subsuming metaphors and metonymies under FIGURATIVE. The expected difference between contexts is clearly there, and statistically highly significant ($\chi^2 = 21.66, \text{df} = 1, p < 0.001, \phi = 0.7182$).

Table 11.12: Literal and figurative utterances containing the sentence adverbials *metaphorically/figuratively speaking* and *technically speaking* (BNC)

		SENTENCE ADVERBIAL		
		MET./FIG.	TECHNICALLY	Total
UTTERANCE	FIGURATIVE	18 (10.48)	4 (11.52)	22
	¬FIGURATIVE	2 (9.52)	18 (10.48)	20
	Total	20	22	42

Of course, the question remains, *why* some metaphors should be explicitly signaled while the majority is not. For example, we might suspect that metaphorical expressions are more likely to be explicitly signaled in contexts in which they might be interpreted literally. This may be the case for *put the boot in* in (11f), which occurs in a description of a rugby game where one could potentially misread it for a statement that someone was actually kicked. Alternatively (or additionally), a metaphor may be signaled explicitly if its specific phrasing is more likely to be used in literal contexts. This may be the case with *hold a gun to sb's head* in (12f): there are ten hits for this phrase in the BNC, only one of which is metaphorical. Again, which of these hypotheses (if any of them) is correct would have to be studied more systematically.

This case study found a clear effect where the authors of the study it is based on did not. This demonstrates the need to formulate specific predictions concerning the behavior of specific linguistic items in such a way that they can be tested systematically and the results be evaluated statistically. The study also shows that the area of metaphoricity signals is worthy of further investigation.

11.2.3.3 Case study: Metaphor and ideology

Regardless of whether metaphor is a rhetorical device (as has traditionally been assumed) or a cognitive device (as seems to be the majority view today), it is clear that it can serve an ideological function, allowing authors suggest a particular perspective on a given topic. Thus, an analysis of the metaphors used in texts manifesting a particular ideology should allow us to uncover those perspectives.

For example, Charteris-Black (2005) investigates a corpus of "right-wing communication and media reporting" on immigration, containing speeches, political manifestos and articles from the conservative newspapers Daily Mail and Daily Telegraph. He finds, among other things, that the metaphor "immigration is a flood" is used heavily, arguing that this allows the right to portray immigration as a disaster that must be contained, citing examples like *a flood of refugees, the tide of immigration*, and *the trickle of applicants has become a flood.*

Charteris-Black's findings are intriguing, but since he does not compare the findings from his corpus of right-wing materials to a neutral or a corresponding left-wing corpus, it remains an open question whether the use of these metaphors indicates a specifically right-wing perspective on immigration. Let us therefore replicate his analysis more systematically. The BNC contains 1 232 966 words from the Daily Telegraph (all files whose names begin with AH, AJ and AK), which will serve as our right-wing corpus, and 918 159 words from the Guardian (all files whose names begin with A8, A9 or AA, except file AAY), which will serve as our corresponding left-wing (or at least left-leaning) corpus. Since Charteris-Black's examples all involve reference to target-domain items such as *refugee* and *immigration*, a metaphorical pattern analysis (cf. Section 11.2.2 above) suggests itself. Figure 11.5 shows all concordance lines for the words *migrant(s)*, *immigrant(s)* and *refugee(s)* containing metaphorical patterns instantiating the metaphor "immigration is a mass of water".

In terms of absolute frequencies, there is no great difference between the two subcorpora (10 vs. 11), but the overall number of hits for the words in question differs drastically: there are 136 instances of these words in the Guardian subcorpus but only half as many (68) in the Telegraph subcorpus. This means that relatively speaking, in the domain of migration liquid metaphor are more frequent than expected in the Telegraph and less frequent than expected in the Guardian (see Table 11.13), which suggests that such metaphors are indeed typical of right-wing discourse. The difference just misses statistical significance, however, so a larger corpus would be required to corroborate the result ($\chi^2 = 3.822, \mathrm{df} = 1, p = 0.0506, \phi = 0.1369$).

This case study demonstrates that even general metaphors such as "immigration is a mass of water" may be associated with particular political ideologies. There is a large research literature on the role of metaphor in political discourse (see, for example, Koller 2004, Charteris-Black 2004, cf. also Musolff 2012), although at least part of this literature is not as systematic and quantitative as it

TELEGRAPH ($n = 68$)

```
Britain would be ` swamped with [[immigrants]] ' under a Labour Government
s country would be swamped with [[immigrants]] of every colour and race ,
support was due to the flood of [[migrants]] and would-be asylum seekers .
t increasing levels of economic [[migrants]] and asylum seekers entering B
nges to the constitution if the [[refugee]] influx was to be curbed . Herr
d open up Britain to a flood of [[immigrants]] and permit the rise of fasc
 the Gulf war and the influx of [[refugees]] from Afghanistan and Iraq . T
 for help to deal with flood of [[refugees]] By Philip Sherwell in Tuzla T
 Sherwell in Tuzla THE FLOOD of [[refugees]] fleeing the escalating confli
an militia groups . Most of the [[refugees]] flowing into Tuzla are escapi
gling to cope with the flood of [[refugees]] and have appealed to the inte
```

GUARDIAN ($n = 136$)

```
mirroring this year 's flood of [[refugees]] . Watched by a demonstration
litary security , migration and [[refugee]] flows on an vast scale . As We
 cope with the current surge of [[refugees]] , her Foreign Secretary , Mr
nd other aspects of large-scale [[immigrant]] absorption . The bureaucracy
he need to control an influx of [[immigrants]] . Rebel troops end siege of
control and manage the flows of [[migrants]] that wars , disasters , and ,
greed that the flow of economic [[migrants]] from Vietnam should be stoppe
e form of an influx of Romanian [[refugees]] . In one case in 1988 a Roman
control and manage the flows of [[migrants]] that wars , disasters , and ,
greed that the flow of economic [[migrants]] from Vietnam should be stoppe
```

Figure 11.5: Selected LIQUID metaphors with *migrant(s), immigrant(s),refugee(s)*

should be, so this remains a promising area of research). The case study also demonstrates the need to include a control sample in corpus-linguistic designs (in case that this still needed to be demonstrated at this point).

Table 11.13: Liquid patterns with the words *migrant(s)*, *immigrant(s)*, *refugee(s)*

		Newspaper		
		GUARDIAN	¬GUARDIAN	Total
Pattern	LIQUID MET.	10 (14.00)	11 (7.00)	21
	¬LIQUID MET.	126 (122.00)	57 (61.00)	183
	Table	136	68	204

11.2.4 Metonymy

11.2.4.1 Case study: Subjects of the verb *bomb*

This chapter was concerned with metaphor, but touched upon metonymy in Case Study 11.2.3.2. While metaphor and metonymy are different phenomena, they are related by virtue of the fact that both of them are cases of non-literal language, and they tend to be of interest to the same groups of researchers, so let us finish the chapter with a short case study of metonymy, if only to see to what extent the methods introduced above can be transferred to this phenomenon.

Following Lakoff & Johnson (1980: 35), metonymy is defined in a broad sense here as "using one entity to refer to another that is related to it" (this includes what is often called *synecdoche*, see Seto (1999) for critical discussion). Text book examples are the following from Lakoff & Johnson (1980: 35, 39):

(13) a. The ham sandwich is waiting for his check

b. Nixon bombed Hanoi.

In (13a), the metonym *ham sandwich* stands for the target expression 'the person who ordered the ham sandwich', in (13b) the metonym *Nixon* stands for the target expression 'the air-force pilots controlled by Nixon' (at least at first glance).

Thus, metonymy differs from metaphor in that it does not mix vocabulary from two domains, which has consequences for a transfer of the methods introduced for the study of metaphor in Section 11.1.

The source-domain oriented approach can be transferred relatively straightforwardly – we can query an item (or set of items) that we suspect may be used as metonyms then identify the actual metonymic uses. The main difficulty with this approach is choosing promising items for investigation. For example, the word *sandwich* occurs almost 900 times in the BNC, but unless I have overlooked one, it is not used as a metonym even once.

A straightforward analogue to the target-domain oriented approach (i.e., metaphorical pattern analysis) is more difficult to devise, as metonymies do not combine vocabulary from different semantic domains. One possibility would be to search for verbs that we know or suspect to be used with metonymic subjects and/or objects. For example, a Google search for ⟨`"is waiting for (his|her|their|the) check"`⟩ turns up about 20 unique hits; most of these have people as subjects and none of them have meals as subjects, but there are three cases that have *table* as subject, as in (14):

(14) Table 12 is waiting for their check. (articles.baltimoresun.com)

Let us focus on the *source-domain* oriented perspective here, and let us use the famous example sentence in (13) as a starting point, loosely replicating the study in Stefanowitsch (2015). According to Lakoff and Johnson, this sentence instantiates what they call the "controller for controlled" metonymy, i.e. *Nixon* would be a metonym for *the air force pilots controlled by Nixon.*[1] Thus, searching a corpus for sequences of a noun followed by the verb *bomb* should allow us to asses, for example, the importance of this metonymy in relation to other metonymies and literal uses.

Querying the BNC for ⟨`[pos=".*NN.*"] [lemma="bomb" & pos=".*VB.*"]`⟩ yields 31 hits referring to the dropping of bombs. Of these, only a single one has the ultimate decision maker as a subject (cf. 15a). Somewhat more frequent in subject position are countries or inhabitants of countries (5 cases) (cf. 15b, c). Even more frequently, the organization responsible for carrying out the bombing – e.g. an air force, or part of an air force – is chosen as the subject (9 cases) (cf. 15d, e). The most frequent case (14 hits) mentions the aircraft carrying the bombs in subject position, often accompanied by an adjective referring to the country whose military operates the planes (cf 15f) or some other responsible group (cf.

[1]Alternatively, as argued by Stallard (1993), it is the predicate rather than the subject that is used metonymically in this sentence, which would make this a metonym-oriented case study.

15g). Finally, there are two cases where the bombs themselves occupy the subject position (cf. 15h).

(15) a. Mussolini bombed and gassed the Abyssinians into subjection.
  b. On the day on which Iraq bombed Larak...
  c. Seven years after the Americans bombed Libya...
  d. [T]he school was blasted by an explosion, louder than anything heard there since the Luftwaffe bombed it in 1944.
  e. ...Germany, whose Condor Legion bombed the working classes in Guernica...
  f. ... on Jan. 24 French aircraft bombed Iraq for the first time ...
  g. ... Rebel jets bombed the Miraflores presidential palace ...
  h. ... Watching our bombs bomb your people ...

Cases with pronouns in subject position – resulting from the query ⟨ `[pos=".*PNP.*"] [lemma="bomb" & pos=".*VB.*"]` ⟩ – have a similar distribution, again, there is only one hit with a human controller in subject position. All hits (whether with pronouns, common nouns or proper names), interestingly, have metonymic subjects – i.e., not a single example has the bomber pilot in the subject position. This is unexpected, since literal uses should be more frequent than figurative uses (it leads Stefanowitsch (2015) to reject an analysis of such sentences as metonymies altogether). On the other hand, there are cases that are plausibly analyzed as metonymies here, such as examples (15d–e), which seem to instantiate a metonymy like MILITARY UNIT FOR MEMBER OF UNIT (i.e. WHOLE FOR PART) and (15f–h), which instantiate PLANE FOR PILOT (i.e. INSTRUMENT FOR CONTROLLER).

More systematic study of such metonymies by target domain could uncover more such facts as well as contributing to a general picture of how important particular metonymies are in a particular language.

This case study sketches a potential target-oriented approach to the corpus-based study of metonymy, along with some general questions that we might investigate using it (most obviously, the question of how central a given metonymy is in the language under investigation). Again, metonymy is a vastly under-researched area in corpus linguistics, so much work remains to be done.

12 Epilogue

In this book, I have focused on corpus linguistics as a methodology, more precisely, as an application of a general observational scientific procedure to large samples of linguistic usage. I have refrained from placing this method in a particular theoretical framework for two reasons.

The first reason is that I am not convinced that linguistics should be focusing quite as much on theoretical frameworks, but rather on linguistic description based on data. Edward Sapir famously said that "unfortunately, or luckily, no language is tyrannically consistent. All grammars leak" (Sapir 1921: 39). This is all the more true of formal models, which have a tendency to attempt to achieve tyrannical consistency by pretending those leaks do not exist or, if they do exist, are someone else's problem. To me, and to many others whose studies I discussed in this book, the ways grammars leak are simply more interesting than the formalisms that help us ignore these leaks.

The second reason is that I believe that corpus linguistics has a place in any theoretical linguistic framework, as long as that framework has some commitment to modeling linguistic reality. Obviously, the precise place, or rather, the distance from the data analyzed using this method and the consequences of this analysis for the model depend on the kind of linguistic reality that is being modeled. If it is language use, as it usually is in historically or sociolinguistically oriented studies, the distance is relatively short, requiring the researcher to discover the systematicity behind the usage patterns observed in the data. If it is the mental representation of language, the length of the distance depends on your assumptions about those representations.

Traditionally, those representations have been argued to be something fundamentally different from linguistic usage. It has been claimed that they are an ephemeral "competence" based on a "universal" grammar. There is disagreement as to the nature of this universal grammar – some claim that is a "mental organ" (Chomsky 1980), some imagine it as an evolved biological instinct (Pinker 1994). But all proponents of a universal grammar are certain that mental representations of language are dependent on and responsible for linguistic usage only in the most indirect ways imaginable, making corpora largely useless for the study of language. As I have argued in Chapters 1 and 2, the only methodological alternative to corpus data that proponents of this view offer – i.e. introspective grammaticality judgments – suffer from all the same problems as corpus data, without offering any of the advantages.

However, more recent models do not draw as strict a line between usage and mental representations. The *Usage-Based Model* (Langacker 1991) is a model of linguistic knowledge based on the assumption that speakers initially learn language as a set of unanalyzed chunks of various sizes ("established units"), from which they derive linguistic representations of varying degrees of abstractness and complexity based on formal and semantic correspondences across these units (cf. Langacker 1991: 266f). The *Emergent Grammar* model is based on similar assumptions but eschews abstractness altogether, viewing language as "built up out of combinations of [...] prefabricated parts", as "a kind of pastiche, pasted together in an improvised way out of ready-made elements" (Hopper 1987: 144).

In these models, the corpus becomes more than just a research tool, it becomes an integral part of a model of linguistic competence (cf. Stefanowitsch 2011). This view is most radically expressed in the notion of "lexical priming" developed in Hoey (2005), in which linguistic competence is seen as a mental concordance over linguistic experience:

> The notion of priming as here outlined assumes that the mind has a mental concordance of every word it has encountered, a concordance that has been richly glossed for social, physical, discoursal, generic and interpersonal context. This mental concordance is accessible and can be processed in much the same way that a computer concordance is, so that all kinds of patterns, including collocational patterns, are available for use. It simultaneously serves as a part, at least, of our knowledge base. (Hoey 2005: 11)

Obviously, this mental concordance would not correspond exactly to any concordance derived form an actual linguistic corpus. First, because – as discussed in Chapters 1 and 2 – no linguistic corpus captures the linguistic experience of a given individual speaker or the "average" speaker in a speech community; second, because the concordance that Hoey envisions is not a concordance of linguistic forms but of contextualized linguistic *signs* – it contains all the semantic and pragmatic information that corpus linguists have to reconstruct laboriously in their analyses. Still, an appropriately annotated concordance from a balanced corpus would be a reasonable operationalization of this mental concordance (cf. also Taylor 2012).

In less radical usage-based models of language, such as Langacker's, the corpus is not a model of linguistic competence – the latter is seen as a consequence of linguistic input perceived and organized by human minds with a particular structure (such as the capacity for figure-ground categorization). The corpus is, however, a reasonable model (or at least an operationalization) of this linguistic input. Many of the properties of language that guide the storage of units and the abstraction of schemas over these stored units can be derived from corpora – frequencies, associations between units of linguistic structure, distributions of these units across grammatical and textual contexts, the internal variability of these units, etc. (cf. Stefanowitsch & Flach 2016 for discussion).

This view is explicitly taken in language acquisition research conducted within the Usage-Based Model (e.g. Tomasello 2003, cf. also Dabrowska 2001, Diessel 2004), where children's expanding grammatical abilities, as reflected in their linguistic output, are investigated against the input they get from their caretakers as recorded in large corpora of caretaker-child interactions. The view of the corpus as a model of linguistic input is less explicit in the work of the major theoretical proponents of the Usage-Based Model, who connect the notion of usage to the notion of linguistic corpora only in theory. However, it is a view that offers a tremendous potential to bring together two broad strands of research – cognitive-functional linguistics (including some versions of construction grammar) and corpus linguistics (including attempts to build theoretical models on corpus data, such as pattern grammar (Hunston & Francis 2000) and Lexical Priming (Hoey 2005)). These strands have developed more or less independently and their proponents are sometimes mildly hostile toward each other over small but fundamental differences in perspective (see McEnery & Hardie 2012, Section 8.3 for discussion). If they could overcome these differences, they could complement each other in many ways, cognitive linguistics providing a more explicitly psychological framework than most corpus linguists adopt, and corpus linguistics providing a methodology that cognitive linguists serious about usage urgently need.

Finally, in usage-based models as well as in models of language in general, corpora can be treated as models (or operationalizations) of the typical linguistic output of the members of a speech community, i.e. the language produced based on their internalized linguistic knowledge. This is the least controversial view, and the one that I have essentially adopted throughout this book. Even under this view, corpus data remain one of the best sources of linguistic data we have – one that can only keep growing, providing us with ever deeper insights into the leaky, intricate, ever-changing signature activity of our species.

I hope this book has inspired you and I hope it will help you produce research that inspires all of us.

13 Study notes

Study notes to Chapter 1

Resources

1. The British National Corpus (BNC) is available for download free of charge from the Oxford Text Archive at http://ota.ox.ac.uk/desc/2554.

2. The Corpus of Contemporary American English (COCA) is commercially available from Mark Davies at Brigham-Young University, who also provides a free web interface at https://corpus.byu.edu/coca/.

Further reading

Although it may seem somewhat dated, one of the best discussions of what exactly "language" is or can be is Lyons (1981).

Study notes to Chapter 2

Resources

1. The Lancaster-Oslo-Bergen Corpus of Modern English (LOB) is available free of charge from the Oxford Text Archive at http://purl.ox.ac.uk/ota/0167.

2. The British National Corpus, Baby edition (BNC-BABY) is available for download free of charge from the Oxford Text Archive at http://purl.ox.ac.uk/ota/2553.

3. The London-Lund Corpus of Spoken English is available free of charge from the Oxford Text Archive at http://purl.ox.ac.uk/ota/0168.

4. The Susanne Corpus is available with some restrictions from the Oxford Text Archive at http://purl.ox.ac.uk/ota/1708.

5. Parts of the Santa Barbara Corpus of Spoken American English (SBC-SAE) are available for download and through a web interface at https://ca.talkbank.org/access/SBCSAE.html.

6. The International Corpus of English, British Component is commercially available from http://ice-corpora.net/ice/; the components for some other varieties (Canada, East Africa, Hong Kong, India, Ireland, Jamaica, Phillipines, Singapore and USA) can be downloaded at that URL after written registration.

7. The Brown University Standard Corpus of Present-Day American English (BROWN), the Freiburg-Brown Corpus of American English (FROWN), The Freiburg–LOB Corpus of British English (FLOB) and the WELLINGTON corpus are available to institutions participating in the CLARIN project at http://clarino.uib.no/korpuskel/.

8. A version of the BROWN corpus can also be downloaded at http://www.nltk.org/nltk_data/, but note that this is not the original version, and some texts are partially missing.

Further reading

Wynne (2005) is a brief but essential freely available introduction to all aspects of corpus development, including issues of annotation; Xiao (2008) is a compact overview of well-known English corpora.

Study notes to Chapter 3

Resources

- The Switchboard Corpus is available free of charge after written registration from the Linguistic Data Consorium, see https://catalog.ldc.upenn.edu/LDC97S62.

- WordNet is available for download free of charge from Princeton University at https://wordnet.princeton.edu.

- Many major dictionaries of English are currently searchable online free of charge. The following are recommended and used in this book:
  - Various Cambridge dictionaries, including the Cambridge Advanced Learners Dictionary (CALD), https://dictionary.cambridge.org

- The Collins Dictionary (fomerly Collins COBUILD Advanced Dictionary), https://www.collinsdictionary.com/
- Longman Dictionary of Contemporary English (LDCE), https://www.ldoceonline.com
- Merriam-Webster (MW), https://www.merriam-webster.com
- Various Oxford dictionaries, including the Oxford Advanced Learners Dictionary (OALD), https://www.oxfordlearnersdictionaries.com

Further reading

A readable exposition of Popper's ideas about falsification is his essay "Science as falsification", included in the collection *Conjectures and Refutations* (Popper 1963). A discussion of the role of operationalization in the context of corpus-based semantics is found in Stefanowitsch (2010), Wulff (2003) is a study of adjective order in English that operationalizes a variety of linguistic constructs in an exemplary and very transparent way. Zaenen et al. (2004) is an example of a detailed and extensive coding scheme for animacy.

Study notes to Chapter 4

Resources

1. The ICE-GB sample corpus is available at http://www.ucl.ac.uk/english-usage/projects/ice-gb/beta/index.htm.
2. The IMS Open Corpus Work Bench (CWB) is a available for download free of charge at http://cwb.sourceforge.net/, it can be installed under all unix-like operating systems (including Linux and Mac OS X).
3. The NoSketch Engine is available for download free of charge at https://nlp.fi.muni.cz/trac/noske for Linux.
4. The Tree Tagger is available for download at http://www.cis.uni-muenchen.de/~schmid/tools/TreeTagger/ for Linux, Mac OS X and Windows.

Further reading

No matter what corpora and concordancing software you work with, you will need regular expressions at some point. Information is easy to find online, I recommend the Wikipedia Page as a starting point (Wikipedia contributors 2018). An excellent introduction to issues involved in annotating corpora is found in Geoffrey Leech's contribution "Adding linguistic annotation" in Wynne (2005). An insightful case study on working with texts in non-standardized orthographies is found in Barnbrook (1996) (which is by now seriously dated in many respects, but still a worthwhile read).

Study notes to Chapter 5

(see Study notes to Chapter 6)

Study notes to Chapter 6

Resources

1. A comprehensive and well-maintained statistical software package is R, available for download free of charge from https://www.r-project.org/ for Linux, Mac OS X, Windows.

2. Especially if you are using Linux or Windows, I also recommend you download R Studio (also free of charge), which provides an advanced user interface to R, https://www.rstudio.com/products/rstudio/.

Further reading

Anyone serious about using statistics in their research should start with a basic introduction to statistics, and then proceed to an introduction of more advanced methods, preferably one that introduces a statistical software package at the same time. For the first step, I recommend Butler (1985), a very solid introduction to statistical concepts and pitfalls specifically aimed at linguists. It is out of print, but the author made it available for free at https://web.archive.org/web/20060523061748/http://uwe.ac.uk/hlss/llas/statistics-in-linguistics/bkindex.shtml. For the second step, I recommend Gries (2013) as a package deal geared specifically towards linguistic research questions, but I also encourage you to explore the wide range of free or commercially available books introducing statistics with R.

Study notes to Chapter 7

If you want to learn more about association measures, Evert (2005) and the companion website at http://www.collocations.de/AM/ are very comprehensive and relatively accessible places to start. Stefanowitsch & Flach (2016) discuss corpus-based association measures in the context of psycholinguistics.

Study notes to Chapter 8

Resources

The Corpus of Late Modern English Texts (CLMET v3.1) is available for download free of charge at https://fedora.clarin-d.uni-saarland.de/clmet/clmet.html.

Further reading

Grammar is a complex phenomenon investigated from very different perspectives. This makes general suggestions for further reading difficult. It may be best to start with collections focusing on the corpus-based analysis of grammar, such as Rohdenburg & Mondorf (2003), Gries & Stefanowitsch (2006), Rohdenburg & Schlüter (2009) or Lindquist & Mair (2004).

Study notes to Chapter 9

Further reading

For a different proposal of how to *evaluate TTRs statistically*, see Baayen (2008: Section 6.5); for a very interesting method of comparison for TTRs and HTRs based on permutation testing instead of classical inferential statistics see Säily & Suomela (2009).

Study notes to Chapter 10

Resources

1. The Corpus of Historical American English (COHA) is commercially available from Mark Davies at Brigham-Young University, who also provides a free web interface at https://corpus.byu.edu/coha/.

2. The *n*-gram data from the Google Books archive is available for download free of charge at http://storage.googleapis.com/books/ngrams/books/datasetsv2.html (note that the files are extremely large).

Further reading

This chapter has focused on very simple aspects of variation across text types and a very simple notion of "text type". Biber (1988) and Biber (1989) are good starting points for a more comprehensive corpus-based perspective on text types. As seen in some of the case studies in this chapter, *text* is frequently a proxy for demographic properties of the speakers who have produced it, making corpus linguistics a variant of sociolinguistics, see further Baker (2010a).

Study notes to Chapter 11

Further reading

Deignan (2005) is a comprehensive attempt to apply corpus-linguistic methods to a range of theoretically informed research questions concerning metaphor. The contributions in Stefanowitsch & Gries (2006) demonstrate a range of methodological approaches by many leading researchers applying corpus methods to the investigation of metaphor.

14 Statistical tables

14.1 Critical values for the chi-square test

1. Find the appropriate row for the degrees of freedom of your data.

2. Find the most rightward column listing a value smaller than the chi-square value you have calculated. At the top, it will tell you the corresponding probability of error.

Significance levels (probabilities of error)											
0.25	0.1	0.09	0.08	0.07	0.06	0.05	0.04	0.03	0.02	0.01	0.001
not sig.	"marginally" significant					sig.				very sig.	highly sig.
1.32	2.71	2.87	3.06	3.28	3.54	3.84	4.22	4.71	5.41	6.63	10.83
2.77	4.61	4.82	5.05	5.32	5.63	5.99	6.44	7.01	7.82	9.21	13.82
4.11	6.25	6.49	6.76	7.06	7.41	7.81	8.31	8.95	9.84	11.34	16.27
5.39	7.78	8.04	8.34	8.67	9.04	9.49	10.03	10.71	11.67	13.28	18.47
6.63	9.24	9.52	9.84	10.19	10.60	11.07	11.64	12.37	13.39	15.09	20.52
7.84	10.64	10.95	11.28	11.66	12.09	12.59	13.20	13.97	15.03	16.81	22.46
9.04	12.02	12.34	12.69	13.09	13.54	14.07	14.70	15.51	16.62	18.48	24.32
10.22	13.36	13.70	14.07	14.48	14.96	15.51	16.17	17.01	18.17	20.09	26.12
11.39	14.68	15.03	15.42	15.85	16.35	16.92	17.61	18.48	19.68	21.67	27.88
12.55	15.99	16.35	16.75	17.20	17.71	18.31	19.02	19.92	21.16	23.21	29.59
13.70	17.28	17.65	18.07	18.53	19.06	19.68	20.41	21.34	22.62	24.73	31.26
14.85	18.55	18.94	19.37	19.85	20.39	21.03	21.79	22.74	24.05	26.22	32.91
15.98	19.81	20.21	20.66	21.15	21.71	22.36	23.14	24.12	25.47	27.69	34.53
17.12	21.06	21.48	21.93	22.44	23.02	23.68	24.49	25.49	26.87	29.14	36.12
18.25	22.31	22.73	23.20	23.72	24.31	25.00	25.82	26.85	28.26	30.58	37.70
19.37	23.54	23.98	24.46	24.99	25.60	26.30	27.14	28.19	29.63	32.00	39.25
20.49	24.77	25.22	25.71	26.25	26.87	27.59	28.45	29.52	31.00	33.41	40.79
21.60	25.99	26.45	26.95	27.50	28.14	28.87	29.75	30.84	32.35	34.81	42.31
22.72	27.20	27.67	28.18	28.75	29.40	30.14	31.04	32.16	33.69	36.19	43.82
23.83	28.41	28.89	29.41	29.99	30.65	31.41	32.32	33.46	35.02	37.57	45.31

14.2 Chi-square table for multiple tests with one degree of freedom

1. Find the appropriate row for the number of tests you have performed (e.g., the number of cells in your table if you are checking individual chi-square components post hoc).

2. Find the most rightward column listing a value smaller than the chi-square value you have calculated. At the top, it will tell you the corresponding probability of error.

No. of Tests	Critical values			
	0.1	0.05	0.01	0.001
1	2.7055	3.8415	6.6349	10.8276
2	3.8415	5.0239	7.8794	12.1157
3	4.5286	5.7311	8.6154	12.8731
4	5.0239	6.2385	9.1406	13.4121
5	5.4119	6.6349	9.5495	13.8311
6	5.7311	6.9604	9.8846	14.1739
7	6.0025	7.2367	10.1685	14.4641
8	6.2385	7.4768	10.4149	14.7157
9	6.4475	7.6891	10.6326	14.9379
10	6.6349	7.8794	10.8276	15.1367
11	6.8049	8.0520	11.0041	15.3167
12	6.9604	8.2097	11.1655	15.4811
13	7.1037	8.3551	11.3140	15.6325
14	7.2367	8.4898	11.4517	15.7726
15	7.3607	8.6154	11.5800	15.9032
16	7.4768	8.7330	11.7000	16.0254
17	7.5860	8.8436	11.8128	16.1402
18	7.6891	8.9480	11.9193	16.2484
19	7.7867	9.0468	12.0200	16.3509
20	7.8794	9.1406	12.1157	16.4481

14.3 Critical values for the Mann-Whitney-Text

There are three tables, one for $p < 0.05$, one for $p < 0.01$ and one for $p < 0.001$ (all for two-tailed tests).

- Starting with the first table, perform the following steps.
  - Find the smaller one of your sample sizes in the rows labelled m and the larger of your sample sizes in the columns labelled n.
  - Find the cell at the intersection of the row and the column.
  - If your U value is smaller than or equal to the value in this cell, your result is significant at the level given above the table.
- Repeat the three steps with the second table. If your U value is larger than the value in the appropriate cell, stop and report a significance level of 0.05. If it is smaller or equal to the value in the appropriate cell, go to 3.
- Repeat the three steps with the third table. If your U value is larger than the value in the appropriate cell, report a significance level of 0.01. If it is smaller or equal to the value in the appropriate cell, report a significance level of 0.001.

Critical Values for the Two-Sided Mann-Whitney Test ($p < 0.05$)

	n																								
	1	2	3	4	5	6	7	8	9	10	11	12	13	14	15	16	17	18	19	20	21	22	23	24	25
m 1																									
2								0	0	0	0	1	1	1	1	1	2	2	2	2	3	3	3	3	3
3					0	1	1	2	2	3	3	4	4	5	5	6	6	7	7	8	8	9	9	10	10
4				0	1	2	3	4	4	5	6	7	8	9	10	11	11	12	13	14	15	16	17	17	18
5					2	3	5	6	7	8	9	11	12	13	14	15	17	18	19	20	22	23	24	25	27
6						5	6	8	10	11	13	14	16	17	19	21	22	24	25	27	29	30	32	33	35
7							8	10	12	14	16	18	20	22	24	26	28	30	32	34	36	38	40	42	44
8								13	15	17	19	22	24	26	29	31	34	36	38	41	43	45	48	50	53
9									17	20	23	26	28	31	34	37	39	42	45	48	50	53	56	59	62
10										23	26	29	33	36	39	42	45	48	52	55	58	61	64	67	71
11											30	33	37	40	44	47	51	55	58	62	65	69	73	76	80
12												37	41	45	49	53	57	61	65	69	73	77	81	85	89
13													45	50	54	59	63	67	72	76	80	85	89	94	98
14														55	59	64	69	74	78	83	88	93	98	102	107
15															64	70	75	80	85	90	96	101	106	111	117
16																75	81	86	92	98	103	109	115	120	126
17																	87	93	99	105	111	117	123	129	135
18																		99	106	112	119	125	132	138	145
19																			113	119	126	133	140	147	154
20																				127	134	141	149	156	163
21																					142	150	157	165	173
22																						158	166	174	182
23																							175	183	192
24																								192	201
25																									211

Critical Values for the Two-Sided Mann-Whitney Test ($p < 0.01$)

	n 1	2	3	4	5	6	7	8	9	10	11	12	13	14	15	16	17	18	19	20	21	22	23	24	25
1																									
2																			0	0	0	0	0	0	0
3									0	0	0	1	1	1	2	2	2	2	3	3	3	4	4	4	5
4						0	0	1	1	2	2	3	3	4	5	5	6	6	7	8	8	9	9	10	10
5					0	1	1	2	3	4	5	6	7	7	8	9	10	11	12	13	14	14	15	16	17
6						2	3	4	5	6	7	9	10	11	12	13	15	16	17	18	19	21	22	23	24
7							4	6	7	9	10	12	13	15	16	18	19	21	22	24	25	27	29	30	32
8								7	9	11	13	15	17	18	20	22	24	26	28	30	32	34	35	37	39
9									11	13	16	18	20	22	24	27	29	31	33	36	38	40	43	45	47
10										16	18	21	24	26	29	31	34	37	39	42	44	47	50	52	55
11											21	24	27	30	33	36	39	42	45	48	51	54	57	60	63
12												27	31	34	37	41	44	47	51	54	58	61	64	68	71
13													34	38	42	45	49	53	57	60	64	68	72	75	79
14														42	46	50	54	58	63	67	71	75	79	83	87
15															51	55	60	64	69	73	78	82	87	91	96
16																60	65	70	74	79	84	89	94	99	104
17																	70	75	81	86	91	96	102	107	112
18																		81	87	92	98	104	109	115	121
19																			93	99	105	111	117	123	129
20																				105	112	118	125	131	138
21																					118	125	132	139	146
22																						133	140	147	155
23																							148	155	163
24																								164	172
25																									180

Critical Values for the Two-Sided Mann-Whitney Test ($p < 0.001$)

		n 1	2	3	4	5	6	7	8	9	10	11	12	13	14	15	16	17	18	19	20	21	22	23	24	25
m	1																									
	2																									
	3																					0	0	0	0	0
	4													0	0	0	1	1	1	2	2	2	3	3	3	3
	5									0	0	1	1	2	2	3	3	4	4	5	5	6	6	7	7	8
	6								0	1	2	2	3	4	5	5	6	7	8	8	9	10	11	12	12	13
	7							0	1	2	3	4	5	6	7	8	9	10	11	13	14	15	16	17	18	19
	8								2	4	5	6	7	9	10	11	13	14	15	17	18	20	21	22	24	25
	9									5	7	8	10	11	13	15	16	18	20	21	23	25	26	28	30	32
	10										8	10	12	14	16	18	20	22	24	26	28	30	32	34	36	38
	11											12	15	17	19	21	24	26	28	31	33	35	38	40	42	45
	12												17	20	22	25	27	30	33	35	38	41	44	46	49	52
	13													23	25	28	31	34	37	40	43	46	49	52	56	59
	14														29	32	35	39	42	45	49	52	55	59	62	66
	15															36	39	43	46	50	54	58	61	65	69	73
	16																43	47	51	55	59	63	67	72	76	80
	17																	51	56	60	65	69	74	78	83	87
	18																		61	65	70	75	80	85	89	94
	19																			70	76	81	86	91	96	102
	20																				81	87	92	98	103	109
	21																					93	98	104	110	116
	22																						105	111	117	124
	23																							118	124	131
	24																								132	139
	25																									146

14.4 Critical values for Welch's t-Test

These are the critical values for a two-tailed t-test. For a one-tailed t-test, divide the significance levels by two (i.e., the values in the column for a level of 0.1 in a two-tailed test correspond to the level of 0.05 in a one-tailed test, etc.)

1. Find the appropriate row for the degrees of freedom of your test.
2. Find the most rightward column whose value is smaller than your t-value. At the top of the column you will find the p-value you should report.

df	0.10	0.05	0.01	0.00	df	0.10	0.05	0.01	0.00
1	6.31	12.71	63.66	636.62	21	1.72	2.08	2.83	3.82
2	2.92	4.30	9.22	31.60	35	1.69	2.03	2.72	3.59
3	2.35	3.18	5.84	12.92	40	1.68	2.02	2.70	3.55
4	2.13	2.78	4.60	8.61	45	1.68	2.01	2.69	3.52
5	2.02	2.57	4.03	6.87	50	1.68	2.01	2.68	3.50
6	1.94	2.45	3.71	5.96	55	1.67	2.00	2.67	3.48
7	1.90	2.37	3.50	5.41	60	1.67	2.00	2.66	3.46
8	1.86	2.31	3.36	5.04	65	1.67	2.00	2.65	3.45
9	1.83	2.26	3.25	4.78	70	1.67	1.99	2.65	3.44
10	1.81	2.23	3.17	4.59	75	1.67	1.99	2.64	3.43
11	1.80	2.20	3.11	4.44	80	1.66	1.99	2.64	3.42
12	1.78	2.18	3.06	4.32	85	1.66	1.99	2.64	3.41
13	1.77	2.16	3.01	4.22	90	1.66	1.99	2.63	3.40
14	1.76	2.15	2.98	4.14	95	1.66	1.99	2.63	3.40
15	1.75	2.13	2.95	4.07	100	1.66	1.98	2.63	3.39
16	1.75	2.12	2.92	4.02	200	1.65	1.97	2.60	3.34
17	1.74	2.11	2.90	3.97	500	1.65	1.97	2.59	3.31
18	1.73	2.10	2.88	3.92	1000	1.65	1.96	2.58	3.30
19	1.73	2.09	2.86	3.88	Inf	1.65	1.96	2.58	3.30
20	1.73	2.09	2.85	3.85					
22	1.72	2.07	2.82	3.79					
23	1.71	2.07	2.81	3.77					
24	1.71	2.06	2.80	3.75					
25	1.71	2.06	2.79	3.73					
26	1.71	2.06	2.78	3.71					
27	1.70	2.05	2.77	3.69					
28	1.70	2.05	2.76	3.67					
29	1.70	2.05	2.76	3.66					
30	1.70	2.04	2.75	3.65					

References

Altenberg, Bengt. 1980. Binominal NP's in a thematic perspective: Genitive vs. of–constructions in 17th century English. In Sven Jacobsen (ed.), *Papers from the Scandinavian Symposium on Syntactic Variation* (Stockholm Studies in English 52), 149–172. Stockholm: Almqvist & Wiksell.

APA, American Psychiatric Association. 2000. *Diagnostic and statistical manual of mental disorders: DSM-IV-TR*. 4th ed., text revision. Washington, DC: American Psychiatric Association.

Aston, Guy & Lou Burnard. 1998. *The BNC handbook: Exploring the British National Corpus with SARA*. Edinburgh: Edinburgh University Press.

Baayen, Harald. 2008. *Analyzing linguistic data: A practical introduction*. Cambridge & New York: Cambridge University Press.

Baayen, Harald. 2009. Corpus linguistics in morphology: Morphological productivity. In Anke Lüdeling & Merja Kytö (eds.), *Corpus linguistics: An international handbook*, vol. 2 (Handbooks of Linguistics and Communication Science 29), 899–919. Berlin & New York: De Gruyter Mouton.

Baker, Carolyn D. & Peter Freebody. 1989. *Children's first school books: Introductions to the culture of literacy*. Oxford & Cambridge, MA: Blackwell.

Baker, Paul. 2010a. *Sociolinguistics and corpus linguistics* (Edinburgh sociolinguistics). Edinburgh: Edinburgh University Press.

Baker, Paul. 2010b. Will Ms ever be as frequent as Mr? A corpus-based comparison of gendered terms across four diachronic corpora of British English. *Gender and Language* 4(1). 125–149. DOI:10.1558/genl.v4i1.125

Barcelona Sánchez, Antonio. 1995. Metaphorical models of romantic love in Romeo and Juliet. *Journal of Pragmatics* 24(6). 667–688. DOI:10.1016/0378-2166(95)00007-F

Barnbrook, Geoff. 1996. *Language and computers: A practical introduction to the computer analysis of language* (Edinburgh textbooks in empirical linguistics). Edinburgh: Edinburgh University Press.

Batygin, Konstantin & Michael E. Brown. 2016. Evidence for a distant giant planet in the solar system. *The Astronomical Journal* 151(2). 22. DOI:10.3847/0004-6256/151/2/22

Bender, Emily M. 2005. On the boundaries of linguistic competence: Matched-guise experiments as evidence of knowledge of grammar. *Lingua* 115(11). 1579–1598. DOI:10.1016/j.lingua.2004.07.005

Berlage, Eva. 2009. Prepositions and postpositions. In Günter Rohdenburg & Julia Schlüter (eds.), *One language, two grammars?*, 130–148. Cambridge: Cambridge University Press.

Berman, Ruth Aronson & Dan Isaac Slobin (eds.). 1994. *Relating events in narrative: A crosslinguistic developmental study.* Hillsdale, NJ: Lawrence Erlbaum Associates.

Biber, Douglas. 1988. *Variation across speech and writing.* Cambridge & New York: Cambridge University Press.

Biber, Douglas. 1989. A typology of English texts. *Linguistics* 27(1). 3–44. DOI:10.1515/ling.1989.27.1.3

Biber, Douglas. 1993. Representativeness in corpus design. *Literary and Linguistic Computing* 8(4). 243–257. DOI:10.1093/llc/8.4.243

Biber, Douglas. 2006. *University language: A corpus-based study of spoken and written registers* (Studies in corpus linguistics 23). Amsterdam & Philadelphia: John Benjamins. OCLC: ocm65978719.

Biber, Douglas, Susan Conrad & Randi Reppen. 1998. *Corpus linguistics: Investigating language structure and use.* Cambridge & New York: Cambridge University Press.

Biber, Douglas, Stig Johansson, Geoffrey N. Leech, Susan Conrad & Edward Finegan. 1999. *Longman grammar of spoken and written English.* Harlow: Longman.

Biber, Douglas & Randy Reppen. 2015. *The Cambridge handbook of English corpus linguistics* (Cambridge Handbooks in Language and Linguistics). Cambridge & New York: Cambridge University Press.

Bock, J.Kathryn. 1986. Syntactic persistence in language production. *Cognitive Psychology* 18(3). 355–387. DOI:10.1016/0010-0285(86)90004-6

Bondi, Marina & Mike Scott (eds.). 2010. *Keyness in texts* (Studies in corpus linguistics 41). Amsterdam & Philadelphia: John Benjamins.

Borkin, Ann. 1973. To be and not to be. In Claudia Corum, T. Cedrik Smith-Stark & Ann Weiser (eds.), *Papers from the ninth regional meeting of the Chicago Linguistics Society*, vol. 9, 44–56. Chicago: Chicago Linguistic Society.

Butler, Christopher. 1985. *Statistics in linguistics.* Oxford & New York: Blackwell.

Caldas-Coulthard, Carmen Rosa. 1993. From discourse analysis to Critical Discourse Analysis: The differential re-presentation of women and men speaking in written news. In John McHardy Sinclair, Michael Hoey & Gwyneth Fox (eds.), *Techniques of description: Spoken and written discourse*, 196–208. London: Routledge.

Caldas-Coulthard, Carmen Rosa & Rosemary Moon. 2010. 'Curvy, hunky, kinky': Using corpora as tools for critical analysis. *Discourse & Society* 21(2). 99–133. DOI:10.1177/0957926509353843

Charles, Walter G. & George A. Miller. 1989. Contexts of antonymous adjectives. *Applied Psycholinguistics* 10(03). 357. DOI:10.1017/S0142716400008675

Charteris-Black, Jonathan. 2004. *Corpus approaches to critical metaphor analysis.* Houndmills & New York: Palgrave Macmillan.

Charteris-Black, Jonathan. 2005. *Politicians and rhetoric: The persuasive power of metaphor.* Houndmills & New York: Palgrave Macmillan.

Charteris-Black, Jonathan. 2006. Britain as a container: Immigration metaphors in the 2005 election campaign. *Discourse & Society* 17(5). 563–581. DOI:10.1177/0957926506066345

Chen, Ping. 1986. Discourse and particle movement in English. *Studies in Language* 10(1). 79–95. DOI:10.1075/sl.10.1.05che

Cheng, Winnie. 2012. *Exploring corpus linguistics: Language in action.* London & New York: Routledge.

Chomsky, Noam. 1957. *Syntactic structures.* The Hague: Mouton.

Chomsky, Noam. 1964. [The development of grammar in child language]: Discussion. *Monographs of the Society for Research in Child Development* 29(1). 35–42. DOI:10.2307/1165753

Chomsky, Noam. 1972. *Language and mind.* Second edition. New York: Harcourt Brace Jovanovich.

Chomsky, Noam. 1980. *Rules and representations.* New York: Columbia University Press.

Christmann, Ursula, Christoph Mischo & Norbert Groeben. 2000. Components of the evaluation of integrity violations in argumentative discussions: Relevant factors and their relationships. *Journal of Language and Social Psychology* 19(3). 315–341. DOI:10.1177/0261927X00019003003

Church, Kenneth Ward, William Gale, Patrick Hanks & Donald Hindle. 1991. Using statistics in lexical analysis. In Uri Zernik (ed.), *Lexical acquisition: Exploiting on-line resources to build a lexicon*, 115–164. Hillsdale, NJ: Lawrence Erlbaum Associates.

Church, Kenneth Ward & Patrick Hanks. 1990. Word association norms, mutual information, and lexicography. *Computational Linguistics* 16(1). 22–29.

Cohen, Jacob. 1960. A coefficient of agreement for nominal scales. *Educational and Psychological Measurement* 20(1). 37–46.

Colleman, Timothy. 2006. *De Nederlandse datiefalternantie: Een constructioneel en corpusgebaseerd onderzoek.* Ghent: Ghent University. (Ph.D. thesis).

Colleman, Timothy. 2009. Verb disposition in argument structure alternations: A corpus study of the dative alternation in Dutch. *Language Sciences* 31(5). 593–611. DOI:10.1016/j.langsci.2008.01.001

Colleman, Timothy & Bernard De Clerck. 2011. Constructional semantics on the move: On semantic specialization in the English double object construction. *Cognitive Linguistics* 22(1). 387–410. DOI:10.1515/cogl.2011.008

Cook, Guy. 2003. *Applied linguistics* (Oxford introductions to language study). Oxford: Oxford University Press. OCLC: 838881088.

Cooper, William E. & John R. Ross. 1975. Word order. In Robin Grossman, L.J. San & Timothy J. Vance (eds.), *Papers from the Parasession on Functionalism*, 63–111. Chicago, IL: Chicago Linguistic Society.

Corley, Martin & Oliver W. Stewart. 2008. Hesitation disfluencies in spontaneous speech: The meaning of *um*. *Language and Linguistics Compass* 2(4). 589–602. DOI:10.1111/j.1749-818X.2008.00068.x

Cowart, Wayne. 1997. *Experimental syntax: Applying objective methods to sentence judgements*. Thousand Oaks, CA: Sage.

Culicover, Peter W. 1999. *Syntactic nuts: Hard cases, syntactic theory, and language acquisition* (Foundations of syntax 1). Oxford & New York: Oxford University Press.

Cutler, Anne, Jacques Mehler, Dennis Norris & Juan Segui. 1986. The syllable's differing role in the segmentation of French and English. *Journal of Memory and Language* 25(4). 385–400. DOI:10.1016/0749-596X(86)90033-1

Dabrowska, Ewa. 2001. From formula to schema: The acquisition of English questions. *Cognitive Linguistics* 11(1-2). 83–102. DOI:10.1515/cogl.2001.013

Dalton-Puffer, Christiane. 1996. *The French influence on Middle English morphology a corpus-based study of derivation*. Berlin & New York: Mouton de Gruyter.

Deane, Paul. 1987. English possessives, topicality, and the Silverstein Hierarchy. In Jon Aske, Natasha Beery, Laura Michaelis & Hana Filip (eds.), *Proceedings of the Annual Meeting of the Berkeley Linguistics Society: General Session and Parasession on Grammar and Cognition*, vol. 13, 65–76. Berkeley: Berkeley Linguistics Society.

Deignan, Alice. 1999a. Corpus-based research into metaphor. In Graham Low & Lynne Cameron (eds.), *Researching and applying metaphor*, 177–199. Cambridge: Cambridge University Press.

Deignan, Alice. 1999b. Metaphorical polysemy and paradigmatic relations: A corpus study. *Word* 50(3). 319–338. DOI:10.1080/00437956.1999.11432491

Deignan, Alice. 2005. *Metaphor and corpus linguistics* (Converging evidence in language and communication research 6). Amsterdam & Philadelphia: John Benjamins.

Deignan, Alice. 2006. The grammar of linguistic metaphors. In Anatol Stefanowitsch & Stefan Th. Gries (eds.), *Corpus-based approaches to metaphor and metonymy* (Trends in Linguistics. Studies and Monographs [TiLSM]), 106–122. Berlin & New York: Mouton de Gruyter. DOI:10.1515/9783110199895.106

Dewey, John. 1910. *How we think.* Boston, MA: D. C. Heath & Company.

Diessel, Holger. 2004. *The acquisition of complex sentences* (Cambridge studies in linguistics 105). Cambridge & New York: Cambridge University Press.

Díaz-Vera, Javier E. 2015. Love in the time of the corpora: Preferential conceptualizations of love in world Englishes. In Vito Pirrelli, Claudia Marzi & Marcello Ferro (eds.), *Word structure and word usage*, 161–165. Pisa: CEUR Workshop Procedings.

Díaz-Vera, Javier E. & Rosario Caballero. 2013. Exploring the feeling-emotions continuum across cultures: Jealousy in English and Spanish. *Intercultural Pragmatics* 10(2). 265–294. DOI:10.1515/ip-2013-0012

Dunning, Ted. 1993. Accurate methods for the statistics of surprise and soincidence. *Computational Linguistics* 19(1). 61–74.

Emons, Rudolf. 1997. Corpus linguistics: some basic problems. *Studia Anglica Posnaniensia* XXXIL. 61–68.

Ericsson, Göran. & Thomas A. Heberlein. 2002. "Jägare talar naturens språk" (Hunters speak nature's language): A comparison of outdoor activities and attitudes toward wildlife among Swedish hunters and the general public. *Zeitschrift für Jagdwissenschaft* 48(S1). 301–308. DOI:10.1007/BF02192422

Evert, Stefan. 2005. *The statistics of word cooccurrences: Word pairs and collocations.* Stuttgart: Institut für maschinelle Sprachverarbeitung, University of Stuttgart. (Ph.D. thesis). http://elib.uni-stuttgart.de/opus/volltexte/2005/2371/.

Evert, Stefan & Andrew Hardie. 2011. Twenty-first century Corpus Workbench: Updating a query architecture for the new millennium. In *Proceedings of the Corpus Linguistics 2011 Conference.* Birmingham: University of Birmingham.

Fellbaum, Christiane. 1995. Co-occurrence and antonymy. *International Journal of Lexicography* 8(4). 281–303. DOI:10.1093/ijl/8.4.281

Fellbaum, Christiane. 1998. *WordNet: an electronic lexical database.* Cambridge, MA: The MIT Press.

Fillmore, Charles. 1992. "Corpus linguistics" or "computer-aided armchair linguistics". In Jan Svartvik (ed.), *Directions in corpus linguistics: Proceedings of Nobel Symposium 82, Stockholm, 4–8 August 1991* (Trends in Linguistics. Studies and Monographs 65), 35–60. Berlin & New York: Mouton de Gruyter.

Firth, John Rupert. 1957. *Papers in Linguistics 1934–1951.* London: Oxford University Press.

Fite, Edward C. 1979. *Residues of lead, mercury, and organochlorine pesticides in whistling swans, 1973.* Missoula, MT: University of Montana. (MA thesis).

Fleiss, Joseph L. 1971. Measuring nominal scale agreement among many raters. *Psychological Bulletin* 76(5). 378–382.

Francis, Gill, Susan Hunston & Elisabeth Manning. 1996. *Collins Cobuild Grammar Patterns 1: Verbs.* London: HarperCollins.

Francis, Gill, Susan Hunston & Elizabeth Manning. 1998. *Collins Cobuild Grammar Patterns 2: Nouns and Adjectives.* London: HarperCollins.

Francis, W. Nelson & Henry Kučera. 1979. *Manual of information to accompany A Standard Corpus of Present-Day Edited American English, for use with Digital Computers.* 3rd edition. Providence, RI: Brown University.

Franz, Alex & Thorsten Brants. 2006. *All our n-gram are belong to you.* Blog. https://research.googleblog.com/2006/08/all-our-n-gram-are-belong-to-you.html.

Fromkin, Victoria. 1973. *Speech errors as linguistic evidence.* The Hague: Mouton.

Fromkin, Victoria (ed.). 1980. *Errors in linguistic performance: Slips of the tongue, ear, pen, and hand.* San Francisco: Academic Press.

Fujioka, Noriko & John J. Kennedy. 1997. *The views of non-native speakers of Japanese toward error treatment in Japanese introductory college classes.* Research report. Chicago, IL.

Garretson, Gregory. 2004. Coding practices used in the project Optimal Typology of Determiner Phrases. Boston, MA.

Georgila, Kallirroi, Maria Wolters, Johanna D. Moore & Robert H. Logie. 2010. The MATCH corpus: A corpus of older and younger users' interactions with spoken dialogue systems. *Language Resources and Evaluation* 44(3). 221–261. DOI:10.1007/s10579-010-9118-8

Gesuato, Sara. 2003. The company women and men keep: What collocations can reveal about culture. In *Proceedings of the 2002 Corpus Linguistics Conference* (UCREL Technical Paper 16), 253–262. Lancaster: UCREL.

Gilquin, Gaëtanelle & Sylvie De Cock. 2011. Errors and disfluencies in spoken corpora: Setting the scene. *International Journal of Corpus Linguistics* 16(2). 141–172. DOI:10.1075/ijcl.16.2.01gil

Givón, Talmy. 1983. *Topic continuity in discourse a quantitative cross-language study.* Amsterdam & Philadelphia: John Benjamins.

Givón, Talmy. 1992. The grammar of referential coherence as mental processing instructions. *Linguistics* 30(1). 5–56. DOI:10.1515/ling.1992.30.1.5

Goddard, Cliff. 1998. *Semantic analysis: A practical introduction* (Oxford textbooks in linguistics). Oxford & New York: Oxford University Press.

Goldberg, Adele E. 1995. *Constructions: A construction grammar approach to argument structure* (Cognitive theory of language and culture). Chicago: The University of Chicago Press.

Goschler, Juliana, Till Woerfel, Anatol Stefanowitsch, Heike Wiese & Christoph Schroeder. 2013. Beyond conflation patterns: The encoding of motion events in Kiezdeutsch. *Yearbook of the German Cognitive Linguistics Association* 1(1). 237–254. DOI:10.1515/gcla-2013-0013

Grafmiller, Jason. 2014. Variation in English genitives across modality and genres. *English Language and Linguistics* 18(03). 471–496. DOI:10.1017/S1360674314000136

Green, Lisa J. 2002. *African American English: A linguistic introduction.* Cambridge & New York: Cambridge University Press.

Greenberg, Steven, Hannah Carvey, Leah Hitchcock & Shuangyu Chang. 2003. Temporal properties of spontaneous speech: A syllable-centric perspective. *Journal of Phonetics* 31(3-4). 465–485. DOI:10.1016/j.wocn.2003.09.005

Greenberg, Steven, Joy Hollenback & Dan Ellis. 1996. Insights into spoken language gleaned from phonetic transcription of the Switchboard corpus. In *Proceedings of the Fourth International Conference on Spoken Language Processing*, vol. 1, 32–35. Philadelphia.

Gries, Stefan Th. 2001. A corpus-linguistic analysis of English *-ic* vs. *-ical* adjectives. *ICAME Journal* 25. 65–108.

Gries, Stefan Th. 2002. Evidence in Linguistics: Three approaches to genitives in English. In Ruth M. Brend & William J. Sullivan (eds.), *LACUS Forum XXVIII: What constitutes evidence in linguistics?*, 17–31. Fullerton, CA: LACUS.

Gries, Stefan Th. 2003a. *Multifactorial analysis in corpus linguistics: A study of particle placement* (Open linguistics series). New York: Continuum.

Gries, Stefan Th. 2003b. Testing the sub-test: An analysis of English *-ic* and *-ical* adjectives. *International Journal of Corpus Linguistics* 8(1). 31–61. DOI:10.1075/ijcl.8.1.02gri

Gries, Stefan Th. 2004. Some characteristics of English morphological blends. In Mary A. Andronis, Erin Debenport, Anne Pycha & Keiko Yoshimura (eds.), *Papers from the 38th Regional Meeting of the Chicago Linguistics Society. Vol. II: The Panels*, 201–216. Chicago: Chicago Linguistic Society.

Gries, Stefan Th. 2005. Syntactic priming: A corpus-based approach. *Journal of Psycholinguistic Research* 34(4). 365–399. DOI:10.1007/s10936-005-6139-3

Gries, Stefan Th. 2013. *Statistics for linguistics with R: A practical introduction.* 2nd revised edition. Berlin: De Gruyter Mouton.

Gries, Stefan Th. & Martin Hilpert. 2010. Modeling diachronic change in the third person singular: A multifactorial, verb- and author-specific exploratory approach. *English Language and Linguistics* 14(03). 293–320. DOI:10.1017/S1360674310000092

Gries, Stefan Th. & Naoki Otani. 2010. Behavioral profiles: A corpus-based perspective on synonymy and antonymy. *ICAME Journal* 34. 121–150.

Gries, Stefan Th. & Anatol Stefanowitsch. 2004. Extending collostructional analysis: A corpus-based perspective on “alternations”. *International Journal of Corpus Linguistics* 9(1). 97–129. DOI:10.1075/ijcl.9.1.06gri

Gries, Stefan Th. & Anatol Stefanowitsch (eds.). 2006. *Corpora in cognitive linguistics. Corpus-based approaches to syntax and lexis* (Trends in Linguistics. Studies and Monographs [TiLSM]). Berlin & New York: Mouton de Gruyter.

Güldenring, Barbara Ann. 2017. Emotion metaphors in new Englishes: A corpus-based study of ANGER. *Cognitive Linguistic Studies* 4(1). 82–109. DOI:10.1075/cogls.4.1.05gul

Guz, Wojciech. 2009. English affixal nominalizations across language registers. *Poznań Studies in Contemporary Linguistics* 45(4). 461–485. DOI:10.2478/v10010-009-0030-6

Halliday, Michael A. K. 1961. Categories of the theory of grammar. *Word* 17. 241–92.

Herrmann, Konrad. 2011. *Hardness testing principles and applications.* Materials Park, Ohio: ASM International.

Heyd, Theresa. 2016. Narratives of belonging in the digital diaspora: Corpus approaches to a cultural concept. *Open Linguistics* 2(1). DOI:10.1515/opli-2016-0013

Hilpert, Martin. 2008. *Germanic future constructions: A usage-based approach to language change* (Constructional approaches to language 7). Amsterdam & Philadelphia: John Benjamins.

Hilpert, Martin. 2015. *Constructional change in English: Developments in allomorphy, word formation, and syntax.* 1st paperback edition (Studies in English language). Cambridge: Cambridge University Press. OCLC: 959270152.

Hoey, Michael. 2005. *Lexical priming: A new theory of words and language.* London & New York: Routledge.

Hoffmann, Sebastian. 2004. Using the OED quotations database as a corpus: A linguistic appraisal. *ICAME Journal* 28. 17–30.

Hoffmann, Thomas. 2014. The cognitive evolution of Englishes: The role of constructions in the dynamic model. In Sarah Buschfeld, Thomas Hoffmann, Magnus Huber & Alexander Kautzsch (eds.), *Varieties of English around the world*, vol. G49, 160–180. Amsterdam & Philadelphia: John Benjamins. DOI:10.1075/veaw.g49.10hof

Hopper, Paul. 1987. Emergent grammar. In *Proceedings of the Thirteenth Annual Meeting of the Berkeley Linguistics Society*, 139–157. Berkeley: Berkeley Linguistics Society. DOI:10.3765/bls.v13i0.1834

Hsu, Hui-Chin, Alan Fogel & Rebecca B. Cooper. 2000. Infant vocal development during the first 6 months: Speech quality and melodic complexity. *Infant and Child Development* 9(1). 1–16. DOI:10.1002/(SICI)1522-7219(200003)9:1<1::AID-ICD210>3.0.CO;2-V

Hundt, Marianne. 1997. Has British English been catching up with American English over the past thirty years? In Magnus Ljung (ed.), *Corpus-Based Studies in English: Papers from the Seventeenth International Conference on English-Language Research Based on Computerized Corpora*, 135–151. Amsterdam: Rodopi.

Hundt, Marianne. 2009. Colonial lag, colonial innovation or simply language change? In Günter Rohdenburg & Julia Schlüter (eds.), *One language, two grammars?*, 13–37. Cambridge: Cambridge University Press.

Hunston, Susan. 2007. Semantic prosody revisited. *International Journal of Corpus Linguistics* 12(2). 249–268. DOI:10.1075/ijcl.12.2.09hun

Hunston, Susan & Gill Francis. 2000. *Pattern grammar: A corpus-driven approach to the lexical grammar of English* (Studies in corpus linguistics 4). Amsterdam & Philadelphia: John Benjamins.

Jackendoff, Ray. 1994. *Patterns in the mind: Language and human nature.* New York: BasicBooks.

Jäkel, Olaf. 1997. *Metaphern in abstrakten Diskurs-Domänen: Eine kognitiv-linguistische Untersuchung anhand der Bereiche Geistestätigkeit, Wirtschaft und Wissenschaft* (Duisburger Arbeiten zur Sprach- und Kulturwissenschaft, Duisburg papers on research in language and culture Bd. 30). Frankfurt am Main & New York: Peter Lang.

Jankowski, Bridget L. & Sali A. Tagliamonte. 2014. On the genitive's trail: Data and method from a sociolinguistic perspective. *English Language and Linguistics* 18(02). 305–329. DOI:10.1017/S1360674314000045

Jespersen, Otto. 1909. *A modern English grammar on historical principles (volumes 1–7).* Heidelberg: Winter.

Johansson, Stig & Knut Hofland. 1989. *Frequency analysis of English vocabulary and grammar: Tag frequencies and word frequencies.* Vol. 1. Oxford: Clarendon Press.

Johnson, Wendell. 1944. I. A program of research. *Psychological Monographs* 56(2). 1–15. DOI:10.1037/h0093508

Jucker, Andreas H. 1993. The genitive versus the of–construction in British newspapers. In Andreas H. Jucker (ed.), *The noun phrase in English: Its structure and variability* (Anglistik und Englischunterricht 49), 121–136. Heidelberg: Winter.

Justeson, John S. & Slava M. Katz. 1991. Co-occurrences of antonymous adjectives and their contexts. *Computational Linguistics* 17(1). 1–19.

Justeson, John S. & Slava M. Katz. 1992. Redefining antonymy: The textual structure of a semantic relation. *Literary and Linguistic Computing* 7(3). 176–184. DOI:10.1093/llc/7.3.176

Kaunisto, Mark. 1999. *Electric/electrical and classic/classical:* Variation between the suffixes *-ic* and *-ical. English Studies* 80(4). 343–370. DOI:10.1080/00138389908599189

Kennedy, Graeme D. 1998. *An introduction to corpus linguistics.* London & New York: Longman.

Kennedy, Graeme D. 2003. Amplifier Collocations in the British National Corpus: Implications for English Language Teaching. *TESOL Quarterly* 37(3). 467. DOI:10.2307/3588400

Kilgarriff, Adam, Vít Baisa, Jan Bušta, Miloš Jakubíček, Vojtěch Kovář, Jan Michelfeit, Pavel Rychlý & Vít Suchomel. 2014. The Sketch Engine: Ten years on. *Lexicography* 1(1). 7–36. DOI:10.1007/s40607-014-0009-9

Kjellmer, Göran. 1986. "The lesser man": Observations on the role of women in modern English writing. In Jan Aarts & Willem Meijs (eds.), *Corpus linguistics II: New studies in the analysis and exploitation of computer corpora*, 163–176. Amsterdam: Rodopi.

Kjellmer, Göran. 2003. Hesitation. In defence of ER and ERM. *English Studies* 84(2). 170–198. DOI:10.1076/enst.84.2.170.14903

Koller, Veronika. 2004. *Metaphor and gender in business media discourse: A critical cognitive study.* New York: Palgrave Macmillan.

Kuhn, Thomas S. 1962. *The structure of scientific revolutions.* Chicago: The University of Chicago Press.

Labov, William. 1996. When intuitions fail. In Lisa McNair, Kora Singer, Lise Dolbrin & Michelle Aucon (eds.), *Papers from the parasession on theory and data in linguistics*, vol. 32, 77–106. Chicago, IL: Chicago Linguistic Society.

Labov, William, Sharon Ash & Charles Boberg. 2006. *The atlas of North American English phonetics, phonology, and sound change: A multimedia reference tool.* Berlin & New York: Mouton de Gruyter.

Lakoff, George. 1993. The contemporary theory of metaphor. In Andrew Ortony (ed.), *Metaphor and thought*, 2nd edn., 202–252. Cambridge: Cambridge University Press.

Lakoff, George. 2004. *Re: Empirical methods in Cognitive Linguistics.* http://listserv.linguistlist.org/cgi-bin/wa?A2=ind0407&L=COGLING&F=&S=&P=2918.

Lakoff, George & Mark Johnson. 1980. *Metaphors we live by.* Chicago: Chicago University Press.

Lakoff, George & Zoltán Kövecses. 1987. The cognitive model of anger inherent in American English. In Dorothy Holland & Naomi Quinn (eds.), *Cultural models in language and thought*, 195–221. Cambridge: Cambridge University Press.

Lakoff, Robin. 1973. Language and woman's place. *Language in Society* 2(1). 45–80.

Langacker, Ronald W. 1973. *Language and its structure: Some fundamental linguistic concepts.* 2d ed. New York: Harcourt Brace Jovanovich.

Langacker, Ronald W. 1991. *Concept, image, and symbol: The cognitive basis of grammar* (Cognitive linguistics research 1). Berlin: Mouton de Gruyter.

Lautsch, Erwin, Gustav A. Lienert & Alexander von Eye. 1988. Strategische Überlegungen zur Anwendung der Konfigurationsfrequenzanalyse. *EDV in Medizin und Biologie* 19(1). 26–30.

Lee, David Y.W. 2001. Genres, registers, text types, domains, and styles: Clarifying the concepts and navigating a path through the BNC jungle. *Language Learning & Technology* 5(3). 37–72.

Leech, Geoffrey N. & Roger Fallon. 1992. Computer corpora: What do they tell us about culture? *ICAME Journal* 16. 29–50.

Leech, Geoffrey N., Roger Garside & Michael Bryant. 1994. CLAWS4: The tagging of the British National Corpus. In *Proceedings of the 15th International Conference on Computational Linguistics*, 622–628. Kyoto.

Leech, Geoffrey N. & Andrew Kehoe. 2006. Recent grammatical change in written English 1961–1992: Some preliminary findings of a comparison of American with British English. In Antoinette Renouf & Andrew Kehoe (eds.), *The changing face of corpus linguistics* (Language and Computers 55), 185–204. Amsterdam: Rodopi.

Levin, Magnus. 2014. The Bathroom Formula: A corpus-based study of a speech act in American and British English. *Journal of Pragmatics* 64. 1–16. DOI:10.1016/j.pragma.2014.01.001

Liberman, Mark. 2005. *What happened to the 1940s?* Blog. http://itre.cis.upenn.edu/~myl/languagelog/archives/002397.html.

Liberman, Mark. 2012. *Historical culturomics of pronoun frequencies.* Blog. http://languagelog.ldc.upenn.edu/nll/?p=4126.

Lindquist, Hans & Christian Mair (eds.). 2004. *Corpus approaches to grammaticalization in English* (Studies in corpus linguistics 13). Amsterdam & Philadelphia: John Benjamins.

Lindsay, Mark. 2011. Rival suffixes: Synonymy, competition, and the emergence of productivity. In Angela Ralli, Geert E. Booij, Sergio Scalise & Athanasios Karasimos (eds.), *Morphology and the architecture of grammar: On-line proceedings of the Eighth Mediterranean Morphology Meeting*, 192–203. Patras: University of Patras.

Lindsay, Mark & Mark Aronoff. 2013. Natural selection in self-organizing morphological systems. In Nabil Hathout, Fabio Montermini & Jesse Tseng (eds.), *Morphology in Toulouse. Selected proceedings of Décembrettes 7*, 133–153. München: Lincom Europa.

Liu, Dilin. 2010. Is it a *chief*, *main*, *major*, *primary*, or *principal* concern? A corpus-based behavioral profile study of the near-synonyms. *International Journal of Corpus Linguistics* 15(1). 56–87. DOI:10.1075/ijcl.15.1.03liu

Lohmann, Arne. 2013. *Constituent order in coordinate constructions: A processing perspective.* Hamburg: Universität Hamburg. (Dissertation).

Louw, Bill & Carmela Chateau. 2010. Semantic prosody for the 21st Century: Are prosodies smoothed in academic contexts? A contextual prosodic theoretical perspective. In Sergio Bolasco, Isabella Chiari & Luca Giuliano (eds.), *Statistical analysis of textual data*, 755–764. Rome: Sapienza Università di Roma.

Louw, William E. 1993. Irony in the text or insincerity in the writer? The diagnostic potential of semantic prosodies. In Mona Baker, Gill Francis & Elena Tognini-Bonelli (eds.), *Text and technology in honour of John Sinclair*, 157–176. Amsterdam & Philadelphia: John Benjamins.

Lyons, John. 1981. *Language and linguistics: An introduction.* Cambridge & New York: Cambridge University Press.

Macmillan, Harold. 1961. House of Commons debate on foreign affairs, 18. October 1961. In *Commons and Lords Hansard, the Official Report of debates in Parliament*, vol. 646, cc177–319. London: UK Parliament.

Mair, Christian. 2004. Corpus linguistics and grammaticalisation theory: Statistics, frequencies, and beyond. In Hans Lindquist & Christian Mair (eds.), *Studies in Corpus Linguistics*, vol. 13, 121–150. Amsterdam & Philadelphia: John Benjamins.

Manning, Christopher D. & Hinrich Schütze. 1999. *Foundations of statistical natural language processing.* Cambridge, MA: MIT Press.

Manning, Susan Karp & Maria Parra Melchiori. 1974. Words that upset urban college students: Measured with GSRs and rating scales. *The Journal of Social Psychology* 94(2). 305–306. DOI:10.1080/00224545.1974.9923225

Marco, Maria José Luzon. 2000. Collocational frameworks in medical research papers: A genre-based study. *English for Specific Purposes* 19(1). 63–86. DOI:10.1016/S0889-4906(98)00013-1

Martin, James H. 2006. A corpus-based analysis of context effects on metaphor comprehension. In Anatol Stefanowitsch & Stefan Th. Gries (eds.), *Corpus-based approaches to metaphor*, 214–236. Berlin & New York: Mouton de Gruyter.

Mason, Oliver & Susan Hunston. 2004. The automatic recognition of verb patterns: A feasibility study. *International Journal of Corpus Linguistics* 9(2). 253–270. DOI:10.1075/ijcl.9.2.05mas

Matthews, Peter H. 2014. *The concise Oxford dictionary of linguistics.* Third edition (Oxford paperback reference). Oxford: Oxford University Press.

McEnery, Tony & Andrew Hardie. 2012. *Corpus linguistics: method, theory and practice* (Cambridge textbooks in linguistics). Cambridge & New York: Cambridge University Press.

McEnery, Tony & Andrew Wilson. 2001. *Corpus linguistics: an introduction.* Edinburgh: Edinburgh University Press.

McHugh, Mary L. 2012. Interrater reliability: The kappa statistic. *Biochemia Medica* 22(3). 276–282.

Merriam-Webster. 2014. *How does a word get into a Merriam-Webster dictionary?* FAQ. http://www.merriam-webster.com/help/faq/words_in.htm.

Meurers, W. Detmar. 2005. On the use of electronic corpora for theoretical linguistics. *Lingua* 115(11). 1619–1639. DOI:10.1016/j.lingua.2004.07.007

Meurers, W. Detmar & Stefan Müller. 2009. Corpora and syntax. In Anke Lüdeling & Merja Kytö (eds.), *Corpus linguistics*, vol. 2 (Handbooks of Linguistics and Communication Science 29), 920–933. Berlin & New York: De Gruyter Mouton.

Meyer, Charles F. 2002. *English corpus linguistics: An introduction* (Studies in English language). Cambridge & New York: Cambridge University Press.

Meyer, David E. & Roger W. Schvaneveldt. 1971. Facilitation in recognizing pairs of words: Evidence of a dependence between retrieval operations. *Journal of Experimental Psychology* 90(2). 227–234. DOI:10.1037/h0031564

Michaelis, Laura A. & Knud Lambrecht. 1996. Toward a construction-based theory of language function: The case of nominal extraposition. *Language* 72(2). 215–247.

Michel, Jean-Baptiste, Yuan Kui Shen, Aviva P. Aiden, Adrian Veres, Matthew K. Gray, The Google Books Team, Joseph P. Pickett, Dale Hoiberg, Dan Clancy, Peter Norvig, Jon Orwant, Steven Pinker, Martin A. Nowak & Erez Lieberman

Aiden. 2011. Quantitative analysis of culture using millions of digitized books. *Science* 331(6014). 176–182. DOI:10.1126/science.1199644

Mondorf, Britta. 2004a. *Gender differences in English syntax*. Tübingen: Niemeyer.

Mondorf, Britta. 2004b. Syntactic variation according to sex: Tag questions. In *Gender differences in English syntax*, 44–75. Tübingen: Niemeyer.

Murphy, Bróna. 2009. "She's a *fucking* ticket": The pragmatics of *fuck* in Irish English – an age and gender perspective. *Corpora* 4(1). 85–106. DOI:10.3366/E1749503209000239

Musolff, Andreas. 2012. The study of metaphor as part of critical discourse analysis. *Critical Discourse Studies* 9(3). 301–310. DOI:10.1080/17405904.2012.688300

Newman, Barry. 2013. *In U.S., apostrophes in place names are practically against the law*. News. http://online.wsj.com/news/articles/SB10001424127887324244304578471252974458308.

Nichter, Luke A. 2007. *Nixon tapes and transcripts*. Archive. http://nixontapes.org.

Noël, Dirk. 2003. Is there semantics in all syntax? The case of accusative and infinitive constructions vs. *that*-clauses. In Günter Rohdenburg & Britta Mondorf (eds.), *Determinants of grammatical variation in English*, 347–378. Berlin & New York: Mouton de Gruyter.

Oakes, Michael P. & Malcolm Farrow. 2007. Use of the chi-squared test to examine vocabulary differences in English language corpora representing seven different countries. *Literary and Linguistic Computing* 22(1). 85–99. DOI:10.1093/llc/fql044

Ogarkova, Anna & Cristina Soriano Salinas. 2014. Emotion and the body: A corpus-based investigation of metaphorical containers of anger across languages. *International Journal of Cognitive Linguistics* 5(2). 147–179.

Or, Winnie Wing-fung. 1994. A corpus-based study of features of adjectival suffixation in English. In *Proceedings Joint Seminar on Corpus Linguistics and Lexicology Guangzhou and Hong Kong*, 72–81. Hong Kong: Language Centre, Hong Kong University of Science & Technology.

Palmer, Stephen E. 1975. The effects of contextual scenes on the identification of objects. *Memory & Cognition* 3(5). 519–526. DOI:10.3758/BF03197524

Partington, Alan. 1998. *Patterns and meanings using corpora for English language research and teaching* (Studies in Corpus Linguistics 2). Amsterdam & Philadelphia: John Benjamins.

Pearce, Michael. 2008. Investigating the collocational behaviour of MAN and WOMAN in the British National Corpus using Sketch Engine. *Corpora* 3(1). 1–29.

Pedersen, Ted. 1996. Fishing for exactness. In *Proceedings of the South-Central SAS Users Group Conference*, 188–200. Austin, TX: South-Central SAS Users Group.

Pedersen, Ted. 1998. Dependent bigram identification. In *Proceedings of the Fifteenth National Conference on Artificial Intelligence and Tenth Innovative Applications of Artificial Intelligence Conference*, 1197. Madison, WI: AAAI Press/The MIT Press.

Pinker, Steven. 1994. *The language instinct.* 1st ed. New York: W. Morrow & Co.

Plag, Ingo. 1999. *Morphological productivity. Structural constraints in English derivation.* Berlin & New York: Mouton de Gruyter.

Popper, Karl R. 1959. *The logic of scientific discovery.* London: Hutchinson.

Popper, Karl R. 1963. *Conjectures and refutations: the growth of scientific knowledge.* London & New York: Routledge & Kegan Paul.

Popper, Karl R. 1970. A realist view of logic, physics, and history. In Wolfgang Yourgrau & Allen D. Breck (eds.), *Physics, logic, and history*, 1–37. Boston, MA: Springer. DOI:10.1007/978-1-4684-1749-4_1

Quirk, Randolph, Sidney Greenbaum, Geoffrey N. Leech & Jan Svartvik. 1972. *A Grammar of contemporary English.* London: Longman.

Quirk, Randolph, Jan Svartvik & Geoffrey N. Leech. 1985. *A Comprehensive grammar of the English language.* London & New York: Longman.

Rayson, Paul. 2008. From key words to key semantic domains. *International Journal of Corpus Linguistics* 13(4). 519–549. DOI:10.1075/ijcl.13.4.06ray

Rayson, Paul, Geoffrey N. Leech & Mary Hodges. 1997. Social differentiation in the use of English vocabulary: Some analyses of the conversational component of the British National Corpus. *International Journal of Corpus Linguistics* 2(1). 133–152. DOI:10.1075/ijcl.2.1.07ray

Read, Timothy R. C & Noel A. C Cressie. 1988. *Goodness-of-fit statistics for discrete multivariate data.* New York, NY: Springer.

Renouf, Antoinette. 1987. Lexical resolution. In Willem Meijs (ed.), *Proceedings of the Seventh International Conference on English Language Research on Computerised Corpora*, 121–131. Amsterdam: Rodopi.

Renouf, Antoinette & John Sinclair. 1991. Collocational frameworks in English. In Karin Aijmer & Bengt Altenberg (eds.), *English corpus linguistics: studies in honour of Jan Svartvik*, 128–143. London: Longman.

Robinson, Andrew. 2002. *Lost languages: The enigma of the world's undeciphered scripts.* New York: McGraw-Hill.

Rohdenburg, Günter. 1995. On the replacement of finite complement clauses by infinitives in English. *English Studies* 76(4). 367–388. DOI:10.1080/00138389508598980

Rohdenburg, Günter. 2003. Cognitive complexity and horror aequi as factors determining the use of interrogative clause linkers in English. In Günter Rohdenburg & Britta Mondorf (eds.), *Determinants of Grammatical Variation in English*, 205–250. Berlin & New York: Mouton de Gruyter.

Rohdenburg, Günter & Britta Mondorf. 2003. *Determinants of grammatical variation in English*. Berlin & New York: Mouton de Gruyter.

Rohdenburg, Günter & Julia Schlüter. 2009. *One language, two grammars? Differences between British and American English*. Cambridge & New York: Cambridge University Press.

Rojo López, Ana María. 2013. Distinguishing near-synonyms and translation equivalents in metaphorical terms: Crisis vs. recession in English and Spanish. In Francisco Gonzálvez-García, M. Sandra Peña Cervel & Lorena Pérez Hernández (eds.), *Metaphor and metonymy revisited beyond the contemporary theory of metaphor recent developments and applications*, 283–316. Amsterdam & Philadelphia: John Benjamins.

Rojo López, Ana María & María Ángeles Orts Llopis. 2010. Metaphorical pattern analysis in financial texts: Framing the crisis in positive or negative metaphorical terms. *Journal of Pragmatics* 42(12). 3300–3313. DOI:10.1016/j.pragma.2010.06.001

Romaine, Suzanne. 2001. A corpus-based view of gender in British and American English. In Marlis Hellinger & Hadumod Bußmann (eds.), *Gender across languages*, vol. 1 (IMPACT: Studies in Language and Society 9), 153–175. Amsterdam & Philadelphia: John Benjamins.

Römer, Ute & Stefanie Wulff. 2010. Applying corpus methods to writing research: Explorations of MICUSP. *Journal of Writing Research* 2(2). 99–127.

Rosenbach, Anette. 2002. *Genitive variation in English: Conceptual factors in synchronic and diachronic studies* (Topics in English linguistics 42). Berlin & New York: Mouton de Gruyter.

Rosnow, Ralph L. & Robert Rosenthal. 1989. Statistical procedures and the justification of knowledge in psychological science. *American Psychologist* 44(10). 1276–1284. DOI:10.1037/0003-066X.44.10.1276

Rudanko, Juhani. 2003. More on horror aequi: Evidence from large corpora. In Archer Corpus Linguistics 2003 Dawn, Dawn Archer, Paul Rayson, Andrew Wilson & Tony McEnery (eds.), *Proceedings of the Corpus Linguistics 2003 conference*, 662–668. Lancaster: UCREL.

Rudolph, John L. 2005. Epistemology for the masses: The origins of "the scientific method" in American schools. *History of Education Quarterly* 45(3). 341–376.

Sacks, Harvey. 1992. *Lectures on conversation*. Oxford & Cambridge, MA: Blackwell.

Sacks, Harvey, Emanuel A. Schegloff & Gail Jefferson. 1974. A simplest systematics for the organization of turn-taking for conversation. *Language* 50(4). 696. DOI:10.2307/412243

Säily, Tanja. 2011. Variation in morphological productivity in the BNC: Sociolinguistic and methodological considerations. *Corpus Linguistics and Linguistic Theory* 7(1). 119–141. DOI:10.1515/cllt.2011.006

Säily, Tanja & Jukka Suomela. 2009. Comparing type counts: The case of women, men and *-ity* in early English letters. *Language and Computers – Studies in Practical Linguistics* 69. 87–109.

Sampson, Geoffrey. 1987. Evidence against the "Grammatical"/"Ungrammatical" distinction. In Willem Meijs (ed.), *Corpus linguistics and beyond*, 219–226. Amsterdam: Rodopi.

Sampson, Geoffrey. 1995. *English for the computer: The SUSANNE corpus and analytic scheme.* Oxford & New York: Clarendon Press & Oxford University Press.

Santorini, Beatrice. 1990. *Part-of-speech tagging guidelines for the Penn Treebank project.* Technical Report MS-CIS-90-47. Philadelphia: University of Pennsylvania, Department of Computer & Information Science. 32.

Sapir, Edward. 1921. *Language: An introduction to the study of speech.* New York: Harcourt, Brace & Co.

Schlüter, Julia. 2003. Phonological determinants of grammatical variation in English: Chomsky's worst possible case. In Günter Rohdenburg & Britta Mondorf (eds.), *Determinants of Grammatical Variation in English*, 69–118. Berlin & New York: Mouton de Gruyter.

Schmid, Hans-Jörg. 1996. Introspection and computer corpora: The meaning and complementation of start and begin. In Arne Zettersten & Viggo Hjørnager (eds.), *Symposium on Lexicography VII. Proceedings of the Seventh Symposium on Lexicography, May 5-6, 1994 at the Unversity of Copenhagen* (Lexicographica, Series Major 76), 223–239. Tübingen: Niemeyer.

Schmid, Hans-Jörg. 2003. Do women and men really live in different cultures? Evidence from the BNC. In Andrew Wilson, Paul Rayson & Tony McEnery (eds.), *Corpus linguistics by the Lune: A Festschrift for Geoffrey Leech*, 185–221. Frankfurt: Peter Lang.

Schmid, Helmut. 1994. Probabilistic part-of-speech tagging using decision trees. In *Proceedings of International Conference on New Methods in Language Processing*, 44–49. Manchester: University of Manchester.

Schmilz, Ulrich. 1983. Zählen und Erzählen: Zur Anwendung statistischer Verfahren in der Textlinguistik. *Zeitschrift für Sprachwissenschaft* 2(1). 132–143. DOI:10.1515/ZFSW.1983.2.1.132

Schütze, Carson T. 1996. *The empirical base of linguistics: Grammaticality judgments and linguistic methodology.* Chicago, Il: The University of Chicago Press.

Scott, Mike. 1997. PC analysis of key words – And key key words. *System* 25(2). 233–245. DOI:10.1016/S0346-251X(97)00011-0

Scott, Mike & Chris Tribble. 2006. *Textual patterns: key words and corpus analysis in language education* (Studies in corpus linguistics 22). Amsterdam & Philadelphia: John Benjamins.

Sebba, Mark & Steven D. Fligelstone. 1994. Corpora. In Ronald E. Asher & James M.Y. Simpson (eds.), vol. 2, 769–773. Oxford: Pergamon.

Semino, Elena & Michaela Masci. 1996. Politics is football: Metaphor in the discourse of Silvio Berlusconi in Italy. *Discourse & Society* 7(2). 243–269. DOI:10.1177/0957926596007002005

Seto, Ken-ichi. 1999. Distinguishing metonymy from synecdoche. In Klaus-Uwe Panther & Günter Radden (eds.), *Metonymy in language and thought*, vol. 4 (Human Cognitive Processing), 91–120. Amsterdam & Philadelphia: John Benjamins.

Shaffer, Juliet P. 1995. Multiple hypothesis testing. *Annual Review of Psychology* 46(1). 561–584. DOI:10.1146/annurev.ps.46.020195.003021

Shankman, Cory, J. J. Kavelaars, Michele T. Bannister, Brett J. Gladman, Samantha M. Lawler, Ying-Tung Chen, Marian Jakubik, Nathan Kaib, Mike Alexandersen, Stephen D. J. Gwyn, Jean-Marc Petit & Kathryn Volk. 2017. OSSOS. VI. Striking biases in the detection of large semimajor axis trans-neptunian objects. *The Astronomical Journal* 154(2). 50. DOI:10.3847/1538-3881/aa7aed

Shih, Stephanie, Jason Grafmiller, Richard Futrell & Joan Bresnan. 2015. Rhythm's role in genitive construction choice in spoken English. In Ralf Vogel & Ruben Vijver (eds.), *Rhythm in cognition and grammar* (Trends in Linguistics. Studies and Monographs 286), 207–234. Berlin, München & Boston: De Gruyter Mouton. DOI:10.1515/9783110378092.207

Simpson, John A. & Edmund S. C. Weiner (eds.). 1989. *The Oxford English dictionary.* 2nd ed. Oxford & New York: Clarendon Press & Oxford University Press.

Sinclair, John. 1991. *Corpus, concordance, collocation.* Oxford: Oxford University Press.

Sinclair, John. 1996a. *EAGLES Preliminary recommendations on corpus typology.* Tech. rep. EAG–TCWG–CTYP/P. Pisa: Expert Advisory Group on Language Engineering Standards.

Sinclair, John. 1996b. The search for units of meaning. *Textus* 9. 75–106.

Sobkowiak, Włodzimierz. 1993. Unmarked-before-marked as a freezing principle. *Language and Speech* 36(4). 393–414. DOI:10.1177/002383099303600403

Stallard, David. 1993. Two kinds of metonymy. In *Proceedings of the 31st annual meeting on Association for Computational Linguistics*, 87–94. Stroudsburg: Association for Computational Linguistics. DOI:10.3115/981574.981586

Standwell, G.J.B. 1982. Genitive constructions and functional sentence perspective. *IRAL: International Review of Applied Linguistics in Language Teaching* 20(1-4). 257–262. DOI:10.1515/iral.1982.20.1-4.257

Steen, Gerard J., Ewa Biernacka, Aletta G. Dorst, Anna Kaal, Clara I. López Rodríguez & Trijntje Pasma. 2010. Pragglejaz in practice: Finding metaphorically used words in natural discourse. In Graham Low, Zazie Todd, Alice Deignan & Lynne Cameron (eds.), *Researching and applying metaphor in the real world*, vol. 26 (Human Cognitive Processing), 165–184. Amsterdam & Philadelphia: John Benjamins.

Stefanowitsch, Anatol. 2003. Constructional semantics as a limit to grammatical alternation: The two genitives of English. In Günter Rohdenburg & Britta Mondorf (eds.), *Determinants of grammatical variation in English* (Topics in English Linguistics 43), 413–444. Berlin & New York: Mouton de Gruyter.

Stefanowitsch, Anatol. 2004. HAPPINESS in English and German: A metaphorical-pattern analysis. In Michel Achard & Suzanne Kemmer (eds.), *Language, culture, and mind*, 137–149. Stanford, CA: CSLI.

Stefanowitsch, Anatol. 2005. The function of metaphor: Developing a corpus-based perspective. *International Journal of Corpus Linguistics* 10(2). 161–198. DOI:10.1075/ijcl.10.2.03ste

Stefanowitsch, Anatol. 2006a. Distinctive collexeme analysis and diachrony: A comment. *Corpus Linguistics and Linguistic Theory* 2(2). 257–262. DOI:10.1515/CLLT.2006.013

Stefanowitsch, Anatol. 2006b. Negative evidence and the raw frequency fallacy. *Corpus Linguistics and Linguistic Theory* 2(1). 61–77. DOI:10.1515/CLLT.2006.003

Stefanowitsch, Anatol. 2006c. Words and their metaphors: A corpus-based approach. In Anatol Stefanowitsch & Stefan Th. Gries (eds.), *Corpus-based approaches to metaphor* (Trends in Linguistics), 61–105. Berlin & New York: Mouton de Gruyter.

Stefanowitsch, Anatol. 2007a. Linguistics beyond grammaticality. *Corpus Linguistics and Linguistic Theory* 3(1). 57–71. DOI:10.1515/CLLT.2007.004

Stefanowitsch, Anatol. 2007b. Wortwiederholungen im Englischen und Deutschen: Eine korpuslinguistische Annährerung. In Andreas Ammann & Aina Urdze (eds.), *Wiederholung, Parallelismus, Reduplikation: Strategien der multiplen Strukturanwendung* (Diversitas Linguarum), 29–45. Bochum: Brockmeyer.

Stefanowitsch, Anatol. 2008. Negative entrenchment: A usage-based approach to negative evidence. *Cognitive Linguistics* 19(3). 513–531. DOI:10.1515/COGL.2008.020

Stefanowitsch, Anatol. 2010. Empirical cognitive semantics: Some thoughts. In Dylan Glynn & Kerstin Fischer (eds.), *Quantitative methods in cognitive semantics: Corpus-driven approaches*, 355–380. Berlin & New York: De Gruyter Mouton.

Stefanowitsch, Anatol. 2011. Cognitive linguistics meets the corpus. In Mario Brdar, Stefan Th. Gries & Milena Žic Fuchs (eds.), *Human Cognitive Processing*, vol. 32, 257–290. Amsterdam & Philadelphia: John Benjamins.

Stefanowitsch, Anatol. 2013. Collostructional analysis. In Thomas Hoffmann & Graeme Trousdale (eds.), *The Oxford handbook of construction grammar*, 290–306. Oxford & New York: Oxford University Press.

Stefanowitsch, Anatol. 2015. Metonymies don't bomb people, people bomb people. *Yearbook of the German Cognitive Linguistics Association* 3(1). 27–50. DOI:10.1515/gcla-2015-0003

Stefanowitsch, Anatol. 2017. A lot of data: Textually distinctive collexemes in a corpus of Scientific Englishes. In *Proceedings of the International Conference "Corpus Linguistics – 2017"*, 85–95. St. Petersburg: St. Petersburg State University.

Stefanowitsch, Anatol. 2018. The goal bias revisited: A collostructional approach. *Yearbook of the German Cognitive Linguistics Association* 6(1). 143–166. DOI:10.1515/gcla-2018-0007

Stefanowitsch, Anatol & Susanne Flach. 2016. The corpus-based perspective on entrenchment. In Hans-Jörg Schmid (ed.), *Entrenchment and the psychology of language learning: How we reorganize and adapt linguistic knowledge* (Language and the Human Lifespan 4), 101–127. Berlin & New York: De Gruyter Mouton.

Stefanowitsch, Anatol & Stefan Th. Gries. 2003. Collostructions: Investigating the interaction of words and constructions. *International Journal of Corpus Linguistics* 8(2). 209–243. DOI:10.1075/ijcl.8.2.03ste

Stefanowitsch, Anatol & Stefan Th. Gries. 2005. Covarying collexemes. *Corpus Linguistics and Linguistic Theory* 1(1). 1–43. DOI:10.1515/cllt.2005.1.1.1

Stefanowitsch, Anatol & Stefan Th. Gries. 2006. *Corpus-based approaches to metaphor and metonymy*. Berlin & New York: Mouton de Gruyter.

Stefanowitsch, Anatol & Stefan Th. Gries. 2008. Channel and constructional meaning: A collostructional case study. In Gitte Kristiansen & René Dirven (eds.), *Cognitive Sociolinguistics*, vol. 39, 129–152. Berlin & New York: Mouton de Gruyter.

Stefanowitsch, Anatol & Stefan Th. Gries. 2009. Corpora and grammar. In Anke Lüdeling & Merja Kytö (eds.), *Corpus linguistics: An international handbook*, vol. 2 (Handbooks of Linguistics and Communication Science 29), 933–952. Berlin & New York: De Gruyter Mouton.

Strömqvist, Sven & Ludo Th. Verhoeven (eds.). 2003. *Relating events in narrative: Typological and contextual perspectives.* Hillsdale, NJ: Lawrence Erlbaum Associates.

Stubbs, Michael. 1995a. Collocations and cultural connotations of common words. *Linguistics and Education* 7(4). 379–390. DOI:10.1016/0898-5898(95)90011-X

Stubbs, Michael. 1995b. Collocations and semantic profiles: On the cause of the trouble with quantitative studies. *Functions of Language* 2(1). 23–55. DOI:10.1075/fol.2.1.03stu

Subtirelu, Nicholas. 2014. *Do we talk and write about men more than women?* Blog. http://linguisticpulse.com/2014/04/09/do-we-talk-and-write-about-men-more-than-women/.

Swaine, Jon. 2009. *Apostrophes abolished by council.* Newspaper. http://www.telegraph.co.uk/news/newstopics/howaboutthat/4388343/Apostrophes-abolished-by-council.html.

Szmrecsanyi, Benedikt. 2005. Language users as creatures of habit: A corpus-based analysis of persistence in spoken English. *Corpus Linguistics and Linguistic Theory* 1(1). 113–150. DOI:10.1515/cllt.2005.1.1.113

Szmrecsanyi, Benedikt. 2006. *Morphosyntactic persistence in spoken English: A corpus study at the intersection of variationist sociolinguistics, psycholinguistics, and discourse analysis* (Trends in linguistics 177). Berlin & New York: Mouton de Gruyter.

Tagliamonte, Sali A. 2006. *Analysing sociolinguistic variation* (Key topics in sociolinguistics). Cambridge & New York: Cambridge University Press.

Taylor, John R. 2003. Near synonyms as co-extensive categories: 'high' and 'tall' revisited. *Language Sciences* 25(3). 263–284. DOI:10.1016/S0388-0001(02)00018-9

Taylor, John R. 2012. *The mental corpus: How language is represented in the mind.* Oxford & New York: Oxford University Press.

The Stationery Office. 1999. *Deceased estates notice, Wilfrid Thomas Froggatt Castle.* https://www.thegazette.co.uk/notice/L-55697-999.

Thompson, Sandra A. & Yuka Koide. 1987. Iconicity and "indirect objects" in English. *Journal of Pragmatics* 11(3). 399–406. DOI:10.1016/0378-2166(87)90139-1

Tissari, Heli. 2003. *Lovescapes: Changes in prototypical senses and cognitive metaphors since 1500* (Mémoires de la Société Néophilologique de Helsinki LXII). Helsinki: Société Néophilologique.

Tissari, Heli. 2010. English words for emotions and their metaphors. In Margaret E. Winters, Heli Tissari & Kathryn Allan (eds.), *Historical cognitive linguistics* (Cognitive linguistics research 47), 298–330. Berlin & New York: De Gruyter Mouton.

Tomasello, Michael. 2003. *Constructing a language: A usage-based theory of language acquisition.* Cambridge, MA: Harvard University Press.

Trips, Carola. 2009. *Lexical semantics and diachronic morphology the development of -hood, -dom and -ship in the history of English.* Tübingen: Niemeyer.

Tummers, Jose, Kris Heylen & Dirk Geeraerts. 2005. Usage-based approaches in Cognitive Linguistics: A technical state of the art. *Corpus Linguistics and Linguistic Theory* 1(2). 225–261. DOI:10.1515/cllt.2005.1.2.225

Turkkila, Kaisa. 2014. Do near-synonyms occur with the same metaphors: A comparison of anger terms in American English. *metaphorik.de* 25. 129–154.

Twenge, Jean M., W. Keith Campbell & Brittany Gentile. 2012. Male and female pronoun use in U.S. books reflects women's status, 1900–2008. *Sex Roles* 67(9-10). 488–493. DOI:10.1007/s11199-012-0194-7

Vosberg, Uwe. 2003. The role of extractions and horror aequi in the evolution of *-ing* complements in Modern English. In Günter Rohdenburg & Britta Mondorf (eds.), *Determinants of Grammatical Variation in English*, 305–328. Berlin & New York: Mouton de Gruyter.

Wallington, Alan, John A. Barnden, Marina A. Barnden, Fiona J. Ferguson & Sheila R. Glasbey. 2003. *Metaphoricity signals: A corpus-based investigation.* Technical Report CSRP-03-05. Birmingham: The University of Birmingham, School of Computer Science. 1–12.

Wasow, Tom & Jennifer Arnold. 2003. Post-verbal constituent ordering in English. In Günter Rohdenburg & Britta Mondorf (eds.), *Determinants of grammatical variation in English* (Topics in English Linguistics 43), 119–154. Berlin & New York: Mouton de Gruyter.

Wasserstein, Ronald L. & Nicole A. Lazar. 2016. The ASA's statement on *p*-values: Context, process, and purpose. *The American Statistician* 70(2). 129–133. DOI:10.1080/00031305.2016.1154108

Widdowson, Henry G. 2000. On the limitations of linguistics applied. *Applied Linguistics* 21(1). 3–25. DOI:10.1093/applin/21.1.3

Wiechmann, Daniel. 2008. On the computation of collostruction strength: Testing measures of association as expressions of lexical bias. *Corpus Linguistics and Linguistic Theory* 4(2). 253–290. DOI:10.1515/CLLT.2008.011

Wiederhorn, Sheldon M., Richard J. Fields, Samuel Low, Gun-Woong Bahng, Alois Wehrstedt, Junhee Hahn, Yo Tomota, Takashi Miyata, Haiqing Lin, Benny D. Freeman, Shuji Aihara, Yukito Hagihara & Tetsuya Tagawa. 2011.

Mechanical properties. In Horst Czichos, Tetsuya Saito & Leslie Smith (eds.), *Springer Handbook of Metrology and Testing*, 339–452. Berlin & Heidelberg: Springer.

Wierzbicka, Anna. 1988. *The semantics of grammar* (Studies in language companion series 18). Amsterdam & Philadelphia: John Benjamins.

Wierzbicka, Anna. 2003. *Cross-cultural pragmatics the semantics of human interaction*. Berlin & New York: Mouton de Gruyter.

Wikipedia contributors. 2018. *Regular expression*. https://en.wikipedia.org/wiki/Regular_expression.

Williams, Raymond. 1976. *Keywords: A vocabulary of culture and society*. New York: Oxford University Press.

Winchester, Simon. 2003. *The meaning of everything: The story of the Oxford English dictionary*. Oxford & New York: Oxford University Press.

Wolf, Hans-Georg & Frank Polzenhagen. 2007. Fixed expressions as manifestations of cultural conceptualizations: Examples from African varieties of English. In Paul Skandera (ed.), *Phraseology and culture in English* (Topics in English Linguistics 54), 399–435. Berlin & New York: Mouton de Gruyter.

Wulff, Stefanie. 2003. A multifactorial corpus analysis of adjective order in English. *International Journal of Corpus Linguistics* 8(2). 245–282. DOI:10.1075/ijcl.8.2.04wul

Wynne, Martin (ed.). 2005. *Developing linguistic corpora: A guide to good practice* (AHDS guides to good practice). Oxford & Oakville, CT: Oxbow Books.

Xiao, Richard. 2008. Well-known and influential corpora. In Anke Lüdeling & Merja Kytö (eds.), *Corpus Linguistics*, vol. 1 (Handbooks of Linguistics and Communication Science 29), 383–483. Berlin & New York: Walter de Gruyter.

Yarowsky, David. 1993. One sense per collocation. In *Human language technology: proceedings of a workshop held at Plainsboro, New Jersey, March 21-24, 1993*, 266–271. Association for Computational Linguistics. DOI:10.3115/1075671.1075731

Zaenen, Annie, Jean Carletta, Gregory Garretson, Joan Bresnan, Andrew Koontz-Garboden, Tatiana Nikitina, M. Catherine O'Connor & Tom Wasow. 2004. Animacy encoding in English: Why and how. In *Proceedings of the 2004 ACL Workshop on Discourse Annotation* (DiscAnnotation '04), 118–125. Stroudsburg, PA: Association for Computational Linguistics.

Name index

Subject index